A GUIDE TO
Microsoft Windows NT
Workstation 4.0

Ed Tittel
LANWrights, Inc.

Christa Anderson

David Johnson
LANWrights, Inc.

COURSE
TECHNOLOGY

ONE MAIN STREET, CAMBRIDGE, MA 02142

an International Thomson Publishing company I(T)P®

Cambridge • Albany • Bonn • Boston • Cincinnati • London • Madrid • Melbourne • Mexico City
New York • Paris • San Francisco • Singapore • Tokyo • Toronto • Washington

A Guide to Microsoft Windows NT Workstation 4.0 is published by Course Technology.

Managing Editor:	Kristen Duerr
Senior Product Manager:	Jennifer Normandin
Production Editor:	Ellina Beletsky
Development Editors:	Deb Kaufmann, Dawn Rader
Composition House:	GEX, Inc.
Text Designer:	GEX, Inc.
Cover Designer:	Wendy Reifeiss
Marketing Manager:	Tracy Foley

© 1998 by Course Technology—I(T)P®

For more information contact:

Course Technology
One Main Street
Cambridge, MA 02142

ITP Europe
Berkshire House 168–173
High Holborn
London WC11V 7AA
England

Nelson ITP Australia
102 Dodds Street
South Melbourne, 3205
Victoria, Australia

ITP Nelson Canada
1120 Birchmount Road
Scarborough, Ontario
Canada M1K 5G4

International Thomson Editores
Seneca, 53
Colonia Polanco
11560 Mexico D.F. Mexico

ITP GmbH
Königswinterer Strasse 418
53277 Bonn
Germany

ITP Asia
60 Albert Street, #15-01
Albert Complex
Singapore 189969

ITP Japan
Hirakawacho Kyowa Building, 3F
2-2-1 Hirakawacho
Chiyoda-ku, Tokyo 102
Japan

Trademarks

Disclaimer

ISBN 0-7600-5098-8

Printed in Canada

5 6 7 8 9   01 00

Brief Table of Contents

TABLE OF CONTENTS

INTRODUCTION

THE INTENDED AUDIENCE

This book is intended to serve the needs of those individuals and information systems professionals who are interested in learning more about Microsoft Windows NT Workstation 4.0, as well as individuals who are interested in obtaining Microsoft certification on this topic. These materials have been specifically designed to help individuals prepare for Microsoft Certification Exam 70-073, "Implementing and Supporting Microsoft Windows NT Workstation 4.0."

FEATURES

Many features in this book are designed to improve its pedagogical value and aid you in fully understanding Windows NT Workstation concepts.

- **Chapter Objectives** Each chapter begins with a detailed list of the concepts to be mastered within that chapter. This list provides you with a quick reference to the contents of the chapter as well as a useful study aid.

- **Illustrations and Tables** Numerous illustrations of networking components help you visualize common networking setups, theories, and architectures. In addition, tables provide details and comparisons of both practical and theoretical information.

- **Chapter Summaries** The text of each chapter concludes with a summary of the concepts it has introduced. These summaries provide a helpful way to recap and revisit the ideas covered in each chapter.

- **Key Terms** Following the summary, a list of new networking terms and their definitions encourages proper understanding of the chapter's key concepts and provides a useful reference.

- **Review Questions** End-of-chapter assessments begin with a set of review questions that reinforce the ideas introduced in each chapter. These questions not only show you whether you have mastered the concepts but are written to help prepare you for the Microsoft certification examination.

- **Hands-on Projects** Although it is important to understand the theory behind networking technology, nothing can improve upon real-world experience. With the exceptions of those chapters that are purely theoretical, each chapter provides a series of exercises aimed at giving students hands-on implementation experience.

- **Case Projects** Finally, each chapter closes with a section that proposes certain networking situations. You are asked to evaluate the situations and decide upon the course of action to be taken to remedy the problems described. This valuable tool will help you sharpen decision-making and troubleshooting skills—important aspects of network administration.

TEXT AND GRAPHIC CONVENTIONS

Wherever appropriate, additional information has been added to this book to help you better understand what is being discussed in the chapter. Icons throughout the text alert you to additional materials. The icons used in this book are described here:

 The Note icon indicates additional helpful material related to the subject being described.

 As experienced network administrators, the authors have practical experience with how networks work in real business situations. Tip icons highlight suggestions on ways to attack problems you may encounter in a real-world situation.

 The authors have placed notes in the margin next to concepts or steps that often cause difficulty. Each Caution anticipates a potential mistake and provides methods for avoiding the same problem in the future.

 The Hands-on icon and a description of the exercise precede each hands-on activity.

 Case Project icons appear at the end of each chapter. They mark more involved, scenario-based projects. In these case examples, you are asked to implement what you have learned.

WHERE SHOULD YOU START?

This book is intended to be read in sequence, from beginning to end. Each chapter builds upon those that precede it, to provide a solid understanding of Windows NT Workstation as a whole. After completing the chapters, you may find it useful to go back through the book and use the review questions and projects to prepare for the Microsoft certification exam— "Implementing and Supporting Microsoft Windows NT Workstation 4.0" (70-073). Readers are also encouraged to investigate the many pointers to online and printed sources of additional information that are cited throughout the book.

ENDMATTER

In addition to its core materials, this book includes an appendix and glossary that are worthy of further investigation.

- **Appendix: Microsoft Windows NT Server 4.0 NET Command Reference** This reference provides a guide to using NET commands to configure Windows NT from the command line.

■   **Glossary** This is a complete compendium of the key acronyms and technical terms used in this book, with definitions.

ADDITIONAL SUPPORT MATERIALS

If you are using this book in an academic setting, materials are available to instructors to assist in teaching this course. All of the supplements available with this book are provided to the instructor on a single CD-ROM.

Electronic Instructor's Manual. The Instructor's Manual that accompanies this textbook includes:

■   Additional instructional material to assist in class preparation, including suggestions for lecture topics and suggested lab activities

■   Solutions to all end-of-chapter materials, including the project assignments

Course Test Manager 1.1. A powerful assessment tool known as the Course Test Manager accompanies this book. Designed by Course Technology, this cutting-edge Windows-based testing software helps instructors design and administer tests and pre-tests. In addition to being able to generate tests that can be printed and administered, this full-featured program also has an online testing component that allows students to take tests at the computer and have their exams automatically graded.

Transcender Certification Test Prep Software. Bound into the back of this book is a disk containing Transcender Corporation's Implementing and Supporting Microsoft Windows NT Workstation 4.0 certification exam preparation software with one full exam that simulates Microsoft's exam.

ACKNOWLEDGMENTS

The authors would like to thank Course Technology for this opportunity to explore a new world for us—that of academic publishing. We deeply appreciate their patience and indulgence, especially that of Kristen Duerr and Jennifer Normandin, during the time when we were climbing their deceptively steep learning curve. Thanks also to Deb Kaufmann, whose yeomanly efforts helped turn these materials into the finely polished form they now take. Also, thanks to Keith Weiskamp of The Coriolios Group, and Fred Grainger of ITP Publishing, who helped us connect with the great team of people at Course Technology, and to Joseph Dougherty of Course Technology, who put us together so effectively with his staff.

The authors would also like to thank the in-house team at LANWrights (*www. lanw.com*) who helped to bring this book to fruition—especially Dawn Rader, who managed the project and handled all the materials that flowed between us and Course Technology. Thanks also to Mary Burmeister, who did much of the scut work on the project and helped us whip things into shape. To Michael, Natanya, and DJ: Thanks for all your efforts in helping out when help was needed. And finally, to our late friend and corporate mascot, Dusty: We miss you, big guy! No more downed machines from your all-powerful, ever-wagging tail makes work a less exciting place to be these days.

Finally, the co-authors would like to thank each other for the camaraderie, hard work, and support that went into making this book. We'd also like to thank Microsoft for making this kind of book not only possible, but necessary.

PREPARING FOR MICROSOFT CERTIFICATION

Microsoft offers a program called the Microsoft Certified Professional (MCP) program. Becoming a Microsoft Certified Professional can open many doors for you. Whether you want to be a network engineer, product specialist, or software developer, obtaining the appropriate Microsoft Certified Professional credentials can provide potential employers with a formal record of your skills. Certification can be equally effective in helping you secure a raise or promotion.

The Microsoft Certified Professional program is made up of many courses in several different tracks. Combinations of individual courses can lead to certification in a specific track. Most tracks require a combination of required and elective courses. The Microsoft Certified Systems Engineer (MCSE) credential is designed for networking professionals who work with Microsoft networks. Having this credential will enable you to leap forward, both professionally and financially.

HOW CAN TRANSCENDER'S TEST PREP SOFTWARE HELP?

To become a Microsoft Certified Professional, you must pass rigorous certification exams that provide a valid and reliable measure of technical proficiency and expertise. The disk contained in this book, Transcender Corporation's Limited Version certification exam preparation software, can be used in conjunction with the book to help you assess your progress in the event you choose to pursue Microsoft Professional Certification. The Transcender CD-ROM presents a series of questions that were expertly prepared to test your readiness for the official Microsoft certification examination, "Implementing and Supporting Microsoft Windows NT Workstation 4.0" (Exam 70-073). These questions were taken from a larger series of practice tests produced by the Transcender Corporation—practice tests that simulate the interface and format of the actual certification exams. Transcender's complete product also offers explanations for all questions. The rationale for each correct answer is carefully explained, and specific page references are given for Microsoft Product Documentation and Microsoft Press reference books. These page references enable you to study from additional sources.

Practice test questions from Transcender Corporation are acknowledged as the best available. In fact, with their full product, Transcender offers a money-back guarantee if you do not pass the exam. If you have trouble passing the practice examination included on the enclosed disk, you should consider purchasing the full product with additional practice tests and personalized feedback. Details and pricing information are available at the back of this book. A sample of the full Transcender product is on the enclosed CD-ROM, including remedial explanations.

System requirements for the Transcender Corporation test preparation software are as follows:

- 8 MB RAM (16 MB recommended)
- VGA/256 color display or better
- CD-ROM drive
- Microsoft Windows 3.1, Windows for Workgroups 3.11, Windows NT 3.51, Windows NT 4.0, Windows 95, or Windows 98.

The Transcender product is a great tool to help you prepare to become certified. If you experience technical problems with this product, please e-mail Transcender at *course@transcender.com* or call (615) 726-8779.

WANT TO KNOW MORE ABOUT MICROSOFT CERTIFICATION?

There are many additional benefits to achieving Microsoft Certified status. These benefits apply to you as well as to your potential employer. As a Microsoft Certified Professional, you will be recognized as an expert on Microsoft products, have access to ongoing technical information from Microsoft, and receive special invitations to Microsoft conferences and events. You can obtain a comprehensive, interactive tool that provides full details about the MCP program online at *www.microsoft.com/train_cert/cert/*. For more information on Course Technology texts that will help prepare you for certification exams, visit our site at *www.course.com*.

When you become a Certified Product Specialist, Microsoft sends you a Welcome Kit that contains:

■ An 8½ × 11 inch Microsoft Certified Product Specialist wall certificate. Also, within a few weeks after you have passed any exam, Microsoft sends you a Microsoft Certified Professional Transcript that shows which exams you have passed.

■ A Microsoft Certified Professional Program membership card

■ A Microsoft Certified Professional lapel pin

■ A license to use the Microsoft Certified Professional logo in your advertisements, promotions, proposals, and other materials, including business cards, letterheads, advertising circulars, brochures, yellow page advertisements, mailings, banners, resumes, and invitations

■ A Microsoft Certified Professional logo sheet. Before using the camera-ready logo, you must agree to the terms of the licensing agreement.

■ A Microsoft TechNet CD-ROM

■ A 50% discount toward a one-year membership in the Microsoft TechNet Technical Information Network, which provides valuable information via monthly CD-ROMs

■ Dedicated forums on CompuServe (GO MECFORUM) and The Microsoft Network, which enable MCPs to communicate directly with Microsoft and one another

■ A one-year subscription to Microsoft Certified Professional Magazine, a career and professional development magazine created especially for Microsoft Certified Professionals

■ A Certification Update subscription—a bimonthly newsletter from the Microsoft Certified Professional program that keeps you informed of changes and advances in the program and exams

■ Invitations to Microsoft conferences, technical training sessions, and special events

■ Eligibility to join the Network Professional Association, a worldwide association of computer professionals, as an associate member

A Certified Systems Engineer receives all the preceding benefits as well as the following additional ones:

■ Microsoft Certified Systems Engineer logos and other materials to help you identify yourself as a Microsoft Certified Systems Engineer to colleagues or clients

■ Ten free incidents with the Microsoft Support Network and a 25% discount on purchases of additional 10-packs of Priority Development and Desktop Support incidents

■ A one-year subscription to the Microsoft TechNet Technical Information Network

■ A one-year subscription to the Microsoft Beta Evaluation program. This benefit provides you with up to 12 free monthly beta software CDs for many of Microsoft's newest software products. This enables you to become familiar with new versions of Microsoft products before they are generally available. This benefit also includes access to a private CompuServe forum where you can exchange information with other program members and find information from Microsoft on current beta issues and product information.

CERTIFY ME!

So you are ready to become a Microsoft Certified Professional. The examinations are administered through Sylvan Prometric (formerly Drake Prometric) and are offered at more than 700 authorized testing centers around the world. Microsoft evaluates certification status based on current exam records. Your current exam record is the set of exams you have passed. To maintain Microsoft Certified Professional status, you must remain current on all the requirements for your certification.

Registering for an exam is easy. To register, contact Sylvan Prometric, 2601 West 88th Street, Bloomington, MN, 55431, at (800) 755-3926. Dial (612) 896-7000 or (612) 820-5707 if you cannot place a call to an 800 number from your location. You must call to schedule the exam at least one day before you want to take it. Taking the exam automatically enrolls you in the Microsoft Certified Professional program; you do not need to submit an application to Microsoft Corporation.

When you call Sylvan Prometric, have the following information ready:

- Your name, organization (if any), mailing address, and phone number

- A unique ID number (e.g., your Social Security number)

- The number of the exam you wish to take (70-73 for the "Implementing and Supporting Microsoft Windows NT Workstation 4.0" exam)

- A payment method (e.g., credit card number). If you pay by check, payment is due before the examination can be scheduled. The fee to take each exam is currently $100.

ADDITIONAL RESOURCES

By far, the best source of information about Microsoft certification tests comes from Microsoft itself. Because its products and technologies—and the tests that go with them—change frequently, the best place to go for exam-related information is online.

If you haven't already visited the Microsoft Training and Certification pages, do so right now. As of this writing, the Training and Certification home page resides at *www.microsoft.com/Train_Cert/default.htm*. Note that it may not be there by the time you read this, or it may have been replaced by something new, because the Microsoft site changes regularly. Should this happen, read the following section titled "Coping with Change on the Web."

The menu options in the home page's left column point to important sources of information in the Training and Certification pages. Here's what to check out:

- **Train_Cert Summaries/By Product and Technology** Use this to jump to product-based summaries of all classroom education, training materials, study guides, and other information for specific products. Under the heading "Implementing and Supporting Microsoft Windows NT Workstation 4.0," you will find an entire page of information about Windows NT Workstation 4.0 training and certification. This tells you a lot about your training and preparation options and mentions all the tests that relate to Implementing and Supporting Microsoft Windows NT Workstation 4.0.

- **Technical Certification/Find an Exam** This feature pulls up a search tool that lets you list all Microsoft exams and locate all exams pertinent to any Microsoft certification (MCPS, MCSE, MCT, and so on)—or those exams that cover a particular product. This tool is useful not only to examine the options but also to obtain specific test preparation information, because each exam has its own associated preparation guide.

- **Site Tools/Downloads** Here, you'll find a list of the files and practice tests that Microsoft makes available to the public. These include several items worth downloading, especially the Certification Update, the Personal Exam Prep (PEP) tests, various assessment exams, and a general Exam Study Guide. Try to peruse these materials before taking your first test.

Of course, these are just the high points of what's available in the Microsoft Training and Certification pages. As you browse through them—and we strongly recommend that you do—you'll probably find other information we didn't mention here that is every bit as interesting and compelling.

COPING WITH CHANGE ON THE WEB

Sooner or later, all the specifics we've shared with you about the Microsoft Training and Certification pages, and all the other Web-based resources we mention throughout the rest of this book, will go stale or be replaced by newer information. In some cases, the URLs you find here may lead you to their replacements; in other cases, the URLs will lead nowhere, leaving you with the dreaded 404 error message, "File not found."

When that happens, please don't give up! If you're willing to invest some time and energy, there's always a way to find what you want on the Web. To begin with, most large or complex Web sites—and Microsoft's qualifies on both counts—offer a search engine. As long as you can get to the site itself, you can use this tool to help you find what you need.

The more particular or focused you can make a search request, the more likely it is that the results will include information you can use. For instance, you can search the string "Training and Certification" to produce lots of data about the subject in general, but if you're looking for, for example, the Preparation Guide for Exam 70-073, "Implementing and Supporting Microsoft Windows NT Workstation 4.0," you'll be more likely to get there quickly if you use a search string such as: "Exam 70-073" AND "Preparation Guide." Likewise, if you want to find the Training and Certification downloads, try a search string such as: "Training and Certification" AND "download page."

Finally, don't be afraid to use general search tools like *www.search.com*, *www.altavista.com*, or *www.excite.com* to find related information. Even though Microsoft offers the best online information about its certification exams, there are plenty of third-party sources of information, training, and assistance in this area that do not have to follow a party line like Microsoft does. The bottom line is: if you can't find something where the book says it lives, start looking around.

READ THIS BEFORE YOU BEGIN

HARDWARE AND SOFTWARE REQUIREMENTS

Students and professionals who wish to get the most from these materials should have access to a networked PC that is running Microsoft Windows 95, Windows NT Workstation 4.0, or Windows NT Server 4.0. If Internet access is also available, students should be able to complete all of the exercises in this book. The following table summarizes the requirements and recommendations (in parentheses) for each of these operating systems:

Item	Windows 95	NT Workstation 4.0	NT Server 4.0
MB RAM	16 (32)	12 (64)	16 (64)
MB disk space	90 (200)	116 (400)	124 (1,000)
CPU	386/16 (486+)	486/33 (Pentium)	486/33 (Pentium)
Display type	VGA (SVGA)	VGA (SVGA)	VGA (SVGA)
Network	Yes	Yes	Yes

When it comes to any of these operating systems, it's wise to meet the recommended configurations, rather than the minimum configurations. Although each will work at the minimum configurations, such systems will be painfully slow. In fact, it's nearly impossible to give any of these operating systems too much memory, disk space, or CPU power.

The full version includes Transcender's new test engine and gives you:
- Three full-length exams, including a Computer Adaptive Testing option
- Detailed Score History - Breaks down your score so you can pinpoint weak areas
- Expanded Printing Options - You can now print by section, string or keyword
- Random Exam Option - Randomize test items from all three tests to create additional exams
- Detailed answer explanations and documented references for every question
- Money Back if You Don't Pass Guarantee*
    - *see our Web Site for guarantee details*

To upgrade to the full version:
1. Install WorkstationCert 4.0a Limited version on the computer system with which you will use the full version.
2. When the program starts, choose "Order Full Version."
3. To upgrade immediately, enable your Internet connection, and go to http://www.transcender.com/upgrade/limited/workstationcert4.
4. Follow the instructions posted at the above listed URL.
5. If you do not wish to purchase your upgrade on-line, mail us the completed coupon below (no reproductions or photocopies please). Enclose a check or money order, payable to Transcender Corporation, for $129, plus $6 shipping ($25 outside U.S.).

Terms and Conditions:
Maximum one upgrade per person. Pre-payment by check, money order or credit card is required. For your protection, do not send currency through the mail.

Send to: Upgrade Program
               Transcender Corporation
               242 Louise Avenue
               Nashville, TN 37203

Please send me the WorkstationCert 4.0a Upgrade. Enclosed is my check or credit card number, payable to Transcender Corporation for $129 plus $6 ($25 outside the U.S.). TN residents add $10.64 for sales tax.

Name_____   School_____

Address_____   Credit Card: VISA   MC   AMEX   DISC

City_____ State_____   CC#_____

Zip_____ Country_____   Expiration Date_____

Phone_____   Name on Card_____

E-Mail_____   Signature_____

                                                       CRS042799

Transcender Corporation
SINGLE-USER LICENSE AGREEMENT

IMPORTANT. READ THIS LICENSE AGREEMENT (THE "AGREEMENT") CAREFULLY BEFORE OPENING THE SOFTWARE PACK. YOU AGREE TO BE LEGALLY BOUND BY THE TERMS OF THIS LICENSE AGREEMENT IF YOU EITHER (1) OPEN THE SOFTWARE PACK, OR (2) IF YOU INSTALL, COPY, OR OTHERWISE USE THE ENCLOSED SOFTWARE. IF YOU DO NOT AGREE WITH THESE TERMS, DO NOT OPEN THE SOFTWARE PACK AND DO NOT INSTALL, COPY, OR USE THE SOFTWARE. YOU MAY RETURN THE <u>UNOPENED SOFTWARE</u> TO THE PLACE OF PURCHASE WITHIN FIFTEEN (15) DAYS OF PURCHASE AND RECEIVE A FULL REFUND. NO REFUNDS WILL BE GIVEN FOR SOFTWARE THAT HAS AN OPENED SOFTWARE PACK OR THAT HAS BEEN INSTALLED, USED, ALTERED, OR DAMAGED.

<u>Grant of Single-User License</u>. **YOU ARE THE ONLY PERSON ENTITLED TO USE THIS SOFTWARE.** This is a license agreement between you (an individual) and Transcender Corporation whereby Transcender grants you the non-exclusive and non-transferable license and right to use this software product, updates (if any), and accompanying documentation (collectively the "Software"). ONLY YOU (AND NO ONE ELSE) ARE ENTITLED TO INSTALL, USE, OR COPY THE SOFTWARE. Transcender continues to own the Software, and the Software is protected by copyright and other state and federal intellectual property laws. All rights, title, interest, and all copyrights in and to the Software and any copy made by you remain with Transcender. Unauthorized copying of the Software, or failure to comply with this Agreement will result in automatic termination of this license, and will entitle Transcender to pursue other legal remedies. IMPORTANT, under the terms of this Agreement:

> YOU MAY: (a) install and use the Software on only one computer or workstation, and (b) make one (1) copy of the Software for backup purposes only.

> YOU MAY NOT: (a) use the Software on more than one computer or workstation; (b) modify, translate, reverse engineer, decompile, decode, decrypt, disassemble, adapt, create a derivative work of, or in any way copy the Software (except one backup); (c) sell, rent, lease, sublicense, or otherwise transfer or distribute the Software to any other person or entity without the prior written consent of Transcender (and any attempt to do so shall be void); (d) allow any other person or entity to use the Software or install the Software on a network of any sort (these require a separate license from Transcender); or (e) remove or cover any proprietary notices, labels, or marks on the Software.

<u>Term</u>. The term of the license granted above shall commence upon the earlier of your opening of the Software, your acceptance of this Agreement or your downloading, installation, copying, or use of the Software; and such license will expire three (3) years thereafter or whenever you discontinue use of the Software, whichever occurs first.

<u>Warranty, Limitation of Remedies and Liability</u>. If applicable, Transcender warrants the media on which the Software is recorded to be free from defects in materials and free from faulty workmanship for a period of thirty (30) days after the date you receive the Software. If, during this 30-day period, the Software media is found to be defective or faulty in workmanship, the media may be returned to Transcender for replacement without charge. YOUR SOLE REMEDY UNDER THIS AGREEMENT SHALL BE THE REPLACEMENT OF DEFECTIVE MEDIA AS SET FORTH ABOVE. EXCEPT AS EXPRESSLY PROVIDED FOR MEDIA ABOVE, TRANSCENDER MAKES NO OTHER OR FURTHER WARRANTIES REGARDING THE SOFTWARE, EITHER EXPRESS OR IMPLIED, INCLUDING THE QUALITY OF THE SOFTWARE, ITS PERFORMANCE, MERCHANTABILITY, OR FITNESS FOR A PARTICULAR PURPOSE. THE SOFTWARE IS LICENSED TO YOU ON AN "AS-IS" BASIS. THE ENTIRE RISK AS TO THE SOFTWARE'S QUALITY AND PERFORMANCE REMAINS SOLELY WITH YOU. TRANSCENDER'S EXCLUSIVE AND MAXIMUM LIABILITY FOR ANY CLAIM BY YOU OR ANYONE CLAIMING THROUGH OR ON BEHALF OF YOU ARISING OUT OF YOUR ORDER, USE, OR INSTALLATION OF THE SOFTWARE SHALL NOT UNDER ANY CIRCUMSTANCE EXCEED THE ACTUAL AMOUNT PAID BY YOU TO TRANSCENDER FOR THE SOFTWARE, AND IN NO EVENT SHALL TRANSCENDER BE LIABLE TO YOU OR ANY PERSON OR ENTITY CLAIMING THROUGH YOU FOR ANY INDIRECT, INCIDENTAL, COLLATERAL, EXEMPLARY, CONSEQUENTIAL, OR SPECIAL DAMAGES OR LOSSES ARISING OUT OF YOUR ORDER, USE, OR INSTALLATION OF THE SOFTWARE OR MEDIA DELIVERED TO YOU OR OUT OF THE WARRANTY, INCLUDING WITHOUT LIMITATION, LOSS OF USE, PROFITS, GOODWILL, OR SAVINGS, OR LOSS OF DATA, FILES, OR PROGRAMS STORED BY THE USER. SOME STATES DO NOT ALLOW THE EXCLUSION OR LIMITATION OF INCIDENTAL OR CONSEQUENTIAL DAMAGES, SO THE ABOVE LIMITATIONS MAY NOT APPLY TO YOU.

<u>Restricted Rights</u>. If the Software is acquired by or for the U.S. Government, then it is provided with Restricted Rights. Use, duplication, or disclosure by the U.S. Government is subject to restrictions as set forth in subparagraph (c)(1)(ii) of The Rights in Technical Data and Computer Software clause at DFARS 252.227-7013, or subparagraphs (c)(1) and (2) of the Commercial Computer Software Act—Restricted Rights at 48 CFR 52.227-19, or clause 18-52.227-86(d) of the NASA Supplement to the FAR, as applicable. The contractor/manufacturer is Transcender Corporation, 242 Louise Avenue, Nashville, Tennessee 37203-1812.

<u>General</u>. This Agreement shall be interpreted and governed by the laws of the State of Tennessee without regard to the conflict of laws provisions of such state, and any legal action relating to this Agreement shall be brought in the appropriate state or federal court located in Davidson County, Tennessee, which venue and jurisdiction you agree to submit to, and the prevailing party in any such action shall be entitled to recover reasonable attorneys' fees and expenses as part of any judgment or award. This Agreement is the entire Agreement between us and supersedes any other communication, advertisement, or understanding with respect to the Software. If any provision of this Agreement is held invalid or unenforceable, the remainder shall continue in full force and effect. All provisions of this Agreement relating to disclaimers of warranties, limitation of liability, remedies, or damages, and Transcender's ownership of the Software and other proprietary rights shall survive any termination of this Agreement.

SULicense.111498.doc

INTRODUCTION TO WINDOWS NT WORKSTATION

Microsoft has developed several operating systems over the years to accommodate everything from standalone desktop computers to huge enterprise networks. The Microsoft networking family includes three major categories or types of computer systems: **servers**, **workstations**, and **clients**. The Windows NT network operating system (NOS) is Microsoft's premier entry for networked computing, competing with Novell NetWare in that arena. At present, there are two basic "flavors" of Windows NT: Windows NT Server and Windows NT Workstation. Windows NT Server is in many respects the same software as Windows NT Workstation, except that NT Server provides more power and control over networked environments. Windows NT Workstation is most often used on workstations and clients, although it can act as a server for small networks.

AFTER READING THIS CHAPTER AND COMPLETING THE EXERCISES YOU WILL BE ABLE TO:

- UNDERSTAND THE DIFFERENCES BETWEEN WINDOWS NT WORKSTATION AND OTHER OPERATING SYSTEMS AND THE RELATIONSHIP OF WINDOWS NT WORKSTATION TO WINDOWS NT SERVER

- DESCRIBE THE FEATURES OF THE WINDOWS NT ENVIRONMENT, INCLUDING THE DIFFERENCES BETWEEN MULTITASKING AND MULTITHREADING

- UNDERSTAND THE WINDOWS NT ARCHITECTURE, INCLUDING DIFFERENT KERNEL MODE AND USER MODE OPERATING SYSTEM COMPONENTS

- DESCRIBE THE HARDWARE REQUIREMENTS FOR WINDOWS NT WORKSTATION

- DECIDE HOW TO IMPLEMENT WINDOWS NT WORKSTATION IN AN ENTERPRISE ENVIRONMENT

In this chapter, you'll learn about the development of Windows NT and the basic features of the NT environment and **architecture** (shared by both NT Server and NT Workstation), as well as the differences between NT Server and NT Workstation. You'll also learn about the relationship of Windows NT to other Microsoft operating systems, such as Windows 95. The chapter concludes with an explanation of the hardware requirements for installing NT Workstation and a discussion of two basic models for constructing enterprise networks.

A HISTORY OF WINDOWS NT

The development of Windows NT began in 1988 when Dave Cutler of Digital Equipment Corporation went to work for Microsoft. With the successful implementation of Windows 3.0 in 1990, Microsoft decided to use the Windows graphical interface for the Windows NT front end, but in a networked environment.

Windows NT 3.1 was released in the fall of 1993. Although there was some response to the product, Microsoft soon realized many improvements would have to be made to the operating system (OS) for it to take on Novell's NetWare, which was the leader in network operating systems at the time.

Windows NT 3.50 was released one year later, in 1994. This version included inherent NetWare connectivity as well as enhanced support for connectivity over different network protocols. This version also reduced the initial overhead required to successfully implement NT.

Windows NT 3.51 was released in May 1995. This version included additional device support, integrated disk compression, and compatibility with Windows 95 applications via the Win32 interface. Most experts regard this version as the first "serious contender" to NetWare, and this release fueled the inroads Windows NT has been able to make into NetWare's market share.

Windows NT 4.0 was released in September 1996 in both Server and Workstation versions. NT 4.0 includes many new features that will be discussed throughout this book.

Underneath its various graphical user interfaces, Windows NT is similar to Digital's VMS and Mach/UNIX systems. The NT server component is based on a Mach kernel architecture, which allows the OS to run across multiple processors and allows other subsystems to be added to the system without changing the Kernel. (Kernel architecture is covered later in the chapter.)

The similarity of NT and VMS results from Dave Cutler's previous experience as a principal developer of the VMS operating system. System mechanisms and terminology are similar to VMS. In fact, although NT officially stands for "New Technology," the Windows NT acronym (WNT) derives from VMS—just add a letter to each character in VMS.

WINDOWS NT SERVER AND NT WORKSTATION

Windows **NT Server** is an NOS that has been built to support mission-critical applications and fast, robust networking services. In addition to standard file and print services, NT Server supports the necessary **application programming interfaces (APIs)** and development tools to permit this platform to host all kinds of networked applications. This explains NT's frequent positioning as a so-called "application server."

Because of its highly modular architecture and its profound support for client/server networking, NT Server supports the best of current technologies and is easy to extend for emerging technologies. As its dramatic increase in market share has demonstrated (from less than 5% of all network OS sales in 1994 to over half of all such sales in 1997), NT now enjoys a significant competitive edge.

 Windows **NT Workstation** allows only local administrative control and restricted remote administration, whereas Windows NT Server provides centralized administrative control across all desktops and servers. Although it doesn't have the power of NT Server, NT Workstation is more powerful and reliable than earlier OSs such as Microsoft Windows for Workgroups, or desktop OSs like Windows 95. NT Workstation is a rock-solid multitasking desktop OS, but it can also function well in a peer-to-peer network or as a high-end client in a Windows NT domain network. (Multitasking, peer-to-peer networks, and domains are covered in later sections of this chapter.)

OTHER MICROSOFT OPERATING SYSTEMS

As you might expect, Windows NT networks can accommodate numerous Microsoft clients (in addition to Windows NT Workstation). Such clients include Windows 95 (and by mid-1998, Windows 98), Windows for Workgroups, Windows 3.x, and MS-DOS. Here's a bit more information about each of these OSs and some of their salient features:

- **Windows 95** is a powerful, versatile client operating system. It supports Plug and Play, numerous system wizards, and a powerful graphical user interface (GUI), which make it much easier to install and use than previous versions of Windows. Although Windows 95 is a true 32-bit OS, it is backward-compatible with earlier Windows and MS-DOS 16-bit applications.

- **Windows 98** is currently available only in beta form, but it promises to extend the capability of Windows 95 to even higher levels. In addition to supporting all the features found in Windows 95, it includes a new 32-bit file system (FAT32), plus extremely tight integration between the local desktop and the view of network resources provided by Internet Explorer in Windows 95 (in Windows 98, the desktop Explorer and the Internet Explorer are welded into one utility that combines local and networked resources under a single view).

- **Windows for Workgroups (Wf W)** includes built-in, peer-to-peer networking capabilities. It was designed primarily to share resources and files among workgroups, which may be defined as a small collection of networked computer users that undertake similar tasks or share common responsibilities. Wf W is a 16-bit OS that remains backward-compatible with MS-DOS. Wf W was also the first Microsoft client OS to include built-in networking capabilities.

- **Windows 3.x** was originally designed as a single-user desktop OS, but its immediate popularity ensured quick release of add-on products that enabled its use as a network client (for a while, this created a large aftermarket for Windows networking add-ons in the early to mid 1990s). Like Wf W, Windows 3.x is a 16-bit system that is backward-compatible with MS-DOS. As with DOS, Microsoft recommends using the Microsoft Network Client 3.0 to add network capabilities to Windows 3.x.

- **MS-DOS** is another single-user desktop OS. As with Windows 3.x, Microsoft recommends using the Microsoft Network Client 3.0 for MS-DOS to permit DOS computers to participate in an NT-based network. MS-DOS cannot execute any Windows applications, unless Windows 3.x or Wf W is installed on a properly equipped DOS machine.

THE WINDOWS NT ENVIRONMENT

Windows NT offers many unique features not found in other NOSs. These capabilities include strong backward compatiblity, in that Windows NT can emulate older 16- and 32-bit Microsoft environments, including "well-behaved" DOS and 16-bit Windows applications and most Windows 95 applications. Windows NT is built around a modular systems architecture that permits easy enhancement and extension and includes powerful security and access controls. These and other important Windows NT features are covered in the sections that follow.

PORTABILITY

Windows NT operates with numerous types of CPUs. This can be advantageous to organizations with existing investments in different kinds of server systems. At present, Windows NT supports these microprocessors (please notice some of the caveats mentioned):

- **PowerPC**: Microsoft announced in June 1997 that this support will not extend to Windows NT 5.0.

- **MIPS R4x00**: Microsoft announced in January 1997 that it will not continue to support the MIPS processor family.

- **Intel Alpha AXP**: Intel has recently purchased this CPU family from DEC, and its future is shrouded in mystery.

- Intel 486, Pentium, Pentium II, Pentium Pro, and clones are all fully supported by Windows NT.

MULTITHREADING

Multithreading refers to code design in which individual tasks within a single process space can operate more or less independently as separate, lightweight execution modules called threads. A **thread** represents the minimal unit of code in an application or system that can be scheduled for execution; threads are called lightweight execution modules because switching among or between threads within the context of a single process involves very little overhead and is therefore extremely fast. Within a process, all threads share the same memory and system resources. A **process**, on the other hand, is a collection of one or more threads that share a common application or system activity focus. Processes are called heavyweight execution modules because switching among processes involves a great deal of overhead, including copying large amounts of data from RAM to disk for outbound processes, and repeating that process to copy large amounts of data from disk to RAM for inbound ones. Under Windows NT, it normally takes upward of one hundred times longer to switch among processes than it does to switch among threads.

Multithreading allows an OS to execute multiple threads concurrently from a single application. If the computer on which such threads run includes multiple CPUs, threads can even execute simultaneously, each on a different CPU. Even on single-CPU computers, threaded implementations speed up applications and create an environment where multiple tasks can be active between the foreground (what's showing on the screen) and the background (what's not on screen). Windows NT is unusually adept and efficient, as multithreaded operating systems go.

MULTITASKING

One of the great features of Windows NT is **multitasking**—a mode of CPU operation that enables a computer to process more than one task at a time. Windows NT supports two types of multitasking—preemptive and cooperative. **Preemptive multitasking** defines a processor scheduling regime in which an OS maintains strict control over how long any execution thread (a single task within a multithreaded application or an entire single-threaded application) may take possession of the CPU. The reason this scheduling regime is called preemptive is because the OS can decide at any time to swap out the currently executing thread should another, higher-priority thread make a bid for execution (the termination of the lower-priority thread is called preemption). NT supports multiple threads and allows multiple duties to be spread among multiple processors. Most native NT applications are written to take advantage of threads, but older applications may not be as well equipped.

Cooperative multitasking defines a processor scheduling regime in which individual applications take control over the CPU for as long as they like (because this means that applications must be well behaved, this approach is sometimes called "good guy" scheduling). Unfortunately, this type of multitasking can lead to stalled or hung systems, should any application fail to release its control over the CPU. Windows 3.x is one of the best examples of this type of environment because it runs on top of DOS, a single-threaded OS. By contrast, native 32-bit Windows NT applications are not hindered by such limitations. In Windows NT, all

16-bit Windows applications run by default within a single virtual machine, which is granted only preemptive CPU access. This guarantees that other processes active on a Windows NT machine will not be stymied by an ill-behaved Windows 3.x application.

SECURITY

Windows NT incorporates a variety of security features, all of which share a common aim: to enable efficient, reliable control of access to all resources and assets on a network. To that end, one key security feature is a protected, mandatory logon system. But these features extend to include memory protection, system auditing over all kinds of events and activities, precise controls on file and directory access, and all kinds of network access limitations. These security features, among many others, permit a suitably modified version of Windows NT to comply fully with the European Economic Community's E2, and the US Department of Defense's C2 security specifications (a special C2 security audit and enhancement module is included as part of the Windows NT Workstation and Server Resource Kits).

Windows NT is an operating environment developed to address the following business security needs:

- Enterprise isolation
- Multilevel security
- Auditing and resource tracking
- Isolation of hardware-dependent code

Also, numerous third-party companies offer security enhancements or extensions to Windows NT that cover everything from biometric authentication add-ons (so fingerprints or retinal scans can control system access) to firewalls and proxy servers to isolate NT-based networks from the Internet or other publicly accessible networks.

FILE SYSTEMS

Windows NT supports two primary file systems:

- **File Allocation Table (FAT)**, the file system used by DOS. The implementation that NT uses is a Virtual FAT, or VFAT, system that adds support for long file names, or LFNs, to FAT's original capabilities.
- **New Technology File System (NTFS)**, a high-performance, secure, and object-oriented file system introduced in Windows NT.

 Versions of Windows NT up through 3.51 supported the High Performance File System (HPFS), originally present in OS/2 and LAN Manager. NT 4.0 no longer supports HPFS.

Chapter 5 covers file systems in detail.

SUPPORT FOR MULTIPLE CLIENTS

Windows NT supports a wide variety of potential client platforms that can interact with resources on a Windows NT-based network. Please note that the following list of clients includes two third-party operating systems, as well as a broad range of Microsoft products.

- Windows 95

- Windows 3.x and Windows for Workgroups

- MS-DOS

- Macintosh

- OS/2

- Windows NT Workstation

 If TCP/IP is used on a Windows-NT based network, any computer that supports this protocol can function as a client, even if with only limited capabilities. Because nearly all versions of UNIX include built-in support for TCP/IP, this extends the reach of Windows-NT based networks considerably.

MULTIPROCESSOR SUPPORT

Windows NT supports true **multiprocessing**—support for up to two CPUs is included in every standard version of Windows NT Workstation, and special OEM versions that can support up to 16 CPUs are available. On multiple-CPU systems, as many processes or threads as there are CPUs can execute simultaneously. This means that multiple applications can execute at the same time, each on a different processor. The network administrator can adjust the priority levels for different processors to make sure that preferred applications get a bigger slice of the CPUs that are available.

COMPATIBILITY

Windows NT is compatible with the following types of applications:

- DOS 16-bit

- Native 32-bit (**Win32**)

- **OS/2** 1.x character based

- POSIX-1-compliant (**POSIX** is a platform-independent OS specification based on UNIX; 1.1 represents the lowest level of recognized POSIX compliance)

- Windows 3.1 or Windows for Workgroups 16-bit (**Win16**)

Any application that attempts direct access to hardware will not work under Windows NT; as soon as such access is attempted, this will cause the program to be halted and its process to be terminated. Unfortunately, such programs include many DOS applications, especially those of older vintage (DOS 5.0 and earlier), but Win16 applications that use virtual device drivers (VXDs) are also subject to this limitation.

STORAGE

Windows NT supports huge amounts of hard disk and memory space:

- *RAM:* 4 GB (Note: only 2 GB are available to any single process, including the OS kernel itself)
- *Hard disk space:* 16 Exabytes (NTFS only; practically speaking, no NT Servers have yet broken past the Terabyte barrier for storage—this reflects limitations on current disk technology and costs, rather than a limitation on Windows NT)

CONNECTIVITY

Windows NT supports a wide variety of networking protocols. The following protocols are included in the core OS:

- **AppleTalk**: The protocol suite developed by Apple for use with Macintosh computers. Note: Windows NT Workstation can use AppleTalk to communicate with Apple printers and similar devices, but (unlike Server) it does not support client services for Macintosh users.
- **Data Link Control (DLC)**: The protocol used to connect to IBM mainframes and network-attached printers.
- **NetBEUI**: An enhanced set of network and transport protocols built in the late 1980s to carry NetBIOS information, when earlier implementations became too limiting for continued use.
- **NWLink**: Microsoft 32-bit implementation for Windows NT of Novell's IPX/SPX protocol stack that's native to NetWare.
- **Transmission Control Protocol/Internet Protocol (TCP/IP)**: The set of protocols used on the Internet, which has been embraced as a vital technology by Microsoft. At present, Windows NT and Windows 95 include outstanding support for TCP/IP.

NT is compatible with many existing network types and environments, and it has native support for:

- TCP/IP intranets/Internet
- Integrated remote access networks

- Macintosh networks
- Microsoft networks (MS–DOS, Windows for Workgroups, LAN Manager)
- Enhanced NetWare connectivity

WINDOWS NT ARCHITECTURE

The internal organization and architecture of Windows NT deeply influences its capabilities and behavior. Understanding its system components helps in understanding differences between NT Server and Workstation as well. Figure 1-1 shows a model of the Windows NT operating system components and its two major modes of operation. The following sections discuss these components and operating modes. Chapter 14 covers NT architecture in more detail.

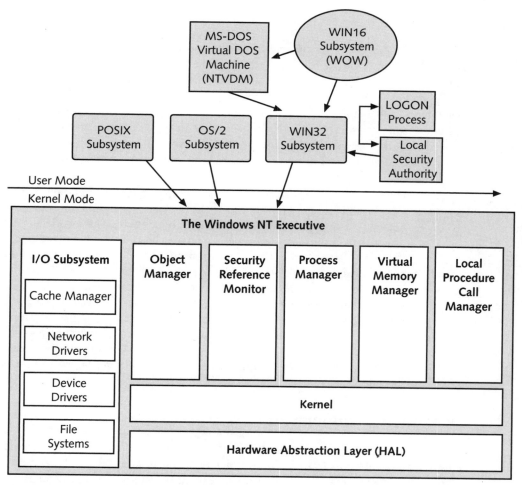

Figure 1-1   Windows NT architecture

MODULAR, COMPONENT-ORIENTED DESIGN

Windows NT is a modular OS. In other words, Windows NT is not built as a single, large program; instead, it consists of numerous small software elements, or modules, that cooperate to provide the system's networking and computing capabilities. Every unique function, code segment, and system control resides in a distinct module, so that no two modules share any code. This method of construction allows Windows NT to be easily amended, expanded, or patched as needed. Furthermore, the Windows NT components communicate with one another through well-defined interfaces, so that even if a module's internals change (or a new version replaces an old one), as long as the interface is not altered, other components need not be aware of any such changes (except perhaps to take advantage of new functionality that was hitherto unavailable).

MODES OF OPERATION

All Windows NT processes operate in one of two modes: **User mode** or **Kernel mode**. A **mode** represents a certain level of system and hardware access and is distinguished by its programming, the kinds of services and functions it is permitted to request, and the controls that are applied to its requests for system resources. Each mode includes only those specific components and capabilities that might be needed to perform the set of operations that is permitted within that mode. The details of what's inherent to User mode and Kernel mode will be explained further in the following sections. Windows NT uses modes very similar to UNIX and VMS, further proof of its modularity and built-in security mechanisms.

Windows NT is an object-oriented operating system; in User mode, any request for a system resource ultimately becomes a request for a particular object. An **object** is an aggregate that consists of a set of attributes with associated data values, plus a set of related services that can be performed on that object. Because objects may be shared or referenced by one or more processes, they have an existence independent of any particular process in the NT environment. Objects are identified by type (which defines what attributes and services they support) and by instance (which defines a particular entity of a certain type—for example, there may be many objects of type "file," but only one object can have a unique combination of directory specification and file-name). Windows NT not only controls access to individual objects, it can even control which users or groups are permitted to perform particular services related to such objects.

User Mode Environments

All user interaction with a Windows NT system occurs through some User mode process or another. User mode is granted only moderate access to Windows NT system resources. In other words, any User mode request for objects or services must pass through the Executive

1

Services components in the Kernel mode to obtain access. In addition to supporting native 32-bit Windows APIs, a variety of User mode subsystems enable NT to emulate Win16 and DOS environments, and even permit OS/2 character mode and POSIX-1-compliant software to be executed.

Windows NT supports three core environment subsystems:

- Win32 supports Windows NT and Windows 95 32-bit applications directly, and through emulation of virtual DOS machines (VDMs) supports both Windows 16-bit and DOS applications.

- POSIX supports POSIX-1 applications, but these have only limited functionality; third-party solutions (most notably, those from SoftWay Systems) offer considerably more powerful and capable POSIX implementations for Windows NT.

- OS/2 provides support for character-mode OS/2 1.1 applications (unfortunately, this makes most modern GUI-based OS/2 applications unusable in this environment; add-ons to extend this functionality are available from Microsoft and third parties).

Each subsystem is built around an API that enables suitable Win16, DOS, OS/2, or POSIX applications to run by emulating their native OSs. But even though other subsystems may be involved in some applications, the Win32 subsystem controls the Windows NT user interface and mediates all input/output requests for all other subsystems. In that sense, it is the core interface subsystem for applications in User mode.

User Mode Security

As part of the NT User mode, the security subsystem is solely responsible for the logon process. The security subsystem works directly with key elements in the Kernel mode to verify the username and password for any logon attempt and permits only valid combinations to obtain access to a system. When a logon attempt occurs, the security subsystem creates an authentication package that contains the username and password provided in the Windows NT Security logon window. This authentication package is then turned over to the Kernel mode, where a module called the Security Reference Monitor (SRM)—the portion of the security subsystem that verifies usernames and passwords against the security accounts database—examines the package and compares its contents to a security accounts database. If the logon request is invalid, the User mode receives a message that the logon was incorrect. For valid requests, the SRM constructs an access token—which contains a summary of the logged-on user's security access rights—that is then returned to the security subsystem and then to the logon process in User mode.

 To gain access to the logon interface of Windows NT, the user must enter a special key combination called the "Windows NT attention sequence." This consists of Ctrl-Alt-Del pressed at once. The attention sequence invokes the Windows NT logon process; because this key sequence cannot be faked, it guarantees that this process (which also resides in a protected memory area) is not subject to manipulation by would-be crackers.

KERNEL MODE

The Kernel mode, which is a highly privileged processing mode, defines the inner workings of Windows NT. All components in Kernel mode take execution priority over User mode subsystems and processes. In fact, some key elements within the Kernel mode (represented by the block labeled "Kernel" beneath the Executive Services modules in Figure 1-1) remain resident in memory at all times and cannot be swapped to disk by the Virtual Memory Manager. This is the part of the OS that handles process priority and scheduling (it's what provides the ability to preempt executing processes and schedule new processes that is at the heart of any preemptive, multitasking operating system, such as Windows NT).

The Kernel insulates hardware and core system services from direct access by user applications. That's why user applications must request any access to hardware or low-level resources from the Kernel mode. If the request is permitted to proceed—and this mediated approach always gives Windows NT a chance to check any request against the access permitted by the access token associated with the requester—the Kernel handles the request and returns any related results to the requesting User mode process. This mediated approach also helps maintain reliable control over the entire computer and protects the system from ill-behaved applications. At a greater level of detail, the Kernel mode may be divided into three primary subsystems: the Executive Services, the Kernel, and the Hardware Abstraction Layer (HAL).

Executive Services

The **Executive Services**, sometimes called the NT Executive, defines the interfaces that permit Kernel and User mode subsystems to communicate. The NT Executive consists of six modules: the I/O Manager, the Object Manager, the Security Reference Monitor (SRM), the Process Manager, the Virtual Memory Manager (VMM), and the Local Procedure Call Manager, as described in the following sections.

I/O Manager   The I/O Manager handles all operating system input and output. The I/O Manager receives requests for I/O services from applications, determines what driver is needed, and requests that driver for the application. The I/O Manager comprises the following components:

- *Cache Manager:* Handles disk caching for all file systems. This service works with the Virtual Memory Manager to maintain performance. It also works with the file-system drivers to keep file integrity.

- *Network drivers:* Actually a subarchitecture in and of itself. This will be discussed later.

- *Device drivers:* Minidrivers that are 32-bit and multiprocessor compatible.

- *File-system drivers:* All disk I/O is handled by a file system, of which Windows NT supports several.

1

Object Manager   The Object Manager manages all system objects by maintaining object naming and security functions. It allocates system objects, monitors their use, and removes them when they are no longer needed. The Object Manager maintains the following system objects:

- Directory objects
- Object Type objects
- Link objects
- Semaphore and Event objects
- Process and Thread objects
- Port objects
- File objects

Security Reference Monitor (SRM)   The Security Reference Monitor compares the access rights of a user (as encoded in an access token) with the Access Control List (ACL) associated with an individual object. If the user has sufficient rights to honor an access request after the access token and ACL are reconciled, the requested access will be granted. Whenever a user spawns a process, that process runs within the user's security context and inherits a copy of the user's security token. This means that under most circumstances, any process launched by a Windows NT user cannot obtain broader access rights than those associated with the account that launched it.

Process Manager   The Process Manager primarily tracks two Kernel-dispatched objects: processes and threads. It is responsible for creating and tracking processes and threads, and then for deleting them (and cleaning up) after they're no longer needed.

Virtual Memory Manager (VMM)   The Virtual Memory Manager keeps track of the addressable memory space in the Windows NT environment. This includes both physical RAM and one or more paging files on disk, which are called virtual memory when used in concert. The operation of the VMM will be discussed in more detail later in this chapter.

Local Procedure Call Manager   The Local Procedure Call Manager controls application communications with server processes such as the Win32 subsystem—the set of application services provided by the 32-bit version of Microsoft Windows. This makes applications behave as if **Dynamic Link Library (DLL)** calls are handled directly, and helps to explain the outstanding abilities of Windows NT to emulate 16-bit DOS and Windows runtime environments.

The Kernel

All processes in NT consist of one or more threads coordinated and scheduled by the **Kernel**. Executive Services use the Kernel to communicate with each other concerning the processes that they share. The Kernel runs in privileged mode (Ring 0) along with the HAL and the other Executive Services. This means that the Kernel is allowed direct access to all system resources. It cannot be paged to disk, meaning that it must run in real memory. A misbehaved Kernel process can stall or crash the OS. That's the primary reason why direct access to this level of system operation is not available to User mode applications.

The Hardware Abstraction Layer (HAL)

The **Hardware Abstraction Layer (HAL)** ultimately controls all direct access to hardware. This is the only module written entirely in low-level hardware-dependent code. Its goal is to isolate any hardware-dependent code in order to prevent direct access to hardware. It is the HAL that helps to make Windows NT scalable across multiple processors and portable across multiple platforms, because the HAL is the only part of the entire OS that must be completely reimplemented to run in different processing environments.

NT MEMORY ARCHITECTURE

The Windows NT memory architecture helps make this operating system robust, reliable, and powerful. As noted earlier, NT can manage as much as 4 GB of RAM (2 for User mode, 2 for Kernel mode); however, most servers available today top out between 1 and 2 GB of RAM. Figure 1-2 illustrates the Windows NT memory architecture.

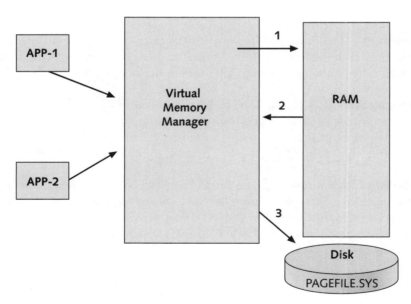

Figure 1-2   Windows NT virtual memory model

Windows NT uses a flat 32-bit memory model. It is based on a **virtual memory**, **demand paging** method that is a flat, linear address space of up to 2 GB allocated to each

32-bit application. Non–32-bit Windows applications such as Win16, MS-DOS, or OS/2 are managed similarly except that all subsystem components including the actual application run within a single 2 GB address space.

The unit of memory that the Virtual Memory Manager manipulates is called a **page**. A page is 4 KB in size. The disk-based files to which pages are stored and retrieved are called page files or paging files. These files are also used for memory reindexing and mapping to avoid allocating memory between non-used contiguous space or to prevent fragmentation of physical memory.

The Windows NT memory model is a flat model that grows based on the demand for memory, as opposed to models in which every section of memory has a fixed role (as in the problematic Conventional, Expanded, HMA, and Extended Memory architecture present in MS-DOS and Windows 3.x).

COMPARISON OF NT WORKSTATION AND NT SERVER

On Windows NT Workstation, the user's foreground application maintains highest priority. All applications are granted minimum memory at startup. An internal Scheduler uses short timeslices for maximum user response. On Windows NT Server, the network services retain the highest system priority, and file cache is preserved above all other services. The NT Server Scheduler uses long timeslices to respond to network requests.

Here are some further differences between NT Server and NT Workstation:

- NT Server can support up to 32 CPUs (only 4 out of the box)—NT Workstation is limited to 2 CPUs (but special OEM—original equipment manufacturer—versions that can support larger numbers of processors are available).

- NT Server supports fault tolerance through disk striping with parity and disk mirroring—NT Workstation does not.

- NT Server gives system priority to network services—NT Workstation gives priority to the foreground application.

- NT Server Internet Information Server (IIS) and NT Workstation Peer Web Services (PWS) are basically the same, but the PWS license prohibits more than 10 simultaneous connections—thus, NT Workstation may not be viable as a low-cost Web server.

COMPARISON OF NT WORKSTATION AND WINDOWS 95

Windows NT Workstation and Windows 95 both offer the benefits of a 32-bit desktop operating system. By implementing a 32-bit desktop architecture in your computing environment, you can take advantage of the new generation of 32-bit applications, exciting new technologies, and more reliable and manageable operating systems. Windows NT Workstation and Windows 95 are the most widely used 32-bit desktop OSs today, for numerous reasons:

- Most of the innovations in graphics, multimedia, productivity, and the Internet occur first on these operating systems.
- All the top-selling applications are written to take advantage of the 32-bit environment.
- The 32-bit architecture is fostering new levels of hardware support.
- 32-bit OSs are less costly to own and maintain than their predecessors, considering setup, maintenance, reliability, support tools, and ease of use.

Increasing numbers of users are choosing Windows NT Workstation over Windows 95 for its improved and expanded memory management capabilities, increased robustness and stability, and its support for preemptive multitasking. Taken together, these factors deliver a system that is more powerful and more capable than its Windows 95 counterpart, especially when power users seek to run numerous applications in tandem.

NT Workstation Hardware Requirements

The hardware requirements defined by Microsoft for Windows NT Workstation on Intel-based systems are:

- 486-based 33 MHz (or faster) or Pentium-based system
- 12 MB of memory (RAM); 16 MB recommended
- 110 MB of available hard disk space
- CD-ROM drive or access to a CD-ROM over a computer network
- VGA (or better) display adapter
- Microsoft Mouse or compatible pointing device

The requirements for NT Workstation on RISC-based systems are:

- Workstation with Alpha AXP, MIPS R4x00 or PowerPC processor
- 16 MB of memory
- 110 MB of available hard disk space
- CD-ROM drive or access to a CD-ROM over a computer network
- VGA or higher resolution display adapter
- Microsoft Mouse or compatible pointing device

Optional hardware for either Intel or RISC-based system includes:

- Network adapter card
- Audio board/sound card

Although it is a good indicator of possible success, simply meeting the list of hardware requirements does not guarantee that all elements of Windows NT Workstation will be fully compatible or operational. Fortunately, Microsoft supplies two additional tools that you can use to validate your hardware: the Qualifier disk and the Hardware Compatibility List (HCL).

THE HARDWARE QUALIFIER DISK

With some OSs, the only way to determine whether a piece of ancillary equipment, or even an entire system, is compatible is to attempt to install it. This is a completely empirical approach: If the software installs, and then runs, only then can you assume that the hardware is acceptable. If installation fails, you may get no feedback about which device or what setting caused the failure. Microsoft has eliminated the need for trial-and-error installations with its Windows **NT Hardware Qualifier (NTHQ)** utility, which is included on the NT CD-ROM.

To make it as simple as possible, NTHQ runs under DOS and checks your computer for potential hardware problems or mismatches. Better yet, NTHQ provides a complete list of all potential problem devices it finds, without requiring a full-blown installation of Windows NT. In fact, you can run this utility on a PC with no OS resident because the Makedisk.bat utility creates a bootable DOS disk on which it places the NTHQ utility. By booting the machine from the disk, you can then run NTHQ, and it will tell you most of what you want to know.

The NTHQ suffers from one important limitation, however: Its hardware list is frozen in time at August 1996—the Windows NT 4.0 release date. Computers with newer components may be compatible with NT because they have current drivers, but those components may not even have existed when the version of the NTHQ on the NT 4.0 CD was built. NTHQ may therefore flag them as potential problems. This is where the tool in the next section comes in handy!

Hardware Compatibility List (HCL)

When it comes to configuring a Windows NT machine, the Microsoft **Hardware Compatibility List (HCL)** is an essential piece of documentation. The HCL supplies a list of all known NT-compatible hardware devices at the time of its creation. The HCL also points to each such device's driver—which may be native (included as part of the NT install program), on a subdirectory on the Windows NT CD, or available only from the device's vendor. Because NT only works properly if a system's hardware is NT-compatible, it's always a good idea to use the HCL as your primary reference when evaluating a prospective NT system or when selecting components for such a system.

Finding the HCL   Finding the HCL is not always easy. The easiest place to look is on your NT CD-ROM, where it resides in the \Support\Help folder as a help file. But the HCL is not a static document—Microsoft Quality Labs are constantly updating this file. The version of the HCL on the Windows NT Workstation CD-ROM is probably dated August 8, 1996, and lots of new drivers and devices have been introduced in the interim.

That's why it's a good idea to look for the most current version of the HCL, especially when you'll be working with new hardware. The most recent version of the HCL is available on the Microsoft Web site for online viewing or it may be downloaded as a help file. The HCL has changed homes (URLs) several times since NT 4.0 was released and it may change homes again. But when last checked, the HCL lived at *http://www.microsoft.com/isapi/hwtest/hsearchn4.idc.*

To find the HCL's current residence, use the search facility at *http://www.microsoft.com*, select Windows NT Server as your product focus, and search on "HCL." On the other hand, if you have access to a copy of the TechNet CD, a new copy of the HCL is published each time it changes, so the most recent copy on a TechNet CD is guaranteed to be less than four months old. Here again, you can use the search facility with the same string "HCL." It's normally located on the one of the Supplemental Drivers and Patches CDs, and its exact whereabouts appears in the Technical Notes for Windows NT Workstation.

Why the HCL Is So Important   Windows NT controls hardware directly; unlike other OSs, it does not require access to a PC's BIOS (as is the case with Windows 95 and earlier versions of DOS and Windows). Although this gives NT a much finer degree of control over hardware, it also means that Windows NT works only with devices that have drivers written specifically for NT. This is especially true for SCSI adapters, video cards, and network interfaces.

Don't be misled into thinking that because a device works with Windows 95 it will work as well (or at all) with Windows NT 4.0. There's no substitute for systematically checking every hardware device on a system against the HCL to determine conclusively if it will work with Windows NT. Please note also that Microsoft's technical support policy is that anything that's not on the HCL is automatically not supported for Windows NT. If you ask Microsoft for support on a system that contains elements not listed in the HCL, it will blame all problems on the incompatible hardware, and may not give you any help at all!

ENTERPRISE MODELS

An enterprise model is a scheme or method of attaching two or more networks together. In an enterprise model, networks are divided into logical groups to determine how network resources may be distributed and to control access. There are two enterprise models to which a Windows NT Workstation can belong: a workgroup or a domain.

WORKGROUP MODEL

The **workgroup model** for networking distributes resources, administration, and security throughout a network. Each computer in a workgroup may be either a server or a client, or both. All computers in a workgroup are equal in stature and responsibility, and are therefore called peers. That's why a workgroup model network is also known as a type of **peer-to-peer** network.

In a workgroup, each computer also maintains its own unique set of resources, accounts, and security information. Workgroups are quite useful for groups of less than 10 computers, and may be used with groups as large as 25 to 50 machines (with increasing difficulty). Table 1-1 lists the pros and cons of workgroup networking.

Table 1-1   Pros and Cons of Workgroup Networks

Advantages	Disadvantages
Easy to share resources	No centralized administration
Resources are distributed across all machines	No centralized account management
Little administrative overhead	No centralized control of resources
Simple to design	No centralized security management
Easy to implement	Inefficient for more than 20 workstations
Convenient for small groups in close proximity	Requires user accounts on each peer
Less expensive, does not require a central server	Requires increased training to operate as both client and server

DOMAIN MODEL

By requiring one or more servers to be dedicated to the job of controlling a domain, the **domain model** adds a layer of complexity to networking. But the domain model also centralizes all shared resources and creates a single point of administrative and security control. In a domain, any member of the domain acts exclusively either as a client or a server. Servers control and manage resources, whereas clients are user computers that may request access to whatever resources are controlled by servers.

Its centralized organization makes the domain model simpler to manage from an administrative and security standpoint, because any changes made to a domain accounts database will automatically apply across the entire network. According to Microsoft, domains are useful for groups of 10 or more computers. Microsoft estimates the maximum practical size of a single domain at somewhere around 25,000 computers, but also describes other multi-domain models that it claims can grow to almost arbitrary sizes. In real-world applications, 3,000 is believed to represent a reasonable upper limit on the number of machines in a single domain.

No matter how many computers it contains, any Windows NT domain requires a single **Primary Domain Controller (PDC)** and zero or more **Backup Domain Controllers (BDCs)** to be present. These domain controllers maintain a database that contains information about and access controls for all the resources and objects known to the network. All other servers and clients on a domain-based network interact with a PDC or BDC to handle resource requests. Table 1-2 summarizes the pros and cons of the domain model.

Table 1-2   Pros and Cons of Domain Networks

Advantages	Disadvantages
Centralized resource sharing	Significant administrative effort and overhead
Centralized resource controls	Complicated, convoluted design
Centralized account management	Requires one or more powerful, expensive servers
Centralized security management	Bullet-proof security is hard to achieve
Efficient for virtually unlimited workstations	Expense for domain controllers and access lags increases with network size
Redundancy of accounts on BDCs	Each BDC imposes extra cost and administration
Users only need to be trained to use clients	Some understanding of domain networks remains necessary
Not restricted to close proximity	Larger scope requires more user documentation and training

CHAPTER SUMMARY

In this chapter, you were introduced to the features and architecture of Windows NT and to similarities and differences between NT Server and NT Workstation. One of the primary features of Windows NT is its robust security. Windows NT is also versatile, with support for multiple application subsystems. Windows NT was designed to support multiple CPUs to establish true multitasking through multithreading. It is an inherently networkable operating system with built-in connectivity solutions for NetWare, Macintosh, and TCP/IP. This allows easy implementation on multivendor networks.

The Windows NT virtual memory model combines the use of both physical RAM and paging files into a demand paging mechanism to maximize memory use and efficiency. Virtual memory is one of the many similarities between Windows NT Workstation and Windows 95 that was pointed out in this chapter along with their differences. The chapter concluded with a discussion of the issues involved in planning a Windows NT Workstation environment, including hardware requirements and enterprise networking models.

KEY TERMS

- **AppleTalk** — This is the network protocol stack used predominantly in Apple Macintosh Networks. It is bundled with Windows NT.
- **application programming interface (API)** — A set of software routines referenced by an application to access underlying application services.
- **architecture** — The layout of operating system components and their relationships with one another.

- **Backup Domain Controller (BDC)** — The network computer that contains a backup copy of the domain's security policy and database. The BDC is able to authenticate network users at logon.

- **client** — A computer used to access network resources.

- **cooperative multitasking** — A computing environment in which an individual application maintains control the entire time any of its threads are using operating time on the CPU.

- **Data Link Control (DLC)** — A low-level network protocol designed for IBM connectivity, remote booting, and network printing.

- **demand paging** — The act of requesting free pages of memory for an active application from RAM.

- **Dynamic Link Library (DLL)** — A Microsoft Windows executable code module that is loaded on demand.

- **domain model** — A centralized enterprise model used in Microsoft networks.

- **Executive Services** — The collection of Kernel mode components designed to act as an oligarchy of operating system management.

- **File Allocation Table (FAT)** — The File Allocation Table file system. The file system used in versions of MS-DOS.

- **Hardware Abstraction Layer (HAL)** — One of the few components of the Windows NT architecture that is written in hardware-dependent code. It is designed to protect hardware resources.

- **Hardware Compatibility List (HCL)** — Microsoft's updated list of supported hardware for Windows NT.

- **Kernel** — The core of the Microsoft Windows NT operating system. It is designed to facilitate all activity within the Executive Services.

- **Kernel mode** — The level where objects can only be manipulated by a thread directly from an application subsystem.

- **mode** — A programming and operational separation of components, functions, and services.

- **MS-DOS** — One of the most popular character-based operating systems for personal computers. Many DOS concepts are still in use by modern operating systems.

- **multiprocessing** — The ability to distribute threads among multiple CPUs on the same system.

- **multitasking** — The ability to run more than one program at the same time.

- **multithreading** — The ability of an OS and the hardware to simultaneously execute multiple pieces of code (or threads) from a single application.

- **NetBEUI** — The NetBIOS Extended User Interface. A common protocol used by Microsoft and IBM for the purpose of small network communication.

- **New Technology File System (NTFS)** — The high-performance enhanced file system introduced by Windows NT.

- **NT Hardware Qualifier Utility (NTHQ)** — A bootable disk used for querying hardware to determine compatibility with Windows NT.

- **NT Server** — A network OS server designed to support mission-critical applications and provide fast and reliable internetworking capabilities.

- **NT Workstation** — An operating system that includes all of the capabilities of Microsoft Windows for Workgroups, but in a more powerful, reliable, and multitasking environment.

- **NWLink** — Microsoft's implementation of Novell's IPX/SPX protocol used for Microsoft networking or for facilitating connectivity with Novell networks.

- **object** — A collection of data and/or abilities of a service that can be shared and used by one or more processes.

- **OS/2** — An operating system currently supported by IBM. NT allows for some OS/2 application support.

- **page** — The unit of memory that the Virtual Memory Manager manipulates.

- **peer-to-peer** — A type of networking in which each computer can be a client to other computers and act as a server as well.

- **POSIX** — A source-compatible subsystem that is sanctioned by the IEEE for maintaining consistency between Windows NT and flavors of UNIX.

- **PowerPC** — A processor architecture co-developed by IBM and Motorola that is one of the RISC-based processors supported by Windows NT 4.0.

- **preemptive multitasking** — A computing environment in which the OS maintains control over the duration of operating time any thread (a single process of an application) is granted on the CPU.

- **Primary Domain Controller (PDC)** — The NT-based networked computer that is responsible for maintaining the domain's SAM database and for authenticating users. The PDC is also in charge of synchronizing security information with the BDCs.

- **process** — A collection of one or more threads.

- **server** — The networked computer that responds to client requests for network resources.

- **thread** — The most basic unit of programming code that can be scheduled for execution.

- **Transmission Control Protocol/Internet Protocol (TCP/IP)** — A suite of protocols evolved from the US Department of Defense's ARPANET. It's used for connectivity in LANs as well as the Internet.

- **User mode** — The area where private user applications and their respective subsystems lie.

- **virtual memory** — An NT Kernel service that stores memory pages that are not currently in use by the system. This frees up memory for other uses. Virtual memory also hides the swapping of memory from applications and higher-level services.

- **Win16** — The subsystem in Windows NT that allows for the support of 16-bit Windows applications.

- **Win32** — The main 32-bit subsystem used by Win32 applications and other application subsystems.

- **Windows 3.x** — An older, 16-bit version of Windows. NT supports backward compatibility with most Windows 3.x applications.

- **Windows 95** — The 32-bit version of Windows that can operate as a standalone system or in a networked environment.

- **Windows 98** — The next version of Windows, currently in beta form, that includes many of the features found in Windows 95, but with a new file system and integrated Explorer utility.
- **Windows for Workgroups (WfW)** — A 16-bit peer-to-peer network operating system that is backward compatible with MS-DOS.
- **workgroup** — A scheme in which resources, administration, and security are distributed throughout the network.
- **workgroup model** — The networking setup in which users are managed jointly through the use of workgroups to which users are assigned.
- **workstation** — A networked computer that requests services from servers. It is also able to service requests in a peer-to-peer networking environment.

REVIEW QUESTIONS

1. Which of the following application environments does Windows NT support?

   a. PICK

   b. SunOS

   c. OS/2

   d. X-Windows

2. Windows NT supports _____ 4 GB _____ of memory and _____ 16 Exabytes _____ of disk space.

3. Which of the following are Kernel mode components in Windows NT? (Choose all that apply.)

   a. virtual DOS machines

   b. security subsystems

   c. Hardware Abstraction Layer

   d. Win16 subsystem

4. Windows NT supports only cooperative multitasking. True or False?

5. Windows NT 4.0 supports the HPFS file system. True or False?

6. Windows NT has inherent support for facilitating connectivity to which of the following networks?

   a. NFS

   b. LANtastic

   c. Novell NetWare

   d. Banyan Vines

7. Memory pages are stored in units of:

   a. 2 KB

   b. 4 KB

    c. 16 KB

    d. 64 KB

8. Which of the following operating systems requires a logon for any local or remote access?

    a. Windows for Workgroups

    b. Windows NT Workstation

    c. MS-DOS

    d. Windows 95

9. If you want users to share resources but have no concern for local security on the system, which operating system would be the best choice?

    a. Windows 95

    b. Windows NT Workstation

    c. Windows NT Server

10. Which of these configuration specifications will allow for the installation of Windows NT 4.0?

    a. Intel 386 DX/25, 32 MB of RAM, 200 MB disk space

    b. DEC Alpha AXP, 8 MB of RAM, 150 MB disk space

    c. Intel Pentium-133Mhz, 16 MB of RAM, 60 MB disk space

    d. Intel 486 DX2/66, 12 MB of RAM, 135 MB disk space

11. An organization is trying to choose an operating system. It is using two, 32-bit applications with the "Designed for Windows 95" logo. It will also be using three, 16-bit applications with application-specific device drivers. Which would be the best operating system to select to establish optimum application support?

    a. Windows NT Workstation

    b. Windows 95

    c. Windows NT Server

12. You are setting up a computer for the purpose of sharing files. Each user connecting will need to have specific levels of access. There will never be more than five users connecting to the share at a time. Which operating system would be the most cost-effective solution?

    a. Windows 95

    b. Windows NT Server

    c. Windows NT Workstation

13. The two enterprise models supported in Windows NT are ____Workgroup____ and ____Domain____.

14. The two file systems supported in Windows NT are FAT and ____NTFS____.

15. When a user presses the Ctrl-Alt-Del key combination in Windows NT, what happens?

    a. The computer reboots.

    b. The Logon Screen appears.

    c. A "Blue Screen of Death" occurs.

    d. A command prompt appears.

16. Windows NT runs on top of DOS. True or False?

17. Which of the following is required to install Windows NT on Intel-based computers?

    a. SCSI CD-ROM drive

    b. tape backup device

    c. network interface card

    d. none of the above

18. Which of the following must be installed on your computer before using the NTHQ utility?

    a. MS-DOS

    b. Windows 3.x

    c. Windows NT

    d. nothing

19. Administrators desiring a centralized model of resource management should consider which network model?

    a. workgroup

    b. domain

20. All direct access to hardware is trapped by which component?

    a. Kernel

    b. Win32 subsystem

    c. Hardware Abstraction Layer

    d. Object Manager

21. Windows NT Workstation supports _____ processors.

    a. 1

    b. 2

    c. 4

    d. 32

CASE PROJECTS

1. You are planning a network in which users need to have a centralized location where discretionary access control is a necessity. This will be an environment in which consistency is a *must*.

Required Result: All users must be able to access the server from any computer within the network through a single logon.

Optional Desired Results: Users must also be required to log on before accessing anything on their local machine; users will have the exact same desktop GUI.

Proposed Solution: Install Windows NT Server as the server platform. Establish a Windows NT domain. On half of the user's desktops install Windows 95, and on the other half, install Windows NT Workstation. Have all computers configured as part of the NT domain.

Which results does the proposed solution produce? Why?

a. The proposed solution produces the desired result and produces both of the optional desired results.

b. The proposed solution produces the desired result but only one of the optional desired results.

c. The proposed solution produces the desired result but neither of the optional desired results.

d. The proposed solution does not produce the desired result.

2. You have been instructed to evaluate the status of the network environment at Site A. Your goal is to evaluate the current network and determine first of all whether upgrading is necessary. If so, then the next step is to determine which operating system will be the migration choice: Windows NT Workstation or Windows 95. Finally, determine what steps need to occur before the migration can proceed.

Site A has 220 computers currently running Windows 3.1. They are running all 16-bit applications from the DOS and Windows environments. They plan on migrating to Microsoft Office 97. Each computer has the following hardware configurations:

- Intel 486 DX4/100

- 8 MB of RAM

- 540 MB hard drive

- NIC (network interface card)

- VGA monitor

Users will not be allowed to share files at the desktop. They will not "roam" from computer to computer, so all of their files can be stored locally on their computers.

Which migration path makes the most sense? Why?

a. No migration

b. Windows NT Workstation

c. Windows 95

If migration is necessary, what steps would be necessary to establish optimum but cost-effective performance?

INSTALLING WINDOWS NT WORKSTATION 4.0

There are a number of issues that must be considered when installing any operating system, and Windows NT Workstation is no exception. This chapter details the various steps that must be taken to get NT up and running. It also examines such issues as whether to perform a fresh installation of NT or to upgrade from an earlier version. It covers the various methods used to install NT (floppy disks, CD-ROM, or network-based), as well as a few things to watch out for along the way.

Although the interfaces are similar, Windows NT 4.0 has more capabilities and more features than Windows 95, and so has greater hardware requirements. Before installing Windows NT Workstation 4.0, you must first ensure that your computer meets the minimum requirements (and, preferably, the recommended requirements) as detailed in Chapter 1 and that all hardware to be used with Windows NT is listed on the Hardware Compatibility List (HCL).

AFTER READING THIS CHAPTER AND COMPLETING THE EXERCISES YOU WILL BE ABLE TO:

- Understand how to install and upgrade Windows NT Workstation 4.0
- Plan an installation or upgrade
- Install Windows NT Workstation using disks, the CD-ROM, or the network
- List the stages of the installation

UPGRADING VERSUS INSTALLING

When installing Windows NT Workstation, you have a choice between upgrading an existing installation or performing a completely fresh installation. Upgrading is an option when you have a version of Windows already installed and wish to preserve some of the settings and information from the previous installation, including password files and some desktop settings.

 Although you can upgrade Windows 3.x or Windows for Workgroups 3.x to Windows NT, you cannot upgrade Windows 95 to Windows NT.

You must perform a complete installation if you want to use a fresh installation of Windows NT, if you want the capability to boot multiple versions of Windows, or are installing Windows NT on several computers and want the installations to be identical.

BOOTING MULTIPLE OPERATING SYSTEMS

It is possible to install more than one operating system on the same computer, allowing you to determine which OS will be used at boot time. Unless you deliberately overwrite or format the **partition** (a space set aside on a disk and assigned a drive letter, which can take up all or part of the space on a disk) where another operating system is located, installing Windows NT will not affect the other OSs. As you add each OS to a Windows NT system, it will be added to the **boot loader** (the software that shows all OSs currently available and provides a menu from which the user chooses which OS should be booted). At boot time, you can choose the OS you want to run, as shown in Figure 2-1.

```
OS Loader V4.00

Please select the operating system to start:

    Windows NT Workstation Version 4.0
    Windows NT Workstation Version 4.0 [VGA mode]
    Microsoft Windows

Use ↑ and ↓ to move the highlight to your choice.
Press Enter to choose.
```

Figure 2-1   Startup screen for a multiple operating system workstation

 The **BOOT.INI** file is a text file that creates the Windows NT boot loader's menu. To remove an OS from the boot loader or edit its entry in the boot loader menu, you have to edit the file BOOT.INI manually (see Chapter 15).

If you plan to use more than one operating system, it's important to consider which **file system** to use and whether data must be accessible to more than one OS on the same machine. Windows NT may be installed to either a FAT partition or an NTFS partition (FAT and NTFS are covered in Chapters 1 and 5). Only NTFS supports the majority of Windows NT file security features, but a partition formatted with NTFS will be invisible to other OSs even when running.

PLANNING THE INSTALLATION

Careful planning is essential to the smooth execution of any operating system, and Windows NT is no exception. The importance of checking hardware against the HCL has already been discussed, but that's only the beginning. It's also important to consider the type of installation you want to perform, as well as the partition on which the OS files will be stored and how that partition is to be formatted.

TYPES OF INSTALLATIONS

For manual installations (unattended installations are covered in a later section), you have a choice between a CD-ROM installation and a network installation. Installing from the CD is quite straightforward: If you have a working hard disk you can ignore the boot floppy disks that come with Windows NT. A network installation requires a bit more preparation.

Installing over the Network

To install Windows NT Workstation over the network, you must copy the Windows NT installation files to the hard disk of a computer on the network. The subdirectory containing the installation files varies depending on the architecture of the computer onto which you're installing Windows NT Workstation. For example, **x86**-based systems require the files found in the \I386 folder on the Windows NT CD-ROM. Hands-on Project 2-1 gives step-by-step instructions for installing Windows NT Workstation over the network.

Installing with or Without Floppy Disks

The Windows NT Workstation installation CD-ROM comes with three floppy disks, but these disks are necessary only if you're installing onto a drive that is not presently bootable (e.g., one that has not yet been formatted). Otherwise, you can use the **/B** switch to **WINNT** or **WINNT32** (the installation command files) to perform a floppyless installation. If the setup disks don't include drivers for your CD-ROM drive (sometimes the case with SCSI drives), you must perform a floppyless installation.

Creating Setup (Boot) Floppy Disks

If the setup floppy disks aren't available for some reason, you can copy the setup files from the CD-ROM to floppy disks by entering commands at the command prompt (also known as the **DOS prompt**). The steps to create setup floppy disks are given in Hands-on Project 2-2.

PARTITIONING THE HARD DISK

You may want to partition your hard disk before installing Windows NT Workstation. Many people create a DOS boot partition that's accessible when booting from a floppy disk. This enables them to run diagnostic software and utilities that only run under DOS and also store data in an NTFS partition that is more secure and is inaccessible unless the system is booted to Windows NT. Although it's possible to install Windows NT to a FAT partition, FAT does not provide the advanced security features and large-partition capabilities of NTFS, so you must determine which file system (or which combination of them) is more appropriate for your needs. Chapter 5, "File Systems," discusses in detail the capabilities and implications of the file systems supported by Windows NT and the criteria for choosing a file system. For now, it is sufficient to say that FAT partitions provide no security; so, if you require the assignment of rights to system resources, NTFS is the file system to use. Other deciding factors are covered in detail in the "Text Mode Windows NT Setup" section of Chapter 5. Right now, it's important to know that the **active partition** is the partition that houses the NT boot files. This is very important: If NT doesn't know where to look for the boot files, it can't start. You can use the DOS **FDISK** utility to partition the hard disk before installation. Hands-on Project 2-3 walks you through the process of breaking a single large partition into two partitions.

UNATTENDED INSTALLATIONS

It's possible to configure an **unattended installation** in which you don't have to respond to installation prompts but instead use a script containing the appropriate answers. Although it can take a little time and practice to set up an unattended installation, this type of installation can save time if you have to install NT Workstation on several machines. To run an unattended installation, you'll run WINNT or WINNT32 with the /U and /S options, to instruct Setup to perform an unattended installation using the files stored in the location you specify with the /S switch. To further customize the installation, you'll specify /UDF to use a **Uniqueness Database File (UDF)** in combination with an **answer file** (the file that provides answers to installation prompts for unattended installations). (UDFs and answer files are covered in detail shortly.)

Each platform–specific directory on the Windows NT Workstation CD-ROM contains a file called UNATTEND.TXT, which is used for configuring unattended installations on that type of platform. For example, if you're preparing an answer file for an unattended installation on an x86–based system, use the copy of UNATTEND.TXT that's found in the \I386 directory. If you must install several instances of NT Workstation that vary slightly (for example, the username differs), then you can use a UDF to supplement the answer file and override its parameters as appropriate.

To make configuring the answer file a little easier, the Windows NT Workstation CD-ROM includes a tool called the **Setup Manager**, stored in the appropriate platform folder in the \SUPPORT\DEPTOOLS folder. This graphical interface to the answer file allows you to configure the General Setup, Network Setup, and Advanced Setup portions of the answer file. Tables 2-1 through 2-3 list the settings you must complete for each section. Hands–on Project 2-4 gives an example of how to create an answer file.

 The *Windows NT Workstation Resource Kit* includes a copy of Setup Manager that's slightly different in appearance from the one on the Windows NT CD-ROM, but its capabilities are essentially identical.

Table 2-1   General Setup Answer File Settings

Tab	Data Required
User Information	Username, organization name, computer name (must be unique on the network) and product ID, found on the installation CD
General	Whether you want to be prompted to confirm hardware settings (for an unattended installation, this should be left blank), the type of upgrade you want to perform (if any), and the name of any programs that should be run during setup
Computer Role	The role of the computer on the network (workstation, domain controller, and so forth), the name of the workgroup or domain to which this computer will belong
Install Directory	The name of the directory to which Windows NT should be installed (or an indication that the default name should be used)
Display Settings	The settings for the display and a preference for whether these settings should be configured at logon during Setup
Time Zone	The time zone in which the computer will be used
License Mode	Does not apply to Windows NT Workstation but is used to specify the number of per-seat or per-connection licenses available for NT Server

Table 2-2   Networking Setup Answer File Settings

Tab	Data Required
General	The type of installation being performed (manual or unattended) and whether the network card should be automatically detected, predetermined, or chosen manually during installation
Adapters	The name of the adapter cards to be installed and their I/O parameters (IRQ, I/O address, and so forth)
Protocols	The names and parameters of transport protocols to be installed during setup
Services	The names and parameters of services to be installed during setup
Internet	The names and storage locations of any Internet services to be installed during setup—applies only to network servers (not workstations)
Modem	Applies only if the RAS service is installed and configured to use one or more ports; needs the type of modem connected to the computer and its configuration information

Table 2-3   Advanced Setup Answer File Settings

Tab	Data Required
General	The name of a new HAL to use, or a special keyboard layout, and any optional parts of Setup to skip
File System	The file system to be used (current or converted to NTFS) and, if the partition is larger than 2 GB, that the OEM partition should be extended
Mass Storage	The names of any mass storage drivers to be used, if not those packaged with Windows NT
Display	The names of any display drivers to be used, if not those packaged with Windows NT
Keyboard	The names of any keyboard drivers to be used, if not those packaged with Windows NT
Pointing Device	The names of any pointing device drivers to be used, if not those packaged with Windows NT
Boot Files	The names and locations of any OEM-supplied boot files
Advertisement	The bitmaps and text that should serve as the background during GUI-mode setup (instead of the blue Microsoft graphics)

CREATING THE UDF

Windows NT 4.0 adds a new twist to unattended installations: the Uniqueness Database File (UDF). The UDF works in conjunction with the answer file already discussed, allowing you to override some settings in the answer file to further streamline the unattended installation. Rather than having to create a new answer file for every change to the installation, you can just specify a separate UDF. Most information will be covered in the answer file, but if a setting exists in both the specified UDF and in the answer file, the UDF takes precedence.

You can create a UDF in a text editor such as EDIT or Notepad. It should look something like the following:

```
[UniqueIDs]
        UserID1 = Userdata,GuiUnattended,Network
        UserID2 = Userdata,GuiUnattended,Network
    [UserID1:UserData]
    FullName = "Hans Delbruck"
    ComputerName = "Monster"
    [UserID1:GuiUnattended]
    TimeZone = " (GMT+01:00) Prague, Warsaw, Budapest)"
    [UserID1:Network]
    JoinDomain = "LabTechs"
    [UserID2:UserData]
    FullName = "Francis N. Stein"
    ComputerName = "Doctor"
    [UserID2:GuiUnattended]
    TimeZone = "(GMT-06:00) Central Time (US & Canada)"
    [UserID2:Network]
    JoinDomain = "MadScientists"
```

When you've finished the UDF, save it as a text file and store it on disk. It's often helpful to name UDFs for the people using them because they're likely to be customized for individuals.

THE OEM DIRECTORY

If you want to include files, components, or applications that are not part of a normal Windows NT installation in your unattended installation, you'll use the **OEM** directory to store them. The locations for these files are important: Hardware-dependent files to be loaded during the text-mode phase of setup should be stored under the directory OEM\TEXTMODE, with a separate directory created for each device to be installed. Network components should be stored under OEM\NET, also with a separate directory created for each device. Applications to be loaded over the network during installation should be stored under OEM\X, where X represents the letter of the drive on the destination computer on which the application will be installed. Once again, each application being loaded needs its own directory subordinate to OEM\X.

USING THE SYSDIFF UTILITY

If you've got a customized Windows NT Workstation installation that you'd like to copy to other machines on your network, you can use the **SYSDIFF** tool (available in the Windows NT Resource Kit) to record the differences between a basic Windows NT Workstation installation and the one you've tweaked.

To use SYSDIFF to customize an installation, follow these steps:

1. If you haven't already, install Windows NT Workstation.

2. Type *SYSDIFF /SNAP* on that computer to create a snapshot of this installation in the filename you specify.

3. Install the software and make the changes you wish to record.

4. Type *SYSDIFF /DIFF* on that computer to record the differences between the original installation and the additions in the file whose name you specify.

5. Install Windows NT on each of the destination computers.

6. Run *SYSDIFF /APPLY* on each destination computer to add the files, naming the file created within /DIFF mode.

To create a text version of the difference file, run SYSDIFF /DUMP on the computer on which you created the SYSDIFF file.

That's the basics of how to perform a SYSDIFF operation. (The switches that may be used with each of these commands are explained in detail in the *Windows NT Workstation Resource Kit*.) You use SYSDIFF in combination with an unattended installation. Specify the SYSDIFF command (and the appropriate switch) when running OEMSetup. Table 2–4 shows what's actually happening when you use each of those commands.

Table 2-4   SYSDIFF Switches

Mode	Function
SNAP	Takes a snapshot of the current Registry and the file system and directories, writing information to a snapshot file
DIFF	Records the differences between the view of the system as recorded with DIFF and its state when SYSDIFF is run again on the same system; the differences are recorded in a difference file
APPLY	Applies the data in the DIFF file to the Windows NT installation on which it's being run; any differences in the OS will be made, and any applications added to the installation
INF	Used to apply differences to installations across the network
DUMP	Creates a text file listing the changes between the original installation and the amended one

BEGINNING THE NT WORKSTATION INSTALLATION

You have now been exposed to the various kinds of possible installations and learned when to use each of them. Now it's time to perform the actual installation; first, using the local CD-ROM drive, and second, over the network.

FLOPPYLESS CD-ROM INSTALLATION FOR A WINDOWS CLIENT

To install Windows NT Workstation locally without using the setup disks, you'll need either a DOS bootable floppy disk or a DOS partition on the hard disk (and, of course, drivers for your CD-ROM). Once you've got one or the other of these, place the CD-ROM in the drive and follow these steps:

1. Boot to DOS.

2. Move to the drive letter of the CD-ROM drive and type *WINNT32 /B*. The installation program should begin.

FLOPPYLESS NETWORK INSTALLATION FOR A DOS COMPUTER

Installing Windows NT onto a DOS machine over the network is quite straightforward:

1. Boot the computer to DOS.

2. Start the network (if it doesn't start automatically during system boot).

3. Map the network drive containing the installation files like this:

```
net use x:\\servername\directory
```

where *x* is the drive letter to which you wish to map the shared network directory, *servername* is the name of the server on which the files are stored, and *directory* is the name of the installation directory. Thus, if you were mapping drive letter E: to the Install directory on the Bigdog server, the command would look like this:

```
net use e:\\bigdog\install
```

4. Once you've mapped the directory, move to the appropriate drive letter and type *WINNT /B*.

 WINNT32 will not run under DOS because it's a 32-bit application and DOS is a 16-bit OS.

FLOPPYLESS NETWORK INSTALLATION FOR A WINDOWS 95 COMPUTER

Installing Windows NT from Windows 95 is even easier because the network will start automatically if it's set up properly.

1. Browse *Network Neighborhood* to find the server sharing the installation files, then double-click that computer to view the list of shared directories.

2. Select *File, Map Network* from the menu, enter a drive letter (such as E:) to map the share to, and press *[Enter]* to connect you to that drive.

3. Once you've mapped the share, click *Start, Run* and type *e: winnt32 /b* to start Setup.

FLOPPYLESS NETWORK INSTALLATION FOR A WINDOWS NT COMPUTER

As with Windows 95, upgrading Windows NT over the network is a simple matter due to the built-in networking capabilities of Windows NT.

1. From the File Manager, map the shared installation directory to a local drive letter (such as E:), as described in the previous section on installing from Windows 95.

2. Once the drive is mapped, choose *File, Run* and type `e: winnt32 /b` to start Setup.

LOCAL INSTALLATION USING INSTALLATION DISKS

Finally, there's the simple method—installing with the floppy disks. To perform this installation, reboot the computer with the Setup disk in the A: drive. Installation files will be copied to a temporary directory, and you'll be prompted to insert disks #2 and #3 as required.

WINNT AND WINNT32

Previously in this chapter, a number of references have been made to WINNT and WINNT32 and some of the switches that may be used with each. You might be wondering, however, what the difference is between the two, why you'd use each, and what the complete set of switches is for each command. Table 2-5 shows command sets for both installation commands.

2

Table 2-5   WINNT and WINNT32 Commands

Switch	Description
/B	Runs the Setup program without requiring the boot floppy disks
/C	Tells WINNT or WINNT32 not to bother checking for free space on the floppy disks you're using to create backup copies of the installation disks
/F	When creating backup copies of the installation disks, copies the files to the disks without verifying the copies
/I	Required to specify a setup information file other than DOSNET.INF
/OX	Used to create a set of installation floppy disks, copying the files directly from the CD-ROM
/S	Specifies the source of the installation files, if not in the path
/T	Forces Windows NT Setup to store the temporary files created during setup in another, specified, directory
/U	On its own, performs an unattended upgrade of Windows NT using the current settings; with an answer file specified, follows the script in the answer file
/X	Prevents Setup from creating boot floppy disks

TEXT MODE WINDOWS NT SETUP

Whether upgrading or installing, all Windows NT installations begin with text-mode setup. At the beginning of this part of the installation, you have four options of how to proceed:

- Press F1 to learn more about installing Windows NT.

- Press Enter to set up Windows NT now.

- Type R to repair a damaged Windows NT installation.

- Press F3 to exit Setup without installing Windows NT.

HARDWARE DETECTION

Once you've pressed Enter, the second step of text-mode setup begins: hardware detection, as shown in Figure 2-2. Identification of the CD-ROM controller is crucial to this stage— Windows NT must be able to access the CD-ROM drive to successfully perform the installation. You can specify the controller yourself by pressing S, but if it is supported (and, if you've checked your hardware against the HCL as recommended, it will be) you can press Enter to let Setup automatically detect mass storage devices.

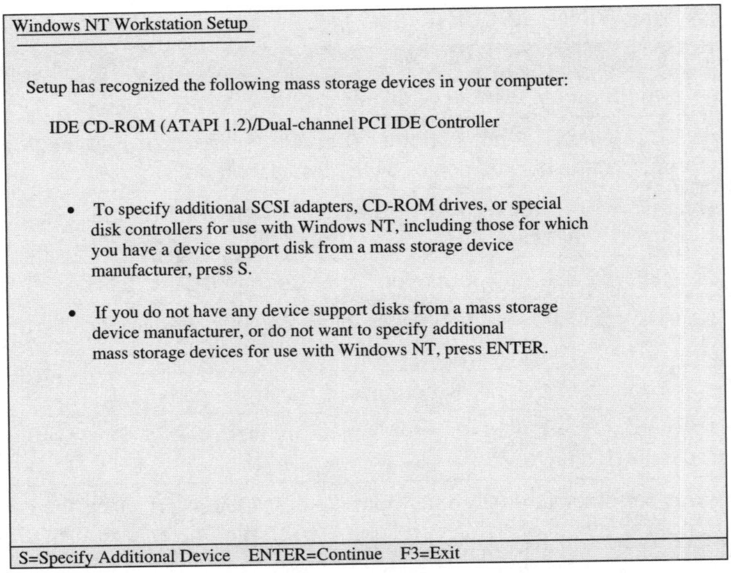

```
Windows NT Workstation Setup

Setup has recognized the following mass storage devices in your computer:

    IDE CD-ROM (ATAPI 1.2)/Dual-channel PCI IDE Controller


      •  To specify additional SCSI adapters, CD-ROM drives, or special
         disk controllers for use with Windows NT, including those for which
         you have a device support disk from a mass storage device
         manufacturer, press S.

      •  If you do not have any device support disks from a mass storage
         device manufacturer, or do not want to specify additional
         mass storage devices for use with Windows NT, press ENTER.

S=Specify Additional Device    ENTER=Continue    F3=Exit
```

Figure 2-2   Setup screen detecting mass storage devices

UPGRADE OR INSTALL?

After displaying the software license agreement, which is accepted by pressing F8, the Setup program checks to see if you've got a version of Windows NT Workstation already on your system, and if there is, asks if you want to upgrade it. To upgrade to version 4.0, press Enter. If you want to install a fresh copy of Windows NT without affecting the one already present, type N, as shown in Figure 2-3.

CHOOSE COMPONENTS

If you're performing a fresh installation, you'll be asked to confirm Setup's identification of the components on your system (mouse, keyboard, video, and so forth). It's generally pretty accurate—the point of this stage is to give Setup something to work with, not necessarily use all the high-tech features of your hardware. Press Enter when you've confirmed that Setup's choices will work.

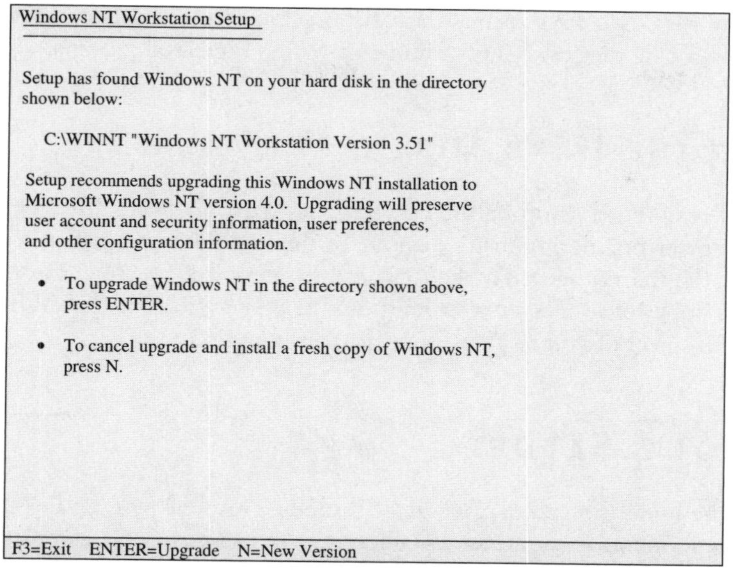

```
Windows NT Workstation Setup

Setup has found Windows NT on your hard disk in the directory
shown below:

    C:\WINNT "Windows NT Workstation Version 3.51"

Setup recommends upgrading this Windows NT installation to
Microsoft Windows NT version 4.0.  Upgrading will preserve
user account and security information, user preferences,
and other configuration information.

    •  To upgrade Windows NT in the directory shown above,
       press ENTER.

    •  To cancel upgrade and install a fresh copy of Windows NT,
       press N.




F3=Exit   ENTER=Upgrade   N=New Version
```

Figure 2-3   Upgrading NT Workstation

PARTITION SELECTION

Next, the Setup program will display the partition information (partition size and format) and, for a complete installation, will ask you where you'd like to install. Select the partition on which you wish to install, and press Enter. You have the option of pressing C to convert the partition to NTFS if it's presently formatted for FAT, but you can also perform the conversion after installation and decide then whether you want your system partition to be unreadable by any OS other than Windows NT. If you choose to install Windows NT into unpartitioned space, you'll have the option of formatting that partition to either FAT or NTFS. To delete a partition and start over, press D.

 Deleting a partition will permanently erase all data on that partition.

How you should arrange your partitions depends greatly on the role of your computer. Although any operating system that can read FAT can read NTFS volumes across the network, those volumes will only be visible to Windows NT installations on the local computer. No problem, perhaps, except in the case of data recovery, when it can be very handy to have access to data when booting from a floppy disk. However, if you use FAT, then you won't be able to use the security options unique to NTFS.

At the very least, it's a good idea to leave a DOS partition on your computer so you can boot to DOS even if Windows NT isn't working. It is preferred for a single-boot machine to leave the system files on a FAT-formatted partition for increased data-recovery capabilities; however, storing data files on NTFS volumes provides increased security.

EXAMINING THE HARD DISK

The final stage of text-mode setup before copying files to your disk is the examination of your hard disk(s) for errors. Although it's possible to instruct Setup to perform only a cursory examination, the full one doesn't take long and it's a good idea. Once the examination is over, Setup will copy some files to your hard disk in preparation for the GUI portion of the installation, then prompt you to press Enter to continue setup.

GRAPHICAL-MODE SETUP

The final part of the installation takes place in GUI mode. This final part has three stages: verifying information about your computer, installing network services, and completing setup.

CONFIGURATION OPTIONS

When performing a full installation, you have the option of performing a typical, portable, compact, or custom installation. (You don't have this option when upgrading because your current configuration will be maintained.) These options are shown in Table 2-6.

Table 2-6   Configuration Options

Configuration	Description
Typical	Installs all optional components and automatically configures your hardware
Portable	Installs the options most likely to be used by portable computers
Compact	Performs a minimal installation to save room, installing no optional components
Custom	Lets you select the options to install

Custom is described as an option for advanced users, but it's fairly simple to look at a list of options and determine which ones you do (or don't) want.

USERNAME, COMPUTER NAME, AND ADMINISTRATOR PASSWORD

When performing a new installation, you'll be prompted for your name, organization, and your computer's name on the network. The latter must be unique on the network and may contain up to 15 characters. Although it can have spaces in it, you'll save yourself trouble when connecting via the command line if your computer's name is a single word—names with spaces must have quotation marks around them when named from the command line.

After choosing a name for your computer, you'll be prompted to select a password for the **Administrator** account. Don't just assign a throwaway password and forget it—if you forget this password before creating another account with administrative privileges, then you'll have to reinstall Windows NT. This password may have up to 14 characters. (Technically, Windows NT can support passwords with up to 128 characters, but there's no room to type more than 14.)

EMERGENCY REPAIR DISK

Next, you'll be prompted to create the **Emergency Repair Disk (ERD)**, the tool you'll need to repair the installation (repairing is an option from the initial setup screen in text-mode installation). The ERD you create now is a copy of some Registry files (all system information is stored in the Registry) needed to restore the system to its original state in case any of the Registry settings are lost or corrupted. You don't have to create an ERD now, but it's strongly recommended that you not only create it now (using a 1.44 MB floppy disk), but also update the disk with the RDISK utility (discussed in Chapter 15) every time you make any changes to the system.

SELECTING COMPONENTS FOR INSTALLATION

If you chose to perform a custom installation, you'll now be prompted to choose the options you want to install. Otherwise, Setup will make the choices for you, based on the configuration you chose earlier.

NETWORK SETTINGS

The second stage of the graphical-mode setup involves network settings. First, you'll specify whether Windows NT should be installed for use on a network. If you don't presently have a network card installed, you can always set up networking later and install the **loopback adapter** in the next step. If you're installing for use on a network, you specify whether the computer is wired to the network directly or is dialing in via remote access. Select the appropriate option.

SELECTING THE NETWORK ADAPTER

After choosing the kind of network access you want, identify the **network adapter** (network interface card) that you want to use with NT Workstation, either instructing Setup to search for it or identifying it yourself by clicking Select from the list, as shown in Figure 2-4. If the card is properly installed and on the HCL but Setup does not find it, then it's worth checking to be sure that the card is installed and seated properly. If you've got vendor drivers to use with the card, be sure to have them handy.

If you don't have a network adapter currently installed, you can choose Loopback Adapter from the list and install a card later.

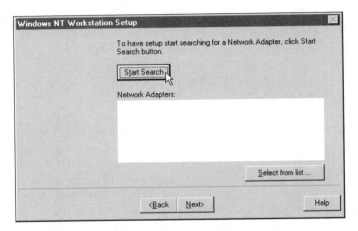

Figure 2-4   Detecting the network interface card

At this stage, you'll also be able to configure the network adapter's hardware settings, including its interrupt and I/O address range. It's important to complete this process, because if the network adapter is not set up according to the vendor's specifications, then network services will not be available.

SELECTING NETWORK PROTOCOLS

After you've got the card installed, it's time to choose a network protocol, as shown in Figure 2-5. Your choice should be based on what's already in use on the network—if everyone else is using TCP/IP, then it won't do you any good to install only NetBEUI.

Which protocol should you use? TCP/IP is the most flexible and is required for some functions such as interoperability with UNIX systems and the Internet. It is, however, a little more difficult to set up because addressing must be configured, and it's also a little slower than the other two protocols. An **IPX/SPX compatible** protocol (called NWLink in Microsoft parlance) is required to gain network access to a machine running true IPX/SPX (often, a NetWare machine). NetBEUI (the advanced set of commands that makes up the NetBIOS Extended User Interface) is the fastest of the three, but is not routable and thus is less often used these days than the other two—as reflected by the fact that it was the default network protocol when Windows NT first came onto the market, but is no longer. Although it's *required* for use with older Microsoft operating systems that don't support any other networking protocols, NetBEUI is really only useful with Microsoft-only networks that are in a single building because it's not routable (except with token ring source routing, which isn't often used). The pros and cons of the various network protocols are discussed in Chapter 8.

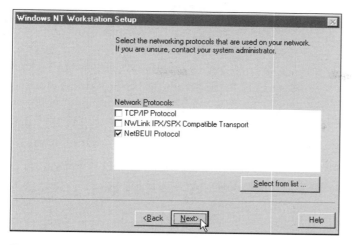

2

Figure 2-5   Selecting network protocols

 These are not the only network protocols available with Windows NT, but they're the ones most often used. If necessary, you can specify AppleTalk and/or DLC after installation.

Choosing Network Services

You now have the option of selecting the network services you want to run. The functions of these services will be described in more detail later in this book, but Table 2-7 gives a quick overview.

Table 2-7   Network Services and Functions

Service	Function
Remote Access Service (RAS)	Required to dial into another computer; not installed by default
Workstation	Handles User-mode requests made over the network and passes them to the Kernel-mode redirector; installed by default
Server	A file-system driver that works with other file-system drivers (such as NTFS) to handle read and write requests; it doesn't do the transferring itself, but passes the request to the transport driver interface (TDI)
NetBIOS Interface	Required for use by NetBIOS applications so that they may pass requests to the TDI
Remote Procedure Call (RPC) Configuration	Required by all Internet Information Server (IIS) services

Generally speaking, stick with the defaults here, unless you want to add RAS. As you can guess from the descriptions, disabling these services will make your network unable to function.

CONFIGURING BINDINGS

The **binding** order determines the sequence in which the installed network protocols will be used by each service. Although it is possible to tweak this order to improve network performance (for example, by binding TCP/IP first if it's the protocol most often used on your network), this generally isn't necessary. Disabling bindings is only done when you're trying to make something inaccessible across the network, so be careful about what you do here.

You are prompted to confirm your settings and the network portion of Setup ends.

ENTERING THE NAME OF A WORKGROUP OR DOMAIN

Now that your network is set up, you'll be prompted for the name of the workgroup or domain to which this computer will belong. If you don't know the name of the domain, you can enter any workgroup name here and join the proper domain later, after installation.

If you're performing a fresh installation of NT Workstation on a computer that previously belonged to a domain, you'll have to ask the network administrator to delete your computer's account on the domain and re-add it, even if it has the same name as it previously did. Windows NT Server will not recognize the computer's membership in the domain for a fresh installation.

CHOOSING FINAL SETTINGS

You're nearly done with the installation. A couple of settings still remain, however:

- *Time/date:* Choose the time zone in which this computer will operate, and set the date.

- *Video settings:* Based on what you know about your video card and monitor's capabilities, set up the system video. Be sure to test all configurations to be sure they work before accepting them. You can also adjust these settings after setup is complete.

Now, you'll be asked to remove all floppy disks and to reboot the computer. Setup will remove all temporary files and install any remaining settings.

REMOVING WINDOWS NT

After installation, it's quite simple to add or remove components via the icons in the Control Panel. However, if you decide to remove Windows NT from your computer altogether, you'll have to be a little more drastic. You'll need a bootable DOS floppy disk with the FDISK, FORMAT, DELTREE, and SYS utilities on it.

Previous versions of WINNT supported a /D option to delete the installation, but this switch is not supported by the Windows NT 4.0 versions of WINNT and WINNT32.

DELETING WINDOWS NT FROM A FAT PARTITION

Removing Windows NT from a FAT partition is essentially a matter of a little housekeeping. To delete NT Workstation from a FAT partition:

1. For the purpose of this example, we are assuming that you installed Windows NT to the WINNT directory on the C: drive (change this reference to the proper letter if it's on any other lettered drive). Open a text editor such as Notepad and create the following batch file to remove Windows NT from your system:

   ```
   @ echo off
   a:
   SYS C:
   DELTREE /Y C:\WINNT
   DELTREE /Y C:\PROGRA~1\WINDOW~1
   DEL C:\PAGEFILE.SYS
   A:\ATTRIB -S -H -R C:\BOOT.INI
   DEL C:\BOOT.INI
   A:\ATTRIB -S -H -R C:\NTDETECT.COM
   DEL C:\NTDETECT.COM
   A:\ATTRIB -S -H -R C:\NTLDR.
   DEL NTLDR.
   A:\ATTRIB -S -H -R C:\BOOTSECT.DOS
   DEL C:\BOOTSECT.DOS
   ```

2. Save the batch file (perhaps as CLEANNT.BAT), run it, and you'll delete Windows NT entirely from your computer.

DELETING WINDOWS NT IF NTFS IS IN USE

Deleting Windows NT from your computer is mostly a matter of deleting the operating system's files. Before you do that, however, be sure to back up any data files that you may have stored to an NTFS partition. Once Windows NT is deleted, that partition will no longer be visible to any other OS—you'll even have to delete the partition and recreate it—and you'll have to reinstall Windows NT to get the data back. Although Windows NT does come with an NTFS-FAT conversion utility, this utility only works in one direction—that is, you can use it to convert a partition from FAT to NTFS, but not the other way around.

To delete Windows NT from your NTFS partition:

1. Back up any data files stored on an NTFS volume. Don't use Windows NT's Backup utility because you won't be able to restore the files. You'll have to use the command line XCOPY to copy the files to a FAT volume either on the computer or accessible from it.

2. Run WINNT32. When you're asked to choose a partition on which to install Windows NT, type *D* to choose to delete the partition. You'll be asked to type *L* to confirm the deletion.

3. Press *[F3]* twice to exit Setup, and when prompted, press *[Enter]* to restart the computer.

At this point, any system files on the NTFS volume will be deleted. If you installed Windows NT to a FAT volume, you can boot from a floppy disk and delete the files with the batch file described earlier.

If the boot volume was formatted to NTFS, you'll need to establish a new boot loader for the computer. If you've already got a FAT C: drive that can become the bootable partition, then follow these steps.

To create a new boot loader if you've already got a FAT:

1. Boot the computer from the MS-DOS Setup disk or from a bootable floppy disk that also contains the SYS utility.

2. From the DOS prompt (you may have to choose to exit to DOS if you use the DOS setup disk), type *a: sys c:*

3. Restart the computer.

If you *don't* already have a FAT partition, you'll need to create one, following these steps:

1. Boot the computer with a bootable floppy disk that has FDISK and FORMAT on it.

2. Using the method described earlier in this chapter, create a DOS primary partition. When asked whether you want to make the partition active, type *Y*.

3. Reboot the computer with the bootable floppy disk still in the drive.

4. Enter *FORMAT C: /S* to format the partition with the system files.

5. When the format is complete, remove the floppy disk from the drive and reboot.

CHAPTER SUMMARY

- In this chapter, you learned how to install and uninstall Windows NT Workstation, including the tools and information you need to make this possible. You should now understand how to choose hardware for a successful installation, how to install Windows NT both locally and across a network, how to use the switches that come with WINNT and WINNT32, and how to run Setup. You should also be familiar with the differences between upgrading and installing Windows NT, and what those differences will mean in terms of the information you must provide during setup.

KEY TERMS

- **OEM** — The folder used to store any files, components, or applications not part of a normal Windows NT installation but which you wish to install in the course of setup.
- **active partition** — The partition that the computer uses to boot.
- **Administrator** — The Windows NT account designed to perform a full array of management functions.
- **answer file** — A text file that contains a complete set of instructions for an unattended installation of Windows NT.
- **bindings** — The connection between a network adapter and a transport protocol so that that adapter may use that protocol to transmit data across the network.
- **BOOT.INI** — The text file that creates the Windows NT boot loader's menu.
- **boot loader** — The software that shows all OSs currently available and, via a menu, permits the user to choose which one should be booted.
- **DOS prompt** — The common name for the command-line window available from DOS and Windows.
- **Emergency Repair Disk (ERD)** — Floppy disk storing crucial Registry settings that may be used to repair a damaged Windows NT installation. This disk should be updated both before and after making any major changes to the Windows NT installation.
- **FDISK** — A DOS utility used to partition a hard disk.
- **file system** — The method used to arrange files on disk and read and write them. Windows NT supports two disk file systems (NTFS and FAT) as well as CDFS, used to read CD-ROMs.
- **IPX/SPX compatible** — A transport protocol not quite identical to NetWare's IPX/SPX protocol but able to communicate with it. Used to network with NetWare networks not using TCP/IP.
- **loopback adapter** — Apparent network adapter that allows you to test network functions without having a network card successfully installed.
- **network adapter** — Another name for network interface card (NIC), the piece of hardware that enables communication between the computer and the network.
- **partition** — A space set aside on a disk and assigned a drive letter. A partition may take up all or part of the space on a disk.
- **Setup Manager** — The Windows NT tool that provides you with a GUI interface for creating an answer file.
- **SYSDIFF** — The Windows NT utility used to take a snapshot of a basic installation and, after changes have been made, record the changes and then apply them to another installation.
- **unattended installation** — A Windows NT installation that uses a previously made script from which to install.
- **Uniqueness Database File (UDF)** — A text file that contains a partial set of instructions for installing Windows NT. Used to supplement an answer file, when only minor changes are needed that don't require a new answer file.
- **WINNT** — The 16-bit Windows NT installation program.
- **WINNT32** — The 32-bit Windows NT installation program.
- **x86** — The chip architecture used by Intel and others to create 386 and later CPUs (including the Pentium).

REVIEW QUESTIONS

1. Which of the following statements best describes the minimum hardware requirements for x86 and RISC-based systems?

   a. They are identical.

   b. x86 systems have slightly more demanding hardware requirements.

   c. RISC systems have slightly more demanding hardware requirements.

   d. Some RISC systems have hardware requirements identical to x86 systems; others have less demanding requirements.

2. Microsoft will only support problems caused by hardware not on the Hardware Compatibility List for an additional fee. True or False?

3. Which of the following operating systems may be upgraded to Windows NT 4.0? (Choose all that apply.)

   a. Windows 3.x

   b. Windows for Workgroups 3.x

   c. Windows 95

   d. Windows NT 3.x

4. Data stored on a partition formatted with NTFS is only accessible to Windows NT. True or False?

5. Which of the following is the correct location for the x86 installation files on the installation CD?

   a. The root directory of the CD

   b. \SUPPORT\I86

   c. \INSTALL\I86

   d. none of the above

6. When sharing an installation folder across the network, you should assign it _____ permission.

7. Which of the following is not a situation likely to require a floppyless installation? (Choose all that apply.)

   a. The network is not yet functioning.

   b. The hard disk for the computer on which Windows NT is being installed is not yet formatted.

   c. No CD drivers exist on the hard disk.

   d. Windows 95 is already installed on the computer.

8. Running the command prompt from Windows NT opens a DOS window. True or False?

9. What is the command used to create setup floppy disks?

   a. WINNT32 /OX

   b. WINNT32 /F

   c. WINNT32 /B

   d. WINNT32 /C

10. The DOS utility used to create and delete partitions on a hard disk is called _____.

11. Windows NT must be installed to an NTFS partition. True or False?

12. Which of the following statements is true? (Choose all that apply.)
   a. The entries in a Uniqueness Database File override those in an answer file, when the two are used together.
   b. An answer file is used to script text-mode setup, whereas a UDF scripts GUI-mode setup.
   c. If you have several installations to complete that differ only in the username, then you can use an answer file to customize the settings in the UDF.
   d. UDFs are new to Windows NT 4.0.

13. List the sections of an answer file that may be configured with the Setup Manager.

14. Which of the following would require you to amend the settings in the Advanced Setup section? (Choose all that apply.)
   a. You want to convert the partition from FAT to NTFS during installation.
   b. You want to specify the name of the directory into which Windows NT will be installed.
   c. You want to select transport protocols to install.
   d. You want to set up RAS during installation.

15. If you want to install other applications while installing Windows NT, you should store those files under the _____ directory.

16. Which of the following commands is used to record the original state of a Windows NT installation?
   a. SYSDIFF /APPLY
   b. SYSDIFF /DIFF
   c. SYSDIFF /INF
   d. SYSDIFF /SNAP

17. Running _____ will create a text record of a SYSDIFF difference file.

18. To map a network drive from a DOS computer, which command will you use?
   a. NET START
   b. NET LOGON
   c. NET USE
   d. NET CONNECT

19. The _____ WINNT32 switch is used to specify a setup information file other than DOSNET.INF.

20. At what point in the installation do you have the option of converting the file system to NTFS?
   a. after selecting the installation partition
   b. after the hard disk has been examined
   c. at the end of text-mode installation
   d. only after setup is completed

21. A password may have up to _____ characters.

22. Which of the following is not a preconfigured set of installation options? (Choose all that apply.)
    a. Custom
    b. Portable
    c. Normal
    d. Compact

23. Which of the following transport protocols is not routable on Ethernet networks?
    a. IPX/SPX
    b. NetBEUI
    c. TCP/IP
    d. DLC

24. You're preparing for a network installation of Windows NT. Which of the following is *not* a step required to accomplish this? (Choose all that apply.)
    a. copy the \SUPPORT directory from the installation CD to the server supplying the installation files
    b. share the installation directory with Read permissions
    c. install a common network protocol on all networked computers
    d. run WINNT32 /N on the network server

25. You want to change the menu description for Windows NT in the boot loader's menu. What file will you edit to make the change?
    a. DOSNET.INF
    b. UNATTEND.TXT
    c. BOOT.INI
    d. WINNT.INI

26. To apply a SYSDIFF difference file to a Windows NT installation, you'd use the _____ switch.

HANDS-ON PROJECTS

PROJECT 2-1

To make the Windows NT x86 installation files available on a Windows NT Workstation computer for network installations:

1. Using an Administrator account, log onto the Windows NT Workstation computer that will be sharing the files.

2. Insert the Windows NT Workstation installation CD-ROM into the drive; it should launch, showing a screen like the one in Figure 2-6.

Figure 2-6   The Windows NT CD-ROM launches automatically

3. Browse the contents of the CD to find the **I386** folder.

4. Launch **My Computer**, locate the folder on the hard disk to which you want to copy the installation files, and drag the I386 folder to that location, as shown in Figure 2-7.

Figure 2-7   Copying the I386 directory

5. In My Computer, right–click the newly created **I386** installation folder on your drive, and select **Sharing** from the menu that appears. You'll see a dialog box like the one in Figure 2-8.

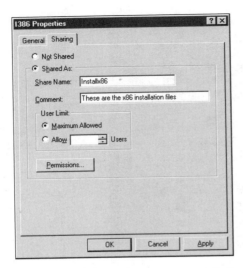

Figure 2-8   Sharing the new installation folder

6. Share the folder by clicking the **Shared As** radio button, entering the Share Name (name it something distinctive, such as **Installx86**) and Comment, then clicking the **Permissions** button. The dialog box shown in Figure 2-9 opens.

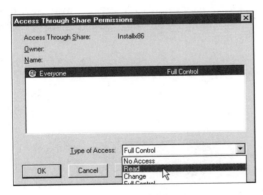

Figure 2-9   Assigning the Everyone group Read permission

7. From the Type of Access: list box at the bottom of the screen, select **Read** to replace Full Control. This will give everyone who connects to the installation files the ability to install from them, but not to change or delete them. Click **OK** to close the dialog box and **OK** again to close the Sharing dialog box and create the share.

8. Click **Yes** on the dialog box that states the name installx86 will not be accessible from some MS-DOS workstations.

9. Close the windows for the CD-ROM, My Computer, and the drive to which you copied the installation files.

PROJECT 2-2

To use a Windows NT Workstation computer to copy the Windows NT Setup files for an x86 installation from the CD-ROM to floppy disks:

1. Set aside three blank, formatted 1.44 MB floppy disks, labeling them **Windows NT Workstation Setup Boot Disk**, **Windows NT Workstation Setup Disk #2**, and **Windows NT Workstation Setup Disk #3**.

2. Open a command-line window (also known as a DOS prompt). From Windows NT 4.0 or Windows 95, select **Start, Programs, Command Prompt**. From a Windows 3.x machine, double-click the **MS–DOS Prompt** icon in the Program Manager. From Windows or Windows for Workgroups 3.x, choose **File**, **Exit Windows**. *Note:* Windows 95 will label the command-line window's icon "MS-DOS Prompt," but it's in the same place as the command prompt accessible from Windows NT 4.0.

3. Once in the command line, move to the CD-ROM drive by typing its drive letter and a colon, then press **[Enter]**. For example, if your CD-ROM is drive E:, type **E:** and press **[Enter]**.

4. Move to the folder containing the installation files (for example, \I386) by typing **cd I386** and pressing **[Enter]**.

5. Place the disk labeled "Windows NT Workstation Setup Disk #3" in the drive.

6. Depending on which operating system you're presently running, choose one of the following commands, and press **[Enter]**:

   - If working from a Windows NT or Windows 95 command prompt, type **WINNT32 /OX**.

   - If working from a true DOS prompt (that is, if you've had to boot to DOS or exit Windows 3.x to get to it), type **WINNT /OX**.

7. Click **Continue**; then click **OK**.

8. The installation program then copies the necessary files to Setup Disk 3. When prompted, insert Setup Disk 2, and then the Setup Boot Disk (Disk 1).

9. Once the files have been transferred to all three disks, remove the Setup Boot Disk from the drive.

10. Close the Command Prompt window.

PROJECT 2-3

To use the FDISK utility to divide the hard disk into two partitions:

Back up any data currently on the disk before repartitioning it! FDISK (or any partitioning utility) will permanently destroy any data currently on the hard disk.

1. Boot the computer to DOS as directed in Project 2-2, step 2.

2. Move to the directory containing the FDISK utility. (To find it, type **DIR FDISK.* /s** to search all subdirectories on the current disk.)

3. Type **FDISK** and press **[Enter]** to start the utility. When FDISK starts, you will see a menu of four options:

   - Create DOS partition or Logical DOS drive

   - Set active partition

   - Delete partition or Logical DOS drive

   - Display partition information

 If your computer has more than one hard disk, you'll see a fifth option: "Change current fixed drive."

4. Type **4** and then press **[Enter]** to view the partitions currently on the hard disk. In this example, it is assumed that you'll see a single primary DOS partition. After reviewing the information, press **[Esc]** to return to the main menu.

5. Once at the main menu screen, type **3** and press **[Enter]** to delete the primary partition. When asked which partition to delete, type **1** and press **[Enter]**.

6. When prompted, type the volume label (if any) for the partition you're deleting. The label will be listed at the top of the screen with other volume information. If there is no volume label, just press **[Enter]**.

7. Type **Y** and press **[Enter]** to confirm the deletion of the selected partition.

8. Press **[Esc]** to return to the main menu.

9. From the main menu, type **1** and press **[Enter]** to create a DOS partition.

10. Type **1** and press **[Enter]** to create a primary DOS partition.

11. Type **N** and press **[Enter]** when asked whether you want to use the maximum available space. When prompted, type in the size (in Megabytes) of the partition you want to create. To have room for both DOS and Windows 95, a partition size of at least 200 MB is recommended.

12. From the main menu, type **2** and press **[Enter]** to set the active partition. When prompted, type **1** to choose the partition you just created.

13. Press **[Esc]** to return to the main menu, then press **[Esc]** again to exit FDISK.

14. Reboot the computer, format the partition, and then reinstall Windows 95 (and DOS, if desired) to the partition you just created.

 It's unnecessary to partition the remaining space on the drive now because you can do that while installing Windows NT.

PROJECT 2-4

To create an answer file for an unattended installation for an x86-based system:

1. Insert the Windows NT Workstation installation CD in the drive and from the **Start** menu, select **Run** and type **D:\SUPPORT\DEPTOOLS\I386\SETUPMGR.EXE** in the text box (replace D:\ with the drive letter where the installation CD is located on your machine, if necessary) and press **[Enter]**.

2. Click the **New** button at the bottom of the dialog box that opens, then click **OK**.

3. Click the **General Setup** button.

4. On the **User Information** tab, enter the names of the user, organization, and computer.

5. On the **Computer Role** tab, indicate the computer's role in the network (including whether it will be part of a workgroup or a domain) and the name of the workgroup or domain to which it will belong. (Workgroups and domains are discussed in Chapter 1.)

 Most other values in General Setup should not need to be adjusted, but page through the tabs to check.

6. Click **OK** to end General Setup.

7. Click the **Networking Setup** button.

8. On the **General** tab, be sure that **Unattended Network Installation** is selected (by default, it will be). Specify the method you wish to use to configure the network adapter or adapters.

9. If you chose to specify the **network adapter** now, move to the **Adapters** tab and click the **Add** button, add the desired adapter or adapters, then click **OK**. To configure card settings, click the **Parameters** button and enter the IRQ and I/O base address values in the dialog box that opens.

10. On the **Protocols** tab, select the network protocols you wish to use and set any applicable parameters (the exact parameters vary with the protocol).

11. Click **OK** to end Network Setup.

12. Ordinarily, you won't need to change most settings in Advanced Setup, but if you wish to convert the file system to NTFS during installation, you'll need to change an advanced setting. To do so, click the **Advanced Setup** button and move to the **File System** tab, where you'll select the **Convert to NTFS** option.

13. Click **OK** to end Advanced Setup.

14. Click the **Save** button at the bottom of the Setup Manager dialog box to save the answer file, then enter the name and desired location for the file. When you've saved the file, click **Exit** to close the Setup Manager.

CASE PROJECTS

1. You're in charge of organizing the installation of Windows NT onto a number of net-worked computers. Some of these computers will have applications in common, but not all of them, and you'll need to set usernames and computer names for each instal-lation. You've got a lot to take care of, so you'd like the installation to go as quickly as possible. Which of the following will you use? Choose all that apply, and justify your choice(s).

   a. An answer file

   b. A Uniqueness Database File

   c. SYSDIFF

   d. The OEM directory

2. You're installing Windows NT onto a single-boot machine that is sharing data with the rest of the network. Some network clients are running Windows NT 4.0, but oth-ers are running Windows for Workgroups, and you've even got a DOS client or two hanging in there. You must come up with some method of making the system files visible when the computer is booted from a DOS floppy disk, but not the data files, yet the data files must be accessible to the network. Which of the following solutions most simply meets your criteria? Explain.

   a. Set aside a separate partition for data, format it with FAT, and password-protect the share.

   b. Set aside a separate partition for data and format it with NTFS, but format the system partition with FAT.

   c. Store both the system and the data files on the same partition and format it with FAT.

   d. Your requirements clash and your criteria may not be met.

 # See back for terms

USERS, GROUPS, AND POLICIES

Most computers are used by more than one person, especially in business or educational environments. Each person is identified to the computer and ultimately the network through a unique user account. Typically, a user account contains details such as what the user can and cannot access, and the user's preferred configuration or environmental settings. To establish such a system where details about each user are maintained, Windows NT uses named access accounts that are protected with password security. Furthermore, access permissions and environmental settings are stored through special mechanisms.

AFTER READING THIS CHAPTER AND COMPLETING THE EXERCISES YOU WILL BE ABLE TO:

- DESCRIBE THE CHARACTERISTICS AND CAPABILITIES OF THE DEFAULT ADMINISTRATOR AND GUEST USER ACCOUNTS

- UNDERSTAND ACCOUNT NAMING CONVENTIONS

- USE THE USER MANAGER TO CREATE AND MANAGE USER ACCOUNTS, INCLUDING COPYING, RENAMING, DISABLING, AND DELETING ACCOUNTS

- CREATE AND MANAGE LOCAL GROUPS

- DESCRIBE THE PURPOSE AND DEFAULT MEMBERS OF THE SIX DEFAULT LOCAL GROUPS AND THE EVERYONE GROUP

- ESTABLISH SECURITY POLICIES FOR ACCOUNTS (PASSWORDS AND LOCKOUTS), USER RIGHTS, AND AUDITS

WINDOWS NT USER ACCOUNTS

On a Windows NT-based network, whether a client/server network or a peer-to-peer workgroup, every person has a unique, named user account and a password that identifies that user to the system. Numerous details about the user's abilities and preferences are tied to this user account.

A Windows NT user account stores details about:

- *Security:* Passwords protect user accounts so only authorized individuals can gain access.

- *Access permissions:* User-specific settings and group memberships define the resources and applications a user has the authority to access and use.

- *Network identification:* The user account identifies the user to the rest of the network, if a network connection is present.

- *User rights:* Actions a user can perform on a computer are defined and limited.

- *Roaming access:* User accounts on a network are stored in a central location (the domain controller on a client/server network) so individuals can gain access to resources via any type of connection, such as local logon, RAS (Remote Access), or gateway access.

- *Preferences:* A user's environmental settings and configuration preferences can be stored as a **profile**, so no matter where a user connects to the network, the pre-ferred desktop and resources are available through the **user profile**.

Networking systems such as Windows NT that can support more than one user are called **multiple-user systems**. Maintaining separate and distinct user accounts for each person is the common feature of all multiple-user systems. Windows NT has taken this common feature and improved it. Windows NT implements its multiple-user system through the following features, which are discussed in this chapter:

- *Groups:* Groups are named collections of users. Each member of a group takes on the access privileges or restrictions defined for that group. Through the use of groups, administrators can manage many users at one time because a group's settings can be defined once and will apply to all members of that group. When the group settings are changed or modified, those changes automatically affect every member of that group. Thus, changing each user's account is not necessary.

- *Resources:* On a network or within a standalone computer, resources are any useful service or object, including printers, shared directories, and software applications. A resource can be accessible by everyone across the network or be limited to one person on a single machine, and at any level in between. The range of control over resources within Windows NT is astounding.

- *Policies:* A policy is a set of configuration options that define aspects of NT security. Security policies are used to define password restrictions, account lockouts, user rights, and event auditing. System policies are defined for a user, computer, or a group to restrict their computing environment.

- *Profiles:* A profile is a stored snapshot of the environmental settings of a user's desktop, Start menu, and other user-specific details. Profiles can exist on a single computer or be configured to follow a user around a network no matter what workstation is used.

3

LOGGING ON TO NT WORKSTATION

Windows NT uses **logon authentication** for two purposes: first, to maintain security and privacy within a network; and second, to track computer use by user account. Each Windows NT user has a unique user account that identifies that user and contains or references all the system preferences for, access privileges of, and private information about that one user. Thus, NT can provide security and privacy for all users through the mandatory requirement of logon authentication.

Logon authentication is the simple process of entering a valid username and password to gain access to an NT-based computer. Pressing Ctrl-Alt-Del at the default NT splash screen brings up, the **Logon Information dialog box**, as shown in Figure 3-1. Here users enter logon information—username, password, and domain—then click OK to have the NT security system validate the information and grant access to the computer. Once users have completed their work, they can log off the computer to make it available for the next user.

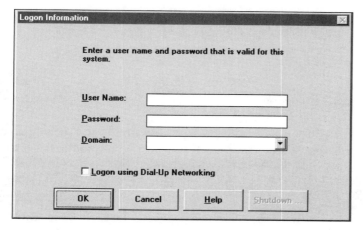

Figure 3-1   Logon Information dialog box

When Windows NT Workstation is installed, it automatically creates two default user accounts: Administrator and Guest.

ADMINISTRATOR

The **Administrator account** is the most powerful user account possible within the Windows NT environment. This account has unlimited access and unrestricted privileges to every aspect of Windows NT. The Administrator account has unrestricted ability to manage all security settings, other users, groups, the operating system environment, printers, shares, and storage devices. Due to these far-reaching privileges, the Administrator account must be protected from misuse. Defining a complicated password for this account is highly recommended. You should also rename this account; this will make it more difficult for hackers to discover a valid username and password.

 The Administrator account cannot be deleted, locked out, or disabled, but can be renamed.

GUEST

The **Guest account** is one of the least privileged user accounts in Windows NT. For security reasons, this account has limited access to resources and computer activities. Even so, you should set a new password for the Guest account and it should be used only by authorized one-time users or users with low-security access. Any configuration changes made to the desktop or Start menu are not recorded in the Guest's user profile. If you do allow this account to be used, you should rename it.

 The Guest account cannot be deleted or locked out, but it can be disabled, renamed, and have a blank password (the default setting).

NAMING CONVENTIONS

Before creating and managing user accounts, you need to understand naming conventions. A naming convention is simply a predetermined process for creating names on a network (or a standalone computer). A naming convention should incorporate a scheme for user accounts, computers, directories, network shares, printers, and servers. These names should be descriptive enough so anyone can recognize which type of object the name applies to. For example, name computers and resources by department or by use to simplify user access.

This stipulation of always using a naming convention may seem pointless for small networks, but it is rare for small networks to remain small. Most networks grow at an alarming rate. If you begin naming network objects at random, you'll soon forget which resource the name corresponds to. Even with the excellent management tools NT offers, you'll quickly lose track of important resources if you don't establish a standard way of naming network resources.

The naming convention your organization settles on ultimately doesn't matter, as long as it can always provide you with a useful name for each new network object. To give you an idea of a naming scheme, here are two common rules:

- Usernames are constructed from the first and last names of the users, plus a code identifying their job title or department, for example, BobScottAccounting.

- Group names are constructed from resource types, department names, location names, project names, and combinations of all four, for example, Accounting01, AustinUsers, BigProject01, and so forth.

No matter what naming convention is used, it needs to address the following four elements:

- It must be consistent across all objects.

- It must be easy to use and understand.

- New names should be easily constructed by mimicking the composition of existing names.

- An object's name should clearly identify that object's type.

MANAGING ACCOUNTS WITH THE USER MANAGER

The **User Manager** is an NT utility that manages local users and groups, meaning those users and groups belonging to the domain on which the User Manager is running. This tool is similar to User Manager for Domains, which manages domain users, global and local groups, and trust relationships. The User Manager is shown in Figure 3-2.

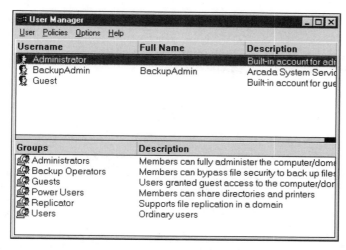

Figure 3-2   NT Workstation User Manager

As you can see, the top pane lists all users that can be managed from this instance of the User Manager. The bottom pane lists all manageable local groups. Through this unpretentious interface, an administrator can perform a wealth of user account management tasks, including:

- Creating, modifying, copying, and deleting user accounts
- Creating, modifying, copying, and deleting group accounts
- Establishing policies for accounts, setting user rights, and auditing

 Creating and modifying user accounts often involves numerous steps. In the Hands-on Projects at the end of the chapter, you'll have a chance to go through these functions step by step. After you've completed the chapter, or even as you're completing the Hands-on Projects, you might want to return to this section and review it.

CREATING A NEW USER ACCOUNT

Creating new user accounts can be accomplished in two ways: from scratch or by copying an existing account. Let's discuss the former first.

Creating a User Account from Scratch

To create a new user account, use the User menu in User Manager to select New User. The New User dialog box opens, as shown in Figure 3-3, where you enter the username (the name by which the user will be known on the system), the user's full name (optional), description (optional), password, and password confirmation (a duplicate entry of the password to confirm it). You can also set various password options or disable the account in this dialog box.

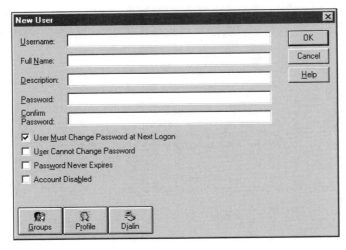

Figure 3-3   New User dialog box

You will see three configuration buttons at the bottom of the New User dialog box: Groups, Profile, and Dialin. Each of these should be used to fully define a user account. Details about the topics found in the dialog boxes accessed through these buttons will be covered later in this chapter.

- Groups adds or revokes group memberships.

- Profile defines the path to a user profile, the path to a login script, and the path to a user's home directory.

- Dialin authorizes a user for dial-in access and specifies callback security if needed.

Copying an Account

As you can see, there are lots of details to work with when creating a user account from scratch. A much simpler and more elegant method of adding new users is to copy an existing account. When you want to add multiple users with similar privileges and settings, you can reduce creation time by copying an account instead of creating a new one. Copying an account is simple; just select the account to be copied from the list of users in the top pane of the User Manager, then choose User, and Copy from the menu. A user properties window, similar to Figure 3-4, will appear with a title of "Copy of <*account name*>." Everything from the previous account will be duplicated into this new account except for the following items:

- Username

- Full name

- Password and password confirmation

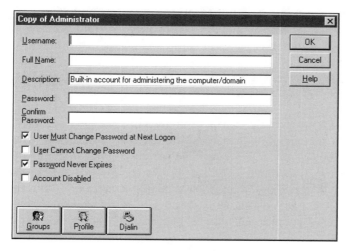

Figure 3-4   Copy of Administrator dialog box

To complete the copy of the account to a new username, fill in those blank fields. In addition, check the boxes beside User Must Change Password at Next Logon and Account Disabled. Once you set these five elements, click the OK button to complete the copy process.

If numerous users are to be created who share the same group memberships and other settings, you should create a template user. The template user is a user account that is not used to log on, but has all the common configuration options preset. By making a copy of the template and customizing it as needed for each user, you can greatly reduce the time involved in creating each account.

DISABLING USER ACCOUNTS

It is common for users to leave an organization and have their computer privileges suspended. Whatever the case, when a user account is no longer needed, it should be disabled. Old user accounts should be disabled instead of deleted so the accounts will be present for future security audits, if the old user requires access again, or if you need to make a copy of the account for someone else.

Disabling user accounts is a wise security practice. Disabled accounts cannot be used to log onto the system. Disabling an account makes no other change to an account other than preventing it from being used to gain access. All other settings and configuration options remain intact. Only administrators can disable (and re-enable) a user account.

Disabling an account is accomplished through the Properties dialog box for the individual user account (accessed through the User, Properties menu selection). If you look back at Figures 3-3 or 3-4, you can see the Account Disabled check box. When an "X" appears in the box, the account cannot be used to log on. Re-enabling or reactivating the account is simply a matter of removing the mark from the Account Disabled check box.

DELETING USER ACCOUNTS

Even though most security advisors and Microsoft recommend disabling accounts rather than deleting them, you can delete user accounts through User Manager. It is just as simple as deleting a file. Select the account to be removed, then select User, Delete from the menu. After a prompt for confirmation, the account will be completely erased from the **security database,** also known as SAM (Security Account Manager). Everything about that user will be erased from the system. Even if you immediately create a new user account with the same settings, you will have to re-establish all the preferences and access privileges the deleted account enjoyed.

Completely removing an account from the security database is an important feature of NT. Each user account is assigned a unique **Security ID (SID)** known only by the system. It is this ID, not the username, that the OS uses to identify users and grant users access to resources. Every user has a unique SID, and SIDs from deleted accounts are never reused.

 As you can see, deleting a user account has some profound consequences, so delete user accounts only when you are absolutely certain the accounts will never be needed again for any purpose.

RENAMING USER ACCOUNTS

Every user account can be renamed, including the default Administrator and Guest accounts. Renaming an account makes no alteration to any other configuration or setting for that account; its SID remains the same.

Renaming user accounts has some efficient uses:

- To move user accounts within the naming convention when a user's job position changes
- To comply with a change in your organization's naming convention
- To change the name of your Administrator account due to a security breach
- To reflect a user's name change

Renaming a user account is simple. In the User Manager, select the account to be altered, then select User, Rename from the menu. In the dialog box, enter the new name for the account.

The username is the only aspect of a user account that is not alterable through the Properties dialog boxes. This is because the Properties dialog boxes use the account name to reference changes made to the account properties.

Now you'll learn how to use the Groups, Profile, and Dialin buttons that appear at the bottom of User Manager dialog boxes when you create, copy, or set properties for a user account.

USING THE GROUPS BUTTON

By clicking the Groups button, you will access the Group Memberships dialog box, as shown in Figure 3-5. Through this dialog box, you can add the user to new groups or remove the user from current group memberships. The usefulness of group memberships will be discussed later in this chapter.

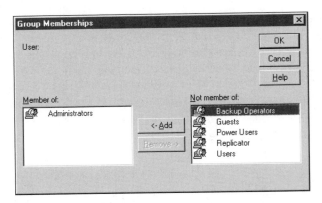

Figure 3-5   Group Memberships dialog box

CREATING A USER PROFILE

By clicking the Profile button, you access the User Environment Profile dialog box, as shown in Figure 3-6. Through this dialog box, you can alter the **User Environment Profile (UEP)**, which is the set of options that define a user's environment.

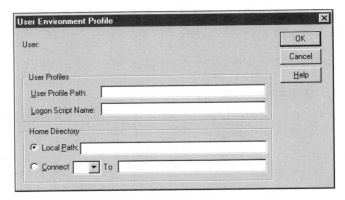

Figure 3-6   User Environment Profile dialog box

User Profile Path

The User Profile Path indicates the location of a user's roaming profile. See Chapter 4 for details on how to create user profiles. A **roaming profile** allows a user to log onto any workstation on the network and retain all of his or her normal desktop and environmental preferences.

Logon Script Name

The Logon Script Name indicates the location of a **logon script**, a set of commands to be executed when the user logs on. Usually, the logon script is a batch file that defines paths, sets environmental variables, maps drives, or even launches other scripts or applications. Logon scripts are necessary for compatibility with legacy (older mainframe) systems or with some DOS applications. The most common use of logon scripts is to retain drive mappings and other settings when migrating from NetWare.

3

Home Directory

The **home directory** is the default save and load directory for a user. This is typically a network share, but it can also be a local drive. Network share home directories allow roaming users to access any files stored in that directory. Local home directories are not accessible when the user is logged onto a different workstation. Typically, a user's home directory has its permissions set so only that user has access to the directory. When establishing a home directory, you should create the directory first, then define the path in the UEP dialog box.

SETTING DIALIN OPTIONS

By pressing the Dialin button, you access the Dialin Information dialog box, as shown in Figure 3-7. Through this dialog box, you can grant or restrict a user's ability to log on over a RAS connection. If you allow such connections, you can also define the level of callback security for that user. Details on RAS and callback security are found in Chapter 11.

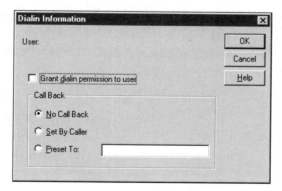

Figure 3-7 Dialin Information dialog box

Managing Users and Resources with Groups

You've seen the level of detail involved in managing users. Just imagine how much work it would be to fill in these details individually for hundreds of users, not to mention granting them access to resources—a topic we've not even covered yet. Fortunately, Windows NT provides a mechanism to make managing users and resources much more reasonable: groups.

As you've learned, a group is just a named collection of users. All members of a group share the privileges or restrictions of that group. Groups are used to give a specific level of access to multiple users through a single management action. Once a group has access to a resource, users can be added to or removed from that group as needed. The group concept is key to managing large numbers of users and their access to any number of resources. In fact, if you use the group concept effectively, there should be little need to assign access rights to an individual user.

A user can be a member of multiple groups. Different groups can be assigned different levels of access to the same resources. In such cases, the most permissive rights will be used, except when access is specifically denied (assigned No Access) to one or more groups.

As you plan your network security (covered in detail in Chapter 5), user base, and resource allocation, remember to keep in mind how you will be managing each group. Think about how groups can be paired with resources to provide you with the greatest range of administrative control. Once your resources are in place and all the required groups have been created, most of your administrative tasks will involve adding users to or removing them from these groups.

To provide the highest degree of control over resources, Windows NT uses two types of groups: local and global. **Local groups** exist only on the computer where they are created. **Global groups** exist throughout a domain. This distinction is very important, as you'll soon see. Local groups can have members who are users or global groups. Global groups can have only users as members.

As you learned in Chapter 1, one of the differences between Windows NT Server and Windows NT Workstation is that the User Manager on a Windows NT Workstation can manage only users and local groups. To create and manage groups across domains, you must have a Windows NT Server in a client/server environment. The User Manager for Domains on Windows NT Server is used to create and manage users, global groups, and local groups. If an NT Workstation is part of a domain, its User Manager can add global groups to local groups, but that is the only activity it can perform with global groups.

With local and global groups, a complete system of links from resources to users can be established. Each resource is assigned to one or more local groups. Each user is assigned to one or more global groups. Global user groups are assigned to local resource groups. Each local group can be assigned different levels or types of access to the resource. By placing a global group in a local group, you assign all members of that global group the privileges of the local group, that is, access to a resource.

PLANNING GROUPS

As stated, you must plan your group management scheme long before you begin implementation. Planning such a scheme involves applying a naming scheme, dividing users into meaningful groups, and understanding the various levels of access your resources offer. For the group method to be effective, you need to manage all access to resources through groups. Never succumb to the temptation to assign access privileges directly to a user account.

Defining group members is often the most time-consuming process of group management. A group should be formed around a common job position, need of resource, or even geographic location. Some existing groupings you can transform into NT groups are:

- Organizational functioning units, workgroups, or departments
- Authorized users of network programs and applications
- Events, projects, or special assignments
- Authorized users of network resources
- Location or geography
- Individual function or job description

Local groups exist only on the computer where they are created. On each computer, all local groups must have a unique name. You can duplicate the names of local groups on different computers, but they will be separate and distinct groups. We don't recommend using the same name twice on any network, even if the architecture allows it.

DEFAULT LOCAL GROUPS

Local groups are defined on each computer hosting a resource. They are used to grant access to resources to users of global groups. Windows NT automatically creates six default groups. These groups and their default members are:

- *Administrators:* Administrator, Domain Administrators
- *Power Users:* None
- *Users:* None
- *Guests:* Guest
- *Backup Operators:* None
- *Replicators:* None

On most NT Workstations, especially those used exclusively for client access and which do not host resources shared with others, no other groups are really necessary. However, you can create new groups (see the section titled "Creating Local Groups") or modify these groups to meet your exact needs.

One additional default group is found on Windows NT—Everyone. The **Everyone** group has every user as a member. This group is not manageable through the User Manager, but it can be used to offer all users access to resources. Service Pack 3 from Microsoft replaces this group with a new group—Authenticated Users. This is to prevent unauthorized access by intruders using the Everyone group. The Everyone group includes absolutely everyone, even non-users. Also, a utility in the Resource Kit removes the Everyone group from the Registry—REGSEC.

Administrators

The **Administrators** local group is a collection of users who have administrative-level privileges on the local computer. All members of this group have the same access privileges as the default Administrator account. The default members of this group include the local Administrator account and the Domain Administrators global group.

Power Users

The **Power Users** local group is a collection of users who have fewer privileges than the Administrator account but more than the common user. All members of this group can share directories and printers, alter environmental elements such as the time and date, and install or remove applications. Power Users can create local user accounts and local groups, but they can manage or delete only those accounts or groups they created. A Power User account should be used for regular system administration instead of a full administrator-level account. This provides the greatest level of security while offering the capability to perform many administrative tasks. Members of the Power Users group are restricted from altering the operating system and many security object settings. This group has no default members.

Users

The **Users** local group is a collection of users who have limited access privileges. All members of this group can log onto the workstation, launch applications, manage owned files, and use both local and network share printers. Members of this group can also create and manage local groups but not users, and they can manage their own profiles (if their profile is not mandatory). Each time a member of the Administrators or Power Users creates a new user account, that account is automatically added to the Users group. All regular users of the network are members of this group. However, it has no default members initially.

Guests

The **Guests** local group is a collection of users who have highly restricted access privileges. All members of this group are limited to application launching, minimal local file management, and printer use. Changes made to the profile by a Guest member are discarded once that user logs off. This group has the Guest account as a default member. If your workstation is attached to a network, anyone may log onto your system as a member of the Guest group.

Backup Operators

The **Backup Operators** group is a collection of users who can access every file on the computer when performing backup operations. All members of the Backup Operators group can use the NT Backup utility to manage file backup and restoration procedures. Backup Operators bypass any and all security restrictions on all resources while performing backup and restore activities. Thus, it is imperative to limit membership to this group. Users can back up any file they can read; Backup Operators can back up every file on the computer. This group has no default members.

Replicators

The **Replicators** group is a special group to be used only by the Replication service and the special replication user created to control that service. All members of the Replicators group can configure the Replication service to act as an import server on the workstation. This service automates file updates from one workstation to another. The Replication service is a feature of NT that is discussed in detail only in Windows NT Server materials because only an NT Server can serve as an export server. This group has no default members.

CREATING LOCAL GROUPS

Creating local groups is even easier than creating user accounts. Once you've settled on a naming convention and a group management organizational scheme, you can create all the local groups you need to manage local resources. Select User, New Local Group from the menu bar of User Manager. The New Local Group dialog box opens, as shown in Figure 3-8.

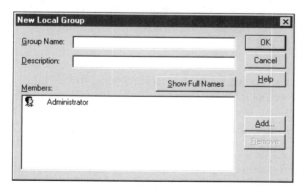

Figure 3-8   New Local Group dialog box

Through this dialog box, you can define the specifics for your group:

- The group must be unique within the local security database.
- The group name may contain both upper- and lowercase letters, numbers, and symbols.
- The name may not contain: " / \ : ; | = + * ? < >

Once you enter a group name meeting these criteria, and a description (optional), click OK. Your new local group will appear in the bottom pane of the User Manager. Notice the icon of a client computer with two user heads floating over it (refer to Figure 3-2); this is the symbol for local groups. The symbol for global groups is a globe with two user heads floating over it.

NT WORKSTATION SECURITY POLICIES

Security policies are important components of the overall security system. Security policies give administrators additional tools to manage and control user accounts and groups. NT has three security policies that are managed through the Policies menu of the User Manager:

- Account policy dictates password settings
- User Rights policy dictates system operation rights
- Auditing policy dictates file access auditing

Administrators are the only users who can work with security policies. It is important to think through any changes to these policies before implementing them. Some changes can prevent users from logging on, others can reduce the privileges of administrators, and yet others can severely affect the system's performance.

THE ACCOUNT POLICY

The **account policy** regulates user account passwords and lockouts. Any changes made to this policy will affect everyone attempting to log onto this workstation. But all users currently logged on are not affected by any new settings until they log off and log back on. To assign an account policy for a user, double-click the username in the User Manager, click the Profile button in the User Properties window, and a screen like that shown in Figure 3-9 appears.

All changes or settings made to the account policy should be made with caution. Frequent expiration of passwords or mandating lengthy passwords may force users to bypass security by writing their passwords down. You need to find a balance between password restrictions and human compliance.

Table 3-1 lists the account policy settings available, the default values, and the range of possible settings.

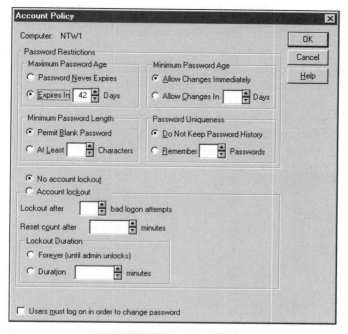

Figure 3-9   Account Policy dialog box

Table 3-1   NT Workstation Account Policy Settings

Policy	Action	Settings	Default
Maximum Password Age	Time period until password change is required	1-999 days or never	42 days
Minimum Password Age	Time period when password change is prevented	1-999 days or immediately	Immediately
Minimum Password Length	Minimum length or blank password	1-14, or blank	Permit blank
Password Uniqueness	Prevents password reuse	1-24 history list or none	No history
Account lockout	Enables failed logon account lockout	Selected or not	No lockout
Lockout after	Number of attempts before lockout	1-999	Blank
Reset count after	Time period until reset of counter	1-99,999 minutes	Blank
Lockout Duration	Duration of lockout	1-99,999 minutes or forever	Blank
Users must log on to change password	Requires users to log on to change password	Selected or not	Not selected

THE USER RIGHTS POLICY

The **user rights** policy controls the system- or computer-specific activities that can be performed on the workstation. User rights set on NT Workstation apply not only to that workstation but to the entire NT Workstation network. Some modifications to user rights can result in undesired effects, so be sure to understand the effects of a right before making changes. You should grant user rights to groups to adhere to the practice of group management, but you can assign user rights to individual user accounts if necessary. To assign a user rights policy, select User Rights from the Policies menu in the User Manager. A screen similar to Figure 3-10 appears.

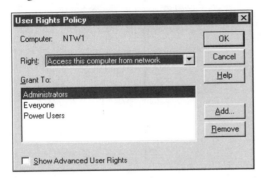

Figure 3-10   User Rights Policy dialog box

There are 10 standard user rights on NT Workstation. Table 3-2 lists these rights, their purposes, and the groups who enjoy these rights by default.

Table 3-2   NT Workstation Standard User Rights

User Right	Description	Default Groups
Access this computer from network	Allows remote access to shared resources on this workstation	Administrators, Everyone, Power Users
Backup files and directories	Allows backups	Administrators, Backup Operators
Change system time	Allows clock changing	Administrators, Power Users
Force shutdown from a remote system	Allows remote system shutdown	Administrators, Power Users
Load and unload device drivers	Allows drivers to be changed	Administrators
Log on locally	Allows the workstation to be used locally	Administrators, Backup Operators, Everyone, Guests, Power Users, Users
Manage and audit Security log	Allows security policy changes	Administrators
Restore files and directories	Allows restoration	Administrators, Backup Operators
Shut down the system	Allows system shutdown	Administrators, Backup Operators, Everyone, Power Users, Users
Take ownership of files or other objects	Allows users to gain authority over system objects	Administrators, Backup Operators, Everyone, Guests, Power Users, Users

In addition to these standard user rights, there are also 17 advanced rights. They are accessible by selecting the Show Advanced User Rights check box at the bottom of the User Rights Policy dialog box, see Figure 3-9. Advanced rights are used for software development and other non–standard system activities; therefore, they are not used for normal workstation administration. Using advanced rights should be considered even more carefully than using standard rights. Table 3-3 lists the advanced user rights, their purposes, and the groups who enjoy these rights by default.

Table 3-3 Advanced User Rights

User Right	Description	Default Groups
Act as part of operating system	Allows users or groups to act like a process with secure trusted privileges to the OS	None
Add workstations to domain	Remotely add new computer accounts to a domain	None
Bypass traverse checking	Allows users or members of groups to traverse directory trees to which they have no other access rights	Everyone
Create pagefile	Allows users or members of groups to create a pagefile	Administrators
Create a token object	Allows users or members of groups to create access tokens	None
Create permanent shared objects	Allows users or members of groups to create permanent shared objects	None
Debug programs	Allows users or members of groups to debug programs	Administrators
Generate security audits	Allows users or members of groups to generate security log audit entries	None
Increase quotas	Allows users or members of groups to increase an object's quotas	None
Increase scheduling priority	Allows users or members of groups to increase an active process's priority	Administrators, Power Users
Lock pages in memory	Allows users or members of groups to lock memory pages in RAM so they are not paged to improve system performance	None
Log on as a batch job	Allows users or members of groups to log on as a batch queue facility	None
Log on as a service	Allows users or members of groups to register with the system as a service	None
Modify firmware environment values	Allows users or members of groups to alter system-wide environment variables	Administrators
Profile single process	Allows users or members of groups to perform performance sampling on single processes	Administrators, Power Users
Profile system performance	Allows users or members of groups to profile system performance	Administrators
Replace process-level tokens	Allows users or members of groups to alter the access token of a process	None

3

THE AUDIT POLICY

The **audit policy** is used to monitor events throughout the system. Auditing records the success or failure of events for every object within the Windows NT environment. It can provide valuable information about security breaches, resource activity, and user adeptness. Auditing is also useful for investigating performance and planning for expansion. To set up auditing, from User Manager, select Auditing from the Policies menu, a screen like that shown in Figure 3-11 appears.

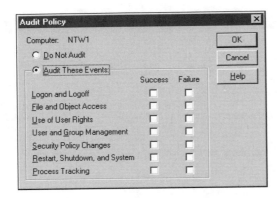

Figure 3-11   Audit Policy dialog box

Events recorded by auditing, called **audit events**, are listed as entries in the **Security log**, which is accessible through the **Event Viewer**. Audit entries in the Security log contain information about the event including user logon identification, the computer used, time, date, and the action or event that instigated an audit.

The auditing system is controlled by three levels of switches or controls. The first or master switch is located on the Audit Policy dialog box shown in Figure 3-11. By default, it is set to Do Not Audit. When you set it to Audit These Events, the seven secondary switches become active.

The second level of switches determines which event types to audit and whether to audit their success and/or failure. The seven audit object types are:

- *Logon and Logoff:* Tracks logons, logoffs, and network connections
- *File and Object Access:* Tracks access to files, directories, printers, and other NTFS objects

- *Use of User Rights:* Tracks use of user rights
- *User and Group Management:* Tracks changes in the accounts of users and groups
- *Security Policy Changes:* Tracks changes of user rights and audit policies
- *Restart, Shutdown, and System:* Tracks server shutdowns and restarts; also logs events affecting system security
- *Process Tracking:* Tracks program activation, program termination, and other object/process access

Third-level switches are relevant only when the second-level switch of File and Object Access is used. Third-level switches are found within the properties of the audited objects themselves. Figures 3-12, 3-13, and 3-14 display the audit dialog boxes for files, directories, and printers, respectively. These screens are accessed by right-clicking an NTFS object and selecting Properties, selecting the Security tab, and then clicking the Audit button.

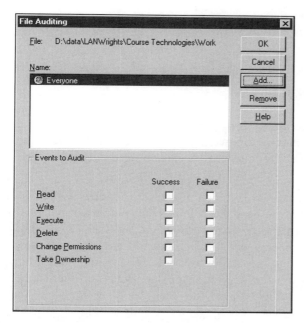

Figure 3-12 File Auditing dialog box

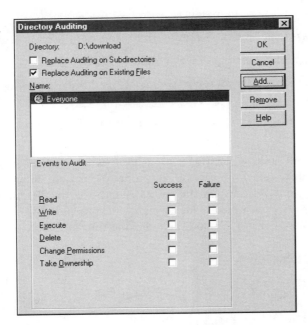

Figure 3-13   Directory Auditing dialog box

Object-level audit switches are all blank or grayed out, and no groups are present in the Name field by default. The Everyone group was added to these dialog boxes before taking these images, so the Events list at the bottom is readable instead of near-invisible gray.

Take notice of the different types of object-level events that can be audited. Each object type has a unique list of possible audit events. File and directory objects have Read, Write, Execute, Delete, Change Permissions, and Take Ownership properties, whereas the printer object has Print, Full Control, Delete, Change Permissions, and Take Ownership properties. These events correspond to an object's services (discussed in Chapter 1). On the object level, the auditing settings apply to all users and groups listed in the Names field. In other words, it's not possible to audit the success of one event for one group and the failure of another event for a different group.

Another important feature that is easily overlooked occurs in the Directory Auditing dialog box (Figure 3-13). The Replace Auditing on Subdirectories and Replace Auditing on Existing File check boxes enable audit control over a directory's contents. These two switches can save hours by eliminating the need to set auditing parameters on every file and directory object separately. However, this convenience should be used carefully. Any current audit settings on content objects will be removed and replaced with only those settings defined.

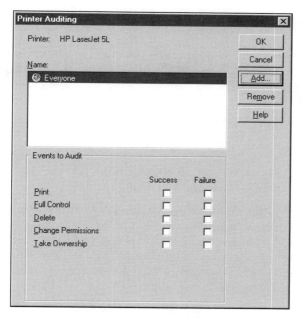

Figure 3-14   Printer Auditing dialog box

 Although auditing is an invaluable resource tool for administrators, it should be used with caution. The system overhead required to watch for, track, and record audit events can cause performance degradation, especially if many events are being tracked and if those events occur often.

One final drawback: Auditing numerous objects or events can result in a large Security log. The Event Viewer (accessed from Start, Programs, Administrative Tools, Event Viewer) can be configured to monitor the size of the Security log and take action when it reaches the target size. The actions are Overwrite Oldest Entries as Needed, Overwrite Entries as Specified Number of Days Old, or Never Overwrite. If the maximum size is reached and Never Overwrite is selected, an alert will appear stating the log needs to be cleared.

SYSTEM POLICIES

System policies are mandatory restrictions imposed on a user's environment by administrators. System policies can be created that affect only a specific user, a specific computer, or everyone within a group. System policies are basically segments of the Registry that overwrite any existing entries in favor of those specified by the system policy creator. System policies can restrict or control customization controls, Control Panel applets, network settings, logon access, and more. The Windows NT Server utility System Policy Editor is required to create, modify, and manage policies. A Windows NT Workstation can be the subject of a system policy, but it does not have the capability to manage system policies in any way.

CHAPTER SUMMARY

- Windows NT user accounts provide individuals with private and secure access to the network or to a standalone computer. A user account contains all the details about a user and is used to offer access to resources. A valid user account and password are required to gain access to a Windows NT computer. Administrator and Guest are the only two default user accounts. The Administrator account has unrestricted access to everything in the NT environment. The Guest account is highly restricted and used only for temporary access.

- A naming convention is a scheme for naming all objects within the NT environment in such a way that the name identifies the resource in a useful manner.

  The User Manager is the administrative utility on Windows NT Workstation used to manage users, groups, and security policies. Management of users includes creating, copying, disabling, deleting, and renaming accounts. Users and groups can be created from scratch, or user accounts can be copied to simplify addition of new users. Each user account can be configured to be a member of one or more groups, to have a user profile defined, and to allow dial-up access.

- Groups are an important design element of Windows NT. They are used to link users to resources and to control each user's level of access. As a client/server system, NT uses global groups to combine users and local groups to manage resources. Only local groups are available for resource management on Windows NT Workstation. Windows NT Workstation has six default groups: Administrators, Power Users, Users, Guests, Backup Operators, and Replicators.

- There are three security policies on Windows NT: account, user rights, and audit. The account policy governs passwords and account lockouts. User rights grant or restrict activities on a computer; there are both standard and advanced user rights. The audit policy is used to track the success or failure of object events.

- System policies are mandatory restrictions placed on a user, computer, or group. NT Workstation can be the subject of system policies, but it lacks the capability to manage them.

KEY TERMS

- **account policy** — An NT security feature that limits and restricts how passwords are defined. An account policy can force password changes, require a minimum length, and prevent password reuse. The account policy also has options for setting the account lockout feature.

- **Administrator account** — The account on an NT system that has complete and unrestricted access to the operating system.

- **Administrators** — A default local group of Windows NT. All members of this group have the same access privileges as the Administrator user account.

- **audit events** — Occurrences within the NT environment that are recorded by the audit system in the Security log. An audit event is the success or failure of an activity with, of, or by an object.

- **audit policy** — An NT security feature in which auditing for the entire system is turned on or off, and the seven audit event types are selected to track success or failure.

3

- **Backup Operators** — A default local group of Windows NT. All members of this group can back up and restore every file on the system in spite of standard security restrictions.

- **Event Viewer** — The NT administrative tool used to view the three logs: system, application, and security.

- **Everyone** — A default group on Windows NT that has every user as a member. This group cannot be managed.

- **global group** — A group that exists throughout a domain.

- **group** — A named collection of user accounts, usually created for some specific purpose (for example, the Accounting group might be the only named entity permitted to use a bookkeeping application; then, by adding or removing individual users from the Accounting group, a network administrator could easily control who may access that application).

- **Guest account** — A default user account on Windows NT that has limited access to basic network resources.

- **Guests** — A default local group on Windows NT. Members of this group have the same access as the Guest default account.

- **home directory** — A user-profile-defined environmental variable; used by NT as the default location to load and save personal data files.

- **local group** — A group that exists only on the computer on which it was created.

- **logon authentication** — The process of validating a user by requiring a matching and valid name and password from a user attempting to gain access to the computer.

- **Logon Information dialog box** — The window that appears on an NT machine when Ctrl-Alt-Del is pressed. A valid username and password must be entered in the fields on this window to gain access to the computer.

- **logon script** — A batch file used to automatically define environmental variables, map drives, or launch applications. Logon scripts are useful only when working with legacy systems or when migrating from NetWare.

- **multiple-user system** — A computing or network operating system that maintains separate collections of information and configuration preferences for more than one user.

- **Power Users** — A default local group on Windows NT. Members of this group have limited administrative privileges.

- **profile** — A collection of user settings and preferences that are automatically saved and loaded when a user logs on to the computer.

- **Replicators** — A default local group on Windows NT. This group is used exclusively for the Replicator service hosted on a Windows NT Server machine.

- **roaming profile** — A user profile that is configured to be downloaded from a server at logon. These types of profiles maintain a consistent user interface for users that must log on to multiple computers.

- **security database** — The encrypted data storehouse of security details within the Windows NT environment. Also called the SAM (Security Account Manager) database, this object stores the names and passwords of all users on a standalone machine for Windows NT Workstation.

- **Security ID (SID)** — The computer-generated identification code used by NT to identify users, computers, groups, and other objects. Every object within the NT environment has a SID, and all SIDs are unique.

- **Security log** — The file where all security-related audit events are recorded. This file is accessed through the Event Viewer.

- **security policies** — The security features of NT defined through the User Manager. There are three security policies: account, user rights, and audit.

- **system policies** — A component of the NT security system. System policies restrict or alter a user's computing environment by directly modifying the Registry. System policies are applied on a user, computer, or group basis. System policies can affect an NT Workstation computer, but they can only be managed from a Windows NT Server computer.

- **User Environment Profile (UEP)** — The name of the collection of data stored within a user account that defines the location of the user's profile, home directory, and logon scripts.

- **User Manager** — The administrative utility of Windows NT Workstation used to manage users, groups, and security policies.

- **user profiles** — The collection of preferences that define the look and use of a user's desktop and computing environments.

- **user rights** — An NT security policy that grants or restricts computer-specific activities to users and groups.

- **username** — The name of a user account used to log onto NT. The username of an account can be changed without modifying the account's SID.

- **Users** — A default local group on Windows NT. Members of this group have normal privileges to launch programs, manage files, and perform low-level administrative tasks.

3

REVIEW QUESTIONS

1. You suspect that a directory containing sensitive information about your organization is being accessed by an unauthorized user. What feature of NT will let you track the use of a directory and its contents?

   a. account policy

   b. user rights policy

   c. audit policy

   d. system policy

2. The User Manager on NT Workstation performs which of the following activities? (Choose all that apply.)

   a. create new users

   b. rename local groups

   c. set account policy

   d. create global groups

   e. add global groups to local groups

3. Bob has been transferred to a new department, but his job description and network responsibilities have not changed. To comply with your organization's naming convention, what is the best and easiest course of action to transfer his user account?

   a. Delete the current account, then create a new account from scratch.

   b. Disable the current account, then create a new account from scratch.

   c. Copy the current account to create a new account, then disable the old account.

   d. Rename the account so its name reflects Bob's new department.

4. One of your administrators has been transferred to another branch of the company in another state. You hire a replacement to take over her responsibilities. What is the best way to create a user account for this new user?

   a. Create a new account from scratch.

   b. Copy the old administrator's account and supply the details for the new person.

   c. Rename the old account for the new person.

5. Which default groups of NT Workstation have the right to log on locally? (Choose all that apply.)

   a. Backup Operators

   b. Guests

   c. Everyone

   d. Users

   e. Power Users

6. Your office has just installed a high–speed color laser printer and has designated your NT Workstation as the printer server. Your boss asked you to track which departments use the printer so the appropriate budgets can be charged for such use. Which of the following steps will enable printer auditing? (Choose all that apply.)

   a. Set the auditing switches on the printer object to record successful print events for the Everyone group.

   b. Grant the Everyone group the auditing right through the User Rights policy.

   c. Set the Audit policy to Audit These Events through the User Manager.

   d. Under Audit These Events, set the audit switch on File And Object Access to Success.

   e. Set the printer priority to 99 (maximum) under the Scheduling tab on the printer's Properties dialog box.

7. Your IS department has installed a new custom application on your NT Workstation. Unfortunately, it seems to conflict with another application, causing both programs to terminate abruptly. Which event type should you audit to record details about the conflict?

   a. File and Object Access

   b. Security Policy Changes

   c. Restart, Shutdown, and System

   d. Process Tracking

   e. Application Environment

8. Which of the following is not a setting found in the Account policy?

   a. Length of passwords

   b. Lockout duration

   c. Maintain password history

   d. Require alphanumeric passwords

   e. Allow blank passwords

9. When creating a new user, which of the following is not an option that appears in the New User dialog box?

   a. User Must Change Password at Next Logon

   b. User Cannot Change Password

   c. User Must Change Password Every X Days (where X can be 0 – 999)

   d. Account Disabled

10. When you make a copy of a user account to create an account for a new user with the same access privileges, what elements of the new account are reset or left blank? (Choose all that apply.)

   a. username

   b. password

   c. profile settings

   d. account Disabled

   e. group memberships

   f. User Must Change Password at Next Logon

   g. Password Never Expires

11. What characteristics do the Administrator and Guest default accounts have in common?

   a. Both give unrestricted access.

   b. Both can have blank passwords.

   c. Neither can be deleted.

   d. Neither can be disabled.

   e. Neither can be locked out.

12. A Windows NT user account stores or references what types of information? (Choose all that apply.)

   a. security through protected privacy

   b. access permissions

   c. network identification

   d. user rights

   e. roaming or remote access

   f. user preferences

13. Windows NT is a multiple-user system because a single user can launch many applications simultaneously. True or False?

14. What elements of NT are used to manage users? (Choose all that apply.)

   a. groups

   b. user accounts

   c. User Manager

   d. Event Viewer

   e. audit policy

   f. account policy

15. Which of the following elements is not part of the user authentication process? (Choose all that apply.)

    a. Ctrl-Alt-Del

    b. username

    c. password

    d. Logon Information dialog box

    e. group memberships

16. Which of the following is not a characteristic of a useful naming convention?

    a. It identifies the department or geographic location of the object.

    b. New names can be created based on the pattern of existing names.

    c. No two objects have the same name.

    d. Each user can name objects at his or her discretion.

    e. An object's name identifies its type.

17. User Manager can be used to manage global groups. True or False?

18. What are the three security policies defined through User Manager? (Select three answers.)

    a. user rights

    b. system

    c. account

    d. audit

    e. roaming

19. When a user account is deleted and a new account is created with the same configuration, the new account has a different SID. True or False?

20. When a user leaves your organization, what should be done with the user account?

    a. nothing

    b. delete it

    c. rename it for a new user

    d. disable it

21. Which of the following elements is not part of a UEP?

    a. profile path

    b. dialin callback settings

    c. home directory definition

    d. logon script location

3

22. Which default local group on Windows NT Workstation does not have any default members? (Choose all that apply.)

   a. Administrators

   b. Power Users

   c. Users

   d. Guests

   e. Backup Operators

   f. Replicators

23. All the default groups of Windows NT Workstation can be managed through the User Manager. True or False?

24. Which groups have the user right to restore files from a backup set?

   a. Administrators

   b. Users

   c. Backup Operators

   d. Power Users

25. On Windows NT Workstation, anyone can shut down the system. True or False?

HANDS-ON PROJECTS

In the following hands-on projects, you will interact with the User Manager to work with user accounts (Projects 3-1 through 3-6), groups (Projects 3-7 and 3-8), and security policies (Projects 3-9 through 3-11).

PROJECT 3-1

To create a new user:

1. Log on as Administrator.

2. Open the User Manager (**Start**, **Programs**, **Administrative Tools**, **User Manager**). See Figure 3-15.

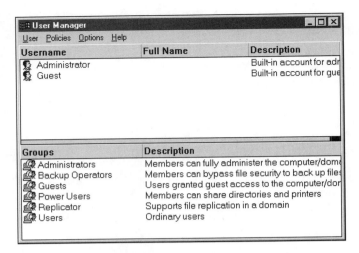

Figure 3-15   User Manager opening screen

3. Select **User, New User** from the menu bar. The New User dialog box opens. See Figure 3-16.

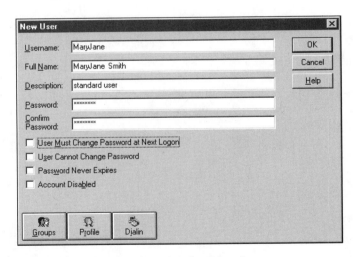

Figure 3-16   User properties for MaryJane

4. Enter the following account details:
   Username: **MaryJane**
   Full Name: **MaryJane Smith**
   Description: **standard user**
   Password/Confirm Password: **password**

5. De-select **User Must Change Password at Next Logon**.

6. Click the **Groups** button at the bottom of the screen. The Group Memberships dialog box opens. See Figure 3–17. Of which group is this user a member by default?
_____

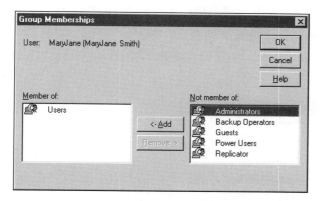

Figure 3-17   Changing group memberships

7. Close this window by clicking **OK**.

8. Click **OK** again to complete the creation of the new user account. The new user, MaryJane, appears in the upper pane of the User Manager. See Figure 3–18.

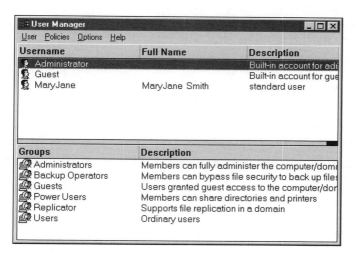

Figure 3-18   A new user is added

9. Keep the User Manager open for the next project.

PROJECT 3-2

To copy a user account:

1. Highlight the user named **MaryJane**.

2. Select **User, Copy** from the menu bar. The Copy of MaryJane dialog box opens. See Figure 3-19.

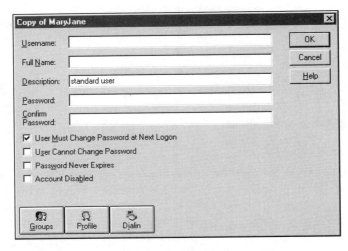

Figure 3-19   Copying a user account

3. Enter the information for the new user in blank fields of Username, Full Name, Password, and Confirm Password.

4. Deselect **User Must Change Password at Next Logon**.

5. Click **OK** to complete the user copy.

6. Keep the User Manager open for the next project.

PROJECT 3-3

To disable a user account:

1. Double-click on the user you created in Project 3-2. The User Properties dialog box for that account opens. See Figure 3-20.

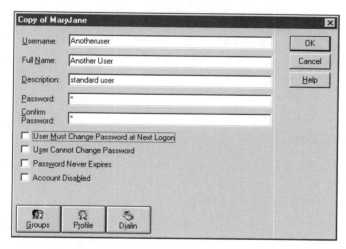

Figure 3-20 Setting user properties

2. Locate and select the **Account Disabled** check box.

3. Close this window by clicking **OK**. This account is now disabled. You can test that this account no longer allows logons by attempting to use this username and password to gain access.

4. To re-enable this account, deselect (uncheck) the **Account Disabled** check box.

PROJECT 3-4

To rename a user account:

1. Highlight the user you created in Project 3-3.

2. Select **User, Rename**.

3. In the Rename dialog box, see Figure 3-21, enter a new name for this account.

Figure 3-21   Renaming a user account

4. Click **OK**. The new name replaces the previous name in the upper pane of User Manager.

5. Leave the User Manager open for the next project.

PROJECT 3-5

To change a UEP:

1. Double-click on the **MaryJane** user account to bring up the User Properties dialog box for that account.

2. Click the **Profile** button. The User Environment Profile dialog box opens. See Figure 3-22.

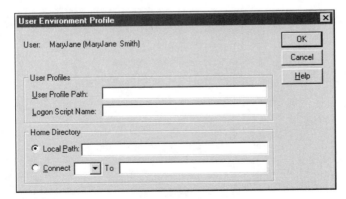

Figure 3-22   Setting the User Environment Profile

3. Select the **Local Path** radio button.

4. Enter **c:\users\%username%** (or the path specified by your instructor).

5. Click **OK** to close this window. *Note:* A warning may appear stating the directory could not be automatically created. See Figure 3-23. (The UEP can create only a single-level directory, so unless the c:\users directory already existed, UEP will not create the specified user directory.)

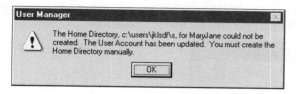

Figure 3-23   UEP cannot create directory

6. Click **OK** in response to the warning.

7. Click the **Profile** button again. Notice the environmental variable of %username% has been replaced with the user's name—MaryJane.

8. Click **OK** to close the UEP dialog box.

9. Click **OK** to close User Properties.

10. Leave the User Manager open for the next project.

PROJECT 3-6

To delete a user account:

1. Highlight the user account you created in Project 3-2.

2. Select **User, Delete**.

3. Click **OK** at the deletion warning.

4. Confirm the deletion by clicking **Yes**.

5. Leave the User Manager open for the next project.

PROJECT 3-7

To create a new local group:

1. Deselect any users currently selected in the upper pane of the User Manager. (Hold down **[Ctrl]** while clicking on a highlighted username to deselect it.)

2. Select **User, New Local Group** from the menu bar. The New Local Group dialog box opens. See Figure 3-24.

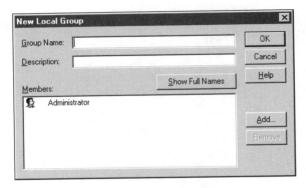

Figure 3-24   Creating a new local group

3. Enter a name for the new group: **SalesForce**.

4. Click **Add**. The Add Users and Groups dialog box opens. See Figure 3-25.

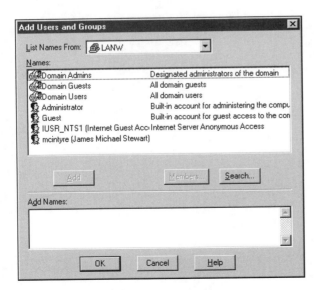

Figure 3-25   Adding a user to a local group

5. Select **MaryJane (MaryJane Smith)**; click **Add**.

6. Click **OK** to close this window. Notice that MaryJane's account now appears in the Members area.

7. Click **OK** to complete the new local group creation. Notice that the SalesForce local group appears in the bottom pane of the User Manager.

8. Leave the User Manager open for the next project.

PROJECT 3-8

To assign an account to a group:

1. Double-click the **MaryJane** user account.

2. Click the **Groups** button in the User Properties dialog box. The Group Membership dialog box opens. See Figure 3-26.

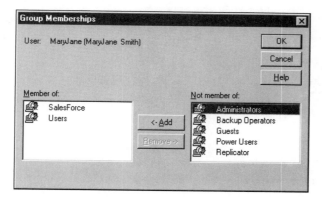

Figure 3-26   Changing group membership

3. Select the **Power Users** group in the Not Member of: field.

4. Click **Add**. MaryJane will be added to the Power Users group.

5. Select the **SalesForce** group in the Member of: field.

6. Click **Remove**. MaryJane will be removed from the SalesForce group.

7. Click **OK** to close Group Membership.

8. Click **OK** to close User Properties.

9. Leave the User Manager open for the next project.

PROJECT 3-9

To set account policies:

1. Select **Policies, Account** from the menu bar. The Account Policy dialog box opens. See Figure 3–27.

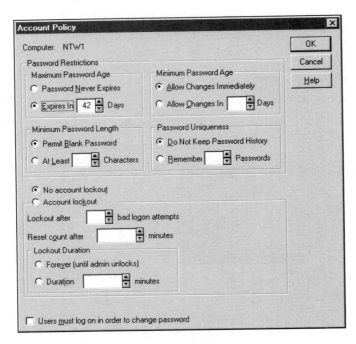

Figure 3-27   Setting account policies

2. Set the Maximum Password Age to **Expires In 25 days**.

3. Set the Minimum Password Length to **At Least 5 characters**.

4. Set the Minimum Password Age to **Allow Changes Immediately**.

5. Set Password Uniqueness to **Do Not Keep Password History**.

6. Select **Account Lockout**.

7. Set the lockout to **Lockout after 3 bad logon attempts**.

8. Set **Reset count after to 10 minutes**.

9. Set Lockout **Duration to 30 minutes**.

10. Click **OK** to save these changes.

11. Leave the User Manager open for the next project.

PROJECT 3-10

To manage user rights:

1. Select **Policies, User Rights**. The User Rights Policy dialog box opens. See Figure 3-28. Notice the right "Access this computer from network" is granted to three groups: Administrators, Everyone, and Power Users.

3

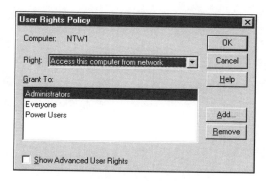

Figure 3-28   Setting user rights

2. From the Right: drop-down list, select **Change the System Time**.
3. Click **Add**.
4. Select the **Everyone** group.
5. Click **Add**. This gives everyone the ability to change the system time.
6. Click **OK**.
7. Click **OK** to close the User Rights window.
8. Leave the User Manager open for the next project.

PROJECT 3-11

To audit user events:

1. Select **Policies, Audit.** The Audit Policy dialog box opens. See Figure 3-29.

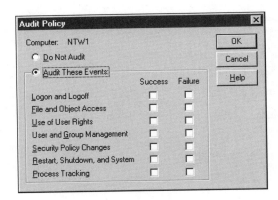

Figure 3-29   Auditing events

2. Select the **Audit These Events** radio button.

3. Check the boxes beside **Logon and Logoff** in both the Success and Failure columns. This will audit successful and unsuccessful logon and logoff attempts.

4. Click **OK** to close the Audit Policy dialog box.

5. Test this audit policy by attempting to log on but mistyping a username or password. Then, log on again as Administrator.

6. Open the Event Viewer (**Start, Programs, Administrative Tools, Event Viewer**). The Event Viewer application opens. See Figure 3-30.

7. Select **Log, Security** from the menu bar.

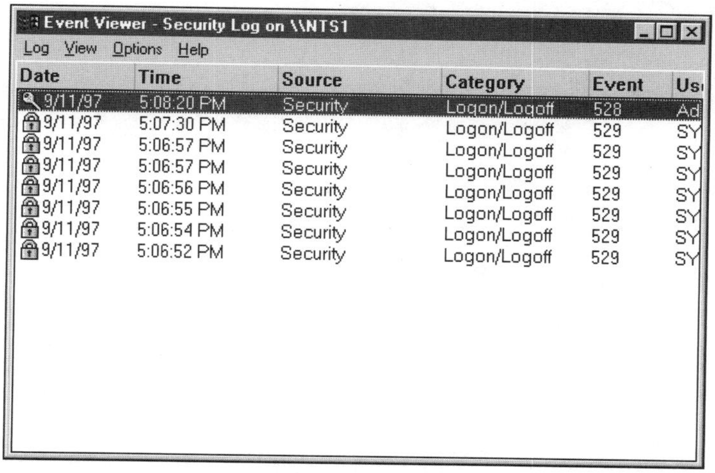

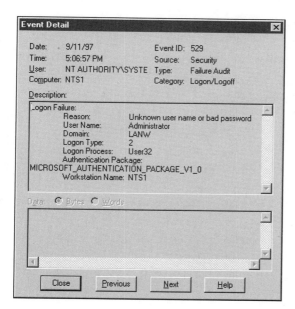

Figure 3-30   Security log in Event Viewer

8. Double-click the top item in the Security log list. The Event Detail dialog box opens. See Figure 3-31.

Figure 3-31   Event Detail dialog box

9. Click **Close** to exit the Event Detail dialog box.

10. Exit Event Viewer.

11. Return to the Audit Policy dialog box and deselect the **Success** and **Failure** for **Logon and Logoff**. Select **Do Not Audit**.

12. Click **OK**.

13. Close the User Manager.

CASE PROJECTS

1. Your organization has recently established a new security policy. As the system administrator, you have been given the task of complying with the new restrictions.

   Required Result: Account users who fail to log on successfully after three tries should be locked out.

   Optional Desired Results: Eliminate the need for an administrator to re-enable user accounts after lockout, and reset the counting of failed logon attempts after five minutes.

   Proposed Solution: Establish an accounts policy; enable account lockouts.   Set failed attempts to three, counter reset to five minutes, and duration to forever.

   Which of the following results does this solution deliver? Explain.

   a. The proposed solution produces the desired result and both of the optional desired results.

   b. The proposed solution produces the desired result but only one of the optional desired results.

   c. The proposed solution produces the desired result but neither of the optional desired results.

   d. The proposed solution does not produce the desired result.

2. Your organization maintains highly confidential accounting reports for many businesses in your area. Your Backup Operators perform daily system-wide backups to protect the data on the network.

   Required Result: Prevent Backup Operators from restoring files from a backup set to a FAT partition.

   Optional Desired Results: Limit restoration of backup set files to Administrators; retain the ability of Backup Operators to create backups.

   Proposed Solution: Revoke the user right of Restore Files and Directories from the Backup Operators group.

    Which of the following results does this solution deliver? Explain.

    a. The proposed solution produces the desired result and both of the optional desired results.

    b. The proposed solution produces the desired result but only one of the optional desired results.

    c. The proposed solution produces the desired result but neither of the optional desired results.

    d. The proposed solution does not produce the desired result.

3. Your company has recently hired 27 college interns to help with data processing. What is the most efficient way to create user accounts for them?

    Required Result: Create separate user accounts for each intern.

    Optional Desired Results: Each user account must have the same configuration settings. You would also like to minimize your administrative time in creating the accounts.

    Proposed Solution: Create 27 user accounts from scratch, making sure to duplicate all settings in each account.

    Which of the following results does this solution deliver? Explain.

    a. The proposed solution produces the desired result and both of the optional desired results.

    b. The proposed solution produces the desired result but only one of the optional desired results.

    c. The proposed solution produces the desired result but neither of the optional desired results.

    d. The proposed solution does not produce the desired result.

4. A new slide printer was added to your network, and your NT Workstation has been designated as the print server. Everyone in the office wants to "test" the printer, but because each slide costs more than $5, this is a waste of money. How do you restrict users from using the slide printer?

    Required Result: Restrict access to the printer to only those users responsible for creating slide presentations.

    Optional Desired Results: Track successful and failed use of the slide printer. Give the boss access to print slides.

    Proposed Solution: Establish an audit policy that tracks usage of the printer object.

Which of the following results does this solution deliver? Explain.

a. The proposed solution produces the desired result and both of the optional desired results.

b. The proposed solution produces the desired result but only one of the optional desired results.

c. The proposed solution produces the desired result but neither of the optional desired results.

d. The proposed solution does not produce the desired result.

5. The receptionist needs the capability to type and print memos using an NT Workstation computer. The receptionist position is a part-time job that six individuals share throughout the week.

What is the most efficient way to create user accounts?

Required Result: Grant limited access rights to the receptionists to accomplish their work tasks.

Optional Desired Results: Maintain privacy for each receptionist. Maintain consistent desktop and environment settings for all receptionist users.

Proposed Solution: Let each receptionist use the default Guest account.

Which of the following results does this solution deliver? Explain.

a. The proposed solution produces the desired result and both of the optional desired results.

b. The proposed solution produces the desired result but only one of the optional desired results.

c. The proposed solution produces the desired result but neither of the optional desired results.

d. The proposed solution does not produce the desired result.

CONFIGURING WINDOWS NT WORKSTATION

Some of the most important activities in the life of any network or system administrator occur when new systems must be installed and configured and when the operating systems of existing systems are updated with newer materials. Especially when working with existing systems, it's essential to understand what's involved when configuring a new OS, and to take appropriate steps to protect existing data and applications. In this chapter, you learn how to approach the post-installation process for Windows NT Workstation and about the many utilities and configuration controls available to create exactly the kind of working environment users will need.

AFTER READING THIS CHAPTER AND COMPLETING THE EXERCISES YOU WILL BE ABLE TO:

- CONFIGURE USER-SPECIFIC SETTINGS USING THE CONTROL PANEL
- CONFIGURE SYSTEM-SPECIFIC SETTINGS, SUCH AS DRIVERS, USING THE CONTROL PANEL
- ADD AND REMOVE HARDWARE ELEMENTS, SUCH AS SCSI ADAPTERS OR CD-ROM DRIVES
- INSTALL OPTIONAL WINDOWS NT ACCESSORIES AND THIRD-PARTY APPLICATIONS
- UNDERSTAND THE REGISTRY AND ITS ROLE IN MANAGING A WINDOWS NT CONFIGURATION
- USE THE WINDOWS NT DIAGNOSTICS SYSTEM STATUS REPORTING UTILITY

THE WINDOWS NT CONTROL PANEL

Working through the **Control Panel** is the easiest way to make changes to the Windows NT environment. From the Control Panel, you can make changes that affect only a single user's **desktop** or **runtime environment** or make changes to a system's configuration that will affect all users of that machine. This section lists the Control Panel icons that belong to each such category, and subsequent sections describe the applications beneath these icons and their settings.

Access the Control Panel by clicking the Start button, Settings, and Control Panel. A screen similar to Figure 4-1 opens with icons for all Control Panel applications, which are commonly called Control Panel **applets** (here, applet is used as a diminutive for application, to indicate a small, tightly focused system utility). Henceforth, these tools will be called Control Panel applets or just applets.

 You can create shortcuts to commonly used Control Panel applets by right-clicking any applet icon on the Control Panel, selecting Create Shortcut from the menu, and placing the shortcut on the desktop for easier access.

Figure 4-1   Windows NT Control Panel

The following Control Panel applets are used to modify individual users' environments. The changes affect the settings for whichever account happens to be open at the time:

- *Display:* Sets colors for Windows' elements such as workspace background, scroll bars, title bars, and so forth; also configures patterns, wallpaper, and, screen savers
- *Mouse:* Deals with mouse sensitivity, button configuration, and settings for double-click speed, cursor shapes and sizes, and so forth
- *Keyboard:* Sets keyboard delay and speed
- *Sounds:* Maps sounds to system events
- *Accessibility Options:* Sets interface options for users with special needs

The following Control Panel applets affect the machine where they're used, so that any users who log onto that Windows NT Workstation, (not just the one who made the changes) will notice the changes introduced by these applets. In many cases, only an administrator will have sufficient access rights to the machine to make such changes.

- *Fonts:* Installs, removes, and views installed TrueType fonts
- *Ports:* Configures serial port settings and defines additional logical ports
- *Printers:* Runs the Print Manager
- *Date/Time:* Sets the system's clock and time zone
- *Network:* Sets network components including protocols, connectivity utilities, and network interface cards (NICs); also determines workgroup/domain status and sets the computer name
- *Server:* Manages resources being accessed by remote users; allows you to determine which users are connected to shared resources and to disallow their further use, or simply break an existing connection between one or more users and any specific shared resource
- *Services:* Allows the manipulation of service startup parameters; used to stop and start services like the Alerter service (which sends warning or status messages across the network to a designated recipient), the Remote Procedure Call service (used to send and receive information across the network), and the Spooler service (handles incoming print jobs on those NT Workstations with printers attached)
- *Devices:* Controls the state of active and inactive device services, such as hard disks, CD-ROMs, tape drives, and their controllers, as well as network interfaces, and other peripherals that may be attached to a particular machine
- *Display:* Installs and removes video drivers, configures video resolution, color palette, font size, and refresh rate
- *Drivers:* Installs, configures, and removes software drivers for add-on multimedia sound boards, video boards, TV boards, and so forth
- *UPS:* Allows interfacing with serial-attached **uninterruptible power supply (UPS)** devices
- *Modems:* Sets up a modem for dial-up networking and/or incoming remote access via data or fax

- *Dial-Up Monitor:* Keeps track of the traffic during an access session
- *Network:* Provides interface for installation and configuration of NICs, plus related protocol configuration and binding information
- *SCSI Adapters:* Scans and resolves drivers for all supported SCSI adapters as well as other mass-storage device drivers
- *Telephony:* Deals with all of the parameters of the Telephony API (application programming interface). The Windows NT Telephony API provides programs with a consistent interface to telecommunications services, and a standard service provider interface makes it easier for hardware developers to write drivers for their hardware to work with Windows NT.

The following Control Panel applets handle both user and system settings. Portions of these applets modify the workstation itself and affect all users thereafter, whereas other portions only modify the profile of the user who's currently logged on.

- *International:* Sets language, currency formats, special characters, and the date/time display—per system for language settings, per user for everything else
- *System:* Sets virtual memory page size, system and application environment variables, system recovery options, and the startup operating system—per system except for user environment variables (per user)
- *MIDI Mapper:* Remaps Musical Instrument Digital Interface (MIDI) key or patch commands to work with MIDI synthesizers that don't comply with Microsoft's general MIDI specifications

The following sections detail specific Control Panel applets and their configurations.

SYSTEM APPLET

The System applet controls Windows NT startup parameters, including the default operating system, timeout period, system environment variables, and user environment variables. As mentioned, the System applet handles both per-user and system settings. The primary interface to the System applet consists of a set of folder-style tabs in the upper portion of its display window. These tabs are labeled: General, Performance, Environment, Startup/Shutdown, Hardware Profiles, and User Profiles.

General Tab

The General tab of the System applet appears by default when that applet is launched. It's an information screen rather than an active system control. The General tab does, however, include some useful information, labeled as follows:

- *System:* Indicates the version and build number of Microsoft Windows NT that's currently running on the machine

- *Registered to:* Reproduces the information about user and company name entered when this instance of Windows NT was installed on the machine

- *Computer:* Indicates what kind of CPU Windows NT detects on the machine and how much RAM is installed on the machine

This is essentially the same information that appears when you select Help, About Windows NT from the Windows NT Explorer menu, except that the Help, About... screen shows the level of service pack that's installed on the computer, and the General tab on the System applet does not. If you want the most useful information about a Windows NT system, use the Help, About... entry.

Performance Tab

The Performance tab includes two control areas: Application Performance and Virtual Memory. Application Performance allows the priority granted to the foreground application—the one that's running on-screen at any given moment—to exceed that given to applications that may be running in the background at the same time. Because this produces snappier performance, especially for screen refresh and mouse tracking, this is the default for Windows NT Workstation and need not be changed, unless a shared printer or some other resource available to the network is installed on some particular NT Workstation machine.

The Virtual Memory area controls how a Windows NT system uses a combination of real RAM and disk space to create a pool of memory for system and application use. By clicking the Change button in the Virtual Memory area on the Performance tab, another window labeled Virtual Memory opens, as shown in Figure 4-2. Before you can explore its details, you must understand the virtual memory model that Windows NT uses.

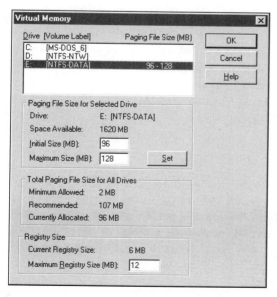

Figure 4-2 Virtual Memory management options

Virtual memory consists of the machine's actual physical RAM plus a **paging file**(s) (PAGEFILE.SYS) that resides on a physical disk attached to the system. The paging file acts like an extension to the system's RAM, which is why it's called virtual memory. Windows NT coordinates the swapping of special 4 KB data units between the paging file and RAM, where such units are called **memory pages**, or more simply, pages. The combination of memory pages in RAM and on disk creates a collection of pages called virtual memory that allows a system to run more and larger applications at any given moment than a system's RAM might physically be able to accommodate. Administrators can change the size of the paging file to help optimize system performance; this usually involves increasing the values assigned to the initial and maximum sizes of this file to give the system more room in which to operate.

The default paging file size for Windows NT equals the amount of physical RAM plus 11 MB. Thus, if a system incorporates 16 MB of RAM, Setup creates a paging file of 27 MB. For a system with 16 MB of RAM, experience indicates that it is a good idea to set the minimum paging file to 32 MB, or double the amount of RAM. If another drive is present on the machine, Microsoft also suggests that a paging file should not reside on the same physical disk as the Windows NT system files. This decreases disk contention between swapping memory pages and accessing system files.

The Windows NT paging file is different from a swap file in that the paging file need not occupy contiguous space on a hard drive. Unlike Windows 95, Windows NT **Virtual Memory Manager (VMM)** maps pages into and out of a paging file as needed and can distribute page writes when a paging file is not contiguous. Figure 4-2 shows the Virtual Memory dialog box, where you can set paging file parameters and view and set the maximum size of a machine's NT Registry database.

Environment Tab

The Environment tab of the System Properties window shown in Figure 4-3 allows **environment variables** to be set. The top pane of the tab controls settings for system-wide environment variables. The bottom pane controls local user environment variables. Only a local user who is currently logged on can set variables on this tab. These variables control how Windows NT operates, but most particularly how older 16-bit Windows or DOS programs behave within the Virtual DOS Machines (VDMs) within which they must run in the Windows NT environment.

Startup/Shutdown Tab

On the Startup/Shutdown tab shown in Figure 4-4, you can configure a system to perform specific actions at startup and if a system STOP error occurs. Startup controls occur in the region of this window labeled System Startup and permit users to assign a startup message that appears when loading Windows NT, to provide a menu of operating system choices. The same area also permits users to vary the delay between displaying this startup message and continuing with the software load. The default is 30 seconds but is often reduced to 5 or 10 seconds to speed system startup.

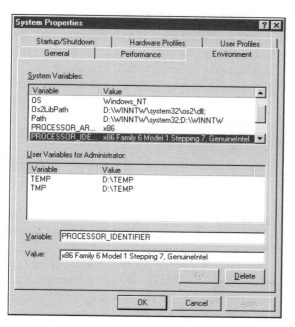

Figure 4-3   Environment tab

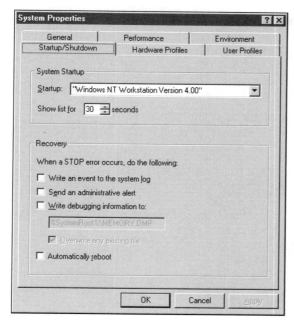

Figure 4-4   Startup/Shutdown tab

The options in the area labeled Recovery in this window are a bit more esoteric. They provide special controls to deal with an outright Windows NT system crash. Normally, when a regular application fails, the application itself generates an error message to the event log while dumping the contents of its address space to a file. When the whole NT system halts due to a STOP error, the entire contents of the computer's virtual memory is dumped to a .DMP file (which resides in the %systemroot% or \winnt folder, by default). Although this dump file is of little use to ordinary mortals and can usually be discarded, this information can be invaluable when debugging system or application problems. There are also options for administrative alerts and for automatic rebooting of the system.

Hardware Profiles Tab

Use the Hardware Profiles tab shown in Figure 4-5 to create and save profiles for different computer hardware configurations. This normally only applies when using a portable computer, to activate particular devices and services, depending on whether the computer is docked or undocked. You can create two hardware profiles for a laptop: docked and undocked. Then at startup, select Device Hardware Profiles from the startup list and boot the system using the hardware profile that reflects current circumstances. This prevents the system from producing startup alerts or errors when a network attachment isn't available (as when operating undocked) and permits users to get to work more quickly without provoking anxiety about errors that aren't really errors.

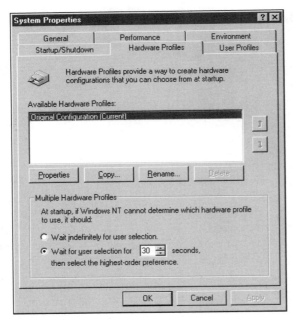

Figure 4-5   Hardware Profiles tab

User Profiles Tab

On the User Profiles tab, you supply settings and preferences that govern desktop layout and appearance, visible icons and applications, associations between file extensions and applications, or events and sounds in special files called **user profiles**. It's typical for individual users to have their own profiles, but it's also possible to create a single profile that services an entire group of users. There are two types of user profiles: local or roaming. A **local profile** resides only on a single computer, whereas a **roaming profile** resides on a networked server, enabling its user to load that profile from any Windows NT machine on the network. Local profiles reside in a file named NTUSER.DAT in the %systemroot%\profiles\%username% folder by default. Local and roaming profiles are covered in more detail later in this chapter.

DATE/TIME APPLET

Double-clicking the Date/Time icon brings up the Date/Time Properties window shown in Figure 4-6. Here you can set the calendar date, clock time, and time zone. When you set the time, the timer clock is set directly on the system's BIOS.

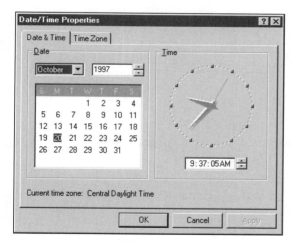

Figure 4-6   Date/Time applet

The Time Zone tab allows you to modify a system's time zone setting by selecting a time zone from a list. Time zone information is stored internally as either a negative or a positive offset to Greenwich Mean Time. This also supports automatic updates for daylight savings time and normal time, in those areas where such seasonal time changes occur.

SERVICES APPLET

Double-clicking the Services icon on the Control Panel brings up the Services dialog box shown in Figure 4-7, where you can start and stop Windows NT system services and specify when they are loaded. In the Windows NT environment, a **service** is a process that runs without requiring a user to be logged on, effectively making such a service act as if it were part of the OS. A service is similar to a UNIX Daemon or a NetWare Loadable Module. It gains the same rights as particular users through the Windows NT API functions named LogonUser and ImpersonateUser. Many services (for example, the Replicator service) require an account name as a part of their installation and configuration.

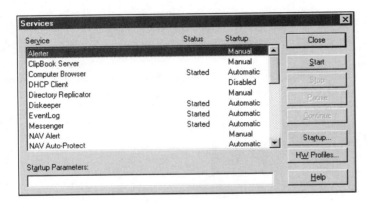

Figure 4-7   Services dialog box

Parameters for services are not easily changed. The Registry should be used to store configuration information, so the service must check for Registry settings. Table 4-1 lists Windows NT Workstation's default services and their functions.

Some of the services that appear in Figure 4-7 do not appear in Table 4-1 because they are not considered to be default services for Windows NT Workstation.

Table 4-1   Windows NT Default Services

Service	Function
Alerter	Along with the Messenger service, generates warning messages about NetBIOS based events, messages, and problems
Clipbook Server	Allows sharing of Clipbook pages among network users
Computer Browser	Allows browsing the network for resources shared by other computers
Directory Replicator	Performs directory replication service for administrators to easily copy complete directories to multiple workstations
Event Log	Monitors a workstation's use by local and remote users and records significant events; also reports internal error conditions such as malfunctioning hardware, etc.
Messenger	Sends and receives messages in conjunction with the Alerter Service; enables use of Service Message Blocks (SMBs) for communications from other networked machines; it uses a username and a workstation name in the NetBIOS name table, with a hex 03 appended to the end of each name
Net Logon	Verifies the identity of users who log onto a workstation, workgroup, or domain
Network DDE (Dynamic Data Exchange)	Required for dynamic data exchange between workstations
Network DDE SDM (Shared Database Manager)	Database manager used by Network DDE
NT LM Security Support Provider	Supplies Windows NT security to RPC Applications that do not use LAN Manager named pipe transports
OLE (Object Linking and Embedding)	Provides OLE support to applications (Microsoft now refers to this service as the Common Object Model (COM), but OLE still appears in the Services window.)
Remote Procedure Call Locator	Used by the RPC to locate available workstations to process remote procedure calls
Remote Procedure Call (RPC)	Primarily used to support client access to the NT machines; also a necessary interprocess communication (IPC) mechanism for Client/Server computing
Schedule	Required for prescheduled commands, such as automated backups, to run at a specified time
Server	Allows a device to accept requests from another computers redirector—MS-NET's network file system mounter
Spooler	Allows a workstation to spool printer files
UPS	Monitors the uninterruptible power supply and instructs the system to issue warnings, save files, and shut down prior to power outages
Workstation	The redirector service that allows access to shared resources

4

TELEPHONY APPLET

The Telephony applet controls settings that permit application programs and communications services to use telephones and **telephony** devices such as faxes and modems. Two tabs appear in the Dialing Properties window shown in Figure 4-8. On the first tab, My Locations, you can describe dialing and area code information about whatever location you are dialing from. This is ideal for traveling users who require a variety of dialing options for telephony-compliant applications. These options include area code, regional location, and how to access outside lines from each location. If a user must charge to a calling card to place a call through the modem, this applet permits such information to be provided as part of the dial string.

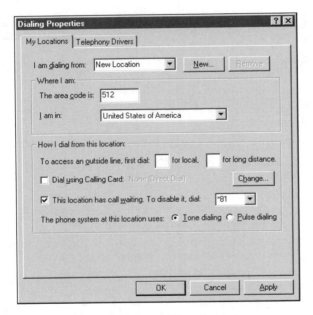

Figure 4-8   Dialing Properties dialog box

To configure a new dial location:

1. Select New and enter the name of the location in the dialog box that opens.

2. Supply the location's area code and country data in the "Where I am:" section.

3. Complete the "How I dial from this location:" section. To add a brief pause to dial string (necessary in some PBX or keyset sytems), enter one or more commas to cause the dialer to delay approximately one-half second per comma.

4. Because call waiting can interrupt modems, you may wish to disable call waiting for lines that support this optional feature (check your local telephone book for your call-waiting disable string). You can choose a disable code from the list, but you must know which entry to choose.

5. To support different types of telephone handsets, you can configure the telephony applet to dial using tones or pulses.

6. If users must charge calls to a credit card, you must check the "Dial using Calling Card" box and then select an entry from the list of calling cards that appears.

Table 4-2 shows options available for calling card dialing.

Table 4-2   Options for Calling Card Dialing

Option	Function
0–9	Dials digits
A–D	Control hexadecimal digits used by some phone companies
E	Country code
F	Area or city code
G	Local phone number
H	Calling card number
* or #	The * and # keys on the telephone
T	Touch-tone dialing
P	Pulse dialing
,	Pause (approximately 0.5 second)
!	Flash hook (activates call waiting, or other optional dialing features)
W	Wait for a second dial tone; required when dialing for an "outside line"
$	Wait for an acknowledgment after dialing calling card access number
?	Solicit user input before continuing

The Telephony Drivers tab includes the two primary drivers needed for Windows NT telephony-compliant applications. Both are installed by default—namely, the TAPI (Telephony API) Kernel service provider and the generic Unimodem Service Provider. This tab is also used to add or remove modem drivers, and other telephony drivers, if needed to support modem-based communications or other telephony applications on a particular Windows NT Workstation.

ADD/REMOVE PROGRAMS APPLET

Double-clicking the Add/Remove Programs Control Panel icon opens the Add/Remove Programs Properties window shown in Figure 4-9. On the Install/Uninstall tab you can install and/or remove optional components that ship with Windows NT as well as third-party software and applications that support this method of installation. (The other method of installation, used with many Windows NT programs, is through an application's setup program, invoked by clicking Start, Run, and entering the path to the installation program.)

If an application is installed through the Add/Remove Programs icon, this utility tracks the various .INF files used to install that application. These .INF files contain instructions that the application's setup program uses to write files and configuration information to various folders in the NT file system and to the Windows NT Registry. Windows NT then uses this information to uninstall the application when instructed to do so. The most common name for any .INF file is OEMSETUP.INF and is usually supplied along with other program files by software vendors on the installation media.

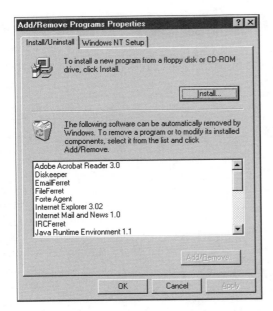

Figure 4-9   Adding and removing applications in Windows NT

Windows NT Setup is the second tab that appears in the Add/Remove Programs Properties dialog box. If you select this tab, it shows the various categories of NT system software for which optional installation selections are available—these include Accessibility Options, Accessories, Communications, and Games, among others. Each category can be further investigated, and elements individually selected or deselected, by clicking the Details button. These controls permit selection of which optional system elements are installed and can be used to install missing elements after an initial installation has occurred or to selectively remove such system elements from an existing installation.

SCSI ADAPTERS APPLET

The SCSI Adapters icon accesses the SCSI Adapters window, shown in Figure 4-10. This applet is used to add, remove, and configure **Small Computer System Interface (SCSI)** devices, such as SCSI adapters, SCSI-based scanners or CD-ROM drives. Depending on how the hardware is configured, Windows NT can boot either from an Integrated Drive

Electronics (IDE) or SCSI hard drive (and even from a CD-ROM drive with the proper CDFS driver installed).

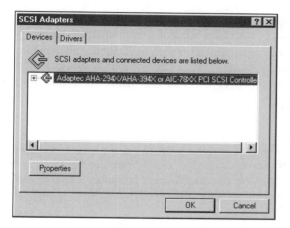

Figure 4-10   SCSI Adapters dialog box

If you install Windows NT on a system where it will boot from a SCSI drive, be sure to set the SCSI ID of that drive to 0 for best results (this is the default boot drive for many SCSI controllers). On the other hand, on a system where IDE and SCSI drives co-reside, if the machine is to boot from an IDE drive, make sure that none of the SCSI drives IDs is set to 0, or the system may try to boot from that SCSI drive rather than the IDE drive you intend it to boot from. As with other Windows NT hardware components, never try to use a disk controller (either IDE or SCSI) that's not on the latest HCL, or for which a current Windows NT driver is not available.

Devices Tab

The Devices tab in the SCSI Adapters window lists all SCSI adapters installed on the system; for each adapter, all attached devices are also listed, in hierarchical fashion. To obtain a description of any device's configuration, double-click the entry for that device in this display. For a similar display for an adapter, you must click the Properties button beneath the list pane, after highlighting the controller of your choice. Either way, this produces a Properties window, for both adapters and their attached devices.

For adapters, the Properties window has three tabs: Cardinfo (indicates the adapter's manufacturer, a device map, and its operational status), Drivers (gives the full name and revision level, plus the name of the file in which it resides), and Resources (shows the adapter's IRQ setting, its I/O range, and its memory buffer addresses). The Properties window for SCSI devices connected to adapters has two tabs: General (lists the device type, manufacturer, and operation status) and Settings (lists target ID, firmware revision, and its SCSI connection information).

Drivers Tab

The Drivers tab in the SCSI Adapters window is where all the real action takes place. This particular tab permits administrators to install **device drivers** for a SCSI device, such as a hard drive, by clicking on the Add button beneath the list of installed drivers. The drivers that appear in the Add list on this tab are organized by manufacturer (left-hand column) and adapter make and model (right-hand column). These listed items include only drivers present on the Windows NT installation CD-ROM. If another device driver has been obtained from the manufacturer, click the Have Disk button beneath the display list and point the applet at the appropriate files.

 The Drivers tab shows all installed drivers in the list area in the center of the display. If the right-hand entry reads "Started" this indicates that the driver was initialized during system startup, which is exactly what's required for a basic system resource like a hard disk or CD-ROM drive.

DEVICES ICON

The Devices icon accesses the Devices dialog box shown in Figure 4-11, where devices can be managed in much the same way as services in the Services applet. To start or stop a device, follow these steps:

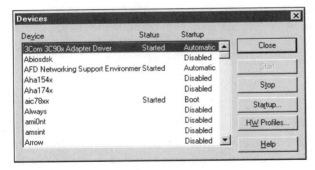

Figure 4-11   Devices dialog box

1. In the Control Panel window, double-click the Devices icon.

2. In the Devices dialog box, select a device. If "Started" appears in the Status column for a device, that device driver is loaded. If the Status column is blank, that device driver is not loaded.

3. Choose the Start or Stop button. (Some devices are essential to system operation and cannot be stopped. When such a device is selected, the Stop button is unavailable.)

4. Click the Close button.

To start up devices, you must be logged onto a user account that has membership in the Administrators local group. To set the startup type of a device:

1. In the Control Panel window, double-click the Devices icon.

2. In the Devices dialog box, select a device.

3. Click the Startup button.

4. Under Startup Type, select Boot, System, Automatic, Manual, or Disabled. *Caution:* Changing the startup type of a Boot or System device can leave the system in an unusable state.

5. Click OK.

6. In the Devices dialog box, click the Close button.

TAPE DEVICES APPLET

The Tape Devices icon accesses the Tape Devices dialog box shown in Figure 4-12, which detects and displays SCSI tape devices and installs and starts the appropriate tape drivers. The computer does not need to be restarted for the tape drivers to start. When you open the Tape Devices icon and click the Detect button, Windows NT automatically detects any tape devices and selects the proper driver for each supported tape device.

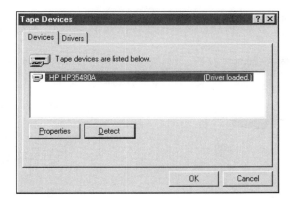

Figure 4-12   Tape Devices dialog box

You can also install, remove, and start tape drivers manually. To add a tape device, the Detect button must register its presence; at that point, device support may be added. To add a tape driver, click on the Drivers tab, click the Add button, and then select the correct driver from the list that Windows NT presents (this requires ready access to the original installation files for Windows NT, or a driver disk from the manufacturer). Once installed, a driver may be started or stopped simply by selecting the appropriate check boxes in the Driver Properties window. The Tape Devices window also provides SCSI tape device information, including information on the SCSI ID number, firmware information, SCSI host adapter, and more. This information may be easily obtained simply by examining the Properties window for the device (by highlighting the device in the device list, then clicking the Properties button).

PCMCIA APPLET

PCMCIA stands for Personal Computer Memory Card International Association and defines a set of interfaces for plugging slim, card-shaped devices into PCs. Although aimed primarily at laptops because of their compact size and powerful functions, PCMCIA adapters are also available for desktop machines. Today, PCMCIA cards are also called PC Cards, but Windows NT still refers to them as PCMCIA. Although a great variety of devices are available in PC Card format, typical PC Card devices include memory modules, modems, network interfaces, SCSI controllers, and floppy drive attachments. PC cards make it easy to attach devices to laptops, and permit such machines to take on flexible configurations to match users' changing needs for computer peripherals.

In Windows NT, the PCMCIA Control Panel applet lists which cards are installed in which sockets, how they are configured, and what resources the PCMCIA controller is using. See Figure 4–13. When you add or remove a PCMCIA card, you must reboot the system before the PCMCIA utility can recognize the change. For many PCMCIA cards, the Windows NT PCMCIA Control Panel applet will suggest the correct device driver when it detects a particular device and allows you to install it immediately thereafter. This helps maintain the flexibility that PC Cards support so well.

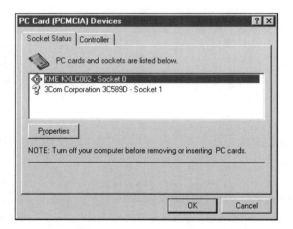

Figure 4-13   PC Card (PCMCIA) Devices dialog box

PORTS APPLET

Windows NT can support up to 256 serial **ports** on a single computer, all of which are configured using the Ports applet. This applet applies only to serial ports; however, it may not be used to configure parallel ports. Most ordinary PCs include two built-in external serial ports, which are normally controlled by the onboard system BIOS (and will be either enabled or disabled, depending on the BIOS settings stored in the computer's CMOS).

The COM ports COM1 and COM2 that usually attach through a PC's motherboard need not be assigned to external ports. Internal communication devices, such as an inport mouse or an internal modem, may claim either or both of these COM port addresses. One of the Ports applet's biggest advantages is that it makes it easy to add COM ports addressed as COM5 or higher on a standard PC.

 A common configuration mistake is to use a modem that requires COM2 while at the same time assigning the COM2 resource to an external serial port. This may cause a serial mouse and an internal modem to conflict. To avoid this mistake, disable COM2's attachment to an external port in the BIOS. This requires that you watch the initial boot-up dialog on a PC and press the appropriate keyboard combination—it is often F1—to launch the BIOS configuration utility. Once launched, you must find the COM port configuration section and explicitly disable the external port for COM2. Then it's safe to install the modem, knowing that the potential for conflict has been eliminated.

The Ports list (the white box that occupies the majority of the Ports applet display shown in Figure 4-14) lists all COM ports that are active and installed on a Windows NT machine. The buttons to the right of the Ports list control the operations that can be performed on COM ports on a machine. These include: Settings (shows existing settings for the selected port and permits them to be changed), Add (permits additional COM ports to be installed one at a time), and Delete (permits existing COM ports to be removed one at a time).

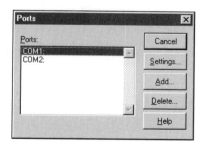

Figure 4-14   Ports dialog box

Adding a COM port in the Ports applet is quite different from enabling or disabling an external serial port on a PC's motherboard. For one thing, because COM1 and COM3 share an IRQ, as do COM2 and COM4, you generally begin adding COM ports numbered 5 and higher. Only if you need a large number of serial devices should you need COM ports with higher numbers; in that event, you must first install a multiport serial card and its driver before the Ports applet will let you complete the settings for any such ports.

USER-SPECIFIC SETTINGS

As mentioned, a user profile is a definition of the Windows NT configuration for a specific user or group of users. By default, each Windows NT computer maintains a profile for each user who has logged onto the computer, except for Guest accounts. Each user profile contains information about a particular user's Windows NT configuration. Much of this information is about things the user can set, such as color scheme, screen savers, and mouse and keyboard settings. Other information covers settings that are accessible only to a Windows NT administrator, such as access rights to common program groups or network printers.

Optionally, an NT administrator can force users to load a so-called mandatory user profile (which can be recognized by its file extension .MAN). Users can adjust this profile while they're logged on, but all changes are lost as soon as they log off. This technique provides a way for administrators to control the look and feel of shared accounts or to restrict non-power users from exercising too much influence over their desktops.

User profiles are accessed through the tab of the same name that appears in the System applet (Start, Settings, System, User Profiles). This tab is shown in Figure 4-15 and lists all profiles for users associated with the particular NT Workstation under examination.

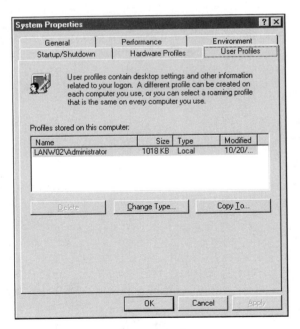

Figure 4-15   User Profiles tab

4

LOCAL PROFILES

A local profile is a set of specifications and preferences for an individual user, stored on a local machine. Windows NT provides users with a folder containing their profile settings. Individual profiles are stored in the Profiles directory. By default, the Profiles directory resides beneath the default Windows NT folder (usually named Winnt, but accessible through the environment variable named %systemroot%). A different location for the Profiles directory may be specified in the User Manager administrative utility. For example, if three user profiles (named Carol, Ted, and Alice) resided on a Windows NT system that adhered to the standard defaults, the resulting directory structure would look like this:

- \Winnt\Profiles\Carol\

- \Winnt\Profiles\Ted\

- \Winnt\Profiles\Alice\

Local profiles are established by default for each user who logs onto a particular machine and reside in the %accountname% subdirectory beneath the %systemroot%\Profiles subdirectory. Although it may seem inevitable that an explicit user profile management utility would exist for Windows NT, user profiles really represent a specialized snapshot of a user's preferences, desktop configuration, and related settings.

There is no single tool that permits all user profile information to be manipulated abstractly. There are only two ways to create a user profile: (1) log on as a user and arrange things as needed; upon logoff this information will become that user's local profile (which may then be transformed into a roaming profile, as you'll learn later), or (2) assign a mandatory profile to a user from an existing definition (but even this must be set up by example, rather than through explicit controls).

ROAMING PROFILES

A roaming profile resides on a network server to make it broadly accessible. When a user whose profile is designated as roaming logs onto any NT Workstation on the network, that profile is automatically downloaded when the user logs on. This avoids having to store a local profile on each workstation that a user uses, but it also has a disadvantage. If a user's roaming profile is large, logging onto the network takes quite a while because that information must be copied across the network each time that user logs on.

The default path designation for a roaming profile is \\Server\%username%; to create a roaming profile, it is necessary to use the "Copy to" button that appears in the User Profile tab of the System applet on a machine where a local profile for the user already exists. The destination for that copy operation must match the path that defines where the roaming profile resides; this is the mechanism that tells the startup module where to find a user's roaming profile.

SOUNDS APPLET

On computers with a properly configured sound card, Windows NT can associate and play sounds with specific system events. Opening the Sounds Control Panel icon displays the Sounds Properties dialog box shown in Figure 4-16, where different types of sound events are listed, such as a Default Beep (which is what plays for events that do not have specific associated sounds). A speaker icon appears beside the event name for each event that has an associated sound.

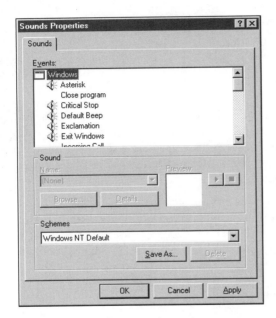

Figure 4-16   The Sounds applet

To associate an event with a sound, select that event and use the Browse button to obtain a path and filename for the desired sound file, such as CHIMES.WAV. To play the sound that's associated with some event, select any event with a speaker icon, and press Play. Some sound files can take a while to finish, so you can stop any sound instantly by pressing the Stop button.

Microsoft permits distinct sound schemes to be defined. These allow users to create named collections of sounds with associations to specific events. To define a sound scheme, select all events for which sounds are needed, and associate desired sound files with each one. Once the collection is complete, choose Save As in the Schemes pane, and enter a unique name for that particular scheme. For convenience, the Windows NT Resource Kit includes a number of predefined schemes that may be used as-is, or further customized. Schemes are accessed by name, through a drop-down list that appears in the Schemes box at the bottom of the Sounds Properties dialog box.

MOUSE APPLET

The Mouse applet governs the behavior of a mouse attached to a Windows NT system. If another pointing device (such as a touchpad or tablet) is used instead of a mouse, it will generally install its own Control Panel applet rather than working through this applet. For "real mice," however, this applet controls how their buttons work, sets speed for mouse clicks (especially for double-clicking), manages the display of cursors on-screen, and controls the motion of the mouse. You can also change mouse or mouse-compatible pointer device drivers in this applet.

Buttons Tab

The Buttons tab of the Mouse Properties dialog box shown in Figure 4-17 allows you to set the functions and speed of the mouse buttons. Because of the preponderance of right-handers in the population, the default mouse button configuration makes the left button the primary control, and the right button the secondary control. Most lefties choose to reverse this order, and all that's needed to switch is to click the radio button that reads "Left-handed" (curiously, this appears as the right-most of these two choices). The lower pane in this tab is where you can adjust Double-click speed with a slider control; a Test area appears in this pane to permit users to test their settings before they exit the applet.

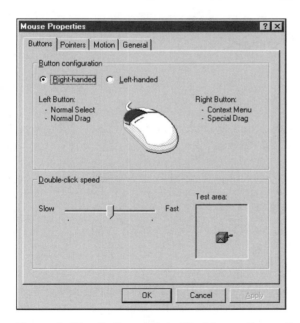

Figure 4-17   Buttons tab in the Mouse Properties dialog box

Pointers Tab

The Pointers tab permits users to associate cursors with particular kinds of on-screen activities. To change any particular cursor, click a category name on the left side of the list box, then click the Browse button to specify a file that contains the cursor you want. Like the Sounds applet, this Pointers applet also supports the scheme concept, so named collections of such associations can be saved and used as needed. Presenters and instructors will find the "Large" and "Extra Large" schemes available on the predefined drop-down list in the Schemes window helpful when projecting computer screens in a classroom or presentation setting.

The Windows NT Resource Kit includes an editing utility named ANIEDIT.EXE that's designed to create animated cursors. Static cursors take a file extension of .CUR (for "cursor"), but animated cursors end in .ANI. Animated cursors place more demands on a CPU and may not be suitable for all occasions.

Motion Tab

Pointer Speed is a slider control on the Motion tab that lets users specify how fast an on-screen cursor moves as compared to the actual movement of a mouse or pointing device; moving the slider to the left makes it lag behind the motion, moving it to the right makes it track or even anticipate the motion. Use this to establish the kind of cursor tracking you want on your desktop. The "Snap to default" checkbox automatically positions your cursor on the default button whenever you open a new dialog box (assuming such a default is assigned, it appears with a darker outline or a drop shadow around it, to distinguish the default from nondefault buttons).

General Tab

The General tab identifies whatever pointing device is currently detected on your system. To change to another device, click the Change button on the right side of this display. This produces a dialog box labeled Select Device, in which you can select from a large collection of predefined devices. If the device you wish to install is not listed, simply click the Have Disk button and define a path to a disk or directory where an appropriate driver may be found.

KEYBOARD APPLET

Double-clicking the Keyboard icon opens the Keyboard Properties dialog box shown in Figure 4-18, where users can change the keyboard configuration and responsiveness.

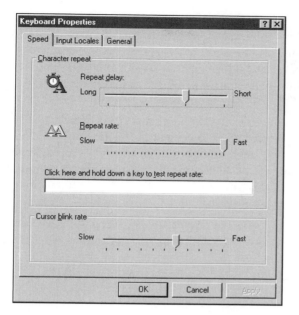

Figure 4-18   Keyboard Properties dialog box

Speed Tab

On the Speed tab in the Keyboard Properties dialog box, the Repeat delay slide control determines how long the system waits when a key is depressed before it begins to repeat that character. This is an important setting because it can prevent electronic key bounce from occurring. Key bounce occurs when you press a key once but two or more corresponding characters appear; this normally happens only when the Repeat Delay setting is too short. The Repeat rate slide control indicates how often the character will appear once the repeat delay has elapsed and the key stays depressed. Once you've established these settings, you can test them in the character entry area at the bottom of the Character Speed pane. A Cursor Blink Rate pane appears beneath this pane, where another slider controls how often the cursor blinks while it's visible on screen.

Input Locales Tab

The Input Locales tab is where alternate keyboard layouts may be selected. Typists who do not wish to use the English QWERTY layout, or who need access to another linguistic scheme, can use this applet to establish their preferred keyboard configurations. Different standard configurations can be chosen from the Input location box. Appropriate fonts must be installed for certain non-English keyboard layouts to appear properly.

Most international characters appear in the Lucida Sans Unicode font, which includes the contents of the ISO 10646 Unicode character set. Because nearly all Microsoft applications, and most other Windows applications, use a Character Map accessory to insert special characters on an as-needed basis (for Microsoft Word, this utility is called Symbol and appears in the Insert menu), users need not change their keyboard layouts to insert special characters.

The Keyboard applet also permits multiple character sets that reflect a particular language or dialect. For example, the US and United Kingdom use different dialects of English, both of which Windows NT supports. These Input Locales can be installed simultaneously. To add another input locale to the existing set of definitions, simply click the Add button beneath the list of input locales in the area of the Keyboard applet that's labeled Installed input locales and layouts near the top of the Input Locales tab.

To switch between multiple locales, define a hot-key sequence using the radio buttons in the Switch locales pane on the Input Locales tab. This lets users switch between any two (but only two) character sets at will.

 Only users with Administrator privileges can add or remove input locales.

General Tab

The General tab lets you determine which keyboard driver is installed and change it if desired. To install a different driver, click the Change button in the Keyboard properties window. To install an updated or unlisted driver, click the Have Disk button after the Select Device dialog box appears, and supply a path to the desired driver. Most keyboards that use nonstandard drivers (for example, Microsoft's Natural keyboard) include a driver disk with the keyboard itself.

DISPLAY APPLET

Use the Display applet to access the Display Properties dialog box shown in Figure 4-19, where you can change settings related to your monitor's resolution, the screen background, its color scheme, and other display elements.

 Because computer users change on-screen displays more than any other system properties, the Display Properties applet is easier to launch than any other Control Panel application. Simply right-click any empty area on your desktop, then choose Properties from the shortcut menu that appears.

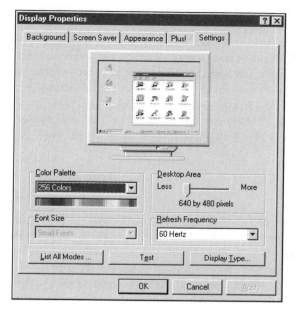

Figure 4-19   Display Properties dialog box

Background Tab

A miniature representation of a computer monitor appears at the top center of the Background tab. Choose desktop patterns from the list on the left, or desktop wallpaper from the list on the right. Your choice appears on the miniature monitor to give you an idea of how it will look on your screen. For wallpaper graphics that cannot fill your entire screen, choose Tile to repeat that graphic to cover the screen entirely, or Center to center a single instance of the graphic on your monitor. Choose Edit Pattern to launch a pixel editor that permits you to change, add, or remove background patterns.

 This utility can be an incredible time-waster. Don't let it suck you—or your users—into a frenzy of fine-tuning and bit-fiddling!

Screen Saver Tab

Screen savers can be a mixed blessing to Windows NT, especially for NT Workstation. Because they are so processor-intensive, 3-D screen savers can swamp a system all by themselves. This can be particularly onerous if such a machine plays any kind of server role on a network. Even though some experts argue against using any kind of screen saver at all, we find that the <None> or Blank Screen options in the Screen Savers menu do the job quite nicely, and do not place more than a 1% load on most CPUs. If you pick some other screen saver, remember that each screen saver has its own specific settings, based on what it depicts or displays.

Appearance Tab

The Scheme concept reappears on this tab, where yet another list is available in the Scheme box. Windows NT offers nearly 30 built-in appearance schemes, and others are available from numerous sources. In addition to such schemes, you can click elements in the display window at the top of this tab to invoke its associated characteristics in the settings at the bottom of the window. This makes it easy to change settings by clicking on elements you wish to alter (which is easier than learning all their specific names). You can also change icon sizes and spacing, buttons, borders, dialog box backgrounds, and all kinds of other user interface elements here as well.

Plus! Tab

The Plus! tab covers the same kind of functions included in Windows 95 with its extra-cost Plus! Pack. Numerous elements from the Windows 95 Plus! Pack are included with Windows NT at no additional charge. You can change default icons for My Computer, Network Neighborhood, and the Recycle Bin. You can also stretch desktop wallpaper to fill your monitor's screen, show window contents while dragging, use large icons, smooth edges of screen fonts, or show icons using all possible colors, simply by clicking in their associated checkboxes.

Settings Tab

The Settings tab permits manipulation of hardware settings for a computer monitor and its associated graphics card. These include the number of colors (Color Palette), the monitor's resolution (Desktop Area), the on-screen font sizes, and the monitor's refresh rate. This last setting is something unique to Windows NT—most other OSs can only adjust a monitor's refresh rate with a driver change or a hardware-level configuration setting change. Finally, the List All Modes button can be quite helpful because it will display all potential settings that are valid for your currently installed monitor and display adapter.

After you change any display option, you'll be asked if you wish to test the change. If elected, the test option displays a test pattern for five seconds that implements the new settings. This permits you to check whether your display settings actually work, and to cancel them if they don't without having to adjust the hardware any further.

 Should you neglect to test a video setting that creates an unworkable configuration, reboot the machine and select the [VGA Mode] option on the boot menu. Then you can run the Display applet again and pick something that works!

(MS-DOS) CONSOLE APPLET

Like most other Microsoft OSs, even Windows NT permits certain DOS applications to run within its environment. All DOS applications run in a console window when launched within Windows NT. The Console applet controls a Console Windows Properties dialog box shown in Figure 4-20, where you can adjust how DOS applications will appear on screen.

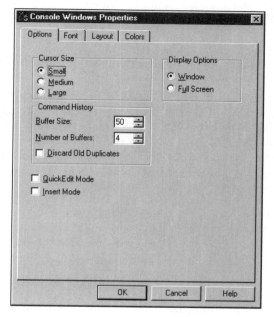

Figure 4-20 Console Windows Properties dialog box

Options Tab

The Options tab allows you to select small, medium, or large cursor size. Windows NT can remember a series of DOS commands; use the Change Buffer size setting to control how many commands it will store (this number can vary from 1 to 999). Press the up arrow on the keyboard and you can scroll through the history list of previous commands. As you begin to peruse the history list, the down arrow permits you to move forward in the list, to view more recent commands. To ignore whatever command history appears, press Esc. When you press Esc, the command monitor remembers its place in the history list, so pressing the up or down arrow permits you to continue navigating the list.

The Number of Buffers entry dictates how many history lists for separate console windows Windows NT will retain in memory; it can be set from 1 to 999.

 Windows NT stores buffer values for all active console windows even if Buffer size and Number of Buffers are set to the absolute minimum. For that reason, there is no good reason for the value to be set higher.

Check QuickEdit Mode so you can use your mouse to highlight text in a console window. This will permit you to copy text without requiring access to Cut and Paste entries in the Edit menu. Because the mouse cannot make menu selections when operating in QuickEdit mode, you must use keyboard equivalents to access menu entries. Although this approach has its advantages, especially if you need to cut and paste text from a console window to some other application, it also requires some concentration and practice to master its use.

To use QuickEdit Mode, launch a DOS program in a console window. Then open the file that contains the text you want to copy. Using the mouse, highlight the text to copy by clicking and dragging what you need on screen. Line returns and graphical elements will all be copied into the paste buffer, so be careful what you grab. To paste this text onto the clipboard, click the right mouse button once. The highlight vanishes but the copy is placed onto the clipboard. This is where things get interesting: you must now use keyboard navigation to position the cursor where the text is to be pasted, whether this is elsewhere in the same document, in another DOS console window, or in any graphical Windows application. To paste the data into a DOS console window, right-click only once. To copy the contents of the paste buffer into a Windows application, either right-click and choose Paste from the shortcut menu, or press Ctrl-V to initiate a paste maneuver from your keyboard.

Insert Mode enables Insert mode for text entry (which inserts characters where the cursor is positioned on screen, as opposed to overtyping or overstriking what's already there) as soon as a console window opens. Please note that certain DOS programs themselves operate in Insert mode, whether or not this option is checked on the Options tab display (most text editors, like EDIT.COM, fall into this category). On the other hand, the command prompt itself defaults to Overstrike mode, which is clearly apparent whenever you try to edit the current command line, or attempt to edit an existing command from the history list. Use the Insert key to turn Insert mode on, and you'll be able to edit commands by positioning the cursor and entering new text.

 Some DOS applications, especially EDIT.COM, interpret Ctrl-V to toggle Insert mode. This is totally different from the native Windows NT environment, where Ctrl-V is equivalent to the Edit, Paste menu entry used to paste text into a document or window from the clipboard!

If the Windows radio button is selected in the Display Options pane of the Options tab, the command prompt will run in a window. This makes the display smaller, but permits users to interact with the Windows NT desktop. Even when expanded to its maximum area, a DOS window may consume the entire screen, depending on what font size is on the Fonts tab in the Console applet.

Selecting the Full Screen radio button in the Display options pane makes the DOS Console window operate in Text-Only mode, and occupies the entire screen. Older DOS applications that assume they own the entire screen often run better in Full Screen Mode. But you can "fool" older applications by setting the properties for individual DOS applications to full-screen, while running the command prompt in a window. Even when a DOS application runs in Full Screen mode, you can still switch to other applications by calling up the task bar and selecting another icon, or by entering Alt-Tab at the keyboard to return to your Windows NT desktop where you can then access other applications.

Font Tab

The Font tab is where you must specify what font appears in a DOS Console window. This tab includes a Selected Font pane at the bottom that indicates what sample text looks like. Above it, a Window Preview pane shows exactly how much of the monitor's visible real estate a DOS console window consumes. As you change font sizes, you'll notice that this display area increases for larger fonts and decreases for smaller ones. On 17" monitors, a font size of 8 × 12 works well, but on 14" or 15" monitors, a font size of 6 × 8 works better.

Layout Tab

The Layout tab also includes a Window Preview pane that shows how a DOS console window will appear on the desktop. To change the default position of a console window, you must first unclick the "Let system position window" checkbox in the Window position pane. The Window size pane is where you can control the horizontal and vertical dimensions of a console window, measured in character widths (not pixels).

For any command console that runs in Full Screen mode, only the entries in the Screen Buffer Size pane will affect this display. These options specify a "virtual" space that is made available to the command console. The actual number of characters that appear on screen depends on the settings in the Window Size pane. When a Screen Buffer Size setting exceeds its Window Size counterpart, this means that the virtual display area is larger than the physical display area. In this case, scroll bars appear in the console window to indicate that more information is available than is showing on screen.

Because the Screen Buffer Size settings define the maximum display area available, settings in the Window Size pane may not exceed their Screen Buffer Size counterparts. If you try to set a Window Size value higher than its Screen Buffer size equivalent, such settings automatically decrease to match the Screen Buffer Size setting. Although the theoretical maximum for Width and Height settings in both panes is 9999, a practical limit is under 100, perhaps much less, and will be determined by the display font you've selected in the Font tab.

 Settings greater than 100 for Screen Buffer Size Width cause some applications to hang.

Colors Tab

The Colors tab in the Console applet permits you to change default assignments for Screen Text, Screen Background, Popup Text, or Popup Background. To change any of these settings, click its radio button, then click any of the color boxes in the row beneath the radio buttons and the Selected Color Values pane. On systems whose monitors and graphics cards can display more than 16 colors—which represents the bulk of most systems in use today—the Selected Color Values pane permits you to select exact colors specified in terms of RGB (Red, Green, Blue) values. Once defined, such custom colors can be assigned to any of the radio button elements at the top of this window, but many DOS applications define and manage their own color schemes and may ignore your custom settings for that reason. However, there is seldom any reason to deviate from the basic color defaults for the DOS console window.

UPS APPLET

The UPS applet controls all options and setting associated with an uninterruptible power supply (UPS) that might be installed on a Windows NT machine. The various panes and settings available through this applet are the following:

- *Serial port:* Establishes where the battery is connected

- *Power Fail Signal:* Sends a signal if your UPS fails

- *Low battery:* Sends a low-battery warning, if your UPS supports it

- *Remote shutdown:* Enables remote shutdown, if supported by your UPS

- *Expected battery life:* Defines the expected battery life, from 2 to 480 minutes with a default of 2 minutes

- *Recharge time:* Defines the recharge time, from 5 to 240 minutes with a default of 100 minutes for each minute of running time

- *Initial warning messages:* Specifies the amount of time after a power failure that warning messages will appear—can be set to 0 to 120 seconds with a default of 3

- *Delay between:* Sets the delay between warning messages, from 30 to 300 seconds with a default of 120 seconds

 The UPS applet depends on two services being started: the Alerter service and the Messenger service.

Third-party software and interface cables are available to enhance the built-in NT UPS service. For example, APC (American Power Conversion—the UPS market leader) provides software that allows you to schedule daily or weekly auto shutdowns and startups. A UPS event log is also included. Some UPS devices also supply software that replaces the NT built-in UPS service. You can activate and deactivate such software through the Services icon in the Control Panel.

 It is a good idea for administrators to shut down servers periodically to increase the battery life of their UPSs (especially for nickel cadmium batteries). You can schedule this with the AT utility—a built-in general-purpose task scheduler included with Windows NT—in a batch script that calls the command-line program named SHUTDOWN.EXE. This program performs a graceful shutdown of any Windows NT system, both for Workstation and Server.

THE REGISTRY

Windows NT uses a system component called the Registry to provide a database that stores data about a system's configuration in a hierarchical form. The information stored in the Registry is comparable to information stored in initialization (.INI) files in Windows 3.1 or Windows for Workgroups 3.11. For native NT applications, the Registry takes the place of .INI files and stores all configuration information in this database. Although the Control Panel applets suffice to cover most Windows NT configuration needs, some Windows NT settings can only be established or changed by editing the Windows NT Registry directly.

Each Registry key is similar to a bracketed heading in an .INI file. Changes made to system configurations through administrative tools such as the Control Panel applets and User Manager are applied to the Registry database. A special kind of administrative tool called a Registry editor allows direct changes to be made to the Registry database. Such tools make use of the hierarchical nature of the Registry and are capable of manipulating its structures within its hierarchy.

The Windows NT Registry consists of a collection of files, each of which represents a major component of the Registry database, called a set of root keys or subtrees. These subtrees form the basis for discussion in the section that follows, where you'll learn about the keys that store information about the local machine, called HKEY_LOCAL_MACHINE. Each Registry subtree is a collection of related values stored in a single file. Registry subtrees are part of the Windows NT OS's structure. Whether you call them root keys or subtrees, these entities occupy the top level of the NT Registry hierarchy. They are similar to the bracketed sub-headings that you may recognize when scanning Windows 3.x .INI files. These root keys reside in a special Windows NT folder named %systemroot%\system32\config.

Under each root key or subtree, you'll find a collection of major keys that aggregate controls around certain kinds of system functions or capabilities; these major keys are sometimes called **hives** to reflect their loose and organic-appearing structure. Other Registry keys appear beneath the hive entries. Within any given key, additional subkeys can occur, as can value entries, which ultimately define the values and settings associated with Registry structures in the Windows NT environment. The complete name of any Windows NT Registry entry consists of a list of all the keys and subkeys of which it is a part, each separated by a backslash. For instance, the full name for the set of parameters that controls Windows NT's logon behavior is:

HKEY_CURRENT_USER\Software\Microsoft\Windows NT\Winlogon

In this example, the subtree is HKEY_CURRENT_USER; the subkeys dive into the Windows NT portion of the Microsoft entries in the Software hive, and the final grouping indicates that the associated values govern the Windows logon settings and characteristics. These can include behaviors like automatic logon, enable/disable the Shut Down button on the WinLogon prompt window, and so on. The values associated with these value entries ultimately define how Windows NT acts when users attempt to log onto a system.

HKEY_LOCAL_MACHINE

HKEY_LOCAL_MACHINE contains information such as bus type, system memory, device drivers, and startup control data. From an administrator's standpoint, the HKEY_LOCAL_MACHINE key contains vital information about a local system. This subtree includes five hives: Hardware, SAM, Security, Software, and System, as shown in Figure 4-21. Table 4-3 lists the types of information that each of these hives contains.

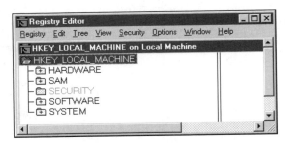

Figure 4-21 HKEY_LOCAL_MACHINE as seen through REGEDT32

Table 4-3 HKEY_LOCAL_MACHINE Hives

Hardware	Installed Devices and Their Current Operational State
SAM (Security Account Manager)	Stores all user, group, and domain information; without going through some special contortions, data is not accessible with a Registry editor
Security	Local security information for use by the security subsystem
Software	Common settings for software; apply to all local users
System	Boot configuration data and related device drivers

The other major subtrees in the Windows NT Registry are as follows:

- *HKEY_CLASSES_ROOT:* Supports backward compatibility with Windows 3.x applications for OLE (a.k.a. COM) and DDE support, and contains OLE and DDE information for Windows NT itself, particularly for shell extension keys and values. This key actually points to another Registry key named HKEY_LOCAL_MACHINE\Software\Classes, and provides multiple points of access to make itself easily accessible to the operating system itself, and to applications that need access to the compatibility information already mentioned.

- *HKEY_CURRENT_USER:* Points to the HKEY_USERS key for whichever user is currently logged onto the Windows NT machine. This provides the user profile information, including application setup, desktop settings, and user interface description that the user expects to encounter when running Windows NT. This also helps explain why user profiles must be available on every machine where a particular user logs on and helps explain the appeal of roaming profiles.

- *HKEY_USERS:* Includes information about and user profiles for all named accounts that log onto a particular Windows NT machine. Most important, this includes the security data for each user who has permission to log onto the machine and the controls over users who haven't yet established their own particular profile, or who have not yet been assigned a mandatory profile.

- *HKEY_CURRENT_CONFIG:* Contains machine-specific information from the HKEY_LOCAL_MACHINE\System subkey that reflects the computer's current configuration. This key makes it easier for applications to access information about a particular Windows NT system.

- *HKEY_DYN_DATA:* A catch-all area that Windows NT uses to store temporary data, application or services buffers, and other temporary information that must be created and managed while a user is active on a particular computer. This information does not persist between logons, however, and acts like a scratch pad for the OS to use while it's working.

Of all these keys, HKEY_LOCAL_MACHINE and HKEY_CURRENT_USER are the most important. These are the areas of the Registry in which you're most likely to be working when direct Registry access is necessary.

THE REGISTRY EDITORS: REGEDIT AND REGEDT32

Because the structure of the Registry is so complex, it requires special tools to edit it directly. In Windows NT 4.0, users have two different Registry editors to choose from: those most familiar with Windows NT 3.51 and earlier versions will probably be most comfortable with REGEDT32, which looks and acts like its namesake from earlier versions. Users more familiar with Windows 95 may find REGEDIT, which shares its name with the Registry editor for that environment, more familiar. Either way, these tools offer direct access into the Windows NT Registry and, therefore, also offer unbeatable ways to mess up a system!

Because of its more recent vintage, you might be inclined to believe that REGEDIT is the logical choice when editing Registry files. To some degree this is true because REGEDIT's user interface is based on the Explorer model. This makes it a bit more user friendly than the File Manager interface implemented in REGEDT32. Then again, REGEDIT's ability to search the Registry for keys, values, and data whereas REGEDT32 can only search for keys makes REGEDIT more appealing to some. In REGEDT32, choose the Find Key entry in the View menu; in REGEDIT, choose the Find command in the Edit menu. Searching for specific keys works in either editor, but searches for specific value names or associated data strings is only possible with REGEDIT.

Why use the older tool at all? REGEDT32 is the only Windows NT Registry editor that can operate on security data. REGEDT32 includes a Security item on its menus, is able to manipulate permission settings, and can even take ownership of certain security keys in the Registry that are otherwise off-limits. This can sometimes provide crucial recovery capabilities when ill-advised or ill-formulated system policies are defined for a Windows NT system, or when security information somehow becomes damaged. That's why there's a good reason to learn and use both of the Windows NT Registry editors.

WINDOWS NT DIAGNOSTICS (WINMSD)

From a configuration management standpoint, Windows NT Diagnostics is one of the more useful administrative utilities that Windows NT offers. This program is often called WinMSD, after the name of its executable file, WINMSD.EXE. To launch this program, you can access it through the Administrative tools menu (Start, Programs, Administrative Tools (Common), Windows NT Diagnostics), or use this shortcut: Start, Run, then enter *WinMSD*.

WinMSD strongly resembles the Microsoft Diagnostics (MSD) utilities for DOS and the Device Manager included with Windows 95. This utility may only be used to inspect system information and offers no active configuration controls. But WinMSD does a great job of bringing lots of important system information together, which makes it a good way to get a quick view of system information and important Registry settings.

The Windows NT Diagnostics main screen appears in Figure 4-22 and includes a large number of tabs, each with its own display that reports on some aspect of system configuration or behavior. This is what makes WinMSD such an outstanding tool for system inspection and analysis. The list that follows explains the purpose of each of these tabs.

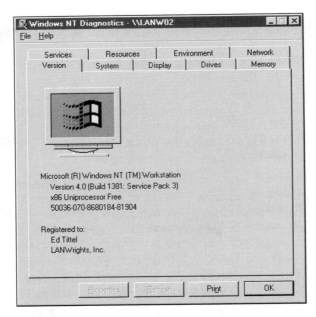

Figure 4-22   Windows NT Diagnostics main screen, with default tab, Version, active

- *Version:* The default display that appears when WinMSD is first launched. Conveys much of the same information as the NT Explorer's Help, About screen—namely, version, serial number, and service pack level

- *System:* In the system area, shows the version of the Hardware Abstraction Layer (HAL) in use, plus BIOS version and date; in the Processor area, lists all CPUs it detects in the machine. Useful for checking multi-CPU configurations, especially after adding another processor

- *Display:* Identifies the BIOS running on the machine's graphics adapter, and reads the vendor name, make and model, memory capacity, and other configuration tidbits from that BIOS. Useful for confirming drivers in use, on-board memory available, and current resolution and color depth settings.

- *Drives:* Provides drill-down displays for all kinds of drives installed on a system: floppy disks, hard disks, CD-ROM drives, and so forth. For each device, shows all the important information about space, file system, and related device settings.

- *Memory:* Shows the same information about memory available in the Task Manager applet (always available with a right-click on the Windows NT task bar). Measures physical and virtual memory use, provides information about paging file location and activity, and includes counts of handles, threads, and processes on a given machine—all of which can be vital indicators of system health and proper functionality.

- *Services:* Provides a list of all services installed on the machine and their status (Stopped or Running). An important initial troubleshooting tool when diagnosing balky or failed services (the same information also appears in the Services applet in Control Panel).

- *Resources:* Shows all system interrupt requests (IRQs) currently defined for the machine. A great pre-installation tool to help locate available IRQs, and an equally good post-installation troubleshooting tool.

- *Environment:* Shows the names and values currently assigned to all Windows NT environment variables. Provides much the same information as the Environment tab in the System applet, but is easier to read and shows current assigned values. Great for debugging scripts or batch files, but also good for diagnosing problems with DOS or Windows 3.x applications running under Windows NT.

- *Network:* Shows current status of network access on the machine, including current access levels, workgroup/domain membership active, and identity of the current user. Great for checking network health and for quickly checking access activity and individuals involved.

In short, WinMSD provides a valuable set of inspection tools that savvy administrators can use to examine a system, either to take its temperature or to begin more formal troubleshooting. You should find the Resources, System, and Display tabs especially useful because they offer the best access to that kind of information on a Windows NT machine.

CHAPTER SUMMARY

This chapter looked at the Control Panel applets that manage a variety of user- and system-specific configuration settings for NT. User profiles can store user preferences either on a local machine or on a server. A local profile is stored on one machine for a specific user, whereas a roaming profile is stored on a server and follows a user from one NT computer to another. A mandatory or default profile is assigned to one or more users and can only be changed by an administrator. Control Panel applets can be used to add and remove Windows NT system components such as SCSI devices, tape drives, PCMCIA cards, or system and application software. The Windows NT Registry plays an all-important role in establishing a system's configuration and runtime environment. Finally, the Windows NT Diagnostics utility is an important inspection tool in any competent Windows NT administrator's toolkit. Throughout, the chapter focused on exploring the tools that support the configuration of the complex collections of hardware and software so necessary to deliver a working Windows NT Workstation environment.

KEY TERMS

- **applet** — Microsoft terminology for a "small application" with specific, focused capabilities. The various applications that appear within the Windows NT Control Panel are often called applets.

- **Control Panel** — The collection of miniature applications that serve as front ends to the Registry for managing user and system configuration.

- **desktop** — The background of your screen on which windows, icons, and dialog boxes appear.

- **device driver** — A program that enables a specific piece of hardware to communicate with Windows NT. Although the device may be physically installed and recognized by Windows NT, the OS cannot use the device properly unless you have installed a device driver.

- **environment variable** — A string consisting of environment information, such as a drive, path, or filename, associated with a symbolic name that can be used by Windows NT.

- **hive** — A term used to describe the major subkeys of the Windows NT Registry.

- **local profile** — The collection of desktop configuration information, application icons, wallpaper, preferences, screen savers, and other user-customizable Windows NT environment information that is automatically stored on each machine where any named user account logs on. This profile is unique and particular to the machine where it resides, which is what makes it local. *See also* mandatory user profile and roaming profile.

- **mandatory user profile** — A user profile created by an administrator and assigned to one or more users. This profile cannot be changed by the user and will remain the same every time they log on.

- **memory pages** — The 4 KB chunks of information that Windows NT Virtual Memory Manager moves between physical RAM and the paging file on hard disk as it handles system and application processing needs.

- **paging file** — A special file on your hard disk. In Windows NT, virtual memory, some of the program code and other information is kept in RAM, and other information is temporarily swapped to a paging file on disk. When that information is required again, Windows NT pulls it back into RAM and, if necessary, swaps other information to disk to make room for incoming memory pages.

- **port** — A connection or socket used to connect a device, such as a printer, monitor, or modem, to your NT computer. Information is sent from your computer to the device or from the device to the computer through a cable.

- **roaming profile** — A user profile stored on a server that follows a user from NT computer to NT computer and provides a consistent user environment across all such systems.

- **runtime environment** — The collection of hardware and software configuration settings, environment variables, system policies, and user profiles that govern a system's actual behavior while it's working—this collection of information effectively describes how the system will act.

- **service** — A process that performs a specific system function and often provides an application programming interface for other processes to call.

- **Small Computer Systems Interface (SCSI)** — A high-speed parallel-bus interface that connects disk drives, optical drives, and other peripherals to a computer.

- **telephony** — The programming interface that maintains information common to any program that uses the telephone system.

- **uninterruptible power supply (UPS)** — A battery-operated power source connected to a computer to keep the computer running during a power outage.

- **user profile** — Configuration information retained on a user-by-user basis and saved into files—these files hold primarily environment and application preferences.

- **Virtual Memory Manager (VMM)** — The service that translates virtual addressing from applications to physical mappings in RAM. This manager hides the memory swapping process from applications and higher-layer services.

REVIEW QUESTIONS

1. A user can modify the data directly in the Registry by using which utility?
   a. Control Panel
   b. REGEDIT.EXE
   c. SYSEDIT.EXE
   d. Explorer

2. The _____ tab of the System icon on the Control Panel is where you can set multiple hardware configurations for an NT Workstation.

   a. User Profiles

   b. Hardware Profiles

   c. Environment

   d. Startup/Shutdown

3. How many subkeys are located beneath HKEY_LOCAL_MACHINE in the Registry?

   a. 3

   b. 4

   c. 5

   d. 6

4. The System icon accesses user environment variables for Windows NT to use, but users can also use environment variables that affect only their account. True or False?

5. The _____ is where NT stores most of its configuration information.

   a. Bindery

   b. Registry

   c. /etc/passwd folder

   d. WinMSD utility

6. When Windows NT is being installed, it calculates how big to make the page file. It chooses a size that is _____ MB bigger than physical memory size.

   a. 10

   b. 11

   c. 20

   d. 21

7. Windows NT uses a technique called _____ to allow your configuration to run more and larger programs than the physical memory in your computer will allow.

   a. virtual memory

   b. SCSI

   c. caching

   d. virtual tuning

8. From where can you delete user profiles?

   a. Services applet

   b. Server Control Panel applet

   c. User Manager

   d. System Control Panel applet

9. The Mouse Control Panel icon can be used to modify _____ settings.

   a. user

   b. system

   c. both user and system

10. The Keyboard Control Panel icon can be used to modify _____ settings.

   a. user

   b. system

   c. both user and system

11. The SCSI Control Panel icon can be used to modify _____ settings.

   a. user

   b. system

   c. both user and system

12. The Telephony Control Panel icon can be used to modify _____ settings.

   a. user

   b. system

   c. both user and system

13. The Add/Remove Control Panel icon can be used to modify _____ settings.

   a. user

   b. system

   c. both user and system

14. The Display Control Panel icon can be used to modify _____ settings.

   a. user

   b. system

   c. both user and system

15. The Server Control Panel icon can be used to modify _____ settings.

   a. user

   b. system

   c. both user and system

16. The Services Control Panel icon can be used to modify _____ settings.

   a. user

   b. system

   c. both user and system

4

17. The System Control Panel icon can be used to modify _____ settings.

   a. user

   b. system

   c. both user and system

18. The Accessibility Options Control Panel icon can be used to modify _____ settings.

   a. user

   b. system

   c. both user and system

19. The Sounds Control Panel icon can be used to modify _____ settings.

   a. user

   b. system

   c. both user and system

HANDS-ON PROJECTS

When working with the Windows NT Registry, it's important to remember that the Registry ultimately controls the behavior—and indeed the workability—of any Windows NT system. That's why it's essential to avoid making permanent changes to values or keys unless you know what you're doing. For the purposes of Project 4-1, this means that if you use REGEDT32, begin your exercise by visiting the **Options** menu, and select **Read-only mode**; if you use REGEDIT, you can do the same thing only by rebooting your machine and hitting the **space bar** when the **Last Known Good Configuration** prompt appears. For that reason, we recommend using REGEDT32 for this exercise.

 You must log onto a Windows NT Workstation with Administrator or equivalent privileges to make changes to system settings. Make sure your user ID is a member of either the Administrators group or the Power Users Group. (Groups were covered in Chapter 3.)

PROJECT 4-1

To use a Registry editor:

1. Open Registry editor by clicking **Start** and selecting **Run**.

2. Type **REGEDIT** and press **Enter.**

3. Minimize the Registry Editor.

4. Open the Control Panel by clicking **Start**, **Settings**, and selecting **Control Panel**.

5. Using the following table, navigate through several of the Control Panel applets. Before you make any changes, examine the related Registry hive from the following table to inspect values. Make changes to one or two settings for at least two applets (System/Performance and Date/Time are good examples). When you make changes to these Control Panel applets, press **[Alt]–[Tab]** to switch to the Registry Editor to check how values change in the Registry. It's easy to see why some experts think of the Control Panel applets as nothing more than "special-purpose Registry editors"!

Control Panel Applet	Primary Registry Hive
Add/Remove Programs	HKEY_LOCAL_MACHINE\SOFTWARE
Console	HKEY_CURRENT_USER
Date/Time	BIOS and HKEY_LOCAL_MACHINE\SOFTWARE
Devices	HKEY_LOCAL_MACHINE\SYSTEM
Display	HKEY_CURRENT_USER and HKEY_LOCAL_MACHINE\SYSTEM
Fonts	HKEY_LOCAL_MACHINE\SOFTWARE
Keyboard	HKEY_CURRENT_USER and HKEY_LOCAL_MACHINE\SOFTWARE
Modems	HKEY_LOCAL_MACHINE\SYSTEM
Mouse	HKEY_CURRENT_USER and HKEY_LOCAL_MACHINE\SOFTWARE
Multimedia	HKEY_CURRENT_USER and HKEY_LOCAL_MACHINE\SOFTWARE
Network	HKEY_LOCAL_MACHINE\SYSTEM and HKEY_LOCAL_MACHINE\SOFTWARE
PC Card (PCMCIA)	HKEY_LOCAL_MACHINE\SYSTEM
Ports	HKEY_LOCAL_MACHINE\SYSTEM
Regional Settings	HKEY_CURRENT_USER and HKEY_LOCAL_MACHINE\SOFTWARE
SCSI Adapters	HKEY_LOCAL_MACHINE\SYSTEM
Services	HKEY_LOCAL_MACHINE\SYSTEM
Sounds	HKEY_CURRENT_USER
System	HKEY_CURRENT_USER, HKEY_LOCAL_MACHINE\SOFTWARE and HKEY_LOCAL_MACHINE\SYSTEM
Tape Devices	HKEY_LOCAL_MACHINE\SYSTEM
Telephony	HKEY_CURRENT_USER and HKEY_LOCAL_MACHINE\SOFTWARE
UPS	HKEY_LOCAL_MACHINE\SYSTEM

PROJECT 4-2

To use the System Control Panel applet to modify system settings:

1. Click **Start**, **Settings**, **Control Panel**.
2. Click the **Startup/Shutdown** tab within the System Properties window.
3. Change the value assigned to "Show list for" to **5** seconds.
4. Click the **Performance** tab in the System Properties window.
5. Click the **Change** button in the Virtual Memory pane.
6. Change the **Initial Size** entry to twice the amount of RAM on your system. If you don't know how much RAM your system has installed, enter **Start**, **Programs**, **Administrative Tools (Common)**, **Windows NT Diagnostics**, and check the **Memory** tab. If you don't have enough disk space, add a value equal to the amount of RAM plus 11 MB.
7. Change the **Maximum Size** entry to three times the amount of RAM on your system. If you don't have enough disk space, add a value equal to the amount of RAM plus at least 12 (up to 22, if space allows).

Experience has taught that twice memory is a better allocation for the paging file, especially on a machine where numerous applications will be launched simultaneously. For the same reason, three times memory is an effective maximum size for the paging file.

8. Click **Close** and then **Yes** to restart the computer.

PROJECT 4-3

In addition to its ability to set the system clock, the Date/Time applet has the important function of permitting you to designate the time zone within which your computer operates. In this exercise, you will attempt to follow the Windows 95 model for time zone selection, and then be instructed on how to make this selection "the right way." Please note that proper time zone selection is important for coordination of Windows NT activities, such as directory replication—if system clocks between replicator and replicatee aren't in substantial agreement, for instance, replication cannot proceed. Likewise, keeping file updates and transactions properly coordinated requires a shared view of time among all computers in a Windows NT Domain—especially Windows NT Domain Controllers.

To use the Date/Time applet to select the time zone:

1. Click **Start**, **Settings**, **Control Panel**, and then double-click **Date/Time**.

2. Select the **Date & Time** tab. Make sure the calendar date is correct. Adjust the month and year entries by using the drop-down lists in the corresponding fields. Select the date by clicking on the number for today's date in the calendar display below. Note the current (or default) time zone appears in text at the bottom of this window.

3. Make sure the time is correct. Adjust hour, minutes, and seconds entries separately by highlighting each of these fields in the numeric time display on the right side of the Date & Time tab, and using the up or down arrows to increase or decrease the associated values. You can also type numeric values from the keyboard into any of these fields.

4. Select the **Time Zone** tab. What happens if you try to pick your time zone by clicking on the world map? Access the drop-down time zone list at the top of the display. Make sure the correct time zone for your machine is selected. Check or uncheck the Automatically adjust for daylight savings changes check box beneath the map, depending on how time flows in your part of the world. Click **OK**.

Although setting date and time may seem somewhat contrived, it's an important set of values upon which machines must agree in order to properly time-stamp files and transactions and to coordinate automatic transfers of data (especially directory replication, for which service Windows NT Workstations can be import servers).

PROJECT 4-4

Because Windows NT is forgiving enough to let us install drivers for some hardware that's not present on a machine, you can use this exercise to go through the steps involved in adding a "fake modem" to a Windows NT Workstation. Here, you use the Modem applet in the Control Panel to install (and then remove) a special kind of modem called a null modem, which is nothing more than a cable that permits two computers to exchange data through their serial ports.

To use the Modem applet to install and remove a null modem:

1. Click **Start**, **Settings**, **Control Panel**, then double-click **Modems**.

2. An installation wizard will guide you through this process. So that you can "fool" Windows NT into installing a modem that's not actually there, check the box on the first Install New Modem screen that reads **Don't detect my modem; I will select it from a list**. Click the **Next>** button at the bottom of this window.

3. The next window has two areas. In the list on the left, make sure the entry labeled **[Standard Modem Types]** is selected; in the list on the right, make sure the entry labeled **Dial-Up Networking Serial Cable Between 2 Computers** is selected. Click the **Next>** button at the bottom of this window.

4. Select an unused COM port on your machine to install the cable. If you're not sure which COM port to pick, check Windows NT Diagnostics Resources tab and see if both IRQs 3 and 4 are assigned. Pick whichever one is available. Click the **Selected Ports** radio button, then pick the unused COM port (IRQ 3 corresponds to COM ports 2 and 4, and IRQ 4 corresponds to COM ports 1 and 3) in the pick list. Click the **Next>** button at the bottom of this window. Click **Next>** after entering the correct location information, click **Finish**, then click the **Close** button.

5. This completes the installation of the null modem. Restart the computer. Elect the **Last Known Good Configuration** prompt on startup, and you bypass these changes, which were purely experimental.

Although hooking up a null modem doesn't involve selecting and installing a specific device driver (that part is handled by the Installation Wizard in the background), it is otherwise exactly the same as installing any real modem. The only difference is that you'd need to supply a pointer to a location where the real modem's drivers resided during the selection process in step 3. Installation Wizards have made administrators' jobs much easier in the Windows NT 4.0 environment (prior to this release, all this work had to be executed without assistance from the OS).

PROJECT 4-5

In this project, you use Windows NT Diagnostics to provide a low-cost solution for inventory of your Windows NT Workstation configurations. This is a simple approach to collecting all of the Windows NT diagnostics output from Windows NT 4.0 machines on your network. It may come in handy in real life! Be sure to get the batch file exactly right, and everything else should flow quite smoothly.

To create a quick inventory of your Windows NT Workstation configuration:

1. Log on as Administrator on your Windows NT Workstation.

2. Create a user in User Manager called **IUSER**. Make sure this user has no password and the User Must Change Password at Next Logon option is unchecked.

3. In User Properties, click **Profile**, and in the Logon Script Property box type **INVRUN.BAT**. Save this new user and close User Manager.

4. Open the Explorer and create a folder called **INV**. Right-click the folder and select **Sharing**. Share the folder as **INV**. (For the purposes of this exercise, the default of Full Control to Everyone is fine.)

5. Navigate to the **\Winnt\system\Repl\Import\Scripts** folder and create a file named **INVRUN.BAT** using Edit or Notepad. Be sure to save the file with a .BAT extension. (*Note*: Notepad saves files with a .TXT extension by default. If you use Notepad, make sure you have not saved your file as INVRUN.BAT.TXT because this can happen if you don't pay sufficient attention.)

6. In the new batch file, type the following (be sure to get the proper value for <classroom-server> from your instructor or technical support person):

Net use Z: \\<classroom-server>\inv
Z:
Winmsd /f
c:
Net use z: /d

7. Save the batch file and log onto a Workstation machine as user IUSER. Because it is the default batch file for user IUSER, this script will run automatically when you log on.

8. Log onto your classroom domain as IUSER; your computer's machine name will appear in the instructor's INV directory with its inventory listed as machine name, ending in a .TXT extension. Thus, for a computer named MACHINE6, the inventory file would be named MACHINE6.TXT.

CASE PROJECTS

1. Immediately following Windows NT installation, there's a great deal of work to be done to finish configuring a machine. Suppose the following is a list of components installed on an NT Workstation. Discuss each of the list elements in terms of which Windows NT Control Panel applet or utility program might be needed to configure the item and what kinds of additional configurations (drivers, configuration settings, port addresses, and so forth) might be required for each one.

Be sure to indicate where drivers will come from (vendor or Windows NT distribution media), what kinds of system settings will be needed to configure these devices, and how you might investigate the availability of necessary settings prior to installing anything. *Hint*: All these vendors have Web sites and offer information about the hardware and their necessary drivers online.

- Two Practical Peripherals PC288MT II V.34 modems

- An Adaptec 2940 PCI SCSI controller and two Seagate 4 GB Barracuda disk drives

- A PC Card CD-ROM drive (Dell model number UJDCD450, with a proprietary Matsushita PC Card interface)

- A Digiboard 4-port high-speed serial card, to enable activation of COM5, COM6, COM7, and COM8 on your machine

2. Part of the process of keeping up with technology is keeping up with new releases of hardware and software. For this case study, assume you are a network administrator, and you've been assigned the job of upgrading 20 identical Windows 95 machines to Windows NT 4.0 Workstation. Given the following configuration, what changes and additions must you make to ensure a successful upgrade process?

- Micron Pentium P90 motherboard with 1996-dated BIOS, 32 MB RAM, 4 PCI slots, 4 ISA slots

- Adaptec 1540 SCSI controllers with two 1.2 GB Toshiba SCSI drives on board, one complete drive will be scrubbed to make room for NT Workstation on each machine

- Proprietary Sony CD-ROM player on board

- Paradise standard VGA graphics interface, with NEC Multisync 3FG monitor

- Standard PC keyboard, Logitech three-button mouse

- Novell NE2000 Ethernet (10Base2) NICs

Be sure to discuss the following topics for each element.

- Does this meet with the Windows NT Workstation minimum system requirements?

- Is the device on the Hardware Compatibility List?

- Are Windows NT drivers available?

- Is the hardware too old or slow to be worth upgrading? If so, what kind of replacement would you suggest?

- What additional configuration work will each item require?

Here again, you should find plenty to help you make your case online of information, not only at the vendors' Web sites, but in online versions of publications like *Windows NT* magazine, *NT Systems Magazine*, *PC Magazine*, and other PC- or NT-related publications. Keep your answers brief and to the point; where alternatives are requested, one or two are sufficient, but be sure to justify such choices in terms of expense and capability.

FILE SYSTEMS

The file system used with Windows NT greatly affects how the operating system works; a number of issues come into play when choosing such a file system. In this chapter, you learn about how Windows NT stores and retrieves files (regardless of what file system is used), how files are named, the pros and cons of the two disk file systems that Windows NT supports, and native and third-party tools you can use to manage disk space.

AFTER READING THIS CHAPTER AND COMPLETING THE EXERCISES YOU WILL BE ABLE TO:

- DESCRIBE HOW WINDOWS NT STORES DATA, BOTH FROM A THEORETICAL STANDPOINT (AS FILE OBJECTS) AND FROM A PHYSICAL ONE (ON THE HARD DISK)
- LIST THE FILE SYSTEMS SUPPORTED BY WINDOWS NT
- DISTINGUISH FAT, FAT32, VFAT, AND NTFS
- DESCRIBE THE CHARACTERISTICS AND CAPABILITIES OF NTFS
- EXPLAIN HOW TO USE DISK ADMINISTRATOR FOR FAULT TOLERANCE AND ENHANCED DISK PERFORMANCE
- LIST THIRD-PARTY SOFTWARE FOR DISK DEFRAGMENTATION

FILE STORAGE

You can examine the way Windows NT stores data on your computer's hard disk from two different perspectives: theoretical and physical. From a theoretical standpoint, Windows NT uses file-system objects as the units written to and read from disk.

FILE-SYSTEM OBJECTS

Windows NT bases much of its operation on objects, which are runtime instances of a particular data type that can be manipulated by an operating system process. Fundamentally, any object is a means of allowing Windows NT to perform an operation. A **file-system object** is any object associated with a file system, such as a file, printer, or folder. These objects are acted upon by the I/O subsystem to write data to and retrieve it from disk, as well as to send data to peripheral devices such as printers.

In the Windows NT 4.0 shell, file-system objects are represented by icons associated with every file, folder, and print device on your system. Figure 5-1 shows the Properties dialog box for the 3dpaint.exe file. Each file-system object has a Properties dialog box and a context menu associated with it; the exact contents of each depend on the characteristics of the particular object (just as the icons vary with the object type as well).

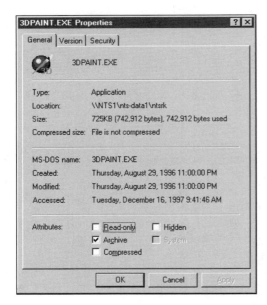

Figure 5-1   File system object Properties dialog box

The objects that Windows NT uses are organized in a hierarchy similar to that of a file system, with some objects responsible for organizing other ones. Thus, folder objects (or directory objects—Microsoft isn't particularly consistent about its own terminology) are higher in the hierarchy than file objects. Actions that affect folder objects will affect those file objects subordinate to that folder object as well. That's why the permissions you set on a shared folder apply also to the objects within that folder (unless you specifically set other file permissions, of course). This is also why, when you delete a folder, all the files within that folder are deleted as well.

HARD DISK STRUCTURE

Windows NT may consider your files and folders to be file-system objects, but these objects also have a physical presence on the hard disk. Let's take a look at the way Windows NT arranges data on your hard disk.

Boot Sector

The **boot sector** partition (a **partition** is a section of a hard disk) contains the information that the file system uses to access the volume (a **volume** is a logical division or partition of a hard disk that's been assigned a name or a drive letter). The **Master Boot Record (MBR)**, discussed shortly, examines the information in the boot sector to load the boot loader.

The Windows NT boot sector consists of the following information:

- A jump instruction

- The name and version of the OS files (such as Windows NT 4.0)

- A data structure, called the BIOS Parameter Block, which describes the physical characteristics of the partition

- A data structure, called the BIOS Extended Parameter Block, which describes the location of the Master File Table for NTFS volumes

- The bootstrap code

 The boot sector is always located on the first 512-byte sector of the disk.

Most of the information in the boot sector describes the physical characteristics of the disk (e.g., the number of sectors per track and clusters per sector), as well as the location of the FAT (File Allocation Table) or the Master File Table (for NTFS volumes). (FAT and NTFS are the two primary file systems used with Windows NT and are covered in detail in this chapter.) The layout and exact information included in the boot sector depends on the disk format used.

NTFS-formatted partitions keep a backup copy of the boot sector. The location of this backup depends on the version of Windows NT in question: Windows NT 3.x NTFS partitions store the backup in the center of the partition; Windows NT 4.0 NTFS partitions store it at the end.

Master Boot Record

If a disk may have more than one partition, how does the right **partition boot sector** get called? The first sector on every disk (whether bootable or not) contains that disk's Master Boot Record. On x86 systems, the MBR contains the partition table for that disk and a small amount of code used to read the partition table and find the **system partition** for that hard disk. It is this code that locates the correct partition where the specified boot sector resides. Once that partition is found, the MBR loads a copy of that partition's boot sector into memory. If the disk is not bootable (has no system partition), then the code never gets used and the boot sector is not loaded.

 A functioning MBR is required to boot a hard disk. Because this record is always in the same location on every hard disk, it is an easy target for viruses. Therefore, it's important to back up your disk's MBR with a disk utility program.

Partition Table

Information about the partitions on a hard disk is located in the **partition table**, a 64–byte data structure located in the first sector on the disk (like the MBR). Because each partition table entry is 16 bytes long, the table may describe up to four partitions (64/16 = 4). Each entry describes one partition, including whether it's a system partition, its starting and ending location on the disk, its total number of sectors, and the file system used to format the partition.

If the partition is part of a volume set or stripe set created in Disk Administrator (volume and stripe sets are covered later in this chapter), then it will have a special bit set to let Windows NT know that it must use the HKEY_LOCAL_MACHINE\SYSTEM\DISK subkey to know how it relates to the other members of the stripe or volume set. Other OSs running on the same computer will not be able to access partitions with this bit set—that is, you can't access a stripe set or volume set from any other OS on the same computer.

A hard disk is basically a stack of round platters with an electromagnetic read/write **head** (like the needle on a record player) for each side of each platter. Each side of each platter is divided into concentric circles called **tracks**. Because the heads of a hard disk always move together, they're always in the same place on each disk platter; if head 0 is positioned over track 45 on surface 0, then head 3 is also positioned over track 45 on surface 3. Because of this synchronized movement, it's possible to envision those tracks as extending downward, making the hard disk into a series of concentric **cylinders** composed of the tracks that lie over each other.

Because the number of tracks per platter and the number of cylinders in the hard disk is equal, it's not necessary to report both, so hard disk manufacturers describe their disks in terms of how many cylinders they have. As shown in Figure 5-2, in addition to being divided into tracks, each surface is figuratively divided into pie-shaped wedges, so each track is divided as well. These wedges are known as **sectors**, and they're the smallest physical division on the hard disk. By industry standard, physical sectors are always 512 bytes in size. To store files, such sectors are chained together with pointers at the end of one sector pointing to the next sector where data resides.

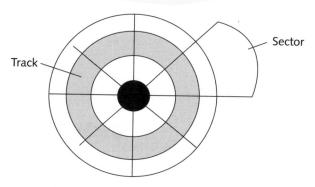

Figure 5-2   Sector division of a hard drive

The number of bits in the pointers at the end of each sector places some constraints on disk size when a disk is formatted outside Windows NT. Because the starting and ending cylinder fields are 10 bits long, they can only describe disks with up to 1,024 cylinders ($2^{10} = 1,024$). Similarly, the partition table's starting and ending head fields are 8 bits long, so only 256 heads can be recognized, and the starting and ending sector fields have 6 bits for a total of 64 numbers. (However, as sectors are numbered beginning with 1, instead of 0, only 63 sectors per track can be recognized.) Thus, because hard disks are low-level formatted with 512-byte sectors, this imposes a theoretical upper limit of 7.8 GB, as you can see from this formula:

Disk Capacity = (sector size) $\times$ (sectors per track) $\times$ (cylinders) $\times$ (heads)

so 512 $\times$ 63 $\times$ 1,024 $\times$ 256 = 8,455,716,864 bytes, or 7.8 GB.

Partitions

If you have experience formatting disks under various operating systems and know that FAT partitions, under normal circumstances, must be no larger than 2 GB, you might be wondering how a theoretical maximum of nearly 8 GB becomes practical under Windows NT. Let's take a look at how partition size is determined, regardless of theory.

You probably know that the function of a file system is to map a section of a hard disk so that data may be retrieved from it. Turn back to the earlier discussion of hard disk structure: Would you really want to have to call up your spreadsheet by identifying the disk head, track, and cylinder it's on? That's the role of the file system, to know the physical location of data on the disk.

A file system doesn't know a physical sector from a hole in the ground, however. To make this work, the file system logically organizes the sectors into groups called **clusters**, the size of the cluster always being a multiple of 512 bytes (the size of a sector) and more specifically determined by the file system being used and the size of the partition. The cluster is the smallest storage unit available. If the cluster size for a partition is 4 KB, then any file will take up at least 4 KB of disk space, even if it's smaller than that. Leftover space in a cluster is wasted. The relationship between cluster size and sectors is illustrated in Figure 5-3.

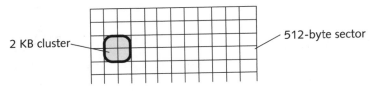

Figure 5-3   Cluster size and sector relationship

 File systems don't have to allocate disk space in clusters. **High Performance File System (HPFS)**, OS/2's file system, does not allocate disk space by clusters— but both NTFS and FAT do.

What does cluster size have to do with partition size? A file system can address only so many clusters, based on the number of bits in each address. A 16-bit file system, therefore, can address 2^{16} (65,536) clusters before it has to start over with another partition. To permit the file system to address as large a partition as possible, cluster size increases proportionately to the size of the partition (as shown in Table 5-1), up to the point at which the clusters are so large that an excess of space is being wasted with each file.

The cluster size proportionate to partition size depends on the file system in use. For example, NTFS follows the rules in Table 5-1:

Table 5-1   Relationship of NTFS Cluster and Partition Size

Partition Size	Number of Sectors/Cluster	Cluster Size
512 MB or less	1	512 bytes (.5 KB)
513 MB–1,024 MB	2	1 KB
1,025 MB–2,048 MB	4	2 KB
2,048 MB or more	8	4 KB

The FAT file system follows the rules outlined in Table 5-2:

Table 5-2   Relationship of FAT Cluster and Partition Size

Partition Size	Number of Sectors/Cluster	Cluster Size
0 MB–15 MB (12-bit FAT)	8	4 KB
16 MB–127 MB	4	2 KB
128 MB–255 MB	8	4 KB
256 MB–511 MB	16	8 KB
512 MB–1,023 MB	32	16 KB
1,024 MB–2,048 MB	64	32 KB
2,049 MB–4,096 MB	128	64 KB
4,097 MB–8,192 MB (Windows NT 4.0 only)	256	128 KB
8,193 MB–16,384 MB (Windows NT 4.0 only)	512	256 KB

Comparing the cluster sizes for the varying drive sizes in Tables 5-1 and 5-2, you can see that NTFS is much more efficient when it comes to allocating space on large partitions than FAT. On large partitions, the cluster size is hopelessly inefficient for any but the very largest files! This isn't quite the end of the story—FAT is actually more efficient in terms of space allocation for small partitions because each entry in the NTFS file-finding database takes up 2 KB, but it's a good initial perspective.

Partitioning Strategies

What can you do to partition your disk space most effectively? For starters, if you've simply got to use the FAT file system (such as if you need the files to be accessible from another OS on the same computer), make partitions smaller. Cluster size is based on logical partition size, not the size of the total hard disk. As such, it's fairly easy to manipulate. Because the Find feature in Windows NT Explorer and My Computer gives you the ability to easily search for files across drives and logical partitions, it's less likely that you'll lose files altogether in your array of drive letters (although you should organize storage so you know where things are). The potential inconvenience is running out of drive letters.

Cluster size isn't the only consideration when it comes to choosing partitions. Should the Windows NT installation become corrupted, it is advisable to create a system partition on which to load OSs and format this partition with FAT so that the computer can be booted from a DOS floppy disk. (Booting from a DOS floppy disk is not a secure configuration, as anyone could thus boot the computer and copy the Registry files, but it's good for troubleshooting and disaster recovery.) Data to be shared may go on an NTFS partition, where it will be more secure, because very specific permissions may be set on the files. It's not necessary to be able to access data when booting from a floppy disk, and in fact, if Windows NT is the only OS running on the local machine, it's probably desirable *not* to be able to access the data. However, this assumes that the data has been backed up regularly and is accessible in backup form. NTFS also comes with its own compression routines, which is handy for data drives that may fill up quickly.

 On RISC-based systems, the system partition *must* be formatted to FAT.

Volumes

Logical partitions are often described as volumes, but a volume is fundamentally any partition or set of partitions organized under a single drive letter and formatted as a unit. Although you can create a group of logical partitions called a **volume set** in Disk Administrator, a volume is not limited to this definition and encompasses single-partition logical drives and fault-tolerant structures as well.

Drive Letters

All volumes are assigned a single drive letter, as are all network shares that are currently connected over the network. Because the drive letters are limited to the 26 letters of the alphabet, this can become a serious limitation in complex networks. If your computer does not have a second floppy drive, you can salvage "B" for use by a network drive.

Windows NT supports the static assignment of drive letters to volumes, network-accessible directories, and CD-ROMs, but until Disk Administrator is used to make these assignments, Windows NT assigns drive letters the same way that MS-DOS does. First, primary partitions are assigned letters (beginning with C), then Windows NT assigns the next available drive letter to each logical drive as it's added.

 When making permanent drive letter assigments, you should be careful to assign letters that correspond to any path information that DOS or Windows applications use.

FAT FILE SYSTEM

Although it doesn't have the advanced features of the NTFS file system, the **File Allocation Table (FAT)** file system is too widely used and, frankly, too important to ignore. Let's take a look at how it works and how that affects when you'll use it—and avoid it.

FAT is a simple file system designed for floppy disks and small partitions with simple structures. It's named for its method of organizing files: the file allocation table. Every file on disk has an entry in the FAT that names the cluster in which it starts and (assuming that the file doesn't fit in a single cluster) the next cluster used, up to the End of File (EOF) entry. So, for example, if a file is stored in clusters 42, 156, and 175, its first entry will be 42, its second

156, its third and final EOF 175—to let the file system know that that's the entire file and the search is complete. Because the FAT is so crucial to the functioning of the file system, two copies are stored on the partition in case the first is corrupted.

CHARACTERISTICS AND LIMITATIONS

FAT is a very simple file system. As such, it has limited capabilities when it comes to setting permissions on files. You can set permissions only on folders shared across the network (you can't share individual files) and cannot set permissions on files available locally. For simple networks, this may not be much of a limitation, but for enterprise networks it's not practical. FAT is also not compressible with the native Windows NT compression software, and you cannot use any DOS-based compression schemes on FAT volumes that you want to be accessible to Windows NT.

BENEFITS

Why use FAT? One obvious reason is cross-platform availability. The FAT file system is compatible with a number of other operating systems: DOS, all Windows from 3.x to Windows 95, and OS/2. Using FAT partitions means that the disk is accessible even if Windows NT isn't bootable. Although this is a potential security risk, it's good for disaster recovery because it gives you a back door to the disk when the front door (Windows NT) isn't available.

Another reason is low overhead. On small volumes (up to about 400 MB), FAT is actually more efficient, because it doesn't need to maintain space for the **transaction log** NTFS uses to maintain volume integrity in the case of an unexpected disk shutdown, as well as some NTFS system files.

 Because the version of FAT implemented on Windows NT and NTFS both support **long filenames (LFNs)**—up to 255 characters, with a closing null character—long filenames are not a consideration when it comes to choosing between FAT and NTFS. However, the original version of FAT introduced with DOS does not support LFNs, so newer versions actually maintain both DOS-style 8.3 filenames (8-character filenames with 3-character extensions) and LFNs, in separate but linked directory entries.

FAT VERSUS VFAT

Windows 95, release 1, uses a FAT-like file system known as **VFAT**. This 32-bit version of FAT works similarly to FAT in terms of organization and cluster allocation, but may use either 32-bit protected mode drivers or 16-bit real mode drivers. The VFAT files may also be compressed and will be readable to both Windows 95 and Windows NT 4.0. That's because the Windows NT implementation of FAT is also based on VFAT.

Like FAT and NTFS, VFAT supports "lazy write," so that applications may send data directly to the cache to be written to disk at a later time.

The major difference between FAT and VFAT is that VFAT supports long filenames (that is, filenames that don't conform to the 8.3 DOS naming conventions). Otherwise, it's FAT with 32-bit drivers that run in protected mode. All the information about cluster sizes applies here. That's why the note that appeared earlier in this chapter indicated that support for LFNs was not an issue between Windows NT implementations of FAT and NTFS.

Like NTFS, VFAT supports filenames of up to 255 characters. It also allows for directory paths of up to 246 characters, including the drive letter, colon, and leading backslash, so that with the final 8.3 filename and terminating null character, it's 260 characters. Table 5-3 describes the differences in naming conventions between FAT and VFAT/FAT32.

Table 5-3   FAT Versus VFAT/FAT32 Naming Conventions

Characteristic	FAT	VFAT/FAT32
Name must begin with letter or number	Yes	Yes
Name cannot contain "/\:;l=,^*?	Yes	Yes
Name cannot contain any spaces	Yes	No
Filename can be only 8 characters long	Yes	No (255 maximum for whole path\name)
File extension can be only 3 characters long	Yes	No (255 maximum for whole path\name)
Only one period map appears in name	Yes	No (text after final period treated as extension)
Device names are reserved*	Yes	Yes
Name is case sensitive	No	No
Name preserves case as entered	No	Yes

* Reserved names are: CON, AUX, PRN, NUL, COMn (n = 1–4), LPTn (n = 1–3)

Both Windows 95 and Windows NT 3.5x and 4.0 use VFAT—Windows 95 OEM Release 2 does not (it's also sometimes referred to as Windows 95 OSR2). It's compatible with FAT and with the Windows NT version of FAT (VFAT) but is not the same thing. VFAT is also included in versions of Linux 1.3.60 and later.

FAT VERSUS FAT32

FAT32 is a derivative of the FAT16 file system, one that supports drives with up to 4 GB of storage (as opposed to 2 GB for 16-bit FAT). Each entry in the FAT32 takes up 4 bytes (32 bits) per cluster, as opposed to the 2 bytes per cluster used by FAT16 or the 1.5 bytes used by FAT12. Any FAT32 partition may have between 65,526 and 268,435,456 clusters.

The four highest bits of each 32-bit entry are not actually part of the cluster number, but are reserved anyway.

FAT32 partitions include more information than FAT16 partitions. To begin with, the BIOS Parameter Block (BPB) for a FAT32 partition is larger than that of a FAT16 partition, so the boot sector is in fact larger than one sector. The boot sector also stores a count of free clusters on the partition and records the cluster number of the most recently allocated cluster. Another difference is that FAT32 partitions don't store the root directory in a set location, as do FAT16 and FAT12 partitions. Instead, it's an ordinary cluster chain, so that it may grow like any other file instead of being limited to a set number of entries.

Another very important difference between FAT16 and FAT32 is cluster size. Not only can FAT32 support larger drives, but it's more efficient in terms of allocating sectors to clusters—each cluster on a FAT32 partition up to 8 GB is 4 KB in size.

The main limitations of FAT32 are that Windows NT 4.0 does not support FAT32 **primary partitions** (a bootable disk partition) or **extended partitions** (a FAT disk partition that may not be bootable, but that can hold up to 32 logical volumes), nor can it recognize FAT32 disk structures of any kind. If you set up a dual-boot machine with Windows 95 OSR2 and Windows NT 4.0 and wish both OSs to share files, you must use FAT16 or VFAT to format such shared partitions.

At this point, only Windows 95 OSR2 supports FAT32. It's not clear at this writing whether Windows NT 5.0 will support FAT32.

LONG FILENAMES AND 8.3 FILENAMES

Both NTFS and VFAT on Windows NT 4.0 support long filenames (LFNs). However, if you're running 16-bit applications, you may not always be able to use those names. This section covers how LFNs work and how and when 8.3 filenames are generated.

8.3 SYNTAX AND LIMITATIONS

The limitations of the 8.3 naming convention are indicated in the name—names must be no longer than eight letters, with a three-letter extension that usually identifies the type of file or the application required to read it. This leads to cryptic filenames and confused muttering as users try to determine what HUYIC.DOC might possibly contain.

5

LONG FILENAME SYNTAX AND LIMITATIONS

LFNs are the response to the cryptic 8.3 filenames. Under Windows NT, files may have names of up to 256 characters including the extension (255 plus a null character to indicate the end of the filename). Using LFNs permits you to name files meaningfully and thus more easily find the files you want.

Long filenames will maintain the cases that you provide for them (that is, if you call a file MyFile.DOC it will be stored as MyFile.DOC), but the names are not case-sensitive. MyFile.DOC is the same name as myfile.doc and MYFILE.DOC.

LFNs aren't a universal panacea, however, because 16-bit applications (and operating systems) can't use them. In fact, some DOS-based disk management applications may destroy long filename entries (although, as long as the 8.3 alias for that file still exists, this doesn't destroy the data). Therefore (as discussed shortly), whenever an LFN is generated for a file, a name that conforms to the 8.3 standard—an **alias**—is also generated.

Another aspect of LFNs is the additional storage space they require. LFNs are stored using a series of linked directory entries, with one for its 8.3 alias and then an additional hidden directory entry for each 13 characters in the name.

CONVERTING LONG FILENAMES TO 8.3 ALIASES

As noted earlier, whenever an LFN is generated, an 8.3 alias is generated along with it. To create this name, the following algorithm is followed:

1. The first six characters of the LFN are stripped off to be used for the name, so that September Report.doc becomes SEPTEM.

2. A tilde (~) and a number are added to the end of the name: SEPTEM~1.DOC. If another file or files with the same first six letters exist, then subsequent files will increment the numbers: SEPTEM~2.DOC, SEPTEM~3.DOC, and SEPTEM~4.DOC.

After the ninth alias has been generated, the remaining files share only the same first five characters, followed by ~dd, where dd starts with 10 and counts up to 99. After the 99th such filename, we drop to four characters followed by ~ddd, starting with 100 up to 999, and so on. In other words, for a set of files named longfilename1.txt, longfilename2.txt, longfilename3.txt, through longfilename50.txt, aliases would be longfi~1.txt, longfi~2.txt, through longfi~9.txt, followed by longf~10.txt through longf~50.txt. The basic principle is to make enough room in the name string to accommodate a unique number suffix, preceded by the tilde (~) character.

The only exception to this rule of creating DOS-compliant aliases for LFNs is the POSIX subsystem: Any files created within this subsystem will not have aliases created for their names, so POSIX filenames that don't comply with the 8.3 standard will be invisible to DOS and Windows applications.

NTFS

Although Windows NT can use FAT, the file system created specifically for this operating system is **New Technology File System (NTFS)**. This file system was designed to be more powerful, more flexible, and more secure than FAT, and largely succeeds in realizing these goals.

5

CHARACTERISTICS AND CAPABILITIES OF NTFS

One of the most salient features of NTFS is its internal structure. Rather than using the flat file table found in FAT, NTFS organizes the data on disk with a relational database called the **Master File Table (MFT)**. Everything on the volume is considered a file (even the MFT itself), and every file stored on the volume is represented in a record in the MFT. The first 16 records of the MFT are reserved for the purposes shown in Table 5-4:

Table 5-4   NTFS Master File Table Entries

Record	Purpose
0	Describes the MFT itself
1	Stores the location of the MFT mirror file, used in case the original is lost or corrupted—this file is stored at the end of the logical volume
2	Log file, used for restoring volume integrity in the case of a crash
3	Volume file, recording the volume name, NTFS version, and other necessary information
4	Attribute definition table, including all attribute names, numbers, and definitions
5	Root folder
6	Cluster bitmap showing which clusters on the volume are currently in use
7	Partition boot sector, if the volume is bootable
8	Bad cluster file, recording the location of any bad clusters on the disk
9	Quota table, showing disk quota usage for each user on a volume—this record is not currently used
10	Upcase table, used to convert lowercase characters to the corresponding Unicode uppercase characters
11–15	Presently unused

All further records in the MFT correspond to files or folders on the volume (folders simply being another type of file). The section in this chapter entitled File and Partition Sizes explains how these records are structured for different kinds of files.

Rather than tacking **attributes** (such as Read Only, Hidden, and so forth) onto data files, NTFS considers all parts of a file as attributes, including the data. Therefore, files on an NTFS volume contain one or more of the attributes shown in Table 5-5:

Table 5-5   NTFS File Attributes

Attribute Type	Function
Standard attribute	Includes time stamps, link count, and other standard attributes
Attribute list	Lists the location of all attributes that don't fit in the MFT
Filename	Includes both short and long filenames; should additional name links be required (perhaps by POSIX), then those links will be listed here
Security descriptor	Shows who has what type of access to the file
Data	Includes the file data; NTFS supports multiple data attributes for a single file, although files typically have a single, unnamed data attribute
Index root	Used to construct the index of a particular attribute over a set of files for the purpose of indexing those files by their attribute value; this attribute is always stored within the MFT
Index allocation	Used to store any indexing information that won't fit in the MFT, if the index stored in the index root becomes too large
Bitmap	Maps the records currently in use on the MFT or folder
Volume information	Used only in the volume system file and includes standard information such as the volume's version and name
Extended attribute information	Used by file servers connected to OS/2 systems; not used by Windows NT
Extended attributes	Used by file servers connected to OS/2 systems; not used by Windows NT

All NTFS data files include standard information, filename, data, and security descriptor attributes. By default, all attributes (including data attributes) are stored within the MFT, or are resident elsewhere in the file.

FAULT TOLERANCE

NTFS is different from FAT in many ways, but one of the most important ways in which it differs is that it's recoverable (changes to files or directories can be redone or undone). Every time the volume's structure or contents changes (such as when files are created or deleted), that change is recorded in a transaction log, noting the state of the volume before and after the change. The size of this log of course depends on the size of the volume, but it may be up to 4 MB in size. Therefore, if a change takes place but is not completed—perhaps the power failed in the midst of a file creation—then the volume is restored to its original state and none of its metadata (the data that describes a volume's file structure, directory organization, and file records) is corrupted. A partition may not be bootable if its boot sector is damaged, but if the computer is booted from another drive (Windows NT is not limited to booting from drive C:) then the partition may be accessed and repaired.

NTFS works in combination with the log file service, the cache manager, and the memory manager to provide transaction logging. Every time a user performs an action that would make a change to the volume structure, the log file service updates all redo and undo information for the transaction. Redo information tells NTFS how to repeat the transaction, and undo information tells how to undo a transaction that was incomplete or otherwise erroneous.

If a transaction is completed successfully, then the file update is committed. If the transaction is somehow aborted, or has an error, then NTFS rolls back the transaction using the undo information. If the file system crashes, then NTFS performs three passes to fix any problems in the volume structure: an analysis pass, a redo pass, and an undo pass. During the analysis pass, NTFS determines exactly which clusters must be updated based on the information in the log file. During the redo pass, it performs all transaction steps performed since the last checkpoint. And during the undo pass, it reverses all uncommitted transactions, those that were not finished.

Note that transaction logging affects only metadata structures and volume integrity—it does not protect you from data loss. The point of transaction logging is to maintain a record of your volume's structure so that the volume remains accessible, not to keep you from losing data.

SECURITY

As discussed earlier, each file stored in an NTFS volume is stored as a set of attributes, of which data is one. Another is the security attribute, which determines which users or groups have what kind of access to the file. It's because of the security attribute that it's possible to set permissions on individual files and not only as part of a shared folder.

A file's security attributes are described in its security descriptor. This security descriptor has four parts:

- The security ID of the file's owner (by default, the creator, although administrators may take ownership of files); the file's owner may change the access permissions for the file

- A group security ID, used only by the POSIX subsystem and ignored by the rest of Windows NT

- A discretionary Access Control List (ACL), identifying the users and groups who are granted specific access permissions; the contents of this ACL are controlled by the file's owner, as identified by the security ID

- A system ACL for controlling the auditing information for that file, unlike the discretionary ACL, the system ACL's contents are controlled by members of the Administrators group

FILE RECOVERY

When used on a fault-tolerant device such as a mirror set or stripe set with parity (see the later section on Windows NT 4.0 Disk Administrator), NTFS may be used to support **hot fixing**. If the file-system drivers encounter a bad sector while reading data from the drive, it can regenerate the data from the fault-tolerant information, passing the data along as though nothing had happened and then noting the bad sector in the MFT's bad sector list. Of course, this advantage is moot to Windows NT Workstation users, because Windows NT Workstation does not support fault-tolerant disk configurations.

FILE AND PARTITION SIZES

The way in which data files are stored in an NTFS volume depends on the amount of space required by the file's attributes. Generally speaking, the MFT contains a 2 KB pointer to each file's location on disk; however, the smaller the file, the simpler the storage process.

Data File Records

Very small files (with a data attribute no larger than 1.5 KB) may be stored entirely within the MFT because the 2 KB slot reserved for the pointer leaves plenty of room for the data and other attributes. According to Microsoft, you can't count on files of this size being stored within the MFT, but it's possible.

If a file is too large to fit within the MFT, then its record looks slightly different. Rather than containing data, its data attribute contains a pointer called the Virtual Cluster Number (VCN) showing the location of the first cluster used to store the data and the number of contiguous clusters in each of the runs.

Extremely large files may have a different record entirely. Recall that all attributes are resident in the MFT by default. What happens when so many pointers exist for a data attribute as to not fit within the MFT? In that case, a special attribute called an extended attribute takes the place of the data attribute in the MFT, pointing to a nonresident data pointer that can then point to the data's VCNs. The very largest files might theoretically require multiple nonresident data pointers, but this is mostly theoretical. The point is that no file is ever too large to fit within the directory structure.

Folder Records

Just as every data file on disk has an MFT record, so do all folders and subfolders on the disk. NTFS considers folders simply to be files that can contain other files, so the structure of folder records is similar to that of data file records.

The placement of the index required to build the folder depends on the number of files in the folder. A small index with only a few entries is resident in the MFT and contains the name of each file and the number of its MFT record.

If an index has too many entries to fit within the MFT, then its record looks slightly different. The index root attribute remains resident within the MFT, but the folder's record now also contains an index allocation attribute that points to other indices for the data. And, of course, just as indices can contain file entries, they can contain other indices to create subfolders, so this structure can get rather complicated. No matter what, however, the basic information needed to construct the index is located within the MFT.

FILE COMPRESSION

Any file or folder on an NTFS volume may be compressed, whether it's part of a larger, compressed folder or not. You can even format entire volumes to be compressed, so that whenever you add files to those volumes the files are compressed automatically. Because compression can be applied to individual files and directories, or even to entire volumes, Microsoft indicates that you need not be cautious about using file compression. In fact, they recommend that infrequently accessed directories be stored in compressed form to help make better use of disk space.

POSIX SUPPORT

Windows NT comes with three environmental subsystems, a sort of suboperating system: Win32 (the one you'll use most often), OS/2 1.x, and POSIX. The POSIX subsystem is designed to run POSIX applications and meets the requirements of POSIX.1.

POSIX (Portable Operating System Interface for Computing Environments) is a set of standards being drafted by the Institute of Electrical and Electronic Engineers (IEEE) that defines various aspects of an operating system, including topics such as programming interface, security, networking, and graphical interface. So far, only one of these standards, POSIX.1, has made the transition from draft to final form. It's not widely in use, but sufficiently so that POSIX compatibility was necessary for Windows NT to be acceptable to the US Department of Defense.

POSIX.1 is based on ideas drawn from the UNIX file system and process model. Because POSIX.1 addresses only API-level issues, most applications written to the POSIX.1 API must rely on non-POSIX operating system extensions (in this case, Win32) to provide services such as security and networking.

POSIX applications need certain file-system functionality, such as support for case-sensitive filenames (to POSIX, there's a difference between MyFile.doc, MYFILE.DOC, and myfile.doc) and support for files with multiple names (or hard links). NTFS supports these POSIX requirements. Any POSIX application requiring access to file-system resources must have access to an NTFS partition, but POSIX applications that do not access file-system resources can run on FAT.

If you install POSIX utilities or file systems on your Windows NT machine, be sure to use native POSIX file management utilities to manage them. Just as older DOS utilities will happily trash LFN information created by VFAT or FAT32, native Windows NT file utilities—namely Explorer, File Manager, and My Computer—will happily trash POSIX file structures, especially when the only difference between two or more otherwise identical filenames is their use of upper- and lowercase characters. For example, POSIX understands very well that MyFile.txt is different from myfile.txt, but NTFS does not (and will actually destroy the directory entry for whichever name appears second in the POSIX-created directory structure).

PERFORMANCE ISSUES

NTFS is designed to be faster at retrieving files—particularly large ones that may be stored in a number of discontinuous clusters—than FAT is. It's hard to tell if it actually is faster at retrieving files, but at least its design is more efficient. Not only can entire files be stored within the MFT itself, but the tree structure is a more efficient pointer to multiple disk locations than is the FAT style of pointing to cluster after cluster until the end of the file is located.

CONVERTING TO NTFS

Windows NT comes with a CONVERT utility to let you convert FAT volumes to NTFS (although not the other way). It works like this: When you begin the conversion process, Windows NT sets aside any data in the partition to be converted, converts the file system from FAT's flat file system to NTFS's tree-based structure, then replaces the data. The only catch—and you knew there'd be one—is that you need room on the volume to do the conversion (perhaps as much as one third of the amount of data you've got) in which to store the data while the conversion is taking place. There's another catch, too: You can't convert the current drive or one with open files. This means that you can't convert the system partition without rebooting.

Whenever you use CONVERT to transform a FAT volume to NTFS, be aware that this is a one-way transformation. There is no UNCONVERT utility that can take an NTFS volume and transform it back into FAT (to do this, you'd have to copy files from NTFS to a FAT partition, then delete the files from the NTFS partition). This means that you'd need enough space to accommodate two sets of files, rather than having recourse to an in-place conversion utility.

The details of the CONVERT process are covered in Hands-on Project 5-1.

CONVERTING A DATA PARTITION

If you've created separate partitions for your data and for your system partition and want to convert the data partition, then the conversion process is relatively easy. Log on using an account with administrative privileges. Make sure all files on the partition are closed, then open a command window and type

```
convert x:/fs ntfs
```

where *x* is the drive letter of the partition you're converting.

CONVERTING A SYSTEM PARTITION

It is not recommended that you convert the system partition to NTFS, because the system files are only shared administratively and converting the system partition to NTFS will make disaster recovery much more difficult (not impossible, but difficult). Instead, if you've got your data and system files on a single FAT partition and feel compelled to convert to NTFS, it's a far better idea to follow these steps instead of a simple conversion:

1. Back up all data, and back up the Registry so that you don't have to reconfigure your computer from scratch.

2. Start reinstalling Windows NT. When you come to the point at which you choose the partition on which you wish to install Windows NT, delete the current partition. You'll have to confirm this several times and in different ways—it's virtually impossible to accidentally delete a partition.

3. Create a new partition big enough for all system files, about 1 GB to be safe (or larger if you've got more than one OS loaded). By default, this partition will be a primary partition. The remaining disk space will be **free space** that you can configure with the Disk Administrator.

4. Install Windows NT onto the system partition as described in Chapter 2, and install any Service Packs that you had installed.

5. Format a data partition with NTFS.

6. Restore your data and Registry files.

This approach lets you separate system files from data files and maintain the kind of structure and organization that you've already built, without risking accidental damage from the conversion process.

OTHER WINDOWS NT-SUPPORTED FILE SYSTEMS

FAT and NTFS aren't the only file systems Windows NT recognizes. This section talks about the other file systems Windows NT uses (and one it no longer does).

COMPACT DISK FILE SYSTEM (CDFS)

Compact Disk File System (CDFS) provides the same directory and file management capabilities for a CD-ROM device as NTFS and FAT do for a hard-disk-based file system. Windows NT Workstation supports the Auto-Run and CD-XA CDFS enhancements.

Auto-Run allows the OS to recognize that a compact disc has been inserted into the drive and to start the application immediately. The application developer puts an AUTORUN.INF file on a compact disc. When that disc is inserted into the CD-ROM drive, Windows NT 4.0 reads the contents and launches the application listed in AUTORUN.INF

CD-XA is an extended format for video compact discs that contain MPEG movies. Whereas regular compact discs have 2,048 byte data blocks, CD-XA compact discs have 2,352 byte data blocks.

NETWORKS AS FILE SYSTEMS

An important network component called the **redirector** can be implemented as a file system. The redirector is a software component through which one computer gains access to the resources of another computer. The Windows NT operating system redirector allows connection to Windows for Workgroups, LAN Manager, LAN Server, and other MS-based network servers. The redirector communicates to the protocols by means of the Transport Driver Interface (TDI). The TDI is a protocol interface that allows developers to sidestep the details of what protocol is used to communicate across a network and makes it much easier for them to use network services abstractly, without having to do as much programming work.

The redirector is implemented as a Windows NT file-system driver, just like NTFS or FAT. Implementing a redirector as a file system has several benefits. First, it allows applications to call a single API (the Windows NT I/O API) to access files on local and remote computers. From the perspective of the I/O Manager, there is no difference between accessing files stored on a remote computer on the network and accessing those stored locally on a hard disk. Second, it runs in Kernel mode and so can directly call other drivers and other Kernel-mode components, such as Cache Manager. (Kernel-mode operation is covered in Chapter 1.) This improves the performance of the redirector. Third, it can be dynamically loaded and unloaded, like any other file-system driver.

HPFS AND WINDOWS NT 4.0

Although Windows NT supported HPFS (the native OS/2 file system) in previous versions, it no longer does so. In fact, the version of the CONVERT utility used to make NTFS partitions no longer works with HPFS at all, although you can use a version of the utility included with an earlier version of Windows NT.

WINDOWS NT 4.0 DISK ADMINISTRATOR

RAID (Redundant Array of Inexpensive Drives) is a catch-all term for a variety of methods of using an array of drives to improve data security and disk performance. Although Windows NT Server supports three of these methods (disk striping, disk striping with parity, and disk mirroring), Windows NT Workstation supports only **disk striping**, a disk arrangement that interleaves data across two or more disks and thus allows data to be read and written to more than one disk at a time.

For both versions of Windows NT (that is, Server and Workstation), Disk Administrator is the tool that must be used to take advantage of its built-in RAID capabilities. For Windows NT Workstation, the only RAID option available is stripe sets (without parity); whereas for Server, the options include stripe sets without parity and also stripe sets with parity, disk mirroring, and even disk duplexing.

Disk Administrator is accessible from the Administrative Tools folder. When you open it, you'll see a screen that looks something like the one shown in Figure 5-4.

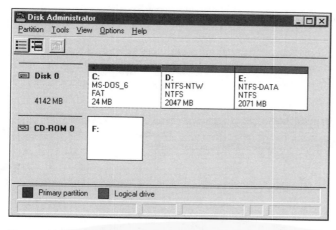

Figure 5-4   Windows NT Disk Administrator main screen

Notice that the layout is divided into both physical and logical drives: the boldfaced labels of Disk 0 and CD-ROM refer to the single physical hard disk in this computer; the partitions set in the long white blocks represent logical partitions on this disk, plus the CD-ROM. From the menus, you can create primary and extended partitions, create stripe sets from free space, format partitions, assign drive letters, and otherwise manipulate your disk configuration.

VOLUME SETS

In addition to RAID options, Disk Administrator for Windows NT Workstation also permits definition of volume sets. A volume set aggregates between 2 and 32 disk partitions (which may be on the same or different drives) and treats them as a single logical volume, with a single drive letter. The primary advantage of a volume set is that it can be expanded at any time without requiring the data to be backed up and then recopied into the expanded set. Thus, volume sets can grow as needed. If, however, you ever need to shrink a volume set, then the existing data must be backed up, the current set deleted, a new (smaller) volume set defined, and the data copied from the backup into the new volume set.

There's a catch to volume sets: they're dependent on the functioning of all disks involved. Should one physical disk fail, you'll lose all the data in the volume set. Be sure to back up volume sets regularly!

You use the Partition menu of the Disk Administrator to create a volume set. Hands-on Project 5-2 gives the steps to create and format a volume set.

You can also delete a volume set from Disk Administrator, by selecting the set and then choosing Delete from the Partition menu. That will delete any data on the volume set and restore it to free space.

SYSTEM AND BOOT PARTITIONS

For the sake of simplicity, this chapter has talked mostly about the system partition; however, the system partition and boot partition are usually but not always the same thing. The system partition is the partition containing the files needed to load Windows NT, whereas the boot partition or boot sector has Windows NT and its support files installed.

On x86-based computers, the system partition must be a primary partition marked as active for startup purposes and must be located on the boot disk. There can only be one primary partition active at any time, which is indicated through color-coding in the Disk Administrator. The **active partition** is the primary partition from which the system will attempt to boot the next time the computer is restarted. If you want to use another operating system without choosing it from the Windows NT boot loader menu, you must first mark its system partition as active in the Disk Administrator before restarting the computer.

Partitions on a RISC-based computer need not be marked active to be bootable. Instead, they are configured using a hardware configuration program supplied by the manufacturer. As opposed to x86-based systems, the system partition on a RISC machine must be formatted for the FAT file system. On either type of computer, the system partition can never be part of a stripe set or volume set, but may be mirrored or duplexed (because Windows NT Workstation does not support mirroring, this applies only to Windows NT Server).

To mark a primary partition as active, click on the partition in question (make sure it's got an operating system on it!) and choose Mark Active from the Partition menu. This change won't be set until you leave Disk Administrator and choose to save the changes, but once you do, the next time you reboot, that partition will be selected. If you realize that you made a mistake before you leave the Disk Administrator, exit and choose not to save the changes. Also note that only primary partitions may be marked active; if you have an extended partition on your drive, Disk Administrator will not permit you to mark it as active.

Mirroring and Duplexing

RAID level 1 is called **disk mirroring**. Basically, mirroring is a way of creating a live copy of all data onto a second disk in the same computer, so that if one disk fails then the other one will always have a copy of the data immediately accessible.

Duplexing is the same thing as mirroring, with one enhancement. By convention, when you speak of mirroring, you're talking about two disks on the same disk controller. If you make the hot backups to a disk on a separate controller, that's known as **disk duplexing**. Duplexing is theoretically more secure than mirroring because it works around any problems occurring in either the disk or the controller, but because a disk is more likely to fail than a controller (more moving parts), practically speaking there's not a lot of difference.

 Unfortunately, Windows NT Workstation does not support mirroring or duplexing as does Windows NT Server.

Stripe Sets with and Without Parity

Two other RAID levels are disk striping (level 0) and **disk striping with parity** (level 5). The two are quite similar. In both cases, data is distributed across two or more (in the case of stripe sets with parity, three or more) partitions on as many disks. Arranging the data this way reduces the time spent both reading and writing to disk, so that throughput is increased. The main difference between striping and striping with parity is one of fault tolerance: stripe sets with parity store both data and parity information to reconstruct data should one of the disks fail, whereas stripe sets store only data, so that if a single disk fails the entire stripe set becomes inaccessible.

Although at first glance it may appear that volume sets and stripe sets accomplish the same thing, this isn't the case. The point of volume sets is to create a single disk larger than all physical disks on the computer, or to create a logical disk of usable size from bits and pieces of disk space. The pieces of a volume set may be of different sizes, and the use of a volume set does not affect throughput. In contrast, the pieces of a stripe set must all be the same size, and the striping technology improves throughput.

Creating a stripe set (Windows NT Workstation does not support stripe sets with parity) is as simple as doing most things with Disk Administrator. The steps to create a stripe set are given in Hands-on Project 5-3.

Drive Letter Assignment

You can use Disk Administrator to statically assign drive letters to volumes so that those letters are reserved. Exercise caution in doing this: If you assign a different drive letter than was originally assigned, you may mess up path information that DOS or Win16 applications need to find their working files. It's really not necessary to manually assign drive letters; Windows NT will assign drive letters for you. An example of a case where you might want to assign a drive letter would be to make it easy for the system to find a specific CD on a CD drive, such as the TechNet CD (Microsoft's monthly information service, and a gold mine of data). Hands-on Project 5-4 gives the steps to assign a static drive letter with Disk Administrator.

RECOVERING DISK CONFIGURATION INFORMATION

Disk configuration information is initially stored on the Emergency Repair Disk (ERD) at system installation. Disk Administrator provides an option for saving and later restoring this configuration information that you can use after making changes such as assigned drive letters, volume sets, stripes sets, and new partitions. This ability to save and restore configuration information is useful both when you're attempting to recover a system with an ERD (unless you wisely updated your ERD every time you made a change) or when you've got a new installation of Windows NT that you'd like to quickly set up with a certain disk configuration.

Saving and restoring the configuration is simple. To save, put your ERD into the A: drive and choose Save from the Configuration option in the Partition menu. To restore a configuration, choose Restore, and choose the file from the ERD.

THIRD-PARTY DISK MANAGEMENT TOOLS

One of the most important disk management tasks is **defragmentation**, the process of taking widely scattered data files on a disk and consolidating them in one contiguous area of the disk. As discussed earlier, both NTFS and FAT keep records of where data is physically stored on the hard disk. Data is always stored in the first available cluster on the disk, not necessarily the one in which it will fit best. Therefore, if you create and delete a lot of files, then you're likely to end up with your file data scattered all over the disk, making it slower to retrieve than it should be.

Thus, you need to regularly run a disk defragmenting tool (defragger) to keep your files as compact as possible and thus keep disk read time up to snuff. Windows NT 4.0 does not come with a such a tool, so it's necessary to turn to third-party software. Today, the two primary third-party defragmentation tools for Windows NT are Speed Disk (see Figure 5-5), one of the Norton Utilities for Windows NT, and Executive Software's Diskeeper (see Figure 5-6) for Windows NT Workstation. More information about these utilities is available at each company's Web sites, which are:

- Norton Utilities for Windows NT: *www.symantec.com*
- Diskeeper for Windows NT Workstation: *www.execsoft.com*

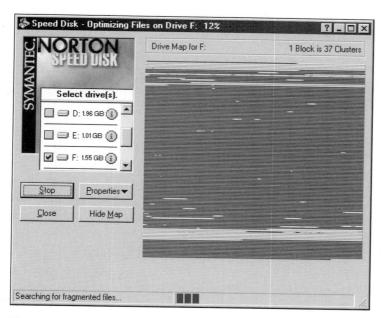

Figure 5-5   Norton Speed Disk

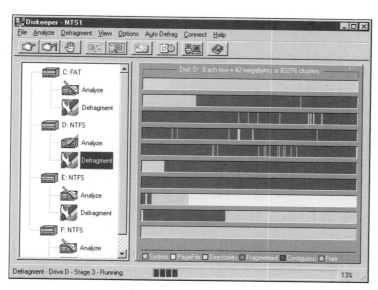

Figure 5-6   Diskeeper Lite

CHAPTER SUMMARY

From a logical perspective, Windows NT views all files and directories as file-system objects, objects that may be manipulated by the file-system drivers. From a physical perspective, all files are stored in groups of sectors called clusters on the disk, and their disk location is described in the file-system directory structure in terms of what cluster or clusters they are in.

There are two major file systems used with Windows NT: FAT and NTFS. FAT comes in three main varieties: FAT16, which uses a 16-bit addressing scheme; VFAT, which permits the use of long filenames instead of just the 8.3 format; and FAT32, which is a 32-bit version of FAT that permits the use of long filenames and may address volumes up to 4 GB in size. All versions of FAT use larger clusters than does NTFS for the same disk size, but they are more efficient on smaller disks than is NTFS because they don't have the complex organizational and logging structures found on an NTFS volume.

NTFS is the native Windows NT file system. It incorporates advanced data security and transaction logging functions not found in FAT. NTFS is necessary to make volumes accessible to some POSIX applications, and it is designed to be more efficient than FAT when retrieving data from large volumes.

In addition to its disk file systems of NTFS and FAT, Windows NT supports CDFS, the CD-ROM File System, with Auto-Run enhancements and network redirectors that behave like other file-system drivers.

Disk Administrator is the main Windows NT tool for managing disk space and configuration after installation. You can use the Windows NT Workstation Disk Administrator to create volume sets and stripe sets, as well as primary and extended partitions. You can also use this tool to define the system partition, if you wish to use an alternate installation of Windows NT.

Although regularly defragmenting disks is an important part of disk maintenance, Windows NT does not include any defragmentation tools. Two defraggers mentioned here are Speed Disk, included with Norton Utilities for Windows NT, and Diskeeper Lite, from Executive Software. Both rearrange the contents of your disk to store files in contiguous clusters.

KEY TERMS

- **active partition** — A primary partition on a PC hard disk that is marked as the partition from which the system must boot.

- **alias** — The 8.3 filename that's generated at the same time as a long filename so that applications and operating systems that can't read long filenames can still access the data.

- **attribute** — To FAT, an attribute is an addition to a data file that describes some feature of the file, for example, that it's hidden, read-only, a system file, or that it's been archived. To NTFS, everything describing a file is an attribute, including the data itself. NTFS has a much larger array of attributes than does FAT.

- **boot sector** — The partition containing Windows NT and its support files.

- **Compact Disk File System (CDFS)** — The file system used to read and write compact disks.

- **cluster** — The storage unit used by FAT and NTFS, it consists of one or more sectors, logically grouped. The number of sectors in a cluster depends on the size of the hard disk partition.

- **cylinder** — All the tracks in a hard disk that are directly in line with each other.

- **defragmentation** — The operation of examining a disk's physical file layout and copying all files that occupy multiple, noncontiguous areas on disk (each part of which is called a file fragment) to areas of disk where all parts are contiguous (thereby eliminating file fragments, resulting in defragmentation).

- **disk duplexing** — A fault-tolerance measure involving linking two disks on the same computer, each using its own controller, so that an exact duplicate of the contents of the first disk are maintained on the second.

- **disk mirroring** — A fault-tolerance measure involving linking two disks on the same computer and using the same controller, so that an exact duplicate of the contents of the first disk are maintained on the second.

- **disk striping** — A method of improving disk read and write performance by distributing data across two or more disks in a stripe set, so that data may be read and written from all disks in the stripe set at once.

- **disk striping with parity** — Disk striping with parity is equivalent to RAID level 5; it spreads data across multiple drives, but also duplicates data from each drive across all the other drives in the parity data for the stripe set. If a single drive fails, the parity data can be used to reconstruct information from the failed drive. If a second drive in the set fails, only then will the stripe set be lost.

- **extended partition** — An area created from free space on a disk and which can be used to create volume sets or fault-tolerant volumes.

- **File Allocation Table (FAT)** — A file system based on the use of a file allocation table, a flat table that records the clusters used to store the data contained in each file stored on disk.

- **FAT32** — The 32-bit version of FAT that supports long filenames (names that don't conform to the 8.3 restriction) and disks up to 4 GB in size. Works only for Windows 95 OSR2.

- **file-system object** — Any object associated with a file system, such as a file, folder, or printer, and that may be manipulated by a file system driver.

- **free space** — An unused and unpartitioned area of a hard disk that is available for the creation of logical drives.

5

- **head** — The part of a hard disk used for reading and writing data.

- **hot fixing** — A technique of recognizing, marking, and avoiding bad sectors on a hard disk supported by some OSs, including Windows NT. Hot fixing basically permits a drive to keep working properly, even if bad sectors are discovered during normal file-system operation.

- **High Performance File System (HPFS)** — OS/2's native file system. Although previous versions of Windows NT supported HPFS, Windows NT 4.0 does not.

- **long filenames (LFNs)** — Filenames that do not conform to the 8.3 standard file-name format used for DOS, where filenames may consist of a maximum of 12 characters, up to 8 for the part before the period to name the file, a period to separate the name from the extension, and up to 3 for the part after the period as an extension to identify a file's type.

- **Master Boot Record (MBR)** — The partition table for a disk and code that permits that partition table to be read. A functioning MBR is required to boot a hard disk.

- **Master File Table (MFT)** — The relational database used by NTFS to locate files on disk.

- **New Technology File System (NTFS)** — The native Windows NT file system, which has a more detailed directory structure and supports data-security measures not found in FAT. It also supports very large disks and long filenames.

- **partition** — A division of an entire hard disk. If not divided, then a hard disk is a single partition.

- **partition boot sector** — The partition that contains the information the file system uses to access the volume, including a physical description of the disk, the name and version of the OS files, the bootstrap code, and an instruction that allows the Master Boot Record to find all this information.

- **partition table** — An on-disk structure on a PC that provides a physical map of the partitions on a hard disk, by indicating their starting and stopping sector addresses. The partition table is a key data structure for disk access, and its damage or loss renders a drive inoperable unless the partition table can be restored, repaired, or rebuilt.

- **POSIX (Portable Operating System Interface for Computing Environments)** — A set of standards under development by the Institute of Electrical and Electronic Engineers (IEEE) that defines various aspects of an OS, including topics such as programming interface, security, networking, and graphical interface. The US Government requires all systems it purchases to be POSIX compliant, to help ensure the portability of the data and applications that such systems contain (theoretically, POSIX compliant software and data formats can migrate from one POSIX compliant system to another with a minimum of effort).

- **primary partition** — The partition on a disk that can be marked for use by an OS. A disk may have up to four primary partitions per disk (or three if an extended partition exists).

- **RAID (Redundant Array of Inexpensive Drives)** — A catch-all phrase for one of a variety of methods of using multiple disks to improve disk performance, data security, or both.

- **redirector** — A part of networking software that permits network transactions to interact directly with the I/O subsystem.

- **sectors** — The 512-byte portions of a hard disk achieved by dividing its surfaces both into tracks and into pie-shaped wedges radiating from the center. The sector is the smallest unit on a disk.

- **system partition** — The partition containing the files needed to run Windows NT. On x86 systems, the system partition must be located on the boot disk and marked as active. On RISC-based systems, they're marked active in hardware and must be FAT-based.

- **Transport Driver Interface (TDI)** — A common API to which Microsoft redirectors communicate to enable applications and services to access the network. This interface handles the details necessary to use one networking protocol or another to communicate, thereby relieving developers of any responsibility to manage protocol-related data in their applications.

- **tracks** — The concentric circles that divide a hard disk's surfaces into one division.

- **transaction log** — The record used in NTFS to note which changes to the file system structure have been completed. This record is used to maintain volume integrity in the case of a disk crash—some data may be lost when the disk is brought back up, but the volume structure will not be corrupted.

- **VFAT** — An implementation of FAT that supports long filenames (LFNs).

- **volume** — Another word for a partition, a logical division of a hard disk that's been assigned its own drive letter.

- **volume set** — A collection of disk partitions that Windows NT treats as a single logical drive. A volume set may be expanded after it's already been created, so administrators can increase the capacity of a logical drive on the fly. To shrink a volume set, however, the data must be backed up, the old volume set deleted, a new (smaller) set defined, and the data restored to that set. If you lose one drive in a volume set, you lose all the data in the entire set, because it offers no fault tolerance.

REVIEW QUESTIONS

1. Identify all of the following (there may be more than one) that are file system objects:
   a. files
   b. directories
   c. modems
   d. printers

2. How many characters may be in a filename on a Windows NT FAT partition?

   a. 8
   b. 11
   c. 255
   d. 256

3. Which of the following is not part of the Windows NT partition boot sector? (Choose all that apply.)

   a. the partition table
   b. the BIOS Extended Parameter Block
   c. a description of the location of the Master File Table
   d. on FAT volumes, the File Allocation Table

4. Where is the backup copy of the partition boot sector stored on Windows NT 4.0 volumes?

   a. partition table
   b. Master Boot Record
   c. middle of the system partition
   d. end of the system partition

5. The partition table is loaded by the ___Master Boot Record___. *operating System*

6. How many partitions can a disk contain?

   a. 4
   b. 3
   c. 2
   d. 1

7. A ___Cluster___ is made up of one or more 512-byte ___sectors___.

8. Unless otherwise specified, what is the largest cluster size that NTFS uses?

   a. 2 KB
   b. 4 KB
   c. 8 KB
   d. 16 KB

9. If your computer has only a single floppy drive, you may assign drive letter B: to a network drive. True or False?

10. Which of the following statements about permissions on a FAT volume is not true? (Choose all that apply.)

    a. FAT volumes cannot set local permissions, only permissions on shares.

    b. You cannot set permissions on files, but only on folders.

    c. By default, permissions set on folders do not apply to the files within those folders.

    d. FAT volumes can only be compressed with DOS compression algorithms.

11. The approximate threshold at which it becomes more efficient to use NTFS than FAT is a disk of ___460 meg___ or greater in size.

12. Under what circumstances are aliases created?

    a. only when the file is created on a volume using the FAT file system

    b. always, to make the data in the file accessible to 16-bit applications and operating systems that cannot read the long names

    c. on shared network drives

    d. none of the above

13. Long filenames are truly case-sensitive; that is, if you create two files with the same name except for the capitalization of the words in the file, the two files will be separate entities. True or False?

14. You've just created the fifth file on the disk with the name Summer 1997 Report.DOC. What will this file's alias be?

    a. Summer~5.doc

    b. Summe~05.doc

    c. Summ~005.doc

    d. Summerrt.doc

15. The first ___16___ records of the Master File Table are reserved.

16. Which of the following attributes will a very large directory have? (Choose all that apply.)

    a. index allocation

    b. index root

    c. index name

    d. none of the above

17. Select names of the three passes that NTFS performs to repair volume structures after a disk crash. (Choose all that apply.)

    a. analysis pass

    b. decoding pass

    c. redo pass

    d. repair pass

    e. undo pass

18. Which of the following parts of the security descriptor are only used by the POSIX subsystem? (Choose all that apply.)

    a. Security ID

    b. Group security ID

    c. Discretionary ACL

    d. System ACL

19. Who controls the contents of a file's system ACL?

    a. the owner of the file

    b. the creator of the file

    c. members of the Administrators group

    d. the operating system

20. The ___*inter allocation*___ attribute is necessary if too many pointers to a file's data exist to fit within the MFT.

21. When you format NTFS volumes to be compressed, all files created within that volume will be automatically compressed, but when you compress FAT volumes only existing files and directories will be compressed. True or False?

22. The ___*HPFS*___ file system was supported in previous versions of Windows NT but is no longer supported.

23. Which method or methods of RAID does Windows NT Workstation support?

    a. disk mirroring

    b. disk striping with parity

    c. disk striping

    d. all of the above

24. If you wanted to get some use out of tiny scraps of free space on your drives, how could you use Disk Administrator to do so?

    a. create a volume set

    b. create a stripe set

    c. create a stripe set with parity

    d. either a or b

25. Which partition must be marked as active to boot an x86-based computer?

    a. primary partition

    b. boot partition

    c. system partition

    d. extended partition

26. What is free space?

   a. empty space within a defined partition

   b. the space in a disk cluster that isn't occupied by file data

   c. unformatted, unallocated space on a disk drive

   d. all of the above

HANDS-ON PROJECTS

PROJECT 5-1

To convert a FAT partition to NTFS with CONVERT.EXE:

1. Launch the DOS box (**Start**, **Programs**, **Command Prompt**).

2. Ask your instructor or technical support specialist to supply the letter identifier for the drive to be converted. Be careful about this, because the conversion routine is irreversible and doesn't ask for confirmation before executing.

3. If the drive's letter is J, then enter **convert j: /fs:ntfs**, with a **/v** on the end if you want verbose output (as in this example). The conversion routine will begin.

4. When it's completed, if you ran the conversion in verbose mode, you'll see output like the following:

```
C:\users\default>convert j: /fs:ntfs /v

The type of the file system is FAT.

Determining disk space required for filesystem conversion

Total disk space:                    3024 kilobytes.

Free space on volume:                2998 kilobytes.

Space required for conversion:       2244 kilobytes.

Converting file system

Conversion complete
```

The conversion takes effect immediately—you don't need to reboot or log off.

5. If for some reason the conversion utility can't get exclusive access to the drive you're converting (this might happen if you're running disk utilities in the background), or if you're currently using the operating system from that drive, then it will inform you of the fact and ask if you want the conversion to take place when you next reboot. Click **Yes** and it will happen automatically, without further prompting from you.

PROJECT 5-2

To use Disk Administrator to build a volume set and format it for use with NTFS:

1. Open Disk Administrator (**Start**, **Programs**, **Administrative Tools (Common)**, **Disk Administrator**). You'll see a screen like the one in Figure 5-7, showing drives, partitions, and free space.

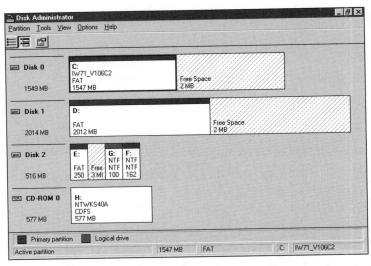

Figure 5-7   Disk Administrator is used to create and manage disk configurations

2. Select the areas of free space that you want to be in the volume set, pressing [**Ctrl**] as you click to select more than one (selected areas are enclosed with a dark line). These areas may be on more than one physical disk, as shown in Figure 5-8 by the presence of regions labeled "Free Space" on both Disks 0, 1, and 2.

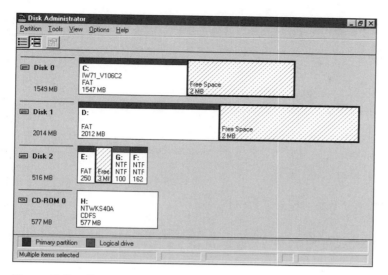

Figure 5-8   Free space on different drives can be selected for a volume set

3. When you've selected all the areas of free space to include in the volume set, choose **Partition, Create Volume Set** from the menu. A dialog box like the one in Figure 5-9 will open.

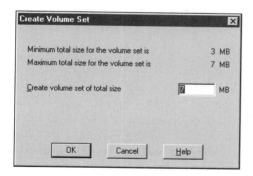

Figure 5-9   You can make the volume set any size up to the amount of free space selected

4. Click **OK** to create the volume set. The set will be created but not yet formatted.

5. Right-click on the new volume set and choose **Commit Changes Now** from the pop-up menu.

6. Now that the change is committed, you can format the volume set. Click the volume set to select it, then choose **Tools, Format** from the menu. The Format dialog box like the one in Figure 5-10 will open.

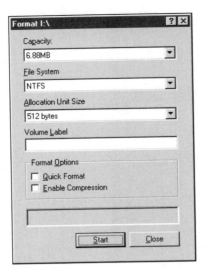

Figure 5-10   Choose a file format and any applicable options before beginning
the format

7. Select **NTFS** as your file system, and click **OK** to begin the format. When the format
is done, your volume set is ready for use.

PROJECT 5-3

In this project, you create the only level of RAID that Windows NT Workstation supports—
RAID level 0, otherwise known as a stripe set (without parity). This permits a set of
same-sized regions across multiple physical disks to be treated as a single logical volume, yet
provides a performance boost to disk access to such a volume, because it puts multiple disk
drives (and perhaps even multiple disk controllers) to work in parallel to read or write the
data in the stripe set. The only thing such a plain-vanilla stripe set lacks is the fault-tolerance
that parity information would provide.

To create a stripe set using Disk Administrator:

1. Open Disk Administrator as described in Hands-on Project 5-2, step 1.

2. Select two or more areas of free space on as many physical disks.

3. Choose **Partition, Create Stripe Set** from the menu. The Create Stripe Set dialog
box opens. See Figure 5-11. By default, the largest possible size for the stripe set will
be chosen.

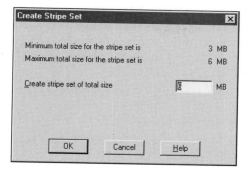

Figure 5-11   Create Stripe Set dialog box

4. Choose the size for the stripe set and click **OK.** The stripe set will appear in bright green.

5. Commit the changes and format the stripe set with the file system you want to use, as described in Hands-on Project 5-2, and you're ready to go.

6. Reboot your system for the changes to take effect.

PROJECT 5-4

To assign a static drive letter with Disk Administrator:

1. Open Disk Administrator as described in Project 5-2, step 1.

2. Select the logical drive to which you want to assign a letter.

3. Choose **Tools, Assign Drive Letter** from the menu. You'll see a dialog box like the one in Figure 5-12.

Figure 5-12   Assigning a static drive letter

4. Choose the letter (or accept the default) and click **OK**.

You can also use the Tools, Assign Drive Letter menu item to stop static letter assignment to a drive. Just choose "Do not assign a drive letter" and click OK.

CASE PROJECTS

1. You're setting up a new workstation/server that will be running Windows NT Workstation. This computer has two hard disks, one 1.5 GB and one 2.1 GB. Windows NT is the only operating system on the computer.

   Required Results: You must be able to set file-level permissions on all shared data files; you must be able to boot the computer from a DOS floppy disk if necessary.

   Optional Desired Result: The data disk on this machine should be as large as possible.

   Proposed Solution: You decide to partition the boot drive to one 1 GB partition and one 500 MB partition for an additional data drive, formatting the boot drive and 500 MB partition with FAT and the large drive with NTFS.

   Which of the following results does the solution deliver? Explain.

   a. You have met both your required results and your optional objective.

   b. You have met both your required results but not your optional objective.

   c. You have met your optional objective, but not your requirements.

   d. You have met one of your requirements (but not the other) and not met your optional objective.

2. As a system administrator, your boss has asked you to take steps to protect the data files that the CAD engineers in the design department create on Windows NT Workstation machines from loss or harm. How can you use the Windows NT Workstation Disk Administrator tools to create a fault-tolerant volume on your computer that uses space as efficiently as possible? What other kinds of approaches can you take to meet your boss's requirements? Explain.

FILE AND DIRECTORY SECURITY

In earlier chapters, you learned how to install Windows NT Workstation and configure the system, how to create user and group accounts, and how to work with hard disks and file systems. In this chapter, you'll learn about the features that Windows NT provides to help you create and maintain a safe, secure network.

AFTER READING THIS CHAPTER AND COMPLETING THE EXERCISES YOU WILL BE ABLE TO:

- DEFINE SECURITY REQUIREMENTS FOR YOUR NETWORK AND CREATE AND IMPLEMENT A SECURITY PLAN

- SAFELY SHARE INFORMATION ON THE NETWORK AND SET APPROPRIATE PERMISSIONS

- USE THE CHANGE ACCESS CONTROL LISTS (CACLS) COMMAND EFFECTIVELY

- EXPLAIN HOW TO PROTECT YOUR WINDOWS NT INSTALLATION FROM VIRUSES

- BACK UP YOUR DATA

SECURITY PLANNING

Data security has two elements. On the one hand, you must protect against unauthorized access or manipulation of data. On the other hand, you must protect against data loss by creating backups of important data that may be restored. A security plan must therefore address both of these concerns—how to protect data against unauthorized access or use and how to avoid losing more data than an organization can afford.

The following questions are pertinent when planning for security:

- What needs to be protected?
- What or whom does it need protection from?
- How likely is it that any particular threat will manifest itself?
- What is the cost of a security breach?
- How can the data be protected most cost-effectively?

DEFINING SECURITY REQUIREMENTS

To effectively protect resources and data, you must first decide what kinds of threats they face. You must also decide how much effort and expense you're willing to expend to achieve any particular level of protection.

Most organizations already have security plans that identify the threats they are prepared to face and specify certain pre-emptive or corrective measures to counter such threats. Such plans derive in part from what security experts call a "risk analysis" that calculates the costs and replacement values for a broad range of security threats or data loss scenarios. Based on the consequences of avoiding such threats, or repairing the kind of damage they can cause, the organization can make a rational decision about what steps are necessary.

In general, if the cost of curing a particular problem is higher than the costs of preventing it, most organizations will choose prevention. The key lies in recognizing threats and assigning them costs. Don't forget that the value of lost employee time and lost business opportunities often outweighs any direct financial losses that a security breach or loss of data can incur. Be sure to figure in the value of such "soft costs" when assessing the financial impact of any particular threat.

Recognizing Potential Security Threats

Begin by creating a list of potential threats: identify these threats and try to assess the consequences if they should materialize. Network security is not the same in every situation and with every bit of data—if it were, then that would imply that the optician's office with a three-node network and a server that stores nothing but a customer database would need to implement the same security measures as the National Security Agency in Fort Meade, MD.

If you read the trade press regularly, or subscribe to any of the security newsgroups or mailing lists, you will probably have a pretty good idea of what constitutes a potential threat to your systems and network. If not, here's a list you can use to stimulate your thinking processes:

- *Being an accessory to copyright violation:* Because the legal and financial consequences of running unlicensed copies of software on a network can be huge (they involve three or more times the cost of such software, plus punitive damages in most cases that go to court), protecting your organization from illicit use of software is a threat that must be analyzed, and countermeasures must be taken. At the least, you'll want to make a statement of company policy that unlicensed software cannot be tolerated and that violators will be found personally liable—if only to protect your organization from having to foot the bill if license violations are discovered.

- *Accidental loss:* Users can do harm by deleting files they didn't mean to delete or by accidentally overwriting good versions of files with bad ones. Regular backups not only prevent loss of entire drives or servers, they also provide the source to restore files that are accidentally lost or overwritten. Be sure to train users about the Windows NT Recycle Bin—in many cases, users can retrieve their own accidental deletions. But to replace damaged or accidentally overwritten files, nothing works better than a recent backup.

- *Accidental or unauthorized disclosure:* Some files (for instance, personnel records or payroll information) that need to be kept confidential must still sometimes be accessed over the network. Whenever you set up network **shares** for such information, be sure to restrict access solely to those with a legitimate need to know. Remember that the default **permission** on NT shares is Full Control for Everyone, so you'll want to reduce the users and groups who can access such resources to the barest possible minimum. Even then, encryption with tight control over decryption keys will sometimes be a good idea.

- *Malicious destruction of data:* System crackers are individuals who delight in breaking into systems; sometimes, they trash what they find. Protecting your data from unauthorized access also protects it from loss or unwanted exposure. Especially if any of your systems attach to the Internet, you'll want to consider the implications of a successful break-in and take steps to eliminate or contain any potential damage that might result from such nefarious activities.

In addition, here are two general pointers when considering threats to security:

- Protect the good stuff, but don't worry about the unimportant stuff. Not all data needs equal security or protection. You probably don't need to worry about protecting everything, but it's essential to recognize what sensitive data assets you must manage and concentrate your security efforts on protecting them (and the systems on which they reside).

- Be ready for the worst: If a meteor takes out your whole building, you'll quickly realize that storing all backup tapes on top of the server is a bad idea. Take steps to identify those data resources that are necessary for continued business operation and be sure to keep a backup copy *offsite*. Many organizations contract with secure, climate-controlled data storage facilities to keep backup copies available within hours of notification.

How Important Is Your Data?

Because your data is so important to your company or organization, it must be protected prudently. You must determine how often you should back up and how much effort you're willing to expend to keep your data safe and protected. The more vital your data, the more fault-tolerance measures you should put in place and the more carefully you should protect such data with regular backup.

In cases of outright system failure, some level of data loss is inevitable, so companies must analyze how much data they can afford to lose. For most companies, this turns out to be a day's worth of data, simply because that's the minimum practical interval between backups. Even so, stock and commodities exchanges; airline, hotel and rental car reservation systems; and other highly profitable online operations maintain active mirrors of all data, or perform continuous, real-time backup to make sure they never lose *anything*.

But it is only when the costs of downtime are sufficiently high that the expense of real-time backup becomes justifiable. Only you (and your management) can decide what levels of loss are acceptable for your organization, and the only way to reach such a decision is to weigh the costs of preventive measures against the costs of the losses that might otherwise occur. For most organizations, a day's worth of productivity is not so staggering a loss that more aggressive measures to protect data must be taken.

Is Protection Cost-Effective?

Calculate how much this protection will cost! Cost considerations include replacement costs, lost opportunity costs, lost employee time, and so forth should a data or service loss occur. Cost-effectiveness might sound niggling, but, as with backups, there really does come a point at which it costs more to protect data than it does to lose it. It's always possible to spend more on data security than you're presently doing, but it may not make financial sense to do so.

Define Your Risks

Examine your physical and security environment. Note physical threats such as evidence of water damage, any history of equipment thefts in the area, fire hazards, outdated or unreliable equipment and the like, but don't forget the threat that users may pose, whether deliberate or unwitting (in the form of novice or poorly trained users who might accidentally damage data).

CREATING A SECURITY PLAN

Based on your answers to the questions in the previous sections, you can create a plan to address the most likely perceived threats. This plan should address the following questions:

- What is the priority of data stores to be protected?

- Who is responsible for managing security breaches/threats to data integrity? When that person is unavailable, who becomes responsible?

- What courses of action will be taken for possible damage control?

- What action will be taken against those who deliberately or unwittingly cause security breaches/data loss?

- Where will backups be stored, and who is responsible for making and maintaining them?

- What mechanisms are already in place for dealing with security breaches/data loss, and what need to be added?

More questions may occur to you, but any security plan must answer these questions at a bare minimum.

COMMUNICATING THE PLAN

Implementing a security plan is a two-stage process: first setting up the security system and making it as foolproof as possible, and then training network users about why the system is in place, how to use it, and the consequences of failing to comply with it. For example, one aspect of network security is password protection. Stage one of implementing passwords is to set passwords for everyone or to set a standard to which passwords must conform. Stage two is explaining this standard to the network users, explaining why it's necessary to follow this standard, and explaining any consequences that violating the standard will have for users. If you make sure users understand why certain policies are in place, the implementation process will be easier.

Maintaining security is similar to any other kind of maintenance: It's pretty much a matter of taking the plan you've developed based on needs identification and making sure that the plan will accomplish its goals and work as intended. It's to be expected that you'll have to make some modifications to the plan after putting it in place, once you see how the security system works in practice and note any deficiencies. Implementing security requires constant vigilance and regular changes to avoid the dangers of a predictable routine.

SHARING INFORMATION ON A NETWORK

The whole point of networking is sharing data and resources. This section talks about how to set up shared resources (shares), maintain their integrity, and access shares that other people have set up. On Windows NT networks, printers and disk directories (folders) are the most common shared resources. For each such shared device or disk area, part of defining the share consists of assigning access rights to individual users and/or named groups on the network.

CREATING A SHARE

You can't protect a share until you create one. Although you can set file-level permissions on NTFS volumes (more about how to do that in a later section), you can't share individual files but must share folders. To share a folder, right-click the folder and select Sharing from the menu. When you do so, you'll see a dialog box like the one shown in Figure 6-1.

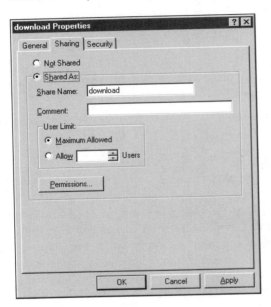

Figure 6-1   Creating a share

Click the Shared As radio button, give the share a name and set permissions or other properties for the share, if necessary, and click OK. The share becomes effective immediately and is marked by the appearance of the "sharing hand" beneath the folder icon in the My Computer or Windows NT Explorer display. The following sections explain the steps to protect and access a share. Hands-on Project 6-1 gives you actual experience with setting up a share.

NAMING THE SHARE

When you share a folder, its default share name is the name of the folder, but you may change that name. Most of the time, this won't be necessary, and it could be confusing because networked users will see the share under its share name even though the local name will be different (and someone has to remember this correspondence). The most likely reason to rename a share is when its name exceeds the eight-character limit recognizable to DOS machines or includes an embedded space. Embedded spaces make it awkward when connecting to a share from a command prompt because the space requires the share name be enclosed in quotation marks. You might also change a share's name if you're sharing it twice, each time with different permissions.

SETTING PERMISSIONS

Now that you've defined a share and given it a name, it's time to protect it. The key to managing share security is establishing proper user access. In the sections that follow, you'll learn how to inspect—and alter—the permissions related to any share over which you have rights to make changes. (Note: If you're a systems administrator, this means most shares on any system to which you have administrative rights.)

The level of permissions that you can set for a share depends on the file format (FAT or NTFS) of the volume on which the share is stored. You may set different permissions for folders and their subfolders (or in the case of NTFS, their files), giving you more control over the permissions attached to the shares.

Only members of the Administrators or Power Users groups may set share permissions, which are accessible through the Properties windows in My Computer or Windows NT Explorer. For example, if you right-click on a folder in either utility, the menu that results includes an entry for Properties, where the **Security tab** controls permissions.

No matter what file system is in place, the same methods work for setting share-level security. Here's another way to set share security: Click the File menu, Properties option, to access the **Sharing tab** of the Properties window for the object, then click the Permissions button. This opens the Access Through Share Permissions dialog box, as shown in Figure 6-2, which shows the currently defined groups and permission levels for a share.

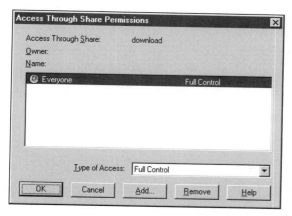

Figure 6-2   Access Through Share Permissions dialog box

Windows NT shares offer four permission levels that apply equally to FAT and NTFS folders and the files and subdirectories they can contain:

- *No Access:* Beyond seeing the name of an object appear in a directory listing, users have no rights to read, write, execute, modify, delete, change permissions, or **take ownership** of the object.

- *Read:* Confers the ability to copy and open an object and to execute its contents (if it's a program or batch file), but not to make any changes.

- *Change:* Adds the abilities to modify or delete file or directory objects to the read and execute abilities conferred by Read (these are called write and delete permissions, respectively).

- *Full Control:* Grants the full collection of rights for Change (read, execute, write, delete) plus the ability to change permissions (permissions) and even to take ownership of an object (once ownership is assumed, any other changes or reassignments become possible).

By default, the Everyone group (whose membership is composed of everyone who accesses a computer either locally or from the network) has Full Control over a share. To change the permissions assigned to Everyone, you'd select a new permission level from the drop-down list at the bottom of the dialog box. To define permissions for a new group, click the Add button to open the Add Users and Groups dialog box shown in Figure 6-3.

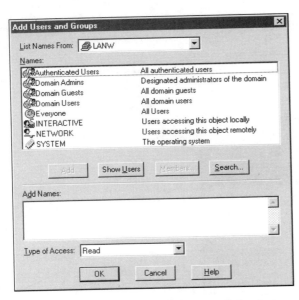

Figure 6-3   Add Users and Groups dialog box

Whenever you create a new share, the default permission granted is Full Control to Everyone. You'll almost certainly want to change this right away because that means that anyone accessing a share can do anything to it, including delete it or take ownership of it. Be aware that, although Windows NT is supposedly set up for security, its default permissions are anything but secure. Also, don't give into the temptation to assign No Access to Everyone (because this all-embracing group includes even administrators)—it's better to add Administrators and explicitly grant them Full Control, and then to remove Everyone; or to grant Read permissions only to Everyone.

Permissions for both folders and the files within them are cumulative—that is, if a user belongs to groups with varying levels of permissions, then the farthest-reaching permissions apply. The only exception to this rule is the No Access permission, which overrides any other permissions garnered from membership in other groups.

Although you're limited to the four folder-level permissions that apply to shares from FAT volumes, file-level permissions for NTFS objects may be more detailed. The lowest level of permissions applies, so that if a folder is shared with one set of permissions but an NTFS-based file within that shared folder has a different set of permissions, whichever set of permissions for that file is the most restrictive establishes the effective controls over that file. For example, if a user has Read rights through the share and Full Control through NTFS, the assigned rights become Read when the file is accessed through the share. If the users had Full Control through the share and only Read through NTFS, the rights would remain Read, because the most restrictive set applies whenever NTFS files are accessed through a share.

 When sharing folders from FAT volumes, you can only set permissions on the folder itself, not on the files within it. You're also limited to the folder-level per-missions of Full Control, Read, Change, and No Access.

The No Access permission normally blocks access altogether. But it is possible to share a folder with No Access permissions for a group, yet set NTFS permissions on a file within that folder to Read, thereby making the group unable to access the file even though NTFS grants them Read permission. However, "Bypass traverse checking" is an advanced user right (set in the User Manager) that permits the Everyone group to get to files to which they have permission even if those files are stored within a No Access folder.

VIEWING SHARED RESOURCES

You can use the Server applet in the Control Panel to view the status of all shares in a single window. From the initial dialog box shown in Figure 6-4, click the Shares button. You'll see a dialog box like the one shown in Figure 6-5, that shows all active shares. Notice the shares that appear at the head of the list in Figure 6-5: Share names that end in a dollar sign ($) are called hidden shares, because they don't normally show up in a browser window (like the information displayed under the Network Neighborhood icon in My Computer or Windows NT Explorer).

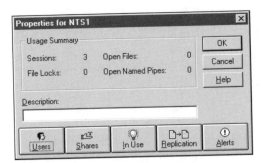

Figure 6-4   Viewing share status in the Server applet

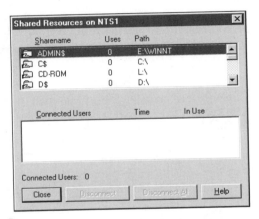

Figure 6-5   Viewing active shared resources

Windows NT establishes a set of special hidden shares, called administrative shares, that show up in this display. They're named ADMIN$, IPC$, plus one for each hard disk drive letter defined on a particular machine (C$, D$, and so forth). These administrative shares are used by the operating system itself but are also available to savvy administrators. Among other things, they make it possible for you to access the entire contents of any hard drive on a Windows NT machine across the network, as long as you have administrative access to that machine. Because they're used by the system, it's not possible to change their permissions, nor is it wise to delete them (but if you do, they'll reappear the next time you reboot the Workstation machine).

You can use the Shared Resources dialog box to view who's using what on your computer or to forcibly disconnect some or all of those users.

ACCESSING SHARES

So far, this discussion has focused on how to create and protect your own shares. Now it's time to examine how to connect to shares that other users have defined. First, you must know how to find them. Once found, you must then create a network link to be able to access their contents—assuming, of course, that you have at least Read-level permissions that allow you to do so.

Browsing the Network

Use the Network Neighborhood applet on the Desktop to browse the network. The information is subdivided into domains or workgroups, depending on how your network is organized. Double-click on any entry, and you'll see what kinds of shared resources are available on that particular machine. Windows NT runs a so-called "browser service" that collects information broadcast by machines as they join the network about what resources they have to share (this service is discussed in detail in Chapter 10). At this point, it suffices to say that the information that drives the Network Neighborhood display comes from a collection of machines whose job it is to gather and report on resources available from the network, so that a timely and accurate listing of such resources—called the **browse list** in Microsoft terminology—appears when you double-click Network Neighborhood.

The browser service provides the information shown in the Network Neighborhood and other browse lists, so it's possible that it may be slightly out of date because the browsers only update this information periodically.

It's also possible to browse the network by opening a command prompt and entering *net view,* then using one of the computers to enter *net view \\computername* to inspect a list of its shared resources (see Hands-on Project 6-4). (See the Appendix for a complete list of net commands.)

Mapping Drives

When you connect to a shared network folder and assign a drive letter to that folder, this is known as **mapping** a drive. To do so from the Explorer, choose Map Network Drive from the Tools menu. You'll see a dialog box like the one shown in Figure 6-6 that displays all the available connections and all the shared folders available from each computer on the network. Hands-on Project 6-3 takes you step-by-step through mapping a network drive.

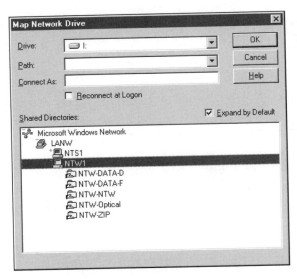

Figure 6-6   Mapping a network drive

 To disconnect a network drive, choose Disconnect Network Drive from the Tools menu in Explorer. Select from the list the drive letter you want to disconnect from, and click OK.

SHARE SECURITY VERSUS NTFS SECURITY

We've covered some of the methods you can use to set file-level permissions on shares on NTFS volumes. However, this isn't the only kind of file security that's available in the Windows NT environment. If you want yet another level of access control, share security can be explicitly applied to any NTFS folder shared across the network.

One of the simpler methods is to create a share but prevent it from appearing on the browse list, so that only those who know that the share is available—and exactly what it's called—can connect to it. To create such a hidden share, end the share name with a dollar sign ($), for example, MYSHARE$ or FOLDER$.

 You can also hide shared printers by adding a dollar sign at the end of their share names.

Another method for applying share-level security is to assign a password to a share, so that no one may connect to a share without first supplying its password. This method of share-level security is not supported in Windows NT 4.0, but it is a common method for controlling access to shares on Windows 95 and Windows 3.x machines.

NTFS SECURITY ADVANTAGES

From your reading so far, it may already be clear why NTFS is a more secure file system than FAT. However, here are some additional details that should make this claim more convincing:

- *Permissions:* As discussed previously, you can set file-level permissions on individual files stored on NTFS volumes, both for local and network access. This is not possible with FAT, with which you can only set folder-level permissions, and then only for network shares.

- *Auditing:* One advantage not yet discussed is **auditing**, which makes it possible to monitor how users access individual files, folders, or volumes. The mechanics of this process are discussed later in this chapter, but audit information is an important component of any file-system object's security properties.

- *Transaction Logging:* Although it's not a user-level security issue, NTFS is superior to FAT in part because of its **transaction logging** scheme, which records each change to the volume structure and also records information that allows any change to be undone if not completed properly. If such a change is not completed before the disk stops operating, any partially completed transactions will be undone automatically when the system next reboots.

- *Ownership:* Files may be owned under NTFS, giving the owner special privileges denied to non-owners. Ordinarily, a file's creator is its owner, although administrators may take ownership (or permission to take ownership may be assigned to someone else). Ownership cannot be granted, however. If you take ownership of a file to read it, for example, you can't give it back and thus cover your tracks.

NTFS PERMISSIONS

NTFS permissions resemble share permissions superficially—that is, the most common set of permissions for files is also No Access, Read, Change, and Full Control. But unlike shares, NTFS files also have an associated set of **special access permissions** that are available for explicit assignment. Because folders are different types of objects than files, they also have special permissions available through NTFS that never appear for network shares.

ACCESS PERMISSIONS

The four basic types of access permissions that you learned for shares also apply to NTFS objects: Full Control, Read, Change, and No Access. The various capabilities attached to each are shown in Table 6-1.

Table 6-1   NTFS Basic Access Permissions

		Permission Level		
	Full Control	Change	Read	No Access
Display subdirectory names and filenames	X	X	X	
Display data files and their attributes	X	X	X	
Move to the directory's subdirectories	X	X	X	
Change the volume structure (adding or deleting files and folders)	X	X		
Change and add to file data	X	X		
Change file attributes	X	X		
Change file permissions (NTFS volumes only)	X			
Take ownership (NTFS volumes only)	X			

USER AND GROUP PERMISSIONS

Each permission level may be assigned to both individual accounts and user accounts, as described in the upcoming section on changing permissions. A user may have one set of permissions assigned personally, another set may derive from one group to which that user belongs, and still another set derive from yet another group. As with user rights, the least restrictive set of permissions prevails. The only exception to this is the No Access permission. If a user is denied access through the permissions assigned to a group or individual account, then No Access cancels out any other permissions.

PERMISSION INHERITANCE

By default, when you set permissions on a folder, those permissions do not apply to any files or folders subordinate to that folder. (They can apply, but by default they don't.) However, any new files or folders created within that folder will inherit those permissions. For that reason, a special checkbox to force inheritance of permission assignments to existing files appears in the Permissions dialog box for NTFS folders (this permits you to reset permissions at the folder level, instead of having to set them on a file-by-file basis).

VIEWING DIRECTORY AND FILE PERMISSIONS

To view the permissions associated with a directory or file, right-click on the object's entry in Explorer and choose Properties from the menu that appears. For folders in FAT volumes, turn to the Sharing tab in the Properties dialog box and click the Permissions button to see who has access to the folder. For folders in NTFS volumes, turn to the Security tab and click the Permissions button to get to the list of who has what permissions for local purposes, or turn to the Sharing tab and click the Permissions button to see who has what permissions across the network—the two don't have to match.

CHANGING PERMISSIONS

6

Changing permissions for a file or folder is a relatively simple process, if you have the necessary permissions (for the set of four common permissions, this means Full Control; in terms of Special Access rights, this means "Change Permissions (P)" or "Take Ownership (O)"). In Hands-on Project 6-5, you change the permissions for a folder. The process is similar whether a volume is formatted with NTFS or FAT, but NTFS offers more options because of its object-level permissions and security controls. Likewise, the process is much the same whether you set permissions for a file or a folder, but again, these NTFS objects differ slightly, so the Special Access permissions differ as well.

Conditions that Must Be Fulfilled

To change permissions for a file or folder, you must have permission to do so. Ordinarily, the only person who can change a file's permissions is the file's owner, unless the file's owner specifically grants someone else permission to change them. Although administrators may take ownership, they cannot change a file's permissions if they don't own the file. Thus, although an administrator can look at a user's folder that is blocked with "No Access," the administrator cannot change permissions without leaving tracks (by taking ownership, which would then be retained and be visible as such to the original owner).

The Change Permissions Permission

Special Access permissions will be discussed in detail shortly. One of them is the Change Permissions permission, which explicitly grants permission to change permissions on a file or folder. The only other conventional permission that grants this level of access is Full Control.

Ownership Has Its Privileges

As just explained, if it's safe to assume that a file's permissions for the Everyone group has been changed from the default—Full Control for Everyone—to something more restrictive, only a file's or directory's owner can change that object's permissions thereafter. Of course, an administrator can always take ownership to make changes afterward, but this is the exception, rather than the rule, in the Windows NT environment. Normally, an administrator would only be called upon to do this if the owner did something to render an NTFS object otherwise inaccessible.

THE CHANGE ACCESS CONTROL LISTS (CACLS) COMMAND

When it comes to changing local-access permissions on NTFS volumes, administrators need not be limited strictly to GUI utilities like Windows NT Explorer or My Computer. Fortunately, administrators may also invoke a Windows NT command-line utility called Change Access Control Lists (**CACLS**) to display or modify the contents of one or more file object's **access control lists (ACLs)**. The ACLs represent the object data structures where permissions information is stored. Because ACLs are only associated with NTFS file objects, CACLS does not work on FAT volumes nor can it be used to edit share permissions.

CACLS DESCRIPTION AND SYNTAX

The syntax for the CACLS commands is as follows:

```
CACLS <filename|folder> [/t] [/e] [/c]
        [/g username:perm] [/r username [...]]
        [/p username:perm [...]] [/d username [...]]
```

Each of its parameters and options is explained in Table 6-2.

Table 6-2 CACLS Options

Option	Function
/t	Specifies that any changes to the directory should apply also to subdirectories and files within that directory
/c	Specifies that, if "access denied" errors are encountered, then CACLS should continue changing the permissions on anything it *can* change
/g	Grants specified user rights to a certain person, replacing the current access control list
/e	Adds the permissions you're setting to the existing access control list
/r	Revokes access rights for the specified user (valid only with the /e switch)
/p	Replaces the specified user's permissions with those newly specified—/g, this will replace the current access control list
/d	Denies a specified user access

If you only specify a file or folder name, then you'll see the current ACL for that object, as shown here:

```
f:\freelnce\QUE MONSTER\Christa:(OI)(IO)N
                MONSTER\Christa:(CI)N
                BUILTIN\Administrators:(OI)(IO)F
                BUILTIN\Administrators:(CI)F
```

CACLS is most helpful when creating large directories and automatically setting permissions, because this method is much faster than using the graphical interface. The following section presents some examples that illustrate CACLS potential uses in such circumstances.

BATCH FILE EXAMPLES

The CACLS definition section defines the command's basic syntax. In the examples that follow, this command appears in forms that administrators could easily use in a batch file to manage files and permissions without requiring direct user interaction.

First, a batch file creates a directory on drive D: and assigns a set of permissions to that directory and all subordinate objects. In this example, the directory will be named MYDIR and everyone who accesses it will have Read permission:

```
MD D:MYDIR

D:

CACLS MYDIR /t /g EVERYONE:R
```

 MD and MKDIR each create directories, just as CD and CHDIR each change file focus to a named directory.

The first line creates MYDIR on drive D:, the second line changes focus to the D: drive, and the third line sets file permissions for the Everyone group to Read.

In the next example, a user named Ed is added to the list of those users with permission to access MYDIR. Ed is a manager, so he is granted permission to change the contents of this directory. However, while adding Ed to that directory, it's important to take appropriate steps so that the resulting permissions don't cut everyone else off from the MYDIR directory. That's why the edit directive (/e) is so important: it adds to an existing ACL, rather than replacing an old one with a new one:

```
CACLS MYDIR /t /e /g ED:C
```

And finally, here's how you might deny a user named Amy access to the MYDIR directory, assuming that she's changed jobs recently and no longer needs access to the information stored there:

```
CACLS MYDIR /t /e /d AMY
```

SPECIAL ACCESS PERMISSIONS

Special access permissions define a set of access permissions you can apply to NTFS objects to fine tune access to volumes, files, and directories. The permissions available depend on whether the object manipulated is a file or a directory (a volume is treated the same way as a directory, to all intents and purposes), as shown in Tables 6–3 and 6–4.

Table 6-3   Special Directory Access Permissions

	Read	Write	Execute	Delete	Change Permissions	Take Ownership	Full Control
Display directory file names	X						X
Display directory attributes	X		X				X
Change the volume structure		X					X
Change directory attributes		X					X
Move to subdirectories of the directory			X				X
Display directory owner and permissions	X	X	X				X
Change directory					X		X
Delete directory				X			X
Take ownership of the directory						X	X

Table 6-4   Special File Access Permissions

	Read	Write	Execute	Delete	Change Permissions	Take Ownership	Full Control
Display file owner and permissions	X	X	X				X
Display file data	X						X
Display file attributes	X		X				X
Change file attributes		X					X
Edit file data		X					X
Run file (if executable)			X				X
Delete file				X			X
Change file permissions					X		X
Take ownership of the file						X	X

Notice that special access rights are not necessarily cumulative; that is, the right to write to a file does not imply the right to read it. This helps to explain why the normal aggregate file and folder permissions—No Access, Read, Change, and Full Control—are so important and why special access rights are seldom used.

HOW TO SET SPECIAL ACCESS PERMISSIONS

Setting special access permissions works very much like setting the normal permissions. You begin by selecting a file or directory and then accessing its permission information in the Properties window. But once you've selected the Security tab, and the Permissions button, you'll notice a new entry appears in the drop-down list of named permissions. It's called Special Directory Access (for volumes or folders) or Special File Access (for files). Picking this selection produces a set of special access permissions that appears in its own window, as shown in Figure 6-7. You can select individual entries using the checkboxes on the left and combine permissions in any way you like. Once you've made your selections, simply click the OK button to exit the Directory (or File) Permissions dialog box, and whatever permissions you've set will take effect.

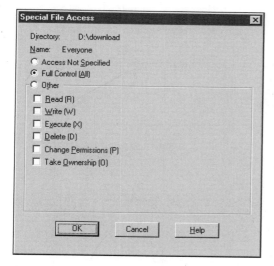

Figure 6-7 Assigning special file access

DEFAULT PERMISSIONS

The default permissions assigned for a volume depend on the file system in use. By default, the Everyone group (everyone logged onto the computer both locally and across the network) has Full Control over the file objects accessible to them on a FAT volume or one converted to NTFS from FAT: they can read, change, and delete those file objects. If you install Windows NT onto an NTFS partition (without using CONVERT after installation), then the default permissions for system files and directories are as shown in Table 6-5.

Table 6-5   NT Default Permissions

	F	C	RWXD	R	RWX	L	N
Root directory of all NTFS volumes							
Administrators	X						
Creator/owner	X						
Everyone		X					
\system32							
Administrators	X						
Creator/owner	X						
Everyone		X					
\system32\config							
Administrators	X						
Creator/owner	X						
Everyone						X	
\system32\drivers							
Administrators	X						
Creator/owner	X						
Everyone				X			
\system32\spool							
Administrators	X						
Creator/owner	X						
Power Users		X					
Everyone				X			
\system32\repl							
Administrators	X						
Creator/owner	X						
Everyone				X			
\system32\repl\import							
Administrators	X						
Creator/owner	X						
Everyone				X			
Replicator			X				
Network							X
\users							
Administrators			X				
Everyone						X	
\users\default							
Creator/owner	X						
Everyone					X		
\win32app							
Administrators	X						
Creator/owner	X						
Everyone				X			
\temp							
Administrators	X						
Creator/owner	X						
Everyone				X			

(F=Full Control, C=Change, RWXD=Read/Write/Execute/Delete, R=Read, RWX=Read/Write/Execute, L=List, N=No Access)

WHY EVERYONE GETS FULL CONTROL PERMISSIONS

Believe it or not, Microsoft actually had its reasons to give the Everyone group complete control over file objects. Their primary reason for this decision was to make accessing new storage devices easier. Because fine tuning permissions on a per-volume basis takes time and consideration, Microsoft opted for a permissive default rather than a restrictive one. Granting Everyone Full Control ensures that all users can access the disk resources they need, without being mistakenly blocked. Except on volumes where system files or other sensitive materials reside, this default makes good sense.

IMPLICATIONS AND COUNTERMEASURES

Assigning Full Control to Everyone also relinquishes much of an administrator's control over the network (or computer), and makes the purposeful or accidental corruption of data more likely. Think carefully before leaving data open to anyone who logs on, especially guests who log onto the network without a personal account and password. On the other hand, you must also be careful about changing the default permissions on the system folders outlined in Table 6-5, because those permissions may be necessary to the proper functioning of the network.

Countermeasures to default permissions are pretty straightforward: Remove the Everyone group from the list of groups for whom explicit permissions are defined for a data directory (it is not recommended to do this for a system directory) and then add groups back and assign permissions on a more discrete basis.

Whenever you change the defaults, add the Administrators (or Domain Administrators) group with Full Control before changing (or removing) Everyone. That way, you'll always retain access to file-system objects without having to go through the additional task of taking ownership and changing permissions.

COPYING AND MOVING FILES

NTFS automatically handles permissions when a file is moved or copied from a directory with one set of permissions to one with another set. Any time a file is created or copied in Windows NT, it inherits its initial set of permissions from the parent folder in which it ultimately resides. But when a file is moved in NTFS, one of two outcomes will occur: When a file is moved within the same partition on NTFS, only a pointer to that file is changed (the on-disk information remains otherwise intact). In this case, the file retains its original permissions. When a file is moved across NTFS partitions, however, it is actually copied from one partition to the other, and then the original is deleted. Because this kind of **move** is really a **copy** operation, it too, inherits its permissions from the parent directory in which the moved file ultimately resides. Although this may seem confusing, it enforces these three rules:

- When an NTFS file is copied or created, it inherits permissions from its parent folder.

- When an NTFS file is moved within a partition, it retains its permissions because only the file's location pointer changes.

- Moving an NTFS file across partition boundaries is really a copy operation, so it also inherits permissions from its new parent folder.

To force a copied file to retain its original security settings, you must use the SCOPY (Secure Copy) utility that is included with the Windows NT Resource Kit CD-ROM utilities.

AUDITING NTFS ACTIVITIES

Users who have permission to enable auditing can use the **Security log** in the Event Viewer to monitor file access on NTFS volumes. Auditing system activities of any kind is a three-step process, as the following sections illustrate. First, it is necessary to turn the system's auditing functions on. Second, one or more classes of auditing events must be activated. Finally, specific objects (in this case, NTFS file or directory objects) must then be tagged with an "Audit me!" attribute so that the audit system will keep track of specific activities related to such tagged objects.

ENABLING FILE AND DIRECTORY AUDITING

To enable auditing on a system-wide basis, you must do so within the User Manager: Start, Run, Programs, Administrative Tools (Common), User Manager, Policies, Audit, then click the Audit These Events radio button. Once auditing is enabled, you can select among a group of events to audit; for NTFS object access, select item 2, "File and Object Access." This tells the system it must watch events related to the file system. Note also that you can audit on Success or Failure, through the checkboxes on the right. Because file-system activity can be so intense, audit only those objects that must be tracked. Auditing failures will produce less data than auditing successes.

Once the initial two steps in the auditing process are complete, you must enable file or directory auditing on a per-object basis. To do this, you must return to the Properties dialog box for a file or a directory within My Computer or Windows NT Explorer. Go to the Security tab, and click the Auditing button. You'll see a dialog box like the one shown in Figure 6-8.

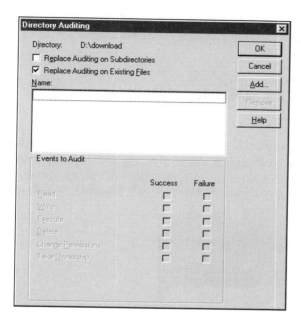

Figure 6-8   Directory Auditing dialog box

By default auditing options are disabled; to enable them, select some user or group you wish to audit. To do so, click the Add button, and choose from the list that appears in the Add Users and Groups dialog box. As you select those users and groups you wish to audit, they will appear in the Add Names box. Once you've finished, simply click OK and you'll return to the Auditing dialog box.

Now you're ready to select audit options. Highlight an appropriate group or user in the list box (it's not necessary to audit the same events for all groups and users), and choose the events you wish to audit and whether you wish to monitor successful events or failed ones. Click OK, and you're done.

SELECTING EVENTS TO AUDIT

The results of any audit are recorded in the Security log, which also records other security information. To avoid becoming swamped with log entries, it's best to choose which events will be audited, based on specific reasons for doing so. Basically, if you wish to determine whether some user or a group is attempting to perform activities that they're not permitted to do, then select audit failures. If you've been fine-tuning file and directory permissions, a brief audit of successes provides a quick way to make sure that everything's working as planned. Once you establish that the permissions are set as needed, turn off the success audit to keep audit files acceptably small.

Generally speaking, failed access attempts are more significant and interesting than successful ones, especially from a security standpoint.

READING AND UNDERSTANDING WINDOWS NT AUDIT LOGS

Security audit logs contain two categories of events: failures (indicated by a closed padlock) and successes (indicated by a key). As shown in Figure 6-9, log entries indicate what type of event is logged, whether it's a failure or success, who attempted the access, and the computer on which it was recorded (which, in the case of Windows NT Workstation, will normally be the local computer).

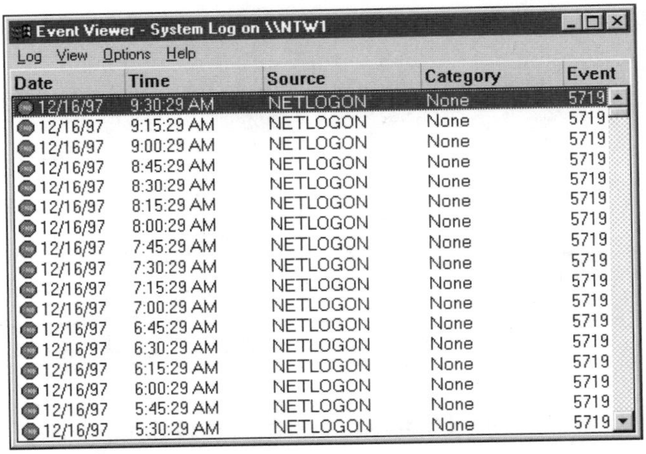

Event Viewer - System Log on \\NTW1				
Log View Options Help				
Date	**Time**	**Source**	**Category**	**Event**
12/16/97	9:30:29 AM	NETLOGON	None	5719
12/16/97	9:15:29 AM	NETLOGON	None	5719
12/16/97	9:00:29 AM	NETLOGON	None	5719
12/16/97	8:45:29 AM	NETLOGON	None	5719
12/16/97	8:30:29 AM	NETLOGON	None	5719
12/16/97	8:15:29 AM	NETLOGON	None	5719
12/16/97	8:00:29 AM	NETLOGON	None	5719
12/16/97	7:45:29 AM	NETLOGON	None	5719
12/16/97	7:30:29 AM	NETLOGON	None	5719
12/16/97	7:15:29 AM	NETLOGON	None	5719
12/16/97	7:00:29 AM	NETLOGON	None	5719
12/16/97	6:45:29 AM	NETLOGON	None	5719
12/16/97	6:30:29 AM	NETLOGON	None	5719
12/16/97	6:15:29 AM	NETLOGON	None	5719
12/16/97	6:00:29 AM	NETLOGON	None	5719
12/16/97	5:45:29 AM	NETLOGON	None	5719
12/16/97	5:30:29 AM	NETLOGON	None	5719

Figure 6-9   Monitoring object accesses in Event Viewer

To examine detailed information about any log entry, double-click the entry. As shown in Figure 6-10, this produces a text record whose contents will vary depending on what kind of entry is examined. The records for security audits are fairly self-explanatory, but basically, all of them report the account name that attempted (or succeeded) in accessing an object, what kind of operation was involved, and what permissions pertain to that specific account in relation to the object concerned.

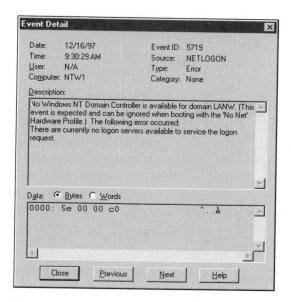

Figure 6-10   Viewing the details of an audit in Event Viewer

6

VIRUS PROTECTION

Viruses present a constant threat to data integrity, particularly if users download files from remote sites or if they import data from floppy disks of unknown origin. Without ongoing virus checks, these are two of the primary sources of potential infection. File attachments to e-mail messages and infections that lurk within .ZIP files and other compressed archives are two of the other most likely sources of viruses for any organization. With so many potential sources of trouble, virus checking is essential in most operations, but where Windows NT is concerned, such checks can present special problems.

Virus scanning is necessary to avoid virus infections or at least clean them up as quickly as possible. Basically, if you or your users work on a network where files from external sources are afforded any points of entry, it's essential to make virus scans part of all system environments. Among other things, this means scanning for viruses on both servers and on client workstations; the former keeps shared files from passing infections inside the network, while the latter helps immeasurably to keep infections from entering the network in the first place.

VIRUS-SCANNING SOFTWARE OPTIONS

DOS-based virus checkers are not effective for Windows NT. Boot viruses, for example, are effectively disabled by Windows NT and cannot propagate as long as Windows NT is running (although they certainly could under another OS). Also, because boot viruses are generally detected by examination of the Master Boot Record and a disk's current boot sector and because those sectors are protected by Windows NT, a DOS-based **virus scanner** run within a command window would not be permitted to access those data structures anyway. Of course, nearly any PC can boot to DOS from a clean floppy disk, and run a DOS-based virus scanner, but that doesn't help if your goal is to continuously scan an NT system for viruses, or check files without booting to DOS.

A broad selection of native Windows NT virus checkers is available today. At last count, there were nearly 20 such products on the market. For an overview of such products, visit Dave Franklin's antivirus software listings (with pointers to demo software) at *http://davecentral.com/virus.html*. One product not listed there is Norton Utilities for Windows NT, which also includes a good virus scanner.

 When choosing an antivirus program, be sure its scans for Word **macro viruses**. At this writing, Word macro viruses are the most commonly found and quickly propagated of all viruses on the Internet.

THE IMPORTANCE OF KEEPING CURRENT

Viruses constantly mutate, and new ones appear all the time, so virus scanners are only as good as their most recent updates. Although some scanners test for viruses by checking for differences between present file sizes and former file sizes or by watching for certain kinds of disk activity, there simply isn't any definite "There's a virus here!" indicator that works for all cases of infection. It's essential to check the Web site or BBS for your chosen virus scanner regularly, and download updates as they appear. Many antivirus vendors publish monthly updates, and some offer automatic delivery of updates via e-mail to their preferred customers.

WINDOWS NT BACKUP UTILITY

Like Windows NT Server, Windows NT Workstation comes with NTBACKUP, a utility you can use to back up data files and the local system Registry.

Once you've installed a driver for the tape drive and ensured that the tape drive is working, you're ready to run the Windows NT Backup utility found in the Administrative Tools folder. As you can see from Figure 6-11, NT Backup consists of two sets of windows organized much like the Explorer (and even more like the old File Manager interface used in Windows 3.x and NT 3.51): One window drives backups, the other drives restoring from tape and appears only if a tape is in the drive. In Hands-on Projects 6-6 and 6-7, you use the Backup utility to back up and restore files.

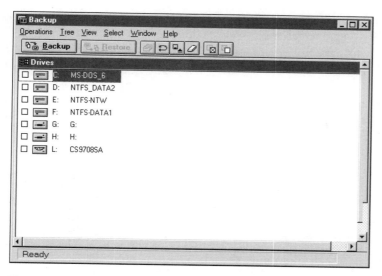

Figure 6-11   Windows NT Backup utility

COMMON BACKUP PROBLEMS AND CONSIDERATIONS

Windows NT Backup is easy to use. Most often, problems encountered while backing up may be traced to either insufficient privilege to back up and restore files (ordinary Users can't do this) or to open files, because Windows NT Backup won't back up open files. As long as the hardware is working and no tapes are damaged, you're not likely to encounter many problems with NT Backup that aren't somehow related to the two issues mentioned here.

WINDOWS NT BACKUP OPTIONS

You can fine-tune the workings of Windows NT Backup, including how the backup is performed, how it's logged, and how you restore files. While in the Backup Information dialog box, you can fine-tune the workings of the backup, including the following:

- *Verify After Backup?* Selecting this option tells Windows NT Backup to compare the files on the tape with the files on the backed-up drive after the backup is complete. Although **verification** is time-consuming and you'll get false alarms if someone has changed a file since it was backed up, this is a good setting to select because it always double-checks the contents of the tape.

- *Tape Name?* Choose a name for the tape that makes it easy to find again. For ordinary backups, the date makes a good name. For special backups, such as one created prior to installing a service pack, name the tape to match the service pack (for example "SP3 10/21/98"). Tape names may include up to 50 characters.

- *Back Up Registry?* The answer to this should always be "Yes." It's not necessary to restore the Registry when restoring the data from a tape, but losing the Registry is not a viable option if a properly configured server is the desired outcome of a restored backup!

- *Append or Replace?* This option tells Windows NT Backup whether to overwrite any data already on the tape or to tack it on to the end of the tape. If the append option is chosen, be sure there's enough room on the tape to contain the backup data. Choose the replace option only if you don't need the old tape any more, because its data will be completely erased.

- *Restrict Access?* You can restrict restoration of the tape to the tape's creator/owner and to administrators. For security reasons, this is a good idea because it limits who can overwrite data on a computer by restoring old files. For practical reasons, such restrictions could involve a bit of pain, simply because they'll require an administrator or owner to be present whenever a restore operation becomes necessary.

- *Tape Description?* In addition to the tape's name, a more detailed text description can be created, to better help identify it in the future.

- *Backup Type?* This tells Windows NT Backup which of the following types of backup to perform:

  - **Full backup**: Copies all selected files to tape and resets their **archive bits**; copies all files.

  - **Incremental backup**: Copies only selected files with the archive bit set, then resets the archive bit for each one; copies all files changed since the last incremental backup.

  - **Differential backup**: Copies all files with the archive bit set, but doesn't reset the archive bit; copies all files since the last full backup.

  - **Copy backup**: Copies all selected files, but doesn't reset the archive bit; copies only selected files.

  - **Daily backup**: Copies all files changed the day of the backup; copies all files created or modified within 24 hours of the program's execution.

Windows NT Backup Log File Options

Logging options also appear within the Backup Information dialog box. You may choose whether to log the backup (logging all backups is recommended, so you can determine if any problems have occurred), where the log should be stored, and the type of log to keep—full or summary only. A full log records everything that happens during the backup process and is not usually as useful as a summary, which records only major events such as errors or discrepancies. The same log options are available to the restoration process and have the same effect.

Windows NT Backup Restore Options

Just as Windows NT Backup permits detailed control over backups, restoration options offer similar controls through the Restore Information dialog box that appears when you instruct the program to restore backed-up data:

- *Which Drive to Restore To?* Any data other than Registry information can be restored to a different drive letter. When rebuilding a server with new drive assignments, this may be necessary.

- *Restore Local Registry?* Choose this option only if it's OK to overwrite any changes made since this backup was performed.

- *Restore File Permissions?* It's probably a good idea to keep files consistent with their original settings, but this will depend on circumstances.

- *Verify After Restoration?* Just as write verification for backup is a good idea, checking restore operations is also recommended, to make sure that everything goes as planned and no errors occur.

When rebuilding a server, be sure to load any Service Packs that were installed when backing up before attempting a restore operation. If the operating system is not exactly as it was when the backup was made, the tapes won't catalog properly and you may not be able to restore the data.

Scheduling Backups

Backups should be scheduled as often as possible—recreating data is time-consuming at best, and impossible at worst. However, because the Windows NT Backup utility cannot back up open files, and even third-party options that can back up open files consume system resources, it's probably best to back up once a day, in the middle of the night when files are less likely to be open.

For smaller collections of data, a full backup every day may be workable (it's always a good idea to keep two or three older tapes on hand in case today's backup fails, and you must restore data from a few days ago). A faster option is to perform a full backup once a week and a differential backup every day. To restore data, all that's needed is to restore the full backup first, then the most recent differential backup.

The AT and WinAT Commands

Unfortunately, the Windows NT Backup utility lacks a built-in scheduler. If you rely on this program as the only means of backup, you as administrator must invoke all backups manually. Not only does this requirement put the onus on you to remember this task, but it requires your physical presence in the office at 3 A.M., if that's when backups occur. Fortunately, a command-line version of NTBACKUP works with one of two scheduling utilities that can automate the backup process. Windows NT includes the plain vanilla version, called **AT** (for Automate Task); a graphical version of AT, called **WinAT** ships with the Windows NT Workstation (and Server) Resource Kit.

 The Scheduler service must be running for WinAT or AT to work, but it doesn't have to be started separately. If the Scheduler is not already running when you invoke either of these utilities, Windows NT will prompt you to start it.

The syntax of the command-line version of the Windows NT Backup utility looks like this:

```
ntbackup backup path options
```

where *path* is the drive and directory to be backed up, and *options* can include one or more of the switches shown in Table 6-6.

Table 6-6 NTBACKUP Command-Line Switches

Switch	Description
/a	Sets the backup mode to append—if omitted, the backup will replace any files presently on the tape
/b	Backs up the local Registry
/d	Adds a description to the backup, enclosed in quotation marks after the /d switch
/l	Writes a summary log of the backup; requires a location where the log will be stored to be specified (in quotation marks)
/r	Restricts access to the tape to the administrator and the tape's creator/owner
/t	Select a backup type other than Full by typing its name after the /t switch—don't use quotation marks around the backup type
/v	Specifies that the tape should be verified after backup is complete

Thus, for example, the command:

```
ntbackup backup c: /d "My Backup Files" /b /l
"c:\backup.log"
```

backs up all files on the C: drive, replaces any existing files on the tape, calls the backup My Backup Files, backs up the local Registry, and writes a log of the backup operation and stores it in c:\backup.log.

Given a working knowledge of the NTBACKUP command-line syntax, you can create a backup job in a batch file and run it using a scheduling utility. Here's an example of how this would look, using the built-in AT scheduler and its specialized syntax:

```
at time /date frequency "name of batch file to run"
```

Here *time* is the time on a 24–hour clock, *date* is the day of the week, *frequency* is specified as "next" or "every," and *name of the batch file to run* is the batch file in which the NTBACKUP job resides. Thus, if the name of the file is BACKUP.CMD and it's supposed to run every Sunday at 2:00 A.M., the AT command syntax is:

```
at 2:00 /every:Su "BACKUP.CMD"
```

To schedule a backup every day, the batch file would have to include all the days of the week like this: M, Tu, W, Th, F, Sa, Su. But because the AT utility may be used to schedule more than one job, you could create one batch file to perform a full backup weekly and another batch file to perform a differential backup daily. With both jobs scheduled, the entire backup schedule can be automated.

WinAT is another common Windows NT scheduler (it's included with the Windows NT Resource Kit). Basically, WinAT is a graphical version of AT. It works much like AT but offers a more intuitive interface, as shown in Figure 6–12.

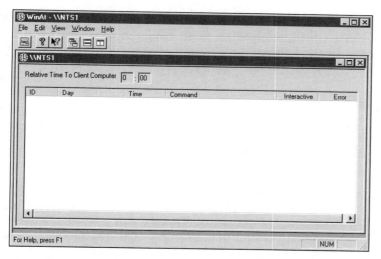

Figure 6-12   WinAT program from the NT Resource Kit

Choose Add from the Edit menu to open a dialog box in which to specify timing and command information. Even if you run the command on a different computer in another time zone, WinAT permits you to indicate the current time on the target machine so you don't have to add or subtract hours from the setup.

  Although AT and WinAT both work with command-line utilities such as NTBACKUP, they're much simpler to use if you specify command-line parameters in a batch file and simply call the batch file from within the scheduling utilities.

THIRD-PARTY BACKUP OPTIONS

Windows NT Backup isn't the only Windows NT-compatible backup utility. Other options include Cheyenne Software's ArcServe for Windows NT, Seagate's Backup Exec for Windows NT, and Software Moguls' SM-arch backup and retrieval software. For many network administrators, the bare-bones capabilities of Windows NT Backup do not suffice; third-party backup utilities offer many features missing from Microsoft's program, including:

- Unattended backups
- RAID support for multiple tape drives
- More backup types and more varied backup options
- Backup for open files

To look for Windows NT-compatible third-party backup utilities, search the Web using "backup" and "Windows NT" as keywords (both Yahoo! at *www.yahoo.com* and Excite at *www.excite.com* produce useful listings for such searches).

CHAPTER SUMMARY

This chapter covered a great deal of ground related to file and directory security, including general security planning, the details of file permissions, how to monitor file object access, and how virus scanning and backups are integral to file security.

When creating a security plan, the first step is to identify potential threats. Once they're recognized, it's easier to make reasonable judgments in regard for countering such threats. Consider how much expense and trouble protecting your data is worth—it may be possible to protect it more comprehensively than at present, but such increased protection may not be cost-effective.

Permissions represent the actions that users or groups are permitted to perform on files or directories. For FAT volumes, permissions may be set only on folders shared across the network. On NTFS volumes, permissions may be set for both files and folders, and for both local and network use. By default, permissions are inherited by all the files in a folder where permissions are set, but are not inherited by any subfolders within that folder.

Permissions are cumulative—that is, if an account belongs to more than one group, and those groups are granted dissimilar access to a particular object, that account obtains the most liberal set of permissions across all possibilities. The only exception to this is the No Access permission, which cancels out any other permissions when it occurs.

Windows NT includes a backup utility to back up and restore data files and Registry information. Although this utility does not include a scheduling component, one of the Windows NT scheduling utilities can automate a batch file that performs a backup. Because Windows NT Backup lacks some of the features that are the most useful in a backup utility, several third-party options are available to back up Windows NT volumes and Registry data.

KEY TERMS

- **access control list (ACL)** — The part of a resource's security descriptor that lists both the permissions applying to that resource and the auditing in place for it.

- **archive bit** — A data attribute that, when set, indicates that a file has been changed since it was last backed up.

- **AT (Automate Task)** — NT's command-line scheduling utility.

- **auditing** — A built-in Windows NT system facility that, when enabled, records successful and/or failed attempts to access objects by certain users or groups of users.

- **browse list** — The list of networked computers and their shared resources, maintained by the Browser service on Microsoft networks.

- **Change Access Control Lists (CACLS)** — A command used to change local security information for NTFS volumes.

- **copy backup** — Copies all selected files, without clearing the archive bit.

- **copy** — Creates a duplicate version of a file in a new location on disk, where it takes on the attributes of the folder in which it resides.

- **daily backup** — Copies all files amended on the day of a backup, without altering the archive bit.

- **differential backup** — Copies all files with the archive bit set, but does not reset their archive bits.

- **full backup** — Copies all selected files and resets their archive bits.

- **incremental backup** — Copies all selected files with the archive bit set, and resets their archive bits.

- **macro virus** — A virus that's attached to an application file as a macro. Word macro viruses are the most common type that occur on networks today.

- **mapping** — The act of assigning a local drive letter to a network connection.

- **move** — Moves a pointer to an NTFS file to a new location within the same partition, so that it retains its original attributes, including permission settings.

- **Net View** — A command-line utility that generates a list of computers on a NetBIOS network, or of resources available from any specified computer.

- **permission** — A setting in an object's access control list (ACL) that indicates which users or groups may access the object and what operations each may perform.

- **Security log** — The log stored in the Event Viewer that contains all audited security events.

- **Security tab** — The tab in a folder's or file's Properties dialog box that controls its availability on a local computer, what auditing options are in force, and that identifies its owner.

6

- **share** — To make resources available to others across the network; when used as a noun, names a shared resource available across the network.

- **Sharing tab** — The tab in a folder's or file's Properties dialog box that controls if and how it's shared with the network.

- **Special Access Permissions** — A superset of special permissions that may be applied to a file or directory, more detailed than normal permissions.

- **take ownership** — Asserting ownership over a system object to obtain access to permissions that are granted only to an object's creator.

- **transaction logging** — Feature of NTFS that notes which changes to the file system structure have been completed. Used to maintain volume integrity in the case of a disk crash—some data may be lost in a crash, but the volume structure will not be corrupted.

- **verification** — In the Windows NT Backup utility, verification means making sure that files on the tape and on the drive match.

- **virus scanner** — Software that monitors a system and watches for signs of virus activity. May run constantly as a background task or be user-driven.

- **WinAT** — A graphical interface scheduling utility included with the Resource Kit; used as a replacement or alternative to the command line AT utility built into Windows NT.

REVIEW QUESTIONS

1. Although you cannot share individual files on FAT volumes, you can on NTFS volumes. True or False?

2. Which of the following is not a reason to rename a share with a space in its name? (Choose all that apply.)

   a. Users connecting to the share from DOS machines won't be able to recognize the name with the space in it.

   b. Anyone connecting to the share from the command line will have to put the share name in quotation marks.

   c. Share names with spaces don't show up on browse lists.

   d. You've already shared the resource once under that name and want to set up a new share.

3. Which of the following Windows NT Workstation groups may set share properties?

   a. Administrators

   b. Account Operators

   c. Power Users

   d. Domain Users

4. Which of the following statements about default permissions is true? (Choose all that apply.)

   a. By default, the Everyone group always has Full Control over the root directory of all NTFS and FAT volumes.

   b. If you convert a system partition from FAT to NTFS, then it will have different permissions than if it were formatted with NTFS from the beginning.

   c. You cannot remove the Everyone group from the list of those with permissions set for a folder or file.

   d. Only the Administrator and the Creator/Owner have Full Control over the directories in the system folder, when Windows NT is installed to an NTFS directory.

5. Which of the following permissions is not available on FAT volumes?

   a. Full Control

   b. Read

   c. Change

   d. No Access

6. What happens if you delete an administrative share?

   a. Administrative shares cannot be deleted.

   b. You will disable networking until it's recreated.

   c. The share will be recreated when you reboot the system.

   d. none of the above

7. Use the ___Network Neighborhood___ applet on the desktop to browse the network.

8. To browse the network from the command line, type _____.

   a. Net Use

   b. Net View

   c. Net Start

   d. Net Logon

9. Which of the following statements describes how connection persistency is determined when connecting from the command line?

   a. Network connections are persistent by default.

   b. Network connections are not persistent by default.

   c. Unless other action is taken, network connections will be persistent or not depending on whether the last one was.

   d. You must indicate each time a connection is made whether it's to be persistent or not.

6

10. To keep shared file objects off the browse list, end their share names with a

    a. @

    b. #

    c. $

    d. %

11. You cannot audit file access on FAT volumes. True or False?

12. The original owner of a file is

    a. its creator.

    b. the system administrator.

    c. the operating system.

    d. the owner of the folder in which it was created.

13. Share permissions and local permissions for the same folder don't have to match. True or False?

14. CACLS does not work on ____Fat____ volumes or edit ___Share___ permissions.

15. Special access rights are not cumulative. True or False?

16. When you ___move___ a file to a new location, it retains its privileges, but if you ___Copy___ it, it adopts the privileges of the folder to which it was moved.

17. To use the SCOPY utility, at a minimum you must have the privileges associated with the _____ group.

    a. Administrators

    b. Power Users

    c. Backup Operators

    d. Users

18. The first step in enabling auditing for a folder is

    a. picking a group or individual for whom you're selecting auditing options.

    b. enabling auditing in the User Manager.

    c. selecting the auditing options.

    d. deleting the Everyone group from the list of groups to audit.

19. What are the categories of Events recorded in the Security log? the primary acess   object acess is

20. It's impossible to run a DOS-based virus scanner on an Windows NT system. True or False?

21. At this time, _____ viruses are the most commonly found type.

MS word macro virus

22. Why should you back up after working hours? (Choose all that apply.)
    a. Windows NT Backup utility won't back up open files.
    b. The backup will add to network traffic.
    c. You won't be able to open files if they're being backed up.
    d. The backup utility consumes system resources.

23. If you choose to restrict access to a tape, only ___administrator___ and ___backup___ can use that tape.

24. To copy to tape only those files with the archive bit set, without clearing it, you'll perform a ___differential___ backup.

25. For security reasons, you cannot restore data to any drive that has a letter different from the original drive containing the data. True or False?

26. To set permissions for a folder that is to be shared but is not yet shared, right-click the folder and choose _____ from the menu that appears.
    a. Sharing
    b. Security
    c. Permissions
    d. Properties

27. When you first begin setting security information for a new volume, permissions are established only for the ___Default___ group(s).

28. What tool will you use to disconnect users from shares on your computer?
    a. User Manager
    b. Server applet
    c. Permissions setting in the Properties dialog box
    d. none of the above

29. JohnM belongs to the Users and Power Users groups. The file MYFILE.DOC has permissions set on it so that Users have No Access to it, Power Users have Full Control over it, and JohnM has Read access to it. JohnM has ___No___ access.

HANDS-ON PROJECTS

PROJECT 6-1

To create and set permissions for a shared directory on an NTFS partition:

1. In the Explorer, select the directory to be shared. Right-click it and select **Sharing** from the menu that appears. A dialog box like the one shown in Figure 6-13 open.

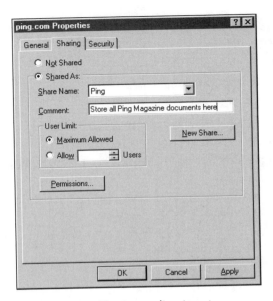

Figure 6-13 Sharing a directory

2. Make sure the **Shared As** radio button is selected, and create a name for your share if you don't want to use the directory's existing name.

3. Click the **Permissions** button to set the permissions for this share. A dialog box like the one shown in Figure 6-14 opens.

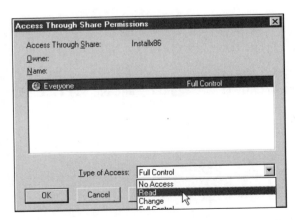

Figure 6-14 By default, the Everyone group has Full Control

4. Select the **Everyone** group in the list, and click the **Remove** button.

5. Click the **Add** button to open the dialog box shown in Figure 6-15.

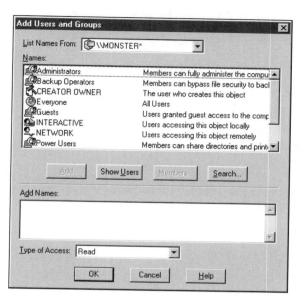

Figure 6-15   Select the groups and individuals for whom you wish to define permissions

6. Select a computer name in the List Names From: list and click **Power Users** in the Names: list. Click the **Add** button to make the group's name appear in the Add Names: box, then choose **Read** from the Type of Access: drop-down list in the bottom of the dialog box. Click **OK**.

7. You are back in the opening Permissions dialog box, which should look like the one shown in Figure 6-16. Click **OK**, then **OK** again in the original Sharing dialog box, and the share is established.

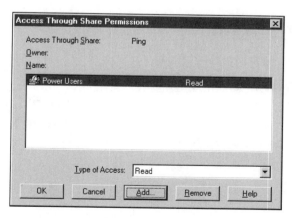

Figure 6-16   Permissions granted only to the members of the Power Users group

Project 6-2

To define file permissions for a particular user account in the Users group, while not permitting anyone else access to the file:

1. Open Explorer and select the file for which you want to set permissions. It must be in an NTFS volume. Right-click on the file and select **Properties** from the menu that appears.

2. Once in the Properties dialog box, move to the **Security** tab, which looks like the one shown in Figure 6-17.

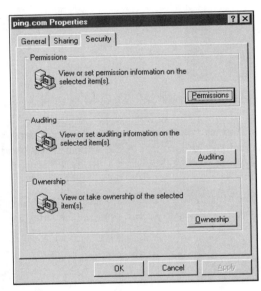

Figure 6-17 The Security tab is available only for files stored on NTFS volumes

3. Click the **Permissions** button to view the permissions currently set for that file. As with shared directories, by default Everyone has Full Control over the file.

4. Select the **Everyone** group and click the **Remove** button to remove the Everyone group from the list, and then click **Add**. This opens the Add Users and Groups dialog box shown in Figure 6-18.

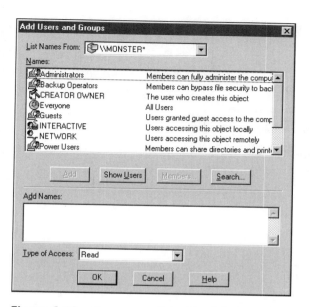

Figure 6-18   Groups are listed in alphabetical order

5. Select a computer name from the List Names From: list, choose the **Users** group in the list, and then click the **Members** button. You see a list of that group's members, as shown in Figure 6-19.

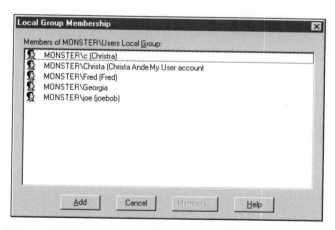

Figure 6-19   Viewing who's in a group

6. Select a name from the list (in this example, we'll pick Georgia), and click **Add**. You return to the Add Users and Groups dialog box. Georgia's name is listed in the Add Names: text box, as shown in Figure 6-20. Choose **Change** from the list of permissions at the bottom, and then click **OK**.

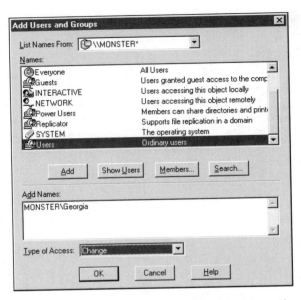

Figure 6-20   Georgia has been selected from the Users group

7. Back in the original Permissions dialog box, Georgia's name is alone in the list of permissions. Click **OK** and **OK** again to close the file's Properties dialog box, and the changes are accepted.

PROJECT 6-3

To map a network drive:

1. In the Windows Explorer, choose **Tools**, **Map Network Drive** from the menu. When you do, you see a dialog box like the one in Figure 6-6 showing the computers in your workgroup or domain, and any other accessible workgroups or domains.

2. Double-click on a computer that has the shared directory you want to connect to. Its shared directories are displayed if they're not already showing.

3. Select the directory to which you wish to connect and make sure that the drive letter being used is the one you want to assign. Check **Reconnect at Logon** to make the connection persistent.

4. Click **OK**. The network drive appears in the Explorer, like any other drive.

PROJECT 6-4

To connect to network resources with the command-line NET VIEW:

1. Open a command prompt and type **net view** to get a list of computers on the network. Identify the computer that has the shared resource to which you wish to connect.

2. Enter **net view \\MachineName** (where MachineName is the name of the machine for which you wish to view shares) to get a list of all folders that machine is sharing with the network.

3. When you've identified the shared resource you want—for example, FOLDER1—then type **net use X: \\MachineName\folder1**. This creates a mapped drive named X: that points to the FOLDER1 share.

6

Connections are persistent (which means they appear each time you log onto the network once they're defined) or not based on what you chose last. To make all future network mappings persistent, type *net use /persistent:yes*.

PROJECT 6-5

To change the permissions on a file or folder:

1. Select the file or folder in Explorer or My Computer, right-click it, and choose **Properties** to open the Properties dialog box.

2. Click the **Security** tab.

3. Click the **Permissions** button. You see a permissions dialog box like the one shown in Figure 6-21.

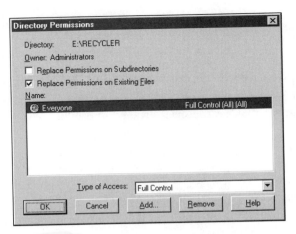

Figure 6-21   Assigning directory permissions

4. If you want to change the permissions assigned to a group already in the list, highlight the group and then choose the new permission from the drop-down list at the bottom of the dialog box, then click **OK**.

5. If you want to set permissions for a new group, click the **Add** button in the dialog box. You see the Add Users and Groups dialog box, as shown in Figure 6-22.

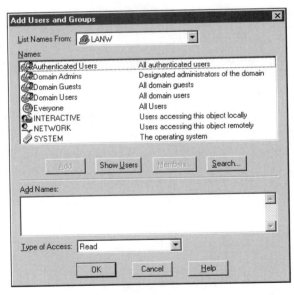

Figure 6-22   Giving users and groups Read permissions to a share

6. Select a computer name from the List Names From: list and select the group or individual for whom you want to assign permissions. Click the **Add** button to make that name appear in the lower box. (You can select more than one group or user.)

7. Choose the permission that you want to assign from the drop-down list at the bottom of the dialog box, and click **OK**.

8. You are back in the initial dialog box, which lists the group or individual account you selected. Click **OK**, then click **OK** again to exit and apply the changes.

PROJECT 6-6

6

To use the Windows NT Backup utility to back up a drive, folder, or file:

1. With a tape in the drive, start the Backup utility by clicking **Start**, **Programs**, **Administrative Tools (Common)**, **Backup**.

2. In the Drives window, select the drive, folder, or file you want to back up. When it's selected, an X appears in the box next to its icon.

3. Click the **Backup** button.

4. Fill out the Backup Information dialog box and click **OK**. The backup should proceed normally.

PROJECT 6-7

To use the Backup utility to restore folders or files from tape:

1. With the tape from which you wish to restore in the drive, start the Backup utility as indicated in step 1 of Project 6-6.

2. In the Tapes window, double-click the icon of the tape to catalog it (index it for restoration).

3. Once the tape is cataloged, select the folder or file you want to restore. When it's selected, an X appears in the box next to its icon.

4. Click **Restore**, and fill out the options in the Restore Information dialog box as necessary. Click **OK**.

5. When prompted as to whether you want to replace files on disk with the same name as files on the tape (if this happens), choose Yes, Yes to All, or No. To be prompted for each such file that occurs, choose **Yes**; to permit all such files to be automatically replaced, choose **Yes to all**; to permit no such files to overwrite existing files, choose **No**. The restoration should proceed normally.

CASE PROJECTS

1. As a systems administrator at XYZ Corp., you're trying to set up security for a folder that contains all employee information, with a separate file for each employee. Each employee may read his or her own file (but may not edit it), and you don't want employees to read each other's files, or even be able to list the contents of the employee information folder because some extremely confidential files with descriptive names are stored therein. How would you set up a share on an NTFS volume so that a user could not access a folder or list its contents but could read his or her own file? How could you set up this share on a FAT volume?

2. Someone with an Administrator account had logged onto a computer. The machine was later left unattended, and someone deleted the C$ administrative share. How might you recover from this?

3. Someone kicks a server's power cord while it's writing a new file to an NTFS volume. What happens to that file? What if the information being written is an update of an existing file? Or one that's being deleted? Does it make any difference if the file is being written to a FAT volume?

CREATING WINDOWS NT SECURITY STRUCTURES

Because of the pivotal role that Windows NT can play on so many networks, the operating system has been constructed to control access to its resources. In fact, Windows NT has been deliberately designed to be able to check permissions for any resource before granting access to that resource. In this chapter, you'll explore the details of the Windows NT security model, its logon process, and the ways in which the operating system associates security information with all objects under its control. Along the way, you'll also appreciate how any user's or program's request for system resources is subjected to close scrutiny at blinding speeds!

AFTER READING THIS CHAPTER AND COMPLETING THE EXERCISES YOU WILL BE ABLE TO:

- UNDERSTAND THE NT SECURITY MODEL AND HOW IT MANAGES SECURITY THROUGH OBJECTS

- UNDERSTAND HOW THE LOGON AUTHENTICATION PROCESS CONTROLS ACCESS

- GRASP THE CONCEPT OF ACCESS CONTROL LISTS (ACLs) AND HOW THEY MANAGE PERMISSIONS

- RECOGNIZE THE COMPONENTS THAT CONSTRUCT ACCESS TOKENS

- CUSTOMIZE THE LOGON PROCESS

- CONFIGURE AUTOMATIC ACCOUNT LOCKOUT

THE NT SECURITY MODEL

Before you attempt to use any Windows NT resource, you must log onto a system, a work-group, or a domain by supplying a valid user ID and **password**. When you successfully log on, you receive an **access token**. This access token includes information about your identity, any permissions specifically associated with your account name, and a complete list of all the groups (including custom groups defined for your network, and Windows NT's predefined **default groups**) to which you belong. This token is represented by a complex string of bits, and is attached to every **process** that you initialize until you log off. In other words, each time you run a program, enter a system command, or access a resource, the resulting system request is always accompanied by a copy of your access token.

For each attempt to access a resource, the requester's access token is compared with a list of permissions associated with the requested resource. This corresponding bit pattern is called an **Access Control List**, or **ACL**. If the access token matches the ACL, the request is allowed to proceed. If the No Access permission occurs anywhere in the user's access token, or if the service requested is not permitted, the request is denied. A match between some portion of the access token and the ACL is very much like finding a key that fits a lock; in fact, many experts explain the access token using the analogy of a ring of keys that are tried one at a time until a match is found or until all the keys have been tried. Such matches may be related to permissions associated to the individual user's account or to permissions that derive from the user's membership in some particular local or global group. Either way, if a match occurs (and No Access doesn't appear anywhere in the picture), the user's request will be allowed to proceed unhindered.

LOGON AUTHENTICATION

Windows NT logon is mandatory and access to applications and resources is suspended during the logon process. This makes it impossible for someone to use an application that could remain resident in memory and steal a user's ID and password from the logon screen. You can log on multiple accounts with multiple configurations and environments at the local machine.

The logon process includes two components: identification and authentication. **Identification** requires that you supply a valid account name (and in a domain environment, the name of the domain to which that **user account** belongs). **Authentication** literally means that you employ some method to verify your identity; by default for Windows NT, possession of the proper password for an account constitutes authentication. However, Windows NT does support third-party authentication add-ins of many kinds, including biometric systems (which check fingerprints or perform retinal scans) and keycard systems (which require physical possession of a unique electronic keycard) to prove a user's identity. Most typical NT systems rely solely on passwords for authentication, so using hard-to-guess passwords is an important aspect of good system security (you'll learn more about this later in the chapter).

When a user logs on successfully to a Windows NT machine, the security subsystem within the Executive Services layer creates an access token for that user. The access token includes all security information pertaining to that user including the user's **Security ID (SID)** and SIDs for each of the groups to which the user belongs. Indirectly, through the user rights policy, this collection of SIDs informs the system of the user's rights. Access to the system is allowed only after the user has received this access token. Each access token is created for one-time use during the logon process. Once constructed, the access token is attached to the user's **shell** process, which defines the runtime environment inside which the user will execute programs or spawn other processes, for as long as the user stays logged onto the system. As far as Windows NT is concerned, a process defines the basic container within which user and system activities reside, and each such container has an access token to define its access rights (that's why each time a user launches a program, enters a command, or otherwise causes another process to be started, NT inherits a copy of that user's access token to define that user's access rights).

To be more specific, an access token includes the following components:

- The unique SID for the account
- A list of groups to which the user belongs
- A list of rights and privileges associated with the user's account

OBJECTS

In Windows NT, access to individual resources is controlled at the **object** level. Requests for resources, therefore, translate into requests for objects. Any individual object is identified by its type, which defines its permitted range of contents and the kinds of operations (called services) that may be performed upon it. Any object is an instance of its type and consists of data and a list of services that may be used to create, manipulate, control, and share the data it contains.

Windows NT is not only able to control access at the object level, but is also able to control which services defined for the object's type a particular security token is allowed to perform or request. All objects are logically subdivided into three parts: a type identifier, a list of services or functions, and a list of named attributes that may or may not have associated data items, called values.

When defining an object, its type describes the kind of entity it is. For example, an object's type may be file, directory, printer, or network share. An object's services, or functions, define how the object may be manipulated. Some possible functions for a directory object are Read, Write, and Delete. An object's attributes are its named characteristics, such as "file name" for an object whose type is file. The value for this attribute would be the actual name of the file.

An Access Control List (ACL) is one of the more important attributes associated with any object. A user's account settings or group memberships as defined in the ACL determine access to that object. The ACL represents the lock on the object and a user's access token represents the ring of keys. Whenever an object is requested, the ACL and the access token are carefully compared, and a request to access an object is granted only when a key fits some lock.

Remember, access or permission to use to an object is determined not only on the basis of the entire object itself, but also for each of the services defined for that object. For example, a user may have access to read a file such as an e-mail program executable, but not to edit or delete it. Thus, a user may have permission to access the object in general, but be subject to more specific controls about what services can be requested in connection with that access.

ACCESS CONTROL

The Windows NT logon process is initiated through the "attention sequence" (the Ctrl-Alt-Del keystroke combination, known to many DOS users as the "three-fingered salute"). This attention sequence cannot be "faked" by a program, and brings up a logon procedure dialog box that is stored in a protected area of memory.

The characteristics of the logon authentication procedure are key to the entire security scheme of Windows NT because all subsequent security features of NT are based upon the level of authority granted a user who has successfully logged on. The Windows NT security structure requires a user to log on to a computer with a valid username and password. Without this step, nothing more can be accomplished in the Windows NT environment.

The Windows NT logon procedure provides security through the use of the following:

- *Mandatory logon:* As mentioned previously, the user is required to log on to access the computer.

- *Restricted User mode:* Until a successful logon takes place, all User mode privileges are suspended. This means that, among other things, the user cannot launch applications, which prevents logon emulation programs from stealing usernames and passwords.

- *Physical logon:* The structure of the logon sequence ensures that the logon occurs from the local keyboard, rather than some other internal or external source. This is because the attention sequence initiates a hardware interrupt that only accepts input from the local keyboard.

- *User profiles:* Windows NT, like Windows 95, allows each user that logs onto a particular machine to save user preferences and environment settings. Each user may have a set of specific preferences restored at logon, or be supplied with a mandatory or default set, depending on how the system that the user is logged onto is configured.

SECURITY INFORMATION IN THE REGISTRY

For Windows NT, security information is hidden from view by design. Even an administrator cannot access such information directly. It is important to understand where this information is stored.

THE SECURITY ACCOUNTS MANAGER (SAM)

The **Security Accounts Manager (SAM)** is a built-in Windows NT facility that maintains a database of security information. The SAM is inaccessible by default, but its database resides beneath the Security key and the **SAM key** in the HKEY_LOCAL_MACHINE Registry key. Usually called the **SAM database**, or just the SAM, this collection of security data contains information on default and post-installation user and group accounts and passwords. Administrators can grant themselves additional access to these keys for exploration purposes. However, it is rare that administrators must actually manipulate these structures directly.

The SAM key contains primarily SID and property information. Policies are not pulled from this key, but rather from the associated Security key that comprises the other main contributor to the SAM database. The main two subkeys for the SAM key are:

- *Domains:* These entries deal with default and post-installation user and group accounts.

- *RXAct:* This a resource identifier relating to the domain that provides the SID for individual elements, and group identifiers for group elements.

 When the term *domain* is used on an NT Workstation configured to function only in a workgroup, it refers to the local machine's database only.

SECURITY SUBSYSTEM KEYS

The Security key is primarily intended for keeping track of the 26 user rights and other database-wide policies.

The access token assigned when a user logs onto Windows NT originates from the Security Accounts Manager process that runs in Windows NT Kernel mode. This token is returned to the generic WinLogon process that always executes in User mode. Once WinLogon receives a valid access token, it launches a so-called shell process (NT Explorer by default) for the user that incorporates the access token supplied from the SAM.

Until this happens, the user has not truly logged on, because no shell process has been created to define a basic runtime environment. Up to this very instant, everything happens within the highly protected process associated with WinLogon. But once a shell process is launched, it takes over on the user's behalf. Thereafter, all processes created by that shell process automatically inherit its access token. Because no Windows NT process can exist without a valid access token, and the only source of such a token is from the parent process that launches it, Windows NT makes it nearly impossible for users to launch processes that exceed whatever permissions and access rights are defined in their access tokens upon logon.

Through strict inheritance of access tokens, NT maintains control over the access level of users based on whatever initial access token they are assigned at logon. The access token that's issued at logon is a snapshot of permissions that exist at the time the shell process is created; Windows NT does not dynamically update access tokens once a user has logged on, so changes don't affect logged on users until they log on again in the future, at which time the new access token they're issued will reflect those changes.

MATCHING ACLs AND ACCESS TOKENS

You've already learned that the entries in an object's ACL act like locks, and entries in the access token act like keys. If a match between a lock and a key occurs, the request will be granted; if no specific match occurs, or the No Access permission for the object appears anywhere in the access token, the request will be denied.

The actual construction of any object's ACL consists of a list of **Access Control Entries (ACEs)**. Each ACE corresponds to a user or group that is explicitly assigned some level of access to the object (including No Access, which means any request that the associated user or group makes for the object will be denied). When an object has no explicit ACE for a particular user or group that requests access, the default access will be granted (and this helps explain why Full Control for the Everyone group can sometimes be a problem).

When a process requests access to an object, which occurs primarily when it requests that some service be performed on that object (Open, Read, Write, Execute, and so forth), this invokes a subsystem within the Windows NT Kernel's Executive Services called the Object Manager. To handle access checks, the Object Manager turns the request over to another subsystem called the Security Reference Monitor, or SRM. The SRM first checks the ACL to see if No Access occurs anywhere where the SID matches that of the requesting account name, or for any of the groups to which that account belongs. If so, the SRM immediately denies the access request and the Object Manager returns an "access denied" message to the requesting process.

If the initial pass through the object's ACL turns up no explicit reference to No Access, the SRM then examines the SID associated with the requesting process and the SIDs for the groups to which that process belongs. If it finds a match with an ACE in the ACL and an entry in the access token, it then compares the requested access with the access that's permitted in the ACE. If the request level falls within or matches the level of access that's granted, the request is allowed to proceed, and the Object Manager is instructed to grant the access request by the SRM. If the request exceeds the level of access that's granted, the SRM checks for other matches, until all possibilities are exhausted.

At the end of this process, one of two conditions will hold:

- The SRM will have instructed the Object Manager to grant the requesting process access because an appropriate match between user permissions and access rights, or group permissions and access rights, has been discovered.

- No explicit match will have been found. In this case, the default access permitted for the object will be checked; if the request falls within or matches that level of access, the request will be granted; if not, it will be denied.

This process takes a great deal longer to explain than it does to execute. Windows NT's use of ACLs and access tokens make it extremely fast for the SRM to determine if a request for an object should be granted or denied. Because both ACLs and access tokens are set up as specially formatted, complex bit patterns, all the SRM has to do is march through the two data structures, looking for specific patterns (No Access), or for matches between ACEs and access token components. Even when no exact matches are found and the default route is taken, the whole process takes a very few milliseconds for most access requests.

In the sections that follow, you'll leave the details of ACLs and access tokens to take a broader look at the environment in which a Windows NT logon occurs and examine some of the options the OS provides to customize and control this process.

CUSTOMIZING THE LOGON PROCESS

The default logon process for Windows NT can be altered in appearance and function by a system administrator. To be specific, the WinLogon process can be customized to display some or all of the following characteristics:

- *Retain or disable the last logon name entered:* If the same user logs onto a single machine consistently, displaying the logon name is convenient; but for shared or public-access machines, this gives away a key piece of information that crackers could use to break into that system.

- *Add a logon security warning:* To successfully prosecute anyone who breaks into a computer system, a logon warning indicating that access may be monitored, that unauthorized access is not permitted, and that unauthorized entry may lead to prosecution must be posted so all would-be users can see it. Windows NT includes a pair of Registry keys to define and label such a warning.

- *Change the default shell:* Once the WinLogon process relinquishes control over a Windows NT machine, it turns control over to a user process that runs within a desktop environment called a shell. For Windows NT 4.0, the default is the Windows NT Explorer, but it is possible to define an alternate shell (for those who prefer the old-fashioned Program Manager shell, or who run POSIX systems on top of Windows NT) by adjusting a Registry entry.

- *Enable/Disable the WinLogon Shutdown button:* The NT attention sequence calls up the Windows NT Security window that runs under WinLogon's control. The right-most entry in the upper row of buttons at the bottom of this window reads Shut Down. By default, this button is enabled for Windows NT Workstation machines, but disabled for Windows NT Server machines. It is possible to change the default by altering the value of its associated Registry key.

- *Enable automated logon:* Some special- or limited-used Windows NT machines—for example an airport kiosk, or an information station in a hotel—may need to be always available, and always logged onto a low-security account for access to some dedicated application. The Registry also supports a set of keys to automate the Windows NT logon process, essentially by reading an account name and password from the Registry to permit the logon process to complete without requiring user input. For obvious reasons, this technique is only recommended for extremely limited use scenarios (the last thing you'd want is to set up an automatic logon with administrator-level system access).

All of the Windows NT settings to control logon are contained in the \HKEY_LOCAL_MACHINE\SOFTWARE\Microsoft\WindowsNT\CurrentVersion\ Winlogon Registry key, as shown in Figure 7-1.

Hands-on Project 7-1 takes you through the steps to open the Winlogon Registry key.

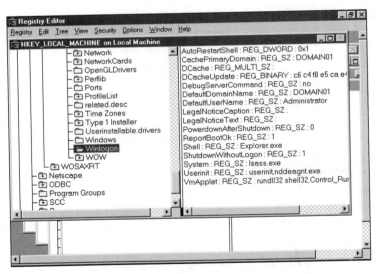

Figure 7-1   The REGEDT32 view of the Winlogon key

 Before editing any Registry entries, be sure to create a backup copy of the Registry. It might also be a good idea to create a log of any Registry settings you change. Warning: Changing entries other than those indicated here may cause your NT Workstation to behave unpredictably or fail altogether.

Several possible configuration changes for the Windows NT logon process are detailed in the following sections.

DISABLING THE DEFAULT USERNAME

By default, the logon window displays the name of the last user to log on. This may aid intruders who seek to gain access through visible user account names that they can attack using easily guessed passwords. Another common form of attack is a dictionary attack, which basically involves supplying the contents of a dictionary one word at a time as a logon password. The need to avoid such systematic break-in attempts also explains why it's a good idea to limit the number of logon attempts permitted. This can be set in the Accounts entry under the Policies menu in the User Manager application.

Disabling this option presents a blank username field at the logon prompt. Please note that the related value and its corresponding assignment do not occur in the Registry by default (which is why it doesn't appear in Figure 7-1). Here, the value is named DontDisplayLastUserName, it's of type "String"; a value assignment of 1 disables the name display and a value of 0 enables it. Hands-on Project 7-2 gives the steps to disable the default username and to turn off the setting, if needed.

ADDING A SECURITY WARNING MESSAGE

Depending on your organization's security policy, you may be legally obligated to add a warning message that appears before the logon prompt appears. In the US, it's a matter of law that you cannot prosecute individuals for unauthorized entry or use of a system if you do not warn them that usage is monitored, that unauthorized access is forbidden, and that they may be liable for prosecution if they do succeed in obtaining access to your system or network.

Two Registry values are used to display warnings:

- LegalNoticeCaption puts a label on the title bar of the legal notice window that appears during logon. This field works best with 30 characters of text or less.

- LegalNoticeText contains text information that provides the details of the warning to be issued to system users. This field may be up to 65,535 characters long, but most warning messages seldom exceed 1,000 characters.

After this feature has been activated and configured, a warning message appears each time a user enters the Windows NT attention sequence. This message requires the user's acknowledgment by pressing OK before the logon window opens. Hands-on Project 7-3 shows how to add a logon security warning.

CHANGING THE SHELL

NT Explorer is the default shell (the application launched by WinLogon after a successful logon). You can change the shell to a custom or third-party application depending on the needs or security policy of your organization. One common change is to use the Program Manager familiar to NT 3.51 and Windows 3.x users. To make this change, for example, you would change the Shell value in the Winlogon key from EXPLORER.EXE to PROGMAN.EXE. (Hands-on Project 7-4 shows you how to do just that.)

If you do change from the Explorer shell to the Program Manager shell, your system will lose its on-screen task bar, and you will no longer be able to use the Start menu to launch programs from your desktop.

DISABLING THE SHUTDOWN BUTTON

By default, the Windows NT logon window includes a Shutdown button. However, in an environment where users have access to the keyboard and mouse on a Windows NT machine, this option has the potential for unwanted system shutdowns. Fortunately, this option can be disabled through the Registry, saving you some headaches. It should be noted, however, that, if the user still has access to the physical power switch on the computer, disabling this option may cause more headaches than it solves. A system that has been shut down or rebooted through the OS has a much higher chance of coming back up successfully than one that has been powered off.

You'll need to edit the value named ShutdownWithoutLogon. It's enabled (set to the value 1) by default. To disable this button, change its value assignment to 0 (zero); to re-enable it, reset its value to 1. The disabled button still appears in the WinLogon window, but it's grayed-out and unusable.

For laptops or other advanced computers with automatic shutdown capabilities, an additional button labeled Shutdown and Power Off will appear. Similar machines may also support a Sleep mode, in which all processing is suspended and all power turned off, except to the computer's RAM. In that case, Sleep also shows up as a shutdown option. This particular setting permits users to eliminate most of a computer's power consumption, yet be ready to resume activity at the push of a single button. Where appropriate, users will find related Registry values in their Winlogon key settings to help handle these functions.

Be aware that leaving the Shutdown button enabled means that anyone with access to the keyboard can enter the NT attention sequence and shut down the machine immediately thereafter!

AUTOMATING LOGONS

Although you cannot bypass the logon process, the values for username and password can be coded into the Registry to automate logons. This is normally of interest only when installing machines for public use, such as for information centers, kiosks, museum guides, or other situations where a computer is used to provide information to anyone who can access the machine. In such cases, it's important to use computer and user policies to prevent NT-savvy users from attempting to break out of the application that the machine is intended to provide and explore other, less public aspects of the system (or worse, of the network to which it may be attached).

To set up an automated logon, the following Registry keys must be defined and set:

- *DefaultDomainName:* Defines the name of the domain to log onto (needed only when logging onto a networked machine that's part of a domain)

- *DefaultUserName:* Defines the account name to log on as

- *DefaultPassword:* Defines the password associated with the default account name

- *AutoAdminLogon:* Instructs the machine to log itself on immediately following each bootup

Automated logon creates a situation in which the computer automatically makes itself available to users without requiring them to know an account name or a password. It's essential, therefore, that this capability be exercised only when security is not a concern (if the machine hosts only a single application and is not connected to the network) or if access to the equipment is otherwise controlled (as for a card catalog or index application in a company library, where only legitimate employees can access the machine).

SECURITY-RELATED REGISTRY SETTINGS

It's probably a good idea to practice customizing the logon process in Windows NT by making additional adjustments to the Registry. Although some the following entries are not as common as the ones already discussed, and knowledge of them is not required for certification, they can add considerably to your abilities to customize security in organizations where security is a priority. For completeness, all applicable entries for the Winlogon key are included in the sections that follow.

All of the Registry values listed can be found under the following Registry key:

HKEY_LOCAL_MACHINE\SOFTWARE\Microsoft\WindowsNT\
CurrentVersion\Winlogon

Be careful to keep a log or a backup copy of the Registry because it is very dangerous to edit the Registry. You might want to consider practicing changing these values on an isolated machine.

Value: AllocateCDRoms/Data Type: REG_SZ /Range: 1

This restricts access to the CDs in the CD-ROM drives to only the user currently logged onto the computer. In this mode, CDs are allocated to the user as part of the interactive logon process, and freed for general use or for reallocation only when that user logs off. This setting satisfies part of the C2 security requirement that removable media must be able to be secured. Without this value entry, the contents of the CDs in the drives will be available to all processes on the system.

Value: AllocateFloppies /Data Type: REG_SZ /Range: 1

This value restricts access to the disks in the floppy disk drives to only the user currently logged onto the computer. In this mode, floppy disks are allocated to the user as part of the interactive logon process and freed for general use or for reallocation only when that user logs off. This setting satisfies part of the C2 security requirement that removable media must be able to be secured. Without this value entry, the contents of the floppy disks in the drives will be available to all processes on the system.

Value: AutoAdminLogon/Data Type: REG_SZ /Range: 0 or 1 /Default: 0

Remember that this specifies automatic logon if this value is 1. For automatic logon to work, you must also add the value entry DefaultPassword with a value for the user listed under DefaultUserName. When AutoAdminLogon is used, Windows NT automatically logs on the specified user when the system is started, bypassing the Logon Information dialog box.

Value: AutoRestartShell /Data Type:REG_DWORD /Range: 0 or 1 /Default: 1 (enabled)

This value specifies whether the Windows NT user interface (usually EXPLORER.EXE) restarts automatically if it stops unexpectedly. If this value is set to 1 and the Windows NT user interface (or one of the third-party components of the user interface) fails, the interface will be restarted automatically. If this value is set to 0, the user must restart the interface by logging off and logging on again.

Value: DefaultPassword /Data Type: REG_SZ /Range: Password

This value specifies the password for the user listed under DefaultUserName. It is used during automatic logon.

Value: DefaultUserName /Data Type: REG_SZ /Range: Username

This value specifies the name of the last successfully logged on user. If values are defined for DefaultPassword and AutoAdminLogon, this is the user who is logged on by default during automatic logon.

Value: DeleteRoamingCache /Data Type: REG_DWORD /Range: 0 or 1 /Default: 0

If the value of this entry is 1, locally cached profiles are deleted when users with domain profiles log off. This setting is designed to conserve disk space.

Value: DontDisplayLastUserName /Data Type: REG_SZ /Range: 0 or 1 /Default: 0 (False)

By default, Windows NT displays the name of the last person to log on in the Username space of the Logon Information dialog box. If you add this value entry and set it to 1, the Username space is always blank when the Logon Information dialog box opens.

Value: KeepRasConnections /Data Type: REG_SZ /Range: 0 or 1 /Default: 0 (Disabled)

By default, at Logoff, Windows NT closes all Remote Access Service (RAS) connections opened during the session. (RAS is covered later in this book.) If this value entry is added and set to 1, the system will not close RAS connections at logoff. This value entry does not appear in the Registry unless you add it.

Value: LegalNoticeCaption /Data Type: REG_SZ /Range: String /Default: (None)

This value specifies a caption for a message to appear when the user presses Ctrl-Alt-Del during logon. Add this value entry if you want to add a warning to appear when a user attempts to log onto a Windows NT system. The user cannot proceed with logging on without acknowledging this message. To specify text for the message, you must also specify a value for LegalNoticeText.

Value: LegalNoticeText /Data Type: REG_SZ /Range: String /Default: (None)

This value specifies the message to appear when the user presses Ctrl-Alt-Del during logon. Add this value entry if you want to add a warning to be displayed when a user attempts to log onto a Windows NT system. The user cannot proceed with logging on without acknowledging this message. To include a caption for the logon notice, you must also specify a value for LegalNoticeCaption.

Value: LogonPrompt /Data Type: REG_SZ /Range: 256-character string /Default: "Enter a user name and password that is valid for this system."

This determines the text that appears in the Logon Information dialog box. It is designed to give users additional legal warnings before they log on. This value entry does not appear in the Registry unless you add it.

Value: PasswordExpiryWarning /Data Type: REG_DWORD /Range: Number of days /Default: 14

This value works with the account policy. It specifies the number of days a warning message appears before the user's password expires. This value entry does not appear in the Registry unless you add it.

Value: PowerdownAfterShutdown /Data Type: REG_SZ /Range: 0 or 1 /Default: 0 on Windows NT Server, 1 on Windows NT Workstation

This value determines whether the Shutdown and Power Off options appear in the Shutdown Computer dialog box. (This dialog box opens when you press Ctrl-Alt-Del and then click the Shutdown button.) The option appears only if the value of this entry is 1. See also ShutdownWithoutLogon and NoClose.

It is important to note that this option is only supported on computers with a Plug and Play BIOS.

Value: RASForce /Data Type: REG_SZ /Range: 0 or 1 /Default: 0

You can use this value once you have installed RAS, discussed later in this book. This value determines whether the Logon Using Dial-Up Networking checkbox is selected by default when the system starts. If this value is set to 1, Logon Using Dial-Up Networking is the default. If it is set to 0, the checkbox is cleared. This value entry does not appear unless you add it to the Registry, and it applies only when a Dial-Up Networking (RAS) connection is installed and the workstation is part of a domain.

Value: Shell /Data Type: REG_SZ /Range: Executable names /Default: Explorer.exe

This value specifies executables that are run by USERINIT and that are expected to be in the user's shell program. If for some reason WinLogon cannot start the entries listed in USERINIT, then WinLogon will execute the entries in the Shell value directly. This shell is not per-user; it affects everyone who uses that machine.

Value: ShutdownWithoutLogon /Data Type: REG_SZ /Range: 0 or 1 /Default: 0 on Windows NT Server, 1 on Windows NT Workstation

This value specifies whether the Shutdown button in the Logon Information dialog box is enabled. If the value is set to 1, users can click the Shutdown button to stop the OS without logging on or turning off power to the computer. If it is set to 0, the Shutdown button is disabled.

AUTOMATIC ACCOUNT LOCKOUT

Automatic account lockout is the NT security feature that disables a user account if a pre-determined number of failed logon attempts occur within a specified time limit. This feature is intended to prevent intrusion by unauthorized users attempting to gain access by guessing a password or launching a dictionary attack. The default setting of Windows NT is to allow an unlimited number of failed access attempts to a user account without locking out that account. However, this is not recommended when there is even a remote chance unauthorized people can gain physical access to logon consoles.

The account lockout feature has two key settings: number of attempts and lockout duration. The number of attempts should be set to 3 in a more secure environment, or a maximum of 5. The lockout duration should be set to Forever for those networks where security is crucial, but should be set to no less than 30 minutes even in the most lax environments. You know that there are times when users forget their passwords. Using these security features ensures that when users do forget their password, the administrator is contacted to unlock the account and help make dictionary attack programs harmless.

The **account policies** also include a setting for the length of time failed attempts are counted toward lockout; this should be set in the User Manager application (or in User Manager for Domains, if the Workstation is administered through a Windows NT Server-based **domain controller**) in the Account Policy dialog box, as shown in Figure 7-2. Any changes made to the account policies settings take effect for each user the next time the user logs onto the system. Hands-on Project 7-5 shows how to change the account lockout settings. The User Manager also permits user accounts to be disabled, either in response to an excess number of invalid logon attempts, or by explicit direction from an administrator. Until re-enabled, **disabled user accounts** cannot successfully get past the WinLogon process.

7

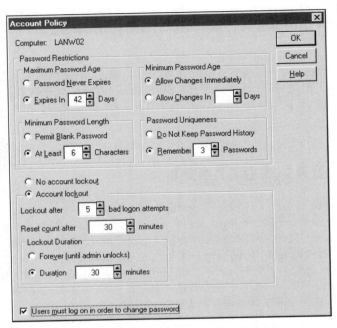

Figure 7-2   The Account Policy window in User Manager

 The Administrator account can't be locked out, so anyone with administrator-level access to a machine can keep trying passwords as long as they like!

There are two ways to solve this problem, both of which are highly recommended by most security experts:

- Rename the default Administrator account to something that's difficult to guess randomly, and always be sure to give administrator-level accounts hard-to-guess passwords as well.

- Set up a "dummy" account named Administrator with only limited system access privileges. If you audit this account, as soon as someone tries to break in through the dummy, you'll be able to start tracking them down! You already learned about Windows NT **event auditing** in Chapter 3, but to audit logon activity, you'd have to enable auditing with an **audit policy** (Start, Programs, Administrative Tools, User Manager, Policies, Audit, click the Audit These Events radio button). Then you'd have to select at least Logon and Logoff under Audit These Events to observe attempts to access the dummy account.

CHAPTER SUMMARY

In this chapter, you've learned about Windows NT object-level access controls that provide the foundation for all NT resource access. By comparing Access Control Entries in the Access Control Lists associated with individual objects to the access tokens that define the rights of any user process within Windows NT, the Security Reference Monitor makes short work of deciding which requests for object access to grant and which to deny.

You also learned about the Windows NT logon process (WinLogon) that strictly controls how users identify themselves and log onto a Windows NT machine. The NT attention sequence (Ctrl-Alt-Del) guarantees that a Trojan horse program can't be used to hijack user account and password information. Likewise, the WinLogon protected memory structures keep this all-important gatekeeper function from being replaced by would-be system crackers.

WinLogon also supports a number of Registry-based logon controls: handling of a default logon name, providing security notices, changing the default shell, handling system shut-down options, and enabling automatic logon. You've also learned about key Account Policy settings in User Manager that can be used to block unauthorized break-in attempts. All in all, Windows NT offers a reasonably secure operating environment that is designed to help administrators keep their important assets safe from harm and unwanted exposure.

KEY TERMS

- **Access Control Entry (ACE)** — A single entry in an object's ACL that identifies whether or not access to the object is permitted for one particular user or group, and if so, which services related to that object the named user or group is permitted to request.

- **Access Control List (ACL)** — A list of security identifiers that are contained by a resource object. Only those processes with the appropriate access token can activate the services of that object.

- **access token** — Object containing the security identifier of an active process. These tokens determine the security context of the process.

- **account policy** — This policy controls the way passwords must be used by all user accounts of a domain, or of an individual workstation.

- **audit policy** — For a domain or for an individual computer, defines the type of security events that are logged and determines what Windows NT will do when the log files become full.

- **authentication** — The process of validating a user's credentials to allow access to certain resources.

- **default groups** — The predefined system and user groups supplied with Windows NT. These groups are granted user rights upon their creation during the installation of Windows NT.

- **disabled user account** — A user account that is not permitted to undergo authentication.

- **domain controller** — For a Windows NT Server, a specified computer role that authenticates domain logons and maintains the security policies and the account database for a domain.

- **event auditing** — This is the process of tracking events by recording selected types of events in a security log of a server or a workstation.

- **identification** — The process of establishing a valid account identity on a Windows NT machine by supplying a correct and working domain name (if necessary) and account name.

- **object** — Any piece of information created by using a Windows-based application with Object Linking and Embedding (OLE), Security, the Component Object Model. This also refers to the operating system process components.

- **password** — A unique string of characters that must be provided before a logon or an access is authorized. Passwords are a security measure used to restrict initial access to Windows NT resources.

- **process** — The primary unit of execution in the Windows NT operating system environment; a process may contain one or more execution threads, all associated with a named user account, SID, and access token. Processes essentially define the container within which individual applications and commands execute under Windows NT.

- **SAM database** — A database of security information that includes security information (such as user account names and passwords) and the settings of the machine's security policies. In both Windows NT Server and Workstation, the SAM database is managed primarily with User Manager for Domains. In nondomain environments, the local User Manager application on an NT Workstation can manage only local security data.

- **SAM key** — The collection of security data that resides under the subkey named SAM in the HKEY_LOCAL_MACHINE hive.

- **Security Accounts Manager (SAM)** — A Windows NT subsystem that maintains the security database and provides an application programming interface (API) for accessing that database. Works in tandem with the Windows NT Security Reference Monitor (SRM) subsystem to handle logons and to arbitrate requests for access to system objects.

- **Security ID (SID)** — A unique name that identifies a logged on user to the security system. SIDs can identify one user or a group of users.

- **shell** — The default user process that is launched when a valid account name and password combination is authenticated by the WinLogon process for Windows NT. The shell process defines a logged in user's runtime environment from this point forward, and supplies all spawned processes or commands with its access token to define their access permissions, until that account logs off.

- **user account** — This entity contains all of the information that defines a user to the Windows NT environment.

REVIEW QUESTIONS

1. The _____ determines which users and groups have access to a particular Windows NT object.
   a. Security Access Manager
   b. User Manager for Domains
   c. Event logger
   d. Server Manager

2. All processes in Windows NT require an access token. True or False?

3. A SID is a unique number and is never duplicated. True or False?

4. Permissions that are changed while the user is actively logged on will not take effect until that user logs onto the system again. True or False?

5. The default NT authentication method is to supply valid domain and account names, plus a valid password. But Windows NT permits use of alternate authentication techniques. True or False?

6. When the SRM scans an ACL for an object, what is the first thing it looks for?
   a. No Access to the object, at which point access is immediately denied
   b. any ACE that provides the requested permission
   c. the default, and if access is permitted thereby, allows the request to proceed
   d. none of the above

7. Windows NT _____ to objects by default.
   a. restricts access
   b. allows access
   c. applies whatever default access has been defined

8. Which of the following reasons is the most likely to cause DontDisplayLastUserName to show up in a Windows NT Registry?
   a. to keep unauthorized users from attacking the Administrator account
   b. to improve security on a shared machine
   c. to reduce burnout on the machine's monitor
   d. to permit only authorized users to log in on the machine

9. The Windows NT authentication process can be automated by adding default user information and the _____ value to the Registry.
   a. DontDisplayLastUsername
   b. AutoAdminLogon
   c. Legal Notice Caption
   d. AutomateLogon

10. Of the following, which is the most likely reason for a security notice to appear when users attempt to log onto a Windows NT machine at the National Security Agency?

   a. to make sure that outsiders don't try to break into the system

   b. to inform unauthorized users that they are subject to legal action if they obtain unauthorized access to the system

   c. to remind valid system users about Acceptable Use Policies

   d. none of the above

11. The default shell process for Windows NT Workstation is called the:

   a. NT Explorer

   b. Program Manager

   c. command shell

   d. C shell

12. The _____ is created by the Security Accounts Manager and identifies the current user to the subsystem.

   a. Access ID

   b. Security ID

   c. Group ID

   d. access token

13. The _____ key sequence initiates the logon process.

   a. Ctrl-Esc

   b. Alt-Tab

   c. Ctrl-Break

   d. Ctrl-Alt-Del

14. An access token is a Windows NT object. True or False?

15. To customize the security structure of your Windows NT system, you can change the behavior of the logon process. True or False?

16. Of the following settings, which is not available from the User Manager Account Policies?

   a. no account lockout

   b. lockout after 5 tries

   c. disable account

   d. lockout duration

17. Which accounts can be locked out? (Choose all that apply.)

   a. Administrator

   b. Guest

   c. Everyone

   d. none of the above

18. The special-purpose application invoked by the Windows NT attention sequence that serves as the logon process is named:

   a. WINPOPUP.EXE

   b. WINLOGON.EXE

   c. The User Manager

   d. EXPLORER.EXE

19. Which of the following Account Policy settings helps prevent dictionary break-ins? (Choose all that apply.)

   a. enabling Account Lockout

   b. limiting the number of bad logon attempts

   c. setting a duration of at least 20 minutes for lockouts

   d. resetting the bad logon count after 2 minutes

20. Why it is important to rename the Administrator account?

   a. to avoid exposing an obvious source of attack, because the Administrator account can't be locked out

   b. to explicitly identify which administrator is logged on

   c. to avoid confusing accounts and passwords across multiple machines

   d. to enable setting up a dummy account named Administrator

21. If the Program Manager shell replaces the NT Explorer shell, which of the following side effects will occur? (Choose all that apply.)

   a. no access to the Start menu

   b. no task bar

   c. no access to the Task Manager

   d. no more DOS command prompt

7

HANDS-ON PROJECTS

For these hands-on projects, you will be editing the Registry on your Windows NT machine. In most real-life circumstances, you would begin this exercise by creating at least a partial Registry backup, in the event that any mishaps should occur during Registry editing.

Windows NT supports only two methods to create complete Registry backups, including all security-related keys (which are not normally accessible to other backup methods). These methods are:

- To use a Windows NT compatible backup program that can back up the entire Registry. Even Windows NT Backup, the built-in program included with the operating system, includes a Backup Local Registry option.
- The Windows NT Resource Kit (both Workstation and Server) includes a utility called REGBACK.EXE. This will also create a complete Registry backup.

The methods for creating partial Registry backups will suffice to capture the information you'll be changing in the following exercises, so any of them will also work:

- Update your current Emergency Repair Disk (ERD), with the command line statement RDISK /S.
- Copy all the files in the \WINNT\SYSTEM32\CONFIG directory. *Warning*: This represents the information from your last successful logon (to supply the data for the Last Known Good Configuration, if needed). If you choose to copy these files, restart your machine before copying them to get the most recent version possible.
- You can use either REGEDIT or REGEDT32 to capture most of the Registry's contents.

Any of these techniques will preserve the Registry settings you're about to change. Ask your instructor or technical support person if creating a backup will be necessary, and if so which method you should use. The RDISK /S approach is recommended.

PROJECT 7-1

To open the WinLogon Registry key:

1. Open the Registry editor by clicking **Start**, **Run**, and entering **regedit** in the Open box.
2. Click **OK**.
3. Double-click the **HKEY_LOCAL_MACHINE** key (or click the **+** to the left of the folder icon for that key).

4. Moving down the hierarchy for the above key, double-click **SOFTWARE**, then **Microsoft**, then **Windows NT**, then **Current Version**.

5. Click the **Winlogon** key in the above hierarchy to display the Winlogon key. Your screen should look similar to Figure 7-1.

PROJECT 7-2

To disable the default username:

1. Open the Winlogon Registry key as shown in Project 7-1.

2. Choose **Edit**, **New** from the menu.

3. Select **String Value** from the menu.

4. Type **DontDisplayLastUserName** in the Name: field of the entry, and press **[Enter]**.

5. Double-click **DontDisplayLastUserName** that you just added. An Edit String dialog box opens, in which you can assign a value for this string.

6. Type **1** (the number one) in the entry field of the Edit String dialog box.

7. Click **OK**.

8. Close the Registry editor.

9. Log off and back on to check the results. The Username: field in the logon dialog box should now be blank.

To restore the system to the original default, replace the 1 in the DontDisplayLastUserName value assignment with a 0 (zero).

PROJECT 7-3

To add a warning message to the logon screen:

1. Open the Winlogon Registry key as shown in Project 7-1.

2. Double-click the value **LegalNoticeCaption**.

3. Type **Warning!** in the entry field of the Edit String dialog box.

4. Click **OK**.

5. Double-click the value **LegalNoticeText**.

6. Type your warning message in the Entry: field of the Edit String dialog box. In his excellent book, Tom Sheldon (*The Windows NT Security Handbook*, Osborne/McGraw-Hill: Berkeley, 1997, p. 71) recommends a warning message that reads something like this, for maximum legal protection:

Authorized Users Only! The information on this computer and network is the property of (name organization here) and is protected by intellectual property law. You must have legitimate access to an assigned account on this computer to access any information. You are permitted only to access information as defined by the system administrators. Your activities may be monitored. Any unauthorized access will be punished to the full extent of the law.

7. Click **OK**.

8. Close the Registry editor.

9. Log off and back on to check the results. Your warning message should appear, and the user must respond to proceed.

PROJECT 7-4

To change the default shell to Program Manager:

1. Launch REGEDIT by clicking **Start**, **Run**, and entering REGEDIT.

2. Open the Winlogon Registry key as indicated in Project 7-1.

3. Double-click the **Shell** value.

4. Type **progman.exe** in the entry field of the Edit String dialog box.

5. Click **OK**.

6. Close the Registry editor.

7. Log off and back on to check the results. After logon, the Program Manager shell should load. (Note that Windows NT does not create Program Manager groups or icons automatically, so you will have to create them.)

To restore Explorer as the default shell, simply follow steps 1-2 above, type **explorer.exe** in the entry field of the Edit String dialog box, and click **OK**. Close the Registry editor, and in the Program Manager, select **File**, **Logoff** from the menu. Click **OK**.

PROJECT 7-5

To change account lockout settings:

1. Log on with Administrator privileges.
2. Open the User Manager by pressing **Start**, **Programs**, **Administrative Tools (Common)**, and **User Manager**.
3. Select **Policies**, **Account** from the menu. The Accounts Policy dialog box shown in Figure 7-2 opens.
4. Click the **Account Lockout** radio button.
5. Set the Account Lockout parameters to the following:

   - Lock out after **4** bad attempts
   - Reset count after **30** minutes
   - Lockout duration **60** minutes

6. Click **OK**.
7. Close the User Manager and log off.
8. To view the effect of the settings, attempt to log on with an incorrect password 5 times. Notice the dialog box that opens on the fifth attempt, telling you that the account has been locked.
9. To unlock the account, log on as administrator and start the User Manager.
10. Double-click the username of the locked-out account.
11. Remove the check from the **Account Locked Out** checkbox.

CASE PROJECTS

1. Your employer, XYZ Corp., has decided to put two kiosk machines in its lobby at corporate headquarters. These machines are intended to be available to all visitors, so they can read the company history and play a video file of the president's latest speech at the shareholders' meeting. Explain how you could use Windows NT Workstation to set up such a kiosk machine. Be specific about what Registry alterations you must make so this machine will log itself into a special account each time it boots up. What other kinds of alterations or limitations should you make to keep this machine from posing any kind of security threat?

2. As the network administrator at Widgets, Inc., you are also responsible for network security. To keep your servers free from unwanted use, your Human Resources Department has asked you to post a security warning on all machines that can log onto the network. What specific Registry changes must you make to set up such a warning on Windows NT Workstation? What elements must appear in such a warning to permit your company to pursue legal remedies against would-be system crackers?

3. To extend your efforts at Widgets, Inc., to keep unwanted users from breaking into your network, what kind of Account Policy changes should you institute to prevent so-called dictionary attacks against your Windows NT machines? What other changes might it be wise to make where default user accounts are concerned? Explain.

WINDOWS NT NETWORK ARCHITECTURE

This chapter begins with a discussion of one of the cornerstones of modern networking terminology—the OSI reference model. This model breaks the tasks involved in communicating across a network into seven distinct and separable peer layers that function as if they were directly connected whenever two computers exchange information. With this foundation firmly in place, you learn about the networking protocols that Windows NT supports and how and when to use them. You also explore the incredible variety of networking tools and utilities that Windows NT includes. You learn about their proper configuration and use and how the relationship among multiple protocols can affect workstation and network performance.

AFTER READING THIS CHAPTER AND COMPLETING THE EXERCISES YOU WILL BE ABLE TO:

- UNDERSTAND HOW THE WINDOWS NT ARCHITECTURE IS DESIGNED
- DEFINE THE OSI REFERENCE MODEL
- DISCUSS NT NETWORKING COMPONENTS
- EXPLAIN NT NETWORK PROTOCOLS
- DEMONSTRATE HOW TO MANAGE NT NETWORK COMPONENTS
- EXPLAIN HOW NETWORK BINDING AFFECTS TRAFFIC PRIORITY

WINDOWS NT NETWORK COMPONENTS

Windows NT is designed for networking and includes all the elements necessary to interact with a network without requiring any additional software. These elements include file and print services, among many others. In fact, many experts assert that Windows NT networking is powerful and efficient, yet relatively easy to configure and use. Its combination of a graphical user interface and wizards for configuration support, and its underlying capabilities make it quite attractive to experts and neophytes alike.

Windows NT works as a network client or as a network server (or both) and can participate in peer-to-peer environments. Windows NT also includes everything needed to access the Internet, including all the necessary protocols and client capabilities that extend from a powerful Web browser (Internet Explorer), to a bundle of IP-based tools and utilities that run the gamut from Telnet to Netstat.

Windows NT consists of a collection of individual software components, each of which is relatively isolated from other components and must be accessed through its own well-defined interface. Figure 8-1 provides an overview of the network architecture; for additional explanation please reread the sections on the Windows NT architecture in Chapter 1. This creates a modular architecture that allows the operating system to readily accommodate new technologies and standards by adding new modules with well-defined interfaces as needed. A component orientation also lets the operating system take advantage of evolutionary change without requiring the entire system to be replaced—an already functioning system can incorporate new modules simply by installing them. It can also accommodate replacements for old modules without requiring a complete reinstallation or a substantial upgrade to the underlying OS.

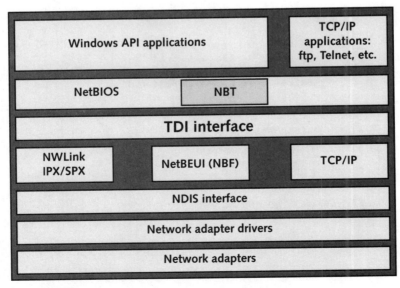

Figure 8-1   The Windows NT network architecture

In Windows NT, numerous components work together to define its networking capabilities. Each component provides one or more individual network functions and also defines an interface through which data moves on its way in from or out to other system components. This is what explains Windows NT's abilities to support multiple protocols easily and transparently. Applications only know that they're communicating because the modular organization of the operating system shields them from having to know anything about the "ugly details" that can sometimes be involved.

In fact, networking components can be added to or deleted from a Windows NT system without affecting the function of other components, unless such components are bound to those other components (binding is discussed in the section entitled "Managing Bindings" at the end of this chapter). Thus, adding new components can bring new services, communications technologies, or other capabilities into existing networks. Likewise, additional protocols can join the mix at any time.

Components exchange data across interfaces that Microsoft calls **boundary layers**. These boundary layers translate data from whatever format is native to a sending component to one that's native to the receiver. Such boundaries also make it easy to use operating system services generically, without requiring one component to understand the details of whichever module sits on the other side of a boundary.

8

OSI REFERENCE MODEL

As part of an attempt to completely standardize networking in the 1980s, the International Standardization Organization (ISO) developed an all-encompassing design for a networking environment called the Open Systems Interconnection (OSI). Perhaps because of its scope, or the overall complexity of the approach it embodied, the promise of OSI never became a reality. But this 10-year effort produced a reference model that describes how networks communicate that's become a standard in its own right. This model is formally known as the **OSI reference model** and is the subject of ISO Standard 9472 (plus several subsequent addenda).

This model for networking describes seven layers that group numerous, related special functions that any operational network must implement. By no coincidence, many modern operating systems often implement their networking components to match the layers in this model, if only to make them easier for users to understand. Windows NT is a typical case in point. The seven layers that comprise the OSI reference model are shown in Figure 8-2 (each is explained in detail shortly).

Each layer in the model provides a set of specific services to the adjacent upper layer. To perform its particular tasks, each layer is endowed with certain built-in capabilities, but also calls the services of the layer below. When two computers communicate across the network, each one moves data through the seven layers of this model; then corresponding layers for the sender and receiver are called peers or peer layers. This is because whatever manipulations and transformations that a peer layer on the sending computer applies to data must be reversed by the peer layer on the receiving computer. In other words, for at least one brief instant, the same data that moves through a layer on the sending machine appears in the corresponding peer layer on the receiving machine.

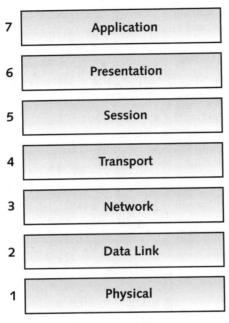

7	Application
6	Presentation
5	Session
4	Transport
3	Network
2	Data Link
1	Physical

Figure 8-2   Layers of the OSI reference model

A layered approach lets developers handle all the complex processing and communications involved in networking by dividing this massive job into a series of separate, but related jobs and then tackling each such job independently. Here again, this approach is entirely consonant with a component-oriented architecture like that implemented in Windows NT. The peer layer relationship is shown in Figure 8-3 and illustrates how peer layers correspond across a network connection.

 It's important to understand that the OSI reference model is an abstract representation of how networks behave. It seldom maps completely into real-world implementations, or directly into many existing protocol stacks (especially those that were developed before the model was created, such as TCP/IP). Nevertheless, this model provides a common frame of reference and associated terminology that makes it easier to describe what networks do, how networks work, and how data makes its way from one computer across a network to another.

Real implementations and protocol stacks also employ layered models that differ substantially from the OSI reference model. This explains why TCP/IP and **Xerox Networking System (XNS)** use four layers, rather than seven—because that's how their designers conceptualized them. For convenience or because different models may be at work, software developers sometimes choose to aggregate multiple OSI layers into single modules when they create individual network components. But the two lowest layers of the OSI model remain consistent across most implementations, probably because they're where hardware makes its way into the picture. Thus, the Physical layer (Layer 1) concerns itself with the equipment and cables necessary for networking, and the Data Link layer (Layer 2) covers those essential elements of software called drivers that permit computers to communicate with external hardware devices.

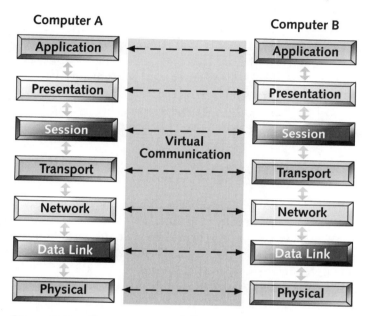

Figure 8-3   How corresponding layers act as peers in the OSI model

To understand the OSI reference model, you must understand what role each layer plays and how those layers interact to enable networking. Figures 8-2 and 8-3 both show all layers of the OSI model; the following sections explain each of these layers.

PHYSICAL LAYER (LAYER 1)

The **Physical layer** handles bits, whether sending or receiving data. This layer is unconcerned with how such bits should be interpreted. It handles the physical connection to the network and the sending and receiving of signals, whether electrical or optical.

As its name suggests, the Physical layer is where the materials that make networking possible are specified, and where the signals that represent communications are dictated. This applies to specifications for network connectors and cables, for transmission and reception devices, and also to signaling, which usually consists of determining how the 1s and 0s that represent individual bits must be represented.

Data Link Layer (Layer 2)

The **Data Link layer** controls how data moves from one device to another, across a so-called logical link. For transmission across the network, this layer accepts **protocol data units (PDUs)** known as **packets** from the Network layer. It performs certain processing, and then repackages packets into its own PDUs, known as **frames**, to be forwarded to the Physical layer for transmission. As part of its unique processing, this layer adds descriptive information, including frame type designators and segment numbers, to outgoing data.

The Data Link layer supports error-checking at the frame level. To ensure correct delivery, the sending computer calculates and adds a Cyclical Redundancy Check (CRC) value to each frame. When that frame is received at its destination, this value is recalculated independently. If both CRC values are the same, the received data is assumed to be correct; if they differ, the receiver may request retransmission of the erroneous frame. By monitoring sequence numbers and delivery times, the Data Link layer also notes when frames get dropped. When that happens, it requests that missing frames be retransmitted.

Network Layer (Layer 3)

The **Network layer** moves data between and among networks. It examines the destination addresses of packets and forwards packets to their intended destinations when sender and receiver are not directly linked. On a single network segment, the Data Link layer handles delivery between machines on that same physical segment, which requires no forwarding. However, crossing segment boundaries automatically requires that at least one third party—that is, a device that is neither the designated sender nor the ultimate receiver of the packet—gets involved in the transmission to forward the packet from one network segment to another. This forwarding may either result in delivery of that packet, or in forwarding it to another third party that may deliver it, or forward it yet again, and so on. The Network layer permits any number of intermediate devices, which are usually called routers, to forward packets from sender to receiver.

Transport Layer (Layer 4)

The **Transport layer** handles reliable delivery of information. It makes sure that packets arrive without errors, assembles them in the proper order, and takes steps to deal with loss or duplication of transmitted data.

To be more specific, the Transport layer takes large outgoing messages from the Session layer and fragments them into a collection of sequenced packets (called disassembly). For incoming messages, it recombines packets by sequence number (called reassembly) to recreate the message in its original form for delivery to the Session layer.

The Transport layer also acknowledges packets received, when required. It manages quality of service data that can recognize prevailing transmission characteristics or network latency for particular network connections. Some Transport layer implementations can even alter maximum packet size settings (which are called "windows" or "sliding windows") to optimize traffic for delivery across links of different speeds, depending on how efficiently communications occur during ongoing communications across the network.

SESSION LAYER (LAYER 5)

The **Session layer** handles any ongoing exchanges of information across the network, called sessions. This handling consists of requesting a connection, setting it up, managing it for as long as it persists, and then bringing it to a graceful conclusion upon its termination (this is called "tear down"). The Session layer also handles whatever name lookup or security services that may need to be accessed or satisfied to allow two applications to find one another on a network, and to establish and maintain ongoing communication. Finally, the Session layer handles whatever exchanges of data occur between the parties involved, and determines which parties may transmit and receive.

8

PRESENTATION LAYER (LAYER 6)

The **Presentation layer** translates data between network-oriented data formats and platform-specific data representations. Because computers on a network may not share common ways of representing character or numeric data (ASCII versus EBCDIC, and "little-endian" versus "big-endian" real numbers are two classic examples of such common mismatches across platform types), it's essential that data sent across the network be as general-purpose or generic as possible. The Presentation layer therefore handles all kinds of data transformations, including protocol conversions, data translations, compression, encryption, and character set mappings. It can even interpret graphics instructions and make format translations for those, if necessary.

A special kind of software that's important in the Windows NT environment, called a redirector, operates at the Presentation layer. Redirectors make files on a server visible to its clients, they also permit remote printers to be used as if they were local. Redirectors work by examining all requests for service, passing on local requests to the local operating system, and redirecting requests for resources that reside elsewhere on the network to the computers where those resources actually reside. Windows NT embeds a redirector into its file-system interface, so that application developers can build programs that simply ask for files, and the operating system can use the redirector to decide if the reference is to the local file system or to some other file system elsewhere on the network.

APPLICATION LAYER (LAYER 7)

The **Application layer** provides services to support user applications, which may involve anything from an e-mail package to a client/server database. The Application layer permits applications to communicate with one another, just as if both were present on a single machine.

It's important to recognize that the OSI Application layer defines an interface to some particular application and does not represent any application by itself. In other words, the Application layer defines those mechanisms through which applications can gain access to network resources, or obtain information from the network, but an external application is required to request or receive such access. If you like, you can think of applications as the eighth layer of the OSI reference model, even though they're not explicitly recognized as such.

THE WINDOWS NT NETWORK MODEL

Microsoft's component architecture means that NT networking services are delivered through a collection of components, and their associated interfaces, which Microsoft calls boundary layers. Sometimes a boundary represents nothing more than a collection of configuration settings that combine to define a desired network service (this is very much how network components visible in the Control Panel Network applet work together). At other times, a boundary layer will consist of some Application Programming Interface (API) designed to permit specific networking components to exchange information within Windows NT (this is where mechanisms like Interprocess Communication (IPC), and RPC come into play). Components deliver services and boundary layers permit components to exchange information and communicate. Figure 8-4 shows some of the most common components and boundary layers that occur within the Windows NT I/O Manager (one of the Executive Services modules that operates as part of the Windows NT Kernel mode environment).

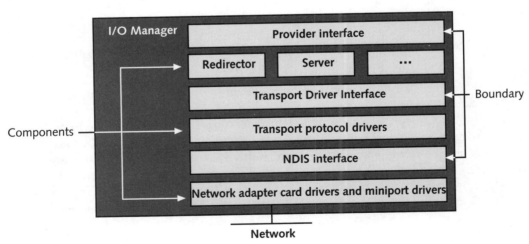

Figure 8-4   Components and boundary layers

BOUNDARY LAYERS

Boundary layers are designed to make it easy for programmers to create drivers for network adapters and to obtain easy access to other network components, such as file systems or network protocols. As indicated in Figure 8-4, boundary layers separate components and provide access between those components they separate; thus, the generic Provider interface permits User mode applications to communicate with one of the NT redirectors (there's one for Microsoft Network resources, another for NetWare-based resources, and so forth), as well as the Server service, the Workstation service, and other high-layer network services.

Likewise, the TDI (Transport Driver Interface) makes it possible for each of these services to interact with one or more available transport protocol drivers. This creates an open-ended networking environment in which services can be indifferent to the transports they will ultimately use, because the boundary layer handles the details of connecting a service to one or more transports. This also helps to explain why Windows NT can deliver NetBIOS-based services so effectively across any or all of its "Big 3" protocols—NetBEUI, NWLink (IPX/SPX), and TCP/IP, either singly or in combination.

The NDIS interface resides beneath the Transport protocol driver components. **NDIS** stands for **Network Driver Interface Specification**; it defines a specification for building network interface card drives that can support multiple interfaces in a single computer and one or more protocols for each such interface. NDIS comes in multiple versions: NDIS 3.0 is the version supported in Windows 4.0; NDIS 3.1 is the version supported in Windows 95 (and in Windows 98 as well; it alone supports the full-blown Microsoft Plug and Play specification).

Because they provide well-documented, rigorously defined interfaces, boundary layers make it easy for Microsoft and third parties to build network components for Windows NT. Boundary layers and components alternate, because boundary layers provide the communications links between the components they separate. That's what makes them such a key ingredient in the Windows NT development world.

PROGRAMMING INTERFACES

Programming interfaces are often referred to generically as APIs (Application Programming Interfaces), but the boundary layer terminology that Microsoft uses emphasizes that such interfaces can—and do—occur at almost any level within an OS. These interfaces traditionally define specific procedure calls or object references that permit applications or drivers to interact with system services. Where Windows NT is concerned, this usually means communicating with file-system drivers or redirectors (which also provide access to network resources as well as local file system capabilities), plus Server and Workstation services.

To be more specific, Windows NT supports the following network programming interfaces, which call upon file-system drivers and transport protocols to perform their functions:

- **Network Basic Input/Output System (NetBIOS)**
- **Windows Sockets (WinSock)**
- **Network Dynamic Data Exchange (NetDDE)**
- **Remote Procedure Call (RPC)**

COMPONENTS: FILE-SYSTEM DRIVERS

The Windows NT file-system components are built so that access to file systems across the network is exactly the same as access to local storage systems. In terms of the OSI reference model, this means that Windows NT provides boundary layers to system components that operate at the Application and Session layers. Because these components look and act like file systems as far as user applications are concerned, any applications access network and local resources in exactly the same way. Here, the redirector services distinguish between what's local and what's not and take appropriate action to see that all requests for resources are satisfied. The Windows NT components that function as file-system drivers are: Workstation services, **named pipes**, Server services, and **mailslots**.

Although "file-system driver" describes the role that the software plays in this situation, these components are also known as redirectors because of their abilities to redirect requests for remote resources elsewhere on the network.

BOUNDARY LAYER: TRANSPORT DRIVER INTERFACE (TDI)

The **Transport Driver Interface (TDI)** operates beneath those software components that provide redirector or file-system driver services to applications. The TDI therefore acts as a boundary layer to shield those software components from encountering the details of whatever transport protocols may be in use for any given service access. In the Windows NT environment, all transport protocols conform to the TDI. Thus, Windows NT services can function as if they were transport independent, because the TDI handles the details necessary to connect those services with their underlying transports. To put this boundary layer in the context of the OSI reference model, it operates between the Session and the Transport layers.

COMPONENTS: TRANSPORT PROTOCOLS

As the discussion of the Transport layer indicated, this layer handles the disassembly of long data streams into a sequence of packets for transmission and then reassembles those sequences into a corresponding data stream on the receiving end. This explains why **transport protocols** deal with activities and services that include packet sequencing, data delivery and integrity checks, and more. In the Windows NT environment, the TDI permits multiple transport protocols to be active simultaneously. In turn, this means that connections made using any of the transport protocols that Windows NT supports—primarily NetBEUI, IPX/SPX, and TCP/IP—can coexist and interoperate effectively and reliably.

BOUNDARY LAYER: NETWORK DRIVER INTERFACE SPECIFICATION (NDIS)

As you learned earlier in this chapter, all Windows NT network drivers must conform to the NDIS 3.0 specification. NDIS defines a standard code interface that permits NDIS-compliant drivers to communicate with one or more of the Windows NT transport protocols. To extend the capabilities of any Windows NT machine, NDIS drivers permit multiple transport protocols to communicate using one or more network interface cards simultaneously. Among other things, this permits a properly configured NT machine to route packets from one network interface to another, or to communicate simultaneously across multiple networks.

All network interface cards (NICs) have unique hexadecimal addresses that allow them to communicate with each other at the lower levels. The NIC is the connectivity device that establishes a physical link between different nodes on a network.

The basis for Windows NT network architecture rests firmly on NDIS. NDIS operates at the Media Access Control (MAC) sublayer of the OSI Data Link layer. Any NIC that is NDIS-compatible can pass data to any protocol that can communicate with an NDIS-based adapter driver. Although this makes Windows NT networking extremely flexible, certain other network operating systems permit only a single protocol at a time to be bound to any single NIC.

In NDIS version 3.0, a piece of code called the NDIS Wrapper replaces the protocol manager, PROTMAN, that was used in previous implementations of NDIS. Like its predecessor, the NDIS Wrapper controls all initial access to the NIC and manages protocol bindings and settings for the adapter. To ensure consistent and reliable operations, the NDIS Wrapper also writes adapter settings to the Registry whenever changes occur (these are part of what's checked against the hardware during the NTDETECT phase of the Windows NT boot process; this process is covered in detail in Chapter 15).

DEFAULT NETWORK COMPONENTS

The default Windows NT installation supplies a collection of components that should meet most users' networking requirements. In other words, a plain-vanilla NT installation delivers a usable network that may need only to be supplemented with some name or address management service (such as WINS, DNS, or DHCP) to create a completely configured internetworking environment. The default networking components are the following:

- *Browser service:* The Browser service creates and distributes a database of all NetBIOS-based resources available on a network; this service provides the data that users peruse to select network resources from within NT Explorer (and in other applications that support a browse function).

■ *NetBIOS interface:* Basic networking in Windows NT can be considered part of a broader Microsoft network environment that rests on NetBIOS-based name services, file and print services, and more. As a fundamental part of Windows NT networking, this interface is the core for much of the NT native built-in networking.

■ *Network adapter drivers:* These software elements create an essential link between NT network services and whatever network interface(s) may be present on a particular computer.

■ *RPC configuration:* Remote Procedure Call is a standard API used in many applications to permit them to exchange data across the network; Microsoft uses this API for some of its NT system utilities and makes it available to external applications as well.

■ *Server services:* As with Workstation services, Server services embrace those capabilities that a Windows NT machine can offer to clients across a network. This also explains why NT Server includes a broader and richer variety of Server services, as compared to NT Workstation.

■ *TCP/IP:* Once an exotic add-on, Microsoft now suggests using TCP/IP as the primary protocol on any Windows NT network.

■ *Workstation services:* The name of these services describes the networking role they play: These services provide all basic network client capabilities for Windows NT for both Windows NT Server and Windows NT Workstation.

NETWORK PROTOCOLS

Windows NT supports three core network transport protocols. Each of these protocols works best on networks of different sizes, where each such network has its own special performance and access requirements. The "Big 3" protocols are:

■ NetBEUI   *Net Bios Extended User Interface*

■ NWLink (IPX/SPX)

■ TCP/IP

Each of these network transports has specific pros and cons, as you'll see in the sections that follow. The list of characteristics that follows sums up the important elements that must be considered when selecting among the three candidates:

■ NetBEUI works best on small networks (defined by Microsoft as 10 computers or fewer), single-server or peer-to-peer networks, where ease of access and use are most important.

- NWLink works best on networks of medium scope (20 servers or less, all in a single facility). Of course, it's also important on networks that include Novell NetWare or IntranetWare servers.

- TCP/IP works on a global scale, as demonstrated by its use on the Internet. According to Microsoft, TCP/IP is a complicated, yet powerful transport that scales well from small networks all the way up to the global Internet. It is the most widely used of all networking protocols.

NetBEUI

The **NetBIOS Extended User Interface (NetBEUI)** implements the simplest of the three basic Windows NT transport protocols. It is also sometimes known as the NetBIOS Frame (NBF) transport protocol. NetBEUI was developed by IBM in the late 1980s for use with the OS/2 and LAN Manager OSs.

Apparently, NetBEUI's developers did not find it necessary to design this protocol so that networked PCs could function in a complex internetworked environment, where routing support is mandatory. Instead, they built NetBEUI to function best within workgroups that ranged in size from 2 to 200 computers. This helps to explain why NetBEUI is not routable, but unfortunately this limitation also constrains NetBEUI to purely local LAN segments that contain either Microsoft or IBM networking clients and servers.

Some networks do indeed use bridges to move NetBEUI traffic across multiple LAN segments. NetBEUI is seldom permitted to transmit across any WAN connections that may otherwise be accessible through network routers. In fact, NetBEUI is known as an excessively "chatty" protocol, which makes it unsuitable for WAN use. This is where Microsoft's TCP/IP implementations of NBT (or NetBIOS over TCP/IP) and NetBIOS over **IPX**, combined with Windows NT mulitprotocol support, make it possible to use nonbroadcast IP or IPX equivalents to provide usable NetBIOS connectivity across router-managed WAN links that routinely block all broadcast traffic.

NetBEUI Pros

The two primary advantages of Net BEUI are that it is both compact and speedy. Although its chatty characteristics make it unsuitable for WAN use, NetBEUI is by far the fastest of all the TDI transports in Windows NT. This makes it ideal on small networks where routing is not required. NetBEUI's most significant features are:

- It is the fastest of all native NT protocols on small networks.

- NetBEUI supports up to 1,023 sessions; earlier implementations supported only 254 sessions.

- NetBEUI has been optimized to perform well across slow serial links.

- Because it relies on NetBIOS naming and delivers automatic addressing, NetBEUI is easy to install and configure.

- NetBEUI is inherently self-tuning, so no analysis or maintenance of its configuration is needed.

- NetBEUI incorporates data integrity checks and retransmission for erroneous or lost packets.

- Of all the major Windows NT protocols, NetBEUI incurs the lowest memory overhead. For older DOS computers, this can make all the difference where RAM space for protocols and drivers is scarce, and larger protocols may not fit into available memory.

NetBEUI Cons

Unroutability and broadcast overhead make NetBEUI unusable on internetworks or on networks that include WAN as well as LAN links. Because of product specificity, NetBEUI is used only seldom outside Microsoft and IBM networks. Possibly because of its insularity, there are hardly any diagnostic or troubleshooting utilities that can interpret NetBEUI internals. In short, NetBEUI is not a contender for deployment in large, complex networks.

NWLink

NWLink is Microsoft's clean-room implementation of Novell's **IPX/SPX** protocol stack (the phrase "clean-room implementation" means that Microsoft built its own version of the Novell protocols by reverse-engineering the stack, rather than licensing the technology from Novell and being forced to pay a fee for its use). Rather than supporting the native Novell Open Datalink Interface (ODI), NWLink works with the NDIS driver technology that's native to Windows NT. NWLink is sufficiently complete to support the most important IPX/SPX APIs, including:

- *Novell's Windows Sockets:* This provides the interface support for existing NetWare applications written to comply with IPX/SPX.

- *NetBIOS over IPX:* This links the NetBIOS interface with the NWLink transport protocol. This is actually the NWNBLink (NetWare-NetBIOS Link) that allows Microsoft networks to use the NetBIOS interface for NetWare connectivity or to facilitate Microsoft networking using the routable IPX transport protocol (instead of NetBEUI which is not routable).

NWLink Pros

In addition to the positive aspects mentioned in the preceding section, NWLink offers some powerful capabilities that are conspicuously lacking in NetBEUI. These include:

- *SPX II:* SPX II is a new version of **SPX** that has been enhanced to support windowing and can also set a maximum frame size.

- *Auto detection of frame types:* NWLink automatically detects which IPX frame type is used on a network during the initial startup and broadcast advertisement phases. When multiple frame types appear, NT defaults to the industry-standard 802.2 frame type.

- *Direct hosting over IPX:* This capability refers to the ability to host ongoing network sessions using IPX transports. Because it eliminates the overhead associated with NetBIOS, this can increase network performance by as much as 20% on client computers. This capability is especially beneficial for client/server applications.

NWLink Cons

IPX may not scale well on large networks. In fact, IPX lacks a built-in facility for centralized address management like the service that DNS provides for TCP/IP. This omission allows address conflicts to occur (especially when previously isolated networks that employed identical defaults or common addressing schemes attempt to interoperate). Novell did establish an address registry in 1994 (IPX was introduced in 1983), but it is neither generally used nor acknowledged. By contrast, the InterNIC and its subsequent assigns have managed all public IP addresses since 1982. Like its other proprietary cousin, NetBEUI, IPX fails to support a comprehensive collection of network management tools like those that are so common for TCP/IP. Finally, IPX imposes a greater memory footprint on DOS machines and runs less efficiently than NetBEUI across slow serial connections.

TCP/IP

This protocol suite takes its name from the Transport and Network layer protocols most commonly associated with its use—that is, the **Transmission Control Protocol (TCP)** and the **Internet Protocol (IP)**. Nevertheless, **TCP/IP (Transmission Control Protocol/Internet Protocol)** represents an all-embracing suite of protocols that cover all layers of the OSI reference model (more than 100 component protocols that belong to the TCP/IP suite have been standardized).

TCP/IP has also been around for a long time. The original version of TCP/IP emerged from research funded by the Advanced Research Projects Agency (ARPA, a division of the U.S. Department of Defense). Work on this technology began in 1969, continued throughout the 1970s, and became broadly available in 1981 and 1982. Today, TCP/IP is the prevalent networking protocol worldwide; it is also the protocol suite that makes the Internet possible.

Some experts believe that TCP/IP's incorporation into UNIX in the mid-1970s is what propelled it into the networking forefront, because it was so widely adopted in academic computing environments worldwide shortly thereafter. Whatever the cause, TCP/IP has become the platform upon which a staggering variety of network services is available. These services include newsgroups (NNTP), electronic mail (SNMP and MIME), file transfer (FTP and

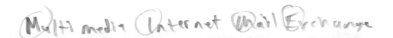
Multi media Internet Mail Exchange

ANS), remote printing (lpr, lpd, lpq utilities), remote boot (bootp and DHCP), and of course, the World Wide Web (HTTP; HyperText Transfer Protocol). That's why Microsoft has made TCP/IP its default protocol for Windows NT—it's what everybody wants.

To provide NetBIOS support using TCP/IP transports, Microsoft includes an implementation of NBT (NetBIOS over TCP/IP) with Windows NT. Microsoft even extended the definition of NBT behaviors by adding a new type of NetBIOS network node to the NBT environment. This type is called an "H" node, and it inverts the normal behavior of the standard NBT "M" node. It looks first for a NetBIOS name service (like a WINS server) and only then sends a broadcast to request local name resolution; whereas, an "M" node sends a broadcast first and then attempts a directed request for name resolution. Microsoft's approach reduces the amount of broadcast traffic on most IP-based networks that use NetBIOS names.

TCP/IP Pros

As network protocols go, TCP/IP is neither extremely fast nor easy to use. But TCP/IP supports networking services better than the other Windows NT protocols through its multiple components, as shown in Figure 8-5 below, and Table 8-1 on page 278. TCP/IP supports multiple routing protocols that can support large, complex networks; it also incorporates better error detection and handling, and works with more kinds of computers than any other protocol (everything from CDPD telephones to full-blown supercomputers). The following list describes the elements of Figure 8-5:

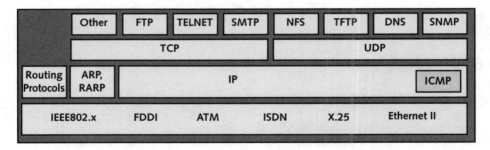

Figure 8-5 TCP/IP protocol stack

- *Other:* Any of the nearly 40 other service/application level protocols defined for TCP/IP

- *FTP (File Transfer Protocol):* The service protocol and corresponding TCP/IP application that permits network file transfer

- *Telnet:* The service protocol and corresponding TCP/IP applications that support networked terminal emulation services

- *SMTP (Simple Mail Transfer Protocol):* The most common e-mail service protocol in the TCP/IP environment (POP3, the Post Office Protocol version 3, and IMAP, the Internet Mail Access Protocol, are also involved in a great deal of Intenet e-mail traffic)

- *NFS (Network File System):* A UDP-based networked file system originally developed by Sun Microsystems but widely used on many TCP/IP networks (Windows NT does not include built-in NFS support, but numerous third-party options are available)

- *TFTP (Trivial File Transfer Protocol):* A lightweight, UDP-based alternative to FTP that was designed primarily to permit users running Telnet sessions elsewhere on a network to grab files from their real "home machines"

- *DNS (Domain Name Service):* An address resolution service for TCP/IP based networks that translates between numeric IP addresses and symbolic names known formally as Fully Qualified Domain Names (FQDNs).

- *SNMP (Simple Network Management Protocol):* The primary management protocol used on TCP/IP networks; used to report management data to management consoles or applications, and to interrogate repositories of management data around a network

- *TCP (Transmission Control Protocol):* The primary transport protocol that helped to give TCP/IP its full name; a robust, reliable, guaranteed delivery, **connection-oriented** transport protocol

- *UDP (User Datagram Protocol):* A secondary transport protocol on TCP/IP networks; a lightweight cousin of TCP; **connectionless**, low overhead, and offers only best-effort delivery rather than the delivery guarantees offered by TCP; used for all kinds of services on TCP networks, including NFS and TFTP

- *Routing Protocols:* Embrace a number of important IP protocols, including the Routing Internet Protocol (RIP), the Open Shortest Path First (OSPF) protocol, the Border Gateway Protocol (BGP), and numerous others including Address Resolution Protocol (ARP)—used to map from a numeric IP address to a MAC-layer address

- *RARP (Reverse Address Resolution Protocol):* Used to map from a MAC-layer address to a numeric IP address

- *IP (Internet Protocol):* The primary network layer protocol that gives TCP/IP the second half of its name, IP includes network addressing information that is manipulated when a packet is routed from sender to receiver, along with data integrity and network status information

- *ICMP (Internet Control Message Protocol):* The network-layer protocol that deals with quality of service, availability, and network behavior information; also supports the Packet Internet Groper (PING) protocol often used to inquire if an address is reachable on the Internet

- *IEEE 802.x:* Includes the 802.2 networking standard, plus standard networking technologies like Ethernet (802.3) and token ring (802.5) among others

- *FDDI (Fiber Distributed Data Interface):* A 100 Mbps fiber-based networking technology

8

- *ATM (Asynchronous Transfer Mode):* A cell-oriented, fiber- and copper-based networking technology that supports data rates from 25 Mbps to as high as 2.4 Gbps

- *ISDN (Integrated Services Digital Network):* A digital alternative to analog telephony; links support two or more 64 Kbps channels per connection, depending on type

- *X.25:* An ITU standard for packet-switched networking; enormously prevalent outside the US where its robust data-handling makes it a good match for substandard telephone networks

- *Ethernet II:* An older version of Ethernet that preceded the 802.3 specification; offers the same 10 Mbps as standard Ethernet but uses different frame formats

Table 8-1   Protocols in the Windows NT TCP/IP Stack

Protocol	Primary Function
Simple Network Management Protocol (SNMP)	Allows monitoring across host computers
Windows Sockets API	The standard interface between TCP/IP socket applications and protocols
NBT	NetBIOS over TCP/IP: Provides NetBIOS Naming Services
Transmission Control Protocol (TCP)	Provides connection-oriented services
User Datagram Protocol (UDP)	Provides connectionless services
Address Resolution Protocol (ARP)	Obtains hardware addresses for communication at the Network layer
Internet Protocol (IP)	Provides addressing and routing functions
Internet Control Message Protocol (ICMP)	Reports messages and errors regarding data delivery

In addition to its many services and capabilities, TCP/IP also supports:

- Direct Internet access from any TCP/IP-equipped computer with a link to the Internet, whether by phone, some kind of digital link (ISDN, frame relay, T1, and so forth), or across any network with routed Internet access

- Powerful network management protocols and services, such as SNMP and the Desktop Management Interface (DMI), which supports interrogation of desktop hardware and software configuration data, among others

- The Dynamic Host Configuration Protocol (DHCP), which provides unique IP addresses on demand, and simplifies IP address management (a vexing problem for many IP network administrators)

- Microsoft Windows Internet Name Service (WINS) to enable IP-based NetBIOS name browsing for Microsoft clients and servers, as well as the Domain Name Service (DNS) that is the most common name resolution service used to map fully qualified domain names to numeric IP addresses throughout the Internet

Unlike IPX/SPX, the InterNIC manages all TCP/IP domain names, network numbers, and IP addresses, to make the global Internet work correctly and reliably.

TCP/IP Cons

Given the glowing portrait that's been painted for TCP/IP, what could possibly be wrong with this environment? For one thing, configuring and managing a TCP/IP-based network requires a fair degree of expertise, careful planning, and constant maintenance and attention. Then too, each of the many services and protocols that TCP/IP supports brings its own unique installation, configuration, and management chores. Finally, there's a huge mass of information and a vast quantity of unforgiving detail work involved in establishing and maintaining a TCP/IP-based network. In short, it's a cruel, demanding, and unforgiving environment, and should always be approached with trepidation and great care. Despite these shortcomings, however, TCP/IP has no equal in capability or reach.

DATA LINK CONTROL (DLC)

8

The **Data Link Control (DLC)** transport mechanism is not really designed for connectivity between computers like the aforementioned transport protocols. Windows NT uses DLC to connect to IBM mainframes (via 3270 terminal emulation) or to access network-attached printers such as the HP 4si.

DLC offers only limited functionality as a network transport. It has been supplanted by TCP/IP in the majority of networks because most direct-attached printers available today rely primarily on TCP/IP-based remote printing protocols instead of DLC. In the same vein, TCP/IP supports IBM host access protocols such as Tn3270 and Tn5250; these protocols not only provide better terminal emulation capabilities, but they are inherently routable and do not rely on extensive broadcast traffic, as does DLC. This makes TCP/IP a better choice for both printing and terminal emulation in most environments.

DLC is subject to the following disadvantages as well:

- It cannot support higher-level file transfer protocols (that is, it's good only for printing and terminal emulation, and that's all).

- It is unroutable and hard to bridge.

- It is nothing more than a simple, primitive network transport and is entirely unsuited for higher-level services.

INTERPROCESS COMMUNICATION (IPC)

In the Windows NT environment, communication among processes is quite important, because of the operating system's multitasking, multithreaded architecture. Here, **Interprocess Communication (IPC)** defines a way for such processes to exchange information. This mechanism is general purpose so that it doesn't matter where such communications occur on the same computer or between two networked computers. IPC defines a way for client computers to request services from some server and permits servers to reply to requests for services. In Figure 8-6, IPC operates directly beneath the redirector on the client side, and the network file system on the server side, to provide a standard communications interface for handling requests and their associated replies.

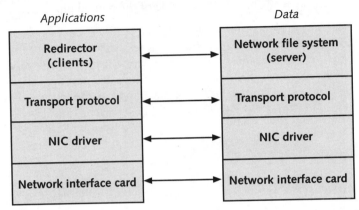

Figure 8-6 Interprocess communication between client and server

In Windows NT, IPC mechanisms are divided into two categories, according to the Windows NT general architecture: programming interfaces and file systems.

Programming interfaces permit general, open-ended client/server dialog to occur as mediated by applications or system services; normally, such dialog is not related strictly to data streams or data files. On the other hand, file systems support file sharing between clients and servers. Where programming interfaces are concerned, individual APIs differ depending on what kinds of client-server dialog they support; but where file systems are concerned, they must behave the same way, no matter how (or where) they employ Windows NT networked file systems and services.

IPC FILE SYSTEM MECHANISMS

Windows NT includes two IPC interfaces for file-system access: named pipes and mailslots. Such mechanisms work through the Windows NT redirector, which distinguishes between local and network resource requests. This permits one simple set of file I/O commands to handle both local and network access to file-system data.

Named Pipes

Named pipes support a connection-oriented message-passing service for clients and servers. In this context, connection orientation requires a message's receiver to acknowledge each message received; thus, named pipes offer a reliable method for clients and servers to exchange requests and replies (and whatever files relate to such message traffic). Named pipes provide their own methods to ensure reliable data transfer, which makes them a good match for lightweight, unreliable transport protocols like the User Datagram Protocol (UDP)—covered in Chapter 9. In short, named pipes' own delivery guarantees make transport-level delivery guarantees less essential.

In addition, the Windows NT version of named pipes includes a security feature called **impersonation**. Impersonation permits the server side of the named pipes interface to masquerade as a client that requests a service. This lets the interface itself check the client's access rights to make sure that the client's request is legal before returning any reply to request for data to this interface.

Mailslots File System

Mailslots are like a connectionless version of named pipes (that is, mailslots offer no delivery guarantees, nor acknowledgment of successful receipts of data). Windows NT uses mailslots as an internal method to support nonessential system–to-system communications. Such communications as registering names for computers, domains, and users across a network, passing messages related to the Windows NT browser service, and providing support for broadcasting text messages to users or computers across the network all fall into this category. Outside such lightweight uses, mailslots are used less frequently than named pipes.

IPC PROGRAMMING INTERFACES

Windows NT offers a number of distinct interfaces to support several IPC mechanisms for various kinds of client/server applications. For communications to succeed, the client and server sides of an application must share a common programming interface. Even though there are numerous such options, software developers normally use whichever interface best fits their particular application or the one with which they're most familiar.

Windows NT supports several programming interfaces (please note that external applications may support other programming interfaces, or even implement their own private interfaces). These well-known programming interfaces include NetBIOS, Windows Sockets, RPC, and NetDDE.

NetBIOS

NetBIOS is a widely used, but simple-minded PC client/server IPC mechanism. Because it is so easy to program, it has remained quite popular ever since its definition was published by IBM in 1985. As you may have already surmised, NetBIOS services are required to permit a Microsoft Windows network to operate. Fortunately, however, NetBIOS works with all TDI-compliant transports, including NetBEUI (NBF), NWLink (NetBIOS over NWLink or NWNBLink), and TCP/IP (NBT).

Windows Sockets

Windows Sockets define a standardized and broadly deployed interface to network transports such as TCP/IP and IPX. This interface was created to migrate UNIX applications written to the Berkeley Sockets specification to the Windows environment. But Windows Sockets also make it easier to standardize network communications used on multiple platforms. That's because one socket interface is much like another, even if one runs on UNIX and the other on some variety of Windows (such as Windows NT, where WinSock 2.0 is becoming the standard sockets API).

Windows Sockets appear in many programs that originated as UNIX programs. They include the majority of Internet utilities, especially the most popular of IP utilities—namely, Web browsers, e-mail software, file transfer programs, and so forth.

Remote Procedure Call (RPC)

Remote Procedure Call (RPC) implements IPC tools that can invoke separate programs on remote computers, supply them with input, and collect whatever results they produce when they've finished execution. This permits a single processing task to be distributed among multiple computers, which can improve overall performance and help balance the processing load across numerous machines.

RPC is actually indifferent to where its client and server portions reside: It's possible for both client and server portions of an application to run on a single computer. In that case, they will communicate using Local Procedure Call (LPC) mechanisms. This makes building such applications easy, because they can be constructed on one computer, but it also permits processing to be distributed on only one machine or across many machines, as processing needs dictate. This creates an environment that is both flexible and powerful.

RPC consists of four basic components:

- A remote stub procedure that packages RPC requests for transmission to a server. It's called a stub because it acts as a simple, extremely compact front end to a remote process that may be much larger and more complex elsewhere on the network

- An RPC runtime system to pass data between local and remote machines, or between client and server processes, to state the same relationship in different terms

- An application stub procedure that receives requests from the runtime RPC system. Upon such receipt, this stub procedure formats requests for the designated target RPC computer and makes the necessary procedure call, which may be either a Local Procedure Call (if both client and server components are running on the same computer) or a Remote Procedure Call (if client and server components are running on two machines)

- One or more remote procedures, which may be called for service (whether locally or across the network)

Network Dynamic Data Exchange (NetDDE)

NetDDE creates ongoing data streams called exchange pipes, or more simply pipes, between two applications across a network. This process works just like Microsoft's local DDE, which creates data exchange pipes between two applications on the same machine. DDE is designed to facilitate data sharing, Object Linking and Embedding (OLE), and dynamic updates between linked applications. Simply put, NetDDE extends local DDE across the network.

NetDDE services are installed by default during the base Windows NT installation, but they remain dormant unless they are explicitly started. NetDDE services must be started using the Services applet in the Network control panel, where they appear under the headings Network DDE (the client side of NetDDE) and Network DDE DSDM (the server side of NetDDE; DSDM stands for DDE Share Database Manager). Once either one of these options is selected, click the Start button to start the service for this particular logon session; to make it part of the normal Windows NT Workstation runtime environment at bootup time, click the Startup button instead.

8

REDIRECTORS

As previously stated, a redirector examines all requests for system resources and decides whether such requests are local (that is, they can be found on the requesting machine) or remote. If remote, the redirector handles transmission of such remote requests across the network so that they may be satisfied.

Among other network services, Windows NT file and print sharing are regarded as the most important functions supplied by any network operating system. Windows NT delivers these services through two critical Application layer components (according to the OSI reference model—that is, these are not themselves applications): the Workstation service and the Server service.

Both of these services are essentially file-system drivers that operate in concert with the FAT, NTFS, and CDFS file-system drivers that can access local file systems on a Windows NT machine. The following NT components are all redirectors that operate at this level:

- Workstation service

- Server service

- **Multiple Universal Naming Convention Provider (MUP)**

- **Multi-Provider Router (MPR)**

All of these system components take client requests for service and redirect them to an appropriate network service provider. Redirectors sit at the top of OSI reference model because they interact and interface directly with user applications. In the sections that follow, you'll learn more about each of these components and its role in the Windows NT networking environment.

WORKSTATION SERVICE

This service supports client access to network resources and handles functions like logging on, connecting to network shares (directories and printers), and creating links using NT IPC options. The Workstation service consists of two elements:

- *User mode interface:* Determines the particular file system that any User mode file I/O request is referencing
- *Redirector:* Recognizes and translates requests for remote file and print services and forwards them to lower-level boundary layers aimed at network access (and delivery)

The Workstation service encompasses a redirector file system. This file system handles access to shared directories on networked computers. This file system acts like a wrapper around all file system requests: It will be used further to satisfy remote access requests; but if any request uses a network name to refer to a local resource, it will pass that request to local FAT, CDFS, or NTFS file-system drivers instead.

The Workstation service requires at least one TDI-compliant transport and at least one MUP to be running. If not, it cannot function properly because the Workstation service supports connections with other Windows NT machines (through their Server services), but also with LAN Manager, LAN Server, and other MS–Net servers (these latter elements are what requires a MUP to be running, as you'll learn shortly). The Workstation service, like any other redirector, communicates with transport protocols through the common TDI boundary layer.

SERVER SERVICE

The Windows NT Server service handles creation and management of shared resources and performs security checks against requests for such resources, including directories and printers. The Server service allows an Windows NT computer to act as a server on a client/server network, up to the maximum number of licensed clients. This limits the number of simultaneous connections possible to a Windows NT Workstation machine to 10, in keeping with its built-in connection limitations.

Just as with the Workstation service, the Server service operates as a file-system driver. Therefore, it also uses other file-system drivers to satisfy I/O requests. The Server service is also divided into two elements:

- SERVER.EXE: Manages client connection requests
- SRV.SYS: The redirector file system that operates across the network and interacts with other local file-system drivers when necessary

MULTIPLE UNC PROVIDER (MUP)

Windows NT supports multiple redirectors that can be active simultaneously. As an example, both the Workstation and Server services and the NetWare redirector built into Windows NT Client Service for NetWare (CSNW) can all be active at the same time. Like the Server service, the NetWare redirector handles Microsoft Windows network shares and exposes them to NetWare clients instead of Microsoft network clients. As with other boundary layers discussed so far, this ability to support multiple clients uniformly is possible because a common provider interface has been defined to allow Windows NT to treat all redirectors the same way.

This particular boundary layer is called the Multiple Universal Naming Convention Provider. The MUP defines a link between applications that make UNC requests for different redirectors. MUP allows applications to remain oblivious to the number or type of redirectors that may be in use. For incoming requests, the MUP also decides which redirector should handle that request by parsing the UNC share name that appears within the request.

8

Here's how this works: When the I/O subsystem receives any request that includes a UNC name, it turns that request over to the MUP. The MUP first checks its internal list of recently accessed shares, which it maintains over time. If the MUP recognizes the UNC name, it passes that request to the required redirector immediately. If it doesn't recognize the UNC name, the MUP sends that request to each registered redirector and requests that it service the request.

Because the MUP chooses redirectors on the basis of each one's highest registered response time that the redirector claims it can connect to a UNC name, this information may be cached until no activity occurs for 15 minutes. This can make trying a series of redirectors incredibly time consuming, and helps to explain why the binding order of protocols is so important (because that also influences the order in which name resolution requests will be handled).

Universal Naming Convention (UNC) names represent the format used in NetBIOS-oriented name resolution systems. UNC names precede the computer portion of a name with two slashes, followed by a slash that precedes (and separates elements) of the share name, and the directory path, followed by the requested filename. Thus this string:

```
\\computer\share\dir-path\filename.ext
```

represents a valid UNC name. In this example, the name of the computer is "computer," the name of the share is "share," the directory path is "dir-path," and the file is named "filename.ext."

MULTI-PROVIDER ROUTER (MPR)

Not all programs use UNC names in the Windows NT environment. Those that call the Win32 API must use a file-system service called the Multi-Provider Router (MPR) to designate the proper redirector to handle a resource request. The MPR lets applications written to older Microsoft specifications behave as if they were written to conform with

UNC naming. The MPR is able to recognize the UNCs that represent drive mappings. Thus, the MPR can decide which redirector can handle a mapped network drive letter like X: and make sure that a request that references that drive can be properly satisfied.

The MPR handles all Win32 network API calls; it passes resource requests from that interface to those redirectors that register their presence through special-purpose Dynamic Link Libraries (DLLs). That is, any redirector that wants to support the MPR must provide a DLL that communicates through the common MPR interface. Normally, this means that whichever network developer supplies a redirector must also supply this DLL. That's why Microsoft implemented CSNW as a DLL that supports this interface—this makes the NetWare redirector able to provide the same kind of transparent file system and network resource access as other Windows NT redirectors.

CONFIGURING NETWORK SETTINGS

Managing Windows NT network configurations is simple, especially when compared with other network operating systems. Making configuration changes does require administrator-level system access, however. In general, most networking components are installed or removed using the Network applet in the Control Panel; some services (for example NetDDE) must be managed through the Services applet instead.

There are many ways to launch the Network applet; for example, using the Start, Settings, Control Panel task bar menu entries, then double-clicking the Network applet. In the hands-on projects at the end of the chapter, you will use the Network applet to configure various network settings.

 Two other quick methods to access the Network applet are double-clicking the Control Panel icon in NT Explorer (right above Network Neighborhood) or in the main window of My Computer. You can also drag the Network applet icon to your desktop from the Control Panel window to put a shortcut to this applet within easy reach at all times.

The tabs in the Network applet, which are shown in Figure 8-7, show how network components are accessed and organized. They also provide a point of access to install or remove network components and to change settings for network components.

The best way to learn about the Network applet is to explore its tabs systematically. These tabs are labeled as follows:

- *Identification:* Contains the NT Workstation computer name and supplies names for domain or workgroup membership
- *Services:* Lists all active network services and provides the interface to remove installed services, change their settings, or install inactive services
- *Protocols:* Identifies all protocols currently installed and provides the interface to remove installed protocols, change their settings, or install protocols that are not currently in use

- *Adapters:* Identifies all network adapters that are currently installed and provides an interface to remove installed adapters, change their settings, or add new adapters
- *Bindings:* Specifies the machine's current binding orders (and existing bindings) for network components and provides an interface to remove, add, or reorder such bindings

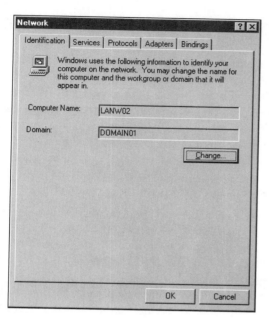

Figure 8-7 Network applet tabs

MANAGING BINDINGS

Binding refers to the order in which Windows NT networking components are linked. These linkages among components, and the order in which multiple components link to a single boundary layer, affect how NT Workstation systems behave, and how well they perform. You'll find this information in the Binding tab in the Network applet.

By default, Windows NT creates as many bindings among networking components as possible. In other words, Windows NT binds any two components that share a common boundary layer, unless such bindings are explicitly removed. In fact, NT binds all components that share a common boundary to the boundary layer they share, unless one or more of these bindings is explicitly removed.

As far as we can tell, Microsoft designed this default to make it as easy as possible to install and use networking services without necessarily understanding all the ins and outs of networking (or the installation and component management processes, for that matter). But because this default is what we can call "complete binding"—that is, all bindings that are possible are created—it can lead to system inefficiencies, especially when bindings are created that will not be used. Even worse, such unused bindings may appear higher in the binding order (as indicated by their position beneath a boundary layer element, where closer indicates higher priority) than bindings that are used. This arrangement can build delays into the system (because the MUP attempts to satisfy UNC requests for names it does not recognize in the order in which bindings appear, and unused bindings must time out before the next binding in the order will be attempted, and so forth).

You will improve system performance, and decrease the likelihood of communication errors, if you disable all protocol bindings that are not needed or used. If remote access with NetBEUI is not required, disable the binding between the NetBEUI transport and the remote access WAN Wrapper (it appears as a "virtual" adapter in the bindings list). It's also important to understand that because clients (in this case Windows NT Workstation machines) initiate communications with NT Servers, changing the binding order of protocols on clients is what matters. Servers only respond using whatever protocol requests appear within, so changing their binding order won't do much to improve performance. Changing a client's binding order, on the other hand, can sometimes deliver dramatic performance improvements.

As already mentioned, binding priority affects network performance. Windows NT makes connections according to the order in which protocols are bound. For two machines that use NetBEUI and TCP/IP, Windows NT uses whichever protocol appears higher in the services binding list. If both computers run NetBEUI and TCP/IP, and NetBEUI ranks higher than TCP/IP in the binding list, then they will establish a faster connection (NetBEUI is faster than TCP/IP) than if the bindings were reversed. To change the priority for any transport protocol, simply highlight that protocol in the Bindings window, then use the Move button to increase (or decrease) its priority level (the details are covered in Hands-on Project 8-3).

CHAPTER SUMMARY

The Windows NT modular architecture follows the same kind of component-oriented approach to networking that the OSI reference model embodies. As you've seen, Windows NT is composed of discrete, individual system components and boundary layers that supply specific network functions, especially for network transports and services, and define the relationships that are possible between such components. Many of these components may be accessed through the Network applet in the Control Panel, through its various tabs.

By default, Windows NT binds all network components that share common boundary layers. It also establishes the protocol priority according to the order in which such components are installed. Particularly where protocols are concerned, it is essential to inspect and manage their binding order, and disable superfluous bindings. This housekeeping activity will allow network administrators to improve network performance and reduce the possibility of communications errors.

KEY TERMS

- **Application layer** — The seventh layer of the OSI model. This is the component that interfaces with User mode applications.
- **binding** — The process of linking network services and protocols in the development of a stack. The binding facility allows users to define exactly how network services operate in order to optimize the network performance of the system.
- **boundary layer** — Microsoft's term for an interface that separates two classes of network or other NT system components. Boundary layers make it much simpler for developers to build general-purpose applications, without requiring them to manage all the details involved in network communications.
- **connectionless** — A class of network transport protocols that makes only a "best-effort" attempt at delivery and includes no explicit mechanisms to guarantee delivery or data integrity in its capabilities. Because such protocols need not be as reliable, they are often much faster and require less overhead than do connection-oriented protocols.
- **connection-oriented** — A class of network transport protocols that includes guaranteed delivery, explicit acknowledgment of data receipt, and a variety of data integrity checks to ensure reliable transmission and reception of data across a network. Reliable, connection-oriented protocols can be slow because of all the overhead and extra communication involved in delivering such a robust level of services.
- **Data Link Control (DLC)** — A network transport protocol that allows connectivity to mainframes, printers, and servers running Remote Program Load software.
- **Data Link layer** — The second layer of the OSI model. This is the layer that provides the digital interconnection of network devices and the software that directly operates these devices, such as network interface cards.
- **Dynamic Data Exchange (DDE)** — A method of interprocess communication within the Windows operating system.
- **frame** — A data structure that network hardware devices use to transmit data between computers. Frames consist of the addresses of the sending and receiving computers, size information, and a Cyclical Redundancy Check (CRC).
- **impersonation** — Permits the server side of a named pipes interface to masquerade as the client that requests some particular service. This lets the interface check the client's access rights, to make sure that the request is legal before returning any reply to that client.
- **Internet Packet Exchange (IPX)** — The network and transport layer protocol developed by Novell for its NetWare product. IPX is a routable, connection-oriented protocol similar to TCP/IP but much easier to manage and with lower communication overhead.
- **Internet Packet Exchange/Sequenced Packet Exchange (IPX/SPX)** — The name of the two primary protocols developed by Novell for its NetWare network operating system. IPX/SPX is derived from the XNS protocol stack, and leans heavily on its architecture and functionality. See also IPX and SPX.
- **Internet Protocol (IP)** — The Network layer protocol upon which the Internet is based. IP provides a simple connectionless transmission that relies on higher layer protocols to establish reliability.
- **Interprocess Communication (IPC)** — The mechanism describing those processes operating in the Application layer. They are foundations for client/server communication.
- **mailslots** — A connectionless messaging IPC mechanism that Windows NT uses for browse requests and logon authentication.

8

- **Multiple Universal Naming Convention Provider (MUP)** — A software component of Windows NT that allows two or more UNC providers, for example, for Microsoft networks and NetWare networks to exist simultaneously. The MUP determines which UNC provider will handle a particular UNC request and forwards the request to that provider.
- **Multi-Provider Router (MPR)** — A file-system service that can designate the proper redirector to handle a resource request that does not use UNC naming. The MPR lets applications written to older Microsoft specifications behave as if they used UNC naming; thus, the MPR is able to recognize those UNCs that correspond to defined drive mappings.
- **named pipes** — An Interprocess Communication mechanism that is implemented as a file system that handles connection-oriented messaging.
- **NetBIOS Extended User Interface (NetBEUI)** — A simple transport protocol developed to support NetBIOS installations. NetBEUI is not routable, and so it is not appropriate for larger networks.
- **Network Basic Input/Output System (NetBIOS)** — A client/server interprocess communication service developed by IBM in 1985. NetBIOS presents a relatively primitive mechanism for communication in client/server applications, but allows an easy implementation across various Microsoft Windows computers.
- **Network Driver Interface Specification (NDIS)** — A Microsoft specification to which network adapter drivers must conform in order to work with Microsoft network operating systems.
- **Network Dynamic Data Exchange (NetDDE)** — An Interprocess Communication mechanism developed by Microsoft to support the distribution of DDE applications over a network.
- **Network layer** — The layer of the OSI model that creates a communication path between two computers via routed packets. Transport protocols implement both the Network and Transport layers of the OSI model.
- **NWLink** — A Windows NT transport protocol that implements Novell's IPX. NWLink is useful as a general-purpose transport for Windows NT and for connecting to NetWare File servers through CSNW.
- **OSI (Open System Interconnection) reference model** — The standard (ISO 9472) that defines a seven-layered model for how networks operate and behave.
- **packet** — A well-defined block of bytes, which consists of a header, a data portion (also known as the payload), and an optional trailer. In layered network architectures, like those described by the OSI reference model, packets created at one layer may be inserted into another header/trailer envelope at lower layers as they make their way down a protocol stack.
- **Physical layer** — The OSI layer that enables communication with cables, connectors, and connection ports of a network. The passive physical components required to create a network.
- **Presentation layer** — The layer of the OSI model that converts and translates information between the Session and Application layers.
- **Protocol Data Unit (PDU)** — OSI terminology for the organization of a packet specific to some particular layer of a protocol stack. In the OSI reference model, the PDU at the Network layer is called a datagram and the PDU at the Data link layer is called a frame.

- **Remote Procedure Call (RPC)** — A network Interprocess Communication mechanism that allows an application to be distributed among many computers on the same network.
- **Sequenced Packet Exchange (SPX)** — A connection-oriented Session-layer protocol used in the NetWare environment when guaranteed delivery is required.
- **Session layer** — The layer of the OSI model dedicated to maintaining a bidirectional communication connection between two computers.
- **Transmission Control Protocol/Internet Protocol (TCP/IP)** — A suite of Internet protocols upon which the global Internet is based. TCP/IP is the default protocol for NT.
- **Transport Driver Interface (TDI)** — A specification to which all Windows NT transport protocols must be written in order to be used by higher layer services such as programming interfaces, file systems, and Interprocess Communication mechanisms.
- **Transport layer** — The OSI model layer responsible for the guaranteed serial delivery of packets between two computers over an internetwork. TCP is the Transport layer protocol for the TCP/IP transport protocol.
- **transport protocol** — A protocol that handles the functions specified at the Transport layer in the OSI reference model (see preceding definition). For TCP/IP, TCP is a transport layer protocol; for IPX/SPX, IPX handles some transport layer functions.
- **Universal Naming Convention (UNC)** — A multi-vendor, multi-platform convention for identifying shared resources on a network.
- **Windows Sockets (WinSock)** — A standard Windows programming interface for networked information exchange, modeled after the Berkeley Sockets interface, designed to make it easy to transport or recreate applications written to the Berkeley Sockets interface in the Windows environment.
- **Xerox Networking System (XNS)** — An early networking protocol stack, XNS was developed at Xerox Parc in the 1970s to network that company's proprietary workstations. A four-layer model informs this protocol stack, which is the progenitor of the Novell IPX/SPX protocol stack, among others.

8

REVIEW QUESTIONS

1. Named pipes are which type of component?

   a. programming interface

   b. file system

   c. transport protocol

   d. Transport Driver Interface (TDI)

2. Which of the following are Windows NT APIs that an application might use to access the network? (Choose all that apply.)

   a. NetDDE

   b. Windows NT redirector

   c. Workstation service

   d. Transport Driver Interface (TDI)

3. Once a software component is installed in Windows NT, it must be removed before it can be reconfigured. True or False?

4. Of the following definitions, which best describes the Windows NT MUP?

    a. handles links between applications and multiple redirectors transparently

    b. resolves UNC names for applications

    c. translates non–UNC references into UNC names

    d. controls bindings between network services and transport protocols

5. Of the following definitions, which best describes the MPR and what it does?

    a. handles links between applications and multiple redirectors transparently

    b. resolves UNC names for applications

    c. translates non–UNC references into UNC names

    d. controls bindings between network services and transport protocols

6. The Programming interfaces use the ___EUI___ interface to exchange data with protocol stacks.

7. NWLink can be used only to attach to NetWare file servers. True or False?

8. More than one redirector can be active in Windows NT. True or False?

9. Programming interfaces are the boundary between the Application layer and user applications. True or False?

10. The NDIS boundary layer allows any number of adapters to be bound to any number of transport protocols. True or False?

11. Of the following choices, which are members of the three primary network transports used with Windows NT? (Choose all that apply.)

    a. NetBIOS

    b. TCP/IP

    c. IPX/SPX

    d. DLC

12. Of the following, which represent valid differences between NDIS 3.0 and previous NDIS versions? (Choose all that apply.)

    a. replaces PROTMAN with the NDIS Wrapper

    b. supports multiple protocols across multiple NICs simultaneously

    c. supports Plug and Play capability

    d. requires NICs to use NDIS 3.0-compliant drivers

13. RPC is a valuable IPC mechanism because (Choose all that apply.)

    a. It permits processes on the same machine, or across the network, to communicate.

    b. It supports development on a single machine, but deployment across a network.

    c. It is powerful and flexible.

    d. It requires using Microsoft's Object Linking and Embedding (OLE) technologies.

14. Which of the following is not installed by default in Windows NT?

    a. TCP/IP

    b. NetBIOS

    c. NWLink

    d. Workstation Service

15. Which of the following transports cannot be routed? (Choose all that apply.)

    a. TCP/IP

    b. NWLink

    c. NetBEUI

    d. DLC

    e. AppleTalk

16. The OSI reference model incorporates how many layers?

    a. five

    b. six

    c. seven

    d. eight

17. Boundary layers serve to facilitate development of network adapter drivers, transport protocols, file systems, and other network components. True or False?

18. The Browser service allows users to peruse and select network resources and objects from within My Computer, NT Explorer, and other windows with browse buttons. True or False?

19. Of the following transport protocols, which is the fastest and best suited for small single-segment LANs?

    a. TCP/IP

    b. NWLink

    c. NetBEUI

    d. DLC

20. The Data Link Control (DLC) protocol supports which two of the following network functions?

    a. direct connection to IBM mainframes

    b. terminal emulation services

    c. network routing

    d. access to network-attached printers

8

Hands-on Projects

Project 8-1

To install a transport protocol:

1. Open the Network applet (**Start**, **Settings**, **Control Panel**, then double-click the **Network** icon).

2. Select the **Protocols** tab.

3. Click the **Add** button. Your computer takes a short time to build a list of options to choose from.

4. Select **NWLink IPX/SPX Compatible Transport** from the Protocols option list and click **OK**. This selection is highlighted in Figure 8-8.

5. Enter the path to your CD-ROM install files and click **OK**. Normally this path will be either the path to the I386 directory on the NT Workstation CD-ROM or a shared directory.

6. Click the **Close** button to complete the operation.

7. Click **Yes** to restart your computer.

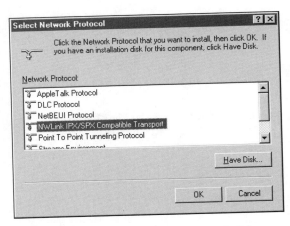

Figure 8-8   Network applet Protocols tab

PROJECT 8-2

To view network bindings:

1. Launch Windows NT Explorer (**Start**, **Programs**, **Windows NT Explorer**), then right-click **Network Neighborhood** and select **Properties**.
2. Select the **Bindings** tab.
3. Double-click **Workstation**. The resulting display appears in Figure 8-9.
4. Select the **NWLink NetBIOS** protocol.
5. Click the **plus sign** to the left of the name. Notice how the NWLink IPS/SPX Compatible Transport listing appears.
6. Click the **Close** button.

8

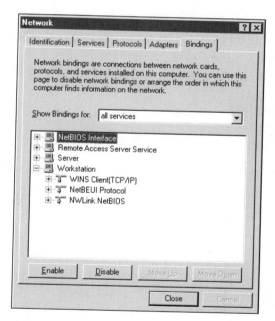

Figure 8-9   Network applets Bindings tab

PROJECT 8-3

To change network bindings:

1. Double-click **My Computer**, double-click the **Control Panel** icon, then double-click the **Network** applet.

2. Select the **Bindings** tab.

3. Click the list arrow for the **show Bindings for:** text box. The resulting display appears in Figure 8-10. Select the **all services** entry in the list.

4. Click the **plus sign** to the left of the **NetBIOS Interface** entry to expand its display.

5. Select the **NWLink NetBIOS** protocol to highlight it.

6. Click the **Move Up** button in the lower-right corner of the Bindings tab window. Notice how this advances the NWLink NetBIOS from the bottom to the middle position in the binding order.

7. Click the **OK** button at the bottom of the window. Notice how the computer saves the updated bindings, and displays a "progress bar" to show it's hard at work.

8. Click **Yes** to restart your computer so the new settings may take effect.

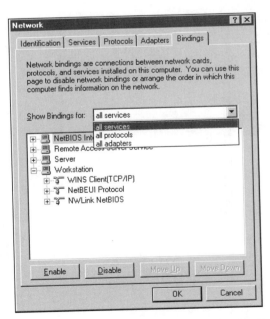

Figure 8-10   Changing binding order for the NetBIOS interface

PROJECT 8-4

To remove a protocol:

1. Double-click **My Computer**, double-click the **Control Panel** icon, then double-click the **Network** applet.

2. Select the **Protocols** tab.

3. Highlight the **NWLink IPX/SPX Compatible Transport** entry, as shown in Figure 8-11.

4. Click the **Remove** button.

5. This produces a warning message that reads "This action will permanently remove the component from the system. If you wish to reinstall it, you will have to restart the system before doing so. Do you still wish to continue?" Click the **Yes** button.

6. You've now removed the same protocol you installed and whose bindings you manipulated in previous exercises.

8

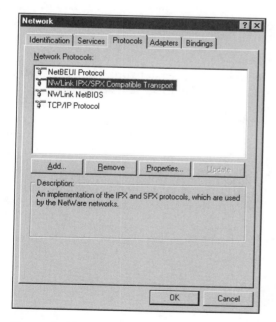

Figure 8-11   Removing a protocol

CASE PROJECTS

1. As a network administrator at XYZ Corp., you always hear about it when performance problems arise on the network. In the past two weeks, you've been involved in switching the network over from using NetBEUI exclusively, to a mixture of NetBEUI and TCP/IP. You've installed TCP/IP on all NT Servers and Workstations, and made sure that all the machines are configured properly.

   Because the network is growing, and an additional cable segment has been added, with more planned for the future, you plan to switch entirely from NetBEUI to TCP/IP over time. Yet, all of a sudden, your users complain that the network has slowed dramatically. What steps can you take that might potentially speed performance, and which machines should you make changes on2 Workstations only, Servers only, or both?

2. You've been hired to consult with Macaroni and Associates, a small pasta factory on the outskirts of town. They have 10 employees, with no immediate plans to grow, and all their computer equipment is located in a single 20 x 20 room, with no plans to expand. Furthermore, they have no full-time network administrator, nor do they plan to hire one.

   Discuss the pros and cons of adopting each of the three primary Windows NT protocols: NetBEUI, NWLink, and TCP/IP. Select the protocol that makes the most sense for their situation, and defend your choice. What happens to your selection if they decide to start selling pasta over the Internet? What protocol should you choose in that case?

3. The Acme Brick Company has decided to install a network. They have offices in two locations in Chicago, a factory in a nearby small town, and another factory in Des Moines. You've been asked to advise them on their choice of networking protocols and have learned that their primary supplier at the Leon Clay Mine uses NetWare servers. Ultimately, the company wants to be able to exchange files and e-mail through a private network link to the mine.

   Discuss the pros and cons of adopting each of the three primary Windows NT protocols: NetBEUI, NWLink, and TCP/IP. Explain why a combination of protocols may make sense. Select those protocols that fit their situation best, and defend your choice.

TCP/IP AND NETWARE CONNECTIVITY

Although Windows NT supports numerous protocols, its two enterprise-scale protocols are TCP/IP and NWLink (the latter is an implementation of the Novell IPX/SPX protocol suite originally developed for NetWare). In this chapter, you learn more about the role these protocols can play in the Windows NT environment. You learn how to understand and assign IP addresses, how to configure and manage the TCP/IP environment on Windows NT Workstation, and about the IP-based tools and utilities available for NT Workstation. In the sections on NWLink, you learn about its addressing and management, and about the various interoperability options available in the Windows NT environment to let Windows NT Workstation clients interact with NetWare-based resources and to let NetWare clients access Microsoft network-based resources.

AFTER READING THIS CHAPTER AND COMPLETING THE EXERCISES YOU WILL BE ABLE TO:

- DISCUSS THE ROLE OF TCP/IP AND TCP/IP-RELATED UTILITIES INCLUDED WITH WINDOWS NT WORKSTATION
- CONFIGURE TCP/IP FOR WINDOWS NT WORKSTATION
- DISCUSS NETWARE CONNECTIVITY FOR WINDOWS NT WORKSTATION COMPUTERS
- TROUBLESHOOT NETWARE CONNECTIVITY PROBLEMS

TCP/IP ARCHITECTURE

As you learned in Chapter 8, the Transmission Control Protocol/Internet Protocol (TCP/IP) is the suite of protocols most widely used today. It supports easy cross–platform communications and provides the technical foundation for the worldwide Internet. However, because TCP/IP predates the OSI reference model by nearly 10 years, their architectures differ a bit.

The TCP/IP suite consists of only four layers compared to the OSI model's seven. These layers are: the Network Interface, Internet, Transport, and Application layers. Figure 9-1 compares the TCP/IP architecture to the OSI model.

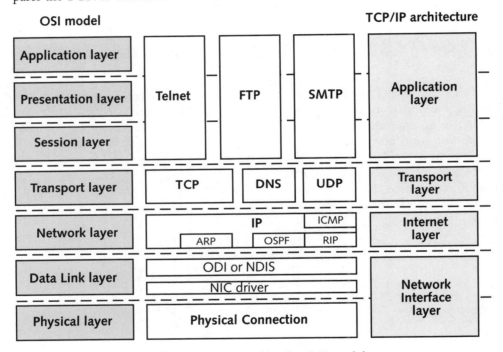

Figure 9-1   TCP/IP architecture compared to the OSI model

TCP/IP NETWORK INTERFACE LAYER

The TCP/IP **Network Interface layer** roughly corresponds to the Data Link and Physical layers of the OSI model. Unlike the OSI reference model, which treats equivalent layers as peers, the TCP/IP suite does not specify how data is passed from the Internet layer on the sending side, through the Network Interface layer, then across the wire to the Network Interface layer on the receiving side, and on to the Internet layer on the receiving end.

In the TCP/IP protocol suite, the Network Interface layer represents a series of steps that must take place for network communications to occur. But, unlike the OSI reference model, this series of steps is not considered part of the protocol suite. Instead, it is the responsibility of developers who build drivers that permit the protocol stack to communicate with networking hardware to gain access to the networking media. Fortunately, this does not impose a threat to interoperability because the series of steps prescribed for the Network Interface layer is detailed enough to more or less guarantee that any successful implementation works with other, similar implementations.

From the TCP/IP perspective, therefore, the Microsoft **Network Device Interface Specification (NDIS)**, which allows multiple protocols to be bound to one or more network adapters, operates at the Network Interface layer.

TCP/IP INTERNET LAYER

As shown in Figure 9-1, the TCP/IP **Internet layer** corresponds to the OSI Network layer. It is responsible for addressing and for internetwork communication. Some of the protocols that operate at the Internet layer are outlined in the following sections.

Internet Protocol (IP)

The **Internet Protocol (IP)** is an OSI Network layer protocol that provides source and destination addressing and routing in the TCP/IP suite. IP is a connectionless datagram protocol that, like all connectionless protocols, is fast but unreliable. It assumes that other protocols will ensure reliable delivery of the data.

IP is responsible for addressing and routing in the TCP/IP environment. IP addresses are logical addresses that are 32 bits (4 bytes) long. Each byte, or octet, is represented by a decimal number from 0 to 255 and separated from those that follow by a period—for example, 183.24.206.18.

Although eight bits have 256 possible combinations, the numbers 0 and 255 are reserved for special purposes. The zero address is reserved to identify the network, and the 255 address is used for broadcasts, which will be read by all IP hosts on the network. Thus, IP network hosts can use only numbers 1 through 254. Note also that "host" is the IP-specific term that identifies any device on an IP network that is assigned a specific address.

Part of the IP address assigned to a computer designates which network the computer is on, and the remainder of the address represents the host ID of that computer. The four bytes (or octets, in IP terms) that IP uses for addresses can be broken up in multiple ways; in fact, several classes of IP addresses have been defined that use different boundaries for the network part and the host ID part. These are shown in Table 9-1.

0 class A

10 Class B

110 Class C

Table 9-1   Classes of IP Addresses

Class	Network IDs	Host IDs	Usable Network IDs
A	126	16,777,214	1–126
B	16,328	65,534	128.1–191.259
C	2,097,150	254	192.0.1–223.255.254

In a Class A address, the first octet identifies the network, and the three trailing octets identify the hosts. This creates a situation where a small number of networks (126, to be exact) is possible, but a large number of hosts (over 16 million per network) may be defined on each one. Class B addresses split the octets evenly, so that the first two identify the network, and the second two identify the host. This permits a relatively large number of networks (over 16,000) with a relatively large number of hosts (over 65,000). Class C addresses use the first three octets for the network portion and the final octet for the host portion of an address. This permits a large number of networks (over 2 million) but only a relatively small number of hosts for each Class C network (254 maximum).

For example, a computer with an address of 183.24.206.18 has a Class B address (because the first two octets fall in the range of 128.1–191.259 as indicated in the fourth column of Table 9-1). Thus, the first two octets represent the network address—namely, 183.24, and the host address portion is 206.18. The computer next to it might have the address of 183.24.208.192, which indicates that it's on the same network (183.24) but has a different host address (208.192).

IP uses a special bit mask called a **subnet mask** to determine which part of an address denotes the network and which part the host. The job of the subnet mask is to block out the network section of the address so that only the host ID portion remains significant. Thus, for the addresses on the 183.24 network mentioned in the preceding paragraph, the subnet mask could be stated as 255.255.0.0: Notice that the two most significant octets are occupied by a binary value that translates into all ones (255 is 11111111 in binary), and the network portion is all zeros (0 is the same as 00000000 in binary).

Sometimes, savvy IP network administrators will actually use part of what the IP address class considers the host portion of an address to further subdivide a single Class A, B, or C network into even smaller partitions. That is why you may see the occasional subnet mask that looks like 255.192 for a Class A, 255.255.192 for a Class B, and 255.255.255.192 for a Class C. Because 192 equals 11000000 in binary, this extends the network portion two digits into the host ID portion of the address and permits two subnets to be defined within a single range of host addresses (because the top and bottom values—0 and 3 in this case—remain reserved to identify the subnetwork and handle broadcasts, respectively).

Another form of addressing is increasingly used on IP networks, especially when individual networks don't need or can't consume an entire Class B or Class C address. This technique is called Classless Interdomain Routing (CIDR, pronounced "sidder" or "cider") and uses the same kind of technique described in the preceding paragraph to let Internet Service Providers carve up their available addresses into more numerous subnetworks, to make better use of the IP address space that's still available.

On the Internet—and in fact, on any IP-based network—all TCP/IP addresses must be unique. If two IP addresses are the same, neither machine that shares that address will be able to access the network. That's why managing IP addresses is quite important. Today, this responsibility falls under the aegis of the Internet Network Information Center (InterNIC). All the Class A addresses were handed out years ago; most Class Bs have been allocated, and even Class C addresses are becoming scarce (if you add all possible numbers of networks allowed by all three address classes, this puts the maximum number of individual networks on the Internet at 2,113,604). Given the vast number of networks on the Internet and the continuing hunger of new organizations to join in the fun, it should be clear that subnet masking tricks and CIDR merely represent stopgap measures to extend the current address space as much as possible. In the meantime, the standards body that governs the Internet (the IAB, or Internet Activities Board) is working frantically to complete a new version of TCP/IP called IPv6 (the current version is IPv4) that will extend the address space significantly (the address space expands to 128 bits, as compared to the current 32 bits; this is enough to support trillions of networks with trillions of nodes per network!).

 All IP-based devices on a single network segment must use the same subnet mask.

Internet Control Message Protocol (ICMP)

The **Internet Control Message Protocol (ICMP)** is an OSI Network layer protocol used to send control messages (such as error messages, quality of service information, and confirmations) between IP hosts. The PING (Packet Internet Groper) utility requests a response from a remote host. It uses the ICMP to return messages regarding this function, such as whether the response was received or timed-out, or the host was not reachable.

Address Resolution Protocol (ARP)

The **Address Resolution Protocol (ARP)** is another OSI Network layer protocol used to associate a logical (IP) address to a physical (MAC) address. When a system begins a conversation with a host for which it does not have a physical address, it sends an ARP broadcast packet requesting a physical address that corresponds to the logical address defined by the numeric IP address. Given this information, the Data Link layer can correctly send the packet across a physical network.

Because Ethernet is the most common form of network in use, the MAC address is identical to the Ethernet address on most networks. The Ethernet address takes a form that's represented as 00:00:00:00:00:00, or six hexadecimal digits separated by colons. In other words, on an Ethernet network, the physical or MAC address is the same as the Ethernet address burned into PROM (Programmable Read-Only Memory) on the network interface card that attaches a computer to a network. On other types of networks, the interfaces also supply unique MAC layer addresses, but their formats vary according to the kind of network in use.

Dynamic Host Configuration Protocol (DHCP)

The **Dynamic Host Configuration Protocol (DHCP)** is used to automatically configure IP addresses. A DHCP server manages a defined block of IP addresses that can be assigned to computers upon request. End users basically take out a "lease" on an address and may use that address only for as long as the lease remains valid. The DHCP server handles granting such leases, renewing, or canceling them. It can also block out reserved IP addresses within a numeric range, permitting certain computers (which may not be able to communicate with the DCHP server) to obtain static, fixed IP address assignments within the same address pool that the DHCP server manages dynamically for computers that can communicate with it.

Using DHCP makes it easy for network administrators to manage IP addresses, and makes it more or less automatic for users to gain access to IP-based resources. DHCP has proven to be a real boon for those reasons. Similarly, one of the best features about Windows NT Workstation is its ability to be configured for TCP/IP by selecting a single radio button in the IP interface that reads Obtain an IP address from a DHCP server.

TCP/IP TRANSPORT LAYER

The TCP/IP **Transport layer** maps to the Transport layer of the OSI model and is responsible for establishing and maintaining host-to-host communication. The primary IP Transport layer protocols are TCP and UDP.

Transmission Control Protocol (TCP)

Transmission Control Protocol (TCP) is the primary Internet transport protocol. It accepts messages of any length from an upper-layer protocol and provides transportation to a TCP peer on a remote network host. TCP is connection-oriented, so it provides more reliable delivery than connectionless-oriented IP. When a connection is established, a TCP port number determines which process on the designated host is to receive any particular packet. TCP is responsible for message fragmentation and reassembly. It uses a sequencing function to ensure that packets are reassembled in the correct order, and it includes mechanisms to acknowledge successful delivery of correct packets and to request retransmission of damaged or lost packets.

User Datagram Protocol (UDP)

User Datagram Protocol (UDP) is a connectionless Transport layer protocol. Due to its reduced overhead, it is generally faster, although less reliable, than TCP. UDP was designed primarily to transport purely local services, where network reliability is relatively safe to assume. That helps explain why it's used for distributed file systems like the Network File System (NFS) and also for the Trivial File Transfer Protocol (TFTP), where the underlying assumption is that access is either purely local (NFS) or that guaranteed delivery is not required (TFTP).

TCP/IP APPLICATION LAYER

The TCP/IP **Application layer** corresponds to all upper layers of the OSI model: Session, Presentation, and Application. Because this layer is responsible for presenting data to the user, its protocols are the most familiar to users. Some of the best-known TCP/IP Application layer protocols include FTP, Telnet, SMTP, and SNMP. These are covered briefly in the sections that follow.

9

File Transfer Protocol (FTP)

File Transfer Protocol (FTP) is an upper-layer protocol that works cooperatively at the OSI Session, Presentation, and Application layers. FTP provides file transfer services, plus directory and file manipulation services (list directory contents, delete file, specify file format, and so on).

Mapping from the OSI reference model to the TCP/IP network model, each of the upper OSI layers provides its specific services to FTP; for example, the Session layer provides connection establishment and release; the Presentation layer provides platform-specific file formatting services, and the Application layer handles the interface between the network and a user's local file system, or a related FTP client application.

A command-line version of FTP is available as part of Windows NT Workstation. To learn more about this command, open a DOS window (Start, Programs, Command Prompt) and enter *FTP ?* at the command line. This produces the Help file for that command.

Telnet

Telnet is not an acronym for anything. **Telnet** is a remote terminal emulation protocol, which also operates across all three upper OSI layers. It is used primarily to provide connectivity between dissimilar systems (PC and VAX/VMS, PC and router, UNIX and VMS), where the remote client works on the Telnet host machine as if it were simply a terminal attached directly to that host. Using Telnet, remote equipment (such as routers and switches) can be monitored and configured, or remote systems can be operated as needed. Despite a primitive, character-oriented interface, Telnet remains one of the most important IP Application layer services.

A 32-bit GUI version of Telnet is available as part of Windows NT Workstation. To learn more about this utility, launch Telnet (Start, Programs, Accessories, Telnet or Start, Run, Telnet) and access its Help utility.

Simple Mail Transport Protocol (SMTP)

The **Simple Mail Transport Protocol (SMTP)** is another protocol that operates across all three upper OSI layers. As its name implies, SMTP is used to provide IP-based messaging services. Although it is not the only e-mail protocol available in the IP environment, most experts regard SMTP as the basis for Internet e-mail. Among other e-mail protocols, the Microsoft Mail application (which shows up as the Inbox icon by default on the Windows NT Workstation desktop) supports SMTP.

Simple Network Management Protocol (SNMP)

The **Simple Network Management Protocol (SNMP)** is a TCP/IP protocol used for network management. It is an industry-standard protocol supported by most networking equipment manufacturers. SNMP supports the ability to query collections of management data, called Management Information Bases (MIBs), on networked devices. This permits management applications to use SNMP to poll devices on the network and obtain regular status updates about their operating conditions and about network utilization and quality of service.

In addition, SNMP supports a "trap" mechanism that permits networked devices to send a message to a management application when specific events or error conditions occur. This latter capability is quite important because it permits networked devices to report potential or actual problems as soon as they're detected, rather than waiting for a management application to poll the device.

SNMP services are not activated by default on Windows NT Workstation. To enable these services, it is necessary to add them to your runtime environment in the Services applet (Start, Programs, Settings, Services, then the Add button) and then to activate them once they appear in the list of installed services in the applet's main display area.

The Berkeley R Utilities

The implementation of TCP/IP present in UNIX in the Berkeley Software Distribution (BSD) in the 1980s included a collection of IP-based network commands collectively known as the "R utilities," where the "R" stands for remote. This includes such commands as **rsh** (Remote shell), which permits a user on one network host to access shell commands on another network host and **rexec** (Remote execution), which permits a user on one network host to execute a program remotely across the network on another network host.

Windows NT Workstation supports both of these R utilities from the client side (but cannot act as a rsh or rexec server to other machines elsewhere on the network).

> To learn more about rsh and rexec, start a DOS window (Start, Programs, Command Prompt) and enter either *rsh ?* or *rexec ?* at the command prompt to access the Help files for these command-line utilities.

Packet Internet Groper (PING)

PING, which stands for Packet Internet Groper, is a command-line utility that uses the ICMP protocol to inquire if a designated host is reachable on the network and also provides information about the round-trip time required to deliver a message to that machine and receive a reply.

PING is actually a very handy utility that will permit you to see if your own machine is properly attached to the network. You can PING yourself by entering the command *PING 127.0.0.1* or *PING loopback*; in the latter case, this special address is defined as the loopback address, or the address of your own machine. You can find out if the network itself is working (by PINGing a nearby machine). Finally, you can determine if some particular machine is reachable (by PINGing either its host name or the equivalent numeric IP address). These capabilities come in handy when installing and testing IP on a new machine, or when you must troubleshoot a network connection.

9

> To learn more about PING, launch a DOS window (Start, Programs, Command Prompt) and enter *PING* (with no arguments) at the command prompt to access its online Help file. Note that PING can also supply all kinds of routing and quality of service data, as well as simply test for reachability.

Trivial File Transfer Protocol (TFTP)

The **Trivial File Transfer Protocol (TFTP)** is a lightweight analog of FTP; it uses UDP as its transport protocol rather than TCP. TFTP is a much more stripped-down version of file transfer services than FTP; all it basically supports is the ability to communicate with a TFTP server elsewhere on the network and to copy files from the workstation to a remote host or vice versa. For directory navigation, file grooming, or format translations, FTP is a much better choice.

> To learn more about TFTP, start a DOS window (Start, Programs, Command Prompt), and enter *TFTP ?* to view its online Help file.

Domain Name Service (DNS)

The **Domain Name Service (DNS)** is a critical component in the Internet's ability to span the globe. DNS handles the job of translating symbolic names like *lanw02.lanw.com* into a corresponding numeric IP address (172.16.1.7). It can also provide reverse lookup services to detect machines that are masquerading as other hosts (a reverse lookup obtains the symbolic name that goes with an IP address; if the two do not match, the DNS server may assume that some form of deception is at work).

DNS is a powerful, highly distributed database that organizes IP names (which for its purposes must take the form of Fully Qualified Domain Names or FQDNs) into hierarchical domains. When a name resolution request occurs, all the DNS servers that can identify themselves to each other cooperate very quickly to resolve the related address. DNS servers include sophisticated caching techniques that permit them to store recently requested name–address pairs, so that users can get to a previously accessed address quite quickly.

 Windows NT Workstation can communicate with DNS servers—only Windows NT Server supports a full-fledged DNS server implementation.

TCP/IP CONFIGURATION

As with many components of Windows NT, TCP/IP configuration is performed through the Control Panel. The Network applet manages the configuration of all networking components, from NICs to services to protocols. Figure 9-2 shows the Network applet Protocols tab. To configure TCP/IP, select TCP/IP Protocol and press the Properties button.

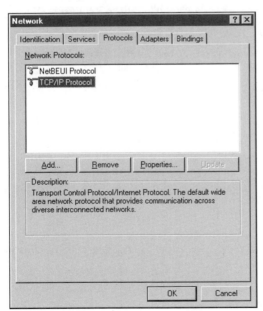

Figure 9-2 Network applet Protocols tab

When configuring TCP/IP for Windows NT Workstation, you may need to know many items of information. If the machine will use DHCP, the DHCP server handles all these details; if not, here's a list of information that you may need to obtain from a network administrator (or figure out for yourself, if that's your job):

- A unique IP address for the computer.

- The subnet mask for the network to which the computer belongs.

- The address of the default gateway, which is the machine that will attempt to forward any IP traffic not aimed at the local subnet (which makes it the gateway to other networks, hence the name).

- The address of one or more DNS servers, to provide IP name resolution services. This is more important on bigger networks than on smaller ones; if you use an Internet Service Provider (ISP) for network access, you'll probably need to get this address from them.

- On Windows NT networks in particular, and IP-based Microsoft networks in general, you may need to provide an address for a WINS (Windows Internet Name Service) server. This permits NetBIOS name resolution requests to be transported across IP networks (and even through routers if necessary). This will be especially important if IP is the only protocol in use on a Windows NT-based internetwork.

You'll learn more about each of these topics in the sections that follow, but this is a good checklist of the information you may need to completely configure TCP/IP on a Windows NT Workstation machine.

IP ADDRESS TAB

IP Address is the first tab displayed when the TCP/IP Properties window opens. Figure 9-3 shows the options available on this tab.

On a multihomed system (a computer with more than one network interface card), the configuration for each adapter can be different. To select the adapter to configure, choose it from the Adapter list.

There are two ways to assign an IP address to a computer: manually or via DHCP. As discussed earlier, DHCP is used to automatically configure the TCP/IP settings for a computer. If a DHCP server is available and it will be used to configure this computer, select the Obtain an IP address from a DHCP server option. If there is no DHCP server available, or the configuration is to be handled manually, select the Specify an IP address option.

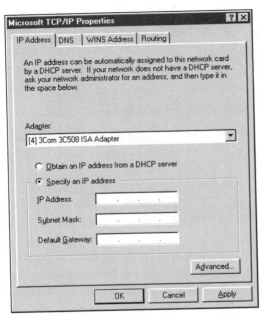

Figure 9-3   IP Address tab in the TCP/IP Properties dialog box

Before you can specify an IP address, however, you must obtain a valid IP address from a network administrator or your ISP. If your network has no requirement to access the Internet directly (or address translation software mediates Internet access on your behalf), you can assign "private IP" addresses from a number of reserved address ranges that the InterNIC has set aside for this purpose. To learn more about these private address ranges and how to use them, download a copy of RFC 1918 from the InterNIC at *ftp://ds.internet.net/rfc/rfc1918.txt* (as an alternative, you can read a hypertext version of this document at *http://www.cis.ohio-state.edu/rfc/rfc1918.txt*).

If you select Specify an IP address, the remaining three boxes become active. When you're finished, the IP Address box should display the correct IP address for that computer.

If you're entering an IP address into an entry box, press the period key to jump from one octet to the next. This comes in handy when an address does not contain a three-digit number in any octet field. You can also use the right arrow key to advance the cursor, but *don't* use the Tab key—it advances the cursor to the next input field and forces you to backtrack to complete the IP address specification!

As described earlier, the subnet mask defines which part of the IP address represents the network and which part represents the host. You must supply this information, or your computer will not be able to communicate using TCP/IP.

The default gateway for a computer defines the host, usually a router, to which the computer should send data that is not destined for the computer's subnet. For example, if a computer's address is 156.24.99.10 with a subnet mask of 255.255.255.0, its host address is 10 and its network address is 156.24.99. If this computer had data to send to a computer whose address was 203.15.13.69, it would send the packets to the default gateway for forwarding to the appropriate network. Thus, whenever connectivity to other networks is required, you must provide an IP address for the default gateway on the machine's network segment. If you don't, no traffic from your machine will be able to get to machines that aren't on the same network segment as your computer.

Pressing the Advanced button opens the window shown in Figure 9-4. The IP Addresses area allows multiple addresses to be assigned to one network adapter, and the Gateways area provides support for multiple router configurations. In addition, Point-to-Point Tunneling Protocol (PPTP) filtering and advanced IP, TCP, and UDP security can be enabled and configured.

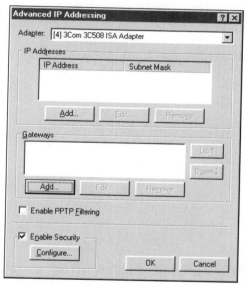

Figure 9-4   Advanced options for IP addressing in Windows NT

DNS TAB

Domain Name Service (DNS) is an OSI Transport layer, name-to-address resolution protocol. A DNS server keeps a list of systems' names and their IP addresses. Through a properly configured workstation, a user can use the system's logical name, such as *microsoft.com*, rather than its numerical address when communicating.

By selecting the DNS tab, shown in Figure 9-5, users are able to configure DNS on their computers. The Host Name: and Domain: settings define the configuration for the local computer. DNS Service Search Order lists all available DNS servers and the order in which the computer will address them when attempting to resolve a name to an address. To add a new DNS server to the list, click the Add button and provide the IP address for the DNS server. Domain Suffix Search Order specifies the order in which the computer will search for a domain name. Configuring this item is optional.

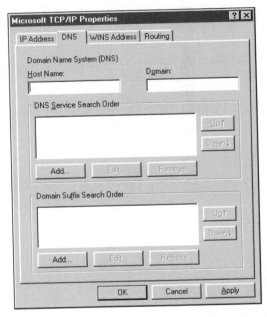

Figure 9-5   DNS tab for TCP/IP properties

WINS ADDRESS TAB

Windows Internet Name Service (WINS) is another resolution service used by Microsoft networks to resolve NetBIOS names to IP addresses. As discussed in Chapter 8, NetBIOS names uniquely identify computers in a Windows NT network. A WINS server maintains a list of NetBIOS names and their associated IP addresses. The WINS Address tab, shown in Figure 9-6, allows users to specify the WINS configuration for their computers.

The Adapter option on the WINS Address tab, like the Adapter option on other configuration tabs, allows separate configurations for each network interface card in a computer.

The Primary WINS Server: and Secondary WINS Server: settings define the IP addresses for the computers from which the system will request NetBIOS name resolution.

It is possible to use a DNS server for Windows name resolution as well. If the DNS server has been properly configured, check the Enable DNS for Windows Resolution box.

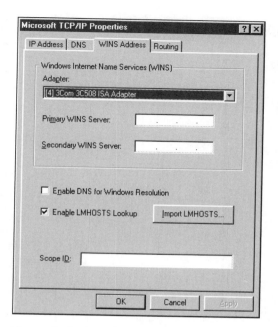

Figure 9-6   WINS Address tab for TCP/IP properties

The **LMHOSTS** file can act as a static alternative to WINS. LMHOSTS stands for LAN Manager HOSTS and supplements the standard symbolic name-to-numeric-IP-address information found in an ordinary HOSTS file with NetBIOS name-to-IP-address information. Because this information resides locally at the client machine, LMHOSTS can act in lieu of (or to supplement) WINS. To enable the computer to use this method for name resolution, check the Enable LMHOSTS Lookup box. Using this option does not interfere with other types of name resolution.

The Import LMHOSTS button will import an LMHOSTS file from a remote location to be stored locally.

The Scope ID box provides a method for limiting network communication. If this setting is used, only computers with the same scope identifier will be able to communicate. This setting should only be used in rare circumstances when it is necessary to limit the traffic between computers.

ROUTING TAB

The final tab–Routing—shown in Figure 9-7, is only used in multihomed systems. By selecting the Enable IP forwarding option, the computer will act as a router, forwarding packets received on one adapter to the other if necessary.

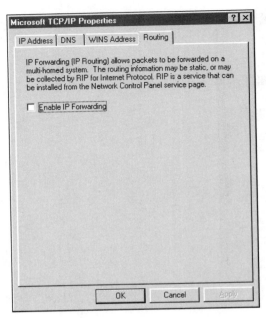

Figure 9-7   IP Routing tab for TCP/IP properties

WINDOWS NT AND THE INTERNET

Windows NT Workstation provides a number of tools used in conjunction with the Internet: Internet Explorer, FTP client, and Peer Web Services.

INTERNET EXPLORER

Microsoft Internet Explorer (IE) version 2.0 is included with the Windows NT Workstation operating system. Because of the many great improvements that have been added to later versions, you should obtain an updated version. Although it's possible to download IE 4.0 from the Microsoft Web site (through the Internet Explorer home page at *http://www.microsoft.com/ie/*), the minimal installation is 13 MB—the standard version is 16 MB, and the complete version is 25 MB! Fortunately, you can order the software on CD from the same Web page for a nominal fee. Unless you have a very fast connection to the Internet, the latter course is recommended.

In a nutshell, IE 4.0 represents the best that a state-of-the-art Web browser can offer. In addition to being powerful and easy to use as a straightforward Web-surfing tool, IE 4.0 is tightly integrated with other Windows applications, so it can invoke Word to open .DOC files or Excel to open .XLS files across the Web. The program also includes advanced support for newsgroups and FTP, and is tightly integrated with Microsoft Mail (or the Exchange client, whichever software you use).

The latest release also includes support for Java and ActiveX controls, which can add powerful interactive features to Web pages that it can exploit. Finally, IE 4.0 includes built-in support for so-called "push" technologies, and you have the option of choosing from numerous incoming channels of information (such as PointCast News, CNN, and other online information services) that can be piped into your browser on an ongoing basis.

FTP Client

As mentioned earlier, FTP is an IP-based Application layer protocol that handles file transfer and remote file system access and manipulation functions. Microsoft includes a command-line implementation of an FTP client as part of the Windows NT Workstation operating system. This client is loaded automatically when TCP/IP is installed.

To learn more about this program, launch a DOS window (Start, Programs, Command Prompt), then enter *ftp* at the command line. When the ftp> prompt appears, enter *help* to read the program's associated list of commands (enter *help <command>* to obtain information about a specific command, where you replace *<command>* with the name of an actual FTP command, like *get* or *put*).

Even though the command-line version of FTP included with Windows NT Workstation is perfectly adequate, there are numerous freeware and shareware GUI implementations of FTP that can take its place and are much easier and friendlier to use. For a complete list of such utilities, visit either of the following Web sites, select Windows NT as the platform, and use *FTP* or *FTP client* as your search string:

- *www.shareware.com*
- *www.download.com*

WS_FTP Professional by IpSwitch combines an Explorer-like file interface with easy controls for uploads and downloads. Visit *http://www.ipswitch.com* to download an evaluation version.

PEER WEB SERVICES

Microsoft includes Internet Explorer and the FTP client with other operating systems as well as Windows NT Workstation. However, one special set of tools is available only for the Windows NT Workstation environment. The **Peer Web Services (PWS)** provide Internet-style services in a peer environment including an FTP service, a Gopher service, and a World Wide Web server.

In fact, PWS is the NT Workstation equivalent of **Internet Information Server (IIS)**, which is part of Windows NT Server. IIS is designed to provide Internet services on a large scale, such as to a major company intranet or directly to the Internet. PWS, on the other hand, provides these services on a much smaller scale (like Windows NT Workstation in general, PWS is limited to a maximum of 10 simultaneous connections). Microsoft positions PWS as a "personal Web service" but also as an environment that is geared toward Web application development.

Rather than run Windows NT Server and IIS on a computer purely for development purposes, you can run NT Workstation and PWS to design and test your Web content. After you're ready to go public with your materials, you can transfer the same files to an NT Server running IIS. At the same time, you can continue to use NT Workstation to develop further enhancements to the site, and as your local workspace for maintenance and improvements.

WORLD WIDE WEB SERVICE

Perhaps the most important, and in fact most widely recognized, function of PWS is the WWW (World Wide Web) Service. This service allows the user to publish **HyperText Markup Language (HTML)** documents for use on the Web. Web browsers, such as Internet Explorer, use the **HyperText Transfer Protocol (HTTP)** to retrieve HTML documents from servers.

Other than its limitations on the number of simultaneous users and the omission of certain site management tools (such as FrontPage 98, which is included with IIS 4.0, but not with PWS), PWS and IIS are nearly identical. Certainly, they're more than consistent enough to facilitate development on Workstation and PWS, and deployment on Server and IIS.

FTP SERVER

The FTP Server installed with PWS is used to transfer files from the server to remote computers. Most installations of FTP on the Internet are used to download drivers and other data or software files.

This code module represents the server side of FTP, whereas the software mentioned earlier in the chapter covers the client side of FTP. In other words, this module permits other machines elsewhere on the network to upload files to an NT Workstation, or to download files from that same Workstation. The client-side software only permits the Workstation to perform the same activities with other FTP servers elsewhere on the network.

GOPHER SERVER

Gopher is a text-oriented document search and retrieval system that was developed at the University of Minnesota (home to the Golden Gophers). Gopher uses a menu-driven, text-based interface to display lists of information for one or more Gopher servers (the total collection of all Gopher servers and the data they contain is called "Gopherspace"). Microsoft includes a Gopher server as part of the PWS environment.

The lists presented to a Gopher client can be expanded (drilled down into) or contracted (details abstracted, one level at a time) at will. Any listing element can therefore represent an entire collection of data that can be further expanded, an individual directory or container for files and information that can be perused for items of interest, or any of a variety of files that can be perused online or downloaded for local access and use.

In a sense, Gopher acts like a kind of remote document management system in that it provides ready abilities to navigate within large document collections and also to peruse or download documents that are found to be of interest to the user. In the wake of the Web, Gopher no longer has the appeal it once did. But it's still a great way to provide organized collections of files for users to browse and remains a popular tool in academic environments. It's worth investigating if your organization wants to make document archives or other large file collections available across the network.

NETWARE NETWORKS

In an effort to more easily integrate into existing networks, Microsoft includes a variety of protocols and utilities that can permit Windows NT Workstation computers to access NetWare-based network resources. This represents a bold market move for Microsoft—even though sales of Windows NT Server currently outpace sales of new NetWare servers, NetWare remains the network operating system in broadest use worldwide. By providing built-in integration capabilities, Microsoft makes it easy for existing networks to accommodate Windows NT, giving that OS a "foot in the door" that may ultimately lead to further deployments of Windows NT on such networks. Recent history appears to indicate that this strategy is not only sound, but working very well for Microsoft. This section describes what kinds of NetWare access Windows NT Workstation can provide and mentions numerous other NT Server software components that can deliver even more sophisticated forms of NetWare-NT network integration.

WINDOWS NT WORKSTATIONS AND NETWARE

The modular design of Windows NT makes it easy to connect to any network operating system. When configured correctly, a Windows NT Workstation computer can use network resources on a NetWare network the same way it uses resources on a Windows NT network. Connecting a Windows NT Workstation client to a NetWare server is accomplished by loading the **Client Service for NetWare (CSNW)** on the workstation (CSNW is discussed later in this chapter).

WINDOWS NT SERVERS AND NETWARE

Two services included with the Windows NT Server 4.0 software, **Gateway Service for NetWare (GSNW)** and **File and Print Service for NetWare (FPNW)**, provide easy integration between NetWare file servers and clients and Windows-based file servers and clients. By loading these services on the Windows NT Server, workstations attached to that NT Server do not need CSNW to access NetWare-based resources. Instead they—like other MS network clients—need to use only standard components to connect to the Windows NT Server, which in turn creates a connection to a NetWare server through its gateway.

GATEWAY VERSUS CLIENT SERVICES

Although the GSNW sometimes makes an attractive alternative to CSNW for Windows NT Workstation users, GSNW is subject to several limitations that are worth noting. For one thing, all users who go through the gateway do so through a single virtual NetWare account—this means that everyone who uses that gateway has the same access rights and account privileges on the NetWare side of the connection. Furthermore, GSNW supports only a single gateway per NT Server machine; to set up two gateways, each with different access rights and account privileges, it is necessary to use two separate NT Server machines. Also, it's well recognized that any gateway can also become a bottleneck, because it is designed to aggregate multiple logical connections through a single physical connection across the network. This means that GSNW can bog down if 10 or more users try to access NetWare resources at the same time. On the plus side, however, NetWare "sees" GSNW as a single user, no matter how many users from the NT side of the network share a gateway connection. This provides a perfectly legal way to extend a limited number of NetWare connections to a larger user population. But because of the performance and access limitations that pertain to a gateway, many NT Workstation users prefer CSNW because it gives them direct, unmediated access to NetWare resources.

A workstation that uses CSNW will be faster than those connected through GSNW. But if multiple NT Workstation computers must be configured to connect to a NetWare environment, it is significantly easier to perform an installation only once, using GSNW on the server. When speed is essential or where no Windows NT Servers are available on a network, CSNW may be the only method to connect with NetWare resources on your network.

NETWARE COMPATIBILITY COMPONENTS

You've learned how the Client Service for NetWare provides connectivity for Windows NT Workstation computers to Novell NetWare servers. The NWLink protocol is another necessary element in NT Workstation–NetWare server communication.

NWLINK

NWLink is the Microsoft NDIS-compliant implementation of Novell's IPX/SPX protocol. Although it was developed primarily to connect to NetWare servers, NWLink can provide connectivity to any OS running IPX, including OS/2, Windows, and DOS.

NWLink is the choice of many network administrators because it is more robust than NetBEUI and easier to work with than TCP/IP. NWLink is routable, which NetBEUI is not, and, unlike TCP/IP, the computer's network and host address are configured automatically.

Installing NWLink

As with all protocols in the Windows NT environment, NWLink is added through the Network applet in the Control Panel. Select the Protocols tab and click the Add button. From the list of available protocols, select NWLink IPX/SPX Compatible Transport. You will then be asked to provide the NT installation files, generally from Windows NT installation CD.

Configuring NWLink

Figure 9-8 shows the NWLink IPX/SPC Properties window with the configurable parameters. Like most protocols in Windows NT, the NWLink parameters can be configured for each network adapter installed in the computer. Choose a particular NIC to configure from the Adapter list.

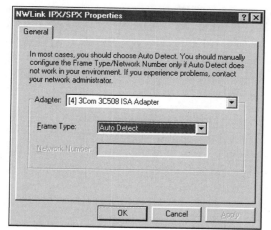

Figure 9-8 NWLink IPX/SPX Properties window

The **frame type** used by the protocol is one very important aspect of IPX/SPX and NWLink. The frame type for a packet specifies the fields and the order of the fields in the packet structure. IPX/SPX and, consequently, NWLink support four standard Ethernet frame types:

- Ethernet 802.2
- Ethernet 802.3
- Ethernet II
- Ethernet SNAP

By default, NetWare 3.11 and older servers use the 802.3 frame, and 3.12 and 4.x servers use the 802.2 frame.

When the frame type is set to Auto Detect, Windows NT will listen to the traffic on the network and determine which frame type is being used. This is generally the best frame type setting in the NWLink Properties window.

 NT automatic frame type detection detects only Ethernet 802.2 frames; all others must be configured manually. Whenever other frame types are present on your network, you must manually configure those used by NWLink and provide corresponding network addresses. To start this process, select the proper frame type from the list. If multiple frame types are in use, you'll want to get all the necessary details from your local NetWare or network administrator.

 It is important for all computers that communicate with IPX/SPX or NWLink to use the same IPX frame type. If any computer appears unable to communicate through NWLink, the first thing to check is that its designated frame type(s) is (are) compatible with actual local conditions.

Network Number is the remaining configuration field. If you manually configure the NWLink frame type, you must also supply an IPX Network Number for the network to which the computer is connected. When the NWLink Frame Type is set to Auto Detect, NT will also automatically discover the network number. As with frame type, each computer on a network must share a common network number in order to communicate successfully. You'll have a chance to experiment with this in Hands-on Project 9-3, where you install and configure NWLink on an NT Workstation machine.

CLIENT SERVICE FOR NETWARE (CSNW)

Client Service for NetWare (CSNW) provides connectivity for Windows NT Workstation computers to the following Novell NetWare resources:

- File and print servers
- NetWare utilities and functions
- Bindery and NetWare Directory Services (NDS)

File and Print Servers

CSNW works by adding a NetWare-focused Windows NT redirector that acts as an extension of the Windows NT file system, in the same way that the native NT redirector adds support for Microsoft Network-based resources to a workstation's local file systems. The primary difference between the two is that the NetWare redirector implements NetWare Core Protocol (NCP) requests for file and print services, whereas the native NT redirector uses the Server

Message Block (SMB) protocol. In other words, a NCP redirector works with NetWare the same way that the SMB requests work with the native Windows NT redirector.

CSNW uses IPX, so NWLink must be present for CSNW to work. If it is not already installed when you install CSNW, NWLink will be installed during the CSNW installation.

NetWare Utilities and Functions

Because it is so closely integrated with NetWare, CSNW supports most NetWare utilities and functions. For example, CSNW provides support for SYSCON (the NetWare 3.x administrative control application) and PCONSOLE (a NetWare administrative print management utility), as well as Burst mode for IPX. Burst mode is an IPX enhancement designed to support bulk data transfer. It allows routed connections to negotiate the largest possible packet size to improve bandwidth utilization.

> To provide maximum interoperability, NetWare servers must load the OS/2 name space to permit support for long filenames (LFNs) in the files that they store. To avoid unpleasant surprises or loss of important name information, be sure that any NetWare servers that handle files for Windows NT or Windows 95 users are able to handle LFNs properly.

Bindery and NDS Support

One of the benefits of CSNW is that it supports both **bindery** and **NetWare Directory Services (NDS)** connections, providing easy connectivity to both newer (4.x) and older (3.12 and earlier) versions of NetWare. The bindery style connection works with older versions of NetWare; NDS works only with newer 4.x versions of NetWare and IntranetWare.

The bindery acts as the primary database for all user, group, and printer information in versions of NetWare prior to 4.x. When users log onto a bindery-based NetWare server, they access the bindery for password validation, rights assignments, and so forth. To maintain backward compatibility and permit an environment in which older versions of NetWare mix with newer ones, Novell includes a Bindery Emulation mode in NetWare 4.x servers that permit them to behave as if they were bindery based, so that older clients and servers can interact with them freely and predictably.

NetWare 4.0 introduced NDS—a more dynamic database that can be shared across multiple servers throughout an enterprise. Centralized administration is its primary benefit. NDS also allows users to log onto the network only once, even if they access multiple servers—a feature that was not available in bindery-based versions of NetWare.

Windows NT Workstation supports both bindery-style logon and NDS. The configuration for each mode is different, as described shortly.

INSTALLING AND CONFIGURING CLIENT SERVICE FOR NETWARE

CSNW is installed for Windows NT through the Network applet, Services tab. (You go through this installation in Hands-on Project 9-4.) Because CSNW relies on IPX/SPX for communication, NWLink will be loaded automatically during the CSNW installation. Once CSNW is installed and your system is rebooted, you can configure the service. Unlike most networking features, CSNW has its own Control Panel applet. Double-clicking the CSNW Control Panel icon opens the window shown in Figure 9-9 where you can configure CSNW properties.

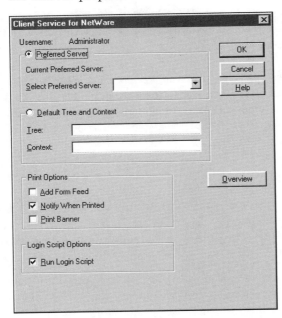

Figure 9-9   CSNW configuration window

Assigning Preferred Server or Default Tree and Context Using CSNW

You can specify either Preferred Server or Default Tree and Context, depending on the version of NetWare the server is running. Preferred Server is used for bindery servers (NetWare 3.12 and before) and Default Tree and Context is used for NDS servers (NetWare 4.0 and above).

Other Configuration Settings

The CSNW properties window shown in Figure 9-9 also provides settings for Print Options and Login Script Options. The Print Options determine whether the computer will send a

Form Feed command to the printer when the job is finished (in most laser printers this sends a blank page), send a notification to the user when the job is finished, or print a banner page at the beginning of the print job.

The Run Login Script Options run a login script when the user logs onto the NetWare server. This helps preserve investments in complex, powerful login scripts that many organizations have built and refined over the years. Windows NT is unique among network operating systems in support for a rival vendor's login scripts!

Changing Redirector Order

When you view the Services Settings tab in the Network applet and press the Network Access Order button, the window shown in Figure 9-10 opens. This shows the order in which the services (redirectors) are searched. You can change this order so that the services to which you connect most often appear first. To change the order, highlight the service whose rank you would like to change, and press the Move Up or Move Down button accordingly.

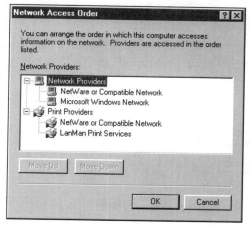

9

Figure 9-10 Network Access Order window

CONNECTING TO NETWARE RESOURCES

When properly configured with CSNW, connecting to a NetWare resource from a Windows NT Workstation computer should be the same as connecting to a Microsoft network resource. When browsing the Network Neighborhood, you will see a separate icon labeled NetWare Networks at the same level in the search hierarchy as Microsoft Networks.

Double-click the NetWare Networks icon to investigate that side of the world. After that, you can access a NetWare resource such as a printer or directory by double-clicking its icon; you can also investigate whatever NetWare servers appear in the Network Neighborhood listing under the NetWare Networks heading. If you are not currently logged onto a

NetWare server, you will be prompted to enter a username and password. This procedure applies to printers and print queues as well as volumes and directories on a NetWare server.

NETWARE-AWARE APPLICATIONS

Many applications fall into the category of "NetWare-aware"; this means they are usually client/server applications (for example the client software used with the popular Platinum accounting package) that have built-in abilities to access NetWare servers and other NetWare-based resources. The good news is that most NetWare-aware applications are supported on a Windows NT computer with CSNW installed, because these applications can use the DLLs that are included with CSNW.

In addition, there are some NetWare applications that require a connection to a NetWare server be established before running the program. The best way to find out if any particular application works is to test it. Unless the application uses nonstandard DLLs or attempts to access hardware directly (which will not be tolerated in a Windows NT environment), odds are good that it will work just fine.

There are a few NetWare client commands that are not supported by CSNW. These are command-line utilities that you would normally need to execute inside a DOS Console window. Table 9-2 lists the commands that have Windows NT command prompt equivalents. (Refer to the Appendix for more information on NET Commands.)

Table 9-2　Unsupported NetWare Commands and NT Equivalents

Unsupported NetWare Command	NT Equivalent
Attach	net use
Capture	net use
Login	net logon
Logout	net logoff
Slist	net view

There are many NetWare commands that will function normally in a Windows NT Workstation DOS window. These include: chkvol, colorpal, flag, flagdir, fconsole, filer, grant, help, listdir, map, ncopy, ndir, pconsole, psc, pstat, rconsole, remove, revoke, rights, security, send, session (except for search mapping), setpass, settts, slist, syscon, tlist, userlist, volinfo, and whoami.

TROUBLESHOOTING NETWARE CONNECTIONS

The following steps can be followed if a user is having trouble connecting to a NetWare server, and the problem has been isolated to NetWare or its components.

- Make sure the NetWare server is up and working properly. Can other users attach?

- Verify that the NT Workstation can attach to other Microsoft network resources.

- Verify that CSNW is installed correctly on the Workstation or that GSNW is installed correctly on the Windows NT Server.

- Check that the Preferred Server and Default Tree and Context settings are correct.

- Verify that the frame type and network numbers configured for the workstation match those configured on the NetWare server.

CHAPTER SUMMARY

Windows NT Workstation provides network access primarily by using TCP/IP and NWLink. These protocols are both routable and can support enterprise-level networks. In particular, TCP/IP has been designed to interconnect dissimilar types of computers, which helps to explain why it's the protocol of choice on the Internet.

TCP/IP is an industry-standard protocol that provides easy cross-platform communication. It can be set as the default protocol for Windows NT, which ensures easy connection to other types of computers and the Internet. The architecture of the TCP/IP protocol stack is different from that of the OSI model, mostly because it predates the OSI model by nearly 10 years. Rather than seven layers, the TCP/IP architecture includes only four: Network Interface, Internet, Transport, and Application.

Windows NT Workstation includes a number of applications that utilize TCP/IP and provide Internet connectivity. Microsoft Internet Explorer and an FTP client are included with most Windows OSs. In addition, Microsoft Peer Web Services can be used to provide Web, FTP, and Gopher services on an NT Workstation.

Windows NT Workstation also connects easily to Novell NetWare networks. NWLink is Microsoft's implementation of Novell's IPX/SPX protocol, which can be used not only to connect to NetWare servers but as the standard protocol for Windows NT as well.

NWLink is easier to configure than TCP/IP and more dynamic than NetBEUI. Once installed on an NT Workstation, the Client Service for NetWare (CSNW) supports all NetWare functions and most applications. It provides connectivity to NetWare servers using either the bindery or NDS for user and group information. This ensures an easy connection for a Windows NT Workstation to NetWare servers and resources.

Finally, several steps can be taken to identify NetWare access or NWLink protocol problems. To begin with, it's important to ensure that all software is properly installed and configured (to make sure that all machines agree on IPX network addresses and frame types in use). Beyond that, it's a matter of checking that connectivity exists, that services are working, and that all the pieces of the puzzle fit together as they should.

KEY TERMS

- **Address Resolution Protocol (ARP)** — The IP Network layer protocol used to resolve numeric IP addresses into their MAC layer physical address equivalents.
- **Application layer** — TCP/IP architecture layer that roughly corresponds to the Session, Presentation, and Application layers of the OSI model.
- **bindery** — Database in NetWare servers prior to version 4.0 in which user, group, and printer information is stored.
- **Client Service for NetWare (CSNW)** — Service included with Windows NT Workstation that provides easy connection to NetWare servers.
- **Domain Name Service (DNS)** — TCP/IP service that is used to resolve names to IP addresses.
- **Dynamic Host Configuration Protocol (DHCP)** — An IP-based IP address management protocol that permits clients to obtain IP addresses from a DHCP server, thereby enabling network administrators to control and manage IP addresses centrally, rather than on a per-machine basis.
- **File and Print Service for NetWare (FPNW)** — Service included with Windows NT Server that is used to connect NetWare clients to NT Servers.
- **File Transfer Protocol (FTP)** — The Application layer protocol and service that provides TCP/IP-based file transfer to and from remote hosts and confers the ability to navigate and operate within remote file systems.
- **frame type** — The structure of a packet that defines what fields are included in the packets and in what order those fields appear.
- **Gateway Service for NetWare (GSNW)** — Service included with Windows NT Server that provides connectivity for Windows-based computers to NetWare servers.
- **HyperText Markup Language (HTML)** — Language used to create documents for viewing on the World Wide Web.
- **HyperText Transfer Protocol (HTTP)** — The Application layer protocol used to ferry client requests for Web documents to Web servers and to carry server replies to those requests back to those clients.
- **Internet Control Message Protocol (ICMP)** — The Network layer protocol in the TCP/IP suite that handles communication between devices about network traffic, quality of service, and requests for specific acknowledgments (like those used in the PING utility).
- **Internet Information Services (IIS)** — Service included with Windows NT Server that provides Web, FTP, and Gopher services on a large scale.
- **Internet layer** — TCP/IP layer that roughly corresponds to the Network layer of the OSI model.
- **Internet Protocol (IP)** — The Network layer protocol that handles routing and addressing information for the TCP/IP protocol suite; this protocol is important enough to the overall collection that it contributes half the name of the group of over 100 protocols that make up the full TCP/IP suite.
- **LMHOSTS** — File used in Microsoft networks to provide NetBIOS name-to-address resolution.

- **NetWare Directory Services** — Advanced database used by NetWare 4.0 servers and higher to store resource information.

- **Network Device Interface Specification (NDIS)** — Microsoft specification that defines parameters for loading more than one protocol on a network adapter.

- **Network Interface layer** — TCP/IP layer that roughly corresponds to the Physical and Data Link layers of the OSI model.

- **NWLink** — Microsoft's implementation of Novell's IPX/SPX protocol suite.

- **Packet Internet Groper (PING)** — An IP-based utility that can be used to check network connectivity, or to verify reachability of a specific host elsewhere on the network.

- **Peer Web Services (PWS)** — Service included with Windows NT Workstation to provide Web, FTP, and Gopher services on a small scale.

- **rexec (Remote execution)** — The IP-based utility that permits a user on one machine to execute a program on another machine elsewhere on the network.

- **rsh (Remote shell)** — The IP-based utility that permits a user on one machine to enter a shell command on another machine elsewhere on the network.

- **Simple Mail Transport Protocol (SMTP)** — The IP-based Application layer messaging protocol and service that supports most Internet e-mail.

- **Simple Network Management Protocol (SNMP)** — The IP-based Application layer network management protocol and service that makes it possible for management applications to poll network devices and permits devices to report on error or alert conditions to such applications as soon as they're detected.

- **subnet mask** — The number used to define which part of a computer's IP address denotes the host and which part denotes the network.

- **Telnet** — The TCP/IP-based terminal emulation protocol used on IP-based networks to permit clients on one machine to attach to and operate on another machine elsewhere on the network, as if they were terminals locally attached to a remote host.

- **Transmission Control Protocol (TCP)** — The reliable, connection-oriented IP-based transport protocol that supports many of the most important IP services, including HTTP, SMTP, FTP, and so forth.

- **Transport layer** — TCP/IP layer that roughly corresponds to the Transport layer of the OSI model.

- **Trivial File Transport Protocol (TFTP)** — A lightweight alternative to FTP that uses UDP to provide only simple get and put capabilities for file transfer on IP-based networks.

- **User Datagram Protocol (UDP)** — A lightweight, connectionless transport protocol used as an alternative to TCP in IP-based environments to supply faster, lower-overhead access, primarily (but not exclusively) to local resources.

- **Windows Internet Name Service (WINS)** — Service that provides NetBIOS name to IP address resolution.

9

REVIEW QUESTIONS

1. The ___Subnet mask___ for an IP address defines which part of the address represents the host and which part represents the network.

2. ___DNS___ is a TCP/IP protocol used to resolve names to addresses.

3. The TCP/IP _____ layer encompasses the Data Link and Physical layers of the OSI model.
   a. Application
   b. Transport
   c. Internet
   d. Network Interface

4. _____ is a connectionless Transport layer protocol of the TCP/IP suite.
   a. Application
   b. User Datagram Protocol
   c. Internet
   d. Network Interface

5. If NWLink is not already installed on a computer, the CSNW installation will automatically install it. True or False?

6. NetWare servers using 4.0 or later use ___NOS___ to maintain user and group information.

7. Which two print options in CSNW are known to waste paper?
   a. place form feed after print job
   b. print banner page
   c. output printer status
   d. capture terminal output

8. The _____ protocol can be used to automatically assign IP configurations to a computer.
   a. WINS
   b. DHCP
   c. NWLink
   d. SNMP

9. What Web-based service is included with Windows NT Server that expands the abilities of PWS?
   a. Internet Information Server (IIS)
   b. FTP Server
   c. Gopher Server
   d. NetMeeting interactive chat facility

10. ___Gateway Services for Network___ and ___NFNW___ are provided only with Windows NT Server but are used to assist NetWare integration.

11. The _____LmHost_____ file provides NetBIOS name to IP address resolution.

12. _____ is an upper layer TCP/IP protocol that is used for file manipulation.
    a. Telnet
    b. Gopher
    c. FTP
    d. SMTP

13. _____NWLink_____ is the Microsoft implementation of Novell's IPX/SPX.

14. By changing the _____Binding order_____, you alter the order in which services are accessed.

15. What is the usable range of numbers available for any octet in a numeric IP address?
    a. 0–256
    b. 1–255
    c. 2–254   1–254
    d. 2–256

16. The NWLink _____Frame Type_____ setting defines how the information is placed in the packet.

17. The TCP/IP _____ layer encompasses all upper layers of the OSI model.
    a. Application
    b. Transport
    c. Internet
    d. Network Interface

18. _____WINS_____ is the Microsoft service that provides name to address resolution.

19. The _____Gopher_____ service supplied with Microsoft Peer Web Services provides menu-based document presentation.

20. Most often, NWLink communication problems can be traced to _____frame type miss match_____

21. A NetWare 3.11 server uses _____ to maintain user and group information.
    a. domains
    b. bindery
    c. workgroups
    d. NDS

HANDS-ON PROJECTS

PROJECT 9-1

To install Peer Web Services on a Windows NT Workstation:

1. Log onto the Windows NT Workstation as Administrator or equivalent and start the Network applet by right-clicking **Network Neighborhood** and selecting **Properties**.

2. Select the **Services** tab.

3. Press the **Add** button.

4. Windows NT builds a list of available services. Select **Microsoft Peer Web Services** from this list and press the **OK** button.

5. You are prompted to provide the path to the Windows NT Workstation files, in this case, **C:\I386** (or the directory indicated by your instructor or technical support person).

6. The Peer Web Services install window opens. Press **OK**.

7. From the PWS setup screen, select the applications you want to install. The Internet Service Manager and the Internet Service Manager (HTML) are the configuration and management applications for Peer Web Services. The World Wide Web, FTP, and Gopher services were described earlier in this chapter. You are also able to install Web samples and ODBC drivers for database support. To change the directory to which to install PWS, press the **Change Directory** button. Select all available applications and press **OK**.

8. The Publishing Directories window opens. This defines the locations for the files that will be served by each of the services. For now, accept the defaults and press **OK**. Click **Yes**.

9. Setup installs the necessary files to the computer.

10. If you do not have an Internet domain name declared for your machine, the Gopher installation prompts you to add one to the TCP/IP configuration for the computer. This is not done automatically but must be completed before the Gopher Service will operate correctly. Enter the information and press **OK**.

11. You are asked to select the ODBC drivers to install. Select **SQL server** and press **OK**.

12. When PWS is successfully installed, a window opens and informs you that Microsoft Peer Web Services setup was completed successfully. Press **OK**.

13. Press the **Close** button to close the Network applet.

14. To start PWS, restart the computer and log on as Administrator.

PROJECT 9-2

To view and configure Peer Web Services via the Internet Service Manager:

1. Start the Peer Web Services manager by selecting **Start**, **Programs**, **Microsoft Peer Web Services**, **Internet Service Manager**. The Internet Service Manager opens, which displays the status of each service, as shown in Figure 9-11.

2. To change the status of any particular service, select the service, open the **Properties** menu and choose **Start**, **Stop** or **Pause Service**, or press the Start, Stop, or Pause icons.

3. To configure a particular service, select the service and open the **Properties** menu, and choose **Service Properties**, or press the **Properties** button.

4. When finished, close the Services applet.

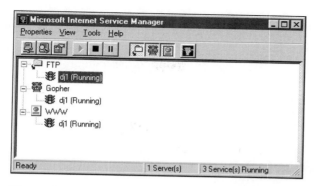

Figure 9-11   Microsoft Internet Service Manager

PROJECT 9-3

To install and configure NWLink on a Windows NT Workstation:

1. After logging onto the Windows NT Workstation as Administrator or equivalent, start the Network applet by right-clicking **Network Neighborhood** and selecting **Properties**.
2. Select the **Protocols** tab.
3. Press the **Add** button.
4. Windows NT builds a list of available protocols. From this list, shown in Figure 9-12, select **NWLink IPX/SPX Compatible Transport** and press **OK**.

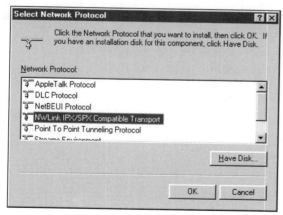

Figure 9-12   Select NWLink from the list of available protocols

5. You are prompted to provide the path to the Windows NT Workstation files, in this case, **C:\I386** (or the directory indicated by your instructor or technical support person).
6. After Windows NT installs the appropriate files, the Network applet appears again. Notice that, along with NWLink IPX/SPX Compatible Transport, NWLink NetBIOS was installed. This is to provide NWLink support for Microsoft networks.

7. Press the **Close** button to complete the installation.
8. You are prompted to restart the computer for the changes to take effect. Click **Yes**. When the computer restarts, log on as Administrator.
9. After logging on, start the Network applet again using the method in step 1.
10. Select the **Protocols** tab.
11. Select **NWLink IPX/SPX Compatible Transport** and press **Properties**.
12. The window shown in Figure 9-13 opens. Notice that, by default, Frame Type is set to Auto Detect, and the Network Number field is unavailable.

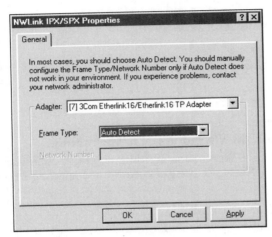

Figure 9-13 NWLink IPX/SPX Properties window

13. Change the Frame Type from Auto Detect to **Ethernet 802.3** by selecting it from the list box. At this point, the Network Number field becomes active.
14. Type **A101B202** in the Network Number field. Remember that, only 0-9 and A-F are available because the Network Number is hexadecimal.
15. The Workstation is now ready to communicate using IPX/SPX with the Ethernet 802.3 frame and network number A101B202. Remember that computers must have the same frame type and network number to communicate across the network.
16. Press **OK** for the changes to take effect.
17. Press **Close** to close the Network applet.
18. Click **Yes** to restart the computer.

PROJECT 9-4

To install and configure Client Service for NetWare (CSNW) on a Windows NT Workstation:

1. After logging onto the Windows NT Workstation as Administrator or equivalent, start the Network applet by right-clicking **Network Neighborhood** and selecting **Properties**.
2. Select the **Services** tab.

3. Press the **Add** button.

4. Windows NT builds a list of available services. Select **Client Service for NetWare** from this list and press **OK**.

5. You are prompted to provide the path to the Windows NT Workstation files, in this case, **C:\I386** (or the directory indicated by your instructor or technical support person).

6. Press the **Close** button to complete the installation.

7. You are prompted to restart the computer for the changes to take effect. Click **Yes**. When the computer restarts, log on as Administrator.

8. After logging on, open the Control Panel (**Start**, **Settings**, **Control Panel**). Notice that CSNW has its own configuration program icon, shown in Figure 9-14.

Figure 9-14   CSNW icon in the Control Panel

9. Double-click the **CSNW** icon. The window shown in Figure 9-15 opens.

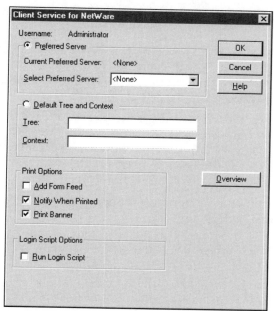

Figure 9-15   CSNW properties window

10. Notice that either Preferred Server or Default Tree and Context can be active. As mentioned in the chapter, the Preferred Server option is used to connect to NetWare 2.x and 3.x servers, and the Default Tree and Context option is used to connect to NetWare 4.x servers.

11. Press the **Overview** button to bring up the Help applet relating to CSNW. This Help file provides detailed information on all options of the Client Service for NetWare.

12. After perusing the Help file, press **Cancel** to close the Help applet.

13. Enter a **Preferred Server** name in the space provided.

14. Press **OK** to invoke the changes.

15. Notice that unless the server is connected to the network, an error appears stating that the server is unavailable and asking if you really want to set the preferred server. Press **No**.

16. Press **Cancel** to close the CSNW configuration program.

CASE PROJECTS

1. After returning from a conference in Las Vegas, the information technology director of your company has decided that all company information, such as phone lists, department goals, and so forth, should be published via the Web for internal use only. There is no version of Windows NT running on your network, either Server or Workstation. Instead, all six employees use Windows 95 on a peer-to-peer network. Of course, your manager wants to keep costs down, even though these new services are to be added to the existing environment.

   Outline the decisions that need to be made concerning audience and content. Recommend what platform to use and how to configure the computer that will serve this information. What difference does it make to your choice if your company plans to add another half-dozen employees before the end of the year?

2. Your network is being combined with another department's network and you have been assigned to the integration team. The other department runs three Novell NetWare servers; your department runs Windows NT Workstation computers in a peer-to-peer environment with a few Windows 95 machines thrown in for good measure. Your department uses TCP/IP as its standard protocol.

   Outline what steps must be taken on both networks to support full connectivity and interoperability between the two networks.

WORKGROUPS, DOMAINS, AND NETWORK BROWSING

A networked Windows NT Workstation can belong either to a workgroup or a Windows NT domain. In this chapter, you learn about the differences between the peer-to-peer oriented workgroup networking model and the centrally administered and controlled domain workgroup model.

> **AFTER READING THIS CHAPTER AND COMPLETING THE EXERCISES YOU WILL BE ABLE TO:**
>
> - DISTINGUISH BETWEEN A WORKGROUP AND A DOMAIN
> - EXPLAIN THE ROLES OF PRIMARY DOMAIN CONTROLLERS, BACKUP DOMAIN CONTROLLERS, AND MEMBER SERVERS ON THE NETWORK
> - DESCRIBE HOW BROWSING WORKS

You also learn how to configure an NT Workstation to participate in one or the other of these environments, and what benefits and liabilities attach to each of these two networking models. Finally, you learn about the browser service that underlies the NT Explorer, My Computer, and any application that offers a Browse button that permits you to look through your local file system and shared network resources for particular files to open or execute. You'll probably be surprised by the richness and complexity underlying the point-and-click browser service.

WORKGROUPS AND DOMAINS

Windows NT networks may be logically organized into either workgroups or domains. A **workgroup** is a set of computers that are logically grouped together for resource sharing and where all the computers appear on the same **browse list** (this is the list of computers and resources that appears when you inspect the Network Neighborhood in NT Explorer, or whenever you click the Browse button in a suitably equipped application). When you browse the network, you won't immediately see every machine on the network, but you will see all the resources in your workgroup.

Each computer in the workgroup maintains its own security information, without sharing it with other computers in the workgroup, so every time users attempt to access a shared resource on a different computer, they will have to supply a username and password for that specific machine. Workgroups are useful when few user accounts exist, or when a network includes a mix of Microsoft clients but has no Windows NT Server computers (which are required to create a domain). Workgroups are impractical for networks with more than 25 users, or for networks that require tight security—in those cases, a domain model is a better choice.

A **domain** is a set of computers that share a common security database, maintained on a Windows NT Server computer known as a **Primary Domain Controller (PDC)**. Domains include servers, workstations, Primary Domain Controllers, plus optional but recommended **Backup Domain Controllers (BDCs)** that store the security information for the entire domain and also authenticate user logons and control access to all domain resources.

WORKGROUPS

In terms of security, Windows NT workgroups differ from the workgroups found with other Microsoft products, such as Windows for Workgroups or Windows 95. Windows for Workgroups and Windows 95 use share-level security, which means that resources are protected by assigning passwords for the resources themselves. Anyone who knows the password can connect to the resource. For example, if JoeBob wants to connect to a shared network printer, all he has to do is provide the password—it's irrelevant that you don't actually want JoeBob to use that printer.

In a Windows for Workgroups- or Windows 95-based workgroup, you'd have two choices at this point: change the password, inconveniencing everyone else who uses the printer, or prevent the printer from appearing on the browse list by attaching a dollar sign ($) to the end of its share name. Windows NT workgroups offer you another choice: workgroups are set up for user-level rather than share-level security. For JoeBob to be able to use your printer, you would have to set up an account for him in the User Manager utility. If JoeBob doesn't have an account with the appropriate permissions, he can't access the printer.

Of course, this greater refinement of security means more work for the administrators. Every time a new user joins the network and needs to be able to access a shared resource, you need to create an account in the User Manager. If one network administrator is in charge of adding and fine-tuning all these accounts on all these individual computers, you can see how this could quickly become a major headache as the network gets larger. And that is where domains come into play.

 Windows NT workgroups cannot span more than one subnetwork. If a single workgroup is defined where two or more subnets exist, it may look like a single workgroup, but in fact it is really two (or more) workgroups with identical names and different browse lists.

10

DOMAINS

Working in a domain is much simpler. Basically, a domain is a collection of computers, defined by a Windows NT administrator, that share a common security database. Logging onto the domain provides access and authentication for all shared domain resources. The members of a domain are computers, not users; users just have accounts in the domain. Log on once to a domain, and you have access to any shared resource in that domain for which you have appropriate rights and permissions.

Only Windows NT computers—Servers or Workstations—can provide domain-level resources within a Windows NT domain. Although Windows for Workgroups, DOS, and Windows 95 can be domain clients, these computers cannot act as repositories for domain resources. Although shared resources on these computers may appear on the same browse list that contains domain resources, their resources function as if they were part of a workgroup. Thus, to access resources shared by non-Windows NT computers, whether in a domain or a workgroup model network, you must supply whatever security information those machines demand when you attempt to access those resources.

WINDOWS NT SERVERS IN THE DOMAIN

Let's take a minute to examine the three possible roles of Windows NT Servers in the network: **domain controllers** (primary and backup) and **member servers** (indicated as standalone servers in the Windows NT Server installation program).

Primary Domain Controller (PDC)

Every domain must have one Primary Domain Controller (PDC), which keeps the master copy of the domain's account and security information. In fact, a domain is established when Windows NT Server is installed on a computer and the administrator chooses to declare it a PDC and gives the domain a name.

The PDC stores the security information, but other computers in the domain may also be servers. These other machines must consult the domain database to determine which accounts are permitted to access their resources. Every so often (by default, every five minutes), certain servers, called Backup Domain Controllers (BDCs), query the PDC, asking whether any changes have been made to the security database since the last time they asked. If any changes have been made, those changes (not the entire security database) are sent to these servers, to add to the copy of the database they received on joining the domain.

Only the domain's Backup Domain Controllers (not member servers), query the PDC for changes to the security database.

If a PDC fails and there's no BDC available, no security information is accessible and user logon authentication is not possible, which renders the network completely unusable. Thus, it's important to have a Backup Domain Controller that can take over user authentication if the need should arise. This explains why Microsoft recommends at least one BDC be created for every domain on a Windows NT network.

Backup Domain Controller (BDC)

When installing Windows NT Server, you specify whether a computer is a domain controller or a member server. The first domain controller you identify becomes the Primary Domain Controller, and additional domain controllers become Backup Domain Controllers (BDCs). Although it's not required in a domain, a BDC is a good thing to have around. First of all, because BDCs maintain copies of the security database, they can help the PDC authenticate user logons, and thus reduce the amount of work the PDC must do. Second, if the PDC fails, then no server on the network can handle the security information and no network resources will be available. If the PDC is the only domain controller for the domain and that PDC goes down, you're out of luck until you get the PDC fixed. If you've got a BDC available, however, then you can promote it to PDC using the Server Manager and get the network back up and running.

If you know that you're going to power down a PDC, you can arrange things ahead of time. First, you must manually synchronize the databases—(ordinarily, this is done every five minutes automatically). To synchronize the databases manually, use the Server Manager utility from the current PDC: Select the PDC from the list of machines it displays, then pick the Synchronize entire domain entry under the Computer menu. Next, you must promote a BDC to become the PDC (which automatically demotes the original PDC to a BDC) before shutting down the original PDC.

If BDCs maintain a relatively up-to-date copy of a domain's security data, you might wonder why it's necessary to designate one machine as the PDC in the first place. The answer hinges on how updates to the security database occur, and how they're propagated around the network. The primary consideration depends on what kind of security information is involved. Domain security information resides in the Registry on a domain controller, just like all other configuration information, but it's broken into two major components and is subject to some very special access restrictions:

- The Security Accounts Manager (SAM) contains the user accounts database of information about users and groups and provides user validation services. Backup domain controllers don't have their own SAM, but instead maintain a copy of the PDC's SAM.

- The Security Reference Monitor (SRM) is in charge of permissions on the network; it enforces account validation and generates audit information as determined by whatever auditing policy may be in place. But the Security hive of the Registry is computer-specific, so this will differ between a PDC and a BDC.

BDCs can't update information in the SAM; they can only use what they've been given by the PDC, and they do not store the permissions information for the domain, because that's stored in the Security hive on the PDC. Thus, if the PDC dies and you don't promote a BDC to take its place, you can use the Server Manager or the User Manager for Domains on a BDC to:

- Create, delete, and modify directory shares for the local computer

- Edit file and directory permissions for the local computer

- Access shared resources (contingent on the permissions in place for those resources)

But because there's no PDC available, you will not be able to:

- Change passwords, or any other user account settings such as name and logon hours

- Create, modify, or destroy global groups, or any groups local to the domain

- Change any user's rights

Therefore, if the PDC dies, not only will no shares that existed on the PDC persist, but although domain logons will still work (if you've got a BDC in place) and existing sessions will be maintained, no computer will be able to play the PDC's role, and the security and accounts database will remain frozen in time, unable to change until a new PDC is appointed or the old PDC resumes working.

It's often a matter of concern for organizations to decide how many BDCs are necessary on a network. Because BDCs can help the PDC with the task of authenticating user logons, it might seem like the more the merrier, but this isn't necessarily true. First, every time a BDC has to ask the PDC whether any changes have taken place and then download those changes, network traffic increases. Second, acting as a BDC takes a certain toll on a server because the SAM must be maintained in physical memory. Thus, if the SAM consumes 10 MB, that's 10 additional megabytes of RAM that you'll need beyond what the server needs for its other duties. RAM is cheaper than it used to be, but it's not free.

Calculating the size of a SAM is an interesting exercise. The SAM requires 1,024 bytes for each user account. For each computer that appears in the Server Manager list for a domain, the SAM requires 512 bytes. It requires 12 bytes for each user that belongs to each global group, plus 512 bytes for the group itself and 36 bytes for each user in each local group, plus 512 bytes for the group itself. Do the math with your own domain, and you can see how much memory your domain's SAM consumes on each domain controller.

Microsoft's general recommendation is that you have at least one BDC per domain, but only one for every 2,000 users. If you believe that a large number of users might all log on at about the same time every day, you might want to increase slightly the number of BDCs. Also, if your domain extends beyond the main office and uses WAN links, a local BDC can significantly reduce the delay involved in authenticating user logons.

Member Servers

Because not every server in the domain can be a domain controller, other servers fall into the member server category. A member server, called a standalone server in the Windows NT Server installation program, is any computer that runs Windows NT Server but does not function as a domain controller of some kind. Such member servers can share resources with the network—and, because they're not burdened with the task of authenticating user logons, they're admirably suited to this job—but they do not maintain any copies of the SAM, nor do they query the PDC about changes to the SAM. Thus, they're able to get on with the task of providing resources to network users.

Windows NT Server computers are not the only member servers that can exist on a Windows NT 4.0 network; LAN Manager 2.x servers can also act as member servers.

Domain controllers can administer member servers, because when member servers are added to the domain, the PDC's global group, Domain Administrators, is automatically added to the server's local Administrators group.

NETWORK BROWSERS

Now that we've clarified the roles of the primary and backup domain controllers and have explained what services they provide to a Microsoft network, it's time to tackle the activities that underlie the Browse service. This service provides the elements that inform the Network Neighborhood in NT Explorer and My Computer (and in any other application that supports a Browse button) about network resources.

The computer that supplies the data for a browse list is called a **browser**. Like PDCs and BDCs, browsers fall into two active service categories: For each domain or network segment there's one master browser (for the domain, it's called a domain master browser) and from one to three backup browsers for any given network segment (there really isn't any such thing as a domain backup browser).

There's a considerable amount of communication from network devices involved in supplying the information that appears in browse lists. There's also a fair amount of data collection and coordination work underway to distribute and share this data among master browsers and backup browsers (not to mention the domain master browser), so that when you browse the network, you're likely to see a reasonably accurate snapshot of the resources that it can make available to you.

BROWSER ROLES

According to Microsoft, a computer in a Windows NT network may take one of five possible browser roles:

- Nonbrowser
- Potential browser
- Backup browser
- Master browser
- Domain master browser

10

Nonbrowsers

A nonbrowser is a computer that has been configured not to maintain a browse list. This doesn't necessarily mean that this computer could not maintain a browse list, but that it has been specifically instructed not to do so. As you will learn later in this chapter, in the section that covers the rules that govern browser elections, it's typical to find Windows NT Workstation or Windows 95 machines configured as nonbrowsers because it's unlikely they would ever be picked as browsers.

Potential Browsers

A potential browser is configured so that it can be instructed to maintain a browse list and become a backup browser if necessary and so ordered by a master browser. Normally, this would involve only Windows NT Server machines, but on network segments where only one NT Server is present, one or more NT Workstations might be designated as potential browsers to fill that role, should the server ever go down.

Backup Browsers

Backup browsers maintain a copy of the browse list, as copied from the master browser, and on request will provide its contents to computers in a domain or workgroup. Any domain controller is automatically designated as a backup browser. Windows NT Workstation, Windows 95, and Windows for Workgroups machines may become backup browsers if fewer than three Windows NT Server computers exist in a domain or on a single cable segment.

Backup browsers get their copies of the browse list from the master browser, whom they call every 12 minutes to get an updated copy of the browse list and a list of all known domains. This updated browse list includes information about which computers have joined the network, which have left, and what resources all known active computers currently share. Then the backup browser caches those browse lists and sends them to every computer that requests browse information through the NetServerEnum API.

If backup browsers cannot find a master browser to supply a browse list, then they force an election to choose a new master browser from the available pool of backup browsers.

Master Browser

The **master browser** (or browse master; Microsoft uses both terms) is responsible for collecting the data to create the browse lists sent to backup browsers. This list consists of all servers in a master browser's domain or workgroup, as well as a list of all domains on the network that are known to that master browser.

The master browser doesn't poll the network to see what's out there. Instead, all servers on the network send a datagram (unacknowledged message) called a server announcement to the master browser of the domain or workgroup. When the master browser receives a server announcement from a server, it adds that server to its browse list. Thereafter, each server announces itself every 12 minutes.

 Workgroup or domain browsers aren't limited to computers running Windows NT Server, but may also be computers running Windows NT Workstation, Windows 95, Windows for Workgroups, or LAN Manager 2.x.

Browsing of subnetworks (**subnets**) depends on what protocol is used. TCP/IP networks maintain a master browser and attendant backup browsers for each subnet, with a **domain master browser** to keep track of the whole structure. NWLink subnets send messages across routers to make sure that only one master browser exists for each domain. There's no subnet-related danger of multiple master browsers when it comes to NetBEUI networks, because NetBEUI isn't routable and so domains always consist of a single subnet.

The master browser is also responsible for selecting backup browsers for the network. As described later, when a computer joins the network as a potential browser, the master browser makes a determination whether or not that machine will be designated a backup browser. Here again, this determination springs from the rules that govern browser elections.

If more than one transport protocol is running in a domain, a master browser will be named for each protocol in use.

Here's how a computer becomes the master browser: When a server starts up, it seeks to locate a master browser. If it doesn't find one, that server calls for a browser election to determine which machine should become the master browser. The browser election process is decided according to the following criteria:

- Windows NT Server computers beat out Windows NT Workstation computers, which beat out anything else (the practical implication for any Windows NT network is that only Windows NT computers will become master browsers).

- If two or more Windows NT Server computers participate in an election, the PDC becomes the master browser if it's a candidate.

- If there is still a tie (which means that no PDC is a candidate for master browser because there's always only one PDC in any domain), then the computer that runs WINS becomes the master browser.

- If more than one candidate runs WINS, then the current master browser wins the election.

- If there is no current master browser, then the **preferred master browser** (a setting explained a little later in this chapter) wins.

- If there's still a tie, then if an NT Workstation has the value of MaintainServerList set to Yes then that workstation wins.

- If there's still a tie, then the present backup browser wins.

- And if there's still a tie, the computer that's been running the longest or (in the case of a tie) the one with the name that appears first in alphabetical order (for example, the computer named BIGDOG beats one named MONSTER) wins.

Elections may also be called under these circumstances:

- When a master browser is powered down properly

- When a server powers up and discovers that it ranks higher in the master browser pecking order just described than does the present master browser

- When an NT Server with the MaintainServerList variable set to Yes is powered up

In every such case, the entrance or exit of a machine causes the pecking order to be revised, and forces an election to occur.

10

Domain Master Browsers

The domain master browser maintains the browse list for an entire domain and provides a list of domain resources to master browsers. The domain master browser is always a domain's PDC. The PDC already has preference to become the master browser in any browser election, but in addition to its role as a domain's master browser, the browser service that runs on the PDC also serves as the domain master browser.

Domain master browsers are not always necessary—in fact, only subnetted TCP/IP networks use them, because the NWLink and NetBEUI protocols use only a single master browser for the entire network. The domain master browser comes into play when a domain spans several subnetworks, each with its own master browser. When master browsers start up, and then every 15 minutes thereafter, they send a datagram announcing themselves to the domain master browser, which then reciprocates with a request for each master browser's browse list. The domain master browser then merges these server lists with its own, to create a comprehensive browse list for the entire domain. The master browsers then contact the domain master browsers to get *their* copies of the entire list.

A domain master browser may also be a master browser—it's just first among equals in a subnetted TCP/IP domain.

THE BROWSING PROCESS

Previous sections explored which computers maintain browse lists and which don't, and what data those browse lists contain. Which computers read those lists—and how accurate those lists are—is another matter entirely.

To view a browse list, a network client (which may be a Windows NT Workstation or Server, or any other Microsoft client computer) must do the following:

1. Find a master browser. This requires sending a broadcast (or a directed packet) to the local subnet to which a master or backup browser must respond. The ultimate result is the network address of the nearest master browser.

2. Retrieve a list of backup browsers from that master browser.

3. Contact a backup browser.

4. Retrieve the browse list from the backup browser.

You'll have a chance to try this out for yourself in Hands-on Project 10-4, where you'll browse the network to see what resources are available.

Unfortunately, the information that a client gets may not necessarily be up to date because of the time lags involved in synchronizing domain master browsers, master browsers, and backup browsers. Recall that servers publish a list of their resources once at the beginning of the day and then every 12 minutes thereafter and that master browsers subordinate to a domain master browser announce themselves every 12 minutes. Furthermore, backup browsers query the master browser every 12 minutes to get the latest copy of the browse list.

When a resource leaves the network, no mechanism exists to let the master browser know that it is leaving. Although a server must announce itself periodically to remain on the browse list, the master browser gives servers a grace period of three announcement periods before it gives up if it doesn't hear from them. Thus, it can take as long as 36 minutes for a master browser to realize that a server has left the network.

Added to that 36 minutes is the time it takes to get changes to the backup browsers, so we're up to 48 minutes. If the network is a TCP/IP subnet, add up to 12 minutes more for updates to get from the master browsers to the domain master browser, so a server could potentially leave the network without its loss being published until an hour after its departure actually occurred.

New services are announced immediately, and thereafter at increasing intervals of 1, 4, 8, and 12 minutes until stabilizing at 12 minutes, so the initial 36-minute delay only applies to servers that leave the network. However, the 12-minute delay still applies to get changes to the domain master and then to backup browsers.

Browser Configuration

Not every computer in the domain or workgroup is a potential browser, and some make better browsers than others. To simplify the election process, or prevent some computers from becoming browsers at all, you can make the following configuration changes.

Nonbrowsers

You may need to tweak system settings to prevent computers from becoming backup or master browsers. The method you use depends on the operating system on the machine in question.

- *Windows NT:* Open the Registry and move to HKEY_LOCAL_COMPUTER\ SYSTEM\CurrentControlSet\Services\Browser\Parameters. To prevent the computer from becoming a master browser, set the value of IsDomainMaster to False. To prevent the computer from maintaining a browse list at all, set the value of MaintainServerList to No.

- *Windows 95:* Windows 95 computers can't be master browsers, so all you have to configure is whether the computer can become a backup browser. Hands-on Project 10-2 takes you through the steps to configure a Windows 95 computer as a backup browser.

- *Windows for Workgroups:* Windows for Workgroups computers can only be backup browsers. To prevent them from becoming so, open the SYSTEM.INI file and add the following entry to the [networks] section: MaintainServerList=No. (To make the computer a backup browser, you'd set the value to Yes, and to make it able to become a backup browser, you'd set the value to Auto.)

Preferred Master Browsers

To make a Windows NT computer a preferred master browser, so that it will become the master browser in case of an election, go to the Registry, to the HKEY_LOCAL_COMPUTER\SYSTEM\CurrentControlSet\Services\Browser\Parameters key. If not already present, you must create the key IsDomainMaster; whether present or not, that key must be set to True. Hands-on Project 10-1 shows how to make a Windows NT Workstation a preferred master browser.

BROWSER COMMUNICATIONS

The types of browser traffic that may be generated in the course of maintaining and distributing browse lists, have been mentioned briefly. The following sections provide a comprehensive description of all the kinds of browser-related communication you're likely to encounter on a Windows NT network.

Browser Announcements

This class of browser traffic is concerned with allowing network members to view clients and servers on the network.

Host Announcements   When a server joins the network, it issues a host announcement to the master browser, announcing its availability and identifying what kind of server it is: Windows NT (Workstation or Server), Windows 95, or Windows for Workgroups. Once the host is up and running, it continues to broadcast its availability to the master browser.

Announcement Requests   When a browser computer starts up, it must determine the identity of the master browser for its domain or workgroup. To do so, it broadcasts an announcement request on its local subnet. When the master browser detects this request, it responds with a local master announcement (as described in the following section).

Announcement requests are also generated by a newly elected master browser computer to force host announcements from local servers and build the master browse list, if empty. At the same time, the new master browser issues another announcement request to other connected master browsers, so that they'll tell the new master browser about their domains or workgroups.

Local Master Announcements   As noted in the previous section, when a backup browser joins the network, it announces itself to the network and receives confirmation from the master browser for the workgroup or domain. This local master announcement not only lets all computers on the network know the identity of the master browser, but it identifies itself (whether it's a Windows NT Workstation or Server computer, and whether it's a PDC), and permits other browsers to determine if they outrank the new master browser, and should therefore call a browser election.

Local master announcements are also issued by master browsers to the master browsers of other domains or workgroups, so that those other master browsers know where their peers are located on the network.

Workgroup Announcements   When more than one domain or workgroup exists on a local subnet, the master browser must make its presence—and that of its domain or workgroup—known to the other master browsers on that subnet. It does this with a browser announcement called a workgroup announcement. This announcement includes the announcement interval (12 minutes), the name of the domain or workgroup, and whether the group announced is a domain or a workgroup.

Election Packets

If an election must be called (based on the criteria explained earlier, then the calling server issues a broadcast called an election packet. This notifies the domain or workgroup that an election is in progress and publishes the election criteria and the running time for the network. Thus, in the case of a tie, the system that has been running longest can be named. Those machines in the domain or workgroup that are capable of becoming master browsers then respond. As soon as the highest-ranking browser responds, the other browsers stop announcing themselves and the election is over.

 Windows NT Server computers respond more quickly to an election announcement than Windows NT Workstation computers. This normally prevents Workstations from participating in elections.

Subnet Browsing

If a domain spans more than one subnet, this complicates the browsing process because browsing is dependent on broadcasts to the entire domain. This is why computers running WINS (Windows Internet Name Service) rank so high in master browser elections, because WINS simplifies moving broadcast messages across routers—it's basically a directory service for reconciling NetBIOS names with TCP/IP addresses. (If the WINS server isn't the domain master browser, then the master browser queries the WINS server for the domain master browser, and the WINS server responds with the domain master browser's IP address.)

 Domain master browsers that are WINS-incompatible (that is, those using Windows NT 3.1) will not use WINS.

Once the IP address of the domain master browser is known, then the master browsers send a message known as a master announcement to the domain master browser to inform it of their existence and download a list of master browsers in the domain and the servers within those domains. As noted earlier, this process repeats every 12 minutes.

Browser Queries

For network clients to display resources in a workgroup or domain, they need access to a browse list, which will normally be obtained from a backup browser. Here's what's involved in obtaining that information.

Finding a Backup Browser   The first step is to locate a master browser, because it lists all known backup browsers. The client doing the searching issues a broadcast to the domain asking for a backup browser list. If the domain spans several subnets and WINS is available, then if no master browser replies to the request, the WINS server responds with the IP address of the domain master browser. The domain master browser always knows the address for each master browser on every subnet—and it may even have a list of backup browsers itself.

When the master browser receives the client's request for a backup browser list, it responds with a list of backup browsers for that domain (or subnet, if the domain extends over more than one subnet).

Viewing the Browse List   Once a network client obtains the list of backup browsers for a subnet, it picks three backup browsers at random from the list and caches their names. When it needs to view the browse list, the client retrieves one of those three names (again, at random) and queries the designated backup browser. Then, the client establishes a network session with that backup browser and sends it a message requesting its browse list (this explains the delay you'll sometimes encounter when expanding entries in the Network Neighborhood listing—you're waiting for the backup browser to respond to your request). The backup browser responds with a list of domains and of the machines with resources to share in the local domain (these are called servers in a generic way, and need not be Windows NT Server machines; actually they can be any machine with a shared network resource to offer) and then terminates that session.

 Each time a network client uses the browser service, it must establish a communications session across the network with another computer. This session may involve the domain master browser or a master browser (when requesting a list of backup browsers), a backup browser (when requesting a list of machines with resources to share), or some machine that appears on the browse list (which presumably has one or more resources to share).

The final step, where the network client views a list of whatever resources are available on the selected server, is handled by establishing yet another session between the network client and a designated server (or, more precisely, some machine with a resource to share). The client requests a list of all shared resources from that machine and is answered with a list of such resources, at which time the session between the network client and the so-called server is terminated. To connect to any shared resource, yet another session must be established to access its contents.

BROWSER NUMBERS AND USAGE

Specific rules govern how many browsers, and of what kind, may exist in any domain:

- One domain master browser (if the domain extends over more than a single subnet)
- One master browser for each domain
- One backup browser for every 15 servers
- A maximum of three backup browsers for any given subnet

CHAPTER SUMMARY

This chapter has distinguished between workgroups and domains, discussed the roles of domain controllers on a network, and explained the browsing process.

Workgroups are logical groupings of computers in a network, formed for the purpose of segmenting browse lists into manageable chunks. Domains are logical groupings of network resources that also share a common security database, so that a single logon to the network provides access to the shared resources of the domain. Domains require domain controllers to manage this security information. A Primary Domain Controller (PDC) is required to provide user account information and store permissions information for the network, although the domain can function to a limited extent without a PDC as long as a Backup Domain Controller (BDC) remains operable.

Shared resources on the domain are made visible to domain clients through the use of browse lists. Browse lists are created as servers join the network and announce to a computer called the master browser that they've got resources available. The master browser combines all these announcements into the browse list, which it then disseminates to the backup browsers on the network, which make these lists available to domain clients. In domains that extend over more than a single subnet, a browser called a domain master browser exists to organize the master browsers for each subnet and let them communicate with each other. You can configure computers to either prevent them from becoming browsers at all or to make them more likely to become master browsers.

Browser communications are largely a matter of broadcasts to the domain. As servers announce their presence, the master browsers let the backup browsers know what servers are active on the network, and (where applicable) the domain master browsers supply complete browse lists to the master browsers for each subnet.

10

KEY TERMS

- **backup browser** — A computer in a domain or workgroup that maintains a list of domain/workgroup resources to provide to clients browsing the network. The backup browser periodically receives updates to the browse list from the master browser.

- **Backup Domain Controller (BDC)** — A Windows NT Server computer that downloads a copy of the Security Accounts Manager (SAM) from the Primary Domain Controller (PDC). This copy is periodically updated and may be used to help the PDC authenticate user logons. Multiple BDCs may exist in a single domain.

- **browse list** — A collection of information about shared resources on a network.

- **domain** — A collection of computers, defined by a Windows NT administrator, that share a common security database. Logging onto the domain provides access and authentication for all shared domain resources.

- **domain controller** — The Windows NT Server computer in a domain that manages the security database, authenticates user logons to the domain, and controls access to shared domain resources based on their permissions. A domain always has one Primary Domain Controller (PDC), and may have several Backup Domain Controllers (BDCs).

- **domain master browser** — In a domain/workgroup that spans more than one subnet, the domain master browser compiles and maintains a list of master browsers in the domain or workgroup.

- **master browser** — The computer in a single-subnet domain or workgroup that maintains a list of all servers to the domain, disseminating this list regularly to the backup browsers in the domain for distribution to clients. The master browser is responsible for making any change to the browse list.

- **member server** — Also known as a standalone server, any computer that runs Windows NT Server but is not a domain controller. Member servers do not receive copies of the domain security database.

- **preferred master browser** — A Windows NT computer with a Registry setting that requests that the computer be made a master browser if not outranked by another potential master browser.

- **Primary Domain Controller (PDC)** — The Windows NT Server computer in a domain that authenticates user logons and maintains the domain's security database. Only the PDC will directly accept changes made to the security database, and only one PDC exists per domain.

- **subnet** — A portion of a network, which may or may not be a physically separate network, that shares a network address with other parts of the network but is distinguished by a subnet number.

- **workgroup** — A collection of computers grouped for viewing purposes, but not sharing any account information.

REVIEW QUESTIONS

1. Which of the following will require the use of a workgroup rather than a domain? (Choose all that apply.)

   a. the need for a segmented browse list

   b. a network with no Windows NT computers on it

   c. a network comprising a mix of network operating systems

   d. none of the above

2. In a Windows NT workgroup, you must provide a password to access shared resources. True or False?

3. Your domain consists of two Windows NT Server computers, three Windows NT Workstation computers, and five Windows 95 computers. Given this information, the domain maintains a total of _____2_____ security database(s).

4. Domains are groups of _____.

   a. user accounts

   b. computer accounts

   c. networked computers

   d. resources

5. A ___member server___ is any Windows NT Server computer that is not a domain controller.

6. Windows NT workgroups cannot span multiple subnets. True or False?

7. If your domain has resources from 5 Windows NT Server computers, 30 Windows NT Workstation computers, 30 Windows 95 computers, and 15 Windows for Workgroups computers, how many computers are members of the domain?

   a. 5

   b. 35

   c. 65

   d. 80

8. Every five minutes, the Primary Domain Controller downloads a new copy of the SAM to the domain's backup controllers. True or False?

9. Which of the following is not a job of the domain's Backup Domain Controllers? (Choose all that apply.)

   a. help authenticate user access to the domain

   b. authenticate user access to shared resources on the network

   c. take over the job of updating the security database if the Primary Domain Controller fails

   d. manage user directory replication

10. The ___Sam___ contains the user accounts database, whereas the ___Srm___ contains information about permissions and controls auditing as specified.

11. If the domain's PDC fails and you don't promote a BDC, which of the following can you still do? (Choose all that apply.)

    a. edit file and directory permissions for the local computer

    b. edit user rights

    c. add users to the domain

    d. none of the above

12. Which of the following is not a reason why it's best not to make a computer a BDC unnecessarily? (Choose all that apply.)

    a. The SAM must be maintained in memory, so being a BDC will require a computer to have more memory than it would otherwise require.

    b. The PDC must periodically review the BDCs' copies of the security database and make updates, so network traffic will increase in line with the number of BDCs.

    c. BDC queries about changes to the security database add to network traffic.

    d. BDCs cannot share information across routers.

13. Each user account in the domain makes the SAM ___1029___ bytes bigger.

14. When a member server joins the domain, the PDC's ___domain___ global account joins the server's ___Administrator___ local account so that the PDC may manage the member server.

15. How many BDCs does Microsoft recommend that you have? (Choose all that apply.)

    a. one per domain

    b. one for every 15 user accounts in the domain

    c. 15 per network

    d. One for every 2,000 user accounts in the domain

16. Which of the following computers may not be browsers?

    a. Windows NT Workstations

    b. Windows 95 computers

    c. Windows for Workgroups computers

    d. none of the above

17. Backup browsers maintain a copy of the browse list as needed. True or False?

18. A server joined the network at 12:00 and announced its presence. What time will it be when it next makes an announcement?

    a. 12:01

    b. 12:04

    c. 12:08

    d. 12:12

19. How often does the master browser poll the network for new servers?

    a. every 12 minutes

    b. every 15 minutes

    c. every 36 minutes

    d. none of the above

20. A domain master browser will only be used on _____ .

    a. TCP/IP subnetted networks

    b. IPX/SPX subnetted networks

    c. both TCP/IP and IPX/SPX subnetted networks

    d. neither TCP/IP nor IPX/SPX subnetted networks

21. Which computer is more likely to become a master browser?

    a. PDC

    b. WINS

    c. none of the above

22. The name of the computers vying to become master browsers can play a part in determining which one gets the job. True or False?

23. From whom does a client computer get a list of resources on a domain server?

    a. the domain master browser

    b. the master browser

    c. the backup browser

    d. the server

24. If a server leaves the network, the change may not show up in the master browser's browse list for up to _____ minutes.

25. Which Registry branch controls whether a Windows NT computer becomes a browser or not?

    a. HKEY_LOCAL_MACHINE

    b. HKEY_LOCAL_USER

    c. HKEY_CLASSES_ROOT

    d. HKEY_LOCAL_SERVICES

26. Setting the Windows NT Registry value _____ equal to True will make that computer a preferred master browser.

10

Hands-on Projects

Project 10-1

To edit the Registry so that a Windows NT Workstation computer is made a preferred master browser:

1. Open the Registry editor by clicking **Start**, **Run**, and entering **REGEDT32**.
2. Dig down into the Registry until you're at HKEY_LOCAL_MACHINE\System\ CurrentControlSet\Services\Browser\Parameters.
3. As shown in Figure 10-1, three values are set for this key: DirectHostBinding, IsDomainMaster, and MaintainServerList. To make the Windows NT Workstation computer a preferred server, IsDomainMaster needs to be set equal to Yes or True.

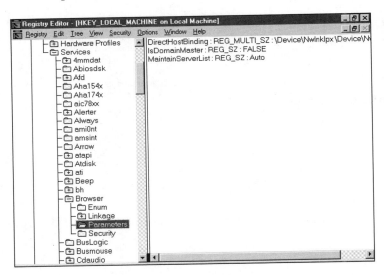

Figure 10-1   Three parameters for the browser service

4. Double-click **IsDomainMaster** to open the String Editor shown in Figure 10-2, and change the value to **TRUE** or **YES** (either will work). Click **OK**.

Figure 10-2 Set IsDomainMaster to YES or TRUE

5. Exit the Registry editor.

PROJECT 10-2

To configure a Windows 95 computer to be a backup browser:

1. From the Windows 95 Control Panel (**Start**, **Settings**, **Control Panel**), open the **Network** applet and click the **Configuration** tab, shown in Figure 10-3.

10

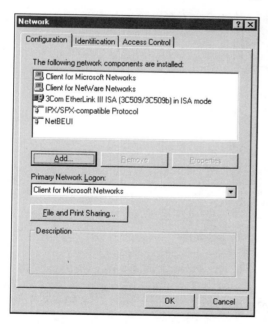

Figure 10-3 Configure browser settings in the Network applet

2. Click the **File and Print Sharing** button. A dialog box like the one shown in Figure 10-4 opens. Check the boxes for file or print sharing or both, and click **OK** to return to the Configuration tab. Only Windows 95 machines set up to share resources can be backup browsers.

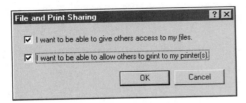

Figure 10-4 Setting file and print sharing

3. Select **File and printer sharing for Microsoft Networks** in the list of installed network components, and then click the **Properties** button to access the browser configuration options shown in Figure 10-5.

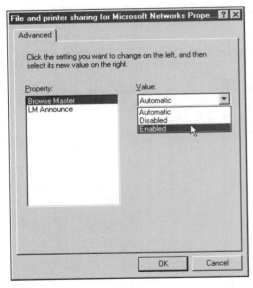

Figure 10-5 Enabling the Browse Master property

4. Select the **Browse Master** property. The Browse Master property specifies whether the computer may be a backup browser, not whether it's a master browser. You'll see that it has three options: Enabled, Disabled, and Automatic. The default is Automatic; set it to **Enabled** to make the computer a backup browser.

5. Click **OK** to exit, and then **OK** again to make the changes and close the Network applet. Click **Yes** to restart the computer so the changes will take effect.

PROJECT 10-3

To examine (or change) a Windows NT Workstation's membership in a domain or a workgroup:

1. Open the Network applet in Control Panel (**Start**, **Settings**, **Control Panel**, double-click the **Network** applet).

2. The default tab that appears is the Identification tab. If the workstation you're logged onto is a member of a domain, the entry beneath Computer Name will read Domain:, otherwise it will read Workgroup: In either case, the associated text box shows the name of the domain or workgroup to which this machine currently belongs.

3. To change membership, click the **Change** button beneath the domain or workgroup text box. This produces the Identification Changes dialog box shown in Figure 10-6, where you can change a Workstation's membership from workgroup to domain, and vice versa.

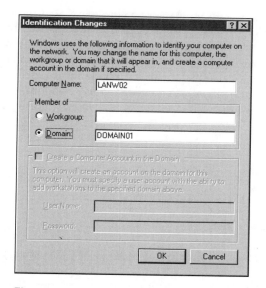

Figure 10-6   Identification Changes dialog box

4. To switch from domain membership to workgroup membership, click the radio button next to the **Workgroup** entry; to switch from workgroup membership to domain membership, click the radio button next to the **Domain** entry. In either case, you must also supply the name of the domain or workgroup you're joining (but the software copies the previous name by default, so be careful).

5. When switching from a workgroup to a domain, a computer must be added to the domain database. To change the database, this switch must have knowledge of an administrative account. This is the intent behind the dialog box at the bottom of the Identification Changes window. If you wish to join a domain, you must therefore obtain an administrative logon and password (or ask an administrator to enter them for you).

6. Because changing a Windows NT Workstation from domain to workgroup membership, or vice versa, can cause all kinds of Registry changes and drastically change the resources that the computer can access, click the **Cancel** button at the lower-right corner of the Identification Changes window to instruct the applet to ignore whatever data you've entered here.

7. Exit the Network applet by clicking the **Cancel** button at the lower right corner again.

8. If you accidentally accepted the changes to your membership status, you must restart your computer (press **[CTRL]-[ALT]-[DEL]**, then click the **Shut Down** button, and choose **Shutdown and Restart Computer** in the Shutdown dialog box that ensues). Watch carefully while Windows NT Workstation reboots. When the character prompt that reads "Strike the space bar to invoke Last Known Good Configuration" appears, press the **space bar**. This will restore the Registry to its configuration the last time the machine booted successfully, and ignore the changes you accidentally accepted in this exercise.

PROJECT 10-4

To view a Microsoft network browse list:

1. Launch Windows NT Explorer (**Start, Programs, Windows NT Explorer**).

2. Select **Network Neighborhood** in the left pane (it usually appears near the bottom of this list, so scroll down in the left pane until you see it). Click the **plus sign** (+) that appears to the left of the icon. This causes your computer to request a list of backup browsers.

3. Notice the delay before a list of entries appears (like that shown in Figure 10-7).

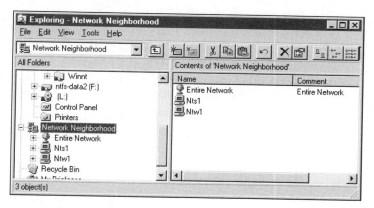

Figure 10-7   The initial browse list

4. The entries that appear beneath the Entire Network icon represent the machines with shared resources that appear on your local network (within your workgroup or domain). The delay that occurs between clicking the plus sign in step 2 and the appearance of the list in step 3 represents the delay involved in obtaining the browse list from a backup browser on the network. Next, click the **plus sign** to the left of whatever element appears directly beneath the Entire Network entry (in Figure 10-7, this is Lanw01).

5. Once again, notice the delay before a list of network shares appears. This time, the delay arises from the time required to contact that machine and request a list of its shares. Ensure that the top share in the list is highlighted, then right-click to produce a shortcut menu. Select the **Map Network Drive** entry. The resulting window appears in Figure 10-8, where you can assign a drive letter to a network file share.

Figure 10-8   Map Network Drive dialog box

10

6. Notice that this window automatically enters the next available drive letter for assignment in the Drive: box, but you may override this default manually. If a password is required to access this resource, a dialog box to provide a password is provided (this indicates that this machine is a Windows 95 device and may require a separate password; for a domain resource, you'd only be permitted to run this command if you had permission to at least read files in the share). This sequence of events is how you can create a persistent network drive mapping, so that you can access remote files as if they were mounted on a local volume on your system.

7. Click the **Cancel** button to close the Map Network Drive dialog box, then close the Windows NT Explorer window.

CASE STUDIES

1. You're installing a Windows NT Server computer onto an existing domain. A Primary Domain Controller and one Backup Domain Controller are already in place. The domain security database holds about 3,000 users. For best network performance, how should you configure the new Windows NT Server computer, and why?

   a. As a Primary Domain Controller

   b. As a Backup Domain Controller

   c. As a member server

   d. As a domain master browser

2. Explain why reducing the number of transport protocols in use on the network can improve browser performance.

3. What happens when a network client tries to obtain information about resources available from its local Browser service? Explain what happens first, what kind of browser responds, then what happens next, and what kind of browser responds. Finally, explain what happens when a machine in a browse list is double-clicked to display its shared resources.

REMOTE ACCESS SERVICES

Not all network access occurs from computers that are physically attached to the network where resources and data reside. Especially for roving workers, such as salespeople and field engineers, but increasingly for telecommuters as well, the ability to gain remote access to a network—that is, from some location other than where the network itself resides—is an important capability. This is an area in which Windows NT shines: It is the only major network operating system that includes remote access capabilities with the core software, at no additional charge.

For Windows NT Workstation, this means that a single dial-in or dial-out connection that can use a **modem**, an ISDN line, frame relay, or other more exotic digital remote link technology is part of the package. Windows NT Server includes a complete multiuser remote access server with its core offering and it can support up to 256 simultaneous dial-in/dial-out connections. Since the release of Windows NT 3.51 in 1995, remote access services have played a crucial role in Windows NT's burgeoning popularity and widespread acceptance.

AFTER READING THIS CHAPTER AND COMPLETING THE EXERCISES YOU WILL BE ABLE TO:

- Understand the Remote Access Service (RAS)
- List improvements new to RAS 4.0
- Discuss RAS WAN connectivity protocols
- Explain the telephony features of RAS
- Install and configure RAS ports and protocols
- Configure dial-up networking (DUN)
- Describe RAS security options
- Understand other RAS connections including direct cable connection, X.25, ISDN, and scripts

REMOTE ACCESS SERVICE (RAS)

You can use the **Remote Access Service (RAS)** to log onto a Windows NT system for user or administrative access. You can log on remotely to access a server or workstation system while you're away from the office. For example, a user can access the system from a hotel room while traveling on business.

The Remote Access Service initiates and maintains the access information from the client systems that initiate connections. A client system may be defined as any NT or Windows 95 workstation that initiates access to an NT system established as a remote access server.

 On Windows NT Workstation, most remote access is dial-out; such access is managed through the Dial-Up Networking applet, available through Start, Programs, Accessories, Dial-Up Networking. To handle dial-in connections, it's first necessary to install RAS on the Workstation; once installed, its behavior is managed through the Network Control Panel applet, by highlighting Remote Access Service in the Services list, then clicking the Properties button beneath that list to access its detailed definitions and setup information.

A Windows NT RAS configuration includes the following components:

- *Clients:* Windows NT, Windows for Workgroups, MS–DOS (with Microsoft network client software installed), and LAN Manager RAS clients can all connect to a Windows NT RAS server. Clients can also be any Point-to-Point Protocol (PPP) client.

- *Protocols:* Windows NT version 3.5 RAS servers support PPP, enabling any PPP client to use TCP/IP, IPX, or NetBEUI. Windows NT version 3.5 clients can also access the large installed base of Serial Line Internet Protocol (SLIP) remote access servers. The Microsoft RAS protocol allows any Microsoft RAS client to dial in.

- *WAN connectivity:* Clients can dial in using standard telephone lines and a modem or modem pool. Faster links are possible using ISDN. You can also connect RAS clients to RAS servers using **X.25** or an RS-232C null modem. Windows NT 4.0 also permits multiple links of the same type to be aggregated and treated like a single virtual connection using **Multilink PPP**. (This means that two or more modem connections, ISDN links, and so forth can be treated as a single connection where the bandwidth of that single connection is equal to the sum of the bandwidths of the individual links involved.)

- *Security:* Windows NT logon and domain security, support for security hosts, data encryption, and callback provide secure network access for remote clients. With Windows NT 4.0 you also have the option of separating LAN traffic from RAS traffic with the Point-to-Point Tunneling Protocol (PPTP).

- *Server:* Windows NT Server RAS permits up to 256 remote clients to dial in. Windows NT Workstation permits one remote client to dial in. The RAS server can be configured to provide access to an entire network or restrict access to the RAS server only.

- *LAN protocols:* IP protocol support permits access to a TCP/IP network, such as the global Internet. IPX protocol support enables remote clients to access NetWare servers and printers. You can also use NetBIOS applications over IPX, TCP/IP, or NetBEUI. In addition, Windows Sockets applications over TCP/IP or IPX, named pipes, Remote Procedure Call (RPC), and the LAN Manager API are supported.

 Remote control and RAS are two control technologies that work in different ways. Remote control employs a remote client as a dumb terminal for the answering system, whereas RAS establishes an actual network connection between a remote client and the answering computer system, using a link device (such as a modem) as a network adapter. RAS keyboard entries and mouse movements occur locally; with remote control, these actions are passed to a host system. Using RAS, computing operations are executed on the client; remote control computing operations are executed on the host with the resultant video signal sent to the client.

IMPROVEMENTS TO RAS IN WINDOWS NT 4.0

RAS 4.0 comes bundled with Windows NT 4.0 and has been significantly improved over the RAS bundled with NT 3.51. The RAS 4.0 improvements include:

11

- *Multilink PPP* (or PPP Multilink Protocol) allows you to increase overall throughput by combining the bandwidth of two or more physical communication links such as analog modems, ISDN, and other analog/digital links. Multilink PPP is based on IETF standard RFC 1717, "The PPP Multilink Protocol" (view it at *http://www.internic.net/rfc/rfc1717.txt*). **RFC** stands for **Request for Comment**, designating official standards documents published by the Internet Engineering Task Force (IETF).

- *Point-to-Point Tunneling Protocol (PPTP)* is a new networking technology that allows users to access corporate networks securely via the Internet because it supports multiprotocol **virtual private networks (VPNs)**. A VPN, as its name suggests, uses encryption to transport private data across public links. This maintains privacy for all communications carried through that transport. Using PPTP, you can shift the burden of hardware support for such devices as modems and ISDN cards from the NT RAS server to an Internet Service Provider (ISP), where the clients will initially connect to the Internet. Clients using PPTP can access a corporate LAN by dialing an ISP or directly through the Internet. In both cases, the PPTP tunnel is encrypted and secure and works with any protocol.

- *Restartable file copy,* a feature that automatically retransmits file transfers that are incomplete due to RAS connectivity interruption. This feature reduces the time it takes to transmit large files over lower quality-connections, reduces cost because it avoids retransmission of entire files, and reduces the frustration that attends interrupted transfers.

- *Idle disconnect*, a feature that breaks off a RAS connection after a specified period of time has gone by with no activity. This feature reduces the costs of remote access, helps you troubleshoot problems by closing dead connections, and frees up inactive RAS ports for reuse.

- *Autodial and Log-on Dial.* You can configure RAS access to automatically connect and retrieve files and applications stored on a remote system. Users do not have to establish a RAS connection manually each time they want to access a remote object; NT handles all RAS activities automatically, providing quick and efficient access.

- *Client and server enhancements.* NT 4.0 RAS includes a number of client and server components that allow third-party vendors to develop RAS and **Dial-Up Networking** (**DUN**) applications.

- *Updated interface.* Windows NT 4.0 RAS and DUN wizards, interfaces, and applications look and feel much like those in Windows 95. If you are already familiar with Windows 95, this will help you master RAS and DUN in NT 4.0.

WAN CONNECTIVITY AND INTERNET ACCESS PROTOCOLS

As you know, wide area networks (WANs) link sites that are often a considerable distance apart. Using RAS and Windows NT 4.0 enables you to create a WAN by connecting existing LANs via RAS over telephone, ISDN, or other communication lines. This is an inexpensive and cost-effective WAN solution if you have minimal to moderate network traffic between sites. You can improve the performance of RAS-based WANs in one of three ways:

- Increase the RAS connection bandwidth.

- Aggregate multiple communication links using Multilink PPP.

- Implement PPTP over the Internet.

NT 4.0 RAS supports all standard protocols for remote Internet access as well as Multilink PPP, which enables creation of a single aggregated connection by linking multiple PPP channels together. The RAS protocol that is used to establish and maintain a WAN link is dependent on the client and server OS and LAN protocols in use. The complete spectrum of RAS protocols supported in Windows NT 4.0 is described in the sections that follow.

POINT-TO-POINT PROTOCOL (PPP)

Point-to-Point Protocol (PPP) is the current remote access standard. Remote access protocol standards are defined in RFCs published by the IETF and other working groups. The RFCs supported in Windows NT 4.0 RAS are:

- RFC 1548: "The Point-to-Point Protocol (PPP)"

- RFC 1549: "PPP in HDLC Framing"

- RFC 1552: "The PPP Internetwork Packet Exchange Control Protocol (IPXCP)"

- RFC 1334: "PPP Authentication Protocols"

- RFC 1332: "The PPP Internet Protocol Control Protocol (IPCP)"

Microsoft recommends using PPP because it is flexible and an industry standard, which assures continued compatibility with client and server hardware and software in the future. Remote clients connecting to third-party PPP servers may need to use a postconnect terminal script to log onto a PPP server. This server will inform users that it is switching to PPP framing mode (this is a mode of communications that allows PPP to transport an arbitrary mix of protocols across a point-to-point link; it is used as soon as a persistent connection is set up between the client and a PPP server). Sometimes users must start the terminal and enter an account name and password to complete the logon process.

When using a PPP stack other than Microsoft's to dial into an NT Server and that stack is a part of a domain but not a PDC or BDC, the server looks only to its local accounts for the account name and password you specify on dial-in. If the server doesn't find a local account name with matching password, it won't check any domain accounts; it will simply deny access. A PDC or BDC does not have local accounts that it uses for verification; it can check logons only in the domain accounts in its database. This explains why you'll sometimes see BDCs also used as RAS servers (it doesn't make sense to load a PDC down this way, except on small, lightly loaded networks).

 The Windows for Workgroups RAS client supports only asynchronous NetBEUI; if you wish to use PPP or SLIP from such clients, you must use a third-party application to make that connection.

POINT-TO-POINT TUNNELING PROTOCOL (PPTP)

Point-to-Point-Tunneling Protocol (PPTP) is one of the most exciting new features of NT 4.0: it allows you to establish a secure RAS pipeline over the Internet and to "tunnel" IPX, NetBEUI, or TCP/IP traffic inside PPP packets. PPTP can provide real benefits for companies with numerous remote users who now subscribe to a local Internet Service Provider (ISP) for e-mail and Internet access, because they can use the same connection to access the corporate LAN. PPTP creates a virtual private network (VPN) that can support the IPX, TCP/IP, and NetBEUI LAN protocols and provides secure, private network access from any Internet connection.

Significant features of PPTP include:

- *Lower transmission costs:* PPTP uses the Internet as the primary long-distance connection medium rather than leased lines or long-distance telephone lines, reducing the cost of establishing and maintaining a RAS connection.

- *Lower hardware costs:* PPTP requires less hardware by letting you locate modems and ISDN hardware on a network rather than directly attaching them to the RAS server.

- *Less administrative overhead:* PPTP permits centralized management of RAS networks and users.

- *Improved security:* PPTP connections over the Internet are encrypted and secure.

PPP Multilink Protocol (PPP-MP)

The **PPP Multilink Protocol (PPP-MP)**, sometimes called just Multilink or Multilink PPP, combines two or more physical RAS links (modem, ISDN, or X.25 links) into one logical bundle that delivers the aggregated bandwidth of all the links involved. For the Windows NT implementation, Multilink PPP can combine up to 32 links of the same type (analog or digital, of the same speed) to create a single logical link.

 Multilink terminology is an area where Microsoft usage diverges somewhat from standard TCP/IP terminology. In RFC 1717, this technology is consistently called PPP Multilink or the Multilink Protocol, and is abbreviated MP. In various Microsoft documents, it is called Multilink PPP, PPP Multilink Protocol (abbreviated PPP-MP), but never simply MP. For that reason it is called Multilink PPP throughout this chapter, in keeping with the most common usage.

 Because only one phone number can be stored in a user account, Multilink does not work with the callback security feature. That's because callback does not know how to recognize or negotiate a Multilink PPP link.

Microsoft RAS Protocol (Asynchronous NetBEUI)

The Microsoft proprietary RAS protocol supports NetBEUI; any RAS client dialing into a Windows NT 3.1 or Windows for Workgroups system must use this protocol. When a connection has been established, the RAS server acts as a **gateway** to the remote client and can provide access to resources via NetBEUI, TCP/IP, or IPX protocols.

NetBIOS Gateway

Microsoft includes the **NetBIOS Gateway** in NT 4.0 to enable backward compatibility with earlier versions of Windows NT, Windows for Workgroups, and LAN Manager. Remote clients connect using NetBEUI and the RAS server translates packets as necessary between clients and local IPX or TCP/IP resources and servers. The NetBIOS Gateway also allows client access to LAN resources without requiring them to support IPX or TCP/IP directly.

SERIAL LINE INTERNET PROTOCOL (SLIP)

Serial Line Internet Protocol (SLIP) was one of the first protocols developed specifically for TCP/IP support over dial-up connections. SLIP is currently falling out of use, due to its limitations compared to PPP. SLIP does not support DHCP, so a static IP address must be assigned to every SLIP client; this makes IP address administration more difficult. Unlike PPP, SLIP supports neither IPX nor NetBEUI. SLIP's biggest drawback is that it does not support encrypted passwords and passes SLIP passwords as plain text. RAS does not include a SLIP server; thus, RAS 4.0 supports SLIP only as a client, which allows NT 4.0 clients access to the large installed base of UNIX servers that do support SLIP.

 SLIP works only for dial-out connections with RAS 4.0; RAS 4.0 will not support dial-in clients who seek to establish connections using SLIP.

The RFCs relevant to RAS SLIP are:

- RFC 1144: "Compressing TCP/IP Headers for Low-Speed Serial Links"
- RFC 1055: "A Nonstandard for Transmission of IP Datagrams over Serial Lines: SLIP"

TELEPHONY FEATURES OF RAS

11

The RAS **Telephony API (TAPI)** supplies a uniform way to access fax, data, and voice communications through an analog or digital telephone connection. TAPI is part of the Windows Open System Architecture (WOSA), developed to aid third-party vendors in designing powerful, integrated telephony applications. TAPI handles all communication between a TAPI-aware computer and a PBX (private branch exchange, or the brains of most larger private telephone systems), including basic phone functions (hold, transfer, conferencing, and so on). TAPI treats a telephone network as a system resource using standard APIs and device drivers, so once installed, TAPI applications gain seamless access to phone features and server-based communications.

Here are some of the benefits and improvements of TAPI 2.0:

- *Comprehensive solution:* TAPI is packaged with Windows 95, Windows NT 4.0 Server, and Windows NT 4.0 Workstation.

- *Native 32-bit:* TAPI 2.0 core components are 32-bit and have additional full support for symmetrical multiprocessing, multithreaded applications, and preemptive multitasking.

- *Application portability:* 32-bit TAPI applications designed for Windows 95 run without modification on Windows NT 4.0.

- *Device sharing:* Separate applications for inbound and outbound calls can control a single device, reducing hardware costs and enlarging communications capacities of small businesses.

For more information about TAPI 2.0, refer to Windows Telephony (TAPI) Support in the Windows NT 4.0 white paper at *http://www.microsoft.com/win32dev/network/tapiwp.htm*.

INSTALLING RAS

RAS is installed through the Services icon in the Control Panel or by choosing the Remote access to the network option during NT installation. Hands-on Project 11-2 takes you through installing the Remote Access Server step by step. If you do not already have a modem or some other TAPI-compatible device installed on your machine, RAS will require you to install one during its installation process (Hands-on Project 11-1 takes you through these steps). You must also collect some important pieces of information before you can install RAS:

- The exact type(s) of modem(s) installed in your NT Workstation
- The interrupt settings, COM port assignments, and baud rates for every communications adapter installed in your NT Workstation for use with RAS
- Whether this modem (or modems) will be used for dial-in, dial-out, or both
- Which protocols you want to load on each RAS adapter

CONFIGURING RAS PORTS

To configure RAS ports, use the Remote Access Setup dialog box, accessed by clicking Properties when Remote Access Service is highlighted on the Services tab of the Network applet in the Control Panel. Click Add to add necessary device drivers for new modems, ISDN adapters, X.25 PADs, and multi-modem adapters. Once an adapter is installed, click Configure to specify whether you want this port to be dial-in, dial-out, or both. Repeat these steps for each RAS device/port.

CONFIGURING NETWORK SETTINGS

To configure network protocol information for a RAS server, you must use the Network Control Panel applet. After launching the applet, go to the Services tab, then select the Remote Access Service element in the Services listing. Next, click the Properties button, then click the Network button to obtain access to protocol configuration information.

Once RAS is installed on a system, you will note that a new utility named Remote Access Admin appears in the Administrative Tools menu for Windows NT. Although you might be inclined to try this tool (which may be launched from the Start, Programs, Administrative

Tools (Common) menu), this utility provides only real-time monitoring information for active RAS connections. For protocol configuration, or dial-in/dial-out access controls, use the Services tab in the Network applet instead. Its Network Configuration dialog box is shown in Figure 11-1 and allows you to specify dial-out protocols and to configure server protocol settings.

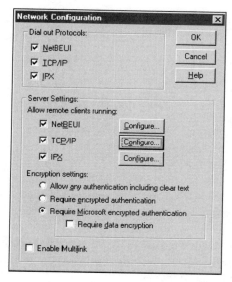

Figure 11-1 Configuring Remote Access Service network settings

CONFIGURING IPX SETTINGS

When you click the Configure button next to the IPX selection, the RAS Server IPX Configuration dialog box opens, as shown in Figure 11-2. By default, IPX clients will be set with a number of 00000000 (this number is the equivalent of the subnet portion of an IP address and identifies a node on a particular network). When set to this particular null value, IPX clients can receive numbers based on the networks they connect to. You can also specify a range of node numbers to assign by selecting the Allocate network numbers radio button. Manual assignments can be useful if you want more control of network number assignments for security or monitoring purposes. If you choose to allocate network numbers manually, type the first network number in the From box. RAS automatically determines the number of available ports and inserts the ending network number for you.

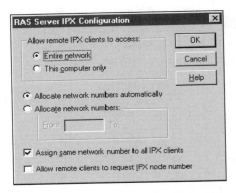

Figure 11-2 RAS Server IPX Configuration dialog box

CONFIGURING NetBEUI SETTINGS

When you select the Configure button for NetBEUI in the Network Configuration dialog box, the RAS Server NetBEUI Configuration options open, as shown in Figure 11-3. The NetBEUI options are limited to Entire network (which means the RAS server will pass traffic out to the LAN and provide access to network resources) or This computer only (which means the RAS server will allow dial-in users to access resources only on the machine where it resides and block them from any access to the network).

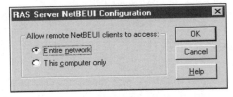

Figure 11-3 RAS Server NetBEUI Configuration dialog box

CONFIGURING TCP/IP SETTINGS

Selecting the Configure button for TCP/IP in the Network Configuration dialog box calls up the RAS Server TCP/IP Configuration dialog box shown in Figure 11-4. This dialog box allows the most flexibility over configurations. Administrators can use a local or available DHCP server on the network to allocate TCP/IP parameters. They can also use a static address pool or "RAS Scope" of IP addresses to assign addresses to their users, or allow clients to use locally assigned static IP addresses.

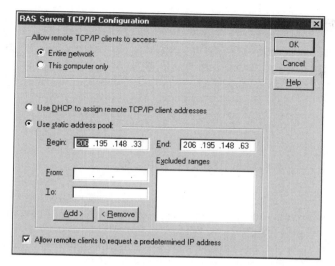

Figure 11-4   RAS Server TCP/IP Configuration dialog box

DIAL-UP NETWORKING

11

Many dialing properties that govern the operation of telephony activities are controlled via the Dialing Properties dialog box. This dialog box can be accessed using two methods:

- Launch the Telephony applet from the Control Panel.
- Launch the Modem applet from the Control Panel, then press the Dialing Properties button.

Using either method delivers access to the My Locations tab of the Dialing Properties dialog box, but only the Telephony applet also reveals the Telephony Drivers tab.

MY LOCATIONS

Telephony parameters can be defined for one or more unique locations via the My Locations tab of the Dialing Properties dialog box. A location is a collection of dialing information that TAPI uses to dial correct numbers when placing telephone calls. For notebook computers, TAPI simplifies mobile telephony by allowing users to predefine call-related variables. Users can define area codes and country prefixes, disable call waiting, and select tone or pulse dialing for each location.

Although a location is usually just a phone number, it can also include the prefixes or suffixes necessary to disable call waiting or to complete calls charged to calling cards. There are numerous predefined calling card types and settings as well as a utility to define new entries. To prevent unauthorized calls from being charged, a calling card number cannot be viewed once it is entered.

TELEPHONY DRIVERS

The Telephony Drivers tab is accessed through the Telephony application and lists the drivers used by Windows NT telephony applications. In most cases, these drivers are installed automatically whenever a modem is added and configured. The two drivers listed on the Telephony Drivers tab—the TAPI Kernel-Mode Service Provider and the Unimodem Service Provider—provide generic interface compatibility with a wide range of RAS modems.

CONFIGURING DIAL-UP NETWORKING

Client dial-out RAS service has a new name in Windows NT 4.0: Dial-Up Networking (DUN). NT 4.0 DUN represents a considerable improvement over dial-out services in earlier versions of NT and is similar to DUN in Windows 95. DUN makes it possible for an NT 4.0 computer to gain client access to other RAS-enabled networks or computer systems using a modem as a NIC and phone lines as network cabling.

DEFINING DUN PHONEBOOK ENTRIES

Dial-out connections are easily defined through the RAS phonebook. You create a Dial-Up Networking connection in the phonebook for each dial-up server to which you will connect. To create a phonebook entry, click Start, Programs, Accessories, Dial-Up Networking; the Dial-Up Networking dialog box opens. To create a new phonebook entry, click New in that dialog box; to edit an entry, click More (see Figure 11-5). Hands-on Project 11-3 shows the steps to create a Dial-Up Networking connection.

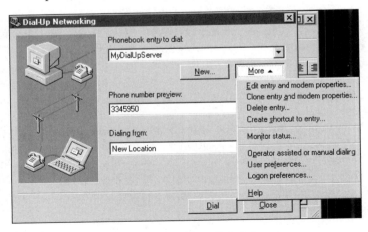

Figure 11-5   Dial-Up Networking dialog box

Once you have an entry in your phonebook, you can edit its properties, which include LAN protocol settings, security, logon scripts, server type, and X.25 connections. For example, to connect to an NT domain over a RAS connection, you might enter the following configuration settings in the Edit Phonebook Entry dialog box shown in Figure 11-6:

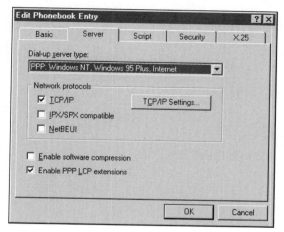

Figure 11-6   Edit Phonebook Entry dialog box

- *Server tab:* Select PPP: Windows NT, Windows 95 Plus, Internet as the server type and TCP/IP as the LAN protocol. You can also predefine the IP address using the TCP/IP Settings button on this tab.

- *Script tab:* This tab allows you to specify commands that will execute at logon. Most NT RAS configurations do not require postconnection logon scripts. Scripts are covered later in this chapter.

- *Security tab:* This tab defines security settings, such as whether a user wants to use the current username and password, as well as encryption options.

In addition, when users are authenticated under RAS, they must have appropriate RAS dial-in permissions. Dial-in permission may be granted by an administrator from either the User Manager or the Remote Access Admin utilities. Figure 11-7 shows the Remote Access Permissions dialog box. To get to this dialog box using User Manager, launch the utility (Start, Programs, Administrative Tools (Common), User Manager); select a user from the Users list in the top list box, click the Properties entry in the User menu, then click the Dialin button at the bottom-right corner of the resulting User Properties window. To get to this dialog box using the Remote Access Admin utility, launch the utility (Start, Programs, Administrative Tools (Common), Remote Access Admin), select a User from the Users list, then click the Permissions entry in the User menu.

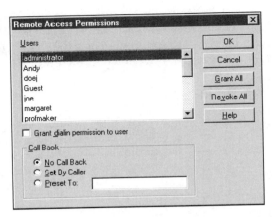

Figure 11-7   Remote Access Permissions dialog box

NETWORK SETTINGS

RAS supports IPX/SPX and TCP/IP in addition to NetBEUI. All three support the Point-to-Point Protocol (PPP). TCP/IP can use both PPP and Serial Line Internet Protocol (SLIP). RAS supports up to 256 connections inbound and/or outbound on a Windows NT Server. Windows NT Workstation only supports one inbound connection.

When you click the Server tab in the phonebook entry, you have the option of configuring for SLIP or PPP. When configuring for PPP, no additional protocol configuration is necessary unless you are connecting via TCP/IP. If you are connecting via TCP/IP, it is recommended to check the box to Enable PPP LCP extensions.

When the TCP/IP Settings button is clicked in a Phonebook Entry dialog box (refer to Figure 11-6), the PPP TCP/IP Settings dialog box opens where you can specify configuration options at the client end, as shown in Figure 11-8. These options include:

- *IP address:* Server-assigned or manually specified

- *DNS:* IP address for preferred DNS server (where applicable)

- *DNS backup:* IP address for backup DNS server (where applicable)

- *WINS:* IP address for preferred WINS server (where applicable)

- *WINS backup:* IP address for backup WINS server (where applicable)

- *IP header compression:* Permits use of compressed IP headers for more efficient connections (must be supported on both ends of the connection to work; check with your ISP)

- *Use default gateway on remote network:* Points IP forwarding activity to a router on the other side of the RAS connection (use this to have the ISP's router forward IP traffic for you; this is absolutely necessary if you want to access the Internet through a RAS connection)

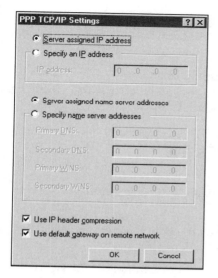

Figure 11-8   PPP TCP/IP Settings dialog box

The dial-up client has the option of specifying that IP addresses be assigned by the server, or to manually specify an IP address. In either case, the subnet mask will never be manually configured.

AutoDial

RAS AutoDial maps network addresses to RAS phonebook entries and maintains those address mappings so that a RAS phonebook entry can be automatically dialed whenever the same address is referenced, either from an application or from the command line. A network address can be an Internet host name, an IP address, or a NetBIOS server name. AutoDial also learns about every connection made over a RAS link for possible automatic reconnection later.

The AutoDial feature of RAS is enabled by default. Thus, no additional configuration is necessary to take advantage of AutoDial. You can obtain a list of DNS entries currently "known" by RAS AutoDial by executing *rasautou -s* from a command prompt. Furthermore, you can view and delete addresses from this list by editing the Registry. Use REGEDT32 to locate the HKEY_CURRENT_USER\Software\Microsoft\RAS\Autodial\Addresses key. By deleting any of the items under this key, you are effectively disabling AutoDial for that address until it is accessed again and returned to this list. You can disable AutoDial by deselecting the Enable auto-dial by location option on the Dialing tab of User Preferences, accessed by clicking More on the Phonebook list dialog box.

There are two possible scenarios when AutoDial attempts to make a connection:

- If you are disconnected from a network, AutoDial attempts to create a network connection whenever an application references a remote address or resource.

- If you are connected to a network, AutoDial attempts to create a network connection only for those addresses it has previously learned. Incorrectly typed server or Internet host names will not cause an AutoDial attempt.

CONNECTION SEQUENCE VIA PPP

Once you are connected to a remote computer, PPP negotiates a persistent connection according to the following steps:

1. PPP establishes framing rules between the remote computer and server, allowing frame transfers (communications) to continue.

2. The RAS server uses the PPP authentication protocols—**Password Authentication Protocol (PAP), Challenge Handshake Authentication Protocol (CHAP), and Shiva Password Authentication Protocol (SPAP)**—to authenticate the remote user. Which protocols are invoked depends on the remote client and server security configurations.

3. Once the user is authenticated, Network Control Protocols (NCPs) enable and configure the server for the LAN protocol used by the remote client.

4. After the PPP connection sequence is successfully completed, the remote client and RAS server begin to transfer data using any supported protocol (e.g., Windows Sockets, RPC, or NetBIOS).

RAS SECURITY

Microsoft declares that RAS security is actually preferable to a local network connection, because with RAS data is fully encrypted both ways. As mentioned earlier, one of Microsoft's design goals for RAS was to allow remote computers to behave as if they were locally connected. This goal is accomplished by allowing RAS to use the same domain database for establishing security that domain controllers use for local network access. This method is an almost certain guarantee that users will experience a consistent network environment, whether they are logged on locally, or remotely via RAS.

In addition, Microsoft had the foresight to include full RAS audit capabilities, allowing you to track remote connection events, including successful (and unsuccessful) authentications and logons. RAS writes audit events into the Application Log, so the Event Viewer should be one of the first places to check when you are trying to troubleshoot a remote connection problem.

RAS supports third-party intermediary security devices that require a password or identification code before permitting a RAS server logon, providing another layer of security to your system.

RAS fully supports callback features on a per-port basis, using a predefined number or extracting the number from the initial contact.

SECURITY TAB

Authentication and encryption settings are defined for Windows NT Workstation in the Security tab. The purpose of these settings is to restrict a hostile third party from intercepting a logon name and password or whatever data is transferred between a RAS client and a RAS server. On this tab, you set the level of security your client will request from the RAS server when a connection is initially established. If the server can provide the requested level of security, any logon to that system will use the designated security setting. If the server cannot provide the requested level of security, the connection will terminate.

The Security tab offers three levels of security:

- *Accept any authentication including clear text:* Provides no protection.

- *Accept only encrypted authentication:* Uses any one of the five supported encryption protocols (covered later in this section).

- *Accept only Microsoft encrypted authentication:* Uses only **MS-CHAP**. Two additional check boxes determine whether or not to encrypt all communication or to use the same name and password used to log onto the client.

The five supported encryption methods are:

- *CHAP (MD5):* The Challenge Handshake Authentication Protocol, a common encryption protocol for more non-Microsoft PPP connections

- *MS-CHAP (MD4):* The Microsoft version of CHAP, used only by Microsoft Windows NT and Windows 95

- *DES:* **Data Encryption Standard**, an older standard with support for legacy systems such as LAN Manager

- *PAP:* Password Authentication Protocol, a non-secure plain-text protocol used for compatibility with older UNIX SLIP connections

- *SPAP:* A version of PAP created by Shiva for its remote client software (also known as Shiva-PAP); Microsoft supports SPAP only as a dial-in encryption type

The Security tab also offers a button to "forget" the password currently used for the phonebook entry to connect to a server. If you select this button, you will be prompted for a new password before the next dial-out connection is attempted.

CALLBACK SECURITY

You can control access to the system from specified phone numbers by using the Call Back radio button, which forces calls to originate from predefined phone numbers, or the remote access client can set the callback number dynamically. This radio button is located on the Dialin Information dialog box, shown in Figure 11-9. It is accessed by pressing the Dialin button on the User Properties dialog box of a user account from User Manager. Setting the number dynamically allows you to access the system from different phone numbers even with the callback feature enabled and negates the callback feature security because remote access can be accomplished from any phone number. If you need to be able to access the system from different phone numbers, ask a local administrator to add phonebook entries at the server, and the server administrator can verify your identity by phone before allowing the remote access. Although this is cumbersome, it is more secure than allowing virtually unchecked callback access.

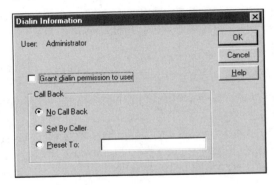

Figure 11-9   Callback security settings

USING RAS TO CONNECT DIRECTLY

You can use a direct connection for remote access, that is, use a null modem cable to connect the serial ports of two computers, a client and server. This kind of connection is limited by the length of the cable, requires one dedicated communication port on each system, and the client and server must be located near each other; for example, in the same room or on the same floor of a building. Hands-on Project 11-3 includes options for setting up a null modem direct RAS connection.

X.25 Support

An X.25 network transmits data with a packet-switching protocol. This protocol relies on an elaborate worldwide network of packet-forwarding nodes (DCEs) that can participate in delivering an X.25 packet to its designated address. RAS allows you to access an X.25 network in two general ways:

- *Client (Windows or NT):* Asynchronous Packet Assemblers/Dissemblers (PADs)

- *Server and client (NT only):* Direct connections

Access the X.25 tab by clicking the More button and selecting Edit and then Modem Properties from the Phonebook dialog box.

 X.25 cannot be configured for callback security.

Other X.25 configuration options shown in Figure 11-10 include:

- *Network:* The Type of PAD that you will be using; if using a Dial-Up PAD, select the name of your provider

- *Address:* The X.25 equivalent of a telephone number

- *User Data:* Any additional information that the X.25 host computer needs to complete the connection

- *Facilities:* Any additional parameters to your provider such as Reverse Charging, which permits the call's receiver, rather than its originator, to be billed

11

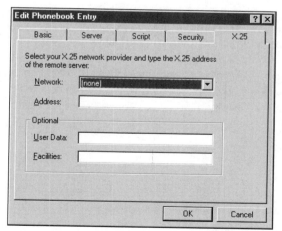

Figure 11-10 X.25 network access settings

TERMINALS AND SCRIPTS

You can use the SWITCH.INF file (or PAD.INF on X.25 networks) to automate the logon process instead of using the manual RAS Terminal that appears automatically on your screen when user input is required to complete a RAS connection. Basically, an automated script takes over the tedium of providing an account name, a password, and whatever else the host on the other side of the connection expects the user to enter.

 All RAS-related files, including the various .INF files mentioned in this chapter, reside in the Windows NT directory named %SystemRoot%\system32\ras. This is where you should look for these files, RAS logs, and other items of interest related to this service.

Automated scripts are especially useful when a constant connection to a remote computer is needed because they make it unnecessary for users to manually enter text at the keyboard in the RAS Terminal window. If a remote connection fails, RAS automatically redials the number and re-establishes the connection if the RAS entry is configured to use a script. However, this is only true for non–SLIP connections.

The SWITCH.INF file is like a set of small scripts, all contained in a single file. The SWITCH.INF file can contain a different script for each intermediary device or online service that the RAS user calls. A SWITCH.INF script has six elements: a section header, comment lines, commands, responses, response keywords, and macros. Hands-on Project 11-4 explains the steps necessary to activate a script in Windows NT.

MANUAL MODEM CONFIGURATION

If you are using a modem that is not explicitly supported in MODEM.INF, you can append a new section to that file that contains whatever command strings may be required by your modem. The name of the section should match the name of your modem and should also be enclosed in square brackets (for example, [PracticalPeripheralsPC288LCD]). The detailed steps required to add another modem section to the MODEM.INF file are not covered in this book; please refer to the *Windows NT Workstation Resource Kit* or other Microsoft documentation.

CHAPTER SUMMARY

This chapter introduced the Windows NT Remote Access Service, including improvements to RAS in Windows NT 4.0. These improvements encompass a pretty sizable laundry list, including support for new protocols like Multilink PPP (permits multiple connections to be aggregated and treated as a single logical link) and PPTP (permits a public network to carry secure, private traffic), and a variety of interface enhancements and installation wizards that make RAS look and act like the Windows 95 Dial-Up Networking environment.

RAS WAN connections and protocols and RAS support for the Windows Telephony API (TAPI) were also covered. These include full-blown support for all the major Windows NT protocols, including TCP/IP, NetBEUI, and NWLink (IPX/SPX), plus a NetBIOS Gateway option that permits clients who lack IPX or TCP/IP support to use the RAS server to permit them to access IPX- or TCP/IP-based resources. The Windows TAPI supports the hardware and drivers that make remote access possible and provide a variety of connection creation and configuration controls (largely through the RAS Phonebook), as well as support for modems, ISDN, X.25, and other digital communications technologies.

The chapter also explained how to install and configure RAS, and how to take full advantage of RAS's advanced Dial-Up Networking and security features. These include support for a variety of authentication methods (such as PAP, CHAP, MS-CHAP, and DES) as well as the ability to control whether RAS clients can access network resources or only files and resources located on the RAS machine itself. After digesting all this information, you should be ready to dial into your NT Workstation or Server or use it to dial out to a service provider.

KEY TERMS

- **Challenge Handshake Authentication Protocol (CHAP)** — An encrypted handshake protocol designed for standard IP- or PPP-based exchange of passwords, CHAP provides a standard, cross-platform method for sender and receiver to broker a connection in a reasonably secure manner.

- **Data Encryption Standard (DES)** — An encryption protocol designed by the US National Bureau of Standards, DES supports compatibility with other clients and servers, such as OS/2 LAN Server and LAN Manager systems. RAS supports DES encryption for dial-in use only.

- **Dial-Up Networking (DUN)** — Digital connections made at the OSI Data Link layer over various serial-based media. The term *dial-up* refers to temporary connections as opposed to leased connections.

- **gateway** — A computer that serves as a router, a format translator, or a security filter for an entire network.

- **modem** — A Data Link layer device used to create an analog signal suitable for transmission over telephone lines from a digital data stream. Modern modems also include a command set to negotiate connections and data rates with remote modems and to set their default behavior.

- **MS-CHAP (Microsoft CHAP)** — A Microsoft-enhanced version of the CHAP RSA Message Digest 4 (MD4) protocol that can negotiate encryption levels and that uses the highly secure RSA RC4 encryption algorithm to encrypt all communications between client and host. This is the highest level of security (and authentication) that RAS has to offer, but works only with Windows 95 and Windows NT machines.

11

- **Multilink PPP** — A capability of RAS to aggregate multiple data streams into one network connection for the purpose of using more than one modem or ISDN channel in a single connection. Also known as PPP Multilink Protocol.

- **NetBIOS Gateway** — A service provided by RAS that allows NetBIOS requests to be forwarded independent of transport protocol. For example, NetBEUI can be sent over the network via NWLink.

- **Password Authentication Protocol (PAP)** — A non-encrypted plain-text password authentication protocol, this represents the lowest level of security for exchanging password data via PPP or TCP/IP.

- **Point-to-Point Protocol (PPP)** — A Network layer transport that provides connectivity over serial or modem lines. PPP can negotiate any transport protocol used by both systems involved in the link and can automatically assign IP, DNS, and gateway addresses when used with TCP/IP.

- **PPP Multilink Protocol (PPP-MP)** — *See* Multilink PPP.

- **Point-to-Point Tunneling Protocol (PPTP)** — Protocol used to connect to corporate networks through the Internet or an ISP.

- **Remote Access Service (RAS)** — The dial-up service in Windows NT that allows users to log onto the system remotely over phone lines.

- **Request for Comment (RFC)** — Any of a series of standards documents controlled by the Internet Engineering Task Force (an arm of the Internet Activities Board that governs the entire Internet) that describe Internet protocols, technologies, principles, or practices. Although RFCs may not sound important, an official RFC standard carries the same weight on the Internet that the code of law carries in a courtroom.

- **Serial Line Internet Protocol (SLIP)** — An implementation of the IP protocol over serial lines. SLIP has been made obsolete by PPP.

- **Shiva Password Authentication Protocol (SPAP)** — A version of PAP implemented by Shiva (a networking equipment vendor) for remote client access that sends passwords in encrypted form. Windows NT RAS Server supports SPAP to permit Shiva clients to gain access to its resources.

- **Telephony API (TAPI)** — A set of application programming interfaces that defines the way that telecommunications equipment works with 32-bit Windows environments, TAPI provides a way for equipment vendors to create drivers easily, and for application writers to take advantage of hardware, without either side being forced to encounter the details from the other side directly.

- **virtual private network (VPN)** — A connection between a client and a remote access server, or even between two networks, across some kind of public network where encryption is applied at the protocol level to create a connection that is secure—and hence private—between sender and receiver. This creates a network that acts as if it were private, hence the name.

- **X.25** — A standard that defines packet-switching networks.

REVIEW QUESTIONS

1. You have configured a Windows NT Workstation client to dial up and establish a connection to a Windows NT Server computer. The user adds a phonebook entry, sets the proper network configuration, and the modem is functioning properly. The user submits the username and password correctly. Unfortunately, the user is unable to authenticate properly. What might be causing this problem?

   a. The user did not configure the NetBIOS Gateway properly.

   b. The user was not granted the appropriate dial-in permissions.

   c. The user was not added to the dial-in users group.

   d. none of the above

2. DHCP is the option for assigning IP configuration to TCP/IP dial-up clients. True or False?

3. Windows NT Workstation supports PPP scripts. True or False?

4. The SWITCH.INF file is the location for X.25 PAD configuration. True or False?

5. Windows NT Workstation supports the following encrypted authentication options through RAS. (Choose all that apply.)

   a. PAP

   b. SPAP

   c. DES

   d. MS-CHAP

6. The special protocol _____ allows multiple channels to be aggregated to increase bandwidth.

   a. Multilink PPP

   b. PPTP

   c. PPP

   d. SLIP

7. Where in NT Workstation do you specify which users have dial-in permissions to the RAS server?

   a. User Manager

   b. Control Panel

   c. Remote Access Admin Tool

   d. My Computer

11

8. Which RAS security option also has an additional option to encrypt data?

   a. Require encrypted authentication

   b. Require C2 encrypted authentication

   c. Require B encrypted authentication

   d. Require Microsoft encrypted authentication

9. Which RAS callback option provides the greatest level of security?

   a. Set By Caller

   b. Set By Server

   c. Preset To

   d. Callback and confirm RAS password

10. Which of the following protocols are supported by both RAS clients and RAS servers?

    a. SLIP

    b. PPP

    c. none of the above

    d. all of the above

11. Which WAN connections are supported by RAS? (Choose all that apply.)

    a. PSTN (modem)

    b. ISDN

    c. X.25

    d. PPTP

12. Which LAN protocols are supported by RAS? (Choose all that apply.)

    a. AFP

    b. TCP/IP

    c. NetBEUI

    d. DLC

    e. IPX

13. Which LAN protocol requires the least amount of configuration for use with RAS?

    a. AFP

    b. TCP/IP

    c. NetBEUI

    d. DLC

    e. IPX

14. Of the following protocols, which ones work with SLIP?

    a. TCP/IP

    b. NetBEUI

    c. IPX/SPX

    d. AppleTalk

15. Where is the Remote Access Service installed?

    a. Modems applet in the Control Panel

    b. WinMSD

    c. Dr. Watson

    d. Network applet in the Control Panel

16. The telephony options in RAS allow users to share location information across multiple entries. True or False?

17. Windows NT Workstation supports direct cable connections under RAS using _____ .

    a. null modem cables

    b. APC UPS cables

    c. LapLink cables

    d. parallel cables

18. RAS is the same thing as remote control for Windows NT. True or False?

19. You can set RAS permissions for individual users and groups. True or False?

20. You can connect to another computer from a RAS client using RAS in the same manner as if it were connected on a LAN. True or False?

HANDS-ON PROJECTS

PROJECT 11-1

To install a modem with RAS:

1. Click **Start**, **Settings**, **Control Panel**.

2. Double-click the **Modems** icon.

3. If no modem is installed, you can let Windows NT detect your modem. Click **Next** to detect your modem. If you do not want Windows NT to detect your modem, then you may opt to select the modem from a list. Detection will take a few minutes.

4. Accept the settings shown in the detected modem windows by clicking **Next**, unless you are absolutely sure these settings will not work. If you know they won't work, you must obtain valid settings from the modem's manufacturer, or from some other reliable source. Checking the manufacturer's Web site for the latest drivers and configuration information works reasonably well as a strategy here.

5. Click **Finish** to complete the modem installation process.

6. Click **Dialing Properties** in the Modem Properties dialog box.

7. Enter the country and area code information that is appropriate for you. Also configure any other settings you may find necessary to complete your RAS connection properly, such as call-waiting options, outside line options, and so forth.

8. Click **OK**.

9. Click **Close**.

Project 11-2

To install the Remote Access Server:

1. Right-click **Network Neighborhood** and select **Properties**.

2. Click the **Services** tab.

3. Click **Add**.

4. Select **Remote Access Service** from the Services tab.

5. Click **OK**. Provide the path to your NT Workstation installation files.

6. Select the modem you would like to use for RAS and click **OK**, then click Continue. In the Add RAS Device dialog box, if your modem does not appear in the Modem list, click **Install Modem** and complete the process to install your modem (refer to Project 11-1).

7. Click **Configure**.

8. Select the dial-out and receive calls options if you wish to also be able to dial out using the modem line, otherwise select **Receive calls only** and click **OK**.

9. Click **Continue**, select **Entire network** or **This computer only**, and click **OK**.

10. Configure your settings in the RAS Server TCP/IP Configuration dialog box, and click **OK**. Complete your configuration settings, click **OK**, then click **OK** again.

11. Close the **Network** dialog box.

12. Answer **Yes** when asked if you want to restart your computer.

PROJECT 11-3

To create a dial-up networking connection:

1. Click **Start, Programs, Accessories, Dial-Up Networking**.
2. Click **OK** when you see the message that informs you the phonebook is empty. If the message doesn't appear, there is already at least one entry in the RAS phonebook.
3. Click **New**. The New Phonebook Entry Wizard opens. Type the name of the new phonebook entry. Click **Next**.
4. In the Server Dialog box, enter the name of the server to which you will be connecting, and select your modem in the Dial using: list. (If you are using a null modem cable to connect two computers, select **Dial-Up Networking Serial Cable between 2 PCs** for the appropriate COM port.)
5. Click **Use Telephony dialing properties**.
6. Enter the area code and phone number of the RAS server in the Phone number box. (If you are using a null modem, leave this blank.)
7. If your RAS server has alternate phone numbers, click the **Alternates** button to enter these numbers.
8. Click **OK** to accept the settings. Click **Next**, then click **Finish**.
9. Click **Close**.

11

PROJECT 11-4

To activate a script in Windows NT:

1. Click **Start, Programs, Accessories, Dial-Up Networking**.
2. Select any entry to which you want to connect (ask your instructor or technical support person for details).
3. Click the **More** button and select **Edit entry and modem properties**.
4. Choose the **Script** tab.
5. In the Scripts dialog box, use the **Before dialing** button to select the name of the script to be run after dialing or one to be launched before dialing. Click **OK**.
6. Click **OK**, then click **Close**.

CASE PROJECTS

1. At XYZ Corp., the field salespeople and field sales engineers have just been equipped with Windows NT Workstation-based laptops, along with modems. Your task is to provide these users with remote access to your network through a Windows NT Server running the full-blown version of RAS. Describe two possible options to establish modem-based access to your network: one for direct dial-in to the RAS server, the other through the Internet. Explain what hardware and software is necessary on both ends of the connection for each approach, then compare and contrast the two approaches.

2. Assume that you're still working on Case 1, but add these assumptions to your working set:

   ■ All salespeople and field engineers always dial in from the same four area codes; long-distance charges from these area codes to the home office come at a low negotiated rate.

   ■ No ISP is available in any of these area codes through a local call.

   ■ Security of the information communicated between the remote staff and the home office is not an issue because the applications they use include their own built-in encryption modules.

   Given these new assumptions, which of the two options (direct dial-in to a RAS server or RAS over the Internet) makes the most sense for providing remote access to the network. Why?

3. Instead of the set of assumptions for Case 2, restate your case for remote access based on these assumptions (which actually represent most organizations' needs for remote access):

   ■ Field salespeople and engineers will be dialing in from all over the country, and sometimes from international locations.

   ■ Long-distance charges become increasingly expensive with distance.

   ■ The company maintains a relationship with a global ISP (such at AT&T Worldnet, WorldCom, MCI, Sprint, and so forth). Most ISP access is through a local call; all other ISP access is through a moderately inexpensive toll call (outside the US and Canada) or a toll-free call (inside the US and Canada).

   Reassess your choice between direct dial-in to the RAS server and ISP-based access using PPTP. In addition to reductions in long-distance charges, what other benefits can result from using the Internet to connect remote users to your network? Explain.

PRINTING

Printing is an integral part of any operating system. In this chapter you are introduced to some of the concepts associated with Windows NT printing, then you learn what's involved in installing and configuring printers for Windows NT. Because of the many options that are possible when accessing printers in the Windows NT environment, this topic is more complex that it may appear at first. For example, it's important to understand the distinction between printers that are directly attached to a computer and those with built-in network interfaces that are attached directly to some networking medium. Finally, you learn about how to troubleshoot common printing-related problems on Windows NT-based networks and systems.

AFTER READING THIS CHAPTER AND COMPLETING THE EXERCISES YOU WILL BE ABLE TO:

- DESCRIBE THE COMPONENTS OF THE NT WORKSTATION PRINTING PROCESS AND HOW THEY FIT TOGETHER
- CREATE, SHARE, AND CONNECT TO PRINT DEVICES
- CONFIGURE A PRINT DEVICE
- FINE TUNE THE PRINTING PROCESS FOR VARIOUS SITUATIONS
- CONNECT TO REMOTE PRINT PROVIDERS
- TROUBLESHOOT COMMON PRINTING PROBLEMS

WINDOWS NT PRINTING

As in other areas of Windows NT system architecture and behavior, Microsoft uses its own unique and specialized terminology to describe and explain how printers interact with the Windows NT system and how its overall printing capabilities work. For best results with the Microsoft certification tests, therefore, it's important to understand Microsoft's printing subsystem concepts, architecture, and behavior. Thus, this chapter begins with a "vocabulary list" of Microsoft print terminology before the key components of the Microsoft print architecture and behavior are discussed.

WINDOWS NT PRINTING TERMINOLOGY

The language of printing in the Windows NT environment is full of specific terms that you must learn. For convenience, we present these terms in alphabetical order:

- **Client application**: An application or service that creates print jobs for output, which may be either end-user originated or created by a print server itself. *See also* print client.

- **Connecting to a printer**: The negotiation of a connection to a shared printer through the browser service, from some client or service across the network to the machine where the shared printer resides.

- **Creating a printer**: Using the Add Printer wizard in the Printers folder (Start, Programs, Printers) to name and define settings for a print device in an NT-based network.

- **Direct-attached printer**: A print device attached to a computer, usually through a parallel port (see *also* network interface printer).

- **Network interface printer**: A print device attached directly to the network medium, usually by means of a built-in network interface integrated within the printer, but sometimes by means of a parallel-attached network printer interface.

- **Print client**: A network client machine that transmits print jobs across the network to a printer for spooling and delivery to a designated print device or printer pool.

- **Print device**: In everyday language, a piece of equipment that provides output service—in other words, a printer. But in Microsoft terminology, a printer is a logical service that accepts print jobs and delivers them to some print device for output when that device is ready. Thus, in Microsoft terminology, a print device is any piece of equipment that can produce output, so this term would also describe a plotter, a fax machine, or a slide printer, as well as a text-oriented output device like an HP LaserJet.

- **Print job**: The contents of a completely or partially interpreted data file that contains text and control characters that will ultimately be delivered to a print device to be printed, or otherwise rendered in some tangible form.

- **Print resolution**: A measurement of the number of dots per inch (dpi) that describes the output capabilities of a print device; most laser printers usually produce output at 300 or 600 dpi. In general, the larger the dpi rating for a device, the better-looking its output (and high-resolution devices cost more than low-resolution ones).

- **Print server**: A computer that links print devices to the network and shares those devices with client computers on the network. In the Windows NT environment, both NT Workstation and Server can function as print servers.

- **Print Server services**: A collection of named software components on a print server that handles incoming print jobs and forwards them to a print spooler for post-processing and delivery to a print device. These components include support for special job handling that can enable a variety of client computers to send print jobs to a print server for processing.

- **Print spooler**: A collection of Windows NT Dynamic Link Libraries (DLLs) used to acquire, process, catalog, and dispense print jobs to print devices. The spooler acts like a holding tank, in that it manages an area on disk called the spool file on a print server, where pending print jobs are stored until they've been successfully output. The term *despooling* refers to the process of reading and interpreting what's in a spool file for delivery to a print device.

- **Printer**: In Microsoft terminology, a printer is not a physical device but rather a named system object that communicates between the operating system and some print device. The printer handles the printing process for Windows NT from the time a print command is issued until a print job has been successfully output. In the Windows NT world, the focus is on printers, not print devices. Printers are logical constructs—named combinations of output ports, a print driver, and configuration settings that may involve one or more print devices. All the configuring and manipulation you'll do in Windows NT is done to printers, not to print devices. The settings established for a printer in the Add Printer wizards in the Printers folder (Start, Programs, Printers) indicate which print device (or devices, in the case of a printer pool) will handle print output, and also provide controls over how print jobs will be handled (banner page, special post-processing, and so forth).

- **Printer driver**: Special-purpose software components that manage communications between the Windows NT I/O Manager and some specific print device. Ultimately, printer drivers make it possible for Windows NT to despool print jobs and send them to a print device for output services. Modern printer drivers also permit the printer to communicate with Windows NT, to inform it about print job status, error conditions (out of paper, paper jam, and so forth), and print job problems.

- **Printer pool**: A collection of two or more identically configured print devices to which one or more Windows NT printers direct their print jobs. Basically, a printer pool permits two or more printers to act in concert to handle high-volume printing needs.

12

- **Queue** (or **print queue**): A series of files stored in sequential order waiting for delivery from a spool file to a print device.

- **Rendering**: Windows NT produces output according to the following sequence of steps: (1) A client application or some service sends file information to a software component called the Graphics Device Interface (GDI). (2) The GDI accepts the data, performs any necessary local processing, and then sends the data to a designated printer. (3) If this printer is local, the data is directed to the local print driver; if the printer is remote (located elsewhere on the network), the data is shipped to a print server across the network. (4) Either way, the driver then takes the print job and translates it into the mixture of text and control characters needed to produce output on the designated print device. (5) This file is stored in a spooling file until its turn for output comes up, at which point it's shipped to a print device. (6) The target device accepts the input data and turns it into the proper low-level format for *rendering* on that machine, on a page-by-page basis. (7) As each page image is created, it's sent to the printer's print engine, where it is output on paper (or whatever other medium the print device may use).

- **Spooling**: One of the functions of the print spooler is the act of writing the contents of a print job to a file on disk so that they will not be lost if the print server is shut down before the job is complete.

Familiarity with these terms will be helpful when interpreting questions about Windows NT printing on the certification exam, and in selecting the proper answers to such questions. Testing considerations aside, some familiarity with this lexicon will make it much easier to understand Microsoft's Help files and documentation on this subject as well. The section that follows describes the Microsoft printing architecture.

WINDOWS NT PRINT SUBSYSTEM ARCHITECTURE

Given all this specialized terminology, it's absolutely essential to put it into context within the Windows NT environment. Thus, the architecture of this subsystem is described next. The Windows NT print subsystem architecture consists of several components that turn print data into a printable file, transfer that file to a printer, and manage the way in which multiple print jobs are handled by a printer. These components are:

- Graphics Device Interface (GDI)

- Printer driver

- Print spooler

Graphics Device Interface

The **Graphics Device Interface (GDI)** is the portion of Windows NT that begins the process of producing visual output, whether that output is to the screen or to the printer—it's the part of Windows NT that makes WYSIWYG (What You See Is What You Get) output possible. In the case of screen output, the GDI calls the video driver; in the case of printed output, it calls a printer driver and provides information about the targeted print device and what type of data must be rendered for output.

PRINTER DRIVER

As explained earlier, a printer driver is a Windows NT software component that enables an application to communicate with a printer, through the IP Manager in the Executive Services module in the Windows NT Kernel. A printer driver consists of three subcomponents that work together as a unit:

- Printer graphics driver
- Printer interface driver
- Characterization data file

Printer drivers are not compatible across hardware platforms, so although Windows NT Workstation and Windows 95 can print to a Windows NT Server print server without first installing a local printer driver—they'll download the driver from the print server—you must make sure that necessary drivers are available for the proper platforms. For example, if the print server is an Alpha machine running Windows NT, and the clients that connect to it are x86 PCs, you must also install the x86 drivers on the print server, even though the print server itself won't need them.

 Windows NT 4.0 clients can't use the same printer drivers included with earlier versions of Windows NT, although Windows NT 4.0 print servers can supply appropriate drivers for earlier versions of Windows NT.

12

Printer Graphics Driver

The **printer graphics driver** is responsible for rendering the GDI commands into **Device Driver Interface (DDI)** commands that can be sent to the printer. Each graphics driver renders a different printer language, so that PSCRIPT.DLL handles PostScript printing requests, PLOTTER.DLL handles the HPGL/2 language used by many plotters, and RASDD.DLL deals with printer languages based on raster images (that is, those based on bitmapped images—collections of dots). RASDD.DLL is used by PCL (printer control language) and most dot matrix printers.

Printer Interface Driver

The **printer interface driver** enables you to interact with the printer by providing the interface you see when you open the Printers window (Start, Settings, Printers).

Characterization Data File

The role of the **characterization data file** is to provide information to the printer interface driver about the make and model of a specific type of print device, including its features—such as double-sided printing, printing at various resolutions, and accepting certain paper sizes.

PRINT SPOOLER

The print spooler (SPOOLSS.EXE) is a collection of DLLs and device drivers that receive, process, schedule, and distribute print jobs. It's implemented as part of the Spooler service, which is required for printing. By default, the Spooler service is installed as part of the Windows NT installation process (to check its status look at the Spooler entry in the Services Control Panel applet, or look for SPOOLSS.EXE in the list on the Processes tab in the Task Manager). The Spooler includes the following components:

- Print router
- Local print provider
- Remote print provider
- Print processors
- Print monitor

The print spooler can accept data from the print provider in two **data types**: either **enhanced metafile (EMF)** or **RAW**. EMF spool files are device-independent files used in Windows NT 4.0 to reduce the amount of time spent processing a print job—all GDI calls needed to produce the print job are included in the file. RAW spool files are device-dependent output files that have been completely processed (usually by their sending application or service) and are ready for output on the targeted print device. Once a spool file has been created, control is restored to the application that created the print job and other processing can resume in the foreground.

 EMF spool files are normally smaller than RAW spool files.

RAW spool files are used for local print jobs, encapsulated PostScript print jobs, or when specified by the user. Unlike EMF spool files, which still require some rendering once it's determined which printer they're going to, RAW spool files are fully defined when created. Only Windows NT 4.0 uses EMF spool files over the network; although Windows 95 uses EMF files for local printing, it sends RAW data when printing via a print server. Windows NT 3.x uses RAW data in either case. The Windows NT print processor also recognizes plain ASCII text files that may be submitted by other clients (especially UNIX machines); the name of this spool file type is TEXT.

Print Router

The **print router** sends print requests from clients to the print server, so that the requests can be routed to the appropriate print provider. When a Windows NT client computer connects to a Windows NT print server, communication takes place in the form of remote procedure calls from the client's print router (WINSPOOL.DRV) to the server's print router (SPOOLSS.DLL), at which point the server's print router passes the print request to the appropriate print provider: the local print provider if a local job, and either the Windows NT print provider or the NetWare provider if sent over the network.

Print Provider

The **print provider** is server-side software that sends a print job to the proper server in the format that the server requires. When a client sends a print job to a remote printer, the print router polls the remote print providers on the client computer and passes control of the print job to the first computer that recognizes the name of the specified printer. Windows NT uses one of the two following print providers:

- Windows NT print provider (WIN32SPL.DLL), used to transfer print jobs to Windows network print servers

- NetWare print provider (NWPROVAU.DLL), used to transfer print jobs to NetWare print servers

If the Windows NT print provider recognizes the printer name, it will send the print job along in one of two ways, depending on the operating system on the print server. If the print server is running a Windows NT 4.0-compatible OS (such as Windows NT 3.x, Windows for Workgroups, or LAN Manager), then the print job will be routed by NetBIOS to the print server. If the print server is running Windows NT 4.0, then the print provider contacts the spooler service on the print server, which will then pass it to the local print provider.

The local print provider writes the contents of the print job to a spool file (which will have the extension .SPL) and tracks administration information for that print job. By default, all spool files are stored in the %systemroot%\system32\printers\spool directory. You can change that location (perhaps if you've installed a faster drive) by adjusting the print server settings in the Printers applet in the Control Panel. (You can practice changing the location of the spool file in Hands-on Project 12-1.)

Because spool files only exist to keep the print job from getting lost in case of a power failure, they are normally deleted after the print job is complete. However, you can enable spooler event logging to monitor spool file information for such data as the amount of disk space required by spool files and what printer traffic is like.

To enable such logging, you must first enable auditing in the User Manager (Start, Programs, Administrative Tools (Common), User Manager, Policies, Audit, then click the Audit These Events radio button) and then enable print auditing by checking the File and Object Access Success and Failure check boxes. Finally, you must locate the print spooler file and turn auditing on for that particular file. You'll also need to set up Performance Monitor to establish a threshold on the drive where the spool file resides and set an Alert to be issued when that threshold is exceeded (this technique is described in Chapter 13).

If the NetWare print provider recognizes the printer name, it passes the print job along to the NetWare workstation service, which then passes control of the print job to the NetWare redirector for transfer to the NetWare print server.

 To send print jobs from a Windows NT client to a NetWare server, you must have Client Services for NetWare (CSNW) installed on the client computer. To route print jobs through a Windows NT Server computer to a NetWare print server, the Windows NT Server must have the Gateway Services for NetWare (GSNW) installed.

Print Processor   *Just Know the term*

A **print processor** works with the printer driver to despool spool files during playback, making any needed changes to the spool file based on its data type. Windows NT Server supports two print processors: one for Windows clients (WINPRINT.DLL) and one for Macintosh clients (SFMPSPRT.DLL), which is normally installed only after Services for Macintosh is installed. Remember that Services for Macintosh is only included with Windows NT Server, which is why this won't be an issue on Windows NT Workstation machines.

For both Windows NT Workstation and Server machines, the built-in Windows print processor understands EMF data files, three kinds of RAW data files, and TEXT files. But the Macintosh print processor that's installed on Windows NT Server when Services for Macintosh is installed understands only PSTSCRPT1, which signifies that the spool file contains PostScript code from a Macintosh client but that the output is not destined for delivery to a PostScript printer. In actuality, this data type lets the print processor know that post-processing to translate the PostScript into the equivalent RAW data for output on the target printer must be performed before the print job can be spooled to the targeted print device.

 Although the limitations of the Windows NT raster image processor that Windows NT Server uses to send print jobs from a Macintosh client to a printer mean that print jobs can have a maximum resolution of 300 dpi and that they must be printed in monochrome (regardless of the capabilities of the targeted print device), third-party raster image processors are available for those who want to get the full capabilities of their printers even when printing via Services for Macintosh.

Print Monitor

The **print monitor** is the final link in the chain of the printing process. It's actually two monitors: a language monitor and a port monitor. The **language monitor**, created when you install a printer driver if a language monitor is associated with the driver, comes into play only if the print device is bidirectional—messages about print job status may be sent both to and from the computer. Bidirectional capabilities are necessary to get meaningful error messages from the printer to the client. If the language monitor has a role, then it sets up the communication with the printer and passes control to the port monitor. The language monitor supplied with Windows NT uses the Printer Job Language. If a manufacturer creates a printer that speaks a different language, it would need to define another language monitor, because the computer and print device must speak the same language for communication to work.

The **port monitor** transmits the print job either to the print device or to another server. It controls the flow of information to the I/O port to which the print device is connected (a serial, parallel, network, or SCSI port). The port monitor supplied with Windows NT (LOCALMON.DLL) controls parallel and serial ports. If you want to connect a print device to a SCSI port or network port, you must use a port monitor supplied by the vendor. Regardless of type, however, port monitors interface with *ports*, not printers, and are in fact unaware of the type of print devices to which they're connected. The print job is already configured by the print processor before it ever hits the output port.

Windows NT 4.0 supports the following port monitors:

- Local print monitor (LOCALMON.DLL)
- Hewlett-Packard network port print monitor (HPMON.DLL)
- Line printer (LPR) port print monitor (LPRMON.DLL)
- Macintosh print monitor (SFMMON.DLL)
- Digital network port print monitor (DECPSMON.DLL)
- LexMark Mark Vision print monitor (LEXMON.DLL)
- NetWare print monitor (NWMON.DLL)

12

 By default, only the local print monitor is installed. To use another monitor, you have to create a new port when configuring a printer from the Printers icon.

At this point, you've now been exposed to Microsoft's unique printing terminology and to the architecture of the Windows NT print subsystem. At this point, you learn how to define and configure printers. After all this preparation, the details are quite anticlimactic.

PRINTING SOFTWARE

The function of printing software is to provide an interface between the client and the print device, whether that device is connected to a print server or directly to the client. In other words, the job of printing software is to insulate applications from having to incorporate the logic and understanding necessary to communicate with a large collection of print devices. That's why the functions that take application-specific file data and translate them into formats suitable for printing are included in the print drivers themselves.

Because selecting a particular print device for output is part of the Windows printing process, it makes perfect sense to put this intelligence into the driver. That's because you must indicate to what kind of device you wish to send a print job as a part of instructing an application to print to some specific printer. Because print devices differ so much from manufacturer to manufacturer, and even from model to model, the right place to bury the details is in the driver itself. Not only does this shield application developers from having to write code to drive each and every kind of print device imaginable, it puts the onus on the device manufacturer to build the file translation routines, because they're the usual source of driver software.

PRINTING ACROSS THE NETWORK

No organization can afford to give each user a printer. That's why printing to a print device across the network is by far the most common print scenario on Microsoft networks (in fact, many experts argue that sharing printers is one of the primary justifications for networking). Two typical options for printing across the network exist for Microsoft network clients, including Windows NT Workstation clients:

- You can print to a print device connected to a print server via a parallel or serial port.
- You can print to a print device connected directly to the network.

The main reason to connect a print device directly to the network is for convenience because the device doesn't have to be located near the print server. Any Windows NT-based print server (be it NT Workstation or NT Server) must still provide drivers and print job management.

THE PRINTING PROCESS

Now that you're familiar with the components of the printing process, here's how they fit together when printing from a Windows NT Workstation 4.0 client:

1. The user chooses to print from an application, causing the application to call the GDI. The GDI, in its turn, calls the printer driver associated with the target print device. Using the document information from the application and the printer information from the printer driver, the GDI renders the print job.

2. The print job is next passed to the spooler. The client side of the spooler makes a remote procedure call to the server side, which then calls the print router component of the server.

3. The print router passes the job to the local print provider, which spools the job to disk.

4. The local print provider polls the print processors, passing the print job to the processor that recognizes the selected printer. Based on the data type used in the

spool file (EMF or RAW), any necessary changes are made to the spool file in order to make it printable on the selected print device.

5. If desired, the separator page processor adds a separator page to the print job.

6. The print job is despooled to the print monitor. If the print device is bidirectional, then the language monitor sets up communications. If not, or once the language monitor is done, the job passes to the port monitor, which handles the job of getting the print job to the port to which the print device is connected.

7. The print job arrives at the print device and prints.

INSTALLING AND MANAGING PRINTERS

The Printers window is the starting point for all printer installation and management. To reach it, choose Start, Settings, and then Printers. If there are no printers installed, you see only the Add Printers icon, which you double-click to create a printer (add a local printer definition) or to connect to one across the network. Once you've created or connected to a printer, it will appear in this window with its own icon, as shown in Figure 12-1. To set its properties, right-click it and choose Properties from the menu that appears.

Figure 12-1   The Printers window includes the Add Printer wizard plus all defined printers

MANAGING PRINT JOBS

The Printers window comes into play not only when managing printers, but when managing print queues. To manage print jobs, just open the Printers window and double-click the icon for the printer in question. When you do so, you'll see a window similar to the one shown in Figure 12-2, which displays all current print jobs for the selected print device.

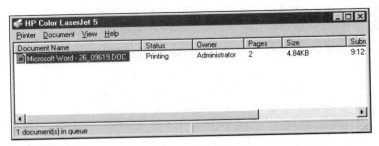

Figure 12-2   Reviewing print jobs

To manage a print job, select it and then choose the appropriate option from the menu. For example, to delete a print job, choose Cancel from the Document menu, and the print job will be deleted, allowing the next job in the queue to begin. Alternatively, you can right-click the print job's list entry and select Pause or Cancel. If the job has already been partially or completely spooled to the printer, it will continue printing until the print device has finished with the spooled data, but no more data will be sent to the printer once you choose to cancel the job.

To delete print jobs, you'll need Full Control over the printer or ownership of the print job. By default, Administrators, Server Operators, Print Operators, and Power Users all have Full Control over printers.

CREATING A LOCAL PRINTER

In the argot of Windows NT, creating a printer means that you're setting up a printer for local use. To do so, double-click the Add Printers icon in the Printer window and answer the questions as prompted, including the following:

- Which port will the printer be connected to?

- What is the make and model of the printer?

- What do you want the printer to be named?

- Do you want the printer to be the default for all print jobs?

- Should the printer be shared with the network?

If you're not sure whether your printer will require some fine tuning (such as port configuration), you can go ahead and create the printer and adjust its properties later.

Once you've answered all the questions and supplied the needed files for the installation, you can choose to print a test page to make sure you've set up the printer properly. You practice creating a printer for local use and sharing it with the network in Hands-on Project 12-3.

CONNECTING TO A REMOTE PRINTER

Connecting to a remote printer is even simpler than creating a printer. Once again, double-click the Add Printer icon in the Printers window, but this time choose to connect to a network printer instead of creating one locally. You'll be presented with a list of shared printers to connect to, and will have the option of making that printer the default. Connect to it, and your work is done. As Windows NT Workstations download printer drivers from the print server, you won't have to install local drivers.

 If the print server is running a version of Windows NT prior to 4.0, you have to install the 4.0 printer drivers onto the server; Windows NT 4.0 systems can't use the drivers from previous versions of Windows NT.

CONFIGURING A PRINTER

Once the printer is created or connected to, configuring it is easy. The following sections explain the options on each tab of the printer's Properties dialog box that opens when you right-click a printer in the Printers window and choose Properties.

 You can set up different configurations for the same print device by creating more than one printer for a single device. Just be sure to tell users which one to connect to so that they get the configuration they need.

12

GENERAL TAB

The General tab in a printer's Properties window contains a variety of controls that you can use to create a text comment that will show up in the Browse list entry for that printer. You can create a separate entry to identify the printer's location. The General tab also provides a point of entry to associate a specific driver with the underlying print device, to define a separator page between print jobs, to associate one or more print processors with print jobs delivered to that print device, and to force the device to print a test page (this comes in handy after you've configured a print device and want to make sure it's working properly).

When you turn to the General tab, it should be similar to Figure 12-3. Here you can specify the various elements just mentioned, each of which is discussed in more detail in the following sections.

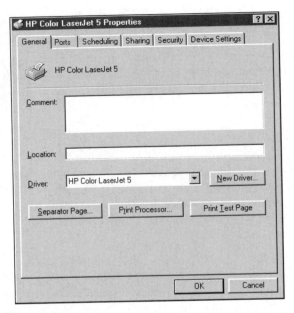

Figure 12-3   General tab in a printer's Properties window

Separator Page

Separator pages can be handy when several people are using the same computer and you want to be sure that the documents don't get mixed up. Windows NT comes with three separator page files: PCL.SEP, PSCRIPT. SEP, and SYSPRINT.SEP, but you can create custom pages in Notepad. Start off the document by putting a character on a line of its own, then use the codes in Table 12-1 to create separator files with the information that you need.

You can define any character as the lead character for the codes, but for the sake of the examples in Table 12-1, the exclamation point (!) is used.

Save the separator page file with a .SEP extension in the %systemroot%\system32 directory, and it will be among the options available when you choose Separator Page from the General tab.

Print Processor

If more than one print processor is installed in your computer, you can specify it by clicking the Print Processor button on the General tab and opening the dialog box shown in Figure 12-4. You can also specify the data type you want spool files to use.

Table 12-1   Separator Page Codes

Code	Function
!B!M	Prints all characters as double-width block characters until the !U code is encountered
!B!S	Prints all characters as single-width block characters until the !U code is encountered
!D	Prints the date the job was printed, using the format in the Regional settings in the Control Panel
!E	Ejects a page from the printer
!F*pathname*	Prints the contents of the file specified in *pathname*, without any formatting
!H*nn*	Prints a printer-specific control sequence, indicated by the hexadecimal number *nn*. Check your printer manuals to get the numbers
!I	Prints the job number (every print job is assigned a number)
!L	Prints all the characters following it until reaching another escape code (!)
!N	Prints the username of the person submitting the job
!*n*	Skips a certain number of lines, where *n* is a number between 0 and 9
!T	Prints the time the job was printed, using the format specified in the Regional settings in the Control Panel
!U	Turns off block character printing
!W*nn*	Specifies a certain width for the page (counted in characters); the default is 80, the maximum 256

12

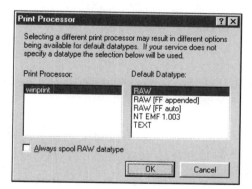

Figure 12-4   Print Processor dialog box

Print Test Page

When you click Print Test Page on the General tab, a test page consisting of SYSPRINT.SEP prints out, so that you can check that your printer is set up properly.

PORTS TAB

On the Ports tab shown in Figure 12-5, you can adjust settings (including interrupts and base I/O addresses) for the ports selected for use with a particular print device. You can also add port monitors by clicking the Add Port button. The bidirectional printing option should be checked for printers that are able to send status information back to the print monitor, where it can provide the basis for user notifications (print job complete, out of paper, paper jam, and so forth).

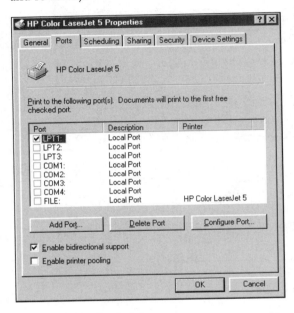

Figure 12-5   Ports tab

This tab can also set up a printer pool, in which more than one print device (the physical printer) is assigned to a single printer (the logical printer construct). This option, which works best with identical print devices with identical amounts of memory installed in each, can reduce waiting time on heavily used printers by sending jobs to whichever print device is least busy.

Select printers that are in close physical proximity to each other for pooling. Users will not be able to tell to which pooled print device a print job went, and they're not going to like chasing all over to find their print jobs. Also, if there's any difference in speed among the pooled printers, pool the fastest printer first, because the pooling software will check the first-pooled printer first.

Scheduling Tab

Use the Scheduling tab shown in Figure 12-6 to set the hours during which the printer is available and to determine how spooling works. You can set printer priority and spooling options on this tab.

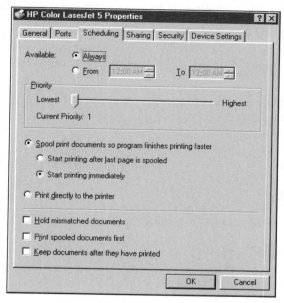

Figure 12-6 Scheduling tab

Priority

Regardless of what the online documentation says (and still says after a correction was posted for Windows NT Advanced Server 3.1), the priority setting available on the Scheduling tab applies to **printer priority**, not document priority. This setting is only used when more than one printer name is associated with a single print device. For example, suppose you've created two printer names (ALPHA and OMEGA) for the HP5P in the office. If you want to be sure that the short print jobs from ALPHA are sent to the printer first, you can increase ALPHA's priority so that the long print jobs normally sent to OMEGA have to wait.

The higher the number, the higher the priority, ranging from 1 to 99. The default is 1.

Spooling Options

Generally speaking, the default spooling options will work well for you because they'll start the printing process quickly and restore control to the application as fast as possible. However, here's what the options mean:

- If you choose to print directly to the port instead of spooling documents, then your application won't regain control until the print job is fully sent to the printer.

- Waiting to print until the document has completely spooled to the printer does not hold up the application as printing to ports does, but it will delay the printing process relative to the size of the print job.

- **Mismatched documents** are those for which the page setup and printer setup are incompatible. Specifying to hold mismatched documents prevents only those documents from printing, without affecting any other.

- If you choose to print spooled documents first, then the order in which documents spool to the print device will override any print priorities that you have in place. By default, this option is disabled, so printer priority controls the order in which jobs print.

- If you want to be able to print a document again without resubmitting it from the application, choose to keep documents in the spooler after they've printed.

SHARING TAB

The Sharing tab shown in Figure 12-7 works much like the one in place for sharing directories, with the addition of a list from which you can choose to install additional drivers for any Windows NT or Windows 95 computers that will be connecting to the printer.

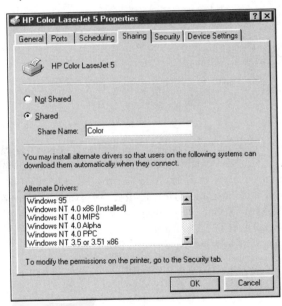

Figure 12-7 Sharing tab

Remember to install drivers for the appropriate client platform when sharing the printer! An x86 system running Windows NT cannot use the drivers installed for an Alpha print server.

Notice that, like shared directories, printers may have share names different from the local name.

SECURITY TAB

The Security tab shown in Figure 12-8 is also quite similar to that used for setting up secure files and directories. Here you can set permissions, auditing, and ownership for printers.

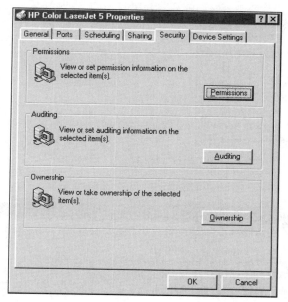

Figure 12-8   Security tab

Permissions

When you click the Permissions button on the Security tab, you'll see a dialog box like the one shown in Figure 12-9. Notice that it looks very similar to the one used for setting permissions on files and directories, but with two differences. First, the default permissions are more detailed and somewhat more restrictive for printers than for directories, and second, the permissions are different: You've got a choice of Full Control, Print, Manage Documents, and No Access, as defined in Table 12-2.

To add to the list of users for whom printer permissions are defined, click the Add button and add them as you would for setting file and directory permissions.

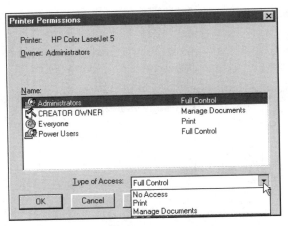

Figure 12-9   Printer permissions include settings unique to print devices

Table 12-2   Printer Permissions

Access	Description
No Access	User/group cannot do anything with the printer, including print to it
Print	User/group may print documents
Manage Documents	User/group may control document settings and manage print jobs, including pausing, resuming, restarting and canceling queued jobs
Full Control	User/group may do anything with the printer or print job, controlling document settings and print jobs, changing printing order, and changing printer properties

It makes no difference whether the file system in use is NTFS or FAT because these are printer permissions, not file permissions.

Auditing

Click the Auditing button on the Security tab to keep track of who's using the printer and what they're doing with it. When you do, you'll see a dialog box like the one shown in Figure 12-10.

The set of auditing options available for printers are, of course, distinct from those available for files or directories. Otherwise, this dialog box works much like the one used to set up other object auditing: To start auditing, choose an account or group for which you wish to choose options, and then select the events you want to record. To make the audit entries appear in the Event Viewer security log, you'll have to enable auditing in the User Manager.

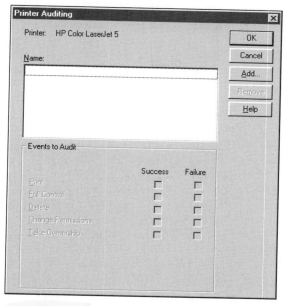

Figure 12-10 Printer auditing manages printer usage tracking

Ownership

Click the Ownership button on the Security tab to determine who owns a printer or to take control of it. Ownership is required to set permissions for a printer. Those with Full Control of a printer may take ownership of it.

12

DEVICE SETTINGS TAB

The Device Settings tab is the final tab in the Properties dialog box, as shown in Figure 12-11. It is used to make sure the print device itself is configured properly.

Most of these settings shouldn't need to be adjusted if you chose the proper printer driver, but these items may be subject to change as you upgrade your printer:

- *Memory:* Be sure that the amount of memory listed on this tab is equal to that installed in the printer. Too little, and you won't be able to utilize it to its full capacity. Too much, and the printer may try to take on more than it can handle.

- *Paper trays and other accessories:* Some printers may be upgraded with particular paper trays. If you install one, or rearrange existing ones, you'll need to update the settings here.

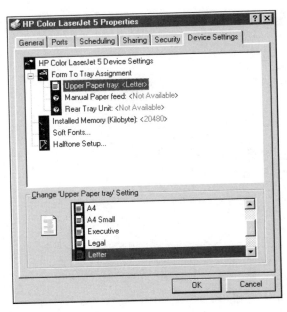

Figure 12-11   Device Settings tab

NETWORK PRINTING WITH WINDOWS NT WORKSTATION

You can use one of two scenarios when it comes to making a Windows NT Workstation machine a print server: workgroup printing and server printing.

WORKGROUP PRINTING

The **workgroup printing** model shown in Figure 12-12 assumes that the print device is connected directly to the network and is created on each individual machine in the workgroup, without sharing it. All users install their own printer drivers and configure their own settings.

Although workgroup printing can work reasonably well in very small workgroups in close physical proximity, for a number of reasons, it can easily become an administrative and troubleshooting nightmare:

- Individuals may change the printer physical configuration without informing others.

- Error messages (such as paper outages) will be sent only to the person initiating the print job during which the error occurred, so if that person doesn't see the error message, no one else will either.

- Print queues are separate, so that users cannot tell where in the print queue their jobs lie.

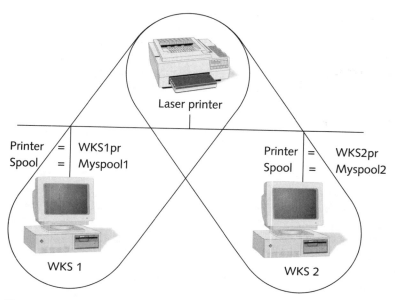

Figure 12-12   Workgroup printing

SERVER PRINTING

The **server printing** model illustrated in Figure 12-13 is much easier to administer. In this model, one Windows NT Workstation computer is attached to the printer and acts as a print server, sharing the printer with the network. The other workstations connect to the print server. Everyone works from the same print queue, error messages go to everyone who connects to the shared printer, and all audited events are recorded in a single log.

Using a Windows NT Workstation machine as a print server is similar to making a Windows NT Server machine a print server, with the following restrictions:

- Windows NT Workstation machines are legally limited to no more than 10 concurrent connections within the same LAN.

- Gateway Services for NetWare and the Services for Macintosh are not available with Windows NT Workstation.

- Spooling on a Windows NT Workstation computer has a lower priority than spooling on a Windows NT Server computer.

- If the Windows NT Workstation computer acting as a print server is also being used as a workstation, the competition for computer resources will slow both printing and user applications.

Thus, Windows NT Workstation is good as a print server only in fairly small and limited environments, but if you're going to use it in that environment, it's best to follow the model of server printing.

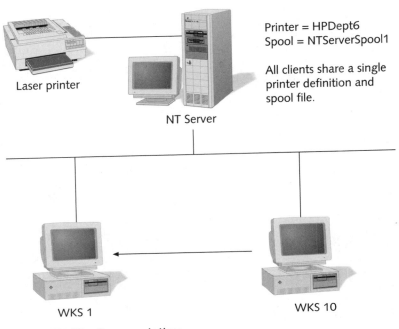

Printer = HPDept6
Spool = NTServerSpool1

All clients share a single
printer definition and
spool file.

Laser printer

NT Server

WKS 1

WKS 10

Figure 12-13   Server printing

TROUBLESHOOTING PRINTING PROBLEMS

Printing from Windows NT is usually a trouble-free process, but something can always go wrong. Microsoft recommends following these steps when troubleshooting printing problems:

1. Identify which of the seven components of the printing process is failing (printer creation and configuration, connecting to a shared printer, creating a print job, sending the print job to the spooler, processing the spooled job, sending the processed job to the print device, or printing at the device). To find the correct one:

   a. Analyze the symptoms of the problem.

   b. Change the configuration as applied to that part of the process.

   c. Test the configuration to see if the print job works.

   If the print job now works, you found the problem. If not, then it's time to start over.

2. Once you identify the problem, then look for documented problem solutions online, in the manuals that ship with Windows NT Workstation or the printer, or in the Microsoft Knowledge Base.

3. Implement a short-term solution.

4. Implement a long-term solution, if possible.

TROUBLESHOOTING NETWORK PRINTING

When troubleshooting network printing problems, add the following steps to your troubleshooting checklist:

1. Verify basic network connectivity, making sure you can see and connect to the print server. Try copying a file to or from the server. If you can't do this, then the print server itself may be inaccessible.

2. Create a local printer and redirect its port to a network printer. This will determine whether there's a problem copying files from the server to the workstation, as is done when you connect to a shared printer.

3. Print from a DOS-based program, using the NET USE command to connect to the printer. If the print job works, this may indicate that the connection to the printer is not persistent and needs to be adjusted. (See the Appendix for more information on NET commands.)

4. If using TCP/IP printing or connecting to a printer attached directly to the network, try PINGing the printer's IP address to make sure it's functioning (the PING utility is covered in Chapter 9). Also, create an LPR port to the printer and connect to that so as to allow the computer to act as the printer's queue.

STOPPING AND RESTARTING THE PRINT SPOOLER

The Spooler service is required for printing. Like other services, it's stopped and started—and its startup configured—from the Services applet in the Control Panel, as shown in Figure 12-14.

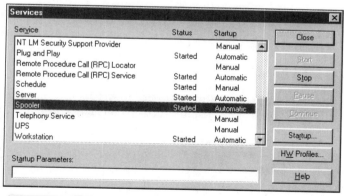

Figure 12-14   Stop and restart the print queue in the Services applet

By default, the Spooler service is set to begin automatically when the system starts. To stop it, select it from the list of services and click the Stop button. To start it again, select it from the list (it will remain on the list even when stopped) and click Start.

CHAPTER SUMMARY

This chapter explained the parts of the Windows NT printing model and how they fit together. The special vocabulary that Microsoft uses for printing-related services, software and hardware components, and activities was outlined. The Microsoft printing architecture and its various subsystems and capabilities was described.

You learned how to use the Add Printers wizard in the Printers folder to create, share, and connect to print devices, whether directly attached to a local machine or to use a shared printer elsewhere on the network. The Add Printer wizard exhibits many capabilities to configure a print device—including driver selection, output configuration, post-processing selections, and working with two or more identically configured printers to establish a printer pool.

The printing process can be fine tuned for various situations, including managing priorities for print jobs and setting up multiple printers with differing priorities so that multiple user communities can share a single print device, yet give one community preferential access to the device. Finally, the most common causes of printing problems in the Windows NT environment were reviewed, along with suggestions for how to isolate and identify these causes and take corrective actions to resolve them. Hopefully, you absorbed an appreciation for the simplicity and power of Windows NT's printing facilities, which are widely regarded as among the best available in any network operating system.

KEY TERMS

- **characterization data file** — The part of the printer driver that provides information about the make, model, and capabilities of the printer in question.

- **client application** — An application or service that creates print jobs for output, which may be either end-user originated or created by a print server itself. *See also* print client.

- **creating a printer** — Setting up a printer for local use.

- **data type** — The format in which print jobs are sent to the spooler. Some data types are ready for printing (RAW) and some require further preparation (EMF).

- **Device Driver Interface (DDI)** — A specific code component that handles translation of generic print commands into device-specific equivalents immediately prior to delivery of a spool file to a print device.

- **direct-attached printer** — A print device attached to a computer, usually through a parallel port. See *also* network interface printer.

- **enhanced metafile (EMF)** — Device-independent spool data used to reduce the amount of time spent processing a print job. Once it's queued, EMF data requires additional processing to prepare it for the printer.

- **Graphical Device Interface (GDI)** — The portion of the Windows NT operating system responsible for the first step of preparing all graphical output, whether to a monitor or to the printer.

- **language monitor** — The part of the print monitor that sets up bidirectional messaging between the printer and the computer initiating the print job.

- **mismatched document** — A document with incompatible printer and page settings (that is, the page settings are impossible to produce given the existing printer settings).

- **network interface printer** — A print device attached directly to the network medium, usually by means of a built-in network interface integrated within the printer, but sometimes by means of a parallel-attached network printer interface.

- **port monitor** — The part of the print monitor that transmits the print job to the print device via the specified port. Port monitors are actually unaware of print devices as such, but only know that something's on the other end of the port.

- **print client** — A network client machine that transmits print jobs across the network to a printer for spooling and delivery to a designated print device or printer pool.

- **print device** — In everyday language, a piece of equipment that provides output service—in other words, a printer. But in Microsoft terminology, a printer is a logical service that accepts print jobs and delivers them to some print device for output when that device is ready. Thus, in Microsoft terminology, a print device is any piece of equipment that can produce output, so this term would also describe a plotter, a fax machine, or a slide printer, as well as a text-oriented output device like an HP LaserJet.

- **print job** — The contents of a completely or partially interpreted data file that contains text and control characters that will ultimately be delivered to a print device to be printed, or otherwise rendered in some tangible form.

- **print processor** — Software that works with the printer driver to despool files and make any necessary changes to the data in order to format it for use with a particular printer.

- **print provider** — The server-side software that sends the print job to the proper server in the format that it requires. Windows NT supports both Windows network print providers and NetWare print providers.

- **print resolution** — A measurement of the number of dots per inch (dpi) that describes the output capabilities of a print device; most laser printers usually produce output at 300 or 600 dpi. In general, the larger the dpi rating for a device, the better looking its output (but high-resolution devices cost more than low-resolution ones).

- **print router** — The software component in the Windows NT print subsystem that directs print jobs from one print server to another, or from a Windows NT client to a remote printer.

- **print server** — A computer that links print devices to the network and shares those devices with client computers on the network. In the Windows NT environment, both NT Workstation and Server can function as print servers.

12

- **Print Server services** — A collection of named software components on a print server that handles incoming print jobs and forwards them to a print spooler for post-processing and delivery to a print device. These components include support for special job handling that can enable a variety of client computers to send print jobs to a print server for processing.

- **print spooler** — A collection of Windows NT Dynamic Link Libraries (DLLs) used to acquire, process, catalog, and dispense print jobs to print devices. The spooler acts like a holding tank in that it manages an area on disk called the spool file on a print server where pending print jobs are stored until they've been successfully output. The term *despooling* refers to the process of reading and interpreting what's in a spool file for delivery to a print device.

- **printer** — In Microsoft terminology, a printer is not a physical device but rather a named system object that communicates between the operating system and some print device. The printer handles the printing process for Windows NT from the time a print command is issued until a print job has been successfully output. The settings established for a printer in the Add Printer wizards in the Printers folder (Start, Programs, Printers) indicate which print device (or devices, in the case of a printer pool) will handle print output and also provide controls over how print jobs will be handled (banner page, special post-processing, and so forth).

- **printer driver** — Special-purpose software components that manage communications between the Windows NT I/O Manager and some specific print device. Ultimately, printer drivers make it possible for Windows NT to despool print jobs, and send them to a print device for output services. Modern printer drivers also permit the printer to communicate with Windows NT, to inform it about print job status, error conditions (out of paper, paper jam, and so forth), and print job problems.

- **printer graphics driver** — The part of the printer driver that renders GDI commands into device driver interface commands that may be sent to the printer.

- **printer interface driver** — The part of the printer driver that provides an interface to the printer settings.

- **printer pool** — A collection of two or more identically configured print devices to which one or more Windows NT printers direct their print jobs. Basically, a printer pool permits two or more printers to act in concert to handle high-volume printing needs.

- **printer priority** — The setting that helps to determine which printer in a pool will get a given print job. The printer with the higher priority is more likely to get the print job.

- **queue** (or **print queue**) — A series of files stored in sequential order waiting for delivery from a spool file to a print device.

- **RAW** — Device-dependent spool data that is fully ready to be printed when rendered.

- **rendering** — Graphically creating a print job.

- **server printing** — A Windows NT Workstation printing model in which a print server shares the printer with the network. All printer and job administration takes place via the print server.

- **spooling** — One of the functions of the print spooler; this is the act of writing the contents of a print job to a file on disk so that it will not be lost if the print server is shut down before the job is completed.

- **workgroup printing** — A Windows NT Workstation printing model in which all workgroup members connect directly to the printer. Printer and job administration are performed from the individual workstations.

REVIEW QUESTIONS

1. In the Windows NT print model, the physical hardware used to produce printed output is called a _____.

2. Which of the following components of the Graphic Device Interface (GDI) is responsible for rendering commands into DDI language for the printer?

   a. the printer graphics driver

   b. the printer interface driver

   c. the characterization data file

   d. none of the above

3. A _____ is software that enables an application to communicate with a printer.

   a. Printer driver

   b. Print provider

   c. Print monitor

   d. Print router

4. The _____ service implements the part of the printing software that receives, processes, schedules, and distributes print jobs.

5. Because they're device independent, EMF spool files are generally smaller than RAW spool files. True or False?

6. Which of the following operating systems use EMF data to send print jobs over the network? (Choose all that apply.)

   a. Windows for Workgroups

   b. Windows 95

   c. Windows NT 3.5x

   d. Windows NT 4.0

7. Spool files are normally deleted after the print job they prepared is completed. True or False?

12

8. What software must you have installed in order to access a NetWare print server via a Windows NT Server machine? (Choose all that apply.)

   a. Client Services for NetWare

   b. File and Print Services for NetWare

   c. NWLink

   d. Gateway Services for NetWare

9. When is SFMPSPRT.DLL normally installed?

   a. when the Spooler service is started

   b. when the Services for Macintosh is installed

   c. when the Gateway Service for NetWare is installed

   d. when the Client Service for NetWare is installed

10. The ___Language Monitor___ prepares the printer for bidirectional communication with the client computer, if the printer supports such communication.

11. Using Windows NT jargon, when you initially set up a printer for local use, you're ___creating___ it.

12. What is the function of the three .SEP files stored in the \system32 directory?

    a. to create custom graphics banner pages for print jobs

    b. to provide templates for separator pages

    c. to provide standard separator pages for immediate use

    d. none of the above

13. When you've got more than one printer set up for the same print device, this is known as

    a. print sharing

    b. printer pooling

    c. printer porting

    d. none of the above

14. One printer (APRINTER) in a printer pool has a priority of 50. The other (BPRINTER) has a priority of 10. BPRINTER has a queued print job. To which printer will the job go?

    a. APRINTER

    b. BPRINTER

    c. none of the above

15. If you choose to print directly to ports, what will happen?

    a. The job will only be able to print if it can fit all at once into printer memory.

    b. The application will stall until the print job is complete.

    c. The application will stall until the print job is fully spooled to the printer.

    d. Complex pages may not print correctly.

16. The ___Scheduling___ tab contains the option that allows you to keep documents in the spooler after they've printed.

17. What additional permissions exist when you share a printer from an NTFS partition?

    a. No Access

    (b.) Access

    c. Full Control

    d. none of the above

18. It's better to overestimate the amount of memory installed in the printer when you're configuring it on the Device Settings tab than it is to underestimate it. True or (False?)

19. When pages will only print after being fully loaded into printer memory, page protection is ___enabled___.

20. Choose all models that Microsoft recognizes for printing with Windows NT Workstation.

    a. workgroup

    b. domain

    c. server-based

    (d.) server printing

21. To most easily administer and troubleshoot the printer, you'll want to use the ___Server___ printing model.

22. Windows NT Workstation print servers may have up to _____ concurrent sessions.

    a. 5

    b. 10

    c. 20

    d. as many as are licensed

23. Print spooling on Windows NT Server is lower priority than print spooling on Windows NT Workstation. True or (False?)

24. Which of the following is/are not one of the seven parts of the printing process as detailed by Microsoft?

    a. connecting to a shared printer

    (b.) printing a separator page

    c. processing a spooled print job

    d. none of the above

25. You're connecting a Windows NT Workstation x86 computer to a Windows NT Server Alpha print server. The Windows NT Workstation must use the Alpha driver. True or (False?)

12

HANDS-ON PROJECTS

PROJECT 12-1

To change the location of the spool file (for all printers) from its default location on the C: drive to a directory on the D: drive, and stop and restart the Spooler service:

1. Start the Registry Editor (**Start**, **Run**, and enter **REGEDIT**). Click **OK**.

2. In the HKEY_LOCAL_MACHINE window, move to \SYSTEM\CurrentControlSet\Control\Print\Printers\<specific printer>\SpoolDirectory and select the **Printers** key, as shown in Figure 12-15.

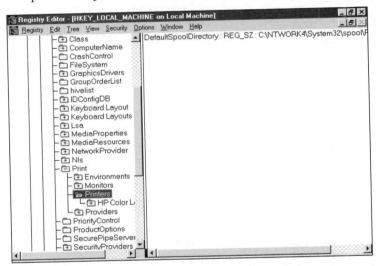

Figure 12-15   The Printers key in the Windows NT Registry

3. Double-click on the value of the Printers key and type the new path name in the dialog box that opens, as shown in Figure 12-16.

Figure 12-16   Changing the spool file location

4. Exit the Registry editor.

5. Open Explorer and add the new directory if it doesn't already exist, being sure to spell the directory's name exactly as you did in the Registry editor.

6. If the directory is part of an NTFS volume, assign the Creator/Owner, Everyone, the System, and the Administrators Full Control over the directory.

7. Open the **Services** applet in the Control Panel, as shown in Figure 12-17, and stop and restart the Spooler service.

8. Close the Services dialog box and the Control Panel window.

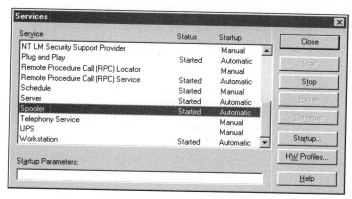

Figure 12-17   The Services applet

PROJECT 12-2

To create a separator page file that labels each print job with the name of the user who created the job and the date and time the job was printed, each on separate lines separated by a blank line:

1. Open Notepad or some other text editor.

2. On the first line of a new document, type a character to use as a control character (e.g., **@**), and press **[Enter]**.

3. Add the username to the document: **@N**.

4. Add a blank line: **@1**.

5. Add the date: **@D**.

6. Insert a blank line: **@1**.

7. Add the time: **@T**.

8. Save the file as **SEPARATOR.SEP** and store it in the \system32 directory.

Project 12-3

To create a new printer for local use and share it with the network:

1. Open the Printers window (**Start**, **Settings**, **Printers**) and double-click the **Add Printer** icon. A dialog box like the one shown in Figure 12-18 opens.

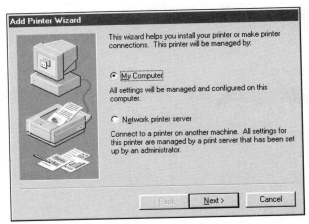

Figure 12-18   Adding a printer using the Add Printer Wizard

2. Choose **My Computer** as the printer manager. Click **Next**.

3. Choose a port to connect the printer to, as shown in Figure 12-19. The default is LPT1. Click **Next**.

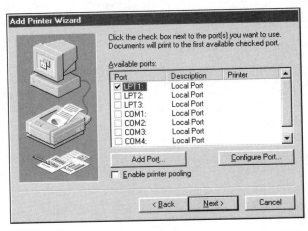

Figure 12-19   Selecting a printer port in the Add Printer Wizard

4. Choose a manufacturer and printer driver from the list that appears. The list of drivers changes depending on the manufacturer you select. Click **Next**.

5. In the next dialog box, shown in Figure 12-20, type in the name of the printer share, or leave the default name. For the sake of your users, choose a name that tells them something about where the printer is or what its capabilities are. Click **Next**.

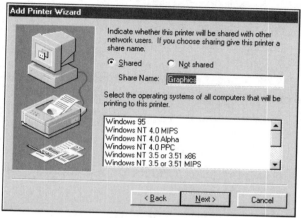

Figure 12-20   Naming the printer share in the Add Printer Wizard

6. In the Sharing dialog box that appears next, click the **Shared** button and assign it a share name. If the name you assign to the printer is more than eight characters long, Windows NT will automatically truncate it, but you can change the name. Install all drivers for the computers that will be connecting to the printer via the network. Click **Next**.

7. To be sure that the printer creation was successful, in the next dialog box that opens choose to create a test page.

8. Insert the Windows NT CD-ROM into the drive and provide the system with the location of the system files (this is usually not necessary because the Wizard knows where to look for these files).

9. The Wizard informs you when the installation is complete and closes itself. It may take as long as a couple of minutes for the new printer icon to appear in the Printers folder, but once it appears, check the printer to be sure the test page has printed properly.

CASE PROJECTS

1. Your workgroup has a single physical printer. One person in the workgroup generates a great many memos and other short documents, and another produces very long documents that are (usually) less time sensitive than the memos. You can't add another printer to the network, and both users must be able to print throughout the workday. How can you set printer priorities to accomplish this?

2. You've got a shared printer attached to your machine that other people can't print to. Your network's running IPX/SPX as its sole protocol. Which of the following would be valid steps in troubleshooting the problem? Explain.

   a. PINGing the printer's IP address to make sure the printer can be found on the network

   b. attempting to print locally

   c. attempting to connect to the print server from the print client and copy or move files on it

   d. none of the above

CHAPTER THIRTEEN

PERFORMANCE TUNING

Once you have installed and configured Windows NT Workstation, connected it to the network, and set up printers, you are ready to optimize the performance of your computer. Windows NT Workstation 4.0 includes several tools to monitor the performance of your computer and tune it for the best output. The most important of these tools are discussed in this chapter, including Performance Monitor, the Task Manager, and others.

Once these tools have been introduced and explored, you learn about specific system objects and counters that are worth monitoring. You also learn what combinations of counters can be used to analyze system slowdowns and how to isolate, identify, and correct system bottlenecks. Very few operating systems include the kinds of tools that Windows NT offers to help inspect and analyze system performance; in this chapter, you'll learn how to use them to good effect.

AFTER READING THIS CHAPTER AND COMPLETING THE EXERCISES YOU WILL BE ABLE TO:

- DESCRIBE THE TOOLS AVAILABLE IN WINDOWS NT TO MONITOR SYSTEM PERFORMANCE
- UTILIZE THESE TOOLS TO DEFINE AND ELIMINATE SYSTEM BOTTLENECKS

MONITORING AND PERFORMANCE TUNING

When it comes to system analysis, there are two primary components involved in tackling performance-related issues:

- *Monitoring:* This requires both a thorough understanding of system components and their behavior and observing those components and how they behave on a regular basis.

- *Performance tuning:* This activity consists of changing a system's configuration systematically, and carefully observing performance before and after such changes. Those changes that improve performance should be left in place, those that make no difference—or that make things worse—should be reversed. There are many well-known ways to improve Windows NT system performance; the most useful of these approaches or configuration changes are covered in this chapter.

In many ways, Windows NT does a remarkable job of tuning itself. It is capable of managing its memory, both physical and virtual, quite well. It also adjusts how it allocates memory across a variety of uses including file caching, virtual memory, system Kernel use, and applications use in a dynamic and effective way. Whereas older operating systems are nearly infinitely tunable, Windows NT offers a more limited set of tools and utilities to monitor and alter system performance. In this chapter, you learn what kinds of things you can do to improve NT performance, but you'll also notice that changing the operating system's configuration is seldom necessary. Instead, you'll learn how to recognize and react to system bottlenecks that can limit the system's overall performance.

BOTTLENECKS

A **bottleneck** is a condition in which a limitation of a single component slows down an entire system. The first thing to remember about bottlenecks is that they will always exist in every computer. Applications, hard drives, operating systems, or network interfaces may all inhibit the system from time to time, but for any given configuration, it is always possible to identify one component that slows the others down. Such components are called bottlenecks.

There is no single "bottleneck monitor" that can easily identify all possible problems. However, by using the monitoring tools included with Windows NT Workstation, you can identify possible bottlenecks and make adjustments. The goal of performance tuning a workstation is to make bottlenecks unnoticeable for everyday functions performed on a system. A computer used for CAD requires much greater throughput than a computer used primarily for word processing. Ideally, a computer should be waiting for user input, rather than making users wait for the computer's response. When the former happens, the user becomes the bottleneck (because computers can do much to speed up humans, this is regarded as an ideal situation).

Although the details will vary from situation to situation, the process of finding and fixing computer system bottlenecks follows a reasonably consistent process that usually works something like this:

1. Create a profile of normal performance for a computer. This is called a "baseline" and establishes how the system behaves under normal conditions. Key elements in a baseline include recorded observations about the characteristics and behavior of the computer system. For Windows NT, this includes observations of memory usage, disk usage, CPU usage, OS resource usage and activity, and network utilization, at the barest minimum.

2. Over time, a system's performance may begin to degrade, sometimes gradually, at other times dramatically. When this happens, the first step in determining potential bottlenecks is to compare baseline observations to current system behavior. In most cases, one or more of the baseline values will have changed for the worse. These changes indicate further areas of investigation that should prove fruitful.

3. Once potential areas of investigation are determined, the first thing to do is consult your knowledge of well-known causes for system problems (some of these for Windows NT Workstation are documented later in this chapter) and see if the symptoms match any of these common system maladies. In that case, the causes of bottlenecks will be easy to identify, and fixes easy to apply.

4. If the list of "usual suspects" does not produce an obvious culprit, further analysis will be required. Part of using Performance Monitor, and other NT system tools, is knowing how to use them to obtain more detailed statistics on system behavior, and then to analyze their reports and statistics to pinpoint potential bottlenecks. Some general analytical techniques, and some interesting combinations of objects and counters that will help in isolating and identifying such bottlenecks are covered in this chapter.

5. Once a potential bottleneck is identified, you will attempt changes to the system's configuration to ameliorate its constricting influences. Sometimes, this will involve software configuration changes; other times it may involve adding or replacing specific hardware components or subsystems to improve their performance characteristics.

6. Whenever a fix is attempted, it's essential to test its impact on the system. A new set of statistics should be compiled and then compared to the same system metrics measured before the fix was applied. Sometimes, the fix will do the trick and values will return to normal, or come closer to acceptable levels. At other times, the fix will not make a difference. In that case, further analysis, other fixes, and subsequent testing will be required. It's important to keep at the job until some action improves conditions.

13

It's essential to understand that bottlenecks can always be fixed but that some fixes are more expensive than others. Remember that an overloaded server or workstation can always be replaced with another, bigger, faster system, or that a single overloaded system can have its load spread across multiple systems to reduce the impact on any single machine. These kinds of fixes are a great deal more expensive than tweaking system settings, or adding more memory or disk space to a machine, but in some cases, drastic solutions become necessary. If you do your job of monitoring performance correctly, such radical changes needn't take anyone by surprise.

TASK MANAGER

The Windows NT Task Manager, shown in Figure 13-1, provides a nice overview of the current state of a computer. Task Manager can be accessed either by pressing Ctrl-Alt-Del and clicking the Task Manager button on the Windows NT Security windows or by right-clicking any unoccupied area on the Windows NT taskbar and selecting Task Manager from the list of shortcuts that appears.

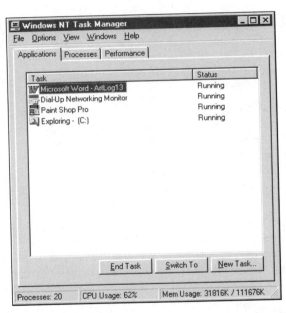

Figure 13-1   Windows NT Task Manager Applications tab

The Applications tab is the first tab that appears in Task Manager. It displays all programs currently running on the computer and the status of those programs (usually running). You can use this tab to halt an application (highlight an entry in the list, and click the End Task button), switch to a specific task (highlight an entry and click the Switch To button), or launch a new application (click the New Task button, and provide the name of an executable program or command in the Create New Task dialog box that opens).

The Processes tab shows all processes that are currently active on the computer, and includes information about each one, including its Process ID number (PID), CPU usage (CPU), CPU time, and Memory Usage. This display makes an excellent instant diagnostic tool whenever ill-behaved applications steal an inordinate amount of CPU time (if it's happening at the moment you use Task Manager, you'll see its CPU usage spike above 90 percent; even if it's not currently hogging the CPU, the CPU time entry may be high enough to stick out like a sore thumb).

The columns displayed on the Processes tab can be changed by choosing Select Columns from the View menu. This tab lists all processes that contribute to the operation of Windows NT, including such processes as SERVICES.EXE and SYSTRAY.EXE. Any particular process can be stopped by selecting it from the list, then clicking the End Process button.

 Be wary of ending Windows NT processes because you can cripple or disable a system by ending processes that are required for normal operation.

The Performance tab, shown in Figure 13-2, provides a graphical representation of cumulative CPU usage and memory usage. The four text windows at the bottom of the screen provide detailed information on the total number of **handles**, **threads**, and **processes** (Totals) active on the system, the amount of memory allocated to application programs or the system (Commit Charge), the amount of physical memory installed on your computer (Physical Memory), and the memory used by the operating system for internal processes (Kernel Memory).

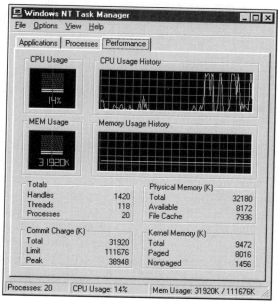

Figure 13-2   Performance tab of Windows NT Task Manager

The Performance tab in Task Manager can be used to quickly identify whether a computer is performing optimally. If the total CPU usage shown in the status bar is consistently high, over 70%, you can use the Processes tab to identify which process is monopolizing the CPU and take corrective action.

PERFORMANCE MONITOR

Performance Monitor (PM), which is included with Windows NT 4.0 Workstation and Server, is able to monitor and track many different areas of server performance. As Figure 13-3 shows, it is a graphical tool that can monitor many different events concurrently. By using Performance Monitor, you will be able to analyze network operations, identify trends and bottlenecks, determine system capacity, notify administrators when thresholds are exceeded, track the performance of individual system devices, and monitor either local or remote computers. To start Performance Monitor, select Programs from the Start menu, then select Administrative Tools (Common), then select Performance Monitor.

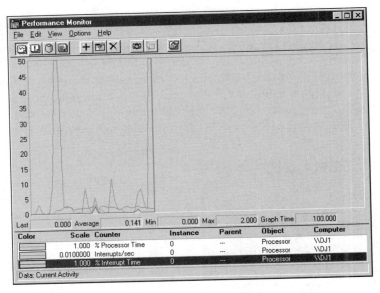

Figure 13-3   Performance Monitor

Although it can consume an appreciable amount of system resources, Performance Monitor is the best built-in tool available to track Windows NT performance over time. To begin monitoring a particular **counter** (each of which counts or reports on performance-related attributes for Windows NT system objects), select Add to Chart from the Edit menu, press Ctrl-I, or press the Add button on the toolbar (which looks like a plus sign). You will be presented with the Add to Chart screen shown in Figure 13-4. To begin monitoring a particular counter, first select the appropriate performance object, then select the related counter from the Counter: list and press Add.

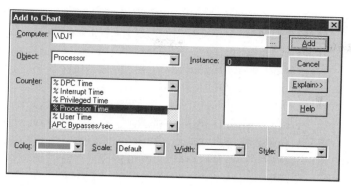

Figure 13-4 Counters are added via the Add to Chart window

The counters that can be tracked are grouped by objects. The Processor object is the default object that appears when the Add to Chart screen first opens. Other objects that can be tracked are accessed in the Object: list. Some of the most important Windows NT objects that Performance Monitor can track include Memory, Logical Disk, Physical Disk, Process, RAS Port, Server, and Thread. To download a complete list of all PM objects and their associated counters, visit this Web site: *http://www.lanw.com/training/pmnm/*, and click the download link labeled "Performance Monitor: List of All Counters (MS Word 97 .doc format) 159 KB."

The counters presented in the Counter: box vary from object to object. For example, the Disk Reads/sec. counter is available for both the Physical Disk object and the Logical Disk object, but not for the Memory object. If more than one object can be tracked, the Instance: box displays all available occurrences of the counter. For example, if two hard drives are installed in the computer and the Logical Disk object is selected, the Instance: box will display options for Total (a cumulative counter for all hard drives), C:, and D:.

The Explain button is perhaps the single most user friendly function in any Microsoft application. If you have a question about any particular counter, select the counter and press Explain. A Counter Definition screen opens at the bottom of the Add to Counter window describing the counter in plain English. This makes using Performance Monitor almost enjoyable.

Another exceptionally useful feature of Performance Monitor is its ability to monitor other computers. Using this feature, you can monitor a Windows NT Server from a workstation and not take the resource hit on the server itself. To monitor a particular computer, type its UNC path in the Computer: box (a UNC is a NetBIOS name that takes the form *node-name;* for example, \\lanw02 is the name of the computer being used to create this document), or press the ellipisis button (...) to browse the network.

OTHER PERFORMANCE MONITOR VIEWS

The default, and perhaps most helpful, view displayed by Performance Monitor is the Chart view. However, three other views are available: Alert, Log, and Report. The Alert view allows the user to set performance thresholds, either over or under a specified number, and display an alert when the threshold is exceeded. The Alert Interval displays the number of seconds between updates. The Log view provides the user with a mechanism to create log files that may be reviewed later, either to define a baseline or as a collection of evidence to be used when troubleshooting. The Report view displays the counters in text format, which can then be printed. You'll have a chance to try out the different views in the Hands-on Projects at the end of the chapter.

To select a particular view, choose it from the View menu, or press the appropriate button on the menu bar. The buttons appear in the following order, from left to right: Chart, Alert, Log, and Report. When the Options menu is selected, the options for the view appear as the first selection in the list. For example, if the Alert view is the current view and the Options menu is invoked, the Alert view properties can be set; if the Chart view is the current view, the Chart properties are available.

Performance Monitor is a powerful tool to track computer performance over time. The logging features can be used to establish a performance baseline against which measurements can be made when there are problems. Thus, PM acts as a measurement tool, a proactive investigative utility to preempt potential sources of trouble, and as a post-symptom diagnostic instrument.

USING PERFORMANCE MONITOR

When using PM to monitor one or more aspects of any Windows NT system, you must supply the following information to chart or log the data that this program produces:

- *Computer:* By default, PM always monitors whatever computer you run the program on. But it is possible to invoke PM to monitor the behavior of some other Windows NT machine by browsing the network in the various Add to dialog boxes for Charts, Logs, Alerts, and Reports.

- *Object:* Any instrumented object in the Windows NT environment can be monitored. For a complete list of the objects available for monitoring, check the list in the Object: entry in any of the Add to dialog boxes in PM. The Processor object is selected by default.

- *Instance:* In some cases, certain objects may have multiple instances. For example, a machine with multiple CPUs will have as many instances of the Processor object as it has CPUs. One with multiple logical drives will have one instance of the Logical Disk object for each such drive, as shown in Figure 13-5, where all three logical disks corresponding to the C:, D:, and E: drives appear in the Instance: box). When monitoring such objects, it's necessary to select the desired instance. By default, the first element in the list of instances is chosen (which is Total for logical disks).

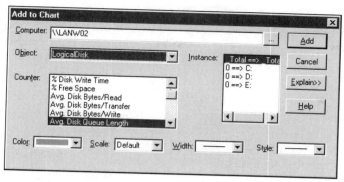

Figure 13-5 Multiple instances of an object appear in the Instance list

- *Counter:* Each instrumented Windows NT object includes one or more counters, which gather information about some particular attribute of the object being monitored. These counters form the basis for PM's various displays and logs, and provide the foundation for PM's various capabilities.

As you'll discover if you spend any time with PM, it has a multitude of counters—a plain-vanilla Windows NT installation will make it possible for you to monitor many hundreds of such counters. In practice, however, you will work with only a handful of objects and associated counters regularly (some more regularly than others). These are covered in the section that follows.

Important PM Objects and Counters

The following list presents those object and counter pairs that you are most likely to encounter on a Microsoft certification test, as well as several others that you may find useful when evaluating performance on your own systems and networks. For convenience, they appear in alphabetical order, in the form object—counter.

- *Logical Disk—Current Disk Queue Length:* If your system includes an older SCSI hard disk, or any kind of EIDE or other controller type, measure this counter. It indicates how many system requests are waiting for disk access. If the queue length is greater than 2 for any logical drive, that drive is suffering from congestion. If you can't redistribute the load across multiple logical disks, you should consider upgrading your disk subsystem. Always check the corresponding Physical Disk counter when examining Logical Disk counters.

- *LogicalDisk—%Disk Time:* This counter measures the percentage of time that a disk is busy handling Read or Write requests. On an NT Workstation, it's unusual for this percentage to hit 100; it's also unusual for this level to be sustained at 80% or higher. If this occurs, you'll want to redistribute files to try to spread the load across multiple logical drives. Always check the corresponding Physical Disk counter.

- *LogicalDisk—Disk Bytes/Transfer:* This counter measures the average number of bytes transferred between memory and disk during Read and Write operations. If the value hovers at or near 4 KB (4,096 bytes) this might indicate excessive paging activity on that drive. In general, a larger number indicates more efficient transfers than a smaller one, so look for declines against your baseline here, too.

- *Memory—Available Bytes:* This counter measures the number of bytes of memory available for use on the system at any given moment. Microsoft recommends that this value always be 4,096 KB or higher. If values hover at or below this threshold, it's a definite indicator that your system will benefit from additional RAM. You can also obtain this number from Task Manager's Performance tab (it's the Available entry in the Physical Memory pane) without having to run PM.

- *Memory—Cache Faults:* This counter measures the number of times the Windows NT cache manager must ask the system to bring a file's page in from disk or locate it elsewhere in memory. Higher values indicate potential performance problems, because a system's performance is best when cache hit rates are low. If you establish a baseline on a lightly loaded system, this will help you recognize when this counter begins to climb into risky regions (which are double or more the values that appear in the baseline). As with other memory counters, the proper response is to add more memory; in this case, adding more L2 cache is even better than adding main RAM.

- *Memory—Page Faults/sec:* This returns a count of the average number of page faults per second for the current processor instance. A page fault occurs whenever a memory page is referenced that is not already loaded in RAM; when this happens, the Virtual Memory Manager (VMM) must bring that page in from disk, and perhaps even make room for that page by swapping an old page out to disk first. This phenomenon helps to explain how memory congestion may manifest itself through excessive disk activity. If this value increases to more than double what you observe in a light-load baseline, it can indicate a need for more RAM.

- *Memory—Pages/sec:* This tracks the number of pages that are written to or read from disk to satisfy requirements of the VMM, and also includes paging traffic for the system cache that occurs to access file data for applications. This is an important counter to watch if paging activity seems high, because it can indicate that paging levels are slowing the system down. If this value increases to more than double what you observe in a light-load baseline, it strongly indicates a need for additional RAM.

- *Network—Bytes Total/sec:* This counts the total amount of traffic through the computer's network adapter, including all inbound and outbound data (framing characters, as well as payload data). It measures the absolute amount of traffic moving through the adapter. When it begins to approach the practical maximum for the type of media in use, trouble lies ahead. When that happens, it may require contemplating a switch to a faster type of network or indicate a need to distribute the machine's load across multiple network segments (and therefore, multiple adapters).

- *Network—Current Bandwidth:* This measures the current utilization levels of the network medium, and provides a background count against which to evaluate the machine's adapter. The same observations about loading and distribution apply to this counter as to the preceding one, except that it may indicate the need to partition the network to which this machine is attached, to lower the total traffic on individual cable segments.

- *Network—Output Queue Length:* This measures the number of packets queued up for transmission across the network, pending access to the medium. As with most other Windows NT queues, if this value approaches or exceeds 2, it indicates that network delays are likely and that the bottleneck should be removed, if at all possible.

- *Network—Packets/sec:* This measures the number of packets sent and received across a specific network adapter. Comparison with a baseline will indicate when this value is getting out of hand. The same observations that apply to the Bytes Total/sec counter apply to this counter as well.

- *Physical Disk—Current Disk Queue Length:* Physical disk counters track activity on a per hard-disk basis, but provide much of the same kind of information that the logical disk counters do. But calculating abnormal queue lengths for physical disks is different than for logical ones: here, the threshold for trouble is between 1.5 and 2 times the number of spindles on the hard drive. For ordinary drives, this is the same as for logical disks. But for RAID arrays (which Windows NT treats as a single drive), the number is equal to 1.5 to 2 times the number of drives in the array.

- *PhysicalDisk—%Disk Time:* This counter measures the percentage of time that a hard drive is kept busy handling Read or Write requests. For NT Workstation machines, although you may see peaks as high as 100%, the sustained average should not exceed 80%. But even if sustained averages are high, this value is not worrisome unless the corresponding queue length numbers are in the danger zone as well.

- *PhysicalDisk—Disk Bytes/Transfer:* This counter measures the average number of bytes that Read or Write requests transfer between the drive and memory. This is a case where smaller values are more worrisome than larger ones, because they can indicate inefficient use of drives and drive space. If this behavior is motivated by applications, try increasing file sizes. If it's motivated by paging activity, an increase in RAM or cache memory is a good idea.

- *Processor—%Processor Time:* This counter measures the percentage of time since PM started that the CPU is busy handling non-idle threads—in other words, real work. Sustained values of 80% or higher indicate a heavily loaded machine;

13

consistent readings of 95% or higher indicate a machine that needs to have its load reduced, or its capabilities increased (for a new machine, a motherboard upgrade, or a new CPU, see "Eight Worthwhile Ways to Improve Windows NT Performance" at the end of this chapter for a discussion of these various performance improvements).

- *Processor—Interrupts/sec:* This counter measures the average number of times per second that the CPU is interrupted by some device requesting immediate processing. Network traffic and system clock activity establish a kind of background count against which this number should be compared. Pathological increases occur when a malfunctioning device begins to generate spurious interrupts, or when excessive network traffic overwhelms a network adapter. In both cases, this will usually create a count that's at least five times greater than a lightly loaded baseline situation.

- *System—Processor Queue Length:* This counter measures the number of execution threads that are waiting their turn for access to some CPU. If this value increases to more than double the number of CPUs present on a machine (which means 2 for most normal NT Workstations), it indicates a need to distribute this machine's load across other machines, or to increase its capabilities—usually by adding an additional CPU (where possible) or by upgrading the machine or the motherboard (increasing CPU speed does not increase performance as much as you might think because it does nothing for the machine's cache or its memory and bus transfer capabilities).

When more than one counter is worth watching for a particular object (for instance, there are four network-related counters), it's more significant when all counters experience a dramatic change in status simultaneously than when only one or two such counters show an increase. Across-the-board changes are more likely to indicate a bottleneck than are more localized ones (which are more likely to be caused by applications or by shifts in local conditions, traffic levels, and so forth).

Establish a Baseline

To recognize when bottlenecks exist, it's first necessary to establish some feeling for what's normal on your system. You can do this by creating a log in PM, establishing monitors on the counters recommended in the preceding section, and then collecting data for those counters at regular intervals over a period of time (like a weekend, when a system is likely to be most lightly loaded). This helps you establish a collection of data that defines what a light load looks like and provides a point of comparison against which you can measure system behavior when things are not going as quickly as you'd like.

Of course, you'll want to make sure that what's normal for a system doesn't itself indicate existing bottlenecks. If you do discover unacceptably long queues or evidence of memory problems when you create a baseline, you'll want to address whatever bottlenecks you discover right away. The next section describes how you can do this for common Windows NT subsystems.

RECOGNIZING AND HANDLING COMMON BOTTLENECKS

Now that you know which counters are most likely to be worth watching, here are tips on how to use them, either alone or in various combinations, to help determine what kinds of bottlenecks might be present on a system. Some steps you might consider taking to correct such bottlenecks, should they be found to exist, are also provided.

Disk Bottlenecks

Disk bottlenecks are most likely when disk counters increase more dramatically than other counters on your system, as compared to your baseline, or when queue lengths become unacceptably long. To monitor disk activity in Windows NT, you must turn disk monitoring on at the Windows NT command line. Here's how: Launch the DOS Command Prompt (Start, Programs, Command Prompt), then enter the string *diskperf -y* at the command line. This turns disk monitoring on and causes the PhysicalDisk and LogicalDisk counters to begin displaying non-zero values. To turn disk monitoring off, follow the same procedure but enter the string *diskperf -n* instead. On older 486 systems, Microsoft recommends that you enable disk counters only while using PM; on newer systems, it's OK to leave disk monitoring on at all times.

If Disk Queue Length and %Disk time values remain consistently high (1.5 or higher and more than 80%, respectively), it's probably time to think about adding more disk controllers or drives, or perhaps even replacing existing drives and controllers with newer, faster SCSI equivalents. This costs money but can provide dramatic performance improvements on systems with disk bottlenecks. Where disk bottlenecks exist, adding a controller for each drive can substantially improve performance, as can switching from individual drives to disk (RAID) arrays. Because high-end disk controllers often include on-board memory, which functions as yet another level of system cache, they too can confer measurable performance benefits.

Sometimes software can contribute to disk bottlenecks, often because of poor design or configuration settings that impact disk performance. Because tweaking an application's source code is beyond the reach of most system administrators, inspect the application to see if you can increase the size of the files it manipulates directly, or the size of data transfers it requests. This may also be one case in which you would want to make sure that disk monitoring has been turned off to remove this extra source of potential system overhead.

13

Memory Bottlenecks

Windows NT is subject to several different kinds of **memory bottlenecks**. To begin with, it's important to make sure the paging file is working as efficiently as possible. This translates into a size between two-to-three times the amount of physical RAM on a machine, and optimal location of the paging file itself. On machines with more than one drive, Microsoft recommends situating the paging file on the boot drive (where the Windows NT system files reside). Likewise, if multiple such drives are available, it's a good idea to spread the paging file evenly across all such drives (avoid the boot drive). Better yet, each such drive should have its own disk controller, because this allows Windows NT to access all those drives in parallel.

Excessive paging activity can be detected by watching the page-related counters mentioned earlier, and by observing the lowest number of Available Bytes encountered over time (remember, Microsoft recommends that this number never dip below 4 MB or 4,096 KB). Likewise, excessive disk time and disk queue lengths can often mask paging problems, so be sure to check paging-related statistics when disk utilization soars. Adding more memory can fix such problems, and improve overall system performance.

Processor Bottlenecks

Processor bottlenecks are indicated when the Processor object's %Processor time counter stays consistently above 80%, or when the System object's Processor Queue Length counter remains near a value of 2 or greater. In both cases, the CPU is being overworked. However, occasional peaks of 100% for processor time are not unusual (especially when processes are being launched or terminated). Therefore, the combination of high utilization and overly long queues is more indicative of trouble than is an occasionally high utilization rate.

Even on machines where multiple CPUs are supported, it's important to recognize that performance doesn't scale arithmetically as additional CPUs are added. Although a second CPU gives a much more dramatic incremental improvement in performance than a third, or fourth, and so on, two CPUs do not double performance (neither do three, for that matter). You're often better off responding to CPU bottlenecks by redistributing a machine's processing load, or by replacing the machine or upgrading its CPU, memory, and motherboard than by upgrading or adding another CPU. In both of these latter cases, these changes do not increase the amount of cache memory on a system, nor do they improve the system's underlying CPU-to-memory data transfer capabilities. Because these often play a crucial role in improving system performance, CPU-only changes cannot deliver the kinds of dramatic performance improvements that outright replacements or motherboard-level upgrades can.

Network Bottlenecks

Network bottlenecks are not typical on most NT Workstation machines because end users seldom load the network sufficiently to experience performance problems of their own making. However, it is worth monitoring how much traffic is passing through a workstation's network adapter as compared to the networking medium to which it is attached. Excessive activity can sometimes indicate either a failing adapter (sometimes called a "jabbering transceiver") or an ill-behaved application. In both cases, the fix is relatively straightforward (replace the NIC or the application, respectively). But sometimes, the network itself may be overloaded. This is indicated by utilization rates that exceed the recommended maximum for the medium in use (for example, Ethernet should not be loaded more heavily than 56% utilization, but token ring can function adequately at loads as high as 98%). When this kind of thing happens, you have two options: Divide the network into multiple segments and balance traffic so that no segment is overloaded, or replace the existing network with a faster alternative. Neither of these options is especially fast, cheap, or easy, but the former is cheaper than the latter and may give your network—and your budget—some breathing room before a wholesale upgrade is warranted.

This concludes the discussion of PM and its many diagnostic and investigative capabilities. The sections that follow cover other tools that you can use to observe NT system behavior or tune its performance.

EVENT VIEWER

The Windows NT **Event Viewer** is another useful tool that can be configured to log **events** that occur on the computer. Event Viewer tracks all events generated by the operating system, as well as security and application events. Failure of a device to load, an unsuccessful logon, or a corrupt database file can all be recorded by Event Viewer and viewed through one of three log files: System, Application, or Security. The Event Viewer is included in the Administrative Tools (Common) group accessed from Programs on the Start menu. Figure 13-6 shows a typical Event Viewer displaying the System log.

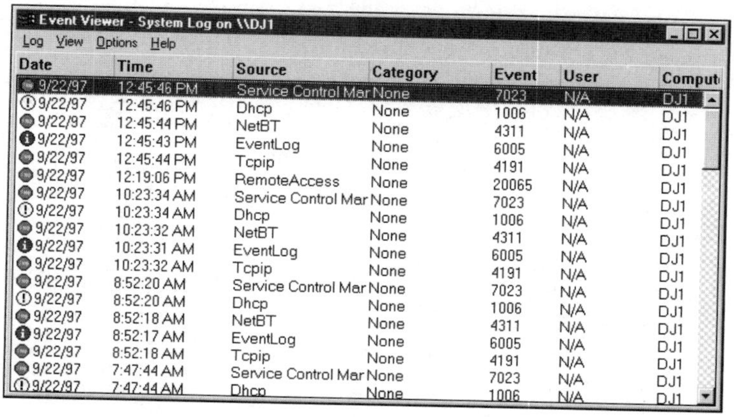

13

Date	Time	Source	Category	Event	User	Comput
9/22/97	12:45:46 PM	Service Control Mar	None	7023	N/A	DJ1
9/22/97	12:45:46 PM	Dhcp	None	1006	N/A	DJ1
9/22/97	12:45:44 PM	NetBT	None	4311	N/A	DJ1
9/22/97	12:45:43 PM	EventLog	None	6005	N/A	DJ1
9/22/97	12:45:44 PM	Tcpip	None	4191	N/A	DJ1
9/22/97	12:19:06 PM	RemoteAccess	None	20065	N/A	DJ1
9/22/97	10:23:34 AM	Service Control Mar	None	7023	N/A	DJ1
9/22/97	10:23:34 AM	Dhcp	None	1006	N/A	DJ1
9/22/97	10:23:32 AM	NetBT	None	4311	N/A	DJ1
9/22/97	10:23:31 AM	EventLog	None	6005	N/A	DJ1
9/22/97	10:23:32 AM	Tcpip	None	4191	N/A	DJ1
9/22/97	8:52:20 AM	Service Control Mar	None	7023	N/A	DJ1
9/22/97	8:52:20 AM	Dhcp	None	1006	N/A	DJ1
9/22/97	8:52:18 AM	NetBT	None	4311	N/A	DJ1
9/22/97	8:52:17 AM	EventLog	None	6005	N/A	DJ1
9/22/97	8:52:18 AM	Tcpip	None	4191	N/A	DJ1
9/22/97	7:47:44 AM	Service Control Mar	None	7023	N/A	DJ1
9/22/97	7:47:44 AM	Dhcp	None	1006	N/A	DJ1

Figure 13-6   Event Viewer

There are three types of System and Application log events and two types of Security log events that Event Viewer records; they are all listed in Table 13-1.

Table 13-1 Event Viewer Event Types

Event Type	Description
Information	Signifies rare but significant events about successful operation of internal services and drivers. For example, when a database program loads successfully, it may generate an Information event.
Warning	Signifies potential problems may be imminent although there is no present danger. For example, if disk space is running out, a Warning event may be logged.
Error	Signifies that significant and immediate problems exist that require immediate attention. For example, if a driver fails to load correctly, an Error event is issued.
Success Audit	A Security log event that indicates that an event selected for audit has occurred. For example, when a user successfully logs onto a system, a Success Audit event is logged.
Failure Audit	A Security log event that indicates when an audited event has failed. For example, an unsuccessful attempt to access a network drive is logged as a Failure Audit.

All Event log entries include the date and time of the event, its source, its category (such as Logon or Logoff), an event number, the name of the account that generated the event, and the name of the computer on which the event occurred.

As with Performance Monitor, Event Viewer can be used to view logs on other computers. To access log files on other computers, use the Select Computer option in the Log menu.

FILTERING EVENTS

In addition, all events can be filtered. By selecting the Filter Events option from the View menu, the window displayed in Figure 13-7 opens. This window allows you to select a range of dates from which to view events, the type of event to view, the Source, Category, User, Computer, or the event ID.

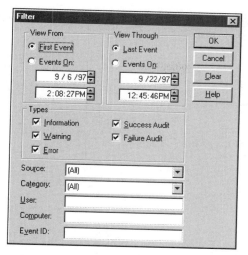

Figure 13-7   The Filter window in Event Viewer

SYSTEM LOG

The System log is the primary log file for most NT system services, drivers, and processes. As mentioned earlier, typical System log events occur when device drivers fail to load or load with errors, when system services fail to start, when system service errors or failures occur, or when auditing is enabled, and system-related events flagged for auditing occur.

APPLICATION LOG

The Application log contains event messages that may be generated by Windows NT Applications, or by certain Windows NT services (such as the Replicator service, which writes its messages to this log). For example, each time Autochk verifies the structure of a disk, its activities are logged in the Application log.

SECURITY LOG

Unlike the System and Application logs, the Security log does not automatically track events. Instead, it is configured via User Manager to track specific successful and unsuccessful events, such as logon, resource access, and computer restart and shutdown. To begin auditing these events, start User Manager by choosing Start, Programs, Administrative Tools (Common), and User Manager. To invoke the Audit Policy screen shown in Figure 13-8, select Audit from the Policy menu in User Manager.

13

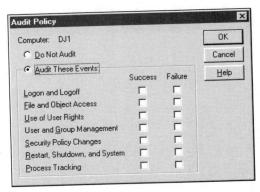

Figure 13-8   The Audit Policy window in User Manager

Users can track success or failure of Logon and Logoff; File and Object Access; Use of User Rights; User and Group Management; Security Policy Changes; Restart, Shutdown, and System; and Process Tracking. File and Object access tracking includes Read, Write, Execute, Delete, Change Permissions, and Take Ownership.

LOG EVENT DETAILS

Although browsing event logs themselves is an excellent way to spot trends and to monitor computer operation in general, you can also view event details. By pressing Enter after highlighting an event, double-clicking on an event, or selecting Detail from the View menu, you can inspect the kind of Event Detail shown in Figure 13-9.

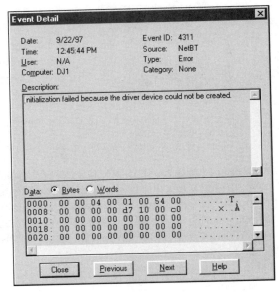

Figure 13-9   The Event Detail window

The Event Detail screen gives the user information that is useful in determining bottlenecks in the system. By pressing the Next or Previous button, the user is able to easily step through a sequence of events.

WINDOWS NT DIAGNOSTICS

The **Windows NT Diagnostics (WINMSD)** tool displays Registry configuration information in an easy-to-read format. It displays hardware, resource, and service information that can be used to identify conflicts or configuration errors. Figure 13-10 shows the Windows NT Diagnostics tool, which is accessed by clicking Start, Programs, Administrative Tools (Common) from the taskbar. It can also be executed by using the Run command from the Start menu and entering *WINMSD*.

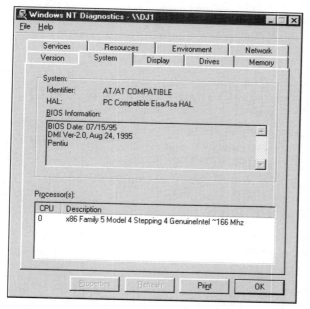

Figure 13-10   Windows NT Diagnostics displays Registry information

Each of the nine tabs of Windows NT Diagnostics displays specific information about the computer's current configuration. These tabs are listed in their default order of appearance:

- *Version:* Displays the software version and registration information
- *System:* Shows more detailed general information about the computer, such as BIOS revision, and number and type of processors installed
- *Display:* Describes the video adapter and its driver
- *Drives:* Shows information about all drives connected to the computer by drive type or drive letter; detailed properties for each drive can be viewed by pressing the Properties button

- *Memory:* Describes the physical memory in the system and pagefile information; the four boxes displayed—Totals, Physical Memory, Commit Charge, and Kernel Memory—are the same boxes displayed in the Task Manager, Performance tab

- *Services:* Displays the current status of all services and devices

- *Resources:* Provides information on all IRQs, I/O ports, DMA channels, and memory addresses used in the system; detailed properties for any setting can be viewed by pressing the Properties button; in addition, the Devices button displays a list of all devices—select the device and press the Properties button to display all information for a specific device

- *Environment:* Displays System and Local User environment settings

- *Network:* Displays configuration information and statistics

Please note that WINMSD is designed as a system inspection tool and does not include any abilities to alter the settings it shows. To change the settings you find in this utility, you must use the appropriate Control Panel applet, or some other system utility, to effect whatever changes are necessary.

WINDOWS NT HARDWARE QUALIFIER (NTHQ)

The **Windows NT Hardware Qualifier (NTHQ)** is an exceptionally useful utility that checks the hardware installed in your computer and creates a report that documents the configuration this program discovers. This report can be printed and used as a hard copy reference as part of your permanent system documentation, for comparison if operational problems occur after a change is made, or to troubleshoot hardware related problems, even when no changes have occurred.

The NTHQ is an MS-DOS-based program that must be run from a floppy disk at system startup. To create the disk, run the MAKEDISK.BAT file located in the \Support\Hqtool folder on the Windows NT CD.

Once you have created the disk, restart the computer with the floppy disk still in the drive. The disk boots the system into DOS, after which it loads NTHQ and the opening screen, which describes the basic steps the program will take once initialized, and prompts you to continue detection. Press the Yes button to continue to the next screen.

NTHQ has two detection options: comprehensive and safe. The next screen asks you whether to perform a comprehensive detection. The first time you run the NTHQ, press Yes for comprehensive detection. However, if you have experienced problems with hardware detection before, press No to perform a safe detection.

Once NTHQ has completed your system inventory, you will be presented with a screen that gives you the opportunity to view the hardware it found, save the report, or exit. Even if you choose to exit, the report will automatically be saved to NTHQ.TXT. The README.TXT file that is created is a Help file that provides information on the report that was created.

The following is a sample of a NTHQ.TXT file.

```
Hardware Detection Tool For Windows NT 4.0

Master Boot Sector Virus Protection Check
Hard Disk Boot Sector Protection: Off.
No problem to write to MBR

ISA Plug and Play Add-in cards detection Summary Report

Number of ISA PnP cards detected: 1


Summary for ISA PnP card number 1
-----------------------------------------------
Vendor ID: TCM5094
Friendly name: 3Com EtherLink III ISA (3C509b-Combo) in PnP mode
Serial Number: AF092206
Reported Checksum: 0xEC
PNP Version:    1.0
Vendor Ver.:    10
Device Description:
Device ID: TCM5094
Supports I/O Range Checking
Vendor Defined Logical Device Control Registers:
None

Compatible Device ID:PNP80F7
IRQ lines supported:
0x3 0x5 0x7 0x9 0xA 0xB 0xC 0xF
I/O Descriptors:
Card decodes full 16-bit ISA Address
Minimum base I/O Address: 0x210
Maximum base I/O Address: 0x3E0
Base I/O Address requires 0x10 byte alignment
Device requires 16 Continuous ports

The current configuration for ISA PnP card number 1
-----------------------------------------------

Logical Device 0 - ID 0x94506D50
```

13

THE SYSTEM RECOVERY UTILITY

At first, it might seem that this utility has nothing to do with performance tuning a Windows NT system. But because some of the changes that you might introduce from time to time might render a system unbootable, the **System Recovery Utility** lets you configure NT for various debugging and restart options in the event of a system crash. This can help restore operation after all kinds of trouble, of course, but comes in especially handy when you're deliberately manipulating your system's configuration and performance characteristics. The System Recovery utility is configured via the Startup/Shutdown tab in the Control Panel System applet, shown in Figure 13-11.

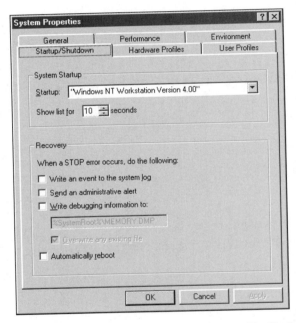

Figure 13-11 The System Recovery utility Startup/Shutdown tab

When a STOP error occurs, the system refers to the settings for the System Recovery utility to decide what to do next. There are four possible actions the computer can take:

- Write an event to the system log

- Send an administrative alert

- Write debugging information to a file—the filename and path for the debug file must be defined; if an existing file is to be overwritten, the appropriate box must be checked

- Automatically reboot the computer

The debugging information provided can then be used by support personnel to determine the problem and possible solutions.

 If you configure the System Recovery Utility to copy the contents of virtual memory to disk after a STOP error, the Windows NT paging file *must* be located on the Windows NT boot drive, or the file will not be properly saved. That's because a failing system can usually write only to the drive where the system files reside before it shuts itself down. This makes it impossible to move the paging file to another hard disk, which is also recommended for performance reasons.

OPTIMIZING APPLICATIONS

Windows NT includes a rudimentary method to adjust system performance between foreground and background applications. Activate this in the Performance tab in the System applet in the Control Panel, as shown in Figure 13-12.

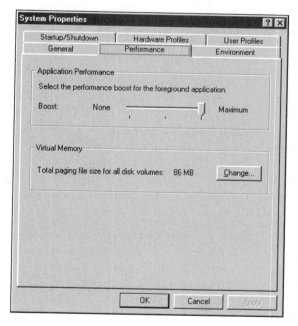

Figure 13-12   The Performance tab in the System applet

The Performance tab provides a slider to adjust the priority of system resources for foreground and background applications. With the slider set to Maximum, the foreground applications receive a higher priority than all background applications. Setting the slider to None gives all applications equal priority, regardless of whether they are in the foreground or background. For Windows NT Workstation, which is designed for a single end user, the default setting is Maximum. As long as such a machine serves only a single user, it's perfectly OK to leave this setting alone. But if this machine plays a role on the network as a print server (or some other shared network resource), you might want to back the slide off to None to give incoming network tasks an equal share of system access compared to local tasks.

This tab also includes settings for the paging file size used in the Windows NT virtual memory subsystem. Pressing the Change button presents the user with configuration options to define paging file settings for each hard drive. As discussed in Chapter 1, the virtual memory paging file is used to swap pages of memory in and out of RAM.

Although there may be no obvious connection between this file and system performance, because the size of the paging file essentially limits the upper bound of the virtual memory space within which Windows NT can work, it is quite true that increasing paging file size or changing its location can often have a profound impact on Windows NT system performance.

For one thing, the default maximum size for a paging file is the number of megabytes of RAM plus 11 MB on Windows NT Workstation. But on systems where users may have five or more applications open simultaneously, a paging file equal in size to twice the amount of physical memory often works better. On especially heavily loaded systems, this ceiling may sometimes need to be set as high as three times the amount of RAM on a system. By using Task Manager to observe the values for the Limit and Peak readings in the Commit Charge pane on the Performance tab, you can tell when the size of the paging file needs a boost: any time the Peak comes within 4,096 KB (4 MB) of the Limit value, it's time to increase the size of the paging file.

If multiple hard disks are installed on a Windows NT Workstation machine, it's also possible to obtain a performance boost by moving the page file to a separate hard drive other than the Windows NT system or boot drives. Windows NT uses the boot drive (which is where the Windows NT system files reside) to continuously access system files and related information. By moving the paging file to a separate hard disk, paging access can often occur in parallel with system access. This too can provide a boost to performance because Windows NT can access important resources simultaneously without having to switch between accessing the paging file and accessing system files.

Windows NT offers a more explicit way to set priority levels for applications than in the Performance tab in the System applet. To begin with, it's important to understand that Windows NT recognizes 32 levels of application priority, numbered from 0 to 31. This is broken into a series of numeric ranges, as follows:

- 0–15: User-accessible process priorities
- 16–31: System-accessible process priorities
- 0–6: Low user range
- 4: Low value (as set in Task Manager, or with /low parameter to start command)
- 7: Normal (default setting for user processes in Windows NT)
- 8–15: High user range
- 13: High value (as set in Task Manager, or with /high parameter to start command)

- 16–24: Real-time values accessible to Administrator-level accounts

- 24: Real-time value (as set in Task Manager, or with /realtime parameter to start command)

- 25–31: Real-time values accessible to operating system only

There are two techniques available to users or administrators to manipulate process priorities: (1) already-running processes can be managed using Task Manager, or (2) the Windows NT Start command can be used to launch processes with specific priority settings from the command line.

To use Task Manager, right-click on any unoccupied region of the taskbar, and select Task Manager from the resulting menu. In Task Manager, select the name of the desired process (usually this is the name of some .EXE file that corresponds to the process), then right-click that process to produce another menu. From this menu, select Set Priority, which produces the menu shown in Figure 13-13. This is where you can pick one of the predefined priority settings—namely Low, Normal, High, or Realtime (the current setting is the entry marked with a bullet symbol to the left, Normal in Figure 13-13). Remember that you must be logged on with Administrator privileges to use the Realtime setting.

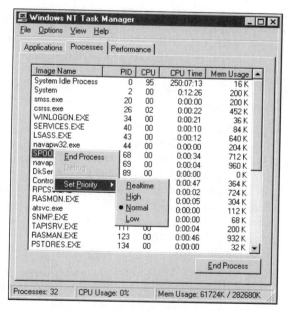

13

Figure 13-13   Task Manager Processes tab

The other alternative is to use the Windows NT Start command from the command line. Use this approach to launch a new application at some priority level other than the default. To begin with, you must open a DOS window (Start, Programs, Command Prompt). Then, at the command line, the Start command follows this general syntax:

```
start /<priority-level> <program>
```

where /<priority-level> must be one of /low, /normal, /high, or /realtime, and <program> is a valid path plus filename for the program you wish to launch at the specified priority level. Thus, to launch a program named pkzip.exe located in the d:/programs/pkz204g directory at high priority, you'd enter the following command at the command prompt:

```
start /high d:/programs/pkz204g/pkzip.exe
```

Eight Worthwhile Ways to Improve Windows NT Performance

As mentioned throughout this chapter, you can do many things to deal with specific system bottlenecks. Here are eight particularly useful system components, elements, approaches, or configuration changes that are likely to result in improved performance. They are listed in approximate order of their potential value, so always try elements higher in the list first when seeking to boost Windows NT performance. But all elements on this list are worth considering when performance improvements are needed.

- *Buy a faster machine:* It only takes about two years for a top-of-the-line, heavily loaded PC to become obsolete these days. Whenever you find yourself considering a hardware upgrade to boost performance, compare the price of your planned upgrades to the cost of a new machine. If you're planning on spending more than half the cost of a newer, faster computer (and can afford to double your expenditure), buy the newer, faster machine. Otherwise, you may be facing the same situation again next year—in other words, the extra cost will buy you at least another year before you must go through this exercise again.

- *Upgrade an existing machine:* Sometimes, you may decide to keep a computer's case, power supply, and some of the adapter cards it contains. As long as the price stays below half the cost of a new machine, replacing a motherboard not only gets you a faster CPU and more memory capacity (both cache and main memory), it may also get you more and faster bus slots for adapter cards. While you're at it, be sure to evaluate costs to upgrade the disk controller and your hard drives, especially if they're more than twice as slow as prevailing access times (at this writing, garden-variety drives offer average access times of 10 milliseconds or so, and fast drives offer average access rates of 6–7 milliseconds).

- *Install a faster CPU:* As long as you can at least double the clock speed of your current CPU with a replacement unit, such upgrades can improve performance for only a modest outlay. Be sure to review your memory configuration (cache and main) and your disk drives at the same time—a faster CPU on an otherwise unchanged system can't deliver the same performance boost as a faster CPU with additional memory and faster drives.

- *Add more L2 cache:* Many experts believe that the single most dramatic improvement possible for an existing Windows NT machine comes from adding more L2 cache or buying only machines with the maximum amount of L2 cache installed. L2 cache can be accessed by the CPU in two CPU cycles, whereas access to main RAM usually takes 8 to 10 CPU cycles; this explains why adding L2 cache to a machine can produce dramatic performance improvements. Although cache chips are quite expensive, they provide the biggest potential boost to a system's performance, short of the more drastic—and expensive—entries that precede this suggestion in this list.

- *Add more RAM:* As operating systems go, Windows NT is smart about how it uses main memory. NT can handle large amounts of RAM effectively, and it's widely observed that the more processes are active on an NT machine, the more positive the impact of a RAM increase becomes. For moderately loaded workstations (six or less applications active at once), 64 MB of RAM is recommended. For heavily loaded workstations, 128 MB or more may improve performance significantly. Note: Whenever you add RAM to an NT machine, make sure to resize the paging file to equal two to three times the amount of RAM present on that machine.

- *Replace the disk subsystem:* Because memory access occurs at nanosecond speeds, whereas disk access occurs at millisecond speeds, disk subsystem speeds can have a major impact on Windows NT performance. This is particularly true in cases where applications or services make frequent accesses to disk, when manipulating large files, or when large amounts of paging activity occur. Because the controller and the drives both influence disk subsystem speeds, you should use only Fast Wide SCSI drives and controllers on Windows NT Workstation machines (or the latest of the EIDE drives and controllers). But it's important to recognize that a fast drive may be limited by a slow disk controller, or vice-versa. That's why upgrading the entire subsystem is often necessary to realize any measurable performance gains.

- *Increase paging file size:* Whenever Performance Monitor indicates that over 10% of disk subsystem activity is related to paging, check the relationship between the Limit and Peak values in the Commit Charge pane in Task Manager (right-click on any empty portion of the taskbar, then select the Performance tab, and check the lower right corner of the display). If the Peak is coming any closer to the limit than 4,096 KB, it's time to increase the size of this file. Use a figure somewhere between twice and three times the amount of RAM installed in the machine.

- *Increase application priority:* On machines in which lots of background tasks must be active, you can use Task Manager's Processes tab to increase the priority of any already-running process by highlighting its entry, then right-clicking to produce a menu that includes a Set Priority entry. This entry permits you to set the priority to High or Realtime, either of which can improve a foreground application's performance. It is recommended that you set only critical applications to Realtime, simply because they can interfere with the operating system's ability to do its job. To launch an application with an altered priority level use the Windows NT Start command at the command line with the following syntax:

```
start /high /Programs/MSOffice/MS-Word/word.exe
```

13

Only users with Administrator-level access to Windows NT can run processes at a Realtime priority level. Ordinary users can set priorities only for processes of low, normal, or high. Also, it's important to be aware that raising the priority of a single process will cause other background processes to run more slowly. The other performance improvements in the list should improve system performance across the board; this one is limited to those processes whose priorities are increased.

CHAPTER SUMMARY

Windows NT Workstation 4.0 provides a number of tools to monitor system performance. By using these tools, it is easy for a user to alleviate the effects of bottlenecks and to improve system response time.

Task Manager can be used to view applications, processes, and overall system performance. Applications and processes can be stopped from the Task Manager, which provides an efficient way to recover control from an application that is experiencing problems.

Performance Monitor is an exceptionally useful tool. Its default display is a chart that can be used to track many system counters concurrently. An enormous number of system counters, grouped by system object, monitor anything from Disk Reads/sec. to RAS Port CRC Errors. Along with the graphical Chart view, Performance Monitor includes Alert, Log, and Report views, which are configured with the same system counters but represent the data in different formats.

Event Viewer is a less dynamic, but equally important, tool that is used to track logs generated by the system. Event Viewer monitors three different logs: System, Application, and Security.

The Windows NT Diagnostic Tool (WINMSD) is used to view Registry information pertaining to the current configuration of the computer. It organizes the information found in the Registry into a more manageable format, generally by device type.

The Windows NT Hardware Qualifier (NTHQ) is an MS-DOS-based tool that creates a hardware configuration report that can be used to provide a permanent record of the system's configuration. It can also be used in troubleshooting after new hardware is added by comparing previous reports against current reports.

The System Recovery Utility defines what the system does when it experiences a STOP error. Along with sending an alert message to the Administrator, writing an entry into the system log, and possibly rebooting the computer, the System Recovery Utility can create a debug file that is very useful to support engineers in diagnosing system problems.

Finally, the system's performance can easily be modified by changing the settings in the Control Panel, System applet Performance tab. By changing the Application Performance setting, the user is able to define roughly what percentage of system processing the foreground application is given. Adjusting the Virtual Memory settings changes the way in which Windows NT handles its paging file, which is used to swap pages of memory to the hard disk.

KEY TERMS

- **bottleneck** — A system resource or device that limits a system's performance. Ideally, the user should be the bottleneck on a system, not any particular component in a system.

- **counter** (or **performance counter**) — A named counter in the Windows NT Performance Monitor utility that measures or monitors some aspect of a registered system or application object within that utility.

- **disk bottleneck** — A system bottleneck caused by some limitation in a computer's disk subsystem, such as a slow drive or controller or a heavier load than the system can really handle.

- **event** — A system occurrence that is logged to a file.

- **Event Viewer** — A Windows NT system utility that displays one of three Event logs: System, Security, or Applications, where logged or audited events appear. Event Viewer is often the first stop when monitoring a system's performance or seeking evidence of problems because it is where all untoward or extraordinary system activities and events will be recorded.

- **handle** — A programming term that indicates an internal identifier for some kind of system resource, object, or other component that must be accessed by name (or through a pointer). In Task Manager, the number of handles appears on the Performance tab in the Totals pane; a sudden increase in the number of handles, threads, or processes can sometimes indicate that an ill-behaved application is running on a Windows NT system.

- **memory bottleneck** — A system bottleneck caused by a lack of available physical or virtual memory that results in system slowdown or (in extreme cases) outright crashing.

- **network bottleneck** — A system bottleneck caused by excessive traffic on the network medium to which a computer is attached, or when the computer itself generates excessive amounts of such traffic.

- **Performance Monitor (PM)** — The Windows NT utility used to track registered system or application objects, where each such object offers one or more counters that can be logged for later analysis, or tracked for immediate information about system behavior.

- **process** — On a Windows NT system, a heavyweight runtime construct that corresponds roughly to an entire application, to the Windows NT Kernel itself, or to some other major NT system component. Each Windows NT process includes its own complete, private 2 GB address space and related virtual memory allocations.

- **processor bottleneck** — A system bottleneck that occurs when demands for CPU cycles from currently active processes and the operating system cannot be met, usually symptomized by high utilization levels or processor queue lengths greater than or equal to 2.

- **System Recovery Utility** — A Windows NT system utility included on the System Control Panel applet that instructs Windows NT how to behave in the event of a fatal STOP error.

- **thread** — In the Windows NT runtime environment, the minimal unit of system execution, and corresponding roughly to a task within an application, the Windows NT Kernel, or within some other major Windows NT system component. Any task that can execute in the background can be thought of as a thread (for example, runtime spell or grammar checking in newer versions of MS Word), but it's important to recognize that

13

applications must be written to take advantage of threading (just as the Windows NT operating system itself is).

- **Windows NT Diagnostics (WINMSD)** — The Windows NT utility that provides information about a machine's current hardware configuration, its runtime environment, memory configuration, and much more.
- **Windows NT Hardware Qualifier (NTHQ)** — The Windows NT hardware detection utility used to document a PC's current hardware configuration for comparison with the requirements of the Windows NT Hardware Compatibility List (HCL).

REVIEW QUESTIONS

1. _____ is an MS-DOS-based application.
2. Windows NT Diagnostics (WINMSD) can be used to change the system's configuration. True or False?
3. Which of the following can be monitored via Task Manager?
   a. Application CPU percentage
   b. Total CPU percentage
   c. Process CPU percentage
   d. all of the above
4. The user is able to access information on another computer by pressing the _____ button or entering the UNC pathname.
5. Which of the following can be set in the User Manager?
   a. automatic reboot
   b. log successful device initialization
   c. write an event to the System log
   d. log successful logons
6. In Performance Monitor, the counters are the same for all objects. True or False?
7. A(n) _____ event is issued when a driver fails to load.
8. The _____ provides a detailed description of a counter.
9. An event's details can be accessed by highlighting the event and pressing Enter. True or False?
10. Which of the following displays a device's IRQ information?
    a. Task Manager
    b. Performance Monitor
    c. Windows NT Diagnostics
    d. Event Viewer
11. A _____ occurs when a system resource causes slow performance.
12. NTHQ performs which of the following functions?
    a. log file viewer
    b. hardware configuration utility
    c. system performance tracking
    d. system resource allocation tracking

13. The way in which log files are displayed in Event Viewer cannot be changed. True or False?

14. The _____ tab in the Control Panel System applet is used to change virtual memory assignments.

15. Which of the following tools are able to monitor other computer's information? (Choose all that apply.)
    a. Performance Monitor
    b. Task Manager
    c. Windows NT Diagnostics
    d. Event Viewer

16. The Task Manager displays application performance and resource utilization. True or False?

17. The _____ is used to generate system performance reports.

18. Which of the following cannot be viewed by Windows NT Diagnostics?
    a. % CPU time
    b. total Kernel memory
    c. display driver version
    d. user environment settings

19. The Security log is automatically used when Windows NT is loaded. True or False?

20. The _____ and _____ event types are available only in the Security log.

21. Of the following commands, which will give the TEST.EXE application the highest priority level available to ordinary users (not administrators)?
    a. start /low test.exe
    b. start /normal test.exe
    c. start /high test.exe
    d. start /realtime test.exe

13

HANDS-ON PROJECTS

PROJECT 13-1

To use Performance Monitor Chart view to monitor memory performance:

1. Log on as Administrator or equivalent.
2. Launch Performance Monitor (**Start**, **Programs**, **Administrative Tools (Common)**, **Performance Monitor**). A screen similar to Figure 13-14 opens.
3. Select **Edit**, **Add to Chart** from the menu. The Add to Chart dialog box opens.
4. From the Object: list, select **Memory**.
5. From the list of counters, select **Page Faults/sec.** and press the **Add** button.
6. From the list of counters, select **Page Reads/sec.** and press the **Add** button.

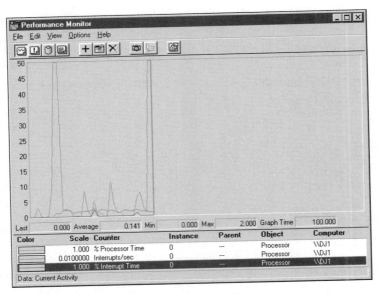

Figure 13-14   Windows NT Performance Monitor

7. From the list of counters, select **Page Writes/sec**. and press the **Add** button. Close the Add to Chart dialog box. You now have a running graph displaying important memory information in realtime. Click **Done**.
8. To see the effects an application has on system performance, open and close Windows NT Explorer three times. Notice how the graphs generally follow similar paths.
9. Select **Options**, **Chart** from the menu to open the Chart Options dialog box, as shown in Figure 13-15.

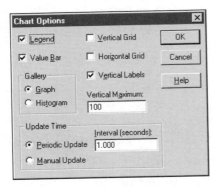

Figure 13-15   Performance Monitor's Chart Options window

10. Change the Vertical Maximum to **40** and click **OK**.
11. Notice that the scale has changed and the metrics are easier to read. Open and close Explorer again to view the information with the new scale.
12. Close Performance Monitor or leave it open for the next Hands-on Project.

PROJECT 13-2

To use Performance Monitor Alert view to set alert on given system events or thresholds:

1. In Performance Monitor, select **View, Alert** from the menu.
2. Choose **Edit, Add to Alert** from the menu. The Add to Alert dialog box opens, as shown in Figure 13-16.

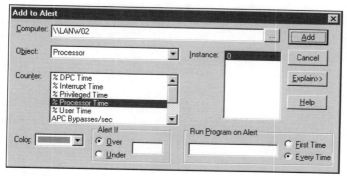

Figure 13-16   Performance Monitor's Add to Alert window

3. From the Object: list, select **Processor**.
4. From the list of counters, select **% Processor Time**.
5. In the Alert If: box, select **Over**, type **20**, and press the **Add** button.
6. Press the **Done** button.
7. Select **Options, Alert** from the menu to open the Alert Options dialog box.
8. Select **Send Network Message** and enter **Administrator** in the Net Name: field. Press **OK**.
9. Launch and close Windows NT Explorer twice.
10. A warning message dialog box should open with the alert information. Click **OK** to clear the dialog box. (For this to appear, Alert Service must be running, and the workstation and account must be designated as the message targets. Be sure to log in with a unique Administrator-level account. The alert message may not appear here, but will appear in the Event Viewer Application log, with a red alert marker.)
11. To disable the Alert, highlight it in the Alert Legend and select **Edit, Delete Alert** from the menu.
12. Close Performance Monitor or leave it open for the next Hands-on Project.

13

PROJECT 13-3

To use Performance Manager Log view to log memory performance:

1. In Performance Monitor, select **View, Log** from the menu.
2. Choose **Edit, Add to Log** from the menu. The Add to Log dialog box opens.

3. From the Object: list, select **Memory** and press the **Add** button.

4. Press the **Done** button. Notice that the Memory object is listed in the log window.

5. Select **Options**, **Log** from the menu.

6. Enter a log filename in the box provided.

7. Press the **Start Log** button.

8. Because the sample time for logs is generally longer than it takes to start and stop an application (the default monitoring interval is 15 seconds), start and stop Explorer or another application a number of times.

9. Select **View**, **Chart** from the menu.

10. Select **Options**, **Data From** from the menu.

11. Select **Log file** and click the ellipsis (...) to find the file created in step 6. Press **OK**.

12. Select **Edit**, **Add to Chart** from the menu.

13. Display the list for Objects. Notice that the only object listed is Memory, as that was the only data captured in the log file.

14. Select **Page Faults/sec**. from the list of available counters and press the **Add** button.

15. Select **Page Reads/sec**. from the list of available counters and press the **Add** button.

16. Select **Page Writes/sec**. from the list of available counters and press the **Add** button.

17. Press the **Done** button.

18. Select **Options**, **Chart** from the menu.

19. Change the Vertical Maximum setting to **20** and press **OK**.

20. Close Performance Monitor after viewing the data.

CASE PROJECTS

1. Performance on the Windows NT Server used for your accounting department has been slowly degrading. You recently added a 100 Mbps network card, thinking that would correct the problem. To your knowledge, nothing new has been added to the server, but you suspect someone has been adding software. Describe the steps you will use to determine what is causing the system to slow down, including which monitoring applications you will use and on which computer they will be run.

2. You are considering an upgrade of your Windows NT Workstation hardware, including memory, hard drive controller, and video card. The only things you are planning on keeping are your hard drive, motherboard, and CPU. Outline the tools and utilities you will use to measure the performance increase or decrease as you add each new component. Include information on expected performance change and actual change.

3. After installing a new custom-built application on your Windows NT Workstation, you notice that the Totals entries in Task Manager for handles and threads have doubled, and that performance on the machine has slowed down noticeably. What might be involved in this slowdown? Explain how you might determine if the new application is at fault and what steps you might take to correct any system deficiencies the new application might expose.

WINDOWS NT COMPONENTS

In this chapter, you encounter the pieces of the Windows NT operating system that endow it with its outstanding power and flexibility. Windows NT supports numerous runtime environments, including DOS and 16-bit Windows applications, as well as more modern 32-bit Windows applications, and provides limited support for OS/2 and POSIX (a portable open systems environment mandated in all operating systems that the US government purchases). You'll have a chance to examine these various subsystems and understand how they work.

Next, you dive under the Windows NT hood to learn more about its Executive Services modules and how they cooperate to support user applications and the many services that this operating system offers its users. Within this context, you'll develop an appreciation for the modular architecture and design of Windows NT, and understand how applications operate within this complex but powerful runtime environment.

AFTER READING THIS CHAPTER AND COMPLETING THE EXERCISES YOU WILL BE ABLE TO:

- Describe the Windows NT system architecture and explain the roles of the various environment subsystems

- Explain the difference between Kernel mode and User mode

- Describe the components of the Windows NT operating system Kernel

- Explain how Win32, Win16, and DOS applications run under Windows NT and use NT system resources

WINDOWS NT SYSTEM ARCHITECTURE

Fundamentally, the Windows NT operating system consists of three main components:

- **Environment subsystems** offer runtime support for a variety of different kinds of applications under the purview of a single operating system. Just like the applications they support, Windows NT environment subsystems run in **User mode**, which means that they must access all system resources through the operating system's **Kernel mode**.

- Windows NT **Executive Services** and the underlying Windows NT **Kernel** define the Kernel mode of this operating system and its runtime environment. Kernel mode components are permitted to access system objects and resources more or less directly and provide the many services and access controls that allow multiple users and applications to coexist and interoperate effectively and efficiently.

- User applications provide the functions and capabilities that make Windows NT the most popular network operating system today. All such applications run within the context of some environment subsystem in the Windows NT User mode.

These three components and their relationship to each other are illustrated in Figure 14-1. To understand how they fit together, the concept of processes and threads (which was introduced briefly in Chapter 1 and also discussed in Chapter 13) must be revisited.

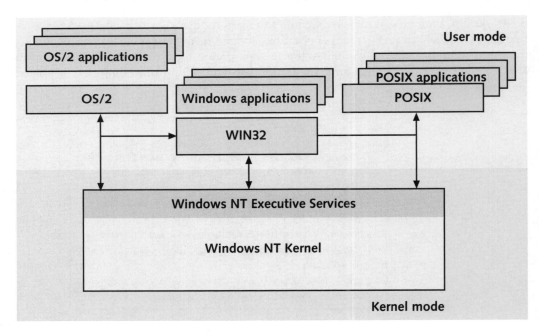

Figure 14-1 Windows NT components

PROCESSES AND THREADS

From a user's point of view, the operating system exists to run programs or applications. But from the view of the Windows NT operating system, the world is made of processes and threads. A **process** defines the operating environment in which an application or any major operating system component runs. Any Windows NT process includes its own private memory space, a set of security descriptors, a priority level for execution, processor affinity data (that is, on a multiprocessor system, information that instructs a process to use some particular CPU), and a list of threads associated with that process.

The basic executable unit in Windows NT is called a **thread**, and every process created includes at least one thread. Within a multithreaded application, each distinct task or any complex operation can be implemented in a separate thread. This explains how Microsoft Word, for instance, can perform spelling and grammar checks in the background while you're entering text in the input window—one thread manages handling input, while another performs those checks.

Applications must be explicitly designed to take advantage of threading. Although it's safe to assume that most new 32-bit Windows applications—and the Windows NT operating system itself—have been built to use the power and flexibility of threads, older 16-bit Windows and DOS applications are usually single-threaded. Also, it's important to understand that threads are associated with processes and do not exist independently. Processes themselves don't run, they merely describe a shared environment comprised of memory, variables, and other system resources; threads represent those parts of any program that actually run.

Processes can create other processes, called **child processes**, and those child processes can inherit some of the characteristics and parameters of the **parent process**. This usually works as follows:

- When a user logs onto Windows NT successfully, a shell process is created inside the Win32 subsystem within which the logon session operates. This process is endowed with a security token used to determine if subsequent requests for system objects and resources may be permitted to proceed (explained in detail in Chapter 7). This shell process defines the Win32 subsystem as the parent process for that user.

- Each time that user launches an application or starts a system utility, a child process is created within the environment subsystem where that application or utility must run. This child process inherits its security token and associated information from the user account, but is a child of the environment subsystem within which it runs. This "dual parentage" (security information from the user account, runtime environment from the environment subsystem) explains how Windows NT can run multiple kinds of applications, yet maintain consistent control over what system objects and resources any user process is permitted to access.

For example, each of the environment subsystems discussed in the following sections is an executable file—a combination of processes and threads running within the context of those

14

processes. When an application runs in one of the Windows NT subsystems, it actually represents a child of the parent process for the environment subsystem, but one that is endowed with the permissions associated with the security token of the account that launches the process. Whenever a parent process halts or is stopped, all child processes stop as well.

ENVIRONMENT SUBSYSTEMS

Windows NT is like a three-in-one operating system. One major part is the **Win32 subsystem** (which includes support for the **DOS subsystem** and the **Win16 subsystem**), but you can also run applications using OS/2 or POSIX environments. As shown in Figure 14-2, all three subsystems run on top of, and separate from, the Windows NT Kernel of the operating system.

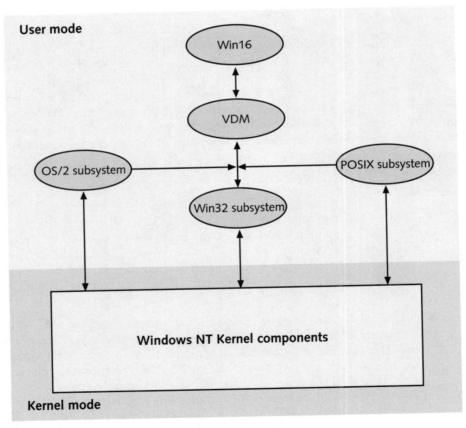

Figure 14-2   NT environment subsystems

Although the concept may seem a bit strange, Windows NT's support for multiple runtime environments, also known as environment subsystems, confers numerous advantages, including:

- It permits users to run more than one type of application, including 32-bit Windows, 16-bit Windows, and DOS applications, as well as OS/2 and POSIX applications.

- It makes maintaining the operating system easier, because the modularity of this design means that changes to subsystems require no changes to the Kernel, as long as interfaces remain unchanged.

- Likewise, modularity makes it easy to add to or enhance Windows NT—if some new OS is developed in the future, Microsoft could decide to add a subsystem for that OS to Windows NT without affecting other environment subsystems.

The catch to using an architecture that supports multiple environment subsystems comes in providing mechanisms to permit those subsystems to communicate with one another when necessary. In the Windows NT environment, each subsystem runs as a separate User mode process, so the subsystems cannot interfere with or crash one another. The only exception to this insulation effect occurs in the Win32 subsystem: Because all User mode I/O passes through this subsystem, the Win32 subsystem must be up and running for Windows NT to function. If the Win32 subsystem's process ends, the whole OS goes down with it. That is *not* true for the POSIX or OS/2 subsystems, which may be shut down without affecting anything but their child processes.

Applications and the subsystems in which they run have a client/server relationship, in that the client application asks the server subsystem to do things for it, and the subsystem complies. For example, if a Win32 client application needs to open a new window (perhaps to create a Save As dialog box) it doesn't create the window itself, but asks the Win32 subsystem to draw the window on its behalf.

The client issues the request via a mechanism known as a **local procedure call (LPC)**. The serving subsystem makes its capabilities available to client applications by linking them to a **Dynamic Link Library (DLL)** that includes procedure stubs to those capabilities. By analogy, you could think of a DLL as a set of buzzers, where each one is labeled with the capabilities it provides. Pushing a specific buzzer tells the server subsystem to do whatever the label tells it to. This form of messaging is transparent to the client application (as far as it knows, it's simply calling a procedure). Thus, when a client pushes one of those buzzers (requests a service), it appears as if the act is handled by the DLL; no explicit communication with a server subsystem is needed. If a service isn't listed in the library, an application can't request it; thus, a word processor running in a command-line environment inside the OS/2 subsystem can't ask that subsystem to draw a window.

The inability to provide functions that aren't offered by a subsystem can occasionally present problems. For example, the POSIX subsystem includes no networking capabilities, so POSIX applications can't access the network. Microsoft has no plans to change this arrangement because doing so would complicate its subsystem design.

14

Message-passing is a fairly time-consuming operation, because any time the focus changes from one process to another, all the information for the calling process must be unloaded and replaced with the information for the called process. In operating system lingo, this change of operation focus from one process to another is called a **context switch**. To permit the operating system to run more efficiently, Windows NT avoids making context switches whenever possible. To that end, Windows NT includes the following "efficiency measures":

- Attributes are cached in DLLs to provide an interface to subsystem capabilities, so that (for example) the second time Microsoft Word requests a window to be created, this activity may be completed without switching context to the Win32 subsystem.

- Executive Services (the collection of Kernel mode Windows NT operating system components that provide basic system services like I/O, security, object management, and so forth) are called directly to perform tasks without requesting help from an underlying environment subsystem. Because the Kernel is always active in another process space in Windows NT, calling for Kernel mode services does *not* require a context switch.

- Messages are batched so that when a server process is called, several messages can be passed at once—the number of messages has no impact on performance, but a context switch does. By batching messages, a single context switch can handle multiple messages in sequence, rather than requiring a context switch for each individual message.

When LPCs must be used, they're handled as efficiently as possible. Likewise, their code is optimized for speed, and special message-passing functions can be used for different situations, depending (for example) on the size of the messages passed, or the circumstances in which they're sent.

That's a broad view of how environment subsystems interact with client applications. Now, let's take a closer look at these subsystems themselves.

The Win32 Subsystem

The Win32 subsystem is the only subsystem required for the functioning of the operating system—it handles all major interface capabilities. In previous versions of Windows NT, the Win32 subsystem included graphics, windowing, and messaging support; but in Windows NT 4.0, these have been moved to the Kernel and are now part of Executive Services.

In Windows NT 4.0, User-mode components of the Win32 subsystem consist of the console (text window support), shutdown, hard-error handling, and some environment functions to handle such tasks as process creation and deletion. The Win32 subsystem is also the foundation upon which **virtual DOS machines (VDMs)** rest, which permit Windows NT to deliver both DOS and Win16 subsystems, so that well-behaved DOS and Win16 applications can run on Windows NT unchanged (more information about VDMs and the DOS and Win16 subsystems is provided later in this chapter).

OS/2 Subsystem

Unlike the Win32 subsystem, which starts on system startup, the **OS/2 subsystem** begins only when a user launches an application that requires its services, at which point it remains resident in memory until the system is shut down and restarted—logging off and logging back on again will not restart the OS/2 subsystem.

The Windows NT OS/2 subsystem is limited in several ways. First, it runs only on x86 machines, because the x86 emulation provided on the Intel Alpha AXP processor only supports 80286-level functionality, and OS/2 requires 80386-level functionality or better. Second, the OS/2 subsystem is limited to OS/2 1.x, so out of the box this subsystem can run only command-line OS/2 applications.

 Real-mode OS/2 applications can run in a DOS box on a RISC machine, such as an Intel Alpha AXP.

POSIX Subsystem

POSIX (the Portable Operating System Interface for Computing Environments) is a set of standards owned by the IEEE that defines various aspects of an operating system. So far, only one of those standards has been adopted: POSIX 1. The Windows NT **POSIX subsystem** (POSIX.EXE) is POSIX 1-compatible.

POSIX defines only API (application programming interface) calls between applications and the operating system, so in general, any application written for POSIX must rely on other operating systems for functions such as security and networking. Also, any POSIX application that accesses files must have access to an NTFS partition, because that file system provides functionality that FAT cannot deliver and POSIX applications need (such as the ability to support multiple names for a single data file).

KERNEL MODE VERSUS USER MODE

Before delving further into the Windows NT architecture, it is important to clarify the distinction between Kernel mode and User mode. The main difference lies in how components of each mode use memory.

In User mode, each process perceives the entire 4 GB of virtual memory available to Windows NT as its exclusive property—with the understanding that the upper 2 GB of addresses are always reserved for system use. This perception remains unaltered no matter what kind of hardware Windows NT may run on. Note also that this address space is entirely virtual and must operate within the confines of whatever RAM is installed on a machine and the amount

14

of space reserved for the paging file's use. Although the theoretical upper bound for Windows NT addresses may be 2 GB (or 4 GB, for system purposes), the real upper bound for Windows NT addresses will always be the sum of physical RAM size plus the amount of space in the paging file.

Although processes that operate in User mode may share memory areas with other processes (for fast message passing or sharing information), by default, they don't. This means that one User-mode process cannot crash another or corrupt its data. This is what creates the appearance that applications run independently and gives each one the illusion that it has exclusive possession of the operating system and the hardware it controls.

 If a User-mode parent process crashes, it will take its child processes down with it.

Processes running in User mode cannot access hardware or communicate with other processes directly. On the other hand, when code runs in the Windows NT Kernel mode, it may access all hardware and memory in the computer. Thus, when an application needs to perform tasks that involve hardware, it calls a User-mode function that ultimately calls a Kernel-mode function.

Because all Kernel-mode operations share the same memory space, one Kernel-mode function can corrupt another's data and even cause the operating system to crash. This is the reason why the environment subsystems contain as much of the operating system's capabilities as possible, so that the Kernel itself is rendered less vulnerable. For this reason, some experts voiced concern about the change in the Windows NT 4.0 design mentioned earlier that moved graphics handlers to the Kernel. But because those graphics components were originally part of the Win32 environment subsystem, which must be available for Windows NT to operate properly anyway, a crash in either implementation could still bring down the system. That's why this change has had little effect on the reliability or stability of NT.

The composition of Kernel mode and User mode is illustrated in Figure 14-3. These components are covered in detail in the next section.

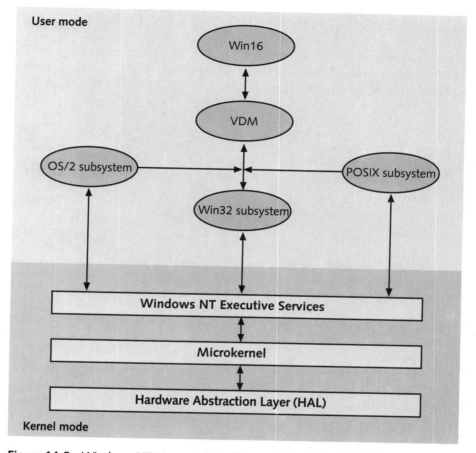

Figure 14-3   Windows NT User mode and Kernel mode components

COMPONENTS OF THE WINDOWS NT KERNEL

As shown in Figure 14-4, the Windows NT Kernel consists of three parts: Windows NT Executive Services, the Windows NT Kernel itself (also known as the **microkernel**), and the **Hardware Abstraction Layer (HAL)**.

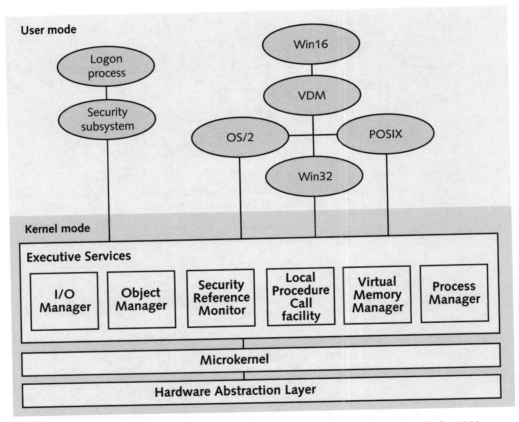

Figure 14-4   NT Kernel includes Executive Services, the microkernel, and the HAL

WINDOWS NT EXECUTIVE SERVICES

The hardware-independent portion of the Kernel is called the Executive Services, shown in detail in Figure 14-5. This is the part of the OS that provides basic services to the environment subsystems, and includes the following components:

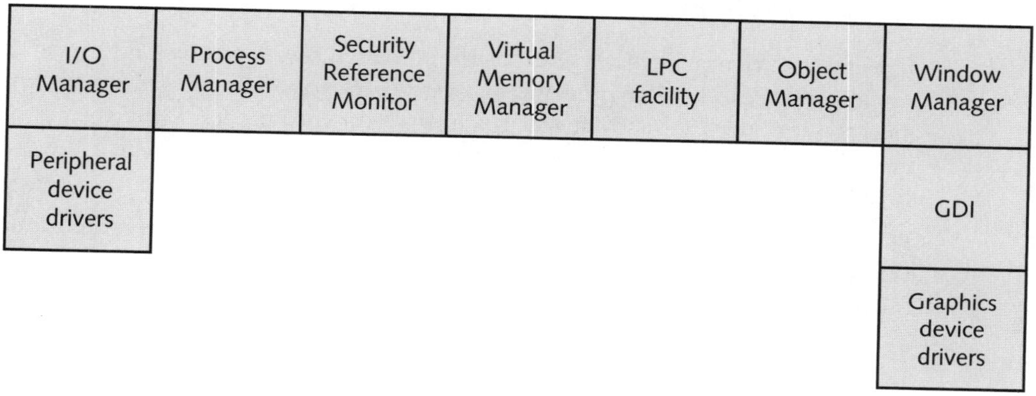

I/O Manager	Process Manager	Security Reference Monitor	Virtual Memory Manager	LPC facility	Object Manager	Window Manager
Peripheral device drivers						GDI
						Graphics device drivers

Figure 14-5   NT Executive Services include numerous independent modules

- Object Manager
- Process Manager
- Virtual Memory Manager
- Security Reference Monitor
- I/O Manager
- Graphical Device Interface (GDI) and Window Manager
- Device drivers
- Local Procedure Call (LPC) facility

Although they share the same 4 GB virtual memory area, these components exist and operate independently of each other, so that modifying one service does not mean that the rest of the services must also be modified as a result.

Object Manager

The Object Manager provides a set of protocols by which objects (software components that include a data type, a set of attributes, and a defined set of operations that they can perform) are named, retained, and protected. The Object Manager also creates handles that can be used to identify unique instances of objects, so that processes may manipulate them.

14

The Object Manager keeps track of all objects in the local computer environment, including directory objects, file objects, process and thread objects, and so forth. Just about everything under Windows NT is treated as an object—it's a convenient way to provide a consistent interface to manage all the User-mode-accessible parts of the operating system.

Process Manager

The Process Manager creates and deletes processes, tracks process and thread objects, and provides services to create processes and threads. Beyond providing these tracking and creation services, the Process Manager has little to do with processes and threads once they're created—this becomes the job of the environment subsystem for which the processes and threads were created.

The Process Manager works with the Security Reference Monitor and the Virtual Memory Manager to provide interprocess protection. Each process has an object called an access token associated with it; this token is used by access-validation routines to determine which threads may reference process objects.

Virtual Memory Manager

The Virtual Memory Manager (VMM) maps virtual addresses on a process's 4 GB address space (2 GB for the process's use, and 2 GB for system use) to the addresses of the physical memory installed in the computer, and to individual memory pages within the paging file (PAGEFILE.SYS). The VMM makes sure that no process overwrites any address space allotted to another process, and manages traffic between the paging file and physical memory so that processes can retrieve any data that they've stored in memory upon demand, regardless of where that data might reside when the demand is made.

Memory is allocated to processes in two stages: reservation and committal. During the reservation stage, a block of memory is set aside for a process to use, but that block is not yet linked to any physical or virtual memory. Reservation permits the operating system to ensure that contiguous virtual addresses will be available for the process when they're needed. When a process actually needs to use memory, however, the memory must be committed, or mapped to physical or virtual memory. Because committal is more time-consuming and resource-intensive than reservation, addresses are only committed when necessary. The difference between the two stages is roughly equivalent to the difference between setting a budget for yourself (allocating so much money for food, the mortgage, the car payment, and so forth), and then writing checks to pay for those items. Even though the money isn't yet out of your account when you write the check, it's as good as out because you've committed those funds at that point.

The most interesting part of the VMM's job is to make 4 GB of memory addresses available to a process on a computer with only 64 MB of RAM installed. If a process requires more storage than is available in physical memory, then the VMM must move (or page) data between physical memory and the paging file on a hard disk as needed. The VMM stores data on the hard disk until it's requested, and thereupon transfers that data back to physical memory. Within the Windows NT environment, all memory (whether physical RAM or paging file on disk) is organized into 4 KB segments called pages. This explains why Windows NT memory is accurately described as a "demand-paged, virtual memory system": The data is organized into fixed-size pages, and the VMM manages the traffic between physical memory and one or more paging files to accommodate requests for specific memory pages, once a process requests such pages be delivered.

Local Procedure Call (LPC) Facility

Recall that applications and the environment subsystems in which they run are both User-mode processes and that User-mode processes are separate entities protected from each other. The only problem with such protection is that processes can't communicate with each other or share information without taking extra steps to interact.

One means for User-mode processes to communicate is through the use of LPCs. When an application needs its environment subsystem to do something on its behalf (perhaps create a process), that application calls a Dynamic Link Library (DLL) that's a stub to the real service. When the application calls this stub, the message is delivered through an LPC to whatever serving subsystem can provide that service.

Security Reference Monitor

The Security Reference Monitor (SRM) is an Executive Services component that fields all requests for system objects or resources from other Windows NT processes, be they User-mode or Kernel-mode processes. It matches security tokens provided by the requesting processes against the access control lists associated with objects and their operations to determine if such requests can be satisfied or must be denied. Also, the SRM generates access audit records if auditing has been enabled, and particular objects' auditing flags are turned on.

14

I/O Manager

The I/O (input/output) Manager provides a consistent interface for the majority of I/O operations on a Windows NT computer (except for screen- and keyboard- or mouse-related I/O, which is handled by the GDI). This confers Windows NT with the ability to interact with any installed device drivers without requiring the operating system itself to understand how such hardware works. The I/O Manager supports I/O drivers for file systems, network adapters, and other peripheral devices (tape drives, scanners, and so forth).

The I/O Manager's interaction with device drivers is layered, so that one driver actually manipulates the hardware and another driver handles communications between the "real" driver and the process that's making I/O requests. Using this layered scheme means that any of the Windows NT Executive Services modules can be replaced or changed without affecting how the system works or how applications must interact with device drivers.

Graphics Managers

The graphics drivers are controlled by two Kernel components: the Graphical Device Interface (GDI) and the Window Manager. The Window Manager is the part of Windows NT that handles user interaction with the Windows NT GUI, moving and resizing windows, selecting icons, and moving the cursor. It also handles requests that go to the interface without necessarily changing it. All requests that go to the Window Manager are passed to the GDI for processing.

The GDI, or graphics engine, provides a set of standard interfaces that applications can use to communicate with graphical output devices such as printers and monitors without knowing anything about them. It intercepts requests for graphical output and translates them for the appropriate graphical driver, which then sends them to the hardware. The flow of information goes both ways, as the GDI is also the means by which graphics drivers communicate with the OS and applications.

Prior to the release of Windows NT 4.0, both the Window Manager and the GDI were part of the Win32 subsystem, but with NT 4.0 they were moved to the Kernel to speed up the graphical display and reduce memory requirements caused by excessive LPCs.

Device Drivers

Device drivers supply the necessary software that permits the operating system (and by extension, applications) to communicate with hardware. For graphics drivers, the graphical components of the Kernel (the GDI and the Window Manager) provide a special-purpose interface for communications between drivers and user applications. A conventional device driver interface is used with other hardware. But for both situations, the I/O Manager defines a standard interface between device drivers and User-mode applications.

MICROKERNEL

A special component called the microkernel lies beneath the Executive Services in the Kernel. The microkernel (or more simply, the Kernel) is the part of Windows NT responsible for scheduling threads and handling interrupts and exceptions. It is also responsible for synchronizing activities among the various components of the Windows NT Executive Services. If more than one processor is installed in a computer, the microkernel also synchronizes processor activity and runs simultaneously on all processors. The microkernel is one of a small number of Windows NT components that always remain resident in memory because it can be called on at any time to manage the rest of the system.

To perform all its scheduling tasks, the microkernel relies on two kinds of objects: dispatcher objects and controlling objects. Dispatcher objects control the dispatching and synchronization of system objects, and include a set of timing objects as follows:

- *Semaphore:* A special flag used to control access to a resource, a semaphore takes a value to indicate how many simultaneous accesses a resource can handle. As threads access that resource, the value decreases. When a semaphore's value reaches zero, all subsequent access requests are denied until a thread releases that resource, at which point the value increases.

- *Mutex:* The special Kernel-mode flag controls mutually exclusive access to a resource (so that only two threads can share the resource associated with each mutex).

- *Thread:* Any object that represents an active execution task in Windows NT is a thread. The microkernel tracks threads and manages their access to the CPU.

- *Timer:* This object records the passage of time and triggers events and actions when specific intervals have elapsed, or when a specific time value is reached.

Controller objects, on the other hand, control how the microkernel works but have no effect on dispatching; they include such events as interrupts and processes.

When scheduling or managing multiple threads, the microkernel thinks in terms of thread priority (all threads have an associated priority, in part inherited from the process in whose context they run) to use processor time as efficiently as possible. This means that the microkernel will preempt any running threads if a thread with higher priority becomes ready to run. This behavior explains why Windows NT is sometimes described as a preemptive, multithreaded operating system.

HARDWARE ABSTRACTION LAYER

14

The Hardware Abstraction Layer (HAL) is the foundation of the Windows NT Kernel. This component is written in a specific machine language so it can communicate with the computer's CPU as quickly as possible (in fact, it's not unreasonable to think of the HAL as a "CPU driver" for Windows NT). The HAL is the main hardware-dependent portion of Windows NT, and its job is to make all CPUs look alike to the rest of the operating system; thus, it is what enables Windows NT to work on computers with different types of CPUs.

WIN32 APPLICATIONS

So far, the components of the Windows NT operating system Kernel have been examined. Now, it's time to see how applications run under that operating system.

ENVIRONMENT SUBSYSTEMS

The Win32 subsystem is the main environment subsystem under Windows NT, and the only one required for operation. Strictly speaking, even the other environment subsystems are Win32 applications that run as child processes to the main Win32 process, although they are full-blown operating systems and not just application environments like the virtual DOS machines (VDMs) that run under Win32 to support Win16 and DOS applications. (VDMs, Win16, and DOS application support are covered in more detail later in this chapter.)

MULTITHREADING

When a program's process contains more than one thread of execution, it's said to be a **multithreaded process**. The main advantage of multithreading is that it provides multiple threads of execution within a single memory space without requiring messages to be passed between processes or use of local procedure calls. Threads are easier to create than processes because they don't require as much context information, nor do they incur the same kind of overhead when switching from one thread to another within a single process.

Some multithreaded applications can even run multiple threads concurrently among multiple processors (assuming a machine has more than one). One more advantage to threading is that it's *much* less complicated to switch operation from thread to thread than to switch from one process to another. That's because every time a new process is scheduled for execution, the system must be updated with all the process's context information. Also, it's often necessary to remove one process to make room for another, which may require writing large amounts of data from RAM to disk for the outgoing process before copying large amounts of data from disk into RAM to bring in the incoming process.

 As a point of comparison, a thread switch can normally be completed in somewhere between 15 and 25 machine instructions, whereas a process switch can take many thousands of instructions to complete. Because most CPUs are set up to handle one instruction for every clock cycle, this means that switching among threads is hundreds to thousands of times faster than switching among processes.

The big trick with multithreading, of course, is that the chances that one thread could overwrite another are increased with each additional thread, so this introduces the problem of protecting shared areas of memory from intraprocess thread overwrites. Windows NT handles this by managing access to memory carefully, and locking out which sections of memory any individual thread can write to, as explained in the next section.

MEMORY SPACE

Multithreaded programs must be designed so that threads don't get in each other's way; this is done by use of Windows NT **synchronization objects**. A section of code that modifies data structures used by several threads is called a **critical section**. It's very important that a critical section never be overwritten by more than one thread at a time. Thus, applications use Windows NT synchronization objects to prevent this from happening, and create such objects for each critical section in each process context. When a thread needs access to a critical section, the following occurs:

1. A thread requests a synchronization object. If it is unlocked, the request proceeds. Otherwise, go to step 2.

2. The thread is suspended in a thread queue until the synchronization object is unlocked for its use. As soon as this happens, Windows NT releases the thread and locks up the object.

3. The thread accesses the critical section.

4. When the thread is done, it unlocks the synchronization object so that another thread may access the critical object.

Thus, multithreaded applications avoid accessing a single data structure with more than one thread at a time by locking its critical section when it's in use and unlocking it when it's not.

INPUT MESSAGE QUEUES

One of the roles of the Win32 subsystem is to organize user input and get it to the thread to which that input belongs. It does this by taking user messages from a general input queue and distributing them to the **input message queues** for each individual process.

As discussed later in this chapter, Win16 applications normally run within a single process, so they share a message input queue, unlike Win32 or DOS applications that have their individual queues.

14

BASE PRIORITIES

When a program starts under Windows NT, its process is assigned a particular priority class, generally Normal, but Idle, High, and Realtime are also options (priority levels and settings are discussed in detail in Chapter 13). The priority class helps determine the priority at which threads in a process must run, on a scale from 0 (lowest) to 31 (highest). In a process with more than one active thread, each thread may have its own priority that may be greater or lower than that of the original thread, but that priority is always relative to the priority assigned to the underlying process, which is known as the **base priority**. As mentioned in Chapter 13, massaging priorities may be accomplished in several ways and can sometimes improve application performance.

DOS AND THE VIRTUAL DOS MACHINE

DOS and Win16 applications work somewhat differently from Win32 applications. Rather than each running in the context of its own process, these applications run in a special environment process called a virtual DOS machine (VDM), which simulates a DOS environment so that non–Win32 Windows applications can run under Windows NT. In fact, it's reasonable to describe two separate operating environments that can run within a VDM: one supports straightforward DOS emulation and may be called the **DOS operating environment**, the other supports operation of Win16 applications within a VDM and may be called a **Win16 operating environment**. Each of these operating environments and its features, characteristics, and components are described in the sections that follow.

The environment created in a VDM is not the same as that available to Win32 applications. Instead, it's equivalent to the environment of Windows 3.x Enhanced mode, in which each DOS application has access to 1 MB of virtual memory, with 1 MB of extended memory and expanded memory if necessary.

 VDMs on RISC machines emulate only a 286 machine.

By default, all DOS applications run in their own VDM, and all Win16 applications share a single VDM (just as they do in "real Windows 3.x" environments).

VDM COMPONENTS

The VDM runs using the following files:

- NTIO.SYS, the equivalent of IO.SYS on MS-DOS machines, runs in **Real mode**. It provides "virtual IO" services to the DOS or Win16 applications that run in a VDM.

- NTDOS.SYS, the equivalent of MSDOS.SYS, runs in Real mode. It provides basic DOS operating system services to the DOS or Win16 applications that run in a VDM.

- NTVDM.EXE is a Win32 application that runs in Kernel mode. This is the .EXE file that provides the runtime environment within which a VDM runs. If you look at the list on the Processes tab of the Task Manager, you'll see one such entry for each separate VDM that's running on your machine.

- NTVDM.DLL is a Win32 DLL that runs in Kernel mode. It provides the set of procedure stubs that fool DOS and Win16 programs into thinking they're talking to a real DOS machine with exclusive access to a PC, when in fact they're communicating through a VDM with Windows NT.

- REDIR.EXE is the virtual device driver (VDD) redirector for the VDM. This software forwards I/O requests from programs within a VDM for I/O services through the Win32 environment subsystem to the Windows NT I/O Manager in Executive Services. Whenever a DOS or Win16 program in a VDM thinks it's communicating with hardware, it's really communicating with REDIR.EXE.

VIRTUAL DEVICE DRIVERS

DOS applications do not communicate directly with Windows NT drivers. Instead, a layer of **virtual device drivers (VDDs)** underlies these applications, and they communicate with Windows NT 32-bit drivers. Windows NT supplies VDDs for mice, keyboards, printers, and communications ports, as well as file system drivers (which include one or more network drivers, each of which is actually implemented as a file system driver).

AUTOEXEC.BAT AND CONFIG.SYS

When a DOS application starts, Windows NT runs the files specified in the application's program information file (PIF) or in AUTOEXEC.NT and CONFIG.NT, the two files that replace AUTOEXEC.BAT and CONFIG.SYS for VDMs. AUTOEXEC.NT installs CD-ROM extensions, the network redirector, and can even provide DOS Protected Mode Interface (DPMI) support, to permit DOS and Win16 applications to access more than 1 MB of memory within a virtual (or real) DOS machine. CONFIG.NT loads into an upper memory area for its VDM and can support HIMEM.SYS to enable extended memory; it also sets the number of files and buffers available to DOS or Win16 programs and provides necessary details to configure expanded memory. Hands-on Project 14-2 shows how to change the location of these configuration files.

CONFIG.SYS isn't used at all by Windows NT; AUTOEXEC.BAT is only used at system startup to set path and environment variables for the Windows NT environment. Neither file is consulted when it comes to running applications or initializing drivers; those settings must exist in the system Registry to work at all.

Once read from AUTOEXEC.BAT, path and environment variables are copied to the Registry, to HKEY_LOCAL_MACHINE\System\CurrentControlSet\Control\Session Manager\Environment.

14

WIN16 CONCEPTS AND APPLICATIONS

Like DOS applications, Win16 applications also run in a VDM, although unlike DOS applications, which by default run in their own individual address spaces, all Win16 applications run in the same VDM unless otherwise specified. This permits them to act like Win32 applications and lets multiple Win16 applications interact with one another in a single VDM. This creates the appearance that multiple applications are active simultaneously (usually, only one Win16 application in a VDM can be active at any given moment, but this form of **multitasking**—which Microsoft calls cooperative multitasking—creates a convincing imitation of the more robust and real multitasking available to Win32 applications). The **Win16-on-Win32** VDM—usually called **WOW**—runs as a multithreaded application, with each Win16 application being one thread.

WIN16-ON-WIN32 (WOW) COMPONENTS

The WOW subsystem consists of the following components:

- WOWEXEC.EXE: Handles the loading of 16-bit Windows-based applications
- WOW32.DLL: The DLL for the WOW application environment
- NTVDM.EXE, NTVDM.DLL, NTIO.SYS, and REDIR.EXE: Run the VDM
- VDMREDIR.DLL: The redirector for the WOW environment
- KRNL386.EXE: Used by WOW on x86-based systems
- KRNL286.EXE: Used by WOW on RISC-based systems
- GDI.EXE: A modified version of Windows 3.10 GDI.EXE
- USER.EXE: A modified version of Windows 3.10 USER.EXE

Calls made to 16-bit drivers are transferred ("thunked") to the appropriate 32-bit driver without the application being aware of it. Similarly, if a driver needs to return information to an application, it must be thunked back again. This back and forth translation helps explain why many Win16 applications run more slowly in a VDM on Windows NT than they do on other versions of Windows (even Windows 95), where no such translations are required.

MEMORY SPACE

By default, all Win16 applications run as threads in a single VDM process. However, it might be a good idea not to permit this, because multiple threads running in a single process can impact the performance of each individual application. This admixture of applications can also make tracking applications more difficult because most monitoring in Windows NT takes place on a per-process basis, not on a per-thread basis. Finally, running all Win16 applications in a single VDM means that if one of those applications goes astray and causes the VDM to freeze or crash, all applications in that VDM will be affected ("just like real Windows 3.x!").

Separate and Shared Memory

The "lose one, lose them all" effect of a single shared VDM explains why you might choose to run Win16 applications in separate VDMs. That way, you'll increase the reliability of those applications as a whole, and one errant application won't take down all the other Win16 applications when it crashes. Likewise, you'll make preemptive multitasking possible (that is, one busy application won't be able to hog the processor), and you'll be able to take advantage of multiple processors if you have them, because all the threads in a single VDM process must execute on the same processor.

The disadvantages of running Win16 applications in separate memory spaces focus on memory usage and interprocess communications: Each additional process running on a machine requires about 2 MB of space in the paging file and 1 MB of additional working set size, or the amount of data that the application has in memory at any given time. Also, those older Win16 applications that don't support Dynamic Data Exchange (DDE) or Object Linking and Embedding (OLE) won't be able to communicate with each other. Additionally, running Win16 applications as processes instead of threads increases the time it takes to switch from one application to another, because each such switch requires a full context change from one process to another. The best way to observe the impact of this separation is to try it the default way (where all Win16 applications share a single VDM), and then set up those Win16 applications in separate VDMs and compare the performance that results from each such scenario. Hands-on Project 14-1 shows the steps required to run a Win16 application in its own memory space.

Message Queues

As mentioned earlier, the Win32 subsystem is responsible for collecting user input and getting it to those applications that need it. However, unlike Win32 applications, all Win16 applications running in a single process share a message queue. Therefore, if one application becomes unable to accept input, it will block all other Win16 applications in that VDM from accepting further input as well.

Threads

As mentioned earlier, Win16 threads that run in a VDM do not multitask like threads running in the Win32 subsystem. Instead of being preemptively multitasked, so that one thread can push another aside if its priority is higher, or any thread that's been taking up too much CPU time can be preempted, all application threads within a WOW VDM are cooperatively multitasked. This means that any one thread—which corresponds to any Win16 application—can hog the CPU. This is sometimes called the "good guy scheduling" algorithm, because it assumes that all applications will be well-behaved and relinquish the CPU whenever they must block for I/O or other system services. The net effect, however, is that WOW VDMs behave as if they have only one execution thread to share among all applications within the VDM.

14

Well-behaved DOS and Win16 Applications

Many DOS applications, as well as numerous older Win16 applications, take advantage of a prerogative of DOS developers—namely, the ability to access system hardware directly, bypassing any access APIs or drivers that the system might ordinarily put between an application and the underlying hardware. Although such applications will work fine in DOS, Windows 3.x, and even on Windows 95, the Windows NT division of the world into User mode and Kernel mode means that any application that attempts to access hardware directly will be summarily shut down with an error message to the effect of "illegal operation attempted."

In Windows NT terminology, any application that attempts direct access to hardware is called "ill-behaved." Such applications will not run in a VDM. On the other hand, any Win16 or DOS application that uses standard DOS or Windows 3.x APIs instead of attempting direct access to hardware will work in a VDM. Such applications are called "well-behaved." Unfortunately, there is no registry of well-behaved applications available, so the only way to tell the difference is to test the ones you'd like to use with Windows NT and see what happens. It is wise to use only well-behaved applications with Windows NT and consider replacing any ill-behaved applications you may find in your current collection of programs.

OS/2 SUBSYSTEM

The Windows NT OS/2 subsystem provides a way to run character-mode OS/2 applications on x86 computers (but not on RISC machines, which support only a 286-equivalent DOS services and access). Unlike the VDMs and WOW, the OS/2 subsystem is indeed a separate operating system, albeit one that runs like a Win32 application. It works just like the OS/2 operating system would if it were running independently, although some of its features (such as its ability to share information between processes) are implemented through Windows NT, not as they would be in OS/2. One thing that *doesn't* work the same as in the original version of OS/2 is the amount of memory available, because the OS/2 subsystem sees the 4 GB of memory normally available to Win32 processes, rather than the 16 MB with which OS/2 was designed to work. Because this represents a substantial improvement over the original, this difference has not occasioned too many complaints.

OS/2 VERSION 1.X

OS/2 1.x doesn't look much like any version of OS/2 you're likely to see, because it's completely character based and doesn't include the familiar graphical workplace shell. Character-based applications that call the OS/2 Presentation Manager will not run under Windows NT. This characteristic makes the OS/2 subsystem of limited use in most organizations, because most OS/2 applications require graphical interface support.

OS/2 COMPONENTS

The OS/2 subsystem consists of the following components:

- OS2SS.EXE: The main component of the OS/2 subsystem and the one started when the first OS/2 application is loaded

- OS2DLL.DLL: Shares address space with each OS/2 application and handles the communication between the application and the subsystem, OS2SS.EXE

- OS2.EXE: A Win32 program that passes the name of the OS/2 application and any command line parameters to OS2SRV.EXE. This portion of the OS/2 subsystem only starts once, no matter how many OS/2 applications are running

- OS2SRV.EXE: The component that actually starts each OS2 application for the OS2 subsystem

These parts of the OS/2 subsystem interact as illustrated in Figure 14-6. They don't start up until the first OS/2 application starts, at which point the OS/2 subsystem comes up and isn't shut down until the system is rebooted. Logging off and logging back on to a Windows NT machine will not reset the OS/2 subsystem; that requires an actual system shutdown or restart.

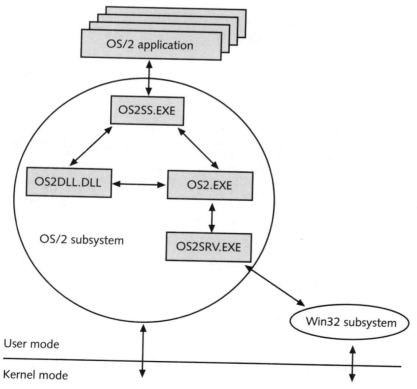

Figure 14-6   OS/2 environment subsystem

BOUND APPLICATIONS

Bound applications, or those that can run under either OS/2 or in a VDM, will run in the OS/2 subsystem on an x86 machine if one is available because they'll run faster. The only way to prevent an application that can go either way from running within the OS/2 subsystem (perhaps because that application won't run in OS/2), is to run FORCEDOS.EXE. This utility appears in the \system32 directory and forces bound applications to run in a VDM instead of in the OS/2 subsystem environment. Because they do not provide the right level of DOS emulation to support OS/2, bound applications *always* run in a VDM on RISC machines.

OS/2 CONFIGURATION

When the OS/2 subsystem starts up for the first time, it checks the Registry for OS/2 setup information. If it doesn't find any, it checks CONFIG.SYS. If CONFIG.SYS does not exist, then the subsystem adds shell initialization information to the Registry.

To update the OS/2 configuration information, you must edit CONFIG.SYS with an OS/2 text editor (Notepad won't do, it must be an OS/2 editor). Open the file, which will be a temporary copy of the configuration information in the Registry. Make the changes, save them, and those changes will be stored in the Registry and take effect after you next restart your computer.

When configuring OS/2, you can use the commands shown in Table 14-1. If you use a command not found in this table, it will be ignored.

Table 14.1   OS/2 Subsystem Configuration Commands

Command	Description
protshell	Specifies the command interpreter, although only the Windows NT interpreter CMD.EXE is supported
devicename	Specifies a user-defined Windows NT device driver used by OS/2 applications
libpath	Specifies the location of the 16-bit OS/2 DLLs
set	Sets environment variables
country	Lets you provide a country code that specifies time, date, and currency conventions
codepage	Specifies the code page the system will use
devinfo=KBD	Specifies the information the keyboard needs to use a particular code page

POSIX SUBSYSTEM

As already mentioned, POSIX is a set of APIs intended to permit UNIX applications to run on a variety of OSs without requiring reimplementation. At this point, only one POSIX standard of the twelve proposed has been formalized: POSIX 1.x. Because POSIX is only an API, the list of what POSIX can't do is as long as the list of what it can. Because POSIX was designed for use in a very simple operating environment, it supports only local input and output and does not even support networking (although you can get to network-accessible files via other parts of Windows NT). Although POSIX technically doesn't support printing, you can pipe information to another NT subsystem for output if you connect or redirect a serial or parallel port and access it with the NET USE command. (See the Appendix for more information on the NET USE command.)

CHAPTER SUMMARY

This chapter provided an overall picture of the Windows NT architecture, its various environment subsystems, and operating environments. At this point, you should understand that Windows NT is divided into two main parts: the environment subsystems, which run in a protected mode called User mode and maintain separate address spaces, and the system Kernel, which runs in a privileged mode called Kernel mode that permits all components to address the same 4 GB memory area and share information.

You should also understand that three environment subsystems (Win32, OS/2, and POSIX) run under Windows NT, plus two special-purpose operating environments (VDM and WOW) that provide backward compatibility within the Win32 subsystem for Win16 and DOS applications. Of these subsystems, only Win32 is crucial to the functioning of Windows NT as a whole. The other subsystems only start up as they're needed; but once launched, these subsystems persist (as do VDMs) until the machine is shut down and restarted.

14

KEY TERMS

- **base priority** — The bottom priority that a thread may be assigned, based on that assigned to its process.

- **bound application** — An application capable of running under the OS/2 subsystem or in a virtual DOS machine. If the OS/2 subsystem is available, it will be used by default.

- **child process** — A process spawned within the context of some Windows NT environment subsystem (Win32, OS/2, or POSIX) that inherits operating characteristics from its parent subsystem, and access characteristics from the permissions associated with the account that requested it to be launched.

- **context switch** — The act of unloading the context information for one process and replacing it with another, when the new process comes to the foreground.

- **critical section** — In operating system terminology, this refers to a section of code that can only be accessed by a single thread at any one time, to prevent uncertain results from occurring when multiple threads might attempt to change or access values included in that code at the same time. Access to critical sections is controlled by special flags called semaphores that guarantee exclusive access.

- **DOS operating environment** — A general term used to describe the reasonably thorough DOS emulation capabilities provided in Windows NT virtual DOS machine (VDM).

- **DOS subsystem** — *See* DOS operating environment.

- **Dynamic Link Library (DLL)** — A collection of virtual procedure calls, also called procedure stubs, that provide a well-defined way for applications to call on services or server processes within the Windows 32 environment. In fact, DLLs have been a consistent aspect of Windows since Windows 2.0.

- **environment subsystem** — A mini-operating system running within Windows NT, providing an interface between applications and the Kernel. Windows NT has three environment subsystems: Win32, OS/2, POSIX, but only Win32 is required for Windows NT to function.

- **Executive Services** — A set of Kernel-mode functions that control security, system I/O, memory management, and other low-level services.

- **Hardware Abstraction Layer (HAL)** — A hardware-dependent piece of software, written in machine language instead of in C, which the rest of the operating system is written in, that creates a standard interface between whatever hardware happens to be in place and the operating system.

- **input message queue** — A queue for each process, maintained by the Win32 subsystem, that contains the messages sent to the process from the user directing its threads to do something.

- **Kernel** — The part of Windows NT composed of system services that interact directly and control all application contact with the computer.

- **Kernel mode** — The portion of Windows NT that operates within a shared memory space and has access to hardware. The Windows NT Executive Services operates in Kernel mode.

- **Local Procedure Call (LPC)** — A technique to permit processes to exchange data in the Windows NT runtime environment, LPCs define a rigorous interface to let client programs request services, and for server programs to reply with responses to such requests.

- **microkernel** — The portion of the Windows NT Executive Services that synchronizes threads and service interaction.

- **multitasking** — Sharing processor time between threads. Multitasking may be pre-emptive, in which one thread may bump another one if the thread really needs the processor, or cooperative, in which one thread will retain control of the processor until its turn to use it is over. Windows NT uses preemptive multitasking except in the context of the WOW operating environment; Windows 3.x applications expect cooperative multitasking.

- **multithreaded process** — A process with more than one thread running at a time.

- **OS/2 subsystem** — The Windows NT subsystem used for running OS/2 applications; an emulation of OS/2 version 1.x (character mode only).

- **parent process** — The Windows NT environment subsystem that creates a runtime process and imbues that child process with characteristics associated with that parent's interfaces, capabilities, and runtime requirements.

- **POSIX subsystem** — The Windows NT subsystem used for running POSIX applications.

- **process** — An environment in which the executable portion of a program runs, defining its memory usage, its processor affinity, its objects, and so forth. All processes have at least one thread. When the last thread is terminated, the process terminates with it. Each User-mode process maintains its own map of the virtual memory area. One process may create another, in which case the creator is the parent process and the created process is the child process.

- **Real mode** — A DOS term that describes a mode of operation for x86 CPUs wherein they can address only 1 MB of memory, broken into 16 64 KB segments, where the lower 10 such segments are available to applications (the infamous 640 KB) and the upper six segments are available to the operating system or to special application drivers—or for Windows NT, to a VDM.

- **synchronization object** — Any of a special class of objects that occur within the Windows NT environment (such as semaphores, timers, threads, mutexes, and so on) that are used to synchronize and control access to shared objects and critical sections of code.

- **thread** — The executable portion of a program, with a priority based on the priority of its process—user threads cannot exist external to a process. All threads in a process share that process's context.

- **User mode** — The portion of Windows NT that operates in private virtual memory areas for each process, so that each process is protected from all others. User-mode processes may not manipulate hardware but must send requests to Kernel-mode services to do this manipulation for them.

- **virtual device driver (VDD)** — A device driver used by virtual DOS machines (VDMs) to provide an interface between the application, which expects to interact with a 16-bit device driver, and the 32-bit device drivers that Windows NT provides.

- **virtual DOS machine (VDM)** — A Win32 application that emulates a DOS environment for use by DOS and Win16 applications.

14

- **Win16-on-Win32 subsystem (WOW)** — The formal name for the collection of components, interfaces, and capabilities that permit the Win32 subsystem to provide native support for well-behaved 16-bit Windows applications.

- **Win16 operating environment** — The collection of components, interfaces, and capabilities that permit Win16 applications to run within a VDM within the Win32 subsystem on Windows NT.

- **Win16 subsystem** — *See* Win16 operating environment.

- **Win32 subsystem** — The Windows NT subsystem that provides the usual Windows NT interface.

REVIEW QUESTIONS

1. Which of the following is not an environment subsystem? (Choose all that apply.)

   a. Win32

   b. Win16

   c. OS/2

   d. none of the above

2. If the threads in a process will always run on one processor in a multiprocessor system, that process is said to have a(n) _____ for that processor.

3. Which of the following statements about process termination is/are true? (Choose all that apply.)

   a. When a process's last thread terminates, the process will terminate as well, unless it creates another thread in a certain interval.

   b. When a process terminates, all of its child processes terminate with it.

   c. A process must have at least one thread at all times.

   d. If a parent process terminates, its threads may be taken over by a child process.

4. Which of the following is not a reason to use the environment subsystem/Kernel model? (Choose all that apply.)

   a. speed

   b. modularity

   c. subsystem protection

   d. ease of communication

5. The _____ subsystem is required for the functioning of the Windows NT operating system.

6. Applications and the subsystems in which they run have a _____ relationship, in that the client application asks the server subsystem to do things for it, and the subsystem complies.

7. When an application stops operating in User mode and begins operating in Kernel mode, this is called a context switch. True or False?

8. Which of the following is not an attempt to speed up subsystem/user application communications?

   a. LPCs

   b. caching services provided by the subsystem

   c. batching messages

   d. calling Kernel services directly

9. What two parts of the Kernel were part of the Win32 subsystem prior to Windows NT 4.0?

   a. GDI

   b. I/O Manager

   c. Device drivers

   d. Windows manager

10. User applications always operate in User mode. True or False?

11. To restart the OS/2 subsystem, you must:

    a. log off and log back on

    b. stop OS2.EXE and then start a new OS/2 application

    c. restart the computer

    d. none of the above

12. Why can't the OS/2 subsystem run on a RISC computer?

    a. because OS/2 was never implemented for RISC

    b. because RISC machines only support 80286 level DOS emulation

    c. because Windows NT doesn't run on RISC machines

    d. none of the above

14

13. POSIX applications must always run on an NTFS partition. True or False?

14. Each time you start a DOS application under Windows NT, it runs in its own VDM. True or False?

15. What are the three parts of the Windows NT Kernel? (Choose all that apply.)

    a. Executive Services

    b. microkernel

    c. HAL

    d. device drivers

16. The Process Manager is responsible for thread scheduling. True or False?

17. Which of the following is not one of the Windows NT Executive Services under Windows NT 4.0?

   a. I/O Manager

   b. GDI

   c. Window Manager

   d. microkernel

18. With which component(s) does the Process Manager work in order to provide inter-process protection? (Choose all that apply.)

   a. Object Manager

   b. Security Reference Monitor

   c. I/O Manager

   d. Virtual Memory Manager

19. When a block of virtual memory addresses is set aside but not backed with any physical storage, this is known as ――――――――.

   a. translation

   b. reservation

   c. committal

   d. block creation

20. A Local Procedure Call (LPC) occurs when a user application requests a service by interacting with the DLL stub for the service so that the environment subsystem knows it has to do something. True or False?

21. In the hierarchy of graphical output, which is closest to (interacts directly with) the user application?

   a. device drivers

   b. GDI

   c. Window Manager

   d. I/O Manager

22. An interrupt is an example of a(n) ―――――――― object used by the microkernel for scheduling.

23. All multithreaded applications running under Windows NT could be designed to operate on multiple processors for greater efficiency. True or False?

24. A ―――――――― 16-bit application always runs in a separate memory space by default; whereas, a ―――――――― 16-bit application runs by default in the same memory space as other applications of its kind.

25. A section of code that modifies data structures used by several threads is called a ――――――――.

26. Neither AUTOEXEC.BAT nor CONFIG.SYS have any role in determining Windows NT system configuration. True or False?

HANDS-ON PROJECTS

PROJECT 14-1

To start a Win16 application in its own address space:

1. From the **Start** menu, choose **Run**. You'll see a dialog box like the one shown in Figure 14-7. Enter the path and filename of the application you want to run.

Figure 14-7   Check Run in Separate Memory Space to run
Win16 applications in their own VDMs

2. Make sure the **Run in Separate Memory Space** box is checked. If it's checked but disabled, then the application you've selected is not a Win16 application.

3. Click **OK** to run the application. It will run in a VDM separate from the other running Win16 applications.

14

PROJECT 14-2

To change the location of system configuration files for a DOS application:

1. Launch the Windows NT Explorer (**Start**, **Programs**, **Windows NT Explorer**). Navigate to the directory specified by your instructor or technical support person to access a DOS application (for example, EDIT.COM).

2. Right-click the entry for this application, then choose **Properties** from the menu that appears. You'll see a dialog box similar to the one shown in Figure 14-8.

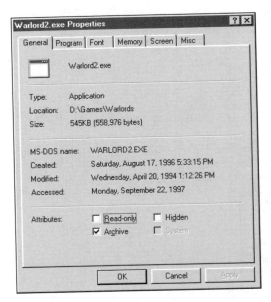

Figure 14-8   Properties window, General tab

3. Move to the **Program** tab and click the **Windows NT** button. A small dialog box showing the location of the NT configuration files opens, as shown in Figure 14-9. You can use this to invoke customized AUTOEXEC.NT and CONFIG.NT files for individual DOS applications in the Windows NT environment. (*Note*: You must copy these files from the default location, edit them as desired, and point to their new location in the two text entry boxes in this window.) Otherwise, all DOS applications share a single system–supplied default.

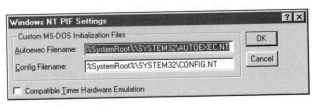

Figure 14-9   Changing configuration information

4. Click **OK** to close this window, then click **OK** again to close the Properties window. Then close Explorer.

PROJECT 14-3

To view the effects of various VDM-based applications on Windows NT:

1. Restart your Windows NT machine by entering the NT attention sequence (**[Ctrl]–[Alt]–[Del]**), then click the **Shut Down** button, and select the **Shutdown and Restart** radio button. This terminates any open VDMs that might otherwise be present on your machine. Click **OK**.

2. Launch the Windows NT Task Manager (right-click on the **taskbar**, then select **Task Manager** from the menu), and select the **Processes** tab. Scroll through the list of entries, looking for NTVDM.EXE, and other VDM components. (You should not find any.)

3. Launch the DOS application EDIT.COM (**Start**, **Run**, then type the information provided by your instructor or technical support person that will permit you to access this file).

4. Return to the Windows NT Task Manager (you should be able to enter **[Alt]–[Tab]** and return to it immediately; if that doesn't work, select its icon on the taskbar).

5. Rescan the list of entries, you should see a single instance of NTVDM.EXE.

6. Now, launch the Win16 Solitaire (SOL.EXE) application (**Start**, **Run**, then type the information provided by your instructor or technical support person that will permit you to access this file).

7. Return to the Windows NT Task Manager (you should be able to enter **[Alt]–[Tab]** and return to it immediately; if that doesn't work, select its icon on the taskbar).

8. Rescan the list of entries, you should now see two instances of NTVDM.EXE (one for EDIT.COM, the other for SOL.EXE, which includes a subentry that reads wowexec.exe).

9. Launch the Win16 Mines (WINMINE.EXE) application (**Start**, **Run**, then type the information provided by your instructor or technical support person that will permit you to access this file).

10. Return to the Windows NT Task Manager (you should be able to enter **[Alt]–[Tab]** and return to it immediately; if that doesn't work, select its icon on the taskbar).

11. You should still see only two instances of NTVDM.EXE, because SOL.EXE and WINMINE.EXE share a common VDM.

12. Return to the Mines game, and close it (**[Alt]–[Tab]** until you get to that application, then press **[Alt]-F**, **X** to exit). Return to the Solitaire game and close it in the same manner. Press ESC to close the dialog box. Return to the DOS Edit application and close it in the same way.

13. Return to the Windows NT Task Manager (**[Alt]–[Tab]** until you get to that application). Notice that both VDMs are still running. Select each one, then click the **End Process** button in the lower right corner of the display to shut each one down. Close the Windows NT Task Manager.

14

CASE PROJECTS

1. To avoid the need to reimplement old code for your user community, which is in the process of upgrading from Windows 95 to Windows NT Workstation machines, you decide to allow your users to run your company's home-grown application, TELLER.EXE on their machines. TELLER.EXE is a well-behaved 16-bit Windows application. Because this program sometimes hangs for as much as 2 or 3 minutes while computing end-of-day balances, it may cause problems for other 16-bit Windows applications that your users might need to run. What can you do to insulate these other applications from TELLER.EXE? How might you launch this program to accomplish this goal?

2. At XYZ Corp., the company has decided to switch from its OS/2 Warp machines to Windows NT Workstation 4.0. Your manager informs you that this will be a snap because Windows NT includes an OS/2 subsystem that supports the company's home-grown graphical OS/2 applications. What must you tell your manager about his assumptions about Windows NT's support for OS/2? Why is this a problem?

3. Given a list of DOS and 16-bit Windows applications that you may wish to use on a Windows NT 4.0 Workstation machine, what is the proper method to ensure that each of them will (or won't) work with this operating system? What happens if any of these applications is ill-behaved?

BOOTING WINDOWS NT

On the surface, booting a computer seems like the simplest thing in the world. In reality, booting is a complex and convoluted process. In fact, it is important to understand each step in the transformation of an inert hunk of metal into a computer running Windows NT. This understanding is essential for the Microsoft certification exam and for troubleshooting a system that won't boot properly.

In this chapter you learn the steps that Windows NT takes a computer through as it begins initial operation of the hardware, then finds pointers to the software that ultimately leads to choosing which operating system to run, goes through the process of loading and starting Windows NT, and finally completes a successful user logon. It is only at this point that the Windows NT boot process is considered to be complete.

AFTER READING THIS CHAPTER AND COMPLETING THE EXERCISES YOU WILL BE ABLE TO:

- Understand the boot process for Windows NT
- Explain the role of the BOOT.INI file and its settings
- Discuss the boot process for computers with multiple operating systems
- Understand the Registry settings involved in the boot process

THE BOOT PROCESS

All computers, whether Intel (x86) or RISC, Windows NT or another operating system, go through a similar **boot process** when they are turned on. In Windows NT, the process is broken down into two major phases, the **boot phase** and the **load phase**.

The NT boot process (including the boot phase and the load phase) varies slightly between Intel and RISC systems, but the principles are the same. The boot process takes place not only when the computer is first powered on, but also when you choose Shutdown and Restart from the Shutdown Computer dialog box (which appears when you select Shut Down from the Windows NT Security dialog box that takes over your screen any time you enter the Windows NT attention sequence, Ctrl-Alt-Del) or when you select Restart Computer from the Shut Down Windows dialog box (Start, Shut Down).

WINDOWS NT BOOT PHASE

The six steps of the Windows NT boot phase are as follows:

1. Power On Self Test (POST)
2. Initial startup
3. Boot loader
4. Selecting the operating system
5. Detecting hardware
6. Selecting a configuration

POWER ON SELF TEST (POST)

The **Power On Self Test (POST)** is the first step in the boot sequence for any computer with any operating system. The POST determines the amount of real memory and whether all necessary hardware components, such as a keyboard, are present. The software for the POST resides in a special, battery-powered chip called the **Complementary Metal-Oxide Semiconductor (CMOS)** that can store not only the software necessary to conduct the POST, but also basic configuration information that the POST uses to check the amount of RAM installed in a system, the number and type of hard drives, the type of keyboard and mouse, and so forth. Figure 15-1 shows a typical screen that results from the successful completion of the POST on an Intel PC.

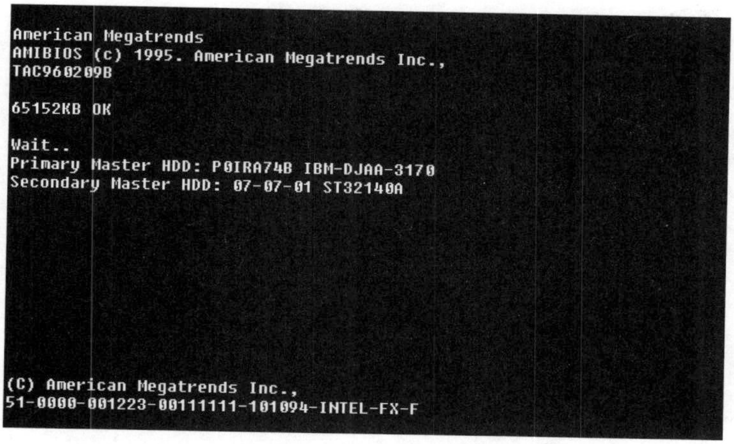

```
American Megatrends
AMIBIOS (c) 1995. American Megatrends Inc.,
TAC960209B

65152KB OK

Wait..
Primary Master HDD: P0IRA74B IBM-DJAA-3170
Secondary Master HDD: 07-07-01 ST32140A




(C) American Megatrends Inc.,
51-0000-001223-00111111-101094-INTEL-FX-F
```

Figure 15-1   The POST display on a PC

After the system POST is complete, each adapter card in the system performs its own self-test. For example, if a computer has a SCSI card in addition to its own built-in adapter cards, it will check its internal configuration and any related devices it sees when it runs its own POST. At the same time, a report on what it finds during this process will appear on the computer monitor in text-only form (because there is no real operating system running at this point, screen output at this stage of the boot process is kept as simple and direct as possible). The screen shown in Figure 15-2 adds the report from an Adaptec 2940 SCSI controller to the information already supplied by the POST routine.

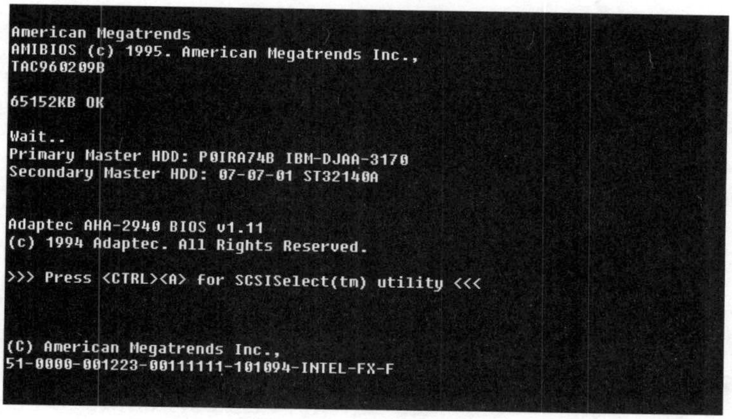

```
American Megatrends
AMIBIOS (c) 1995. American Megatrends Inc.,
TAC960209B

65152KB OK

Wait..
Primary Master HDD: P0IRA74B IBM-DJAA-3170
Secondary Master HDD: 07-07-01 ST32140A

Adaptec AHA-2940 BIOS v1.11
(c) 1994 Adaptec. All Rights Reserved.

>>> Press <CTRL><A> for SCSISelect(tm) utility <<<


(C) American Megatrends Inc.,
51-0000-001223-00111111-101094-INTEL-FX-F
```

15

Figure 15-2   Output from the BIOS on an Adaptec 2940 SCSI controller

INITIAL STARTUP

The initial startup sequence is a bit different for x86 and RISC systems, but much is the same on either platform. For both systems, the first sector of the hard disk contains the **Master Boot Record (MBR)** and the partition table. If you are booting from a floppy disk, the first sector contains the **partition boot sector**. For more information on the MBR, the partition table, and partition boot sector, consult Chapter 5.

x86 Startup

When the POST has successfully completed on an x86-based computer, the BIOS tries to locate the startup disk. **BIOS** stands for **Basic Input Output System** and represents a chip-based set of routines that DOS and Windows 95 use to drive all system input and output, including access to peripheral devices of all kinds. Windows NT, on the other hand, uses its own built-in input/output logic and drivers and ignores whatever BIOS is installed in a computer; this permits NT to manage I/O much more carefully than earlier Windows and DOS operating systems, and also helps to explain why applications that attempt direct access to hardware are treated as ill-behaved in the NT environment (in most cases, they're attempting to access drivers or the computer's BIOS directly, without requesting I/O services from the operating system).

If a floppy disk is in the A: drive when the BIOS checks that drive, it may decide to use that drive as the startup disk (this decision depends on how the boot sequence has been configured in the CMOS). If there is no floppy disk in that drive, or the CMOS has been configured to boot only from a hard disk, it will use the first hard disk it finds as the boot disk. Of course, if drive A: is enabled for booting and you have a floppy disk inserted in that drive that does not have a partition boot sector, you will get a "Non-system disk or disk error: Replace and press any key when ready" message, and the system won't start. This is one of the most common causes of "boot failure" in the Windows NT environment!

If this happens, remove the floppy and cycle the power off and on again. It is important to do this to avoid transferring boot-sector viruses to the computer. By turning it off, rather than rebooting with Ctrl-Alt-Del, you reduce the risk of virus infection.

When the BIOS uses the hard disk as its startup disk, it reads the Master Boot Record and loads that into memory. The BIOS then transfers system control to the MBR. The MBR scans the partition table to locate the system partition. When the MBR locates the system partition, it loads sector 0 of the partition into memory and executes it. Sector 0 can contain a diagnostic program, a utility such as a virus scanner, or a partition boot sector that contains the startup code for the operating system. Should the computer boot from a floppy, only the partition boot sector is used.

Generally, the MBR is independent of the operating system. For example, the same MBR is used in x86 systems to boot to Windows 95, MS-DOS, Windows NT, or Windows 3.x.

Unlike the MBR, the partition boot sector is completely dependent on the operating system and file system in use. For example, the partition boot sector in a Windows NT computer is responsible for a number of operating-system-specific functions. It must understand enough of the file system in use to find **NTLDR**, which is the program that locates and loads the Windows NT operating system files, in the root folder. On a hard drive with a FAT partition, the partition boot sector is generally one sector long and points to another location on disk that will ultimately permit the computer to find and launch NTLDR. On an NTFS partition, because the partition boot sector can be as many as 16 sectors long, it can contain all the necessary file system code needed to locate and launch NTLDR, without requiring transfer of control to another area on disk. Thus, the partition boot sector is responsible for loading a boot loader, which for Windows NT is called NTLDR.EXE, into memory and initiating boot loader execution.

At this point, on x86 computers, the **system partition**, which contains the MBR and partition boot sector, must be on the first physical hard drive in the system. The **boot partition**, the partition that contains the Windows NT files, however, can be on the same partition, a different partition on the same drive, or on another drive entirely. In other words, you boot Windows NT from the system partition and run the operating system from the boot partition.

Because this terminology is counterintuitive and because it appears on numerous Windows NT-related Microsoft exams, it's important to remember this reversal of terminology.

On x86 PCs, the first partition on the first hard drive, called the system partition, must be a file system that Windows NT recognizes. If your computer currently runs Windows 95 OSR2 and the system partition is formatted as FAT32, Windows NT will not install, nor will it be able to run, even if you plan to install Windows NT to another disk. In other words, the first partition on the first hard drive on a system that is to run Windows NT must be formatted with FAT, VFAT, or NTFS, or you won't be able to install or run Windows NT on that system!

RISC Startup

15

The initial startup sequence for a RISC-based computer is more streamlined and simpler than for Intel computers. Once the POST has been completed on a RISC system, its ROM firmware selects a startup disk (the ROM plays the same role on a RISC system that the CMOS plays on a PC). The ROM figures out which startup disk to use by reading a boot precedence table from **non-volatile random access memory (NVRAM)**, RAM that is not erased when the system is powered off. NVRAM also contains the location for the OSLOADER (the RISC equivalent of NTLDR), the path to the boot partition, and the folder that contains the Windows NT operating system.

Unlike x86 computers, the system partition for a RISC computer can be on any hard disk. By using the **boot selection menu**, you are able to set up or change the system partition. The system partition in a RISC system must be formatted with the FAT file system. This is because the ARC standard, which will be discussed later in this chapter, requires that the firmware have the SCSI miniport and FAT file system stub drivers built into it.

When a RISC–based computer is booted, all processing is handed off from the firmware directly to OSLOADER. Because of this, the firmware takes over the function of the partition boot sector, and the partition that contains OSLOADER must also be formatted as FAT. Once OSLOADER has control of the system, it is able to access an NTFS partition as the boot partition.

Table 15-1 outlines the startup files for Windows NT for both Intel (x86) and RISC computers.

Table 15-1   Windows NT x86 and RISC Startup Files

x86/RISC	Filename	Location	Explanation
x86	NTLDR	Root of startup disk	Windows NT boot loader for Intel machines
RISC	OSLOADER	\Os\<winnt>	Windows NT boot loader for RISC machines
x86	BOOT.INI	Root of startup disk	Windows NT PC boot menu information
RISC	No equivalent file		OSLOADER handles this on RISC machines
x86	BOOTSECT.DOS	Root of startup disk	Provides DOS boot information for dual-boot PCs
RISC	No equivalent file		DOS doesn't run on RISC machines by itself
x86	NTDETECT.COM	Root of startup disk	Windows NT hardware detection program
RISC	No equivalent file		OSLOADER handles this on RISC machines
x86	NTBOOTDD.SYS	Root of startup disk	Lets NT access SCSI drives on PCs with SCSI controller with onboard BIOS disabled
RISC	No equivalent file		Not required on RISC machines
x86	NTOSKRNL.EXE	%systemroot%\System32	Windows NT operating system Kernel
RISC	NTOSKRNL.EXE	%systemroot%\System32	Windows NT operating system Kernel
x86	HAL.DLL	%systemroot%\System32	Hardware Abstraction Layer code (CPU driver for x86 chips)
RISC	HALL.DLL	%systemroot%\System32	Hardware Abstraction Layer code (CPU driver for RISC CPU in use)
x86	No equivalent file		Not used on PC machines
RISC	.PAL files	\Os\<winnt>	Special configuration files for Alpha-based RISC machines
x86	SYSTEM key	%systemroot%\System32	Key Windows NT Registry data
RISC	SYSTEM key	%systemroot%\System32	Key Windows NT Registry data
x86	Device drivers	%systemroot%\System32	PC-specific device drivers for NT use
RISC	Device drivers	%systemroot%\System32	RISC-specific device drivers for NT use

BOOT LOADER

Boot loader processing and files are different on x86 and RISC, but they perform the same general functions: they select an operating system to boot and load the related operating system files from the boot partition. On PCs, this happens once the boot OS is selected from the BOOT.INI menu. On RISC machines, OSLOADER handles this function along with other initial bootup tasks.

x86 Boot Loader—NTLDR

NTLDR controls the operating system selection and hardware detection processes before the Windows NT Kernel is initialized. The following files must all be present in the root directory of the startup disk:

- NTLDR

- BOOT.INI

- BOOTSECT.DOS: This file appears only if the machine has been configured to dual-boot between Windows NT and DOS, Windows 3.x, or Windows 95.

- NTBOOTDD.SYS: This file appears only when a SCSI controller has its built-in BIOS controller disabled; this file supplies the necessary controller driver that the hardware would otherwise provide.

Of this collection of files, NTLDR and BOOT.INI must always be present for Windows NT to boot (the other two are optional and depend on the configuration of the particular machine in use).

When NTLDR begins execution, it clears the screen and displays the following message:

```
OS Loader V4.0
```

At this point, NTLDR switches the processor into 32-bit Flat Memory mode. When x86 computers start, they are running in "Real mode," which means they are functioning as an old-fashioned 8088 or 8086 computer. Because NTLDR is a 32-bit program, it must change the processing mode to support the 32-bit flat memory model it uses before it can perform any further processing.

Next, NTLDR starts the appropriate file system. The code to access both FAT (or VFAT) and NTFS file systems is programmed into NTLDR so that it can read, access, and copy files on either type of file system.

Then, NTLDR reads the BOOT.INI file and displays the operating system selections it contains. The screen that appears at this point is usually called the boot loader screen and represents the point at which users may select which operating system they would like to load (or which form of Windows NT graphics operation they would like to use).

15

A typical boot loader screen appears in Figure 15-3; notice how it includes two varieties of Windows NT Workstation:

```
OS Loader v4.00

Please select the operating system to start:

Windows NT Workstation v4.00
Windows NT Workstation v4.00 [VGA Mode]
MS-DOS 6.22

Use up and down arrows to move the highlight to your choice.
Press Enter to choose.
```

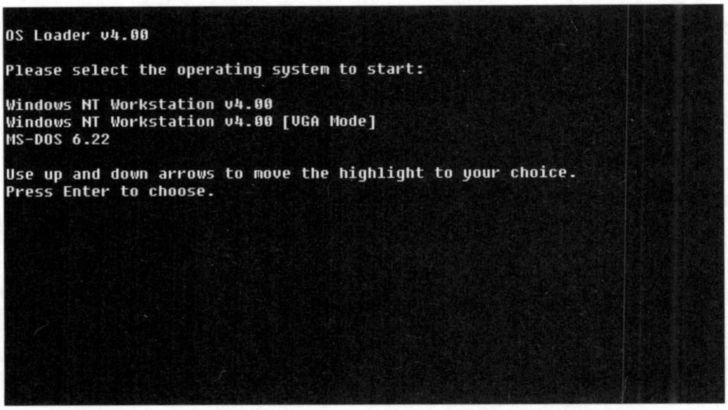

Figure 15-3   A typical Windows NT boot selection menu

- An unadorned listing that will invoke whatever VGA driver is currently installed in the current set of Registry entries
- A second listing that ends with [VGA Mode]—this mode provides a built-in way to boot to a 640 × 480 plain-vanilla VGA driver

Should any problems arise with the VGA driver in your Windows NT environment, this second entry provides a safe mode in which to boot Windows NT so that you can repair whatever misconfiguration has been applied to the display settings (this is absolutely necessary, because Windows NT will happily boot and run without any working screen interface at all; although this may not be a problem for the computer itself, it makes things quite difficult for the computer's would-be operator!).

In fact, Windows NT will coexist with numerous other operating systems, including those that depend on DOS for their underpinnings. Evidence of such a system appears in the third line of the BOOT.INI menu which reads "MS-DOS 6.22," indicating that this is a dual-boot machine that can boot either into Windows NT or DOS.

If a selection is not made before the counter reaches zero, the highlighted operating system will start automatically. To change the default operating system to load or to change the amount of time to wait before automatically loading the highlighted operating system, change the settings in the BOOT.INI file—this will be discussed in greater detail later in this chapter.

If the user selects an operating system other than Windows NT, the boot loader loads BOOTSECT.DOS and hands over control of the system. The other operating system then starts normally because BOOTSECT.DOS contains the partition boot sector for that operating system. However, if the user selects a version of Windows NT, the boot loader executes NTDETECT.COM to gather hardware information.

The remaining functions of NTLDR (operating system selection, hardware detection, and configuration selection) are discussed later in this section. For now, note that NTLDR maintains control of the computer until it loads NTOSKRNL.EXE and passes the hardware information and system control to that program.

RISC Boot Loader—OSLOADER

For RISC-based computers, the program OSLOADER.EXE performs all the functions of the x86 components NTLDR, NTDETECT.COM, and BOOTSECT.DOS. The NVRAM in the RISC system includes the information supplied by the BOOT.INI file for x86 computers.

RISC Operating System Selection

For a RISC-based computer, the boot menu contains the boot options. The first selection is the default operating system, which is the most recently installed version of Windows NT unless you change the order of the selections. If there are other operating systems installed, the boot menu will have the option: Boot to an alternate operating system. By selecting this option, the user will be shown a list of other operating systems that are installed on the computer.

DETECTING HARDWARE

On RISC-based computers, OSLOADER.EXE retrieves hardware information from the firmware. Because of this, the process is rather short and doesn't merit discussion.

However, on x86 computers, the procedure is more detailed. NTDETECT.COM is executed by the boot loader and is used to collect a list of hardware currently installed in the computer. When NTDETECT is identifying the installed hardware, a screen like that shown in Figure 15-4 appears.

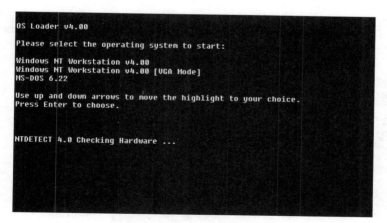

15

Figure 15-4 NTDETECT checks hardware

NTDETECT checks the computer ID, bus/adapter type, video, keyboard, communication ports, parallel ports, floppy disks, and mouse or pointing devices. It creates a system profile that will be compared to Windows NT Registry entries that describe the system later during the boot process, at which point the operating system will look for discrepancies or potential problems.

SELECTING A CONFIGURATION

For both RISC and x86 hardware platforms, the boot loader next presents users with an opportunity to choose which configuration to load as it displays the information shown in Figure 15-5.

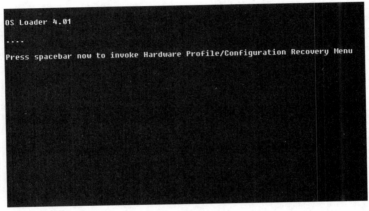

Figure 15-5   Users can stop the boot process and select an alternate configuration

The boot loader then waits five seconds for the user to press the spacebar. If the spacebar is not pressed, the boot loader uses the default **control set**, which represents those key Registry entries that describe the system and that were saved the last time the system was shut down. However, if the user presses the spacebar, a screen like the one shown in Figure 15-6 appears.

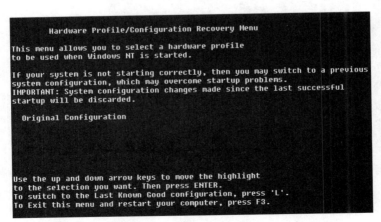

Figure 15-6   Choosing a different hardware profile (where applicable) or using the LKGC to boot

By default, the Original Configuration option is highlighted. If a user has configured multiple hardware profiles, these hardware profiles will also be available here. The user also has the option to select the **Last Known Good Configuration (LKGC)**, rather than the default Original Configuration. By choosing the default configuration, Windows NT uses the Registry information that was saved the last time Windows NT was shut down. The LKGC, on the other hand, uses the Registry information that was saved at the completion of the last entirely successful startup. To load the LKGC, press *L* and then *Enter*.

WINDOWS NT LOAD PHASE

The Windows NT load phase begins when the Kernel assumes control of the machine. It consists of the following five steps:

1. Loading the Kernel

2. Initializing the Kernel

3. Services load

4. Windows NT system start

5. Logging on

LOADING THE KERNEL

Several dots appear on the screen as the boot loader loads the Windows NT Kernel (NTOSKRNL.EXE) and the Hardware Abstraction Layer (HAL; file HAL.DLL) into memory. However, these programs are not executed at this time. Before executing the programs, the boot loader loads the Registry key HKEY_LOCAL_MACHINE\SYSTEM from the *%systemroot%*\System32\Config\System directory.

At this point, the boot loader retrieves the configuration you selected from the Registry subkey HKEY_LOCAL_MACHINE\SYSTEM\Select. Based on the ControlSet00x setting in the subkey, the boot loader knows which ControlSet00x to use. For example, if you chose the Last Known Good Configuration during the configuration selection process, the control set may be ControlSet003 rather than ControlSet001, the default configuration.

Then the boot loader loads the drivers listed in the Registry subkey HKEY_LOCAL_MACHINE\SYSTEM\CurrentControlSet\Services. These drivers are loaded and/or initialized according to their settings in the Registry.

15

INITIALIZING THE KERNEL

It is evident that the Kernel is initializing and that it has accepted control when the following message appears:

```
Microsoft ® Windows NT ™ Version 4.0 (Build 1345)
1 System Processor (32 MB Memory)
```

After its initialization, the Kernel creates the Registry key HKEY_LOCAL_MACHINE\ HARDWARE using the information received from the boot loader. This key contains the hardware information that is computed when the system is started up and includes information about components on the system board and the interrupts used by specific hardware devices.

The Kernel also creates the CloneControlSet by making a copy of the CurrentControlSet. The Clone set is never modified, because it is intended to be an identical copy of the data used to configure the computer and should not be modified during the startup process.

The Kernel now initializes the drivers that were loaded by the boot loader. If drivers experience errors as they load, they send conditions to the Kernel that determine how the error is treated. The error levels are:

- *Ignore:* The error is ignored and no message appears.
- *Normal:* The boot process continues, but a message appears.
- *Severe:* The management of this error depends on whether Last Known Good Configuration is in use. If the LKGC is not being used, then the error message appears and the boot process restarts using the LKGC. If the LKGC is already in use, then the message appears and the boot process continues.
- *Critical:* The management of this error message depends on whether LKGC is in use or not. If not, then the error message appears and the boot process restarts using the Last Known Good Configuration. If the LKGC is already in use, then the message appears and the boot process fails.

All such events are automatically saved in the System log and invoke on-screen messages as well. The System log is available as one of the views in the Windows NT Event Viewer (Start, Programs, Administrative Tools (Common), Event Viewer) and should always be checked whenever errors are reported during the boot process. Because that process cannot be interrupted, however, it will be necessary to wait and inspect the log after the boot phase is complete.

SERVICES LOAD

During the services load phase, the Kernel starts the Session Manager. The Session Manager reads the entries that are stored in the Registry key:
HKEY_LOCAL_SYSTEM\CurrentControlSet\Control\Session Manager.

It then starts programs that correspond to the key entries under this Registry key: HKEY_LOCAL_SYSTEM\CurrentControlSet\Control\Session Manager\BootExecute.

The default entry for this key is *autocheck autochk* *. Autocheck makes sure that the files stored on your hard drive are always consistent. It detects and attempts to repair damaged files and directories. As with any repair utility, it cannot guarantee that all files can be fixed or retrieved.

Once Autocheck is complete, the paging files are set up. These are stored under HKEY_LOCAL_SYSTEM\CurrentControlSet\Control\Session Manager\Memory Management.

The Session Manager then writes the CurrentControlSet and the CloneControlSet to the Registry and finally loads the subsystems that are defined in the Registry.

HKEY_LOCAL_SYSTEM\CurrentControlSet\Control\Session Manager\Subsystems contains the subsystem information. The Windows (Win32) subsystem is the default subsystem for Windows NT and is also the subsystem within which the default user shell always executes (consult Chapter 14 for a discussion of Windows NT architecture and its User mode subsystems).

WINDOWS NT SYSTEM STARTUP

Once the NT services have started up and the elements in the group of processes that are configured to launch on startup are fired off, the Windows NT system may be considered to be fully started. This brief, but meaningful, phase of the process is signaled by the appearance of the Windows NT logon screen as the Win32 subsystem starts WINLOGON.EXE, and that process automatically launches the Local Security Administration (LSASS.EXE) process.

LOGGING ON

The Begin Logon dialog box instructs the user to press Ctrl-Alt-Del to log on. Until a user successfully logs on, the boot process is not complete. Once a user logs on, the Clone control set is copied to the Last Known Good control set. This will provide the values that will be used the next time the machine is powered up, if the user elects to invoke the Last Known Good Configuration.

15

BOOT CONFIGURATION

As you may have noticed, the Windows NT boot configuration can be controlled through its configuration files. To understand how this works, look at the boot configuration file for an x86-based computer, which is called BOOT.INI.

BOOT.INI

As mentioned earlier, the BOOT.INI file is located in the root directory of the system partition and is used by the boot loader to display the list of available operating systems. This file consists of two sections: [boot loader] and [operating systems]. A typical BOOT.INI file is shown in Figure 15-7.

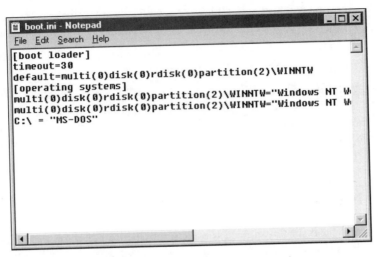

Figure 15-7　BOOT.INI as it appears in Notepad

[BOOT LOADER]

The [boot loader] section of the BOOT.INI file contains two items: timeout and default.

The timeout setting defines the number of seconds the system will wait for the user to select an operating system before loading the default operating system. If timeout is set to zero, NTLDR immediately loads the default operating system without displaying the boot loader screen. To cause the system to wait indefinitely for a selection, set the timeout to –1. This setting, however, can only be altered using a text editor, because it is an illegal value for the setting from the System icon in the Control Panel. (See the section later in this chapter on editing the BOOT.INI, which explains how to edit this file and what kind of text editor to use.)

The default setting lists the path to the default operating system.

[OPERATING SYSTEMS]

The [operating systems] section lists the available operating systems. Each listing contains the path to the boot partition for the operating system, the text displayed in the boot loader screen, and optional parameters. The text is clipped in the screen capture in Figure 15-7, so here's what it looks like in its entirety:

```
multi(0)disk(0)rdisk(0)partition(2)\WINNTW="Windows NT Workstation
Version 4.00"

multi(0)disk(0)rdisk(0)partition(2)\WINNTW="Windows NT Workstation
Version 4.00 [VGA mode]"
```

Remember, the first entry will invoke Windows NT using whatever graphics drivers and settings are specified in the Windows NT Registry; the second entry invokes Windows NT using a plain-vanilla 640 × 480 generic VGA driver (which works with nearly every known VGA-capable graphics card or better) to permit graphical configuration errors to be corrected.

Table 15-2 lists the switches that can be added to the end of entries in the [operating systems] section of the BOOT.INI.

The switches used in the BOOT.INI are not case-sensitive.

Table 15-2   BOOT.INI [operating systems] Optional Settings

Switch	Description
/BASEVIDEO	Starts Windows NT in standard VGA mode (640 × 480)
/BAUDRATE=*nnnn*	Specifies the baud rate for debugging; using this switch will automatically force /DEBUG mode
/CRASHDEBUG	Enables the debugger if a Kernel error occurs
/DEBUG	Loads the debugger and allows access by a host debugger connected to the computer
/DEBUGPORT=com*x*	Defines the communications port to be used for debugging; using this switch will automatically force /DEBUG mode
/MAXMEM:*n*	Defines the maximum amount of memory Windows NT can use
/NODEBUG	No debugging information is being used
/NOSERIALMICE=com*x*	Disables serial mouse detection on the specified communication port
/SOS	Displays the device driver names when they are loaded

15

ADVANCED RISC COMPUTING (ARC) PATHNAMES

In the BOOT.INI file, the path pointing to files and directories is written using the **Advanced RISC Computing (ARC)** naming conventions. These pathnames are described as follows:

- *scsi(n)* or *multi(n)*: This portion of the path indicates the type of the device on which the operating system resides. *scsi* is used if the operating system is on a SCSI hard disk that is connected to a SCSI adapter whose built-in BIOS is disabled. *multi* is used for other hard disks including IDE, EIDE, and SCSI with a built-in BIOS. The *(n)* indicates the hardware adapter from which to boot. It is replaced with a number corresponding to the correct hardware adapter, numbered ordinally (starting with zero).

- *disk(n)*: This portion of the path indicates which SCSI bus number should be used. The *(n)* always equals zero when the adapter is a multi-adapter; otherwise, it is an ordinal number.

- *rdisk(n)*: This portion of the path indicates the SCSI LUN number or selects which of the hard disks attached to the adapter contains the operating system. *(n)* always equals zero when the adapter is SCSI; otherwise, it is an ordinal number.

- *partition(n)*: This portion of the path selects the disk partition that contains the operating system files. Partition is a cardinal number (starting with 1).

- *\path*: The final portion of the path indicates the directory on the partition in which the operating system files are found. The default path for Windows NT is \Winnt.

SAMPLE BOOT.INI FILE

A simple BOOT.INI file follows; this file includes a pointer to the default OS selection, timer information, and the typical Workstation versions. Its inclusion of the C:\= "Microsoft Windows" entry in the [operating systems] section indicates this is a dual-boot machine that also includes some version of Windows (probably Windows 95).

```
[boot loader]
timeout=15
default=multi(0)disk(0)rdisk(0)partition(1)\NTWKS
[operating systems]
multi(0)disk(0)rdisk(0)partition(1)\NTWKS="Windows NT
Workstation Version 4.00"
multi(0)disk(0)rdisk(0)partition(1)\NTWKS="Windows NT
Workstation Version 4.00 [VGA mode]" /basevideo /sos
C:\="Microsoft Windows"
```

EDITING BOOT.INI

To make changes to a BOOT.INI file, the user has two options: use the Control Panel to edit this file indirectly or use a text editor to change the file directly.

USING THE CONTROL PANEL

Using the Control Panel to make changes to BOOT.INI is the safest way to proceed. By opening the System applet in the Control Panel, you can make certain changes to your setup. The System applet allows you to choose a default boot selection and select a delay interval before the boot selection starts automatically. This delay time corresponds to the timeout value set in BOOT.INI. These options are depicted in the System Startup box on the Startup/Shutdown tab in the System applet shown in Figure 15-8. Notice also that the Recovery options that control debugging output for STOP errors appear on this tab; this information often comes in handy when severe bootup problems may manifest.

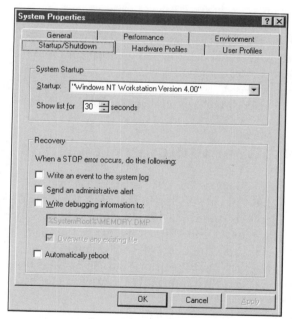

Figure 15-8   Boot options on the Startup/Shutdown tab in the System applet

USING A TEXT EDITOR

Notepad or any other text editor can be used to edit BOOT.INI. As with any initialization file, you should be careful editing the file. If you configure the file incorrectly, Windows NT may not boot.

You should always create an Emergency Repair Disk before making changes to BOOT.INI; if nothing else, create a backup copy of the file and name it BOOT.BAK before you make any changes.

If you decide to edit the BOOT.INI file from a text editor, you must first reset the file's attributes to make it editable. By default, this file has the following attributes set: System, Hidden, Read-only. To edit the file, you must turn off at least the Read-only attribute (you should usually turn off the Hidden attribute as well).

To change the file's attributes, you must locate the file in Windows NT Explorer, right-click its entry, click Properties, and then uncheck the default attribute settings boxes on the General tab. After you make these attribute changes, you can edit the file using any simple text editor (Notepad works fine). Once you've finished editing, you must then return to Windows NT Explorer and reset the Read-only attribute (NT doesn't care if you restore its Hidden status or not, but the system won't boot properly unless you restore the Read-only attribute).

MULTIPLE-BOOT SYSTEMS

One of the biggest advantages of the Windows NT operating system is its ability to peacefully coexist with other operating systems. Each operating system uses one or more file systems to organize the data within the volumes. Some operating systems can use the same file system; others are incompatible. For example, MS-DOS, Windows 95, and Window NT are able to use FAT volumes, but Windows NT and UNIX are not able to share file systems.

MULTIPLE WINDOWS OPERATING SYSTEMS

Windows 3.1, Windows 3.11, and Windows 95 can all exist on the same system as Windows NT. In fact, Windows NT can be installed in the same folder as Windows 3.1 or 3.11 because Windows NT places its important files in the \System32 directory and only uses the %systemroot% directory for .INI files that it maintains for 16-bit applications and backward compatibility. If you install Windows NT to a different directory, you will not be given the option of migrating .INI and Program Manager settings from Windows 3.1x. On the other hand, Windows 95 and Windows NT must be installed in separate directories.

Different versions of Windows NT may also be installed on the same computer, but, again, each must have a separate directory. In addition, if the computer is logging into a domain, each Windows NT installation must have a different computer name.

If you plan to use applications from the different versions of Windows you have installed, you must install the application from each operating system. For example, if you intend to use Microsoft Word from both Windows 95 and Windows NT 4.0, you must run the Word setup program while the computer is booted to each operating system.

MULTIPLE INSTALLATION ORDER

When installing multiple operating systems on x86-based computers, the order in which you install the OSs is important. When installing Windows NT and MS-DOS, it is best to install MS-DOS first, then Windows NT. Windows NT will see the DOS operating system and leave it intact. The same guideline applies to installing Windows NT and Windows 95. At this time, the recommended installation order is Windows 95 first, Windows NT second. If you plan on running all three operating systems (MS-DOS, Windows 95, and Windows NT), they should be installed in that order: MS-DOS, Windows 95, and Windows NT last.

REGISTRY CONTROL SETS

The control sets in the Registry contain configuration information, such as which device drivers to load and start and at what time. All control sets are stored in the Registry as subkeys of HKEY_LOCAL_MACHINE\SYSTEM. A typical Windows NT installation will have five control sets—Clone, ControlSet001, ControlSet002, ControlSet003, and CurrentControlSet—but can have more or less, depending on the number of times the system configuration is changed and whether you have problems with a configuration.

The subkey CurrentControlSet is actually a pointer to one of the ControlSet00x keys. As mentioned earlier, the Clone control set is created by the Kernel and is a clone of the configuration when the computer was initialized, either Default or Last Known Good.

To fully understand how the control sets work, it is important to understand the Registry subkey HKEY_LOCAL_MACHINE\SYSTEM\Select. This key contains the values Current, Default, Failed, and Last Known Good. The settings in these fields contain the corresponding control set number. For example, if the Current setting is 0x1, then the CurrentControlSet is pointing to ControlSet001. Or, if the Last Known Good setting is 0x2, then the Last Known Good control set is ControlSet002.

As mentioned earlier, the control sets contain information on the device drivers that are loaded and/or initialized when the computer is started. The Start value for each driver defines whether the driver will be loaded by the Kernel and, if so, when it will be initialized. The Start values are located in the HKEY_LOCAL_MACHINE\SYSTEM\ControlSet00x\ Services*driver name* key. The Start value for any driver can be set to any of the following:

15

- *0x0 (Boot):* Driver is loaded by the boot loader before the Kernel is initialized, such as a disk device driver.

- *0x1 (System):* Driver is loaded by the I/O subsystem during Kernel initialization, such as a mouse driver.

- *0x2 (Auto load):* Driver is loaded by the Service Control Manager. Devices with this setting are loaded automatically, every time the system is started, such as the parallel port driver.

- *0x3 (Load on demand):* Driver is loaded by the Service Control Manager, but only when the user specifically starts it.

- *0x4 (Disabled):* Driver is not loaded by the Service Control Manager. This setting is generally used if hardware is not installed in the system.

CHAPTER SUMMARY

The Windows NT boot process can be daunting, but it is not nearly as mysterious as one first supposes. It follows the same general boot steps as any other operating system, and in fact, "plays well with others." After the POST (Power On Self Test), the BIOS in an x86 computer loads the Master Boot Record, which then loads the partition boot sector. For RISC systems, this is handled by the firmware.

Then, on both platforms, the boot loader takes control of the system and begins the true Windows NT boot. The users are presented with options for choosing the operating system to load, and, if they choose Windows NT, the configuration to use.

At this point, the Kernel is loaded into memory and it is granted control of the computer. As the Kernel is initializing, it displays several dots across the screen. The Kernel loads the operating system files and device drivers before finally allowing the user to logon. When the user successfully logs onto the computer, it is considered a good startup and the configuration is saved to the Registry.

In x86 computers, the boot process can be altered by changing the BOOT.INI file. This includes information such as the default operating system, its location, and the amount of time to wait before automatically loading the default OS. The type of information displayed and the debugger setting can be changed by adding switches to the configurations in the BOOT.INI.

There are a number of Registry settings that keep track of the state of the boot process. The Last Known Good key records the configuration of the computer the last time a user successfully logged on. Other control sets define the current configuration and other configurations that may have problems.

KEY TERMS

- **Advanced RISC Computing (ARC) pathname** — Naming convention used in the BOOT.INI to define the particular hard disk and partition where Windows NT operating system files reside.

- **Basic Input/Output System (BIOS)** — A special PC ROM chip that contains sufficient program code to let a computer perform a POST routine, to check its hardware components, and to operate basic input and output routines for keyboard or mouse input and screen output.

- **boot partition** — In Windows NT, the disk that contains the Windows NT operating system files.

- **boot phase** — Any of a number of stages in the Windows NT boot process, starting with the Power On Self Test (POST), through initial startup activities, to activation of a boot loader program, to selection of the operating system (or version) to boot, hardware detection (NTDETECT), to selection of a configuration.

- **boot process** — The process of bringing up a completely functional computer, starting from initial power-up (or reboot) through the boot phases and load phases involved in starting the hardware, finding a boot loader, and then loading and initializing an operating system.

- **boot selection menu** — The list of bootable operating systems (or versions) that BOOT.INI provides for display at the end of the Windows NT boot phase.

- **Complementary Metal–Oxide Semiconductor (CMOS)** — A special, battery-powered chip that can store not only the software necessary to conduct the POST, but that also stores basic, nonvolatile configuration information that the POST uses to check the RAM installed in a system, the number and type of hard drives, the type of keyboard and mouse, and so forth.

- **control set** — A special set of Registry values that describe a Windows NT machine's startup configuration that is saved each time a Windows NT machine is shut down (as the current configuration) and each time a user successfully logs on for the first time after boot up (as the Last Known Good Configuration).

- **Last Known Good Configuration (LKGC)** — The control set for Windows NT that is automatically saved by the system in a special set of Registry keys the first time a user logs on successfully to a system immediately after it has booted up. This information provides a "safe fallback" to use when booting the system the next time if changes made to the Registry in the interim cause problems with booting (or simply introduce changes a user does not wish to retain on that system).

- **load phase** — Begins when the Kernel assumes control of the machine and consists of the following five steps: (1) loading the Kernel, (2) initializing the Kernel, (3) services load, (4) Windows NT system start, and (5) logging on. All five steps must complete successfully for a complete load to occur.

- **Master Boot Record (MBR)** — The partition table for a disk and code that permits that partition table to be read. A functioning MBR is required to boot a hard disk.

15

- **non-volatile random access memory (NVRAM)** — Memory in a RISC-based computer that contains hardware and operating system information.

- **NTLDR** — The Windows NT loader program that manages the boot and load phases of Windows NT on a PC, as soon as the MBR passes control to that program, through the load of NTOSKRNL.EXE (the Windows NT Kernel program).

- **partition boot sector** — The partition that contains the information the file system uses to access the volume, including a physical description of the disk, the name and version of the operating system files, the bootstrap code, and an instruction that allows the Master Boot Record to find all this information.

- **Power On Self Test (POST)** — System check performed by all computers when they are turned on.

- **system partition** — In Windows NT, the disk that contains the MBR and partition boot sector.

REVIEW QUESTIONS

1. The _____ contains the files that initialize components of the operating system.

    a. boot partition

    b. system partition

    c. start partition

    c. Kernel partition

2. What program has control of an x86 computer when the user is able to choose which operating system to boot?

    a. NTLDR

    b. boot loader

    c. BOOT.INI

    d. NTBOOTDD.SYS

3. When configuring an x86 computer for multiple operating systems, _____ should always be loaded last.

4. When booting a RISC computer, the boot loader must be installed on a(n) _____ file system.

    a. NTFS

    b. HPFS

    c. FAT

    d. FAT32

5. The _____ setting in the BOOT.INI file defines the operating system that will be loaded automatically.

    a. [operating systems]

    b. [system loader]

    c. [boot loader]

    d. [default]

6. You can tell the Kernel is initializing when the screen displays _____.

7. _____ is the boot loader for RISC-based systems.

    a. NTLDR

    b. OSLOADER.EXE

    c. BOOTDD.SYS

    d. BOOTSECT.DOS

8. The timeout option is in the _____ section of the BOOT.INI file.

9. The control set Registry keys are in the _____ key.
   a. HKEY_LOCAL_MACHINE\SYSTEM
   b. HKEY_LOCAL_MACHINE\SECURITY
   c. HKEY_LOCAL_MACHINE\CONTROL
   d. HKEY_LOCAL_MACHINE\SETTINGS

10. The BOOT.INI file can be changed by two methods. What are they?
    a. using the Control Panel System applet
    b. using the Control Panel Startup applet
    c. using the Windows NT Configuration Manager
    d. changing the file's attributes using a plain-text editor, then changing its attributes back after editing

11. The _____ file is only accessed when SCSI disks are used.
    a. MULTIDISK.SYS
    b. SCSILDR.SYS
    c. RDISK.SYS
    d. NTBOOTDD.SYS

12. At what point in the boot process is the user given the option of selecting a configuration other than the Default configuration?
    a. POST
    b. MBR load
    c. boot selection menu
    d. OS load

13. Which ARC settings are used only for SCSI disks? (Choose all that apply.)
    a. multi(n)
    b. scsi(n)
    c. rdisk(n)
    d. disk(n)

14. The NTOSKRNL.EXE file is located in the _____ directory on a RISC system.

15. The device driver start value _____ indicates the driver should be loaded before the Kernel is initialized.

16. What is the function of NTDETECT.COM on a RISC-based computer?
    a. to check installed hardware components
    b. to compare installed hardware components discovered against prior configuration data
    c. to examine the system for new hardware components and install appropriate drivers
    d. none of the above

15

17. What memory mode does Windows NT operate in?

    a. Real mode

    b. Protected mode

    c. Safe mode

    d. Flat 32-bit mode

18. The _____ BOOT.INI switch displays the names of the device drivers as they are loaded.

    a. /B

    b. /AT

    c. /SOS

    d. /DRV

19. The Last Known Good Registry key is written after _____.

20. The _____ partition contains the Windows NT operating system files.

    a. system

    b. boot

    c. start

    d. Kernel

Hands-on Projects

These projects should be performed on an x86 computer with Windows NT Workstation 4.0 installed.

Project 15-1

To modify the BOOT.INI file by using the Control Panel:

1. Open the Control Panel (**Start**, **Settings**, **Control Panel**).

2. Double-click the **System** applet to start it.

3. Select the **Startup/Shutdown** tab.

4. Notice the Startup option defines the default operating system for the computer. Select another operating system from the list.

5. To modify the amount of time the list appears when the system is booted, change the **Show list for:** setting to **10** seconds by using the **scroll arrows**.

6. The remaining options define what action the Kernel will take when a STOP error occurs. In most situations, these should not be changed.

7. To save the configuration to the BOOT.INI, press the **Apply** button.

8. Press the **OK** button. Close the Control Panel.

9. To see the effect of the changes you made, restart the computer.

PROJECT 15-2

To change the BOOT.INI settings using a text editor:

1. First create a backup copy of the BOOT.INI file: Launch Windows NT Explorer (**Start, Programs, Windows NT Explorer**); right-click the BOOT entry, select the **Copy** entry, then click on the current drive and press **[Ctrl]-[V]** (paste). This creates a file named "Copy of boot.ini" in that directory. Rename the file to **BOOT.BAK**. You may need this if something goes wrong later.

2. Next, to remove the Read-only attribute from the BOOT.INI file, highlight the **BOOT.INI** file in Explorer.

3. Right-click the file and select **Properties**.

4. Deselect the check box next to **Read-only**. This changes the file's attributes so that it can be altered.

5. Press the **OK** button.

6. Open the BOOT.INI file into Notepad: open the **Start** menu, select **Run**, and enter **notepad boot.ini** in the box provided.

7. Press the **OK** button. Notepad opens with the BOOT.INI file displayed.

8. Restore the timeout to 30 seconds by changing the timeout= value to **30**.

9. The /SOS switch displays the drivers names as they are loaded by the boot loader. Add the /SOS switch to the "Windows NT Workstation Version 4.0" value. This is done by typing **[spacebar]/sos** at the end of the line.

10. Save the file by choosing **File, Save** from the menu.

11. Exit Notepad by choosing **File, Exit** from the menu. Close Explorer.

12. Reboot the computer to view your changes. If it doesn't work, you'll need to boot from a set of boot floppy disks and rename the BOOT.BAK file to BOOT.INI, and reboot again.

15

PROJECT 15-3

Rebooting Windows NT in Safe Video Mode:

1. Enter the Windows NT attention sequence **[Ctrl]-[Alt]-[Del]** to invoke the Windows NT Security dialog box. Click the **Shut Down** button, then click the **Shutdown and Restart** radio button.

2. As Windows NT reboots, watch for the boot selection menu. As soon as it appears, hit the **up arrow** key. *Note:* This will pause the boot process until you make a menu selection and press the [Enter] key, so you can take as much time to examine this screen as you like—the default timer is turned off as soon as you strike a key.

3. Select the boot entry that reads:

   `Windows NT Workstation Version 4.00 [VGA mode]`

4. Press the **[Enter]** key, and allow the boot process to continue to completion.

5. Notice the appearance of the video screen on your system. If you've been using higher-color or higher-resolution settings, you'll notice the screen has reverted to standard VGA (640 × 480 resolution, 256 colors or less). This boot option will come in handy should you ever mistakenly make changes in the Settings tab on the Control Panel Display applet that your graphics controller or monitor can't handle—it will allow you to boot successfully and see enough of your screen to run the Display applet again and restore your system to proper operation!

6. Repeat step 1, and allow your machine to reboot normally.

CASE PROJECTS

1. The engineering department in your company has decided to add Windows NT Workstation 4.0 to its computers. It currently has four PCs, two running Windows 3.11 and two running Windows 95. It would like to retain the current configurations and programs. Outline the steps necessary to install Windows NT on all systems and what configurations will be available after the update is complete.

2. After installing a new graphics controller on a Windows NT Workstation machine, you start up the system, but when the boot process is complete, you see nothing on the monitor except a small dot of light in the exact center. What boot option can you use to see enough of the screen to try a different driver or to change display settings in the Display Control Panel applet?

3. By default, the BOOT.INI entry for Windows 95 in the boot selection menu reads "MS Windows." How might you edit BOOT.INI to change this value to read "Windows 95 Rules!" instead? What part of the BOOT.INI file does the appropriate entry reside in, and which entry should you edit?

TROUBLESHOOTING WINDOWS NT WORKSTATION

Troubleshooting Windows NT Workstation is an important and vast arena, not only for real-world network management issues, but for the Microsoft MSCE exam as well. In this chapter, you learn general troubleshooting principles and how to detect, isolate, and eliminate common NT Workstation problems with installation, disks, system crashes, network connectivity, RAS, the boot process, and printing. In addition, a collection of other pertinent issues is discussed, and you are introduced to several types of resources for troubleshooting NT systems.

AFTER READING THIS CHAPTER AND COMPLETING THE EXERCISES YOU WILL BE ABLE TO:

- Identify common troubleshooting techniques
- Deal with installation difficulties
- List native NT utilities for repair and investigation
- Troubleshoot boot and disk problems
- Recover from system crashes
- Troubleshoot printer, RAS, and network problems
- Understand service packs and hot fixes—when, why, and how to use them
- Learn where to obtain more information about using and troubleshooting NT

GENERAL TROUBLESHOOTING PRINCIPLES

Troubleshooting is a tedious process of systematically eliminating computer system problems. You'll soon discover that troubleshooting is more often an art than an exact science. However, there are several common-sense guidelines you should follow to improve your troubleshooting skills and reduce downtime.

Over the years, it has become clear that the two most valuable assets you can possess when troubleshooting are:

- Information about your system, including details about the computer and previous troubleshooting activities
- A basic, common-sense problem-solving technique

INFORMATION ABOUT YOUR SYSTEM

A **Computer Information File (CIF)** is a detailed collection of all information related to the hardware and software products that comprise your computer (and even your entire network). Actually, a CIF is not just a single file but an ever-expanding accumulation of data sheets sorted into related groups that are stored in a fireproof storage vault. Obviously, constructing a CIF from scratch is a lengthy process but one that will be rewarded with averted problems, easy reconfigurations, or simplified replacement of failed components.

The organization of a CIF is not important; what is important is that it contains thorough, specific, and accurate information about the products, configuration, setup, and problems associated with your network. Some method of correlating the data sheets to the actual components needs to be derived, such as an alphanumeric labeling system.

Some of the important items you'll want to include in your CIF are:

- Component details, such as platform type, brand name, and even model number
- The specifications as detailed by the manufacturer
- Product use information, such as the user's guide or manual
- Installation and configuration settings both for hardware and software, including DIP switches and jumpers along with the legend matching the settings to I/O address, DMA, IRQ, port, speed, and so forth.
- Details about all software, including name, version, patches, and configuration settings
- Assigned names and network address assignments
- Drivers and software for each device, with backups on floppy disk (don't forget to include BIOS upgrades, new drivers, and any service releases)
- Details on the warranty and obtaining warranty service

- A printout of the directory structure on each storage device
- Copies of all initialization and configuration files on floppy disk and in print
- Contact information for technical support, both paid and pro bono
- Log book detailing the history of changes, problems, and solutions
- Backup details (date of last backup, location, software used, and so forth.)
- Map of network and cabling

Your CIF is not complete with just hardware and software details. You should also include the nonphysical characteristics of your system, such as:

- Permission settings and use restrictions for each resource
- Schedule for backups, maintenance, upgrades, training
- System administrator contact information: e-mail, phone, pager
- Services key to productivity on the system (for example, if users need e-mail to do their jobs, then e-mail is a critical service for them—this includes the ability to access the services of a working e-mail server, as well as the client software necessary for end users to read e-mail)
- Your organization's content-publishing guidelines
- Security system and structure of authorized access measures

Neither of these lists is exhaustive. As you operate and maintain your systems, you'll discover other important information to add to this collection. Remember, if you don't document it, then you won't be able to find it when you really need it.

 It is wise to maintain both a printed/written version of this material and an electronic version. Every time a change, update, or correction occurs, it should be documented in the electronic version and printed out and stored. Murphy's Law guarantees that the moment when you need your electronic data most is when your system will not function.

16

BASIC PROBLEM-SOLVING SKILLS

Unfortunately, the time when you need to be clear-headed and have plenty of time to solve problems is usually the exact time when you are overworked, stressed, or facing serious deadlines. Troubleshooting is a process that rarely offers satisfactory results when pursued with impatience and hostility. Here are some common-sense rules for getting the most out of your troubleshooting efforts:

- *Be patient:* Anger, frustration, hostility, and frantic impatience usually cause problems to intensify rather than dissipate.
- *Know your system's hardware and software:* If you don't know what the baseline is, you may not know when a problem is solved or when new problems surface.

- *Undo the last alteration:* The simplest fix may be to expunge the most recent alteration, upgrade, or change made to your system.

- *Look for common culprits and repeat offenders:* The most active or sensitive components are the most common points of failure; this includes hard drives, cables, and connectors. As the old axiom goes, history does repeat itself (and usually right in your own backyard).

- *Isolate the problem:* When possible, eliminate segments or components that are functioning properly; thus, you narrow the range of suspects.

- *Change one element at a time:* A long flight of stairs is best traversed one step at a time. Attempting to leap several or all the steps can be a big mistake. A step-by-step process enables you to clearly distinguish the solution when you stumble upon it.

- *Try the easy and quick solutions first:* Why punish yourself early? Try the easy fixes before moving on to the more time-consuming, difficult, or even destructive measures.

- *Let the fault be your guide:* "Where there's smoke there's fire" applies to computer problems just as to real life. Investigate related components and system areas associated with suspected faults.

- *Try to repeat the failure:* The ability to repeat an error is often the only way to locate its source. Transient, inconsistent faults can be difficult to find because they usually exhibit "now you see it, now you don't" behavior.

- *Log all errors and solutions:* Keep track of everything you do to troubleshoot each problem (both successful and failed attempts). This will prove an invaluable resource should that error recur on the same (or a different) system, or should that system experience a related problem.

- *Learn from the mistakes of others:* Studying the mistakes others have made can save you from repeating those same errors. Newsgroups and mailing lists are particularly good sources of such information.

- *Learn from your own mistakes:* A wise person can examine previous mistakes and failures and learn how to become a better network administrator.

As you can see, there is not much in this list of common-sense items that you didn't already know. The hardest part is remembering these tips when you are in the middle of a problem, and the pressure is set to high.

INSTALLATION DIFFICULTIES

Unfortunately, the installation process of Windows NT Workstation is susceptible to several errors: media errors, domain controller communication difficulties, STOP message errors or halt on blue screen, hardware problems, and dependency failures. The following list contains a short synopsis of each error type and common solutions:

- *Media errors:* Such problems can arise from errors in the distribution CD-ROM itself, with copies of the distribution files on a network drive, or with the communication links between installation and distribution files. The only regularly successful solution to media errors is to switch media, such as copying files to a network drive, linking to a server's CD-ROM, or installing a CD-ROM on a workstation. If media errors occur, always restart the installation process from the beginning.

- *Domain controller errors:* Communication with a domain controller is crucial to some installations, especially when attempting to join a domain or to install a BDC. Most often, this problem relates to typing errors (name, password, domain name, and so forth), but network failures and offline domain controllers can be involved as well. Verify the viability of the domain controller directly and from other workstations (if applicable).

- *STOP message errors or blue screen lockup:* Using an incompatible or damaged driver controller is the most common cause of STOP messages and halting on the blue screen during installation. If any information appears about an error, try to determine if the proper driver is being used. Otherwise, double-check your hardware devices and the drivers required to operate them under NT.

- *Hardware failures:* If you failed to verify that your hardware is on the HCL (Hardware Compatibility List) or a physical defect has surfaced in previously operational devices, strange errors can surface. In such cases, replacing the device is the easiest solution. But before you go to that expense, double-check the installation and configuration of all devices within the computer.

- *Dependency failures:* The failure of a service or driver due to the failure of a foundational or prior service or driver is a dependency failure. An example of a dependency failure is when the Server and Workstation services fail because the NIC fails to initialize properly. Often NT will boot with these errors, so check the Event log for more details.

Just knowing about such installation problems can help you avoid them. Unfortunately, successfully installing NT does not eliminate the possibility of further complications. Fortunately, Windows NT includes several built-in troubleshooting tools that can help locate and eliminate most system failures. These are discussed in the next section.

16

WINDOWS NT REPAIR AND INVESTIGATION UTILITIES

You need to familiarize yourself with the repair and troubleshooting tools native to NT. They are applicable to most situations and can save you countless hours of troubleshooting digression. The next few sections detail how to use the Event Viewer, Last Known Good Configuration, Registry, Emergency Repair Disk (ERD), and NT Diagnostics. The use of these utilities and solutions has also been covered under different topics in earlier chapters.

THE WINDOWS NT EVENT VIEWER

The **Event Viewer**, accessed from Start, Programs, Administrative Tools (Common), is used to view the three logs automatically created by NT:

- *System log:* Records information and alerts about NT internal processes
- *Security log:* Records security-related events
- *Application log:* Records NT application events, alerts, and system messages

Each log records a different type of event, but all logs collect the same meta-information about each event: date, time, source, category, event, user ID, and computer. Each logged event includes some level of detail about the error, from an error code number to a detailed description with a memory hex buffer. Most system errors, including STOP errors that result in the blue screen, appear in the System log. This allows you to review the time and circumstances around system failures. Hands-on Project 16-3 shows how to open and use the Event Viewer.

THE LAST KNOWN GOOD CONFIGURATION BOOT OPTION

The **Last Known Good Configuration (LKGC)** is a snapshot of all the Registry settings that exist at the time a user successfully logs onto the computer. Every time a user logs on successfully, NT records a new LKGC. If a system error occurs, a corrupt driver is installed, or the Registry becomes corrupted so that booting or logging on is impossible, the LKGC provides a way to return to an operational state. The LKGC may be accessed during boot-up when the following message appears: "Press the spacebar to boot with the Last Known Good Configuration." Pressing the spacebar causes a menu to appear where the LKGC may be invoked (by pressing *L*). Chapter 15 covers the LKGC in detail.

THE WINDOWS NT REGISTRY

As you know, the Registry is a database that contains the lion's share of configuration and operational settings for NT. It is not an area that should be altered with impunity—in fact, edit the Registry directly only as a last resort. A single, improperly configured Registry entry can cripple NT or render it completely inoperable. There are two Registry editing utilities: **REGEDIT** and **REGEDT32**. Both of these utilities must be launched from the Start, Run command or from a DOS prompt. REGEDIT displays all the hives of the Registry in a single display window, and the entire Registry can be searched at once. REGEDT32 displays each of the five hives in a separate display window and offers more security- and control-related features. It is a good idea to back up your Registry regularly. Here are some potential methods to complete this task:

- NT Backup
- Disk Administrator (SYSTEM key only)

- Either Registry editing tool (REGEDIT or REGEDT32)
- REGBACK utility from the Resource Kit (requires the REGREST utility from the same source to restore its contents)

> You should make a backup of the Registry before and after any significant changes to your system, such as hardware installation, software installation, or **service pack** application. If your alterations render a system inoperable, attempt repairs by restoring the earlier version of the Registry from a backup.

Here are a few additional points to keep in mind when working with the Registry:

- All Registry edits using REGEDIT or REGEDT32 occur in active memory, meaning that changes go into effect immediately.

- Even immediate changes may not be able to alter "static" memory and system configurations. A reboot is often required after editing the Registry (only rarely do the editing tools suggest this action).

- When you save a Registry key, you also capture the contents of all subkeys. When you restore portions of the Registry from backup, all subkeys beneath the point at which restoration occurs will also be overwritten by the saved version. Any and all changes made since the backup will be lost in all sections restored. Be wary of unforeseen side effects that might result!

THE EMERGENCY REPAIR DISK

The **Emergency Repair Disk (ERD)** acts like a miniature first-aid kit for NT. This single floppy disk contains all the files needed to repair most system-partition and boot-partition problems. The ERD is used to repair or replace critical NT boot process files. An ERD can be created during the initial installation of NT, but an ERD is only as useful as it is current. You should create a new ERD after each significant change to your system using the RDISK.EXE utility, as shown in Hands-on Project 16-1. An ERD contains the following files:

- system._: HKEY_LOCAL_MACHINE\SYSTEM compressed
- software._: HKEY_LOCAL_MACHINE\SOFTWARE compressed
- security._: HKEY_LOCAL_MACHINE\SECURITY compressed
- sam._: HKEY_LOCAL_MACHINE\SAM compressed
- ntuser.da_: Default profile, compressed
- autoexec.nt: %winntroot%\system32\autoexec.nt
- config.nt: %winntroot%\system32\config.nt
- setup.log: List of installed files and their checksums
- default._: HKEY_USERS\DEFAULT compressed

16

The ERD does not contain the entire Registry but just enough to fix the most common boot and startup errors. To use the ERD to make repairs, you'll also need the three setup disks used to install NT. If they are not available, they can be created, as detailed in Hands-On Project 16-2. The repair process is launched by performing the following procedure:

1. Boot using the Windows NT setup Disks #1 and #2.

2. Select "R" for Repair.

3. A menu appears containing the following options:

   - Inspect Registry files

   - Inspect startup environment

   - Verify Windows NT system files

   - Inspect boot sector

4. Deselect any options you do not wish to use, then select continue.

5. When prompted, insert Disk #3 and the ERD.

WINDOWS NT DIAGNOSTICS

Windows NT Diagnostics is an inspection tool you can use to extract configuration and environmental details about your system. Its multi-tabbed dialog box offers details about settings, driver versions, services, resources, network activity, and environmental variables. You can access this utility from Programs, Administrative Tools (Common), Windows NT Diagnostics in the Start menu or launch it by clicking Start, Run, and entering *WINMSD*.

CORRECTING BOOT FAILURES

Problems that occur during NT startup are called **boot failures**. The NT boot process was covered in Chapter 15; this section looks at errors that can occur between powering up and logging on.

ERRORS WITH NTLDR

If the NTLDR executable file is missing or if a disk is in the floppy drive at power-up, the following error message may appear:

    BOOT: Couldn't find NTLDR. Please insert another disk.

The ERD (Emergency Repair Disk) can be used to repair or replace the damaged or missing NTLDR.EXE. If there is a floppy disk in the drive, eject it and continue the boot process.

ERRORS WITH NTOSKRNL

If the NTOSKRNL (NT Operating System Kernel) is corrupt, missing, or the BOOT.INI file points to the wrong partition, then the following error message may appear:

```
Windows NT could not start because the following
file is missing or corrupt:

\winnt root\system32\ntoskrnl.exe

Please re-install a copy of the above file.
```

The ERD repair process can correct this problem by repairing the NTOSKRNL. Or, if the BOOT.INI file is wrong, you can edit it to correct the problem (see the discussion on ARC names in Chapter 15).

ERRORS WITH NTDETECT.COM

If the NTDETECT.COM file is not present, then the following error message may appear:

```
NTDETECT V1.0 Checking Hardware...

NTDETECT failed
```

The ERD repair process must be used to resolve this issue.

ERRORS WITH BOOT.INI

If no BOOT.INI file is present, NTLDR will attempt to load NT from the default \Winnt directory of the current partition. If this fails, then the following error message may appear:

```
BOOT: Couldn't find NTLDR. Please insert another disk.
```

Replacing the BOOT.INI file from a backup or using the ERD repair process can solve this problem.

ERRORS WITH BOOTSECT.DOS

If the BOOTSECT.DOS file is not present to boot to MS-DOS or another operating system (not NT), then the following error message may appear:

```
I/O Error accessing boot sector file

multi(0)disk(0)rdisk(0)partition(1):\bootsect.dos
```

Several situations can cause this error, such as an altered BOOT.INI file, a change in the partition order or numbering, or a missing, inactive, or inaccessible partition. The ERD repair procedure may be able to repair or replace the BOOTSECT.DOS file.

16

CORRECTING DISK PROBLEMS

The hard drive experiences more activity than any other component on your computer—even more than your keyboard and mouse. It should not be surprising that drive failures are common. Windows NT is natively equipped to maintain the file system, but even a well-tuned system is subject to hardware glitches. Most partition, boot sector, and drive configuration faults can be corrected or recovered from by using the Disk Administrator (Start, Programs, Administrative Tools (Common), Disk Administrator) and a recent ERD. But the only reliable means of protecting data on storage devices is to maintain an accurate and timely backup.

RECOVERING FROM SYSTEM CRASHES

A system crash can occur for a variety of reasons, including power failure, device failure, and operating system failure. Recovering from a system crash can be as simple as rebooting or as complex as reinstalling the OS and restoring data from backups. In either case, familiarity with your system, a recent ERD, and a solid backup routine are your only means of protection.

ELIMINATING NETWORK PROBLEMS

Network problems can range from faults in the media, to misconfigured protocols, to workstation or server errors. Attempt to eliminate the obvious and easy before moving on to more drastic, complex, or unreliable measures. Cabling, connections, and hardware devices are just as suspect as the software components of networking. Verifying hardware functionality is more than just eyeballing it; you may need to perform some electrical test work, change physical settings, or even update driver/ROM BIOS.

SOLVING RAS PROBLEMS

RAS is another area of NT that offers numerous points of failure—from the configuration of the computers on both ends, to the modem settings, to the condition of the communications line. Unfortunately, there is not an ultimate RAS troubleshooting guide, but here are some solid steps in the right direction:

- Inspect all physical connection points, including network cable connections, phone or other communication lines, and any special interdevice links (for example, many RAS servers employ a special RS-232 or RS-422 cable to connect a PC acting as a RAS server with an external equipment rack or cable management center where numerous modems or other devices may be attached).

- Verify the operation of the communications line itself.

- Double-check the installation and configuration of the RAS service and the modem.

- Review the RAS-related logs: DEVICE.LOG and MODEMLOG.TXT (see Chapter 11).

- Remember that multilink and callback will not work together.

- Verify that the settings and parameters on both ends of the link—client and server—match or are compatible.

- Make sure the user account has the proper privileges to use RAS.

- Autodial and persistent connections may cause the computer to attempt RAS connection on logon.

Most RAS problems are related to misconfiguration. For more details on RAS, refer to Chapter 11.

RESOLVING PRINTER PROBLEMS

Network printers are often the instigators of several affronts to normal productive activity. Printer problems can occur anywhere between the power cable of the printer and the application attempting to print. Systematic elimination of possible points of failure is the only reliable method for solving printing errors. Here are some common and useful tips for troubleshooting printer problems:

- Inspect the physical components and aspects of the printer, such as cables, connectors, power cord, paper, toner, and so forth.

- Reinstall the logical printer on both the server and the client.

- Look for stalled jobs in the print queue (the printer's status folder).

- Reinstall the printer driver to ensure it is not corrupted.

- Try to print from another application on the same client or from another client with the same application.

- Test the print capabilities using an account with Administrator privileges.

- Through the Services applet, stop and restart the print spooler.

- Through the Task Manager, view the CPU and memory usage of the SPOOLSS.EXE. If the value is too high or zero, the spooler is the fault point. Reboot the computer.

- Check the available free space on the drive hosting the spooler file. Provide additional space by removing files or changing its destination.

This list covers most of the more common printer-related problems. If these tips fail to resolve the issue, you may want to review the material in Chapter 12. Understanding how

16

printing functions within the NT networking architecture may help you locate and correct the problem.

MISCELLANEOUS TROUBLESHOOTING ISSUES

Several more troubleshooting tips that don't fit well into the other categories in this chapter are covered here.

PERMISSION PARANOIA

Permission problems usually occur when group memberships conflict or when permissions are managed on a per-account basis. To test for faulty permission settings, attempt the same actions and activities with the Administrator account. Double-check group memberships to verify that No Access settings are not causing the problem. This means examining the ACLs of the objects and the share, if applicable.

It is important to remember that any changes to the access permissions of the individual or groups will not affect that user until the next time he or she logs on. The access token used by the NT security system is rebuilt each time a user logs on.

RECOVERING FROM MASTER BOOT RECORD FAILURES

The **Master Boot Record (MBR)** is the area of a hard drive that contains the data structure that initiates the boot process. If the MBR fails, the ERD cannot be used to repair it. Instead, you'll need to use a DOS 6.0+ bootable floppy and execute FDISK /MBR. This will recreate the drive's MBR and restore the system correctly.

 Sometimes, using FDISK /MBR to repair the MBR on a system drive may alter or remove the NT boot record. If this happens, the repair will appear to have failed, but can be fixed by using the three installation disks and the ERD to correct the NT boot record problem.

DR. WATSON: THE APPLICATION MEDIC

Windows NT has an application error debugger called **Dr. Watson**. This diagnostic tool detects application failures and logs diagnostic details. Data captured by Dr. Watson is stored in the DRWTSN32.LOG file. It can also be configured to save a memory dump of the application's address space for further investigation. However, the information extracted and stored by Dr. Watson is only useful to a Microsoft technical professional who is well versed in its cryptic logging syntax.

NT automatically launches Dr. Watson when an application error occurs. But to configure Dr. Watson, you'll need to launch it from the Start, Run command with DRWTSN32.

COMMAND SWITCHES FOR BOOT.INI

The BOOT.INI file can be used to control or modify the activity of or the operational parameters of NT. By adding command-line switches after an ARC name entry, you can alter the parameters used to boot NT. The options are:

- /BASEVIDEO: The standard VGA video driver, used to boot into 256-color 640 × 480 mode

- /BAUDRATE=*n:* Sets the debugging communication baud rate when using the Kernel Debugger; default is 9,600 for a modem and 19,200 for a null modem cable

- /CRASHDEBUG: Loads the debugger into memory, where it remains inactive unless a Kernel error occurs

- /DEBUG: Loads the debugger into memory to be activated by a host debugger connected to the computer

- /DEBUGPORT=com*x:* Sets the debugging COM port

- /MAXMEM:*n*: Sets the ceiling restriction on RAM usage for Windows NT

- /NODEBUG: Indicates that no debugging information is being used

- /NOSERIALMICE=[COM*x* | COM*x,y,z*...]: Disables serial mouse detection of the specified COM port(s)

- /SOS: Forces NT to display each driver name as it is loaded

By default, an alternative boot menu selection is present in the BOOT.INI that can be used to boot into NT with the standard VGA driver. The entry with the extra "[VGA Mode]" at the end already has the /BASEVIDEO and /SOS switches present. This is useful to get around video driver problems.

16

CORRECTING NTDETECT DEFECTS

During bootup, if the NTDETECT component fails to detect the proper hardware, then you may have a corrupted NTDETECT file or a hardware problem. One way to determine the cause of this error is to use the debugged or checked version of NTDETECT stored on the distribution CD in the Support\Debug\I386 directory. To use this version, follow these steps:

1. Remove attribute settings of Hidden, System, and Read Only on NTDETECT.COM.

2. Rename the existing file to NTDETECT.BAK.

3. Copy NTDETECT.CHK to the system partition.

4. Rename NTDETECT.CHK to NTDETECT.COM.

5. Set attribute settings of Hidden, System, and Read Only on NTDETECT.COM.

6. Reboot the computer.

This version will display verbose information about the detection process, which should help you determine where the problem occurs. Once you have eliminated the problem, restore the original NTDETECT.COM or pull it from an ERD.

POWER PROTECTION PROBLEMS

A UPS (uninterruptible power supply) is an invaluable asset for any computer. A UPS can interact with NT through a serial port. This enables the UPS to inform NT when a power failure occurs and when to power down. There are several manufacturer-dependent configurations for UPSs; but all are controlled through the UPS Control Panel applet. Some of the most common problems with UPSs are:

- If the /NOSERIALMICE parameter is not added to the BOOT.INI, NT will poll the COM ports for a mouse and may cause the UPS to power off.

- If the voltage directions are improperly defined through the UPS applet, the UPS may not be able to communicate with NT. Thus, a power-down signal may not be understood and NT will fail to shut itself down.

- Always be conservative when indicating the battery life and recharge time values for your UPS. Using the exact values provided in the user manual may result in lost power before NT finishes a graceful shutdown.

- The interface between NT and the UPS is a special UPS cable, not a standard RS-232 serial cable as used with modems. Using the wrong cable can prevent communication between the UPS and NT.

PRE-IDE HARD DRIVE DIFFICULTIES

NT does not support all ESDI hard drives. ESDI hard drives are pre-IDE with the special ability to be low-level formatted with various sector-per-track values. This can result in more than 1,024 cylinders. If an intelligent ESDI drive controller is used, NT may be able to use the area of the disk above 1,024 cylinders. The only way to know if NT can use an ESDI disk and its controller is to test it by installing NT on the drive. If a Fatal System Error:0x0000006b occurs, this indicates that the ESDI drive is not supported.

REINSTALLING WINDOWS NT

There is one final troubleshooting technique you can use if you have exhausted all other options—reinstallation. The process of reinstalling NT can resolve many problems, especially those caused by Registry errors. However, reinstallation can cause other difficulties, such as lost application configuration, removal of third-party drivers, and the need to reapply service packs.

There are two types of reinstallation: full and upgrade. A full installation will overwrite everything, just as if you were performing the installation for the first time. All data and configuration settings, including the Security ID, will be lost if a full installation is performed. An upgrade installation retains most of the current configuration settings, data, and the Security ID. However, because not everything is overwritten, the source of the problem may not be corrected.

Always be sure to back up important data before performing either type of reinstallation. Even an upgrade does not guarantee that your data will not be destroyed.

DEATH BY BLUE SCREEN

Even though Microsoft touts NT as a no-failure OS, it is still not uncommon for the system to completely fail. The system failures are no longer called GPFs (General Protection Faults), but their occurrence is no less frustrating. When the Ring 0 layer of the system is compromised (i.e., the protected-mode, CPU-controlled Kernel), NT crashes and the "blue screen of death" appears. This blue screen displays data about the STOP error, such as its memory location and type. Most of the screen is filled with a hex dump of some portion of memory that relates to the failure. This information may be used by a professional technician to determine the cause of the failure, but unless you have such a person on hand, this display is fairly useless. Hopefully, you can return to operation by rebooting the machine. If not, you may need to apply one of the troubleshooting techniques described earlier in this chapter.

DUMPING MEMORY ON STOP ERRORS

At the point of a STOP error, NT can automatically save the contents of active memory to a file. A technical professional can use this memory dump file to determine the cause of the failure. Memory dumps can be configured on the Startup/Shutdown tab of the System applet of the Control Panel. The options are:

- Write the error event to the System log
- Send an Administrative alert
- Write a dump file
- Automatically reboot

16

By default, the dump file is stored in %winntroot%\Memory.dmp. The contents of the memory dump file can be examined with the DUMPEXAM.EXE utility. However, most of the contents will require a Microsoft technical professional to interpret.

 If dump file option is enabled (which it is by default), then there must be sufficient disk space on the system disk to accommodate the memory dump. Otherwise, a reinstallation must be performed. Also, this option will work only if the paging file is located on the system disk (because it's the only disk that NT can find while it's shutting down after a fatal error occurs).

APPLYING NT SERVICE PACK UPDATES

Since the initial release of Windows NT Workstation in August 1996, Microsoft has released several patches to improve and repair the OS. A **service pack** is a collection of code replacements, patches, error corrections, new applications, version improvements, or service-specific configuration settings that correct, replace, or hide the deficiencies of the original product, or preceding service packs or hot fixes. A hot fix is similar to a service pack, except that it addresses only a single problem or a small number of problems and may not be fully tested.

Service packs are cumulative, which means that Service Pack 3 (SP3) contains SP2 plus all post-SP2 hot fixes. Thus, the latest service pack is all you need to install. You should only apply hot fixes if you are experiencing the problem it was created to fix, otherwise the hot fix may cause other problems.

A few important points to remember about patches include:

- Always make a backup of your system before applying any type of patch. This will give you a way to restore your system if the fix destroys the OS.
- Be sure to retrieve the correct CPU type and language version.
- Always read the readme and Knowledge Base documents for each patch before installing.
- Update your ERD.
- Make a complete backup of the Registry using the Registry Editor or the REGBACK utility on the Resource Kit.
- Export the disk configuration data from Disk Administrator.
- Because service packs rewrite many system-level files, you must disconnect all current users, exit all applications, and temporarily stop all unneeded services before installing any service pack or patch.

To locate Knowledge Base documents, visit or use one of these resources:

- Web site: *http://www.microsoft.com/kb/*
- TechNet CD

- Microsoft Network
- CompuServe: GO MICROSOFT
- Resource Kit Documentation (online Help file)

Service packs and hot fixes can be retrieved from:

- Web/FTP: *ftp://ftp.microsoft.com/bussys/winnt/winnt-public/fixes/usa/nt40/*
- By phone: (800) 370-8758
- By fax: (716) 873-0906 US, (905) 374-3855 Canada
- By US mail: Microsoft Service Pack 3; PO Box 810; Buffalo, NY 14207-0810
- By Canadian mail: Microsoft Service Pack 3; PO Box 643; Fort Erie, ON; L2A 6M1 Canada

To install a service pack:

1. Move the SP file into an empty directory.
2. Close all applications, especially debugging tools.
3. Locate and execute UPDATE.EXE with the Start, Run command.
4. Follow any prompts that appear.
5. When instructed, reboot your system.

To uninstall a service pack:

1. You must have selected the "Save uninstall information" during the initial application of the service pack. Whenever it's offered as an option, this is usually a good path to take.
2. Extract the original SP archive into an empty directory.
3. Locate and execute UPDATE.EXE.
4. Select the "Uninstall a previously installed Service Pack" button.
5. Follow the prompts.
6. Reboot.

To determine what service packs have been applied to your system, you can use one of the following techniques:

- Type *WINVER* from a command prompt.
- From the menu bar of NT Explorer, My Computer, Network Neighborhood, the Control Panel, or the Printers folder, select Help, About Windows NT.
- Watch the blue screen where the system version appears during the Kernel initialization phase of the system bootup.

16

- Use the Registry Editor to view the CSDVersion value in the HKEY_LOCAL_MACHINE\SOFTWARE\Microsoft\WindowsNT\ CurrentVersion.

USING MICROSOFT REFERENCES FOR TROUBLESHOOTING

Several Microsoft resources are available to aid you in troubleshooting and working with Windows NT:

- The Microsoft Web site: *http://www.microsoft.com/ntworkstation/*

- *Microsoft Network (MSN):* Microsoft's own online membership service, the Microsoft Network, is a great source for information, but it is not as easy or as fast to use as the TechNet CD.

- *The Knowledge Base:* The predecessor to and a resource for the TechNet CD, an online resource that can be accessed by several means, which were detailed earlier in this chapter.

- *TechNet:* The best periodic publication from Microsoft. This multi-CD collection is an invaluable resource for white papers, FAQs, troubleshooting documents, book excerpts, articles, and other written materials, plus utilities, patches, fixes, upgrades, drivers, and demonstration software. At only $300 for a one-year subscription, it is well worth the cost.

- *Resource Kits (RKs):* The NT Resource Kits are useful information sources. They are available in electronic form through TechNet as a whole and through the online services in portions. RKs include material not found in the manuals, and often include add-on software utilities to enhance product use.

- *Inline books:* The NT distribution CD contains several electronic publications that include additional and expanding information not included in the printed user's manuals.

CHAPTER SUMMARY

No matter what problems or errors are discovered on your computer system, you should always follow several common-sense principles of troubleshooting: Perform one task at a time, avoid panic, isolate the problem, and perform the simplest fixes first. Information is the most valuable tool needed for troubleshooting. This includes maintaining a Computer Information File (CIF) and a detailed history log of troubleshooting activities.

There are five common installation problems: media errors, domain controller communication difficulties, STOP message errors or a halt on blue screen, hardware problems, and dependency failures. NT includes several utilities you can use for troubleshooting: Event

Viewer, Last Known Good Configuration, Registry, Emergency Repair Disk (ERD), and Windows NT Diagnostics. Most boot failures can be repaired through the use of an ERD and the three NT setup floppy disks.

Printer problems are most often associated with physical configuration or spooling problems. RAS and Network problems are caused by several types of problems, but the most common is misconfiguration.

Windows NT has a service pack and several hot fixes that should be applied to your system to improve its operation and eliminate several problems. In addition, Microsoft has provided several avenues to gain access to information about the operation and management of its products, including a substantial collection of troubleshooting documentation.

KEY TERMS

- **boot failures** — Problems that occur between powering on a computer and the logon prompt display.

- **Computer Information File (CIF)** — A detailed collection of all information related to the hardware and software products that make up your computer (and even your entire network).

- **Dr. Watson** — A Windows NT application error debugger. This diagnostic tool detects application failures and logs diagnostic details.

- **Emergency Repair Disk (ERD)** — A miniature first-aid kit for NT. This single floppy disk contains all the files needed to repair most system-partition and boot-partition problems.

- **Event Viewer** — The utility used to view the three logs automatically created by NT.

- **Last Known Good Configuration (LKGC)** — A configuration recording made by NT of all the Registry settings that exist at the time a user successfully logs onto the computer.

- **Master Boot Record (MBR)** — The area of a hard drive that contains the data structure that initiates the boot process.

- **REGEDT32** — A Registry editor that displays each of the five hives in a separate display window but offers security- and control-related features.

- **REGEDIT** — A Registry editor that displays all the hives of the Registry in a single display window and can search the entire Registry at one time.

- **service pack** — A collection of code replacements, patches, error corrections, new applications, version improvements, or service-specific configuration settings that correct, replace, or hide the deficiencies of the original product or preceding service packs or hot fixes.

- **Windows NT Diagnostics** — A system inspection tool used to extract configuration and environmental details about your system.

16

REVIEW QUESTIONS

1. The Computer Information File (CIF) is _____.
   a. a documentation manual distributed by manufacturers
   b. a detailed collection of all information related to the hardware and software products that make up your computer
   c. a branch of the government that collects data on electronic communications
   d. a new publication used to learn how to use a computer

2. Which of the following are important items to include in your CIF? (Choose all that apply.)
   a. name and version of all software
   b. manual, user's guide, or configuration sheets
   c. complete technical support contact information
   d. warranty information
   e. location of backup items and original software

3. When approaching a computer problem, which of the following should you keep in mind? (Choose all that apply.)
   a. how the last problem was solved
   b. what changes were recently made to the system
   c. details from the CIF
   d. ability to repeat the failure

4. If a media error occurs during installation, which of the following are steps you should take to eliminate the problem?
   a. attempt to recopy or reaccess the file that caused the failure
   b. switch media sources or types
   c. open the Control Panel and reinstall the appropriate drivers
   d. restart the installation from the beginning

5. Your NT Workstation experiences a STOP error due to a runaway process from a custom application developed in-house. Where can information about this error be found once the machine has been rebooted?
   a. Kernel Debugger
   b. Performance Monitor
   c. Event Viewer
   d. Windows NT Diagnostics

6. Which of the following NT repair tools can be used to gain information about drivers or services that failed to load?

   a. Event Viewer

   b. Registry

   c. Windows NT Diagnostics

   d. Dr. Watson

7. The Last Known Good Configuration (LKGC) is useful for _____.

   a. returning the system to the state it was in immediately after the initial installation

   b. recording a system state for future use

   c. returning the system to the state it was in at the time of the last successful user logon

   d. loading a configuration file from floppy disk to use as the current boot parameter file

8. Which of the following are valid ways to make full or partial backups of the Registry? (Choose all that apply.)

   a. create an ERD using the RDISK /S command

   b. use NT Backup

   c. copy all of the contents of the \Winnt\System32\Config directory

   d. use the Disk Administrator

   e. use REGEDT32

9. Which Registry editor should you use if you need to modify the access permissions on a specific key?

   a. REGEDIT

   b. REGEDT32

10. Which of the following can be corrected by the repair process using the three installation disks and a recent Emergency Repair Disk? (Choose all that apply.)

    a. boot sector corruption

    b. unable to locate Master Boot Record

    c. NTLDR not found

    d. corrupt NTOSKRNL

11. How can you create an Emergency Repair Disk (ERD)? (Choose all that apply.)

    a. during the initial installation of NT

    b. through the System applet of the Control Panel

    c. through either of the Registry editors

    d. with the RDISK /S command

16

12. Your NT Workstation experiences yet another STOP error. Fortunately, you enabled the memory dump option through the System applet. What utility can you use to view the contents of the .DMP file?

    a. Event Viewer

    b. Debug Inspector

    c. DUMPEXAM.EXE

    d. Windows NT Diagnostics

13. Which of the following are possible troubleshooting techniques for eliminating printer problems? (Choose all that apply.)

    a. check the physical aspects of the printer—cable, power, paper, toner, and so on

    b. check the print queue for stalled jobs

    c. attempt to print from a different application or a different client

    d. stop and restart the spooler using the Services applet

14. Which of the files on the ERD lists the files installed during setup and the checksums of each of these files?

    a. INSTALLED.DAT

    b. CONFIG.NT

    c. DEFAULT._

    d. SOFTWARE._

    e. SETUP.LOG

15. What is the most common cause of RAS problems?

    a. telco service failures

    b. misconfiguration

    c. user error in typing name and password

    d. communication device failure

16. Which two parameter switches are present by default on the [VGA Mode] selection ARC name line in the BOOT.INI file? (Choose two answers.)

    a. /NODEBUG

    b. /BASEVIDEO

    c. /NOSERIALMICE

    d. /SOS

    e. /VGAVIDEO

17. A user's ability to access a resource is controlled by access permissions. If you suspect a problem with a user's permission settings, what actions can you take?

    a. attempt the same actions and activities with the Administrator account

    b. delete the user's account and create a new one from scratch

    c. double-check group memberships to verify that no No Access settings are causing the problem

    d. grant the user Full Access to the object directly

18. How can an MBR error be repaired?

    a. with the three NT setup floppy disks

    b. with an ERD

    c. using FDISK /MBR from DOS 6.0+

    d. through the Disk Administrator

19. During the boot process, you receive the following error message after the Last Known Good Configuration prompt: "Windows NT could not start because the following file is missing or corrupt: \winnt root\system32\ntoskrnl.exe. Please reinstall a copy of the above file." What are the possible explanations for this error? (Choose all that apply.)

    a. NTOSKRNL.EXE is missing

    b. BOOT.INI points to the wrong partition

    c. NTOSKRNL.EXE is corrupt

    d. BOOT.INI file is missing

20. What application automatically loads to handle application failures?

    a. Event Viewer

    b. System applet

    c. Windows NT Diagnostics

    d. Dr. Watson

21. The SYSTEM Registry key contains errors. You do not have a recent ERD, but you do have a copy of the SYSTEM key itself on floppy disk. Which of the following programs should you use to restore the SYSTEM key from the floppy disk?

    a. Disk Administrator

    b. System applet

    c. User Manager

    d. the three NT setup floppy disks

16

22. Performing a full reinstallation of Windows NT to repair a system failure is a drastic solution because of what? (Choose all that apply.)

    a. all system settings and configurations will be destroyed

    b. all applications will need to be reinstalled

    c. it requires the purchase of another user license

    d. it changes the system's Security ID

23. After installing a new SCSI driver, NT will not successfully boot. No other changes have been made to the system. What is the easiest way to return the system to a state where it will boot properly?

    a. use the repair process with the ERD

    b. use the Last Known Good Configuration

    c. configure a memory dump

    d. boot to DOS and run the Setup utility to change the installed drivers

24. Which of the following are important actions to perform before installing a service pack or a hot fix? (Choose all that apply.)

    a. make a backup of your system

    b. read the readme and Knowledge Base documents

    c. make a complete backup of the Registry

    d. update your ERD

25. Your NT Workstation has recently been experiencing numerous STOP errors. Where should you configure NT so that a memory dump will occur before the system reboots to help pinpoint the problem?

    a. the Network applet's properties

    b. the recovery option in Dr. Watson

    c. the Tracking tab of the Task Manager

    d. the Startup/Shutdown tab of the System applet

HANDS-ON PROJECTS

PROJECT 16-1

To create an Emergency Repair Disk (ERD):

A formatted floppy disk is required for this project.

1. Log on as Administrator.
2. Click **Start, Run** to open the Run dialog box shown in Figure 16-1.

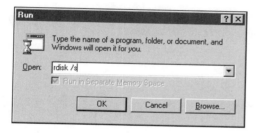

Figure 16-1   The Run dialog box

3. Type **rdisk /s**, then click **OK**.
4. Wait while the system saves the Registry.
5. When prompted about whether to create an ERD as shown in Figure 16-2, click **Yes**.

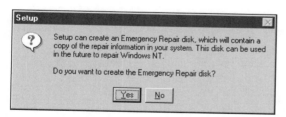

Figure 16-2   Click Yes to create an ERD

16

6. At the prompt shown in Figure 16-3, place a formatted floppy disk into the drive and click **OK**. The utility will create an ERD and close automatically.

Figure 16-3   Place a formatted floppy disk into
the drive and click OK

PROJECT 16-2

To create the three NT Setup floppy disks:

Three formatted floppy disks are required for this project.

1. Log on as Administrator.
2. Open the Run dialog box by clicking **Start**, **Run**.
3. Click the **Browse** button.
4. Locate and select the **Winnt32.exe** file in the \i386 directory of the NT distribution set. Then click **Open**.
5. Add the **/ox** parameter after the Winnt32.exe in the dialog box. Be sure to use a space to separate the parameter from the filename, as shown in Figure 16-4.

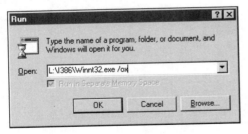

Figure 16-4   Use a space to separate the
/ox parameter from the filename

6. Click **OK** to execute the file.
7. A dialog box opens, as shown in Figure 16-5, requesting you to verify the path to the distribution files. Verify by clicking **Continue**.

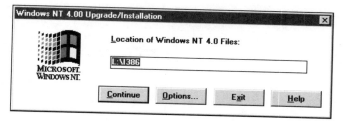

Figure 16-5   Verify the path to the distribution files

8. A dialog box like the one in Figure 16-6 opens, instructing you to label three format-ted floppy disks as Windows NT Workstation Setup Boot Disk, Setup Disk #2, and Setup Disk #3. Place Setup Disk #3 in the drive and click **OK**.

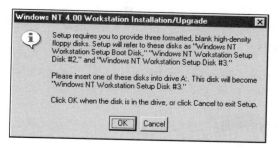

Figure 16-6   Label three formatted floppy disks,
place Disk #3 in the drive, and click OK

9. You are prompted to insert Setup Disk #2 and Disk #1 (the Setup Boot Disk) in turn. Once the floppy disk creation is complete, the utility closes.

PROJECT 16-3

To use the Event Viewer:

1. Log on as Administrator.
2. Launch the Event Viewer from **Start**, **Programs**, **Administrative Tools (Common)**, **Event Viewer**. A screen similar to Figure 16-7 appears.

16

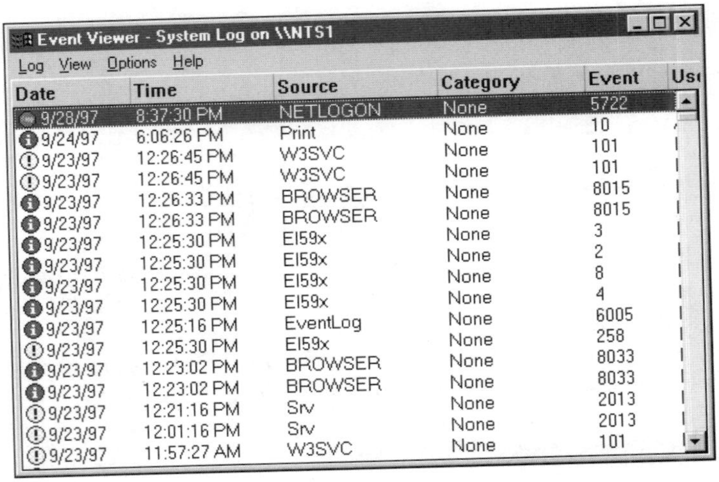

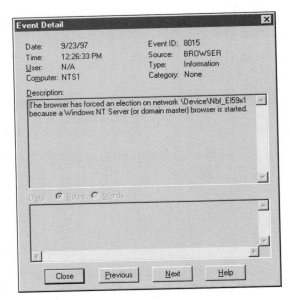

Figure 16-7   Event Viewer System Log

3. Double-click any of the items that appear in the display window to open the Event Detail dialog box, shown in Figure 16-8.

Figure 16-8   Event Detail dialog box

4. Read the information about the event.

5. Close the dialog box by clicking **Close**.

6. View another entry in the Event Viewer by double-clicking it, then close it.

7. Exit the Event Viewer using the **Log**, **Exit** menu command.

PROJECT 16-4

To use Windows NT Diagnostics:

1. Log on as Administrator.
2. Launch Windows NT Diagnostics by clicking **Start**, **Programs**, **Administrative Tools (Common)**, **Windows NT Diagnostics**. The Windows NT Diagnostics window opens, as shown in Figure 16-9.

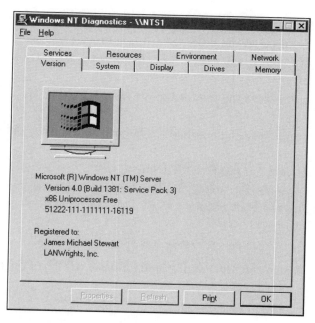

Figure 16-9   Windows NT Diagnostics screen

3. View the data on any of the tabs by clicking the tab name.
4. When finished, click **OK** to exit.

16

CASE PROJECTS

1. After installing a new drive controller and a video card, along with their associated drivers, Windows NT refuses to boot and the LKGC does not result in an operational system.

   Required Result: Return the system to a bootable and operational state.

   Optional Desired Results: Retain the Security ID; retain most, if not all, of the system's configuration.

   Proposed Solution: Perform a complete reinstallation of Windows NT.

   Which of the following results does the proposed solution provide and why?

   a. The proposed solution produces the required result and produces both of the optional desired results.

   b. The proposed solution produces the required result, but only one of the optional desired results.

   c. The proposed solution produces the required result, but neither of the optional desired results.

   d. The proposed solution does not produce the required result.

2. After installing a new drive controller and a video card, along with their associated drivers, Windows NT refuses to boot and the LKGC does not result in an operational system.

   Required Result: Return the system to a bootable and operational state.

   Optional Desired Results: Retain the Security ID; retain most, if not all, of the system's configuration.

   Proposed Solution: Perform an upgrade reinstallation of Windows NT.

   Which of the following results does the proposed solution provide and why?

   a. The proposed solution produces the required result and both of the optional desired results.

   b. The proposed solution produces the required result, but only one of the optional desired results.

   c. The proposed solution produces the required result, but neither of the optional desired results.

   d. The proposed solution does not produce the required result.

WINDOWS NT SERVER 4.0
NET COMMAND REFERENCE

The majority of Windows NT functions can be executed by using graphical utilities; however, there are several reasons to use the NET commands at the command prompt instead. One reason is that inputting a command at the command prompt simply takes less time than starting a graphical utility and searching through its menus—for example, NET USE is a faster way to map a drive than launching Windows NT Explorer, locating the appropriate network share in the Network Neighborhood, then right-clicking to elicit a Map Network Drive dialog, and filling in the appropriate details. Given the breadth of the NET commands, this same observation also applies to using NET commands instead of numerous Control Panel applets or User Manager.

Another, more important reason to use NET commands is that you can import them into batch files. Batch files allow you to set up logon scripts, execute commands at scheduled times, and perform functions when events are triggered. For example, you could use the Windows AT (Automate Task) command to schedule a series of NET commands in a batch file to run every night at 3:00 A.M. and to document the current logons assigned to users and the files they're permitted to access.

This appendix summarizes the NET commands. A description can also be found in online Help by typing *net help syntax* at the command prompt.

NET COMMAND SYNTAX CONVENTIONS

The following conventions are used to represent command syntax:

- **Bold letters** indicate entries that must be typed as they are shown.

- Filenames and variables are represented using *lowercase italic* letters.

- Square brackets—[and]—surround optional command elements.

- Curly braces—{ and }—surround a list of items. Items in the list are separated by the | character, indicating that you can choose only one list item with this command. For example, NET COMMAND [name] {OPTION1 | OPTION2} would mean that the name is optional and either OPTION1 or OPTION2 must be chosen.

- An ellipsis—...—repeats the preceding item, separated by spaces.

  - An ellipsis following a comma or semicolon—,... or ;...—repeats the preceding item, separated by commas or semicolons, respectively.

- If a string includes any spaces, you must put quotation marks around the entire string to quote it as a single argument. For example, you must enter NET PAUSE "FTP SERVER" to pause the FTP Server service.

NET COMMAND DESCRIPTIONS

The following sections describe the most frequently used NET commands.

NET ACCOUNTS

NET ACCOUNTS is the syntax used to maintain the user account database. It is used to modify every user's account password and logon requirement. NET ACCOUNTS shows the domain information for the logged on account, the password's current settings, and the logon limitations when entered without the options.

Syntax

NET ACCOUNTS   [/FORCELOGOFF:{*minutes* | NO}]
                              [/MINPWLEN:*length*]
                              [/MAXPWAGE:{*days* | UNLIMITED}]
                              [/MINPWAGE:*days*]
                              [/uniquepw:*number*]
                              [/DOMAIN]

NET ACCOUNTS [/SYNC] [/DOMAIN]

Options

/FORCELOGOFF:{*minutes* | NO}

Minutes designates how many minutes a user has before he or she is automatically logged off because of account or logon hours lapses. The default value NO ensures that forced logoff will not occur.

/MINPWLEN:*length*

Length specifies the minimum number of characters required for a password.

/MAXPWAGE:{*days* | UNLIMITED}

Days specifies the maximum number of days a password is good for. If you use the UNLIMITED option, there is no limit on the number of days a password can be legitimately used. Ninety days is the default, and you can use any number of days between 1 and 49,710. The /MAXPWAGE number must be more than the /MINPWAGE number.

/MINPWAGE:*days*

Days specifies the minimum number of days that must pass before a user can change his or her password. Zero days is the default, and you can use any number of days between 1 and 49,710. The /MINPWAGE number must be less than the /MAXPWAGE number.

/UNIQUEPW:*number*

This syntax specifies that the user must use a different password every *number* of times a password is changed. The maximum value that can be assigned to this *number* is 8.

/SYNC

/SYNC synchronizes the account's database.

/DOMAIN

This syntax performs the specified action on the Primary Domain Controller of the current domain rather than on the current computer. This option is valid only when the Windows NT computer that it is being performed on belongs to a domain.

A

Example

NET ACCOUNTS is used to make global changes to every user account. The following command will change the minimum password length for everyone to five days:

NET ACCOUNTS /MINPWAGE:5

Notes

The NET ACCOUNT options will not become effective unless the following conditions pre-exist:

- The user accounts must have been set up by the User Manager or the NET USER command.
- Every domain controller must have the Net Logon service functioning on it.

NET COMPUTER

This command is used to add and delete computers in a domain database.

Syntax

NET COMPUTER \\computername {ADD | /DEL}

Options

\\computername	Represents the name of the computer that is going to be added or deleted
/ADD	Adds the computer to the domain
/DEL	Deletes the computer from the domain

Example

To add a computer named BLUE to the domain, type the following:

NET COMPUTER\\BLUE/ADD

Notes

You can use this command only in Windows NT Server.

NET CONFIG SERVER

You use the NET CONFIG SERVER command to show or change the settings of the Server service. This command is relevant only to the server on which it is performed. To be able to configure this server, a user must be logged onto it as a member of the Administrators group.

Syntax

NET CONFIG SERVER   [/AUTODISCONCONNECT:*time*]

[/SRVCOMMENT:*"text"*]

[/HIDDEN:{YES | NO}]

Options

/AUTODISCONNECT:*time*   *Time* specifies the number of minutes an account can be inactive before it is automatically disconnected. By assigning 1 as the value, the account will never be disconnected, no matter how long it remains idle. Fifteen minutes is the default, and you can assign a value from 1 to 65,535 minutes.

/SRVCOMMENT:*"text"*   This option adds a message for the server that can be viewed in Windows NT screens and by using the NET VIEW command. The message has to be contained in quotation marks and can be up to 48 characters long.

/HIDDEN:{YES | NO}   Using this option, you can choose whether the server's computer name appears on the display listings of servers. The default is NO, which makes the server's name visible; YES hides the server's name.

NET CONFIG WORKSTATION

Workstation services are viewed and changed by the NET CONFIG command.

Syntax

NETCONFIG WORKSTATION   [/CHARCOUNT:*bytes*]

[/CHARTIME:*msec*]

[/CHARWAIT:*sec*]

A

Options

/CHARCOUNT:*bytes*	Before data is sent to a communication device, bytes of data are collected. This command specifies how many bytes are collected. If both /CHARTIME and /CHARCOUNT are set, NT acts on the option that is satisfied first. The default number of bytes is 16, and you can enter a range from 0 to 65535.
/CHARTIME:*msec*	Use this option to set the number of milliseconds Windows NT gathers data before it is sent to a communications device. The default is 250 milliseconds, and you can enter a range from 0 to 63,553,500 milliseconds.
/CHARWAIT:*sec*	This option measures the amount of time (measured in seconds) that Windows NT will wait for a communication device to become accessible. The default is 3,600 seconds, and you can enter a number from 0 to 65,535.

Notes

To view the most current configuration of the Workstation service, type *net config workstation* without designating any parameters.

NET CONTINUE

Processes that have been paused by NET PAUSE command can be reactivated by the NET CONTINUE command.

Syntax

NET CONTINUE *service*

Options

service   Any of the following paused services can be designated:

FILE SERVER FOR MACINTOSH, FTP SERVER, LPDSVC, NET LOGON, NETWORK DDE, NETWORK DDE DSDM, NT LM SECURITY SUPPORT PROVIDER, REMOTEBOOT, REMOTE ACCESS SERVER, SCHEDULE, SERVER, SIMPLE TCP/IP SERVICES, WORKSTATION

Notes

Service names that include spaces must be enclosed in quotes.

NET FILE

The NET FILE command is used to remove file locks, close a shared file, and list a file's ID number. You can use this command without options to catalog the files open on a server including their pathnames, usernames, IDs, and number of locks.

Syntax

NET FILE [id [/CLOSE]]

Options

id   The file's identification number.

/CLOSE   Used to close an open file and to unlock locked records. The command will not work unless the command is typed from the server where the file is shared.

Notes

Only computers operating the Server service can use this command.

NET GROUP

The NET GROUP command is used to view, add, and change global groups on servers. Entering the command without parameters will allow you to view the group names on the server.

Syntax

NET GROUP [*groupname* [/COMMENT: *"text"*]] [/DOMAIN]
NET GROUP *groupname* {/ADD [/COMMENT: *"text"*] | /DELETE} [/DOMAIN]
NET GROUP *groupname username* [...] {/ADD | /DELETE} [/DOMAIN]

A

Options

groupname	This parameter signifies the name of the group to be expanded, added, or deleted. By supplying only the groupname, you can display a list of all the users in a group.
/COMMENT: *"text"*	This option allows you to add a comment describing the user's account. The comment can be up to 48 characters, and the text must be enclosed in quotation marks.
/DOMAIN	This syntax performs the specified action on the Primary Domain Controller of the current domain rather than on the current computer. This option is valid only when the Windows NT computer on which it is being performed belongs to a domain.
username [...]	Use this option to specify the users being added or deleted from a group. Multiple-user entries must be separated by a space.
/ADD	This option is used to add users to groups or groups to domains.
/DELETE	This option is used to remove users from groups or groups from domains.

Examples

To view membership of the local group "Server Operators," type the following command:

NET GROUP "SERVER OPERATORS"

By typing the following, you can add users or groups to the Blivet Engineers group:

NET GROUP "Blivet Engineers" /ADD

NET HELP

NET HELP is your key to the Help files for all the NET commands. Use NET HELP by itself to produce a list of commands for which Help is available, or NET HELP *command* to produce the Help file for a specific command. Either way, this is an invaluable key to the whole universe of NET commands.

Syntax

NET HELP *command*
or
NET *command* (/HELP | /?)

Options

You can find Help information for the following commands using NET HELP:

ACCOUNTS	HELP	SHARE
COMPUTER	HELPMSG	START
CONFIG	LOCALGROUP	STATISTICS
CONFIG SERVER	NAME	STOP
CONFIG WORKSTATION	PAUSE	TIME
CONTINUE	PRINT	USE
FILE	SEND	USER
GROUP	SESSION	VIEW

Examples

To obtain a list of all the NET commands, enter the command NET HELP.

To read the Help information for the NET USE command, enter the command NET HELP USE.

Notes

- Using NET HELP *command* | MORE will let you view Help one screen at a time.
- Using NET HELP SERVICES will give you a list of the network services you can start.
- Using the NET HELP SYNTAX command will give you an explanation of how to read NET HELP syntax lines.

NET HELPMSG

This command provides you with an explanation of the Windows NT network messages. The message types you can access are warnings, alerts, and errors.

Syntax

NET HELPMSG *message#*

Options

message#   This is the four-digit number that represents the Windows NT message you want help with.

NET LOCALGROUP

Users who use the network or computers in similar or identical ways are grouped together by this command. When rights are assigned to a local group, the users who belong to that local group are automatically assigned the same rights.

By entering this command without parameters, you can obtain a list of the local groups on the computer.

Syntax

NET LOCALGROUP [*groupname* [/COMMENT:"*text*"]] [/DOMAIN]
NET LOCALGROUP *groupname* {/ADD [/COMMENT:"*text*"] | /DELETE}
  [/DOMAIN]
NET LOCALGROUP *groupname* *name* [...] {/ADD | /DELETE} [/DOMAIN]

Options

groupname	*Groupname* represents the name of the local group that is going to be added, expanded, or deleted. By typing this option without parameters, you can view a list of the users or global groups within a local group. Groupnames that have spaces in them should be contained in quotation marks.
/COMMENT:"*text*"	This option allows a comment describing the local group to be added. This comment can be up to 48 characters of text enclosed in quotation marks.
/DOMAIN	This syntax performs the specified action on the Primary Domain Controller of the current domain rather than on the current computer. This option is valid only when the Windows NT computer on which it is being performed belongs to a domain.
name [...]	This option lists one or more groupnames or usernames that are going to be added or removed from a local group. Multiple entries need to be separated by a space. You cannot use names from other local groups; however, names from other domains or global groups may be used. List the domain name and then the username when listing users from other domains, i.e., ACCOUNTING/LAURA.
/ADD	This option adds a specific global groupname or username to a local group. It is necessary to create an account for the user or global group before it can be added to a local group.
/DELETE	This option removes a groupname or username from a local group list.

Example

The following command should be entered to add the local group ACCT to the local user accounts database:

NETLOCALGROUP ACCT/ADD/DOMAIN

NET NAME

This command is used when adding or deleting a messaging name (also called an alias) or when displaying the list of names for which the computer will receive messages. To use this command, the Messenger service must be enabled.

A computer's list of names comes from one of three sources:

- *Message names:* These names are added with NET NAME.

- *Computername:* This is the computer's computer name. It is added when the Workstation service is started and cannot be deleted.

- *Username:* This name is added when you log on; it cannot be added if the name is being used as a message name elsewhere on the network. Once added, this name cannot be deleted.

Syntax

NET NAME [*name* [/ADD | /DELETE]]

Options

name	You can enter a name of up to 15 characters that is the name of the user account to receive messages.
/ADD	This option adds a name to a computer. By typing NET NAME *name*, you get the same results as typing NET NAME *name* /ADD, making /ADD optional.
/DELETE	This option removes a name from a computer.

A

NET PAUSE

This command is used to pause, or put on hold, a running Windows NT service or resource.

Syntax

NET PAUSE *service*

Options

service   This specifies the service that is to be paused. These are the services that can be paused: FILE SERVER FOR MACINTOSH (Windows NT Server only), FTP PUBLISHING SERVICE, LPDSVC, NET LOGON, NETWORK DDE, NETWORK DDE DSDM, NT LM SECURITY SUPPORT PROVIDER, REMOTEBOOT (Windows NT Server only), REMOTE ACCESS SERVER, SCHEDULE, SERVER, SIMPLE TCP/IP SERVICES, WORKSTATION.

Notes

- Use the NET CONTINUE command to restart a service that has been paused.
- Service names that include spaces must be enclosed in quotes.

NET PRINT

This command lets you view or control print queues and jobs. This command will display the status of the queue, list the number of jobs, and display the size of each job for each printer queue.

Syntax

NET PRINT *computername**sharename*
[*computername*] job# [/HOLD | /RELEASE | /DELETE]

Options

computername   This option specifies the name of the computer sharing the printer queue(s).

sharename   This is the sharename of the printer queue. If using the *sharename* and the *computername*, a backslash must be used to separate the names.

job#   This option specifies the identification number that is given to a print job in a printer queue. Computers with additional printer queues have a unique number for each print job.

/HOLD   When this option is used with *job#*, it puts a hold status on a print job that is waiting at the printer queue. The job stays in the queue, and other jobs bypass it until it is taken off hold or deleted.

/RELEASE   This removes the job from hold status and sends it to the printer.

/DELETE   This removes a job from the queue.

Examples

By typing the following command, you can view the active print jobs from the computer named BONZO:

NET PRINT \\BONZO

To hold job number 214 on the computer named BONZO you would type:

NET PRINT \\BONZO 214/HOLD

NET SEND

This command sends messages to other computers, users, or messaging names on the network.

Syntax

NET SEND {*name* | * | /DOMAIN[:*domainname*] | | /USERS} *message*

Options

name	This option specifies the username, computername, or messaging name to which the message is being sent. Computernames containing blank characters must be contained in quotation marks. An asterisk (*) sends the message to all the names in your group.
/DOMAIN[:*domainname*]	Specifies that the message should be forwarded to all users in the domain. The message is sent to all the names in the specified domain or workgroup if *domainname* is specified.
/USERS	This option sends the message to every user connected to the server.
message	This option specifies the text that is going to be sent as a message.

A

Examples

To send the message "Sell Sell Sell" to everyone in the SALES group, type the following:

NET SEND/DOMAIN:SALES Sell Sell Sell

To send the message "Lunch at 2" to a specific user, type the following:

NET SEND PAMELA Lunch at 2.

Notes

For you to receive a message, your username must be active on the network, and you must be logged on and running the Messenger service.

NET SESSION

Use this command to disconnect or list the sessions occurring between a local computer and the clients connected to this computer. By typing NET SESSION without any parameters, you can view information about every session on the local computer.

Syntax

NET SESSION [*computername*] [/DELETE]

Options

computername	This names the computer that is going to have sessions listed or disconnected.
/DELETE	This function ends the session of the computer with *computername* and closes any open files on the computer for that particular session. If *computername* is left off, every session on the local computer is ended.

Notes

This command can also be typed as NET SESSIONS or NET SESS.

NET SHARE

This command is used to display, create, or delete shared resources between a server's resources and the network users. To display a list of information about the resources to be shared on a computer, use this command without options.

Syntax

NET SHARE   *sharename*

NET SHARE   *sharename=drive:path*

                        [/USERS:*number* | /UNLIMITED]

                        [/REMARK:*"text"*]

NET SHARE   sharename [/USERS:*number* | /UNLIMITED]

                        [/REMARKI:*"text"*]

NET SHARE   {sharename | devicename | drive:path} /DELETE

Options

sharename	This option represents the network name of the resource to be shared. By typing NET SHARE with a *sharename* only, you can view information about that share only.
Devicename	This option specifies one or more than one printer (LPT1–LPT9) that is shared by sharename.
drive:path	This options represents the absolute path of the directory that is going to be shared. Use this option when setting up a directory share.
/USERS:*number*	This option represents the maximum number of users that can access a shared resource at the same time.
/UNLIMITED	This option allows an unlimited number of users to access the shared resource at the same time.
/REMARK:*"text"*	The /REMARK option lets you add a comment describing the resource. The *text* must be contained in quotation marks.
/DELETE	This option deletes the resource from the share list.

Examples

To share a computer's C:\PICS directory with the sharename ARTDEPT, type the following command:

NET SHARE ARTDEPT=C:\PICS

To set the maximum number of simultaneous users:

NET SHARE ARTDEPT=C:\PICS/USERS:7

To stop a share:

NET SHARE LPT6: /DELETE

NET SHARE ARTDEPT /DELETE

A

Notes

You can stop printer shares using the NET SHARE command; however, you can create new printer shares only from the Print folder.

NET START

Use this command to restart services that have been halted by the NET STOP command or to start network services. You can also view a list or services that are currently running by entering NET START without any options.

Syntax

NET START [*service*]

Options

service   The service to be started, including the following:

ALERTER, CLIENT SERVICE FOR NETWARE, CLIPBOOK SERVER, COMPUTER BROWSER, DHCP CLIENT, DIRECTORY REPLICATOR, EVENTLOG, FTP SERVER, LPDSVC, MESSENGER, NET LOGON, NETWORK DDE, NETWORK DDE DSDM, NETWORK MONITORING AGENT, NT ML SECURITY SUPPORT PROVIDER, OLE, REMOTE ACCESS CONNECTION MANAGER, REMOTE ACCESS ISNSAP SERVICE, REMOTE ACCESS SERVER, REMOTE PROCEDURE CALL (RPC) LOCATOR, REMOTE PROCEDURE CALL (RPC) SERVICE, SCHEDULE, SERVER, SIMPLE TCP/IP SERVICES, SNMP, SPOOLER, TCP/IP NETBIOS HELPER, UPS, WORKSTATION

The following services are only available on NT Server:

FILE SERVER FOR MACINTOSH, GATEWAY SERVICE FOR NETWARE, MICROSOFT DHCP SERVER, PRINTER SERVER FOR MACINTOSH, REMOTEBOOT, WINDOWS INTERNET NAME SERVICE

Notes

- To obtain information regarding a specific service, see the online Command Reference (%winntroot%\NTCMDS.HLP).
- When entering the name of a service that contains more than one word separated by spaces, you must enclose the service name in quotes: NET START "WINDOWS INTERNET NAME SERVICE"
- NET START can also be used to start non-native NT services.

NET STATISTICS

Use this command to view the statistics log for the local Workstation or Server service. Enter NET STATISTICS without any options to get a list of services for which statistics are available.

Syntax

NET STATISTICS [WORKSTATION | SERVER]

Options

WORKSTATION	This option lets you view the statistics for the Workstation service.
SERVER	This option lets you view the statistics for the Server service.

NET STOP

Use this command to halt NT services.

Syntax

NET STOP *service*

Options

service   This option stops any native Windows NT service. Use the NET START command to obtain a list of native services.

Notes

- You can also use this command to halt non-native NT services.
- Stopping a service stops all network connections that are associated with that service. Services that are dependent on others will also be stopped if the parent service is halted.
- Only a user with administrative rights can use the NET STOP command.
- You cannot stop the Eventlog service with this command.

A

NET TIME

This command is used to synchronize the local computer's clock with a clock belonging to another domain or computer. When used without the /set option, the time of another computer or domain can be accessed.

Syntax

NET TIME [*computername* | /DOMAIN[:*domainname*]] [/SET]

Options

computername	This option represents the name of the server you are setting or synchronizing with.
/DOMAIN[:*domainname*]	*Domainname* specifies the domain with which you are synchronizing time.
/SET	This option synchronizes the current machine's clock with the time on the indicated machine or domain.

NET USE

Use this command to connect a computer to or disconnect a computer from a shared resource, or to view computer connection information. Enter NET USE without any options to view a list of the current connected shared resources.

Syntax

NET USE   [*devicename* | *]

[*computername**sharename*[*volume*] [*password* | *]]

[/USER:[*domainname*\\]*username*]

[[/DELETE] | [/PERSISTENT:{YES | NO}]]

NET USE   [*devicename* | *] [*password* | *] [/HOME]

NET USE   [/PERSISTENT:{YES | NO}]

Options

devicename	Represents the name to connect to the resource or the name of the device to be disconnected:

- Disk drives (D – Z)

- Printers (LPT1 – LPT3)

To assign the next available devicename, type an asterisk rather than a specific devicename.

computername	This represents the name of the computer in control of the shared resource. Computernames containing spaces should be contained in quotes. The double slashes should also be inside the quotation marks.
sharename	The shared resource's network name.
volume	The NetWare volume on the server. You must have CSNW or GSNW installed and running to use this option.
password	The password that is needed to access the shared resource. The asterisk (*) renders a prompt for the password.
/USER	This option stipulates a different username used to make the connection.
domainname	This option specifies a domain other than the current domain.
username	This option specifies the username that is going to be used to log on.
/HOME	This option allows a user to connect to a home directory
/DELETE	This option deletes a specific network connection to the resource. If the connection is specified by an asterisk, every network connection is canceled.
/PERSISTENT {YES | NO}	This option is used to manage persistent connection use. By specifying YES, the system is instructed to maintain the current connection setting at the next logon. NO does not save the connection being made. This option defaults to the setting used last. Use /DELETE to remove persistent connections.

A

Examples

To create a connection to a shared directory named CONTACTS on the server NTS3 to the devicename of M using the password CHEESE, type the following:

NET USE M: \\NTS3\CONTACTS CHEESE

To make a prompt for the password to appear, type the following:

NET USE M: \\NTS3\CONTACTS *

To prompt for a password and use a different user account, type the following:

NET USE M: \\NTS3\CONTACTS * /USER:M_LARRY

NET USER

Use this command to create and change user accounts. By entering this command without any options, you can view a list of all current user accounts.

Syntax

NET USER [*username* [*password* | *] [*options*]] [/DOMAIN]

NET USER *username* {*password* | *} /ADD [*options*] [/DOMAIN]

NET USER *username* [/DELETE] [/DOMAIN]

Options

username	This option represents the name of the account, 20 characters or less, that is going to be added, deleted, or changed.
Password	The user's password is changed or assigned via this option. The password can be only up to 14 characters, the minimum length set in the /MINPWLEN option of NET ACCOUNTS.
*	The asterisk symbol renders a prompt for the password.
/DOMAIN	By using this option, the specified activity is performed on the PDC in the current domain.
/ADD	Use this option to create a user account in the user accounts database.
/DELETE	Use this option to delete a user account from the user accounts database.
options	This represents any combination of the items listed in the following NET USER [*options*] table.

NET USER [*options*]

/ACTIVE:{YES | NO}

This activates or deactivates a user account. The default is YES, which makes the account active.

/COMMENT:"*text*"

This allows you to enter a comment, of up to 48 characters and enclosed in quotations, that describes the user's account.

/COUNTRYCODE:*nnn*

This option allows you to pick the country code (*nnn*, is the numeric operating system country code) that you want the system's help and error messages to appear in. When *nnn* = 0, the default country code is used.

/EXPIRES:{[*date*] | NEVER}

This option allows you to give a user's account an expiration date. The date can be in one of the following three formats: *mm/dd/yy*, *dd/mm/yy*, or *mmm, dd, yy*.

/FULLNAME:"*name*"

This option lets you specify the user's full name instead of a username. The name has to be enclosed in quotation marks.

/HOMEDIR:*pathname*

This option allows you to designate a path for a pre-existing user's home directory.

/HOMEDIRREQ:{YES | NO}

This option allows you to indicate whether a home directory is required. If YES is entered, you use the /HOMEDIR option.

/PASSWORDCHG:{YES | NO}

This option allows you to decide whether a user has the right to change his or her password. This option's default is YES.

/PASSWORDREQ:{YES | NO}

With this option, you can either assign a password to an account or not. YES is the default.

/PROFILEPATH[:*path*]

This option defines a path for the user's logon profile, which is a Registry profile.

A

/SCRIPTPATH:*pathname*

This option sets the path logon scripts.

/TIMES:{ *times* | ALL}

This option allows you to designate the time frame in which users can access the computer.*times* = day[-day][,day[-day]] ,time[-time][,time [-time]] and hours are the only acceptable increments. You can abbreviate the days or spell them out. Hours can be in either 12- or 24-hour (A.M./P.M.) format. Leaving the value blank prohibits a user from ever logging on. Day and time entries should be separated by commas and multiple day and time entries should be separated by a semicolon (M,5AM–10PM;T12AM–9PM). Never use spaces when you are designating time.

/USERCOMMENT:"*text*"

This allows administrators to modify or add the "User Comment" within accounts. The text must be contained in quotation marks.

/WORKSTATIONS: {*computername*[,...] | *}

This options lets you create a list of up to eight workstations from which users can log onto the network. If this option is blank or if the list is *, users can log on from any workstation. Multiple entries should be separated by a comma.

Examples

If you want to list the information about a user, type the following:

NET USE D_TAYLOR

If you want to create a new user and to be prompted for the password, type the following:

NET USE G_NELSON * /ADD

Notes

- You can also type this command as NET USERS.

- This command can only be used on NT Server.

- You can use this command in a batch file to speed up the creation of many user accounts. Command-line values can be applied when the %1 batch file variable parameter is used. For example, after adding this line to a batch file named

  ACCTNEW.BAT: NET USE %1 PASSWORD /ADD /HOMEDIR:\\users\%1 /PASSWORDCHG:NO

  you can create a new user named T TAYLOR by typing the following:

  ACCTNEW T TAYLOR

NET VIEW

To view a list of domains, computers, or resources shared by a specific computer, use this command. By entering the NET VIEW command without any options, you can view a list of the computers in the present domain.

Syntax

NET VIEW [*computername* | /DOMAIN[:*domainame*]]

NET VIEW /NETWORK:NW [*computername*]

Options

computername	This represents the name of the computer containing the resources you wish to view.
/DOMAIN:*domainname*	This option denotes the domain containing the computer with the resources you wish to view. Leaving out the domain name produces a list of all the domains on the network.
/NETWORK:NW	This option renders a list of the available servers on a NetWare network. If a computername is listed, it lets you view the resources on that machine.

A

Examples

To view a list of the resources available on the NTS5 machine, type the following:

NET VIEW \\NTS5

To obtain a list of the resources of NTS9 that is in the ACCTDOM domain, type the following:

NET VIEW \\NTS9 /DOMAIN:ACCTDOM

To view a list of every domain type:

NET VIEW /DOMAIN

GLOSSARY

OEM The folder used to store any files, components, or applications not part of a normal Windows NT installation but that you wish to install in the course of Setup.

A

Access Control List (ACL) The part of a resource's security descriptor that lists both the permissions applying to that resource and the auditing in place for it.

access token Object containing the security identifier of an active process. These tokens determine the security context of the process.

account policy An NT security feature in which limitations and restrictions for passwords are defined. An account policy can force password changes, require a minimum password length, and prevent password reuse. The account policy also has options for setting the account lockout feature.

active partition The partition that the computer uses to boot.

adapter Any type of hardware device that allows communication to occur on different systems.

Administrator account The account on a Windows NT system that has complete and unrestricted access to the operating system.

Administrators A Windows NT default local group. All members of this group have the same access privileges as those using the Administrator user account.

Advanced RISC Computing (ARC) pathname The naming convention used in the BOOT.INI application to define the location of operating system disks.

alias The 8.3 filename that's generated at the same time as a long filename so that applications and operating systems that can't read long filenames can access the data.

answer file A text file that contains a complete set of instructions for installing Windows NT.

Application layer The seventh layer of the OSI model. This component interfaces with User-mode applications.

archive bit A data attribute that, when set, indicates that the file has been edited since it was last backed up.

Automate Task (AT) The NT command-line scheduling utility.

attribute To FAT, an attribute is an addition to a data file describing some feature of the file; for example, that it has been archived, is hidden, is read-only, or is a system file. To NTFS, everything describing a file is an attribute, including the data itself. NTFS has a much larger array of attributes than FAT does.

audit events Occurrences within the NT environment that are recorded by the audit system in the Security log. An audit event is the success or failure of an activity with, of, or by an object.

audit policy An NT security feature in which auditing for the entire system is turned on or off, and the seven audit event types are selected to track success or failure.

authentication The process of validating a user's credentials to allow access to certain resources.

B

backup browser A computer in a domain or workgroup that maintains a static list of domain/workgroup resources to provide to clients browsing the network. The backup browser periodically receives updates for the browse list from the master browser.

Backup Domain Controller (BDC) A Windows NT Server computer that downloads a copy of the Security Account Manager from the Primary Domain Controller. This copy is periodically updated and may be used to help the Primary Domain Controller authenticate user logons. Multiple BDCs may exist in a single domain.

Backup Operators A default local group of Windows NT. All members of this group can back up and restore every file on the system in spite of standard security restrictions.

base priority The lowest priority that may be assigned to a thread of a process.

bindery A database in NetWare servers prior to version 4.0 in which user, group, and printer information is stored.

binding The process of linking network services and protocols when developing a protocol stack. The binding facility allows users to define exactly how network services operate to optimize the system's network performance.

boot failures Problems that occur between powering on a computer and the logon prompt display.

BOOT.INI The text file that creates the Windows NT boot loader's menu.

boot loader The software that shows all OSs currently available and permits the user to choose which one should be booted, via a menu.

boot partition In Windows NT, the disk that contains the Windows NT operating system files.

boot sector The partition containing Windows NT and its support files.

bottleneck A system resource or device that causes the system to perform below par.

bound application An application capable of running under the OS/2 subsystem or in a virtual DOS machine. If the OS/2 subsystem is available, it will be used by default.

C

Change Access Control Lists (CACLS) A command used to change local security information on NTFS volumes.

characterization data file The part of the printer driver that provides information about the make, model, and capabilities of the printer in question.

client A computer on a network that subscribes to the services provided by a server.

client/server model A model that allows applications to communicate with each other across networks. These models allow for processing to be distributed, resulting in better performance for user applications. The client portion is often referred to as the front end and the server portion is referred to as the back end.

Client Services for NetWare (CSNW) Service included with Windows NT Workstation that provides easy connection to NetWare servers.

cluster The storage unit used by FAT and NTFS; it consists of one or more sectors, logically grouped. The number of sectors in a cluster depends on the size of the hard disk partition.

Compact Disk File System (CDFS) The file system used to read and write compact disks.

Computer Information File (CIF) A detailed collection of all information related to the hardware and software products that make up your computer and even your entire network.

connecting to a printer Connecting to a network-accessible printer.

context switch The act of unloading the context information for one process and replacing it with another when the new process comes to the foreground.

Control Panel The collection of miniature applications that serve as front ends to the Registry for managing user and system configuration.

copy backup A copy of all selected files, without clearing the archive bit.

copying Moving a copy of a file to a new location so that it takes on the attributes of the folder it is moved to.

counter (or performance counter) A certain part of an object that measures some aspect of a registered system or application object. For example, the Processor object has counters such as %Processor Time and Interrupts per second.

creating a printer Setting up a printer for local use.

cylinder All of the tracks in a hard disk that are directly in line with each other.

D

daily backup A copy of all files amended on the day of the backup.

Data Link Control (DLC) A network transport protocol that allows connectivity to mainframes, printers, and servers running Remote Program Load software.

Data Link layer The second layer of the OSI model. This is the layer that provides the digital interconnection of network devices and the software that directly operates these devices, such as network interface cards.

data type The format in which print jobs are sent to the spooler. Some data types are ready for printing (RAW) and some require further preparation (EMF).

desktop The background of your screen on which windows, icons, and dialog boxes appear.

device driver A program that enables a specific piece of hardware to communicate with Windows NT. Although the device may be physically installed and recognized by Windows NT, it cannot be used properly unless the device driver has been installed.

Dial-Up Networking (DUN) Digital Data Link layer connections made over various serial lines; *dial-up* refers to temporary connections as opposed to continuous connections.

differential backup A copy of all selected files that have the archive bit set, but the archive bit is not reset on each.

disk duplexing A fault-tolerance measure involving linking two disks on the same computer, each using their own controller, so that an exact duplicate of the contents of the first disk is maintained on the second.

disk mirroring A fault-tolerance measure involving linking two disks on the same computer and using the same controller, so that an exact duplicate of the contents of the first disk is maintained on the second.

domain A collection of computers, defined by an Windows NT administrator, that share a common security database. Logging onto the domain provides access and authentication for all shared domain resources.

domain controller For a Windows NT Server, a specified computer role that authenticates domain logons and maintains the security policies and the account database for a domain. A domain always has one Primary Domain Controller and may have several Backup Domain Controllers.

domain master browser In a domain/workgroup that spans more than one subnet, the domain master browser compiles and maintains a list of master browsers in the domain or workgroup.

Domain Name Service (DNS) The TCP/IP protocol that is used to resolve names to IP addresses.

DOS prompt The common name for the command-line window available from DOS and Windows.

Dr. Watson A Windows NT application error debugger. This diagnostic tool detects application failures and logs diagnostic details.

Dynamic Data Exchange (DDE) A form of Interprocess Communication implemented in the Microsoft Windows family of operating systems.

Dynamic Host Configuration Protocol (DHCP) A method of automatically assigning IP addresses to client computers on a network.

E

Emergency Repair Disk (ERD) A miniature first-aid kit for NT. This single floppy disk contains all the files needed to repair most system-partition and boot-partition problems.

Enhanced Metafile (EMF) Device-independent spool data used to reduce the amount of time spent processing a print job. Once it's queued, EMF data requires additional processing to prepare it for the printer.

environment subsystem A mini-operating system running within Windows NT that provides an interface between applications and the Kernel. Windows NT has three environment subsystems—Win32, OS/2, POSIX—but only Win32 is required for Windows NT to function.

environment variable A text string made up of environment information, such as a drive, path, or filename, associated with a symbolic name that can be used by Windows NT.

event Any significant occurrence in the system or in an application that requires users to be notified or a log entry to be added.

event auditing This is the process of tracking the success or failure of events by recording selected types of events in a security log of a server or a workstation.

Event Viewer The Windows NT administrative tool used to view the three logs—system, application, and security.

Everyone A default group in Windows NT that includes every user as a member. This group cannot be managed.

Executive Services A set of Kernel-mode functions that controls security, system I/O, memory management, and other low-level services.

extended partition An area created from free space on a disk that can be used to create volume sets or fault-tolerant volumes.

F

FAT32 The 32-bit version of FAT that supports long filenames (names that don't conform to the 8.3 restriction) and disks up to 4 GB in size.

FDISK A DOS utility used to partition a hard disk.

File Allocation Table (FAT) A file system based on the use of a File Allocation Table, a flat table that records the clusters used to store the data contained in each file stored on disk.

File and Print Services for NetWare (FPNW) A service included in Windows NT Server that is used to connect NetWare clients to NT Servers.

file system The method used to arrange, read, and write files onto disks. Windows NT supports two disk file systems—NTFS and FAT—as well as CDFS, used to read CD-ROMs.

file-system object Any object associated with a file system, such as a file, folder, or printer, that may be manipulated by a file-system driver.

format Rewriting the track and sector information on a disk; therefore, removing all data previously on the disk.

frame A data structure that network hardware devices use to transmit data between computers. Frames consist of the addresses of the sending and receiving computers, size information, and a Cyclical Redundancy Check (CRC).

frame type The structure of a packet that defines what fields are included in the packets and in what order those fields appear.

free space An unused and unpartitioned area of a hard disk that is available for the creation of logical drives.

full backup A copy of all selected files and clearing the archive bit on each.

G

gateway A computer that serves as a router, a format translator, or a security filter for an entire network.

Gateway Services for NetWare (GSNW) A service shipped with Windows NT Server that provides connectivity for Windows-based computers to NetWare servers.

Graphical Device Interface (GDI) The portion of the Windows NT operating system responsible for the first step of preparing all graphical output, whether to a monitor or to the printer.

group A named collection of user accounts, usually created for some specific purpose. For example, the Accounting group might be the only named entity permitted to use a bookkeeping application; by adding or removing individual users from the Accounting group, a network administrator could easily control who may access that application.

Guest account A default user account on Windows NT that has limited access to basic network resources.

Guests A default local group on Windows NT. Members of this group have the same access as those using the Guest default account.

H

Hardware Abstraction Layer (HAL) A hardware-dependent piece of software, written in machine language instead of in C (which the rest of the operating system is written in), that creates a standard interface between whatever hardware happens to be in place and the operating system.

head The part of a hard disk used for reading and writing data.

High Performance File System (HPFS) OS/2's native file system. Although previous versions of Windows NT supported HPFS, Windows NT 4.0 does not.

home directory A user profile-defined environment variable. The home directory is used by Windows NT as the default location to load and save personal data files.

hot fix A remedy for system malfunctions that is similar to a Service Pack except that it addresses only a single problem, or a small number of problems, and may not be fully tested.

HyperText Markup Language (HTML) The language used to create documents for the World Wide Web.

I

incremental backup A copy of all selected files that have the archive bit set; and the archive bit is reset on each.

input message queue A queue for each process, maintained by the Win32 subsystem, that contains the messages sent to the process from the user and that directs its threads to do something.

Integrated Services Digital Network (ISDN) A direct, digital dial-up Public Switched Telephone Network Data Link layer connection that operates at 64 KB per channel over regular twisted-pair cable between a subscriber site and a telephone network central office.

Internet Information Server (IIS) A service shipped with Windows NT Server that provides Web, FTP, and Gopher services on a large scale.

Internet layer The TCP/IP layer that roughly corresponds to the Network layer of the OSI model.

Internetwork Packet Exchange (IPX) The Network and Transport layer protocol developed by Novell for its NetWare product. IPX is a routable, connection-oriented protocol similar to TCP/IP but much easier to manage and with lower communication overhead.

Internet Protocol (IP) The Network layer protocol upon which the Internet is based. IP provides a simple, connectionless transmission that relies on higher layer protocols to establish reliability.

Interprocess Communication (IPC) These are the mechanisms describing processes operating in the Application layer. They are foundations for client-server communication.

IPX/SPX compatible A transport protocol not quite identical to NetWare's IPX/SPX protocol but able to communicate with it. Used to network with NetWare networks that do not use TCP/IP.

K

Kernel The part of Windows NT composed of system services that interacts directly and controls all application contact with the computer.

Kernel mode The Windows NT Executive operates in Kernel mode; that is, within a shared memory space and with access to hardware.

L

language monitor The part of the print monitor that sets up bidirectional messaging between the printer and the computer initiating the print job.

Last Known Good Configuration (LKGC) A configuration recording made by Windows NT of all the Registry settings that exist at the time a user successfully logs onto the computer.

LMHOSTS The file used in Microsoft networks to provide NetBIOS name-to-address resolution.

logon authentication The process of validating a user by requiring a matching and valid name and password from a user attempting to gain access to the computer.

logon script A batch file used to automatically define environment variables, map drives, or launch applications. Logon scripts are useful only when working with legacy systems or when migrating from NetWare.

long file name (LFN) A filename that does not conform to the 8.3 standard filename format.

loopback adapter An apparent network adapter that allows you to test network functions without having a network card successfully installed.

M

macro virus A virus that is attached to a Word or Excel document as a macro. Presently the most common virus type.

mailslots A connectionless messaging Interprocess Communication (IPC) mechanism that Windows NT uses for browse requests and logon authentication.

mandatory user profile A user profile created by an administrator and assigned to one or more users. This profile cannot be changed by the user and will remain the same every time the user logs onto the system.

mapping The act of assigning a local drive letter to a network connection.

Master Boot Record (MBR) The information on the first sector of a hard disk that controls system startup.

master browser The computer in a single-subnet domain or workgroup that maintains a list of all servers connected to the domain, disseminating this list regularly to the backup browsers in the domain for distribution to clients. The master browser is responsible for making any changes to the browse list.

Master File Table (MFT) The relational database used by NTFS to locate files on disk.

member server Also known as a standalone server, any computer that runs Windows NT Server but not a domain controller. Member servers do not receive copies of the domain security database.

microkernel The portion of the Windows NT Executive Services that synchronizes threads and service interaction.

mismatched document A document with incompatible printer and page settings; that is, the page settings are impossible to produce given the existing printer settings.

modem (modulator/demodulator) A Data Link layer device used to create an analog signal suitable for transmission over telephone lines from a digital data stream. Modern modems also include a command set for negotiating connections and data rates with remote modems and for setting their default behavior.

move Transferring or copying an existing file to a new location while retaining its original attributes.

Multilink PPP A capability of RAS to aggregate multiple data streams into one network connection for the purpose of using more than one modem or ISDN channel in a single connection.

multiple-user system A computing or network operating system that maintains separate collections of information and configuration preferences for more than one user.

multitasking Sharing processor time between threads. Multitasking may be preemptive (one thread may bump another one if the thread really needs the processor) or cooperative (one thread will retain control of the processor until its turn to use it is over). Windows NT uses preemptive multitasking except in the context of the WOW operating environment, because Windows 3.x applications expect cooperative multitasking.

multithreaded process A process with more than one path of execution (thread) running at a time.

N

named pipe An Interprocess Communication mechanism that is implemented as a file system that handles connection-oriented messaging.

NetBIOS Extended User Interface (NetBEUI) A simple transport program developed to support NetBIOS installations. NetBEUI is not routable so it is not appropriate for larger networks.

NetBIOS Gateway A service provided by RAS that allows NetBIOS requests to be forwarded independently of transport protocols. For example, NetBEUI can be sent over the network via NWLink.

Net Use The command-line utility that is used to connect to network-accessible resources.

Net View The command-line utility that is used to get a list of computers on the network or resources available on a specified computer.

NetWare Directory Services (NDS) An advanced database used by NetWare 4.0 and higher servers to store resource information.

network adapter Another name for network interface card; the piece of hardware that enables communication between the computer and the network.

Network Basic Input/Output System (NetBIOS) A client/server Interprocess Communication service developed by IBM in 1985. NetBIOS presents a relatively primitive mechanism for communication in client/server applications, but allows easy implementation across various Microsoft Windows computers.

Network Device Interface Specification (NDIS) A Microsoft specification that defines parameters for loading more than one protocol on a network adapter.

Network Dynamic Data Exchange (Net DDE) An Interprocess Communication mechanism developed by Microsoft to support the distribution of DDE applications over a network.

Network Interface layer The TCP/IP layer that roughly corresponds to the Physical and Data Link layers of the OSI model.

Network layer The layer of the OSI model that creates a communication path between two computers via routed packets. Transports protocols implement both the Network and Transport layers of the OSI model.

non-volatile random access memory (NVRAM) Memory in a RISC-based computer that contains hardware and operating system information.

NT File System (NTFS) The native Windows NT file system, which has a more detailed directory structure and supports data-security measures not found in FAT. It also supports very large disks and long filenames.

NT Hardware Qualifier Utility (NTHQ) The Windows NT hardware detection utility, commonly used for troubleshooting hardware configuration.

NWLink A Windows NT transport protocol that implements Novell's IPX. NWLink is useful as a general-purpose transport for Windows NT and for connecting to NetWare file servers through CSNW.

O

object Any piece of information created by using a Windows-based application with Object Linking and Embedding (OLE), Security, or the Component Object Model (COM). This also refers to the operating system process components.

OS/2 subsystem An emulation of OS/2 version 1.x (character mode only) that will run OS/2 applications.

P

paging file A special file on the hard disk. In Windows NT virtual memory, some of the program code and other information is kept in RAM, and other information is temporarily swapped to virtual memory. When that information is required again, Windows NT pulls it back into RAM and, if necessary, swaps other information to virtual memory.

partition Space set aside on a hard disk and assigned a drive letter. A partition may take up all or part of the space on a hard disk.

partition boot sector The portion of a hard disk that contains the information the file system uses to access the volume; including a physical description of the disk, the name and version of the operating system files, the bootstrap code, and an instruction that allows the Master Boot Record to find all this information.

password A unique string of characters that must be entered and accepted before a user can log onto the system or access resources. Passwords are a security measure used to restrict initial access to Windows NT resources.

Peer Web Services (PWS) A service shipped with Windows NT Workstation that provides Web, FTP, and Gopher services on a small scale.

Performance Monitor (PM) The Windows NT application that allows users to monitor and view many system objects. Users can view this information in Chart view, Alert view, Report view, and Log view.

permission The setting in a resource's Access Control List (ACL) that indicates which users can access a resource and what they can do to the resource.

persistent connection A network connection that is remade each time the user logs on.

Physical layer The passive physical components required to create a network, such as the cables, connectors, and connection ports.

Point-to-Point Protocol (PPP) A Network layer transport that provides connectivity over serial or modem lines. PPP can negotiate any transport protocol used by both systems involved in the link and can automatically assign IP, DNS, and gateway addresses when used with TCP/IP.

Point-to-Point Tunneling Protocol (PPTP) The protocol used to connect computers and/or networks to the Internet in a secure and reliable manner.

port A connection or socket used to connect a device such as a printer, monitor, or modem to your Windows NT computer. Information is sent from your computer to the device through a cable.

port monitor The part of the print monitor that transmits the print job to the print device via the specified port. Port monitors are actually unaware of print devices as such and know only that something's on the other end of the port.

POSIX subsystem The subsystem used to run POSIX applications.

Power on Self-Test (POST) A system check performed by all computers when they are turned on.

Power Users A default local group on Windows NT. Members of this group have limited administrative privileges.

preferred master browser A Windows NT computer with a Registry setting that requests that it be made a master browser if not outranked by another potential master browser.

Presentation layer The layer of the OSI model that converts and translates information between the Session and Application layers.

Primary Domain Controller (PDC) The Windows NT Server computer in a domain that authenticates user logons and maintains the domain's security database. Only the PDC will directly accept changes made to the security database and there can be only one PDC per domain.

primary partition A partition on a disk that can be marked for use by an operating system. A disk may have up to four primary partitions per disk (or three if an extended partition exists).

print device The actual hardware that performs the printing.

printer In Microsoft terminology, the software interface between the operating system and the print device. The printer's configuration determines how much of the printing process works. More than one printer may be associated with a single print device.

printer driver The software that allows applications to communicate with print devices. Windows NT printer drivers are composed of three parts that work as a unit—one to create the image for printing, one to create an interface for working with the printer, and one to educate the user about how the printer works.

printer graphics driver The part of the printer driver that renders GDI commands into device driver interface commands that can be sent to the printer.

printer interface driver The part of the printer driver that provides an interface to the printer settings.

printer pooling Logically grouping two or more identical print devices under a single printer name, so that a print job sent to the printer will print on whichever print device is available.

printer priority The setting that helps determine which printer in a pool will get a given print job. The printer with the higher priority is more likely to get the print job.

print job Source code that contains the data to be printed and the data that controls the print process.

print processor Software that works with the printer driver to despool files and make any necessary changes to the data to format it for use with a particular printer.

print provider The server-side software that sends print jobs to the proper server in the required format. Windows NT supports both Windows network print providers and NetWare print providers.

print router Software that sends the print request from the client to the server so that it can be routed to the proper print provider.

print server The computer to which the printer is attached and via which all printer and print job management is performed. More rarely, a print server can be a hardware device that connects the printer to the network.

process An environment in which the executable portion of a program runs, defining its memory usage, its processor affinity, its objects, and so forth. All processes have at least one thread. When the last thread is terminated, the process terminates with it. Each User-mode process maintains its own map of the virtual memory area. One process may create another, in which case the creator is the parent process and the created is the child process.

profile A collection of user settings and preferences that are automatically saved and loaded when a user logs onto a computer.

Q

queue The "waiting list" of documents in line to be printed.

R

RAW Device-dependent spool data that is fully ready to be printed when rendered.

redirector The part of networking software that permits network transactions to interact directly with the I/O subsystem.

Redundant Array of Inexpensive Drives (RAID) A catch-all phrase for one of a variety of methods of using multiple disks to improve disk performance, data security, or both.

REGEDIT A Registry editor that displays all the hives of the Registry in a single display window and allows the entire Registry to be searched at one time.

REGEDT32 A Registry editor that displays each of the five hives in a separate display window but offers security and control-related features.

Registry The database with the lion's share of configuration and operational settings for Windows NT.

Remote Access Service (RAS) The dial-up service in Windows NT that allows users to log onto the system remotely over phone lines.

Remote Procedure Call (RPC) A network Interprocess Communication mechanism that allows an application to be distributed among many computers on the same network.

rendering When used in reference to printing, graphically creating a print job.

Replicators A default local group on Windows NT. This group is used exclusively for the Replicator service hosted on a Windows NT Server machine.

roaming profile A user profile that is configured to be downloaded from a server at logon. These types of profiles maintain a consistent user interface for users who must log onto multiple computers.

S

SAM (Security Accounts Manager) database A database of security information that includes security information (such as user account names and passwords) and the settings of the security policies. In both Windows NT Server and Workstation it is managed with User Manager for Domains.

sectors The 512-byte portions of a hard disk achieved by dividing its surfaces both into tracks and into pie-shaped wedges radiating from the center. The sector is the smallest unit on a disk.

Security Accounts Manager (SAM) A Windows NT subsystem that maintains the security database and provides an application programming interface (API) for accessing the database.

security database The encrypted data storehouse of security details within the Windows NT environment. Also called the SAM (Security Accounts Manager) database, this object stores the names and passwords of all users on a standalone machine for Windows NT Workstation.

Security ID (SID) The computer-generated identification code used by Windows NT to identify users, computers, groups, and other objects. Every object within the Windows NT environment has a SID and all SIDs are unique.

security log The file where all security-related audit events are recorded. This file is accessed through the Event Viewer.

security policies The security features of Windows NT defined through the User Manager. There are three security policies—account, user rights, and audit.

Security tab The tab in a folder or file's Properties dialog box that controls how it is available on the local computer, what auditing is available, and who its owner is.

Serial Line Internet Protocol (SLIP) An implementation of the IP protocol over serial lines; SLIP has been made obsolete by PPP.

server printing A Windows NT Workstation printing model in which a print server shares the printer with the network. All printer and job administration takes place via the print server.

service A process that performs a specific system function and often provides an application programming interface (API) for other processes to call.

service pack A collection of code replacements, patches, error corrections, new applications, version improvements, or service-specific configuration settings that correct, replace, or hide the deficiencies of the original product, or preceding service packs or hot fixes.

Session layer The layer of the OSI model dedicated to maintaining a bidirectional communication connection between two computers.

Setup Manager The Windows NT tool that provides you with a GUI interface for creating an answer file.

share To make resources available to other users on a network.

shared directory A folder made accessible (to some degree) over the network, rather than being available just from the local computer.

Sharing tab The tab in a folder's or file's Properties dialog box that controls how it is shared with the network (if it is being shared).

Small Computer Systems Interface (SCSI) A high-speed parallel-bus interface that connects disk drives, optical drives, and other peripherals to a computer.

Special Access Permissions A superset of special permissions that may be applied to a file or directory; it is more detailed than standard permissions.

spooler A collection of Dynamic Link Libraries (DLLs) and drivers that receive, process, and send print jobs to the print device.

spooling One of the functions of the spooler, the act of writing the contents of a print job to a file on disk so they will not be lost if the print server is shut down before the job is complete.

stripe set A method of improving disk Read and Write performance by distributing data across two or more disks, so that data may be read and written from all disks in the stripe set at once.

stripe set with parity A method of providing fault tolerance by writing data across three or more disks, while also writing parity information so that the data may be reconstructed if something happens to one of the disks.

subnet A portion of a network that may or may not be a physically separate network that shares a network address with other parts of the network but is distinguished by a subnet number.

subnet mask The number used to define which part of a computer's IP address denotes the host and which part denotes the network.

SYSDIFF The Windows NT utility used to take a snapshot of a basic installation and, after changes have been made, record the changes and then apply them to another installation.

system log Records information and alerts about Windows NT internal processes.

system partition The partition that contains the files needed to run Windows NT. On x86 systems, the system partition must be located on the boot disk and marked as active. On RISC-based systems, they are marked active in hardware and must be FAT-based.

system policies A component of the Windows NT security system. System policies restrict or alter a user's computing environment by directly modifying the Registry. System policies are applied on a user, computer, or group basis. System policies can affect an NT Workstation computer, but they can only be managed from a Windows NT Server computer.

T

taking ownership The act of taking over a file object so you have access to the permissions normally granted only to that object's creator.

telephony The programming interface that maintains information common to any program that uses the telephone system.

thread The executable portion of a program, with a priority based on the priority of its process; user threads cannot exist external to a process. All threads in a process share the context of that process.

tracks The concentric circles that divide a hard disk's surfaces into one division.

transaction log The record used in NTFS to note which changes to the file system structure have been completed. This record is used to maintain volume integrity in the case of a disk crash—some data may be lost when the disk is brought back up, but the volume structure will not be corrupted.

Transmission Control Protocol/Internet Protocol (TCP/IP) A suite of Internet protocols upon which the global Internet is based. TCP/IP is the default protocol for NT.

Transport Driver Interface (TDI) The specification to which all Windows NT transport protocols must be written to be used by higher-layer services such as programming interfaces, file systems, and Interprocess Communication mechanisms.

Transport layer The OSI model layer responsible for the guaranteed serial delivery of packets between two computers over an internetwork. TCP is the Transport layer protocol for the TCP/IP transport protocol.

U

unattended installation A Windows NT installation that installs from a previously made script.

uninterruptible power supply (UPS) A battery-operated power supply connected to a computer to keep the system from running down during a power failure.

Uniqueness Database File (UDF) A text file that contains a partial set of instructions for installing Windows NT. UDF is used to supplement an answer file when only minor changes are needed that don't require a new answer file.

Universal Naming Convention (UNC) A multivendor, multiplatform convention used to identify shared resources on a network.

user account This entity contains all of the information that defines a user to the Windows NT environment.

User Environment Profile (UEP) The name of the collection of data stored within a user account that defines the location of the user's profile, home directory, and logon scripts.

User Manager The administrative utility of Windows NT Workstation used to manage users, groups, and security policies.

User mode Operating in private virtual memory areas for each process, so each process is protected from all others. User-mode processes may not manipulate hardware; they must send requests to Kernel-mode services to do this manipulation for them.

username The name of a user account used to log onto Windows NT. The username of an account can be changed without modifying the account's SID.

user profiles The collection of preferences that define the look and feel of a user's desktop and computing environments.

user rights An NT security policy that grants or restricts computer-specific activities to users and groups.

Users A default local group in Windows NT. Members of this group have normal privileges to launch programs, manage files, and perform low-level administrative tasks.

V

verification In the backup utility, the act of making sure that the files on the tape match files on the drive.

VFAT An implementation of FAT that supports long filenames.

virtual device driver (VDD) A device driver used by virtual DOS machines to provide an interface between an application that expects to interact with a 16-bit device driver and the 32-bit device drivers that Windows NT provides.

Virtual DOS machine (VDM) A Win32 application that emulates a DOS environment for use by DOS and Win16 applications.

Virtual Memory Manager (VMM) The service that translates virtual addressing from applications to physical mappings in RAM. This manager hides the memory swapping process from applications and higher-layer services.

virus scanner Software that monitors your hard disk and watches for signs of virus activity; may be constantly running or user-driven.

volume Another word for a partition, a logical division of a hard disk that has been assigned its own drive letter.

W

Win32 subsystem The Windows subsystem that provides the usual Windows NT interface.

WinAT The graphical interface scheduling utility that comes with the Windows NT Resource Kit.

WinLogon dialog box The window that appears on a Windows NT machine when Ctrl-Alt-Del is pressed. A valid username and password must be entered in the fields on this window to gain access to the computer.

Windows Internet Name Service (WINS) A service that provides NetBIOS name to IP address resolution.

Windows NT Diagnostics A system inspection tool you can use to extract configuration and environmental details about your system.

WINMSD The executable for the Windows NT Diagnostics Utility. This is the Windows version of the MSD program that performs the same function for MS-DOS-based computers.

WINNT The 16-bit Windows NT installation program.

WINNT32 The 32-bit Windows NT installation program.

workgroup A collection of computers grouped for viewing purposes, but not sharing any account information.

workgroup printing A Windows NT Workstation printing model in which all workgroup members connect directly to the printer. Printer and job administration is performed from the individual workstations.

X

X.25 A standard that defines packet switching networks.

x86 The chip architecture used by Intel and others to create 386 and later CPUs (including the Pentium).

INDEX